张道真

实用英语语法

A PRACTICAL ENGLISH GRAMMAR

[最新版]

张道真　编著

外语教学与研究出版社
FOREIGN LANGUAGE TEACHING AND RESEARCH PRESS
北京　BEIJING

图书在版编目(CIP)数据

张道真实用英语语法(最新版)/张道真编著. — 修订本. — 北京：外语教学与研究出版社，2002（2007.3 重印）
ISBN 978 - 7 - 5600 - 2448 - 6

Ⅰ. 张…　Ⅱ. 张…　Ⅲ. 英语—语法　Ⅳ. H314

中国版本图书馆 CIP 数据核字（2001）第 066370 号

悠游网—外语学习　一网打尽
www.2u4u.com.cn
阅读、视听、测试、交流、共享

封底刮刮卡，获积分！在线阅读、学习、交流、换礼包！

出 版 人：于春迟
责任编辑：杨镇明
出版发行：外语教学与研究出版社
社　　址：北京市西三环北路 19 号 (100089)
网　　址：http://www.fltrp.com
印　　刷：北京大学印刷厂
开　　本：880×1230　1/32
印　　张：21.75
版　　次：2002 年 5 月第 1 版　2010 年 5 月第 22 次印刷
书　　号：ISBN 978 - 7 - 5600 - 2448 - 6
定　　价：37.90 元
＊　　＊　　＊
购书咨询：(010)88819929　　电子邮箱：club@fltrp.com
如有印刷、装订质量问题，请与出版社联系
联系电话：(010)61207896　　电子邮箱：zhijian@fltrp.com
制售盗版必究　举报查实奖励
版权保护办公室举报电话：(010)88817519
物料号：124480001

前　言

　　本书最早在1958年出版，至今已四十余年，总印数可能已超过九百万册。在这段时间里，虽曾作过几次修订，但语法科学的发展非常之快，所以在这世纪之交的时候，我决定作一次彻底的修改，以期更符合读者的需要，使对大家有更大的助益。

　　这次修改主要从以下几方面着手：

1. 更新全书内容，提高例句质量

　　过去书中多少带有一些当时政治运动的痕迹，这次可说是一扫而空。绝大部分例句都是新的，都摘自原著，因此语言质量有所提高。而且例句丰富，很少语法书能与之相比。我们未做统计，但超过万句是可能的。例句多可以更好说明语法现象，可以加深对语言规律的认识。在学习语法的过程中可望提高整个语言的修养。

2. 把语法与词汇揉和在一起

　　语法可说是躯干，词汇可说是枝叶。根深叶茂才能长成大树。在几十年的研究中深深感到语法和词汇密不可分。可说每个词汇中都有语法问题，语法体现在整个词汇之中。孤立研究语法不可能掌握语法。干巴巴的语法条文绝不代表语法，语法要在活生生的语言中体现。语法与词汇是血肉关系，这次修订就是要使语法学习有血有肉，以加深对整个语言的认识。

3. 这次修订时试图抓住纲，纲举则目张

　　动词就是语法的纲，它基本上贯串着全书。从第7章到第13章（共7章）都讲动词。篇幅可能占全书的三分之一。而后面讲句法的各章，也都与它有关系。特别是第13章讨论动词句型，它总结了英语的主要语式，每个句型都有大量例句。这是为了确立句型观念，以后学习时可以对号入座，使语法知识条理分明。附录1列举了大量成语动词。这都是英语的难点所在，掌握动词是掌握英语的先决条件。

4. 研究各家学说，吸取众人之所长

过去研究语法困难很多，主要靠国内影印的语法书。现在我身在国外，可以看到英美最新出版的各类语法书，这就提供了向各家学习的机会。这次修订也算是我这一段学习的汇报。总的看来，我国这些年来形成的语法体系基本上是站得住的。这从附录4中可以看出。从实用英语的角度来说，这样的处理是基本上合适的。希望在未来一段时间内，语法体系比较稳定，这有利于大家学好英语。

*　　　　　*　　　　　*

回顾近三十年的工作，主要是致力于语法与词汇的研究。目的是明确的，就是要帮助读者提高语言的修养，加强语言的实用能力，适应国家发展的需要。在最近一两年中将出版一套词典系列，主要有：

- 《初级英汉词典》（1,700多页，10,000词条，已出版）
- 《中级英汉词典》（1,700多页，20,000词条，即出版）
- 《高级英汉词典》（2,600多页，30,000词条，即出版）

希望中学及大学的青年英语教师能利用这本语法和这几本词典，把英语的基础打得更牢，以培养出更好的学生。也希望大部分大学本科及研究生，以及社会上需要使用英语作工具的人，都能利用这套书从语法及词汇两方面提高自己的素养，把有关工作做得更好。

为了发挥这些书的作用，仅仅阅读一遍作用是不大的，要常伴案头，反复阅读，读通读透，要熟练掌握其内容，并结合进行大量阅读及口、笔语实践，反复印证，年深日久才能见效。

我已年逾古稀，但我仍坚持每天工作七八小时。计划还耕耘十年，为大家提供更多学习英语的工具书和参考书。21世纪是中国振兴的时期。要使国家早日富强，使全国人民都过上幸福生活，我们要举国上下加倍努力，要向全世界表明中国人民勤劳苦干的精神。我们要用一个世纪的时间赶上世界上最先进的国家，推动全世界走向更幸福的未来。

张道真

2002年1月1日

目　录

第5章 代 词

第 10 章 虚拟语气

第13章 动词句型

第14章　形容词

第24章 语　序

第25章 省略句

第26章　句型的转换

第27章　标点符号

第1章 概 论

1.1 语法的内容

1.1.1 词法与句法

语法是研究词形变化和句子结构的科学。研究词形变化的部分称为**词法** (Morphology)，如名词的数、格，动词的时态、语态，都属于词法范畴。研究句子结构的部分称为**句法** (Syntax)，如句子的成分、语序、句子种类等，都属于句法范畴。这两部分虽各有不同内容，中间的关系却非常紧密。在谈词法时不可避免要涉及句法，在句法中也有很多部分与词法有关。因此我们在学习的过程中，既要注意这两者之间的差异，又要注意两者之间的联系，机械地把它们分割开对学习是不利的。

1.1.2 语法与词汇

语法虽有一定的独立性，但它与词汇是密不可分的。语法指遣词造句的规律，但它离不开词汇。语法体现在词汇中，而词汇受语法的制约。语法好比是骨架，而词汇好比是血肉，两者也是枝与叶的关系。要形成有机的躯体和繁茂的枝叶，必须把两者结合在一起。在英语入门阶段，主要学词汇，也学少量语法。等词汇积累到一定水平，例如已掌握三四千词，则有必要多学一些语法。头一遍可学一套简明语法。等词汇积累到 6,000 至 8,000 时，可以学一本比较大型的语法。学语法可以帮助更快地积累词汇和掌握词汇，提高语言学习的自觉性。不论是加强语言理解力或使用的能力，语法都可以发挥重要的作用。比较理想的做法是把语法和词汇交叉学习，经过多次反复，才可更深入掌握语言。学词汇大体上是加强感性认识，学语法则是提高理性认识。只有把两者结合起来才能真正掌握语言。这本语法的特点是对词汇给予充分的重视，脱离了丰富的词汇，语法会是一些干巴巴的条文。只有两者并重，才能学到有血有肉生动的语言。

1.2　词　类

1.2.1　词类

英语中的词可根据词义、句法作用和形式特征，分为十大类，称为**词类** (Parts of Speech)，它们是：

词　类	英语名称	作　　用	例　词
名　词	Noun (n.)	人或事物的名称	girl, history
代　词	Pronoun (pron.)	代替名词、数词等	they, many
数　词	Numeral (num.)	表示数目或顺序	nine, third
形容词	Adjective (adj.)	表示人或事物的特征	brave, small
动　词	Verb (v.)	表示动作或状态	hear, know
副　词	Adverb (adv.)	表示动作特征或性状特征	nicely, very
冠　词	Article (art.)	用在名词前，帮助说明其意义	a(n), the
介　词	Preposition (prep.)	用在名词、代词前说明与别的词的关系	for, from
连　词	Conjunction (conj.)	用来连接词与词或句与句	and, if
感叹词	Interjection (interj.)	表示说话时的感情或口气	oh, ah

在这十种词类中，前六种可以在句子中独立担任成分。如名词可用作主语、宾语等，动词可用作谓语等，称为**实意词** (Notional Words)。介词、连词、冠词都不能独立在句子中担任任何成分，称为**虚词** (Form Words)。感叹词一般不构成句子的成分，可以看作特殊的一类。除了这十大类之外，还有表示肯定与否定的 yes 和 no，还有不定式前的**小品词** (Particle) to。实意词大多数在句子中都重读，只有助动词、情态动词和动词 be 以及人称代词等在某些情况下弱读，而虚词一般都不重读。

1.2.2　限定词

关于词类的区分，大多数语法学家都按上述分法。但有一些英国语法学家把一些词归在一起，称为**限定词** (Determiners)，主要指用在名词前帮助说明词义的词，如：

1）冠词 a，an，the；

2）物主代词 my，your，his 等；

3）用作定语的某些不定代词，如 some, any, many, little, few, both, each 等；

4）用作定语的指示代词、疑问代词、关系代词等，如 this，what，whose，whatever 等。

而美国语言学家不作这种区分，用作定语的代词他们干脆称为形容词，如：

This is Helen's room. (代词)

This room is mine. (形容词)

You can have *either* of them. (代词)

You can have *either* one. (形容词)

这样处理在字典中也比较方便。但从实用角度看，统统称为代词也未尝不可。代词也可用作定语，在本书中基本不作过细的区分，只在必要的地方点一点。

1.2.3   分清词类至关重要

要学好英语，第一件事就是分清词类。每学一个词都要知道它属于哪个词类，是名词还是动词，这样区分至关重要。各种词类都有自己的特点，只有知道一个词属于哪个词类，才能正确使用它。同时还应弄清各个句子成分应由哪类词来担任，例如：

主语、宾语多由名词担任：

The *success* of the play has been a great encouragement to him. 剧本的成功给他很大的鼓舞。(作主语)

She wished him *success*. 她祝他成功。(作宾语)

谓语一般由动词担任：

The experiment has *succeeded*. 试验成功了。(作谓语)

定语常由形容词担任：

He is a *successful* writer. 他是一位成功的作家。(作定语)

状语多由副词担任：

He worked *successfully*. 他工作很顺利。(作状语)

从这些句子中可以看出，不分清词类就寸步难行。

1.2.4　同一个词可用作多种词类

同一个词只用作一个词类的情况是相对较少的，多数词都可兼作不同词类，例如：

after 可用作介词、连词、副词、形容词：

It is easy to be wise *after* the event. （谚）做事后诸葛亮是容易的。(作介词)

I will tell them the news *after* you leave. 你走之后我将把这消息告诉他们。(作连词)

A moment *after* there was a knock at his door. 一会儿之后有人敲他的门。(作副词)

In *after* years I became familiar with it. 在以后的岁月中,我对它熟悉起来。(作形容词)

double 可用作形容词、动词、名词和副词：

He again did *double* work that day. 他那天再次干了双份工作。(作形容词)

The price of vegetables has been *doubled* because of the weather. 由于天气不好, 蔬菜的价格翻了一番。(作动词)

Jane and Tom won the mixed *doubles*. 简和汤姆赛赢了混合双打。(作名词)

Many things now cost *double* what they did a year ago. 许多东西现在的价钱是一年前的两倍。(作副词)

round 可用作形容词、介词、副词、名词和动词：

In the middle was a *round* table. 房间中央有一张圆桌。(作形容词)

She looked *round* her in astonishment. 她惊奇地向四周望望。(作介词)

The children gathered *round* to hear the story. 孩子们聚集在四周听故事。(作副词)

Charles was on his *rounds*. 查尔斯正在巡视病房。(作名词)

We *round* our lips to say oo. 我们发"乌"音时,嘴唇要呈圆形。(作动词)

1.2.5　词尾

有些词从词尾上就可看出属于哪个词类,有些词尾是名词的标志,另一些是副词的标志，例如：

构成名词的词尾	-er (fighter)	-or (sailor)	-ist (artist)
	-ant (assistant)	-ee (employee)	-ian (librarian)
	-tion (action)	-ment (government)	-dom (freedom)
	-ness (eagerness)	-ism (socialism)	-ship (friendship)
	-ure (pleasure)	-ty (cruelty)	-ence (reference)
构成形容词的词尾	-ful (careful)	-less (careless)	-ish (selfish)
	-ive (active)	-ous (famous)	-able (drinkable)
	-ible (audible)	-y (easy)	-ese (Chinese)
	-al (natural)	-ent (different)	-ant (important)
构成动词的词尾	-ize (realize)	-en (strengthen)	-ify (simplify)
构成副词的词尾	-ly (luckily)	-ward(s) (homeward)	-wise (likewise)
构成数词的词尾	-teen (fifteen)	-ty (thirty)	-th (fourth)

关于这方面的情况详见第 2 章构词法。

1.3   句 子

1.3.1   句子

句子 (The Sentence) 是表达思想的基本单位，就像家庭是社会的基本单位一样。只有完整的句子才能表达完整的思想。句子由单词组成，但组成时要遵循一定的规律，这就是语法。违反了这些规律，语言即不正确，也就不能正确地表达思想。因此，每句话都牵涉到语法。就书面语而言，每句话的第一个字母要大写，句末应有句号，若是问句，末尾应加问号。如：

China is a great country.   中国是一个伟大的国家。

We love our motherland.   我们热爱我们的祖国。

What's your nationality?   你是哪国人？

汉语也有语法，有些地方与英语是相似的，但在更多地方是不同的，在学习过程中要注意两种语法的异同。

1.3.2　句子成分

句子主要有下面这些成分:

1)主语 (Subject) —— 是一句话的中心,整句话都谈它的情况:

My sister is a nurse.　我姐姐是护士。

Her room is on the fifth floor.　她的房间在 5 楼。

2)谓语 (Predicate) —— 是主语的主要情况,可表示动作,也可表示状态:

She *works* in a hospital.　她在一家医院工作。(动作)

She *knows* a little English.　她懂一点英语。(状态)

3)宾语 (Object) —— 表示动作的承受者,也可表示动作的结果:

Everybody likes *her*.　人人都喜欢她。(动作承受者)

She is writing *a letter* now.　她在写信。(动作的结果)

4)表语 (Predicative) —— 和系动词一道构成谓语:

She is *a conscientious girl*.　她是一个工作认真的姑娘。

5)定语 (Attribute) —— 修饰名词、代词等:

Her hospital isn't very big.　她的医院不大。(修饰名词)

But everyone *in the hospital* works hard.　但医院里人人工作都很努力。(修饰代词)

6)状语 (Adverbial) —— 修饰动词、形容词或副词:

She goes to work *very early*.　她每天很早上班。(修饰动词,very 修饰副词)

She feels *very* happy.　她感到很快乐。(修饰形容词)

此外还有 **同位语** (Appositive)、**插入语** (Parenthesis) 及 **呼语** (Vocative):

This is my sister *Mary*.　这是我妹妹玛丽。(作 my sister 的同位语)

Mary is a good girl, *they say*.　他们说玛丽是个好姑娘。(作插入语)

Sit down, *Mary*.　玛丽,请坐。(作呼语)

1.3.3　句子种类

1)句子按说话目的可分为四类:

a. 陈述句 (Statement) —— 陈述一个事实,或是表明一个看法等:

Beijing is the capital of China.　北京是中国的首都。(事实)

She may be right.　她可能是对的。(看法)

b. 问句 (Question) —— 提出问题:

Where are you from?　你是哪个地方的人?

c. 祈使句 (Imperative) —— 提出命令、请求等:

Don't be late again. 再不要迟到了。(命令)

Take a seat, please. 请坐。(请求)

Take care! 保重!(叮嘱)

d. 感叹句 (Exclamation) —— 表示赞美、惊异等情绪:

What a nice view from this window! 这窗子外面景色多美!

How silly you are! 你真傻!

2) 从结构上说,又可分为三类:

a. 简单句 (Simple Sentences) —— 句子成分都由单词或短语担任,且只有一个主谓结构:

We love our great motherland. 我们热爱我们的祖国。

b. 并列句 (Compound Sentences) —— 句子成分都由单词或短语担任,但有两个或更多互不依从的主谓结构:

Honey is sweet, but the bee stings. (谚)蜂蜜虽甜,但蜜蜂蜇人。

Don't swear, for I dislike swearting. 别骂人,因为我讨厌骂人。

互不依从的主谓结构可称为分句,分句可由并列连词连起来,也可用逗号隔开:

Hurry up, it's getting late. 赶快,时间不早了。

c. 复合句 (Complex Sentences) —— 有一个或更多成分由从句担任:

Do you see what I mean? 你明白我的意思吗?(宾语由从句担任)

Come again when you're free. 有空再来。(状语由从句担任)

1.3.4 问句种类

问句可以分为四类:

1) 一般问句 (General Questions) 通常以 yes, no 回答:

Are you from China? —— Yes, I am. 你是中国人吗? ——是的,我是中国人。

Do you know Chinese? —— No, I don't. 你懂汉语吗? ——不懂。

这类问题一般多用升调 (↗)。

2) 特殊问句 (Special Questions) 都用疑问词开始:

Where have you been? 你到哪里去了?

How do you like the weather here? 你觉得这儿的天气怎样?

这类问句一般多用降调 (↘)。

3）选择问句 (Alternative Questions) 都提出两种可能，问哪种情况属实：

Are you from the South or from the North? 你是南方人还是北方人？

Would you like coffee or tea? 你喝咖啡还是喝茶？

这类问句的语调，一般前半句升，后半句降（↗ ↘）。

4）反意问句 (Disjunctive Questions)，也称Tag Questions (tag指后面的简短问句)。这种问句由两部分组成，前面是陈述句，后面为简短问句，如果前面是肯定句，后面一般为否定问句 (a)，如果前面是否定句，则后面多为肯定问句 (b)：

a. This is your office, isn't it? 这是你的办公室，对吧？

You come from Britain, don't you? 你是英国人，是吗？

You were born in Beijing, weren't you? 你是北京出生的，对吧？

b. Peter hasn't arrived yet, has he? ——No, he hasn't. 彼得还没到，对吧？ ——是的，还没到。

You don't speak Chinese, do you? ——No, I don't. 你不会讲中文，是吧？ ——是的，不会讲。

Your wife isn't in China now, is she? ——But yes, she is. 你妻子不在中国，对吧？ ——不，她在。

在回答b类问题时要注意，如果是肯定回答，先说yes，如果是否定回答，先说no。这和汉语是不同的 (见上面例句译文)。反意问句的语调有两种：

a. 对自己的看法较肯定时，前后都用降调：

Beijing is a beautiful city（↘），isn't it?（↘）

Mary speaks good Chinese（↘），doesn't she?（↘）

b. 对自己的看法不肯定时，前面用降调，后面则用升调：

He'll be back tomorrow（↘），won't he?（↗）

You're staying in a hotel（↘），aren't you?（↗）

〔注〕在特殊情况下，前后都肯定或否定的情况也是有的，如：

So he won't pay his bills, won't he? We'll see about it. 这样说他不肯付钱，是吗？ 咱们走着瞧。（有威胁的意思）

You sold that lovely bracelet, did you? 你把那只漂亮的手镯卖了，是吗？（表示遗憾）

1.4　单词、短语和从句

1.4.1　单词

担任句子成分的，在很多情况下都是单词，可作任何成分：

We are *proud* of *our* country. 我们为我们的国家感到骄傲。
(主语)　　(表语)　　(定语)

Charles *faxed* the *plans* to *us*. 查尔斯把计划用传真发给了我们。
(主语)　(谓语)　　(宾语)　(介词宾语)

有时可用成语动词作谓语，作用和单个动词一样：

What *are* you *looking for*? 你在找什么？

I'*ll take care of* it. 我来处理这事。

动词有时和助动词或情态动词一起用，构成动词短语，如上面两句中的斜体部分。

1.4.2　短语

句子也有很多成分可用 短语 (Phrases) 担任。最常用的短语有：

1）动词短语 (Verbal Phrases)：

What *have* you *been doing*? 你一直在干什么？

We *had better go* there by boat. 我们最好坐船到那里。

2）不定式短语 (Infinitive Phrases)：

It's time *to go to bed*. 该睡觉了。

She loved *to play the piano*. 她喜欢弹钢琴。

3）动名词短语 (Gerundial Phrases)：

His major interest is *painting pictures*. 他的主要兴趣是画画。

I enjoy *working with you*. 我喜欢和你们一道工作。

4）分词短语 (Participial Phrases)：

There's a freeway *connecting the two cities*. 有一条高速公路把两座城市连接起来。

Is there anything *planned for tonight*? 今晚安排什么活动了吗？

5）介词短语 (Prepositional Phrases)：

The boys went swimming *in the river*. 男孩子们到河里游泳。

Who are you talking *to on the phone*? 你在电话里和谁交谈？

6) 名词短语 (Noun Phrases):

Thanks *a lot*.　非常感谢。

Wait *a minute*.　等一会儿。

1.4.3　从句

还有些成分由类似句子的主谓结构担任，称为 **从句** (Clause)，它们有下面几类：

1) that 引导的从句，称为 **that- 从句** (that-clause)，that 有时可以省略：

I admitted *that I'd been wrong*.　我承认我错了。

I'm sorry *(that) I'm late*.　对不起我来晚了。

2) 连接代词或副词引导的从句，可称为 **wh- 从句** (wh-clauses)，因为引导的词多由 wh- 开头：

Do you know *who he is*?　你知道他是谁吗？

He wasn't sure *whether he ought to laugh or cry*.　他感到啼笑皆非。

3) 关系代词型的 what 引导的从句 (详见第 5.5.3 节)：

That's *what I want to know*.　这正是我想知道的。

Write down *what you want to say*.　把你想说的话写下来。

4) 由各种连词引导的从句：

Send me a postcard *when you get there*.　到那里时给我寄张明信片来。

You may stay with us *if you like*.　如果你愿意可以住我们这儿。

5) 由关系代词或关系副词引导的从句，可称为关系从句，也可称为定语从句 (详见第 5.6.1 — 5.6.5 节，第 15.1.6 节)：

The girl *who won the prize* is my cousin.　获奖的姑娘是我表妹。

That's the town *where I was born*.　这就是我出生的城市。

随着在句中的作用不同，从句也可分为：

- 主语从句 (Subject Clause)
- 宾语从句 (Object Clause)
- 表语从句 (Predicative Clause)
- 定语从句 (Attributive Clause)
- 状语从句 (Adverbial Clause)
- 同位语从句 (Appositive Clause)

关于句子结构，后面再作详细讨论。

第2章 构词法

2.1 概 说

2.1.1 英语的主要构词法

英语主要有下面三种构词法:

1) 转化 (Conversion) —— 即由一个词类变为另一个词类:

    water 水 (名) —— water 浇水 (动)

2) 派生 (Derivation) —— 通过加前缀和后缀构成另一个词:

    happy —— unhappy (加前缀)

             happiness (加后缀)

3) 合成 (Compounding) —— 由两个或更多词构成一个词:

    wood 木 + cut 刻 —— woodcut 木刻

    happy + go + lucky —— happy-go-lucky 无忧无虑

2.1.2 一些次要的构词法

英语还有一些次要构词法, 如:

1) 截短法 (Clipping) —— 即把一个词的一部分去掉, 构成一个新词:

    bicycle —— cycle

2) 混合 (Blending) —— 把两个词各取一部分, 混合成一个新词:

    Europe + Asia —— Eurasia 欧亚大陆

3) 缩写 (Abbreviation) —— 把几个词的首字母连在一起:

    British Broadcasting Corporation —— BBC 英国广播公司

4) 反转构词法 (Backformation) —— 把带词尾的名词去掉词尾构成动词:

    editor 编辑 (名) —— edit 编辑 (动)

2.1.3　掌握构词法的重要性

要学好英语，掌握构词法至关重要。它的主要好处是：

1) 帮助辨认词类——通过一些词尾(即后缀)或词头(即前缀)辨别某些词的词类：

care*ful*　　　(带形容词词尾) 细心 (形)
careless*ness*　(带名词词尾) 粗心大意 (名)
*be*little　　　(带动词词头) 贬低 (动)

2) 帮助了解词义——不少词头有特别意思，可以举一反三：

*kilo*gram 千克，公斤 ⟶ *kilo*meter 公里，　*kilo*watt 千瓦
*im*possible 不可能　⟶ *im*polite 不客气，　*im*moral 不道德
diges*tible* 好消化 ⟶ permis*sible* 容许的, collap*sible* 可折叠的

3) 帮助扩大词汇——掌握几千基础词后，通过构词法，可以比较容易地把词汇量扩大到一万以上。

4) 把有关词组合在一起，形成词群，就像单个人组成一个家庭似的，如：

care　　careful　　careless　　carefully　　carelessly
carelessness　　carefulness

courage　　courageous　　courageously　　encourage
encouragement　　discourage　　discouragement

这对记住这些词和使用这些词都有帮助。

5) 建立清楚的词类概念，每学一个词都要知道它的词类，并掌握与它相关的词，左引右联，很容易形成一个词汇网，这是掌握英语的第一步。

6) 建立词与词的联系，大多数词都可用于几个不同的词类，如果知道各种词类的用法，语言能力会得到更大的发展。

2.2　转　化

2.2.1　动词转化为名词

1) 大量动词可转化为名词，有时意思没有太大的变化：

Let me have a *try*. 我来试一试。
We stopped there for a *swim*. 我们在那儿停下来游了一会儿泳。
Can I have a *read* of your paper? 我能看看你的论文吗？
We heard a *shout* and ran to the spot. 我们听到呼叫声就跑到那里。
She had a *cry* about the sad news. 听了这悲惨的消息她哭了一顿。

We went for a *stroll*. 我们出去蹓了蹓。

She gave the girl a *kiss*. 她吻了那女孩一下。

Let's take a *break*. 咱们休息一会儿。

You could make a *guess* at it. 你可以猜一猜。

She gave a long *sigh*. 她长叹了一声。

2) 有些动词转化为名词时意思有些变化:

They have the same *build*. 他们是同样身材。

The *catch* on the door is broken. 门钩坏了。

It was a clever *move*. 这是一着聪明棋。

I bought a bag of bird *feed*. 我买了一包鸟饲料。

The father has the final *say*. 父亲有最后的发言权。

The game ended in a *draw*. 球赛打成了平局。

Our team has a *lead* of two goals. 我们队领先两球。

I'll give you *leave* to stay. 我将同意你留下。

She passed her test at the first *go*. 她一下子就通过了测试。

His heart *beats* were getting weaker. 他的心跳越来越微弱。

3) 可以转化为名词的动词很多，常见的如:

appeal	beat	bite	break	call	change
charge	chat	cry	dance	dread	dream
fall	feel	fight	giggle	grin	groan
guess	hug	kick	kiss	jog	jump
laugh	lead	lie	look	love	pull
push	quarrel	read	remark	respect	ride
ring	run	scream	search	shave	shout
sigh	sip	sleep	smile	smoke	squeeze
start	stay	stroll	swim	talk	taste
try	walk	wash			

2.2.2　名词转化为动词

1) 许多表示物件的名词可以转化为动词，意思也随着有些改变:

She had *booked* three seats on the plane. 她在飞机上订了三个座位。

The usher *seated* us in the front row. 引座员让我们在前排坐下。

The committee is *chaired* by General Lee.　委员会由李将军任主席。

He *pinned* the notice on the blackboard.　他把通知钉在黑板上。

The expedition will *map* the South Pole.　探险队将绘制南极的地图。

The policeman *bagged* the thief.　警察把小偷抓到了。

How can you *pocket* her insults?　你怎么能忍受她的侮辱？

The results of the experiments are *tabled* at the back of the book.　实验的结果列成了表放在书后。

Picture yourself in his situation.　设想你处于他的地位。

2) 表示身体某部分的名词也可用作动词：

His name *headed* the list.　他的名字列在名单之首。

He *handed* the glass of beer to Grandpa.　他把那杯啤酒递给了爷爷。

Many of his friends *backed* his plan.　他的许多朋友都支持他的计划。

The boy *shouldered* the basket of fruits.　男孩揹那筐水果。

He asked us not to *finger* the tomatoes.　他让我们别摸西红柿。

A policeman *eyed* him suspiciously.　一位警察怀疑地瞧着他。

I can't *stomach* such behavior.　我不能容忍这种行为。

He *elbowed* his way to where we stood.　他推挤着来到我们站的地方。

The puppy *nosed* at my arm.　小狗嗅我的手臂。

We have missed the bus, so we'll have to *foot* it.　我们没搭上汽车，因此我们得步行去。

3) 表示一类人的名词也可用作动词：

Lydia had always *nursed* a grievance against her cousin.　丽迪亚对她的表哥一直怀有抱怨情绪。

Stop *fooling* about and do something useful.　不要胡混了，干点有益的事。

He is paid by the police to *spy* on other students.　他受警方雇用来监视其他学生。

He *doctored* the information on his passport.　他窜改了他护照上的内容。

He *fathered* many inventions.　他发明了许多东西。

It's hard to *pilot* a boat in rough waters.　在汹涌的水域中领航是困难的。

They *pioneered* the Northwest Territory.　他们探察了西北地区。

The older boys *lord* it over the younger ones.　大孩子欺压小孩子。

She *mothered* two children and adopted a third.　她生了两个孩子，又领养了一个。

4）一些其他实物名词也可用作动词：

The library *houses* 600,000 books. 这个图书馆藏书 60 万册。

He is *rooming* with my friend Smith. 他和我的朋友史密斯一起住。

Cherry trees *flower* in the early spring. 樱桃树早春时开花。

The boxer *floored* his opponent. 拳击师把对手击倒在地。

They have *dammed* that river up. 他们在那条河上筑了一道坝。

This money should *bridge* you over till next month. 这笔钱应当可以帮你度过困难维持到下个月。

He got up and *dusted* his trousers. 他站起身把裤子上的尘土掸掉。

She *oiled* herself with suntan lotion. 她在身上擦了防晒油。

I was so hungry that I *wolfed* down my meal. 我饿得狼吞虎咽地吃饭。

Don't *monkey* with the machinery. 不要瞎摆弄机器。

5）甚至某些抽象名词也可用作动词：

The injustice of this *angered* him. 这事的不公平使他气愤。

I am *hungering* for news from you. 我渴望得到你的消息。

The bomb was *timed* to go off at midnight. 那枚炸弹定时在午夜爆炸。

He *thirsted* for knowledge. 他渴望获得知识。

We plan to *winter* in Italy. 我们计划在意大利过冬。

We *summered* by Lake Geneva. 我们在日内瓦湖畔避暑。

Then we *lunched* at the Connaught Restaurant. 然后我们在克努餐馆吃午饭。

I am going to *breakfast* with him tomorrow. 我明天将和他一起吃早饭。

The enemy *stormed* the castle. 敌人猛攻城堡。

The guests *numbered* more than a hundred. 客人有一百多。

2.2.3 形容词等转化为动词

1）有些形容词可以转化为动词：

The city *quieted* down again. 城市又平静下来。

Shelley was unable to *calm* her down. 雪莱没法使她平静下来。

He *slowed* down at the crossroads. 他在十字路口慢了下来。

Please *warm* up the cold meat. 请把冷肉热一下。

In the bright sunlight she had to *narrow* her eyes. 在强烈的阳光下她只得眯上眼睛。

They *idled* away two hours doing nothing. 他们浪费了两小时什么也没干。

He pretends to *busy* himself writing. 他假装忙着写东西。

Don't *dirty* your new dress. 不要把你的新衣服弄脏了。

We must *lower* our expenses. 我们必须降低开支。

Living conditions have *bettered* a great deal. 居住条件改善了许多。

2) 还有少数其他词类也可用作动词:

They *forwarded* his mail to his new address. 他们把他的信件转寄到他的新地址。

This will help to *further* the sciences. 这会有助于发展科学。

The firm's employees have *downed* tools. 公司的雇员都罢工了。

They *upped* the price of petrol. 他们提高了汽油价格。

Truth will *out*. 真相总有大白之日。

I *second* the nomination. 我赞成这项任命。

2.2.4　一些其他转化的情况

1) 有些形容词可以转化为名词:

I enjoy the *quiet* of the country. 我喜欢农村的恬静。

Her *calm* in the face of disaster is amazing. 她在灾难前的冷静态度令人惊讶。

The temperature reached a new *high*. 气温达到了新的高度。

Profits have reached a new *low* this month. 本月的利润降到了新低点。

I think you are in the *right*. 我认为你是对的。

A *single* to London, please. 请给我一张去伦敦的单程票。

There are about 4,000 Chinese *nationals* in the city. 这座城市有四千华裔居民。

This was a custom among the *ancients*. 这是古代人的一种习俗。

He failed his *finals*. 他决赛输了。

Few *whites* live in West Africa. 很少白人住在西非。

2) 有些形容词可以转化为副词:

The eagle flies *high*. 鹰飞得很高。

Her head was bent *low*. 她头垂得低低的。

She had gone *dead* tired. 她极其疲惫。

You can live *cheaper* in the smaller towns. 住在小些的城市里费用低些。

He sells his goods very *dear*. 他的货物卖得很贵。

The blow struck him *full* in the face. 这一拳正打在他脸上。

Spring draws *near*. 春天日益临近。

Come *closer* so that I can see you. 走近一些，让我能看见你。

How *slow* he drives! 他车开得真慢!

Are you staying *long*? 你会待久吗?

3) 还有一些其他转化情况:

They asked him to give a *repeat* performance. 他们让他再表演一次。(动—形)

She was a very *forward* young lady. 她是一个很大胆的年青女子。(副—形)

During the war we had to *black* out all our windows. 在战争期间我们得实行灯火管制。(形—动)

She *paled* when we told her the news. 我们把消息告诉她时，她脸都白了。(形—动)

He walked *north*. 他朝北走。(名—副)

I'll drive you *home*. 我开车送你回家。(名—副)

2.2.5 转化中语音的变化

1) 大多数词转化时语音没有变化，但有些词转化时重音有变化:

	动词(重音多在后面)	名词(重音多在前面)
accent	/æk'sent/ 重读	/'æksənt/ 重音
combine	/kəm'baɪn/ 合并	/'kɒmbaɪn/ 康拜因(收割机)
compress	/kəm'pres/ 压紧	/'kɒmpres/ 止血垫布
conduct	/kən'dʌkt/ 指挥	/'kɒndəkt/ 行为
conflict	/kən'flɪkt/ 与…冲突	/'kɒnflɪkt/ 冲突
contest	/kən'test/ 争夺，竞争	/'kɒntest/ 比赛
contrast	/kən'træst/ 形成对比	/'kɒntræst/ 对比
convict	/kən'vɪkt/ 定罪	/'kɒnvɪkt/ 囚犯
digest	/daɪ'dʒest, dɪ-/ 消化	/'daɪdʒest/ 摘要，文摘
discount	/dɪs'kaʊnt/ 打折扣	/'dɪskaʊnt/ 折扣

escort	/ɪsˈkɔːt/ 护送	/ˈeskɔːt/ 护送人	
export	/ekˈspɔːt, ɪk-/ 出口	/ˈekspɔːt/ 出口(商品)	
extract	/ɪkˈstrækt/ 提取	/ˈekstrækt/ 提取物	
ferment	/fɜːˈment/ 发酵	/ˈfɜːmənt/ 酵素	
import	/ɪmˈpɔːt/ 进口，输入	/ˈɪmpɔːt/ 进口	
misprint	/ˌmɪsˈprɪnt/ 印错	/ˈmɪsprɪnt/ 印错处	
increase	/ɪnˈkriːs/ 增加	/ˈɪnkriːs/ 增加	
insult	/ɪnˈsʌlt/ 侮辱	/ˈɪnsʌlt/ 侮辱	
perfume	/pə(ː)ˈfjuːm/ 洒香水	/ˈpɜːfjuːm/ 香水，香气	
permit	/pə(ː)ˈmɪt/ 允许	/ˈpɜːmɪt/ 许可证	
present	/prɪˈzent/ 赠送，上演	/ˈprezənt/ 礼物	
produce	/prəˈdjuːs/ 生产	/ˈprɒdjuːs/ 农产品	
progress	/prəˈgres/ 前进，进展	/ˈprəʊgres/ 进步，进展	
protest	/prəˈtest/ 抗议	/ˈprəʊtest/ 抗议(行动)	
rebel	/rɪˈbel/ 造反，反抗	/ˈrebl/ 造反者，判乱者	
record	/rɪˈkɔːd/ 记录，录音	/ˈrekɔːd/ 记录，唱片	
refill	/riːˈfɪl/ 加(油)	/ˈriːfɪl/ 笔心	
refuse	/rɪˈfjuːz/ 拒绝	/ˈrefjuːs/ 垃圾	
reject	/rɪˈdʒekt/ 拒不接受	/ˈriːdʒekt/ 不合格产品	
survey	/səˈveɪ/ 斟查，考察	/ˈsɜːveɪ/ 斟查，考察	
suspect	/səˈspekt/ 怀疑，疑心	/ˈsʌspekt/ 嫌疑犯	
torment	/tɔːˈment/ 折磨	/ˈtɔːment, -mənt/ 折磨	
transfer	/trænsˈfɜː/ 转(学)，调往	/ˈtrænsfɜː/ 转学，调动	
transport	/trænˈspɔːt/ 运送	/ˈtrænspɔːt/ 运输	

也有个别词作形容词时重音在前，作动词时重音在后：

作形容词(重音在前)	作动词(重音在后)
absent /ˈæbsənt/ 缺席，不在	/æbˈsent/ 缺席
abstract /ˈæbstrækt/ 抽象的	/æbˈstrækt/ 提取
perfect /ˈpɜːfekt/ 完美的	/pɜːˈfect/ 使完善

个别双音节词作两种词类时重音不变，如：

comment /ˈkɒment/　　contact /ˈkɒntækt/　　debate /dɪˈbeɪt/

2) 另外有些词转换词类时，词尾读音有变化，有时拼法也有变化：

作名词	作动词
abuse /ə'bjuːs/ 辱骂	abuse /ə'bjuːz/ 辱骂
advice /əd'vaɪs/ 劝告	advise /əd'vaɪz/ 劝
belief /bɪ'liːf/ 信仰	believe /bɪ'liːv/ 相信
excuse /ɪk'skjuːs/ 借口	excuse /ɪk'skjuːz/ 原谅
grief /griːf/ 悲痛	grieve /griːv/ 感到悲痛
half /hɑːf/ 一半	halve /hɑːv/ 分为两半
house /haʊs/ 房子	house /haʊz/ 提供住所
mouth /maʊθ/ 嘴	mouth /maʊð/ 装腔作势地说
relief /rɪ'liːf/ 宽慰减轻	relieve /rɪ'liːv/ 减轻(疼痛)
shelf /ʃelf/ 架子	shelve /ʃelv/ 搁置
thief /θiːf/ 小偷	thieve /θiːv/ 偷窃
use /juːs/ 用处	use /juːz/ 用

个别词拼法有差异而读音都不变，如：

practice　练习(名)　　　　　　　　practise　练习(动)

在美国作动词或名词都用 practice 这个形式。

3) 有少数词在转变成另一词类时，元音也发生变化，有的音不变但拼法变了：

名 词	动 词
blood /blʌd/ 血	bleed /bliːd/ 流血
food /fuːd/ 食物	feed /fiːd/ 喂食
gold /gəʊld/ 黄金	gild /gɪld/ 镀金
proof /pruːf/ 证据	prove /pruːv/ 证明
speech /spiːtʃ/ 讲话，发言	speak /spiːk/ 说话
tale /teɪl/ 故事	tell /tel/ 告诉

还有个别词可兼作形容词和动词，词形不变但读音不同：

名 词	动 词
close /kləʊs/ 近	close /kləʊz/ 关上

live /laɪv/ 活的　　　　　　　　　live /lɪv/ 生活
separate /'seprɪt/ 不同的　　　　　separate /'sepəreɪt/ 分开

2.3 派　生

2.3.1 构成名词的后缀

1) 构成名词的后缀很多，常见的有下面这些：

后　缀	例　词			
-ability	stability	availability	advisability	capability
-age	shortage	marriage	leakage	drainage
-al	denial	betrayal	dismissal	withdrawal
-an	American	Russian	Asian	African
-ance	attendance	guidance	performance	assistance
-ant	applicant	consultant	immigrant	participant
-ary	dictionary	missionary	boundary	commentary
-ate	doctorate	consulate	electorate	directorate
-ation	examination	education	decoration	temptation
-cy	accuracy	efficiency	privacy	bureaucracy
-dom	freedom	kingdom	wisdom	boredom
-ee	employee	absentee	refugee	trustee
-eer	engineer	mountaineer	auctioneer	profiteer
-ence	difference	existence	preference	diligence
-er	driver	writer	reporter	dancer
-ery	bribery	embroidery	mockery	machinery
-ese	Chinese	Japanese	Portuguese	Vietnamese
-ess	actress	princess	goddess	hostess
-ful	handful	spoonful	bagful	busful
-hood	childhood	neighborhood	motherhood	knighthood
-ian	magician	musician	historian	mathematician
-ibility	possibility	visibility	responsibility	flexibility
-ing	feeling	shopping	reading	sightseeing
-ion	action	decision	collection	creation

-ism	Marxism	socialism	pessimism	heroism
-ist	capitalist	communist	racist	novelist
-ity	prosperity	equality	formality	majority
-let	piglet	booklet	starlet	bracelet
-man	fireman	policeman	chairman	Englishman
-ment	arrangement	government	development	assignment
-ness	happiness	sadness	weakness	bitterness
-or	actor	sailor	director	visitor
-ry	jewelry	slavery	bribery	bravery
-ship	friendship	leadership	ownership	sportsmanship
-ty	loyalty	safety	cruelty	penalty
-ure	failure	departure	pleasure	pressure
-ware	software	glassware	silverware	hardware
-work	housework	schoolwork	needlework	paperwork
-y	modesty	difficulty	discovery	inquiry

2）还有一些次要的构成名词的后缀：

后　缀	例　词		
-aholic, oholic	bookaholic	workaholic	chocoholic
-archy	anarchy	monarchy	hierarchy
-arian	librarian	vegetarian	humanitarian
-cide	suicide	homicide	genocide
-craft	aircraft	hovercraft	spacecraft
-ette	cigarette	usherette	kitchenette
-folk	menfolk	countryfolk	townsfolk
-gram	diagram	telegram	kilogram
-graph	autograph	paragraph	photograph
-hand	farmhand	factory-hand	garage-hand
-head	spearhead	bridgehead	letterhead
-ial	denial	burial	memorial
-itis	arthritis	hepatitis	appendicitis
-logue	dialogue	monologue	catalogue
-mania	egomania	kleptomania	megalomania
-mate	schoolmate	roommate	playmate

-meter	barometer	speedometer	thermometer
-metre	centimetre	kilometre	millimetre
-monger	fishmonger	warmonger	rumourmonger
-ocracy	autocracy	democracy	bureaucracy
-ocrat	aristocrat	bureaucrat	democrat
-ology	biology	psychology	ecology
-phone	earphone	saxophone	telephone
-scape	landscape	moonscape	riverscape

2.3.2　构成形容词的后缀

1) 构成形容词的后缀也很多，常见的有下面这些：

后　缀	例　词			
-able	valuable	lovable	miserable	comfortable
-al	cultural	national	logical	original
-an	American	Cuban	African	Korean
-ant	important	pleasant	ignorant	tolerant
-ary	momentary	imaginary	honorary	legendary
-ate	fortunate	affectionate	passionate	collegiate
-ed	excited	amazed	bearded	indebted
-en	woolen	golden	wooden	earthen
-ent	different	dependent	existent	consistent
-ese	Chinese	Japanese	Burmese	Portuguese
-ful	beautiful	hopeful	cheerful	useful
-ian	Canadian	Belgian	Jordanian	Palestinian
-ible	permissible	contemptible	negligible	collapsible
-ic	realistic	poetic	historic	economic
-ical	classical	geographical	theatrical	economical
-ing	amusing	convincing	misleading	neighboring
-ish	Irish	childish	selfish	foolish
-ive	active	effective	attractive	expensive
-less	endless	homeless	useless	harmless
-like	childlike	warlike	dreamlike	lifelike

-ly	friendly	orderly	costly	leisurely
-ous	courageous	furious	nervous	dangerous
-some	troublesome	lonesome	tiresome	quarrelsome
-wide	worldwide	nationwide	area-wide	company-wide
-worthy	trustworthy	praiseworthy	noteworthy	respect-worthy
-y	rainy	windy	dirty	muddy

2）还有一些次要的构成形容词的后缀：

后　缀	例　词		
-based	market-based	class-based	home-based
-bound	duty-bound	westbound	London-bound
-conscious	self-conscious	class-conscious	safety-conscious
-fold	twofold	eight-fold	tenfold
-free	carefree	tax-free	pollution-free
-headed	hot-headed	clear-headed	muddle-headed
-made	hand-made	man-made	US-made
-minded	open-minded	absent-minded	liberal-minded
-most	innermost	topmost	foremost
-ological	biological	ecological	ideological
-poor	nutrient-poor	oxygen-poor	resource-poor
-proof	waterproof	soundproof	bullet-proof
-related	job-related	drug-related	race-related
-rich	carbon-rich	fibre-rich	protein-rich
-side	bedside	fireside	riverside
-sized	apple-sized	fist-sized	postcard-sized
-stricken	panic-stricken	horror-stricken	poverty-stricken
-ular	muscular	triangular	molecular

2.3.3 一些构成其他词类的后缀

1）构成副词的后缀：

后　缀	例　词		
-ly	clearly	finally	gradually	suddenly
-down	headdown	belly-down	face-down	palm-down

-first	head-first	nose-first	feet-first	heel-first
-ward(s)	homeward	onward(s)	westward(s)	backward(s)
-wise	likewise	clockwise	length-wise	anticlockwise

2) 构成动词的后缀:

后缀	例　词			
-ate	activate	originate	motivate	hyphenate
-en	widen	sharpen	brighten	sweeten
-ify	simplify	purify	notify	justify
-ize	apologize	emphasize	criticize	modernize

3) 构成数词的后缀:

后缀	例　词			
-teen	thirteen	fourteen	fifteen	sixteen
-ty	twenty	thirty	forty	fifty
-th	fifth	twelfth	eighth	thirtieth

2.3.4　一些较为常见的前缀

1) 可用来改变词类的前缀:

a- 加在名词前构成形容词或副词:

asleep　　aboard　　aside　　ashore　　ablaze

be- 加在名词或形容词前构成动词:

befriend　bewitch　behead　belittle　bedim

em- 加在名词等前构成动词:

embark　embed　embody　empower　embitter

en- 加在名词前构成动词:

endanger　encourage　enrage　enforce　enslave

en- 加在形容词前构成动词:

enrich　enlarge　ennoble　endear　enable

out- 加在名词或形容词前构成动词:

outflank　outnumber　outpace　outwit　outsmart

2）有些前缀可用来构成反义词:

de- (非…)	de-emphasize decolonize	decentralize depoliticize	demilitarize dehydrate	demobilize declassify
dis- (构成动词)	dislike disapprove	disbelieve disobey	distrust displease	disagree disappear
dis- (构成名词)	disbelief discomfort	discontent disobedience	disorder disrespect	dishonour disadvantage
dis- (构成形容词)	disloyal discourteous	dishonest disreputable	disinterested dissimilar	disorderly disproportionate
il-	illegal	illogical	illiterate	illegitimate
im-	impatient	impolite	impossible	immature
in-	incapable inability	informal injustice	inadequate inadequacy	independent insecurity
ir-	irresolute	irresponsible	irresistible	irregular
mal-	malnutrition	maladjusted	maltreatment	maladministration
non-	non-essential non-smoker	non-economic non-specialist	non-profit non-violent	non-resident non-competitive
un- (构成形容词)	unable unconscious	uncertain unfortunate	untidy unlucky	unsafe uncomfortable
un- (构成名词)	uncertainty unacceptability	untidiness unfairness	unhappiness unpleasantness	unwillingness unbelievability
un- (构成副词)	unwillingly uncertainly	unconsciously unluckily	unfairly unofficially	unfortunately untidily
un- (构成动词)	undress unpack	unbutton uncover	untie undo	unlock unwrap
un- (构成分词)	unexpected unchanging	unfinished unhesitating	unprepared uninviting	unprecedented untrusting

3）一些表示特定意思的前缀

大部分前缀都表示特定意思，较常见的有：

前　缀	意　思	例　词	
all-	纯，全是	all-wool	all-steel
		all-female	all-new
	各个	all-age	all-season
		all-purpose	all-weather
anti-	反，抗	anti-fascist	anti-racist
		anti-war	anti-abortion
		anti-aircraft	anti-cancer
		anti-pollution	anti-inflation
		antibiotic	antibody
		antidote	antiseptic
arch-	大的	archduke	archangel
		archbishop	archdeacon
	头号的	arch-enemy	arch-rival
		arch-villain	arch-traitor
auto-	自动的	automatic	auto-timer
		auto-record	auto-reverse
	自己的	autobiography	autograph
		autonomous	autonomy
	汽车的	automobile	auto-industry
		auto work	auto sport
bi-	双，二	bilingual	bilateral
		bigamy	bifocals
bio-	生物的	biochemical	biological
		biologist	biotechnology
centi-	百分之一的	centimeter	centigram
		centiliter	centigrade
co-	共同(做某事)	co-author	co-chairman
		co-pilot	co-founder
		co-direct	co-operate
		co-exist	co-edit
counter-	反	counter-measure	counter-attack

		counter-strike	counter-revolution
double-	双	double-decker	double-barrelled
		double-breasted	double-bed
	哄骗	double-cross	double-dealing
		double-talk	double-dealer
down-	往下	downhill	downward(s)
		downriver	downstairs
	恶化	downturn	downfall
		downgrade	downcast
ever-	一直，不断	ever-present	everlasting
		ever-widening	evergrowing
	越来越	ever stronger	ever-bolder
		ever-greater	ever-faster
ex-	以前的	ex-president	ex-husband
		ex-lover	ex-wife
extra-	特别的，超	extra-bright	extra-strong
		extra-large	extra-thin
	以外的	extra-curricular	extra-mural
		extra-marital	extra-territorial
fore-	前部的	foredeck	forehead
		foreleg	forearm
	预见的	foresight	foretell
		forecast	foresee
free-	自由的	free-flowing	free-moving
		free-floating	free-running
full-	完全	full-scale	full-speed
		full-grown	full-strength
	全部，整个	full-time	full-year
		full-size	full-page
half-	半	half-asleep	half-finished
		half-circle	half-pay
		half-moon	half-empty
		half-French	half-sister
hand-	用手的	hand-made	hand-operated
		handwritten	hand-wash

		handbag	handcart
		handbaggage	handbook
hydro-	水力的	hydro-power	hydro-electric
		hydro-energy	hydrophobia
ill-	不好的	ill-health	ill-humour
		ill-luck	ill-will
		ill-tempered	ill-natured
		ill-mannered	ill-bred
	不适宜的	ill-timed	ill-informed
		ill-educated	ill-chosen
inter-	之间的	international	inter-city
		inter-racial	intercontinental
	相互的	interchange	interact
		interlink	interrelate
kilo-	千	kilogram	kilowatt
		kilometre	kilohertz
mal-	不良的	maladjusted	malnourished
		maladroit	malformed
		malfunction	malnutrition
		malpractice	maldistribution
man-	由人，人	man-made	man-devised
		manpower	mankind
	对人	man-killer	man-eating
		manhunt	manslaughter
mid-	中间(指时间)	midday	mid-summer
		midnight	mid-century
	中部(指空间)	midair	mid-Europe
		midocean	mid-Wales
milli-	千分之一	milligram	millimeter
		milliliter	milliamp
mini-	小的，微型的	minicab	minibus
		mini-computer	miniskirt
mis-	错误地	misjudge	misuse
		misunderstand	misprint
	错误的	misconception	misinformation

		mismanagement	misunderstanding
new-	新近	newborn	newfound
		new-wedded	new-baked
news-	新闻	newscast	newsletter
		newspaper	news-stand
over-	过分地	overeat	over-reach
		over-do	overestimate
	过于	over-anxious	over-eager
		over-cautious	over-confident
	过量的	overdose	overcharge
		overweight	overwork
	压倒	overcome	overpower
		overthrow	overrule
	其他意思	oversee	overseas
		overlook	overcoat
post-	…之后的	post-election	post-medieval
		post-liberation	post-renaissance
	邮(政)的	postmark	postcard
		post-box	postcode
pre-	…之前的	pre-war	pre-birth
		pre-marital	pre-revolution
	预见，在前	prejudge	preview
		predetermine	predecease
	预先…的	pre-arranged	prepaid
		pre-planned	prefabricated
pro-	亲…，支持…的	pro-government	pro-communist
		pro-West	pro-abortion
re-	重新	re-open	rewrite
		remarry	rebuild
	再次	reappear	reconsider
		rediscover	review
self-	自我…的	self-educated	self-appointed
		self-employed	self-imposed
	自(我)的	self-defence	self-criticism

		self-analysis	self-control
	自己…的	self-locking	self-cleaning
		self-winding	self-regulating
semi-	半…的	semi-automatic	semi-naked
		semi-official	semi-liquid
	半	semi-circle	semi-annual
		semi-conductor	semi-darkness
sub-	次…，下一级的	subcontinent	subcommittee
		subdivision	sub-heading
	下面的，潜	subway	subconscious
		submarine	sub-current
	不…够的	subnormal	subfertile
		substandard	sub-literacy
super-	极…的	super-clever	super-cheap
		super-friendly	super-sensitive
	超级的	superpower	supermarket
		superstar	superman
	超…的	supersonic	supernatural
		supernormal	supernational
	其他意思	superfluous	superstition
		supervise	superstructure
tele-	远距离的	telephone	telescope
		television	telecommunication
trans-	从…到	transport	transfer
		transplant	transmit
		translate	transform
		transcribe	transition
	穿越	transAmerica	transatlantic
		trans-Siberian	trans-Alaska
under-	不足的	under-developed	under-financed
		undernourished	underestimate
	下面的	underground	underwear
		underline	undersigned
	下一级的	undergraduate	undersecretary

		underlibrarian	undermanager
	其他意思	understand	undertake
		undermine	underworld
uni-	单一的	unilateral	unisex
		unify	unity
up-	在…上方的	upside	uphill
		upriver	upstairs
	改进，更新	update	upgrade
		uprate	upsurge
	打乱	upset	uproar
		uproot	uprising
	其他意思	upright	uphold
		upheaval	upbringing
vice-	副的	vice-chairman	vice-premier
		vice-minister	vice-consul
well-	…得很好的	well-behaved	well-written
		well-dressed	well-educated
	很…的	well-known	well-deserved
		well-loved	well-respected
	其他意思	well-read	well-informed
		well-paid	well-received

2.3.5　一些用得较少的前缀

还有一些用的较少的前缀，它们也各有自己的意思，如：

前　缀	意　思	例　词		
aero-	空中的	aeroplane	aerodynamic	aeronautics
agro-	农业的	agrology	agronomy	agrochemical
ante-	在…前的	anteroom	antechamber	antecedent
astro-	太空的	astronaut	astrology	astrophysics
audio-	听觉的	audiovisual	audio-tape	audio-cassette
cardi-	心脏的	cardiac	cardiologist	cardiogram
chron-	时间的	chronic	chronology	chronicle

contra-	反，防	contrary	contradiction	contraceptive
cross-	横跨	cross-country	cross-channel	cross-harbour
deci-	十进的	decimal	decimeter	deciliter
eco-	生态的	ecology	ecosystem	eco-technology
electro-	电的	electronic	electrocute	electrode
Euro-	欧洲的	Euro-bank	Euro-currency	Europarliament
fresh-	刚刚…的	fresh-baked	fresh-fried	fresh-made
geo-	与地有关的	geology	geography	geophysics
homo-	相同的	homogeneous	homo-sexual	homonym
hyper-	极为…的	hyperactive	hyper-modern	hyper-alert
mega-	兆，极大的	megahertz	megaton	megastar
micro-	微…的	microscope	microfilm	microcomputer
mock-	假装的	mock-fight	mock-modesty	mock-sadness
mono-	单一的	monologue	monosyllabic	monogamy
multi-	多…的	multilateral	multinational	multi-purpose
neo-	新	neo-classical	neo-colonialism	neo-Nazism
neur(o)-	神经的	neurology	neurobiologist	neurosurgeon
once-	一度	once-famous	once-powerful	once-popular
pan-	泛…	pan-American	pan-Arab	pan-European
para-	副，准	paratyphoid	paramedic	paramilitary
	空降	parachute	paratrooper	paragliding
phon-	声音的	phonetics	phonology	phonograph
poly-	多…的	polysyllabic	polytechnic	polygamy
pseudo-	仿…，假	pseudo-metal	pseudo-friend	pseudonym
quad-	四…的	quadrangle	quadrilateral	quadruped
quasi-	近似…的	quasi-academic	quasi-official	quasi-religious
socio-	社会	socio-economic	socio-political	sociolinguistic
sur-	超过	surcharge	surplus	surpass
sym(n)-	相同的	sympathy	synonym	synchronize
tech-	技术	technical	technician	technique
therm-	热	thermotherapy	thermometer	thermoelectric
tri-	三	triangle	trilateral	trilogy
ultra-	极，外	ultra-secret	ultra-smart	ultraviolet
video-	图像的	videotape	videodisc	video-recorder

2.4　合　成

2.4.1　合成名词

1) 合成名词数量最多，其中大多数由名词＋名词构成：

air conditioner 空调机	air raid 空袭
alarm clock 闹钟	arms race 军备竞赛
assembly line 装配线	baby-sitter 看孩子的人
bank account 银行账户	birth control 节制生育
blood donor 献血者	blood pressure 血压
book case 书柜	bookmark 书签
brain drain 人才流失	burglar alarm 防盗警报器
bus stop 公共汽车站	can opener 开罐器
car park 停车场	contact lens 隐形眼镜
corporal punishment 体罚	cotton wool 药棉
credit card 信用卡	death penalty 死刑
estate agent 地产经纪人	fancy dress (ball) 化装舞会
generation gap 代沟	greenhouse effect 温室效应
health center 医疗中心	heart attack 心脏病发作
heart failure 心力衰竭	hire purchase 分期付款
income tax 所得税	labour force 劳动力
labour market 劳动市场	letter-box 信箱
mail order 邮购定单	mineral water 矿泉水
mother-tongue 母语	nail varnish 指甲油
news bulletin 新闻公报	package holiday 一揽子度假计划
pen friend 笔友	pocket money 零用钱
police station 警察分局	post office 邮局
sign language 手语	soda water 苏打水，汽水
sound barrier 音障	table tennis 乒乓球
tea bag 袋泡茶	tea-table 茶几
telephone number 电话号码	toilet paper 卫生纸
unemployment benefit 失业救济金	welfare state 福利国家
X-ray X 光	youth hostel 青年旅舍

2) 也有不少合成名词由形容词＋名词组成:

central bank 中央银行	civil rights 公民权力
compact disc 激光唱盘	current affairs 时事
dry cleaning 干洗	fast food 快餐
first-aid 急救	French fries 炸薯条
general knowledge 人所共知的事	general public 公众
higher education 高等教育	high heels 高跟(鞋)
high jump 跳高	high school 中学
human being 人	human rights 人权
industrial relations 劳资关系	modern languages 现代语言
musical instrument 乐器	natural history 自然历史
natural resources 自然资源	nervous breakdown 神经失常
old age 老年	old hand 老手
open air 露天	open letter 公开信
personal computer 个人电脑	polar bear 白熊，北极熊
public sector 公营部门	remote control 遥控
social security 社会保险	social services 社会服务(事业)
social studies 社会研究	social work(er) 社会工作(者)
solar system 太阳系	stainless steel 不锈钢
vocal cord 声带	yellow pages (电话簿)黄页部分

3) 有些合成词由动词的 -ing 形式和另一词构成，如:

a. dining room 餐厅	drawing pin 图钉
driving license 驾驶执照	frying pan 煎锅
sleeping bag 睡袋	parking meter 停车计时器
swimming pool 游泳池	washing machine 洗衣机
washing powder 洗衣粉	writing paper 信纸
b. air-conditioning 空调	central heating 集中供暖
data processing 数据处理	family planning 计划生育
food poisoning 食物中毒	sight-seeing 观光
weightlifting 举重	window-shopping 逛商店
wind surfing 风帆冲浪	zebra crossing 斑马线(人行横道)

4）还有些合成名词以其他方式或三个词构成：

by-product 副产品	comrade-in-arms 战友
cover-up 掩盖事实	fork-lift truck 叉车
looker-on 旁观者	one-parent-family 单亲家庭
air-traffic control 空中交通管理	do-it-yourself 自己动手(手册)
women's movement 妇女运动	turnover 营业额
hocus-pocus 愚弄手法	jibbery-pockery 骗局
show-off 爱卖弄的人	passer-by 路旁经过的人
bird of prey 猛禽	bride-to-be 准新娘
bring-and-buy sale 慈善性义卖	merry-go-round 旋转木马
pickpocket 扒手	break-water 防波堤
take-off 起飞	go-between 中间人
breakthrough 突破	get-together 联欢会
downfall 垮台	outbreak 爆发
well-being 福利	back-seat driver 指手画脚瞎指挥者
good-for-nothing 不中用的人	touch-me-not 凤仙花
commander-in-chief 总司令	editor-in-chief 总编

关于合成名词还可参阅第 22.2 节。

2.4.2　合成形容词

1）合成形容词很多由过去分词或带 -ed 词尾的词构成，如：

absent-minded 心不在焉的	air-conditioned 有空调的
bow-legged 弓形腿的	breast-fed 吃人奶长大的
broken-hearted 心碎的	clean-shaven 胡子刮得很干净的
clear-cut 明确的	cold-blooded 冷血的
deep-seated 牢固的	double-barreled 双筒的(猎枪)
double-breasted 双排扣的	duty-bound 义不容辞的
far-fetched 牵强的	full-blown 盛开的
full-grown 已经长成的	gilt-edged 金边的
good-tempered 脾气好的	grey-haired 头发灰白的
hand-picked 精选的	high-heeled 高跟的
home-made 家里制作的	ill-advised 不明智的

kind-hearted 心肠好的　　　　　left-handed 惯用左手的
light-hearted 心情轻松的　　　　long-lost 长期丢失的
low-paid 工资低的　　　　　　　mass-produced 成批生产的
middle-aged 中年的　　　　　　muddle-headed 糊里糊涂的
narrow-minded 心胸狭窄的　　　new-born 新生的
old-fashioned 老式的　　　　　　one-sided 片面的
panic-stricken 惊慌失措的　　　　ready-made 现成的
remote-controlled 遥控的　　　　right-angled 直角的
short-handed 人手短缺的　　　　short-lived 短命的
short-sighted 近视的，眼光短浅的　short-tempered 急躁的
silver-plated 镀银的　　　　　　so-called 所谓的

2）也有不少合成形容词由动词的 -ing 形式和另一词构成：

close-fitting 紧身的　　　　　　easy-going 好说话的
epoch-making 划时代的　　　　　face-saving 护面子的
far-reaching 深远的(影响)　　　　good-looking 漂亮的
hard-wearing 耐磨的　　　　　　hard-working 勤劳的
labor-saving 节省劳动力的　　　　long-lasting 耐用的
long-standing 由来已久的　　　　long-suffering 长期受苦的
man-eating 吃人的　　　　　　mouth-watering 令人垂涎的
never-ending 没完没了的　　　　off-putting 令人不快的
record-breaking 创记录的　　　　smooth-running 运转平稳的
smooth-talking 花言巧语的　　　well-meaning 好心好意的

**3）还有一些合成形容词由"形容词＋名词"(a) 或"名词等＋形容词"(b)
构成：**

a. deep-sea 深海的　　　　　　first-class 头等的
front-page 头版的　　　　　　full-length 全身大小的
full-scale 全力(进攻)　　　　　last-minute 最后一分钟的
late-night 深夜的　　　　　　long-distance 长途(电话)
long-range 远程的　　　　　　loose-leaf 活页的
one-way 单向(通行)的　　　　　part-time 部分时间的
present-day 当今的　　　　　　second-hand 二手的
second-rate 二流的　　　　　　top-secret 绝密的

b. all-mighty 万能的   brand-new 全新的
bullet-proof 防弹的   duty-free 免税的
ice-cold 冰冷的   interest-free 免利息的
knee-deep 水深及膝的   lead-free 无铅的
nuclear-free 无核(区)   top-heavy 头重脚轻的
trouble-free 没有麻烦的   world-famous 世界著名的

4) 还有一些其他形式的合成形容词，特别是一些包含副词的合成词：

a. 动词＋副词：

broken-down 破旧不堪的   built-in 嵌在墙内的(橱柜)
built-up 盖满房子的(地区)   cast-off 扔掉的
drive-in 开车进去的(电影院)   laid-back 冷静放松
run-down 年久失修的   see-through 透明的

b. 副词＋名词：

off-budget 预算外的   off-campus 校园外的
off-guard 失去警惕的   off-hand 不经准备的
off-hour 休息时间   off-peak 非高峰时期
out-door 户外的   up-hill 上山的

c. 其他形式：

all-out 全力以赴的   all-round 全面的
ever-victorious 常胜的   face-to-face 面对面的
out-and-out 彻头彻尾的   ten-minute 十分钟的
third-floor 三层楼上的   three-hour 三小时的
two-year-old 两岁大的   well-off 富裕的

2.4.3　合成动词及合成副词

1) 合成动词主要有下面几类：

a. 名词＋动词：

baby-sit 看孩子   eavesdrop 偷听
ghost-write 为别人代写   proof-read 校对
sleep-walk 梦游   spoon-feed 用勺喂，灌输
tape-record 用磁带录下来   water-ski 滑水

b. 副词＋动词：

overcharge 超额收费   overeat 吃得太多

overhear 听见(别人说话)　　overthrow 推翻

undergo 经历　　underwrite 承担，同意保证

uphold 维护　　uplift 提起，振奋

c. 形容词或副词＋动词：

back-pedal 往后退缩　　backtrack 往回走

black-list 列入黑名单　　cross-examine 盘问

ill-treat 虐待　　short-change 少找钱

short-circuit 发生短路　　white-wash 粉刷

d. 其他形式的合成动词：

blow-dry 吹干　　court-martial 军法审判

deep-fry 炸　　dillydally 浪费时间

pooh-pooh 认为愚蠢可笑　　spin-dry 甩干

stir-fry 翻炒　　tittle-tattle 闲聊

2) 合成副词为数不多，大多用作状语：

She almost did all this *single-handed*. 这一切几乎是她单枪匹马干的。

He returned home *empty-handed*. 他毫无所获地回家了。

They ran *helter-skelter* down the road. 他们沿着公路慌乱地逃走了。

Files were scattered *higgledy-piggledy* about the office. 文件档案杂乱地散落在办公室里。

〔注1〕在构成合成词时，是否加连字号，是一个麻烦问题。有的需加连字号，如 word-formation，letter-writing，boat-ride；有时不加连字号，如 washing machine，dance hall，book review；有时甚至连写，如 handwriting，haircut，input。有时不同字典会有不同处理法，总的说来，美国英语中连字号比英国英语用得少，比较现实的办法是注意观察和多查字典。由三个以上词构成的合成词一般都加连字号，如 a state-of-the-art aircraft design (最新式的飞机设计)。

〔注2〕有一种词，前后两部分声音很近似，称为 **叠声词** (Reduplicatives)：

zigzag 弯弯曲曲(形)　　chit-chat 闲聊(名)

walkie-talkie 步话器(名)　　dillydally 磨蹭，耗费时间(动)

wish-washy 淡而无味(形)　　shilly-shally 犹犹豫豫(动)

hotch-potch 大杂烩(名)　　higgledy-piggledy 乱七八糟(形，副)

criss-cross 纵横交错(形)　　fiddle-faddle 胡闹(动)

helter-skelter 慌乱地(副)　　tittle-tattle 无聊闲谈(动)

tip-top 极好的(形)　　goody-goody 假正人君子(名，形)

2.5 一些次要的构词法

2.5.1 截短语

1) 截短语可以截去前面一部分，如:

telephone —— phone 电话   violincello —— cello 大提琴

aeroplane —— plane 飞机   helicopter —— copter 直升飞机

omnibus —— bus 公共汽车   bicycle —— cycle 自行车

2) 也可截去后面一部分:

advertisement —— ad 广告   exposition —— expo 博览会

gentlemen's —— gents 男厕所   public house —— pub 酒店

professor —— prof 教授   stereophonic —— stereo 立体声的

mathematics —— math 数学   professional —— pro 职业的

co-operative —— co-op 合作社   preparatory —— prep 预料的

examination —— exam 考试   laboratory —— lab 实验室

memorandum —— memo 备忘录   taxicab —— taxi 出租车

television —— telly 电视机   submarine —— sub 潜水艇

rubber-shoes —— rubbers 胶鞋   zoological garden —— zoo 动物园

kilogram —— kilo 公斤   veterinary surgeon —— vet 兽医

有个别词前后各截去一部分，如:

refrigerator —— fridge 冰箱   influenza —— flu 流感

有时几个词合成一个词，如:

a prefabricated house —— prefab 预制房屋

a popular song singer —— pop-singer 流行歌手

2.5.2 混合

混合是从两个词中各取一部分，混在一起构成一个新词:

news broadcast ⟶ newscast 新闻广播

parachute troops ⟶ paratroops 伞兵

television broadcast ⟶ telecast 电视播送

electro + execute ⟶ electrocute 上电刑处死

transfer + resistor ⟶ transistor 半导体

travel catalogue ⟶ travelogue 旅游影片，游记

International Criminal Police ——→ Interpol 国际刑警组织

motorist's hotel ——→ motel 汽车旅馆

teleprinter exchange ——→ telex 电传

breakfast and lunch ——→ brunch 早午餐，早饭午饭一起吃

American Indian ——→ Amerind 美国印第安人

medical care ——→ medicare 美国老人医疗保险

smoke and fog ——→ smog 烟雾

biographical picture ——→ biopic 传记片

psychological warfare ——→ psywar 心理战

multi-university ——→ multiversity 综合大学

2.5.3　缩写

1）缩写词多数按字母读音：

TV /ˈtiː ˈviː/ 电视	TB /ˌtiː ˈbiː/ 肺结核
FBI 联邦调查局	CIA 美国中央情报局
CID 英国刑事调查部	KGB 克格勃(前苏联国家安全委员会)
APEC 亚太经合组织	
EEC 欧洲经济共同体	MIT 麻省理工学院
VIP 重要人物，贵宾	DDT 滴滴涕杀虫剂
CNN 美国有线新闻电视网	CBS 美国哥伦比亚广播公司
PRC 中华人民共和国	U.S.A. 美国
UK 联合王国，英国	UN 联合国
IMF 国际货币基金组织	WHO 世界卫生组织
WTO 世界贸易组织	WB 世界银行
LA 洛杉矶	DC 哥伦比亚特区
Ph D 博士学位	M.A. 硕士学位
B.A.(或 B.S.) 学士学位	MP 英国国会议员

2）缩写词中有少数像单词一样拼读，称为 acronyms（首字母缩拼词）：

NATO /ˈneɪtəʊ/ 北约　　　　　OPEC /ˈəʊpek/ 石油输出国组织

Laser /ˈleɪzə/ 激光　　　　　radar /ˈreɪdə/ 雷达

UFO /ˈjuːfəʊ/ 不明飞行物，即飞碟（亦可读作 /ˌjuː ef ˈəʊ/）

UNESCO /juˈneskəʊ/ 联合国教科文组织

BASIC 或 Basic /ˈbeɪsɪk/ 计算机初学者通用符号指令码

2.5.4   反转构词法

通常是先有词根，再加词尾(后缀)。而有少数词，先有名词，再去掉词尾构成动词，这和通常构词的步骤相反，称为 **反转构词** 法 (Backformation)。例如：

先有名词	去词尾构成动词
editor 编辑	edit 编辑
television 电视	televise 电视播送
typewriter 打字机	typewrite 打字
sleep-walker 梦游者	sleep-walk 梦游
day-dreamer 做白日梦的人	day-dream 做白日梦
housekeeper 管家	housekeep 管家
window-shopping 逛商店	window-shop 逛商店不买东西
sightseeing 观光游览	sightsee 观光游览
mass-production 成批生产	mass-produce 成批生产
dry-cleaning 干洗	dry-clean 干洗

第3章 名 词

3.1　名词的种类

3.1.1　专有名词和普通名词

名词可分为两大类:
- **专有名词**　(Proper Nouns)
- **普通名词**　(Common Nouns)

专有名词主要指人名、地名及某些类人和事物专有的名称, 如:

1) 人名: Diana, Mrs Green, President Clinton, Einstein, Gorky;

2) 地名: Beijing, West Lake, the Yellow River, Bond Street, Broadway;

3) 某类人的名称: Americans, Russians, Democrats, Jews;

4) 某些抽象事物的名称: English, Buddhism, Christianity, NATO;

5) 月份、周日名及节日名称: May, Saturday, Easter, New Year's Day;

6) 书名、电影及诗歌的名称: A Tale of Two Cities, Gone with the Wind, Ode to the West Wind (西风颂), (la) Marseillaise (马赛曲);

7) 对家人等的称呼: Mum, Dad, Auntie, Uncle Tom。

专有名词的第一个字母要大写。

专有名词以外的名词都是普通名词, 普通名词又可分为四类:
- **个体名词**　(Individual Nouns)
- **集体名词**　(Collective Nouns)
- **物质名词**　(Mass Nouns 或 Material Nouns)
- **抽象名词**　(Abstract Nouns)

其中个体名词和集体名词可以用数来计算, 称为 **可数名词** (Countable Nouns), 而物质名词和抽象名词一般都不能用数来计算, 称为 **不可数名词** (Uncountable Nouns)。因此名词的类别可以下表表示:

$$\text{名词}\begin{cases}\text{专有名词}\\[4pt]\text{普通名词}\begin{cases}\text{个体名词}\\\text{集体名词}\end{cases}\Big\}\text{可数名词}\\\phantom{\text{普通名词}}\begin{cases}\text{物质名词}\\\text{抽象名词}\end{cases}\Big\}\text{不可数名词}\end{cases}$$

3.1.2　个体名词

个体名词指作为个体而存在的人或东西，可以指具体的人或物，如：

He has two *aunts*. 他有两个姑姑。

There are hundreds of high-rise *apartments* in the *city*. 这座城市有数以百计的高层公寓楼。

Pandas are found in Sichuan. 熊猫出在四川。

Most *classrooms* have *computers*. 多数教室里都有电脑。

也可指抽象东西，如：

We've lived here for twenty *years*. 我们在这里住了二十年了。

A new *century* has just begun. 一个新的世纪刚刚开始。

She has read lots of *fairy tales*. 她看过大量的童话故事。

I had a *dream* last night. 我昨晚做了一个梦。

个体名词有复数形式，如 weeks, problems；单数形式可以和 a(n) 连用，如 a week，a problem，an old man。

3.1.3　集体名词

集体名词表示由个体组成的集体，下面是一些常见的集体名词：

aristocracy 贵族(总称)	army 军队
audience 听众，观众	bacteria 细菌
cast 演员(总称)	committee 委员会
community 社区	company 公司；全体船员
council 议事机构；理事会	crew 船员(总称)
data 资料	enemy 敌人
family 家，家庭	flock 鸟群
gang 一伙人	government 政府

group 小组，团体	herd 牛群
jury 陪审团；评委会	media 传媒(总称)
navy 海军	nobility 贵族(总称)
opposition 反对派	police 警方
press 新闻界	proletariat 无产阶级
public 公众	staff 全体员工
team 队；组	youth 青年人(总称)

集体名词有时作单数看待，有时作复数看待。一般说来，视为整体时作单数看待，想到它的成员时作复数看待：

作单数看待	作复数看待
His family *is*n't large. 他家人不多。	His family *are* all music lovers. 他家的人都喜欢音乐。
The enemy *has suffered* heavy losses. 敌人遭受严重损失。	The enemy *are* in flight. 敌人正在逃窜。
The government's *planning* to build a dam here. 政府打算在这里建一座水坝。	The government *are discussing* the proposal. 政府在讨论这项建议。
The public *was* unlikely to support it. 公众支持它的可能性不大。	The public *were deceived* by the newspapers. 公众受到报纸的蒙骗。

在不少情况下，集体名词后单复数动词都可以用，没有什么差别：

The school's teaching staff *is (are)* excellent. 该校的师资很不错。

The audience *was (were) excited* by the show. 观众对演出甚感激动。

The local council *are (is)* in charge of repairing roads. 当地的政务会负责道路的维修工作。

The jury *are (is)* about to announce the winners. 评委会将宣布优胜者名单。

有少数集体名词通常用作单数：

The entire community *is* behind the appeal. 整个社区都支持这项呼吁。

The opposition *was* quick to reply to the charge. 反对派迅速对指控作出回答。

Our company *is sending* him to work in Berlin. 我们公司将派遣他去柏林工作。

The gang *is being hunted* by the police. 这伙匪徒正受警察追捕。

个别集体名词则多作复数看待:

Bacteria *are* often a cause of disease.　细菌常引起疾病。

The police *are looking* for him.　警察正在找他。

3.1.4　物质名词

物质名词指无法分为个体的东西,下面是一些常见的物质名词:

beer	brandy	cake	cheese	cloth	coal
coffee	coke	cotton	curry	detergent	disinfectant
dye	fabric	fertilizer	fuel	fur	glue
ice	ink	insecticide	iron	jam	jelly
juice	liqueur	lotion	meat	medicine	metal
milk	oil	ointment	ore	paint	paper
perfume	plastic	poison	preservative	rain	ribbon
salad	salt	sand	sauce	snow	soap
soil	soup	steel	sugar	tea	whisky
water	wine	wood	wool	yarn	yoghurt

一般说来,物质名词是不可数的,因而没有复数形式。但有一些特殊情况:

1) 有些物质名词可用作可数名词,表示"一份"、"一杯":

Two strong black *coffes*, please.　请给我两份浓咖啡,不要加奶。

Three *beers*, please.　请来三杯啤酒。

A chocolate *ice-cream* for me.　给我一份巧克力冰淇淋。

2) 有些物质名词可作可数名词,表示"一种":

It was a special *tea* which tasted of orange blossoms.　这是一种特别的茶,有橘子花味。

It was a delicious Californian *wine*.　那是一种美味的加州红酒。

Stainless *steels* contain about 12% of chromium.　不锈钢含有约百分之十二的铬。

3) 个别物质名词可用于复数形式或有特殊意义:

She forbids any vessels to enter her territorial *waters*.　她禁止任何船只进入其领海。

It was now the time of the spring *rains*.　现在是春天雨季的时候。

Here are the *snows* of last year.　这是去年的积雪。

3.1.5　抽象名词

抽象名词主要表示一些抽象概念，一般不可数，因此没有复数形式，前面也一般不加不定冠词 a(n)。下面是一些常见的抽象名词：

absence	access	age	agriculture	anger
beauty	behaviour	cancer	capacity	childhood
comfort	concern	confidence	courage	death
democracy	depression	design	duty	economy
education	energy	environment	evil	existence
experience	failure	faith	fashion	fear
finance	freedom	fun	growth	happiness
health	help	history	independence	industry
insurance	intelligence	joy	justice	labour
loneliness	love	luck	magic	marriage
mercy	music	nature	patience	peace
philosophy	pleasure	policy	poverty	power
pride	protection	purity	reality	relief
religion	respect	safety	security	silence
sleep	strength	status	technology	time
trade	training	transport	travel	trust
truth	violence	waste	wealth	weather
welfare	work	worth	youth	

在多数情况下，这种名词常用于单数形式，不加任何冠词：

Safety first!　安全第一！

He's learning French for *fun*.　他学法语是为着好玩。

He never had any *education*.　他从未受过教育。

They had *justice* on their side.　正义在他们一边。

I wish you *luck*.　我祝你好运。

It's wonderful *weather*.　天气好极了。

但有时也加定冠词 the (a)，或不定冠词 a 或 an (b)：

a. He works hard for *the welfare* of the poor.　他为穷人的福利努力工作。

The oppressive *weather* lasted only a few days.　闷热天气只持续了几天。

I shall never forget *the beauty* of that lake.　我永远不会忘记那座湖的秀美景色。

She didn't have *the courage* to ask him. 她没有勇气问他。

b. There's *a beauty* in simplicity. 朴实之中有一种美。

He had always had *a warm affection* for me. 他对我一直有一种温馨的情感。

After *a brief peace*, war broke out again. 经过一段短暂的和平时期，战争又爆发了。

Switzerland adopted *a policy* of neutrality. 瑞士采取了中立政策。

关于抽象名词前冠词的用法，下面将作详细的讨论。

3.1.6　可数名词与不可数名词

1) 可数名词与不可数名词的区分是英语中的一个重要问题，因为它牵涉到一个名词的形式和它前面加不加冠词以及加哪种冠词的问题。多数名词情况是比较简单的，例如桌子、椅子、房间、人，在英语及汉语中都是可数名词，使用就比较简单。但也有不少名词在英语中是不可数的，而在汉语中却是可数的，例如下面这些都是不可数名词，在使用时要小心：

furniture: We haven't got much furniture. 我们的家具不多。

equipment: His firm supplies kitchen equipment. 他的公司提供厨房设备。

clothing: There is nothing but clothing in the cupboard. 这柜子里只有衣服。

news: No news is good news. (谚)没有消息就是好消息。

information: His task was to collect information. 他的任务是收集情报。

machinery: How much machinery has been installed? 安装了多少机器?

如果要表示"一件"这类概念，前面得加"a __ of"这类定语：

a piece of furniture　一件家具	a piece of equipment　一件设备
an article of clothing　一件衣裳	a piece of information　一则信息
an item of news　一条新闻	(但 a machine　一台机器)

这类定语是非常有用的，在许多不可数名词前都可以用它：

a cake of soap　一块肥皂	a tube of toothpaste　一管牙膏
a loaf of bread　一只面包	a slice of cake　一块蛋糕
a can of beer　一罐啤酒	a length of cloth　一段布料
a sheet of paper　一张纸	a jar of jam　一罐果酱
a lump of sugar　一块方糖	a bottle of brandy　一瓶白兰地

a ball of wool　一团毛线	a pot of tea　一壶茶
a bar of chocolate　一大块巧克力	a cube of ice　一块冰
a pinch of salt　一小撮盐	a grain of sand　一粒沙子
a stick of candy　一根棒糖	a grain of rice　一粒米
a large sum of money　一大笔钱	a bar of gold　一根金条
a piece of thread　一根线	a small amount of sugar　少量白糖
an expanse of water　一片水域	a stretch of land　一片土地
a portion of soup　一份汤	a bowl of rice　一碗米饭
a blade of grass　一根草	a carton of milk　一盒牛奶
a fit of anger　一顿脾气	a suit of clothes　一套衣服
a stroke of good luck　一阵好运	a burst of applause　一阵掌声
a ray of hope　一线希望	a shower of criticism　一阵批评

这类定语还可修饰复数名词：

a packet of cigarettes　一包香烟	a bunch of keys　一串钥匙
a pair of pants　一条裤子	a pair of spectacles　一副眼镜
a set of books　一套书	a series of problems　一系列问题
a pack of cards　一副纸牌	a host of difficulties　一大堆困难
a pack of wolves　一群狼	a herd of deer　一群鹿
a busful of children　一车孩子	a handful of sweets　一把糖果
a basket of peaches　一筐桃子	a dish of peanuts　一碟花生
a bag of cashew nuts　一包腰果	a swarm of ants　一大群蚂蚁
a packet of envelopes　一沓信封	a pack of lies　连篇的谎言
a pride of lions　一群狮子	a herd of elephants　一群大象

2）有些名词可以兼作可数名词和不可数名词，例如：

a. 有些名词兼作物质名词和个体名词：

物质名词	个体名词
glass　玻璃	a glass　玻璃杯
copper　铜	a copper　铜币(板)
tin　锡	a tin　(英)罐头，听头
paper　纸	a paper　报纸，证件，论文
iron　铁	an iron　熨斗
wood　木头	a wood　树林
gold　金子	a gold　金牌

b. 有些抽象名词可兼作个体名词:

抽象名词	个体名词
youth 青春	a youth 青年人
relation 关系	a relation 亲属
authority 权威	an authority 权威人士
power 力量	a power 大国
necessity 必要性	a necessity 必需品
democracy 民主	a democracy 民主国家
beauty 美	a beauty 美人，美的东西
pleasure 高兴，愉快	a pleasure 使人感到愉快的事

3) 有些个体名词可转而用作抽象名词:

个体名词	抽象名词
The rooms are to let. 房间出租。	There's no room for doubts. 没有怀疑的余地。
They are building a new school. 他们在盖一所新学校。	He finished school at sixteen. 他十六岁中学毕业。
Is there a church round here? 这一带有教堂吗?	Grandpa never went to church. 爷爷从不做礼拜。
There was a big double bed. 有一张大双人床。	Time for bed. 该睡觉了。
Butterflies flattered among the flowers. 蝴蝶在花间飞舞。	The roses are in flower. 玫瑰开花了。
How many holidays do you have in a year? 你们一年有多少节假日?	They went on holiday last week. 他们上星期度假去了。
There's a general hospital in the area. 这地区有一家综合医院。	When did she leave hospital? 她什么时候出院的?

4) 英语中有许多对词，一个可数，一个不可数，例如:

可数名词	不可数名词
a poem 一首诗	poetry 诗歌(总称)
a machine 一台机器	machinery 机器(总称)
a job 一件工作	work 工作

a laugh　一个笑声	laughter　笑声
a permit　许可证	permission　允许
a garment　一件衣裳	clothing　衣裳(总称)
a bag (case)　一件行李	luggage (英)，baggage (美)行李
a loaf　一只面包	bread　面包

从上面例子可以看出，名词的可数与不可数是一个复杂问题。有不少词只有查较好的词典才能弄清有关问题。平常看书时也要留心，有意识地积累这方面的知识。

3.2　名词复数

3.2.1　一般名词的复数形式

1) 一般名词的复数以加 -s 或 -es 的方式构成，构成的方法如下：

情　　况	加　法	例　　词
一般情况	加 -s	brothers　flowers　schools　books
以 s，x，ch，sh 结尾的词	加 -es	buses　foxes　watches　dishes
以"辅音＋y"结尾的词	变 y 为 i 再加 -es	lady → ladies　country → countries (但 boys，toys，ways)

-(e)s 词尾的读法如下：

情　　况	读法	例　　词
在 /p/，/t/，/k/，/f/ 等清辅音后	/s/	cups /kʌps/，hats /hæts/，cakes /keɪks/， roofs /ru:fs/
在 /s/，/z/，/ʃ/，/tʃ/， /dʒ/ 等音后	/ɪz/	glasses /ˈglɑːsɪz/，faces /ˈfeɪsɪz /，roses /ˈrəʊzɪz/， ashes /ˈæʃɪz/，watches /ˈwɒtʃɪz/，ages /ˈeɪdʒɪz /
其他情况	/z/	boys /bɔɪz /，girls /gɜːlz/，ladies /ˈleɪdɪz /， rooms /ru:mz/

以 th 结尾的词，原读 [θ]，加词尾后多读 [ð]，如：

mouth /maʊθ/ —— mouths /maʊðz/

path /pɑːθ/ —— paths /pɑːðz/

但也有些这类词加词尾后读音不变：

length /leŋθ/ —— lengths /leŋθs/

month /mʌnθ/ —— months /mʌnθs/

length /leŋθ/ —— lengths /leŋθs/

另有个别词可变可不变：

youth /ju:θ/ —— youths /ju:θs/ 或 /ju:ðz/

truth /tru:θ/ —— truths /tru:θs/ 或 /tru:ðz/

2）以 -o 结尾的词，许多加 -es 构成复数，特别是一些常用词：

heroes	potatoes	tomatoes	echoes	tornadoes
torpedoes	dominoes	vetoes	mosquitoes	Negroes
mangoes	buffaloes	volcanoes		

但下面几类词只加 -s：

a. 以 "元音 + o" 或 "oo" 结尾的词：

videos   radios   studios   folios   oratorios   embryos

zoos   bamboos   kangaroos   cuckoos   taboos

b. 一些外来词，特别是音乐方面的词：

pianos   concertos   solos   sopranos   tobaccos

commandos   mottos   cellos   banjos   manifestos

c. 一些缩写词和专有名词：

kilos   photos   memos   micros   Eskimos   Filipinos

有个别词加两种词尾都可以，如：

archipelago(e)s   halo(e)s   cargoes (英)   cargos (美)

3）以 -f 或 -fe 结尾的词，通常变 f 为 v，再加 -(e)s，读作 /vz/：

half —— halves	leaf —— leaves	loaf —— loaves
self —— selves	thief —— thieves	wolf —— wolves
shelf —— shelves	calf —— calves	elf —— elves
wife —— wives	knife —— knives	life —— lives
housewife —— housewives		

有些只加 -s，读作 /fs/：

roofs   cliffs   proofs   beliefs   chiefs

有个别词加 -s 或 -es 都可以：

scarf —— scarfs 或 scarves   dwarf —— dwarfs 或 dwarves

wharf —— wharfs 或 wharves   hoof —— hoofs 或 hooves

handkerchief —— handkerchiefs 或 handkerchieves

3.2.2　不规则的复数形式

1) 有些常用名词有不规则的复数形式:

man —— men	woman —— women /ˈwɪmɪn/
tooth —— teeth	foot —— feet
child —— children	goose —— geese
mouse —— mice	ox —— oxen
louse —— lice	

由 man 和 woman 构成的合成名词也有不规则的复数形式:

policeman —— policemen	policewoman —— policewomen
gentleman —— gentlemen	chairwoman —— chairwomen

penny 有两个复数形式:

pennies 指硬币: He had a few pennies in his pocket. 他口袋里有几个一便士的硬币。

pence 指钱数: The apples were 75 pence a kilo. 苹果 75 便士一公斤。

2) 有些外来词有不规则的复数形式 (也就是它们原来的复数形式):

analysis —— analyses /-siːz/ 分析	basis —— bases /-siːz/ 基础
crisis —— crises /-siːz/ 危机	criterion —— criteria 标准
medium —— media 媒体	phenomenon —— phenomena 现象
stratum —— strata 阶层	thesis —— theses /-siːz/ 论文

另外有些外来词有两个复数形式,一是原来的形式,一是英语化的形式:

单数形式	原来的复数形式	英语化的复数形式
sanatorium	sanatoria	sanatoriums 疗养院
formula	formulae /-liː/	formulas 公式
antenna	antennae /-niː/	antennas 天线
index	indices /-dɪsiːz/	indexes 附录
cactus	cacti	cactuses 仙人掌

还有少数外来词已完全英语化, 如 albums, appreratuses, geniuses。

3.2.3　一些其他复数形式

1) 合成词的复数形式:

多数合成词以在末尾加 -(e)s 词尾的方式构成复数:

theatre-goers　　　fire-engines　　　forget-me-nots

有少数合成词，把 -(e)s 词尾加在主体词后面：

editor*s*-in-chief　　　　looker*s*-on　　　　runner*s*-up

以 man 和 woman 构成的合成词变成复数时，把 man 和 woman 改成复数：

fireman ——　firemen　　　　　　chairwoman —— chairwomen

在以 man 和 woman 修饰时，这两个词要连同主体词一起变：

man-servant ——　men-servants　　woman doctor —— women doctors

2) 一些其他复数形式：

a. 年份 —— 加 -s 或 -'s：

the 1990s（或 1990's）/'naɪtiːn 'naɪntɪz/ （二十世纪）九十年代

b. 缩写词 —— 加 -s 或 -'s：

VIPs 或 VIP's （very important persons 贵宾们）

MPs 或 MP's （members of Parliament 国会议员们）

c. 英语字母 —— 加 's：

Dot your i's and cross your t's. 记得在 i 上加点，在 t 上加横。

'Committee' has two m's, two t's and two e's. committee 一词中有两个 m，两个 t 和两个 e。

3.2.4　单复数同形的情况

1) 英语中有少数名词，复数形式与单数形式相同：

a sheep / a flock of sheep　　　　an aircraft / ten aircraft

a goldfish / a few goldfish

常见的单复数同形的词有：

a. 某些动物的名称，如：

bison 野牛　　　deer　　　reindeer　　　cod 鳕鱼

salmon 鲑鱼　　　fish　　　trout 鳟鱼

b. craft 及由它构成的合成词：

craft　　　aircraft　　　hovercraft 气垫船　　　spacecraft 太空船

c. 表示某国人的名词：

He is a *Chinese*. They are all *Chinese*. 他是中国人。他们都是中国人。

I know a *Japanese* (a few *Japanese*). 我认识一个(几个)日本人。

His wife is a *Swiss*. Her parents are both *Swiss*. 他妻子是瑞士人，她的父母都是瑞士人。

d. 还有另外一些词：

species:

　　It's a rare *species* of fish. 这是一种罕见的鱼种。

　　Both *species* live in the lake. 两个品种都生活在这湖中。

means:

　　It's an effective *means* of communication. 它是高效的通讯手段。

　　All possible *means* have been tried. 各种可能的办法都尝试过了。

works（工厂）:

　　There has been an accident at the *works*. 这家工厂出了事故。

　　There are some iron *works* near the river. 江边有几家炼铁厂。

offspring:

　　She's the *offspring* of a scientist. 她是一位科学家的后代。

　　Their *offspring* are all very clever. 他们的后代都很聪明。

2）一些特殊情况:

某些词有特殊情况：

a. hair 通常用于单数形式，是头发的总称：

　　Go and get your *hair* cut. 去把头发理一理。

　　In the *hair* she had pinned a red rose. 她在头发上插了一朵红玫瑰。

可加 -s 词尾表示几根头发：

　　There're *hairs* on your jacket. 你的上衣上有几根头发。

　　He had a few white *hairs*. 他有几根白头发。

b. fruit 通常用单数形式：

　　He does not eat much *fruit*. 他不太多吃水果。

　　Apples, oranges and bananas are *fruit*. 苹果、橘子和香蕉都是水果。

也可加复数词尾表示不同种类的水果：

　　There the most common *fruits* are pear, apple and peach. 那儿最普通的水果是梨、苹果和桃。

用于抽象意义时，可用单数形式，也可用复数形式：

　　I hope your hard work will bear *fruit*. 我希望你的努力会取得成果。

　　We have thus defended the *fruits* of our victory. 就这样我们保卫了自己的胜利果实。

c. fish 通常单复同形，复数后也可加 -es：

　　I caught a *fish* (two fish). 我捕到一条(两条)鱼。

　　He caught three little *fishes*. 他抓到三条小鱼。

在表示不同种类的鱼时多加 -es:

We'll go and look at the *fishes* in the aquarium. 我们到水族馆去看(各种各样的)鱼。

3.2.5　通常用于复数形式的词

1) 有些名词通常用于复数形式, 其中有些由两个对等部分构成 (a), 有些以 -ing 结尾 (b), 还有一些其他情况 (c):

a. scissors 剪刀　　　　　trousers 裤子　　　　　pants 裤子
　　shorts 短裤　　　　　　jeans 牛仔裤　　　　　briefs 三角裤
　　compasses 两脚规　　　scales 天平　　　　　　pliers 钳子
　　tongs 夹钳　　　　　　glasses 眼镜　　　　　　spectacles 眼镜
　　earphones 耳机　　　　braces 背带　　　　　　cords 灯心绒裤
　　binoculars 双筒望远镜　knickers 女内裤　　　　sunglasses 太阳镜
　　tights 紧身裤　　　　　overalls 工装裤　　　　trunks 游泳衣
　　pyjamas 睡衣裤　　　　underpants 内裤　　　　slacks 便装裤
　　specs 眼镜　　　　　　nail-clippers 指甲刀

b. belongings 所有物　　　surroundings 环境　　　tidings 消息
　　winnings 赢得的钱　　　savings 积蓄　　　　　findings 调查结果
　　clippings 剪下的东西　　earnings 挣的钱　　　　writings 作品
　　sweepings 扫拢的垃圾　　doings 行为　　　　　　shavings 刨花

c. contents 目录　　　　　arms 武器　　　　　　statistics 统计资料
　　fireworks 烟火　　　　remains 残余部分　　　assets 资产
　　congratulations 祝贺　thanks 感谢　　　　　oil-colours 油画
　　living-quarters 住宅区　clothes 衣服　　　　　outskirts 城郊
　　valuables 贵重物品　　ashes 灰烬　　　　　　riches 财富
　　amends 修补　　　　　annals 编年史　　　　archives 档案室
　　arrears (未付)尾数　　bowels 肠　　　　　　dregs 渣滓
　　stairs 楼梯　　　　　　guts 胆量　　　　　　particulars 细节
　　dominoes 骨牌　　　　goods 货物　　　　　　greens 青菜
　　tropics 热带　　　　　dues 应交的费　　　　brains 头脑
　　armed forces 武装部队

2) 还有一些名词虽以 -s 结尾，却并不是复数形式，例如：

a. 某些疾病的名称：

diabetes 糖尿病	measles 麻疹	mumps 腮腺炎
rabies 狂犬病	rickets 佝偻病	shingles 带状疱疹
syphilis 梅毒		

b. 某些学科的名称：

physics 物理学	linguistics 语言学	economics 经济学
statistics 统计学	acoustics 声学	aeronautics 航空学
electronics 电子学	genetics 遗传学	mathematics 数学
logistics 后勤学	obstetrics 产科学	mechanics 力学
aerodynamics 空气动力学	thermodynamics 热力学	

c. 某些活动的名称：

acrobatics 杂技	athletics 体育运动	cards 打纸牌
billiards 台球	politics 政治活动	darts 掷镖游戏
draughts 国际跳棋		

3) 有些名词用于某个意义时通常用复数形式，例如：

the authorities 当局	see the sights 观光
go to the pictures 去看电影	put on airs 摆架子
natural resources 自然资源	personal effects 个人用品
in high spirits 情绪高昂	internal affairs 内部事务
working conditions 工作条件	good manners 有礼貌
serve refreshments 用点心招待	hold talks 举行谈判
travel expenses 路费	diplomatic relations 外交关系
show one's papers 出示证件	

3.3 名词所有格

3.3.1 名词所有格构成法

1) 英语中有许多名词可加 's 来表示所有关系，如：

She's my *wife's* cousin. 她是我妻子的表妹。

此形式称为**名词所有格** (The Possessive Case of Nouns)，'s 称为 apostrophes /əˈpɒstrəfi ˈes/。

2）'s 词尾的加法可概括如下：

a. 在单数情况下把 's 直接加上去：

Philip's new address　菲力普的新地址

her sister-in-law's mother　她嫂子的母亲

the editor-in-chief's telephone number　总编辑的电话号码

b. 若名词已有复数词尾，则仅加 '：

workers' resthomes　工人疗养院

the officers' living quarters　军官住宅区

the teachers' reading-room　教师阅览室

c. 如果名词是复数却不以 -(e)s 结尾，仍应加 's：

children's books　儿童读物

the women's movement　妇女运动

the Working People's Palace of Culture　劳动人民文化宫

d. 以 -s 结尾的单数名词后，可加 's，也可加 '，但均读作 /ɪz/：

Engels's（或 Engels'）works　恩格斯的著作

Burns's（或 Burns'）poems /'bɜːnzɪz 'pəʊɪmz/　彭斯的诗

不过以 -ts 结尾的名词只加 '，读作 /ts/，如：

Keats' poems /'kiːts 'pəʊɪmz/　济慈的诗

3）'s 的读音和名词复数词尾的读音一样（可参考第 3.2.1 节）：

情 况	读 法	例 词
在 /p/, /t/, /k/, /f/ 等清辅音后	/s/	Aesop's fables /'iːsəps 'feɪblz/ 伊索寓言 his wife's sister /hɪz 'waɪfs 'sɪstə/ 他妻子的妹妹
在 /s/, /z/, /ʃ/, /tʃ/, /dʒ/ 等音后	/ɪz/	Marx's works /'mɑːksɪz 'wɜːks/ 马克思的作品 George's father /'dʒɔːdʒɪz 'fɑːðə/ 乔治的父亲
其他情况	/z/	the author's name /'ɔːθəz neɪm/ 作者的名字 the girls' dormitory /'gɜːlz 'dɒmɪtəri/ 女生宿舍

3.3.2　名词所有格的用法

1） 名词所有格主要用于表示人的名词，表示"(某人)的"(有时有较灵活的译法)：

Is this Mr. *Black's* office?　这是布莱克先生的办公室吗？

It's one of *Shelley's* best poems.　这是雪莱的最佳诗作之一。

Old Wives' Tales is a good book.　《老妇谈》是一本好书。

Did you visit St. *Paul's* Cathedral?　你去没去看圣彼得大教堂？

2） 也可用于某些高级动物的名称或个别低级动物的名称后：

From the plane we had a *bird's* eye view of Manhatten.　从飞机上我们可以鸟瞰曼哈顿。

It is made from *mare's*, *cow's* or *ewe's* milk.　它是用马奶、牛奶或羊奶做的。

The donkey moved at a *snail's* pace.　驴以蜗牛的速度慢慢行进。

Here is an *ants'* nest.　这儿是个蚂蚁窝。

3） 也可用于一些表示无生命东西的名词后：

a. 表示时间的名词

Today is *yesterday's* pupil.　(谚)昨日是今日之师。

I'll never forget that *night's* experience.　我永远不会忘记那天晚上的经历。

We have two *weeks'* vacation for Christmas.　圣诞节我们有两星期的假。

It was a *summer's* morning.　这是一个夏天的早晨。

b. 表示距离、价格等的名词：

The park is a *stone's* throw from here.　公园离这儿很近。

I bought ten *dollars'* worth of stamps.　我买了十美元的邮票。

It's about an *hour's* drive from here.　开车到那里大约一小时。

c. 表示国家、城市等地方的名词：

The sea covers nearly three-fourths of the *world's* surface.　海水覆盖地球表面近四分之三的地区。

That was the first time I had left *England's* shore.　这是我第一次离开英国海岸。

It's the *city's* finest park.　它是这座城市最美的公园。

She wanted him to climb in the *college's* little world.　她希望他在大学的小小天地里往上爬。

We met at the *hotel's* entrance.　我们在旅馆门口相遇。

d. 表示集体或机构等的名词:

What's your *mission's* attitude towards the problem? 你们代表团对这问题态度如何?

That's the *majority's* view, I think. 我想这是多数人的意见。

We sat in the *station's* waiting-room until evening. 我们在车站候车室等到晚上。

She teaches at *Harvard's* Department of Linguistics. 她在哈佛大学语言学系任教。

4) 还可用在某些固定的词组中:

I'll take the risk *for friendship's sake*. 为了友谊我愿冒这个风险。

Mrs. Howells was *at her wit's end*. 豪威尔夫人已黔驴技穷。

Now they could sing *at their heart's content*. 现在他们可以尽情歌唱了。

We should get the children *out of harm's way*. 我们必须让孩子们不受到损害。

In my mind's eye I can still see my old home, with the roses over the door. 在我心目中我仍能看到我的老家,门上装饰着玫瑰。

We had best keep them *at arm's length*. 我们最好和他们保持距离。

For goodness' sake, stop arguing. 看在上帝的份上,别再争论下去了。

Jane *got the money's worth* out of that coat. 简买那件大衣很合算。

3.3.3 名词所有格的一些特殊意义

1) 名词所有格除了表示"所有关系"之外,还可有一些特殊意义,例如表示:

a. 主动关系 (前面名词表示后面动作的执行者):

John's gift to Marry was a watch. 约翰给玛丽的礼物是一块手表。

The soldier's heroic deed earned him a medal. 那士兵的英勇行为使他获得一枚奖章。

He was pleased by *his teacher's praise*. 老师的称赞使他很高兴。

b. 被动关系 (前面名词表示后面动作的承受者):

The play ends with *Hamlet's murder*. 该剧以哈姆雷特被杀害告终。

Everybody is singing *the fighter's praise*. 人人都赞颂这位战士。

The film star's admirers crowded round her. 这位电影明星被她的崇拜者围住了。

c. 特征：

The young boy has *a man's voice*. 这小男孩有大人的嗓音。

He has *a doctor's degree*. 他有博士学位。

He rose at *cock's crow* and hurried off. 他鸡叫时起身，匆匆离去。

2) 还可和 of 引导的短语结合使用：

a. He's *a friend of Henry's*. 他是亨利的一个朋友

I saw *a play of Shaw's*. 我看了萧伯纳的一出戏剧。

I have only read *four books of Dickens's*. 我只看过狄更斯的四本书。

b. Do you recall *that poem of Byron's*? 你还记得拜伦的那首诗吗？

Have you heard anything of *this new novel of Carleton's*? 你听人提过卡尔顿的这本新小说吗？

That wife of Mr. Brown's is constantly complaining. 布朗先生的那位太太老是抱怨个不停。

of 前面的名词或有不定冠词或数词修饰 (a)，或有 this, that 等词修饰，这时表示欣赏或厌恶的口吻 (b)。

3.3.4　所有格所修饰词省略的情况

1) 所有格修饰的词，如刚刚提过则可以省略，以避免重复：

"Whose seat is this?" "It is *Mary's*." "这是谁的座位？" "是玛丽的。"

This is not my dictionary, but *Xiao Lin's*. 这不是我的字典，是小林的。

She had views quite different from her *father's*. 她有着和她父亲完全不同的看法。

She put her arm through her *brother's*. 她伸手挽住她哥哥的手臂。

2) 可用来表示教堂、商店等：

We visited *St. Paul's* (Cathedral). 我们参观了圣彼得大教堂。

I've been shopping in *Macy's*. 我刚才在梅西百货公司买东西。

He went into a *stationer's* to buy a ruler. 他到文具店买了把尺子。

I am going to the *barber's*. 我去理发店。

He was educated at *Taylor's* (School). 他上的是泰勒中学。

3) 还可用来表示某人的家：

He had to go to his *sister's* for dinner. 他只好去他姐姐家吃晚饭。

We can meet at Aunt *Lucy's*. 我们可以在露希姨妈家碰头。

I went to *Paul's*, but he was at his *cousin's*. 我去了保罗家，但他在他表哥家里。

She's staying at my *Grandma's*. 她住在我奶奶家。

3.4　名词的性

3.4.1　名词的阴阳性

1) 英语不像其他欧洲语言,它的名词一般不分阴阳性。但随着词义不同,有一部分名词也可以分阴阳性,表示男人或雄性动物的名词属于阳性,表示女人或雌性动物的名词属于阴性,主要的这类名词有下面这些:

a. 表示人的名词:

阳性名词	阴性名词
god 神	goddess 女神
emperor 皇帝	empress 女皇帝,皇后
king 国王	queen 女王,王后
prince 王子	princess 公主
actor 男演员	actress 女演员
waiter (餐馆)服务员	waitress (餐馆)女服务员
master 主人(对仆人而言)	mistress 女主人
host 主人(对客人而言)	hostess 女主人
headmaster 中学校长	headmistress 中学女校长
heir 继承人	heiress 女继承人
shepherd 牧羊人	shepherdess 牧羊女
count 伯爵	countess 女伯爵,伯爵夫人
duke 公爵	duchess 女公爵,公爵夫人
marquis 侯爵	marchioness 女侯爵,侯爵夫人
baron 男爵	baroness 女男爵,男爵夫人
viscount 子爵	viscountess 女子爵,子爵夫人
landlord 男房东,地主	landlady 女房东,女地主
chairman (男)主席	chairwoman 女主席
fiancé 未婚夫	fiancée 未婚妻
policeman 警察	policewoman 女警察
wizard 巫师	witch 女巫
priest (男)教士	priestess 女教士

poet (男)诗人　　　　　　　poetess 女诗人

manager 经理　　　　　　　manageress 女经理

widower 鳏夫　　　　　　　widow 寡妇

lad 少年　　　　　　　　　lass 少女

hero 英雄　　　　　　　　　heroine 女英雄

gentleman 先生　　　　　　lady 女士

nephew 侄儿　　　　　　　niece 侄女

bridegroom 新郎　　　　　bride 新娘

monk 和尚　　　　　　　　nun 尼姑

sir 先生(称呼)　　　　　　madam 夫人(称呼)

steward (轮船、飞机上的)招待　　stewardess 女招待

usher (电影院)引座员　　　usheress 女引座员

salesman 售货员　　　　　saleswoman 女售货员

masseur 男按摩师　　　　　masseuse 女按摩师

b. 表示动物的名词:

lion 狮子　　　　　　　　　lioness 母狮子

tiger 老虎　　　　　　　　tigress 母老虎

bull 公牛　　　　　　　　　cow 母牛

stallion 公马　　　　　　　mare 母马

ram 公羊　　　　　　　　　ewe 母羊

cock, rooster 公鸡　　　　hen 母鸡

drake 公鸭　　　　　　　　duck 母鸭

leopard 公豹　　　　　　　leopardess 母豹

dog 狗　　　　　　　　　　bitch 母狗

fox 狐狸　　　　　　　　　vixen 母狐狸

gander 公鹅　　　　　　　goose 母鹅

boar 公野猪　　　　　　　sow 母(野)猪

stag 公鹿　　　　　　　　doe 母鹿

2) 英语大部分名词都分不出阴阳性。如果要表示一个人的性别，可以在
这个名词前加 man 或 woman，如:

a man servant 男佣人　　　a woman worker 女工

a man doctor 男医生　　　a woman wrestler 女摔跤手

也可加 boy, girl 这类词，如:

a boy scout 男童子军　　　a girl scout 女童子军

a boy friend 男朋友　　　a girl cousin 表姐妹

a male guest 男宾	a maid servant 女佣人
a male baby 男婴	a female child 女孩
a male nurse 男护士	a lady friend 女朋友
a male model 男模特	a female singer 女歌手

在动物前可加 male, female, he, she 之类的词来表示性别：

a male monkey 公猴	a female gorilla 母猩猩
a male animal 雄性动物	a female elephant 母象
a he-goat 雄山羊	a she-wolf 母狼

3.5 名词在句中的作用

3.5.1 名词在句中的作用

名词在句中可担任不同成分：

1) 作主语：

Knowledge is power. 知识就是力量。

Where there is a *will*, there is a *way*. (谚)有志者事竟成。

2) 作表语：

Smoking is my only *weakness*. 抽烟是我唯一的缺点。

The affair remained a complete *mystery*. 这件事整个还是个谜。

3) 作宾语 (谓语或非谓语动词的宾语)：

Did you get my *fax*? 你收到我的传真了吗?

They agreed to fax us their *proposals* tomorrow. 他们同意明天把建议传真给我们。

4) 作定语：

We bought a new *color* TV. 我们买了台新彩电。

Would you like to go to the *flower* show tomorrow? 你明天去看花展吗?

5) 作同位语：

This is our department head, *Dr. Owen*. 这是我们的系主任欧文博士。

You *girls* sit on this side. 你们姑娘们坐这边。

6) 作呼语：

Come in, *Mrs. Patterson*. 请进，帕特森夫人。

Morning, *Helen*. 海伦，早上好。

7) 作状语:

Wait a *minute*, I'll call her. 稍等一会儿，我去叫她。

We'll meet *Monday*. 我们星期一碰头。

8) 作介词宾语:

She majored in *physics* at *Yale*. 她在耶鲁大学主修物理。

He was devoted to *pure science*. 他专心致志于纯科学。

9) 构成复合宾语 (作宾语的补语):

They elected James (to be) *chairman*. 他们推选杰姆斯作主席。

He painted the door a brighter *color*. 他把门漆成了更鲜艳的颜色。

3.5.2　名词作定语的情况

1) 在英语中用名词作定语是常见的情况，如:

paper flower 纸花	cotton goods 棉织品
orange juice 橘汁	tomato sauce 番茄汁
eye drops 眼药水	nose drops 滴鼻剂
welcome party 欢迎会	welcome speech 欢迎词
weather station 气象站	weather forecast 天气预报
seat belt 安全带	forest belt 防护林带
import duty 进口税	income tax 所得税
trade deficit 贸易逆差	trade delegation 贸易代表团
fire brigade 消防队	fire extinguisher 灭火器
emergency department 急诊部	inquiry office 问讯处
power plant 电力厂	power politics 强权政治
feature film 故事片	horror film 恐怖电影
identity card 身份证	credit card 信用卡
time table 时刻表	time zone 时区
zip code 邮政编码	area code (电话)地区号
family planning 计划生育	family name 姓
news broadcast 新闻广播	news agency 新闻社
press conference 记者招待会	press release 新闻公报

其中很多已成为合成词。

2) 有少数名词可以复数形式作定语:

goods train (火车)货车	arms depot 军火库

a grants committee 补助金委员会 　an Arts degree 文科学位
machines hall 机器展览厅 　careers guide 就业指导
parks department 园林局 　a two-thirds majority 三分之二多数
examination board 考试委员会 　customs officer 海关人员
sports meet 运动会 　courses committee 课程委员会
commodities fair 商品交易会 　entertainments guide 娱乐指南
savings bank 储蓄银行 　a customs house 海关大楼

3) 有不少名词, 既可用名词作定语, 又可用形容词作定语, 意思上常有一些差别:

用名词作定语	用形容词作定语
gold ring 金戒指	golden sunshine 金色的阳光
silver cup 银质奖杯	silvery hair 银白色的头发
heart disease 心脏病	hearty welcome 热情的欢迎
art circles 艺术界	artistic level 艺术水平
stone house 石头房子	stony heart 铁石心肠
snow mountain 雪山	snowy table-cloth 雪白的桌布
rain drops 雨滴	rainy season 雨季
rose garden 玫瑰园	rosy cheeks 红红的脸颊
color film 彩色电影	colorful costumes 艳丽的服装
mountain village 山村	mountainous region 山区
history exam 历史考试	historical events 历史事实
geography lessons 地理课	geographical terms 地理名词
peace talks 和谈	peaceful construction 和平建设
youth delegation 青年代表团	youthful appearance 年轻的模样
production plan 生产计划	productive labor 生产性劳动
music lessons 音乐课	musical instrument 乐器
drama school 戏剧学校	dramatic changes 戏剧性的变化

第4章　冠　词

4.1　概　说

4.1.1　定冠词和不定冠词

冠词是一种虚词，不能独立担任一个成分，只能附着在一个名词上，帮助说明其词义，英语中有两个冠词：

1）定冠词 (The Definite Article) —— 即 the；

2）不定冠词 (The Indefinite Article) —— 即 a 和 an。

the 通常读作 /ðə/，在元音前读作 /ði/，特别强调或单念时读作 /ðiː/：

Who is the /ði/ author of the /ðə/ book? 谁是这书的作者?

He was the /ðiː/ greatest poet of the /ði/ age. 他是那时代最伟大的诗人。

不定冠词在元音 (指音，不指元音字母) 前用 an 这个形式，读作 /ən/：

an island /ən ˈaɪlənd/   an umbrella /ən ʌmˈbrelə/

an apple /ən ˈæpl/   an ounce /ən ˈaʊns/

an eyewitness /ən ˈaɪwɪtnəs/   an honest man /ən ˈɒnɪst ˌmæn/

an honour /ən ˈɒnə/   an hour /ən ˈaʊə/

在其他情况下一概作 a，读作 /ə/：

a girl /ə ˈɡɜːl/   a red apple /ə ˈred ˌæpl/

a university /ə ˌjuːnɪˈvɜːsɪti/   a one-act play /ə ˈwʌnækt ˈpleɪ/

a European city /ə ˌjʊərəˈpiːən ˈsɪti/   a humble man /ə ˈhʌmbl ˌmæn/

4.1.2　冠词的基本意义

不定冠词 a(n) 与数词 one 同源，表示"一个"的意思，用在可数名词单数前：

She is *a nurse*. She works in *a hospital*. 她是个护士，在一家医院工作。

He is *an Englishman*, with *an Irish wife*. 他是一位英国人，有一个爱尔兰妻子。

　　定冠词 the, 与 this 和 that 同源，有"这(那)个"的意思，但比较弱，表示一(几)个特定的人或东西，有时可译作"这个(些)"或"那个(些)"：

　　　　That's *the book* you want.　这就是你要的那本书。

　　　　Who is *the young man* over there?　那边那个年轻人是谁?

　　　　The old woman in the middle is my grandma.　中间这位老太太是我的祖母。

　　但在很多情况下，"这"或"那"这类词在译文中并不出现：

　　　　Put it on *the table*.　把它放在桌上

　　　　Shut *the door*, please.　请把门关上。

4.1.3　特指和泛指

　　一般来说，名词有特指和泛指两种情况，试比较下面句子：

　　　　Take *a seat*.　请坐。(泛指，随便坐哪把椅子都可以)

　　　　Is *the seat* taken?　这椅子有人坐吗?　(特指，指面前这把椅子)

　　　　Ask *a girl* to dance with you.　请一位姑娘和你跳舞。(泛指，找哪位都行)

　　　　Ask *the girl* to dance with you.　请那位姑娘和你跳舞。(特指，指特定的一位姑娘)

　　　　A gentleman is asking to see you.　有位先生要求见你。(泛指)

　　　　Ask *the gentleman* to come in.　请那位先生进来。(特指)

　　　　Can you lend me *a book* to read?　你能借本书给我看吗?　(泛指)

　　　　Can you lend me *the book*?　你能把那本书借给我吗?　(特指)

　　在特指时一般前面要加定冠词，而泛指时则有三种情况：

1) 在可数名词单数前加不定冠词：

　　　　It was *a lovely garden*.　这是一座漂亮的花园。(表示"类别")

　　　　She sent me *a postcard*.　她寄给我一张明信片。(表示"一个")

2) 在可数名词复数前可不加冠词，而可加 some, any 这类词：

　　　　These are *new words*.　这些是生词。(表示"类别")

　　　　She sent me *some flowers*.　她送给我一些花。(表示"一些")

3) 在不可数名词前多不加什么，有时也可加 some, any 等：

　　　　It's *lovely weather*.　天气真好。(表示"类别")

　　　　It's *pure silk*.　这是纯丝。(表示"类别")

　　　　Do you want *any sugar* in your tea?　你茶里要放点糖吗?　(表示"一些")

　　　　Give us *some help*.　给我们一些帮助。(表示"一些")

这些情况可以下表表示:

意义 冠词用法举例 名词类别	特指	泛指	
		表示类别	表示"一个(些)"
可数名词单数	the book	a book	a book
可数名词复数	the books	□ books	some (any) books
不可数名词	the sugar	□ sugar	some (any) sugar

这可以说明冠词用法的总的情况,但具体用法是比较复杂的,下面将作详细的讨论。

4.2 冠词的基本用法

4.2.1 不定冠词的基本用法

不定冠词主要用在可数名词单数前, 表示:

1) "一个"(意思接近 one):

Rome was not built in *a day*. (谚)罗马不是一天建成的。

There was now not *a minute* to lose. 现在一分钟也不能耽误。

His wages were four hundred pounds *a week*. 他每周工资四百镑。

I can only carry two at *a time*. 我一次只能拿两个。

A thousand people attended the concert. 一千人出席了这次音乐会。

A fifth of the population are young children. 五分之一的人口是儿童。

She is *a friend* of mine. 她是我的一位朋友。

可用在大量表示数量的词组中:

four times *a day* 一天四次		half *a kilo* 半公斤	
one pound *a metre* 一英镑一米		60 km *an hour* 每小时六十公里	
a quarter of a mile 四分之一英里		*a cup of coffee* 一杯咖啡	

2) "某一个"(=a certain, 但仍可译作"一个"):

A car is waiting at the gate. 有一辆车在门口等着。

He was born in *a small city* in Hunan. 他出生于湖南的一座小城。

A scholar is coming to speak to us. 一位学者将来给我们作报告。

She told us *an interesting story*. 她给我们讲了一个有趣的故事。

3) 某类人或物 (可用在表语、同位语等中):

She is *a Canadian (dancer)*.　她是加拿大人(舞蹈演员)。

Is this *a planer* or *a lathe*?　这是刨床还是车床?

The book was written by Dr. Cooper, *a geneticist*.　这书是遗传学家古柏博士写的。

He does not seem to be *a particularly able person*.　他似乎不是一个特别能干的人。

We knew Moses as *an authority* on Wagner.　我们知道摩西是研究瓦格纳的专家。

4) 某类人或物 (可作主语,表示整个这类人或东西):

A child needs love.　孩子需要爱。

An owl can see in the dark.　猫头鹰能在黑夜中看东西.

An upright man should be honest and fair.　正直的人应当诚实公正。

A rattlesnake is a poisonous American snake.　响尾蛇是美洲的一种毒蛇。

在前两种用法中,a 通常译作"一个",在把这名词变为复数时,a 需换作数词或不定代词:

Two fifths of the population are women.　五分之二的人是妇女。

A few scholars are coming to speak to us.　几位学者将来给我们作报告。

They ordered *three cups* of coffee.　他们要了三杯咖啡。

She told us *some interesting stories*.　她给我们讲了几个有趣的故事。

在后两种用法中,译成汉语时常不带"一"字,在把名词变为复数时,前面常不加什么:

Children need love.　孩子需要爱。

They don't seem to be particularly able *person*s.　他们似乎不是特别能干的人。

Rattlesnakes are poisonous American snakes.　响尾蛇是美洲的毒蛇。

Are these *planers* or *lathes*?　这些是刨床还是车床?

4.2.2　定冠词的基本用法

定冠词主要有下面这些用法:

1) 和个体名词的单数或复数连用,表示某个 (些) 特定的人或东西:

Where is (are) *the other girl(s)*?　另外那(几)个姑娘在哪里?

Put *the parcel(s)* on the table.　把那个(些)包裹放在桌上。

Show *the guest(s)* to his (their) room.　带客人去看他(们)的房间。

The bus has left. We had to wait for *the next bus*. 车开走了，我们得等下一班车。

Did you go to *the opening ceremony*? 你参加开幕典礼了吗？

凡属特指的名词(即指特定的人或物)都应加 the，试比较下面的句子：

特　指	泛　指
Pass me *the salt*. 把盐递给我。	Give me *some salt*. 给我点盐。
Take *the medicine* now. 现在就把药吃掉。	You'd better take *some medicine*. 你最好吃点药。
Here are *the records* I bought. 这些是我买的唱片。	I bought *two records* for you. 我给你买了两张唱片。
How do you like *the children's performance*? 你觉得孩子们的演出如何？	I like *children's performance*. 我喜欢孩子们的演出。

在第二次提到某样东西 (甚至与它有关的东西) 时，常在前面加 the：

He bought a TV and a video recorder, but he returned *the video recorder*. 他买了一台电视机和一台录像机，但把录像机退了。

She bought a bicycle, but when she rode it one of *the wheels* came off. 她买了一辆自行车，可骑上去时一个轮子掉了。

He saw a house in the country. He stood outside it for a while before going in. In *the front room* there was a fire burning in *the fireplace*. *The room* was clean, small and very warm. 他在乡下看到一栋房子。他站了一会儿，走了进去。前屋壁炉里生了火。房间很干净，小而暖和。

2) 也可和一个单数名词一道用，表示一类人或东西：

The whale is in danger of becoming extinct. 鲸有灭绝的危险。

The bluebird is the prettiest thing I've ever seen. 蓝知更鸟是我见过的最美的东西。

The eighteenth century was the golden age of *the novel*. 十八世纪是小说的黄金时代。

The aeroplane has made the world a small place. 飞机使世界变小了。

The computer has changed our way of life. 电脑改变了我们的生活方式。

The careful speaker should avoid it. 谨言的人应回避这种说法。

The small shopkeeper is finding life increasingly difficult. 小店主发现生活越来越艰难。

3） 还可和某些名词连用表示整个民族、阶级、阶层、一家人等:

The Chinese people are industrious and brave. 中国人民勤劳勇敢。

The Dutch are very skilful engineers. 荷兰人是能工巧匠。

They represented the interests of *the bourgeoisie*. 他们代表中产阶级的利益。

The Goncourts were careful artists. 龚古尔兄弟是很细致的艺术家。

The Thompsons arrived at 7 o'clock this evening. 汤普森一家今晚七点钟到达。

4） 还可和某些形容词连用，表示一类人 (a) 或某种品质 (b):

a. He never envied *the rich* their luxurious pleasures. 他从不羡慕富人们骄奢淫逸的生活。

Thus *the privileged* numbered less than 600,000. 因此特权阶级不超过六十万人。

In a week or two I'll be among *the unemployed*. 一两周后我将加入失业大军。

These seats are for *the disabled*. 这些座位是留给残疾人的。

b. I was weak, afraid to venture *the unknown*. 我很脆弱，不敢探查未知世界。

She admires *the mystical*. 她喜欢那些神奇古怪的事。

He has a strong dislike for *the sentimental*. 他非常讨厌多愁善感无病呻吟。

Their aim was to discover *the good*, *the beautiful* and *the true*. 他们的目标是发掘真善美。

5） 另外还可和一些表示世上独一无二的东西的名词一道用:

Do you know how big *the universe* is? 你知道宇宙有多大吗?

There was a rainbow in *the sky*. 天上有一道彩虹。

The sun lights and warms *the earth*. 太阳照亮地球并供给能量。

The moon had risen. 月亮已经升起。

The Milky Way is a bright band of stars. 银河系是一条明亮的星带。

The air was full of butterflies. 空中飞满蝴蝶。

此外还有 the Equator (赤道), the outer space (外层空间), the atmosphere (大气层), the solar system (太阳系), the North Pole (北极), the Tropic of Cancer (北回归线), the tropics (热带地区)等。

4.3　各类名词前的冠词用法

4.3.1　专有名词前冠词的用法

专有名词前一般不加冠词，因为它本身就是特指的，即使前面有形容词修饰时通常也不加冠词，如：

人名：Shakespeare，Jack London，Queen Elizabeth，Little Tom，Big Hugh，John Smith junior；

地名：Paris，Los Angeles，Russia，ancient Rome，East Africa，Western Europe，Southern France，North America；

其他：July，Saturday，Easter，English。

但有许多特殊情况：

1）在某些地理名词前要加定冠词：

a. 江，河，海，洋：

the Yangtze River 长江，the Hudson River 哈得孙河，the Pearl River 珠江，the Red Sea 红海，the Mediterranean 地中海，the Indian Ocean 印度洋，the Pacific Ocean 太平洋，the Arctic 北冰洋。

b. 山脉，群岛：

the Tian Shan Moumtains 天山山脉，the Rocky Mountains 洛矶山脉，the Philippines 菲律宾群岛，the Riukiu Islands 硫球群岛，the West Indies 西印度群岛。

但：Mount Emei 峨眉山，Christmas Island 圣诞岛。

c. 海峡，海湾：

the English Channel 英吉利海峡，the Taiwan Straits 台湾海峡，the Bay of Biscay 比斯开湾，the Gulf of Mexico 墨西哥湾。

湖名前一般不加冠词，如：

Lake Success 成功湖，Dongting Lake 洞庭湖，Lake Baikal 贝加尔湖。

但个别湖名前也有加 the 的，如：

the Lake of Geneva 日内瓦湖，the West Lake 西湖，the Great Salt Lake 大盐湖。

另外有少数地名前通常加 the：

the Netherlands 荷兰，the Vatican 梵蒂冈，the Balkans 巴尔干半岛各国，the Middle Esat 中东，the Hague 海牙，the Ukraine 乌克兰，the Caucasaus 高加索，the Crimea 克里米亚半岛，the Sahara 撒哈拉大沙漠，the Sudan 苏丹，

the Yemen 也门。

2）由普通名词构成的专有名词很多要加 the：

a. 某些国名及政治组织名称：

the People's Republic of China，the United States，the United Kingdom，the United Nations，the General Assembly，the Security Council，the People's Congress，the House of Commons，the Republican Party。

（但 Parliament 和 Congress 前不加 the）

b. 某些机构、学校、建筑物等的名词：

the British Museum，the National Gallery，the Philadelphia Orchestra，the Victoria Chest Hospital，the Bronx Zoo，the Midland Bank，the University of Washington，the Royal College of Art，the Harlow Technical College，the Odeon Cinema，the Pentagon 五角大楼，the Hilton (Hotel)，the Phoenix (Theatre)，the Titanic 泰坦尼克号。

（但也有一些不加冠词，如 Buckingham Palace，Westminster Abbey，Brools Hotel）

c. 某些报刊杂志的名称：

the New York Times 纽约时报，the Chicago Tribune 芝加哥论坛报，the Washington Post 华盛顿邮报，the Labour Monthly 劳动月刊，the Daily News 每日新闻，the Observer 观察家报，the Economist 经济学家杂志，the Times 泰晤士报。

（但有些也不加，如 Life 生活杂志，Newsweek 新闻周刊，Harper's 哈珀斯杂志）

3）下面这类名词前通常不加冠词：

a. 多数街名：

Fleet Street 舰队街，Marston Road 玛斯登道，Riverside Avenue 滨河大道，Park Lane 派克巷，Rodeo Drive 罗狄欧路，Sunset Boulevard 日落大道。

（但：the High Street）

b. 多数广场名：

Russel Square 罗素广场，Berkeley Square 贝克莱广场，Times Square 时代广场，Piccadilly Circus 皮卡迪利圆形广场（但：the Red Square）。

c. 车站、机场、公园、桥梁名：

Central Station 中央车站，Kennedy Airport 肯尼迪机场，Central Park 中央公园，Waterloo Bridge 滑铁卢大桥（但：the Golden Gate Bridge）。

d. 大学名：

Harvard University 哈佛大学，Oxford University 牛津大学，Oregon State

University 俄勒冈州立大学，Balliol College 贝里欧学院。

(但：the University of East Anglia，the Institute for Contemparary Arts)

e. 节日名：

National Day 国庆节，May Day 五一节，New Year's Day 新年，Christmas 圣诞节，Easter 复活节，Thanksgiving Day 感恩节，St. Valentine's Day 情人节，International Women's Day 国际妇女节。

(但：the Mid-Autumn Festival，the Spring Festival)

f. 多数杂志名：

Time 时代周刊，New Scientist 新科学家，English Language Teaching 英语教学，U.S. News and World Report 美国新闻与世界报导，Reader's Digest 读者文摘。

4) 人名前一般不加冠词，但在一些特殊情况下也可以加，如：

A Mrs Green is waiting to see you. 一位格林夫人等着见你。

My boss is *a little Napolean*. 我的老板是一个小拿破仑。

I didn't know you were *an ardent Romeo*. 我不知道你是一个热情的罗密欧。

The Smith you're looking for no longer lives here. 你找的史密斯现在不住这儿。

The little Vesta was now eighteen months old. 小薇斯塔现在有十八个月大了。

The theory was advanced by *the great Einstein*. 这理论是伟大的爱因斯坦提出的。

还可以用在某些专有名词前表示一种车、一张某人的画像等：

The car was *a Buick*, not *a Benz*. 那辆车是别克，不是奔驰。

He had *a Van Gogh* in the dining room. 他的餐厅里有一张凡高的画。

What *a strange London* he saw! 他看到的是一个多么奇怪的伦敦!

He ordered *a second Martini*. 他又叫了一杯马提尼酒。

4.3.2 抽象名词前冠词的用法

1) 抽象名词前一般不加冠词：

The music is full of *life*. 这音乐充满活力。

Practice makes perfect. （谚)熟能生巧。

I wish you *joy*. 祝你愉快。

While there is *life* there is hope. （谚)有生命就有希望。

即使前面有形容词修饰，一般也不加冠词：

She cared little for *social life*. 她对社交生活不太有兴趣。

This invitation gave him *particular joy*. 这项邀请使他非常高兴。

He has always been interested in *classical music*. 他一向喜欢古典音乐。

You have given me *fresh hope*. 你给了我新的希望。

2）若抽象名词用于特指（即指特定的内容），特别是有一个限制性定语修饰时，多加定冠词：

Minor accidents can shorten *the life* of a car. 小事故也可能缩短车的寿命。

Her children were *the joy* of her life. 她的孩子是她生活的乐趣。

The younger generation is *the hope* of the nation. 年轻一代是国家的希望。

He went on playing *the music* of Mozart. 他继续演奏莫扎特的乐曲。

特指和泛指相对，试比较下面的句子：

特　指	泛　指
What do you think of *the music*? 你觉得这音乐怎样？	She has a passion for *music*. 她酷爱音乐。
He asked about *the progress* of my book. 他问我书的进展情况。	My research made *slow progress*. 我的研究工作进展缓慢。
She immediately took *the advice*. 她立即接受了这个意见。	*Good advice* is beyond price. （谚)好的意见是无价之宝。
What's *the result* of your investigation? 你调查的结果如何？	I worked all day, but without *result*. 我干了一天，却没有结果。

限制性定语 (Limiting Attributes) 指 of 引导的定语或某些定语从句，它们限制名词的意义，使指特定的内容，和它相对的则是 **描绘性定语** (Descriptive Attributes) (这种定语只描绘，不限定意思)：

限制性定语	描绘性定语
the picture *on p. 2* 第二页上的那张画	a picture *by a child* 一张儿童画的画
the grammar book *you want* 你要的那本语法书	a book *you must read* 你必读的一本书
the girl *sitting there* 坐在那里的姑娘	a hard-working girl 一位勤劳的姑娘
the idea *he put forward* 他提出的意见	a *wonderful* idea 一个好主意

3）抽象名词在一定的情况下可加不定冠词，用来表示：

a. 一种、一场等：

She always had *an affection* for me. 她一向对我有感情。

He had *a strong dislike* for cold weather. 他很讨厌寒冷的天气。

She showed *a certain elegance*. 她表现出一种优雅的风度。

He felt *a great tenderness* for Ruth. 他对露丝感到一种深情。

It was *a just war*. 这是一场正义的战争。

b. 某动作的一次、一例等：

Do you care for *a smoke*? 抽支烟好吗？

The report called for *a public inquiry*. 该报告要求进行一次公开调查。

He made *a careful check* of the accounts. 他对账目进行了仔细检查。

It made *a good analysis* of the situation. 它很好地分析了形势。

c. 引起某种情绪的人或事：

This work has been *a great joy*. 这项工作使人感到很愉快。

He is *a shame* to his family. 他使他的家人蒙羞。

Seeing him so active was *a great encouragement*. 看他这样积极很令人鼓舞。

Her son was *a great disappointment* to her. 她的儿子很让她失望。

d. 表示某种品质的具体行动、人或东西：

Would you do me *a favor*? 你能帮我一个忙吗？

You were *a great help* to us. 你对我们很有帮助。

In some places, white bread is *a luxury*. 在某些地方白面包都是奢侈品。

A forced kindness deserves no thanks. 勉强的善行不值得感谢。

由于每个抽象名词情况都不一样，不清楚时最好查一本较好的词典。

4.3.3 物质名词前冠词的用法

1）物质名词前一般不加冠词：

Do you like *tea* or would you prefer *coffee*? 你要茶还是愿意喝咖啡？

We can't live without *air*. 没有空气我们就不能生存。

We use *water* for drinking and washing. 我们饮水并用水洗东西。

They were digging for *gold*. 他们在挖找金子。

We expect *snow* before morning. 我们预计清晨前会下雪。

即使前面有形容词，一般也不加冠词：

Is that Indian tea or *Chinese tea*?　这是印度茶还是中国茶？

Cold air blew in through the open window.　冷空气从开着的窗子吹了进来。

Is this *fresh water*?　这是淡水吗？

It's made of *pure gold*.　它是纯金打造的。

Heavy snow is reported in the north.　据报导北方下大雪。

2) 物质名词特指时前面也可以加 the：

How do you like *the tea*?　这茶你觉得怎样？

The air was bad.　(房里的)空气很不好。

Someone has fallen into *the water*!　有人掉水里去了！

The gold they found weighed two kilos.　他们找到的黄金有两公斤重。

The visitor disappeared in *the whirling snow*.　客人消失在飞旋的雪花中。

Don't stand in *the rain*.　别站在雨里。

3) 物质名词前间或加不定冠词，表示：

a. 一场，一阵：

A heavy snow was falling.　下着一场大雪。

There was *a light rain* falling.　下着一阵小雨。

Last night there was *a terrible storm*.　昨晚下了一阵可怕的暴雨。

b. 一种：

It was *a wonderful tea*.　这是一种很好的茶。

The bakery makes *a very fine rye bread*.　那家面包房制作一种很好吃的黑麦面包。

A high-grade paper is made from rushes.　有一种高档纸是灯心草做的。

c. 一份：

A large coffee for me.　给我一大杯咖啡。

You may as well bring me *a chocolate* too.　你不妨也给我一份巧克力。

I want *a strawberry ice-cream*.　我要一份草莓冰淇淋。

4.4　不用或省略冠词的情况

4.4.1　零冠词

在不少情况下，名词前不加冠词，可以称作 **零冠词** (Zero Article)。除上面谈到的一些不用冠词的情况，还有下面这些值得注意：

　　1）当一个名词用作表语或同位语等表示一个领导职位时，前面常不加冠词（也可说省略掉冠词）：

In 1993 Bill Clinton became (the) *President* of the United States.　1993年克林顿成为美国总统。

He is still *head* of the organization.　他仍然是这个组织的首脑。

This is Professor Brockbank, *head* of the history department.　这是历史系主任布洛克邦教授。

He succeeded his father as *president* of the company.　他接替他父亲担任公司董事长。

This is Mr. Kirk, *director* of the Department of African Affairs.　这是非洲司司长科克先生。

They appointed him *minister* to a foreign country.　他们任命他为驻外公使。

尽管指普通员工，某些职务名称前也有不加冠词的趋势：

I'm coming back to take the job of *foreign editor*.　我将回来当外语编辑。

She worked as *correspondent* to a local newspaper.　她担任当地一家报纸的记者。

在 turn 后的表语都不带冠词：

He was a Conservative but he turned *Socialist*.　他原是保守党员后来成了社会党人。

He has turned *botanist (Mahammedan)*.　他成了植物学家(回教徒)。

在 title 和 rank 后，名词前也多不带冠词：

I prefer the title of *reporter*.　我更喜欢记者的头衔。

That officer holds the rank of *captain*.　那位军官的官阶为上尉。

　　2）个体名词抽象化后，前面也不加冠词：

He has to get ready for *college*.　他得准备好上大学。

They decided to send their son to *university*.　他们决定送儿子上大学。

We were at *school* together.　我们在一起上学。

It was too early for *bed*.　现在睡觉还太早了一点。

There's *room* for three more.　还可以容纳三个人。

What time does *church* begin?　什么时候开始做礼拜？

You should go into *hospital* at once.　你应当马上去住院。

The trees were all in *flower*.　树都开花了。

The thief was sent to *prison* for a year.　小偷要蹲一年监狱。

She went by *bus* (*boat/plane/car*).　她坐巴士(船/飞机/汽车)去。

在大量短语中的名词前不加冠词，如：

from beginning to end 从头到尾　　　　from head to foot 从头到脚

from day to day 日复一日　　　　　　from time to time 不时地

year after year 年复一年　　　　　　in case of 在…的情况下

in place of 代替　　　　　　　　　　on foot (holiday) 步行(度假)

make fun of 拿…开玩笑　　　　　　　make room for 给…腾地方

3）表示季节、月份、日期的名词前一般不加冠词：

Spring was at hand.　春天即将到来。

She was born in *April*.　她是四月出生的。

He is arriving on *Monday*.　他将于星期一到达。

October 1st is our National Day.　十一是国庆节。

如果有限制性定语修饰，则应加定冠词：

Nanchang Uprising took place on *the 1st* of August, 1927.　南昌起义是1927
年8月1日举行的。

It happened in *the summer* of 1937.　这事发生在1937年夏天。

**4）在 daybreak，dusk，dawn，noon，midnight，sunset，sunrise 这类名
词前通常不加冠词：**

At *daybreak* we started on our journey.　天亮时我们起程了。

The attack came just before *dawn*.　拂晓前进攻开始了。

At *dusk* the lights of the city come on.　黄昏时分城里的灯亮了。

The workers ate fast food at *noon*.　工人们中午吃快餐。

It's getting on for *midnight*.　快到午夜了。

We left home at *sunrise*.　日出时我们离开了家。

After *sunset*, the sky darkened rapidly.　太阳落山后天很快就黑了。

Before *daylight* it started to drizzle.　天亮前开始下起毛毛雨。

偶尔前面可加定冠词：

The dawn here in the mountains is beautiful.　这儿山里的黎明是美丽的。

One cannot see very far in *the dusk*.　暮色中我们看不到很远。

5）在呼语、家人及亲属名称后常不加冠词：

Be quiet, *children*!　安静点，孩子们！

Thank you, *sir*.　谢谢你，先生。

Can I help you, *ma'am* (madam)?　我能为你做点什么，夫人？

Can I get you anything to drink, *father*?　我能给你弄点什么喝的吗，爸?

Mother is with *Grandma*.　妈和奶奶在一起。

Auntie is in the kitchen.　姨在厨房里。

Big sister is playing chess with *uncle*.　大姐在和叔叔下棋。

甚至 cock, nurse 这样的词有时看作家庭成员，前面也可不加冠词：

Come quickly, *nurse*.　奶妈，快来。

6) 在一些并列名词前，常可不加冠词，如：

Mother and child are doing fine.　母子平安。

When *host and guest* appeared, they received a standing ovation.　当宾主出现时，大家长时间起立鼓掌。

Father and son went to New York by a morning train.　父子两人坐早上的火车去了纽约。

It has handed down *from father to son* for many generations.　这东西父传子已传了许多代了。

He went *head over heels* into the water.　他一个跟斗跌进了水里。

I cannot *make head or tail* of your letter.　我看不懂你的信。

此外还有不少这类并列词组，如：

shoulder to shoulder　并肩	side by side　并排
hand in hand　手牵手	arm in arm　手挽手
tit for tat　以牙还牙	step by step　一步步地
back to back　背靠背地	face to face　面对面地
heart and soul　全心全意地	heart-to-heart　推心置腹地

4.4.2　冠词省略的情况

在一些情况下冠词常常省略，如：

1) 新闻标题：

(The) City Congress (is) to be in session Friday　市议会星期五开会

(A) Hotel Fire Disaster　饭店大火成灾

2) 通知说明：

(The) Lift (is) out of order.　电梯坏了。

Cut along (the) dotted line.　沿虚线剪开。

3) 提纲：

(The) Algerian Crisis led to (the) downfall of (the) French government in May 1958.　阿尔及利亚危机导致法国政府于 1958 年 5 月倒台。

(The) Causes of World War Ⅱ: massive re-armament, (the) invasion...　第
· 二次世界大战起因：大规模重新武装，入侵捷克…

4）剧本提示：

Vossilisa (Open door quickly；to Alyushka): You here again?　薇希丽莎
　（迅速开门；对阿留希说）：你又来了？

Exit into garden.　出去进入花园。

5）书名：

(An) Outline Political History of the Americas　美洲政治史纲

(The) BBC English Dictionary　BBC 英语词典

第5章 代 词

5.1 概 说

5.1.1 代词的分类

代词可以分为下面几类：

- **人称代词** (Personal Pronouns)
- **物主代词** (Possessive Pronouns)
- **自身代词** (Self Pronouns)
- **相互代词** (Reciprocal Pronouns)
- **指示代词** (Demonstrative Pronouns)
- **疑问代词** (Interrogative Pronouns)
- **连接代词** (Conjunctive Pronouns)
- **关系代词** (Relative Pronouns)
- **不定代词** (Indefinite Pronouns)

5.1.2 代词的作用

严格地讲，代词是代替名词的，在句子中起名词的作用，可用作：

1）主语：

This is our new home. 这是我们的新家。

Both are from the South. 两人都是南方人。

Who is on the phone? 谁在打电话？

2）宾语：

I have read *neither* of the books. 这两本书我都没看过。

Take good care of *yourself*. 多多保重。

We should help *each other*. 我们应互相帮助。

3）表语：

That's not *mine*. 那不是我的。

Who is it? ——It's *me*. 谁呀? ——是我。

I'm not quite *myself* today. 我今天不太舒服。

4) 同位语:

We *both* live in the dormitory. 我们两人都住宿舍。

You *yourself* are to blame. 这得怪你自己。

He ate them *all*. 他把它们全吃了。

5) 呼语:

You sit here. 你坐这儿。

Get out, *both of you*! 你俩都滚出去!

Be patient, *everybody*. 大家都耐心点。

偶作宾语的补语 (和宾语一道构成复合宾语):

What do you call it? 这个你们叫作什么?

在很多情况下,代词也可用作定语,较早的语法学家仍认为它是代词,如:

It's *my* book. (比较:It's John's book.)

I'll take *that* shirt. (比较:I'll take the blue shirt.)

现在主要有两种说法。美国语言学家多把作定语用的这类词称作形容词,例如下面句子中的斜体部分,他们都称作形容词:

There are *many* reasons why I moved to New York. 我搬到纽约有很多原因。

Few people showed up for the party. 没几个人出席这次聚会。

This watch cost $ 100. 这只表花了一百美元。

Mary washed *each* piece of fruit. 玛丽把每个水果都洗了。

而英国的一些语言学家则把它们称作 **限定词** (Determiners)。

5.1.3 限定词

限定词不是一个单纯的词类,而是用在名词前一些词的通称,它们包括:

1) **冠词** (Article):

Anne is in *the* garden. 安妮在花园里。

You need *a* visa to go there. 你去那里需要签证。

2) **指示形容词** (Demonstrative Adjectives):

This time last year we were in Canada. 去年这时我们在加拿大。

Who owns *those* dogs? 那些狗是谁的?

3) **物主代词** (Possessive Determiners):

The girls are with *their* mother. 姑娘们和她们的母亲在一起。

A tree drops *its* leaves in autumn.　树在秋天会落叶。

4）不定限定词 (Indefinite Determiners)：

Did you catch *any* fish?　你捕到鱼了吗？

There are two sides to *every* question.　每个问题都有两方面。

下面这些词作定语时都可称为不定限定词：

all	another	any	both	each	either
every	few	little	many	more	most
much	neither	no	other	several	some

除了冠词外，大多数限定词都与代词紧密相连，主要差别是代词作主语、宾语等，而限定词作定语。它们的意思也是互相联系的。从实用角度看，这一区分并不重要(美国词典一般都没有限定词这个说法)。为了处理上的方便，我们把两者放在一起讨论。

5.2　人称代词和物主代词

5.2.1　人称代词

1）英语中有下面这些人称代词：

格＼人称	单　数			复　数		
	I	II	III	I	II	III
主　格	I	you	he she it	we	you	they
宾　格	me	you	him her it	us	you	them

2）人称代词在句中可用作：

a. 主语：

I'm sorry *I'm* late.　对不起我来晚了。

Is *he* married?　——No, *he's* single.　他结婚了吗？ ——没有，是单身。

He (She) majors in English.　他(她)主修英语。

We (They) are both from the south.　我俩(他俩)都是南方人。

在口语中有时用宾格，尤其是在 than 引导的从句中：

Who found Gran's watch?　——*Me*.　谁找到格兰的表的？ ——我。

John is smaller than *him*. 约翰个子比他小。

She is cleverer than *me*. 她比我聪明。

b. 宾语 (需用宾格) 或介词宾语:

Tell *him (her)* to call back a little later. 请他(她)过一会再打电话来。

You don't need to thank *me (us)*. 你不需要谢我(们)。

Put *it (them)* on the table, please. 请把它(们)放在桌上。

She has great concern for *us (me/him)*. 她很关心我们(我/他)。

c. 表语 (在口语中常用宾格):

I saw at once it was *her*. 我马上看出是她。

If I were *her (him)*, I'd take the job. 我要是她(他),我会接受这份工作。

Don't blame Tom. It's *me* who broke it. 别怪汤姆,是我打破的。

Did you see who it was? —— *Them*, of course. 你看见是谁了吗?
——当然是他们。

但在笔语中仍宜用主格:

It's *I* (me). 是我。

It was *she* who had been wrong. 是她错了。

3) she 除了指"她"外,还可表示:

a. 雌性动物:

I stroked the cat and *she* rubbed against my leg. 我抚摸猫,它蹭我的腿。

The mare whined when *she* saw her master. 这匹母马见到主人时会嘶叫。

b. 船只,车辆:

She is a fine ship. 这是条很好的船。

Nice car — how much did *she* cost? 好车——买它花了多少钱?

c. 国家:

Spain is a major car manufacturer. *She* exports cars to the UK. 西班牙是
个重要的汽车生产国,它出口汽车到英国。

English has done what *she* promised to do. 英国已履行了它的承诺。

4) we,you 两词可用来泛指一般人:

We all have our weaknesses. 我们(人)都有弱点。

We (You) need to consider all these factors. 我们(你)需要考虑所有这些因
素。

You can never tell what they will do next. 谁也说不上他们下一步会做什
么。

they 也可泛指一般人:

They say prices are going to increase again. 据说物价又要上涨。

They don't make decent furniture nowadays.　现今做不出像样的家具。

5) it 可有许多用法，表示：

a. 某样东西：

Where's my map? I left *it* on the table.　我的地图哪里去了? 我(刚才)放在桌上的。

Look at the bird. *It* always comes to my window.　瞧那只鸟，它老飞到我窗口来。

b. 抽象事物：

You've saved my life. I shall never forget *it*.　你救过我的命，我永远不会忘记的。

"I want to stay." "Your wife won't like *it*."　"我想留下。" "你妻子不会赞成的。"

c. 不知性别的孩子 (婴儿)：

Her new baby is tiny. *It* only weighs 2 kilos.　她刚生的婴儿个头很小，才两公斤。

What a beautiful baby — is *it* a boy?　多漂亮的宝宝呀——是男孩吗?

d. 某种感觉或情况：

Does *it* itch much?　痒得厉害吗?

Where does *it* hurt?　哪儿疼?

How is *it* going with you?　你情况怎样?

e. 是谁：

Who is that (it)?　——*It*'s me.　是谁(来电话)?　——是我。

Is that Tom over there?　——No, *it*'s Peter.　那边是汤姆吗?　——不，是彼得。

f. 时间、日期等：

What time is it?　——*It* is eight o'clock.　现在几点钟?　——八点。

What's the date?　——*It*'s the third of April.　今天几号?　——四月三号。

g. 天气、环境等：

It's raining (snowing).　天在下雨(下雪)。

It's so noisy (quiet) in the room.　房间里很吵(安静)。

In winter *it*'s dark at six o'clock.　冬天六点钟天就黑了。

h. 距离等：

How far is *it* to Chicago?　——*It* is 800 kilometers.　这儿离芝加哥有多远?　——八百公里。

It's 112 miles from London to Birmingham. 从伦敦到伯明翰有112英里。

it还有一些特殊用法, 详见第 19.2.1—19.2.5 和 21.3.1—21.3.3 节。

5.2.2 物主代词

1) 物主代词有下面这些:

词 义 类 型	我的	你的	他(她,它)的	我们的	你们的	他们的
形容词型物主代词	my	your	his, her, its	our	your	their
名词型物主代词	mine	yours	his, hers, its	ours	yours	theirs

2) 形容词型物主代词有些语法学家称为限定词, 主要在句中用作定语:

Is this *your (his/her)* seat? 这是你的(他的/她的)座位吗?

Their (My/Our) house looks on to the sea. 他们(我的/我们)的房子面临大海。

What's *your* nationality? 你(们)是哪国人?

The cat's had *its* dinner. 猫已吃过(它的)饭了。

The swimming club held *its* Annual General Meeting last night. 游泳俱乐部昨晚开了年度会员大会。

The baby threw down *its* rattle. 婴儿把他的拨浪鼓扔掉了。

The government has changed *its (their)* policy. 政府改变了它的政策。

The cuckoo lays *her* eggs in other birds' nests. 杜鹃把蛋下在别的鸟的窝里。

3) 形容词型物主代词还可和 own 连用, 在句中:

a. 作定语:

I always write for *my own* people. 我总是为我自己的人民写作。

Virtue is *its own* reward. (谚)有德便是有报。

He arranged for me to study with *his own* children. 他安排我和他自己的孩子一道学习。

She did it of *her own* free will. 她自愿这样做的。

b. 作表语、宾语等:

My time isn't *my own*. 我的时间不是我自己的。

It's her friend's car, not *her own*. 这是她朋友的车, 不是她自己的车。

Their views are similar to *our own*. 他们的看法和我们自己的看法相似。

c. 和 of 连用：

The accident happened through no fault *of her own*.　事故绝非出于她自己的过错。

We have no children *of our own*.　我们没有自己的孩子。

I wish to God I had a lab *of my own*.　我乞求上帝让我有一个自己的实验室。

4) 名词型的物主代词可以：

a. 作表语：

Is this your book or *mine*?　这是你的书还是我的书？

This suit is *his*.　这套衣服是他的。

Is that old black cat *yours*?　那只老黑猫是你们的吗？

b. 作主语：

That isn't my car; *mine* is being repaired.　这不是我的车，我的车在修。

Ours is the only garden in the lane.　我们的花园是这条巷子里唯一的花园。

Yours is on that shelf.　你的在那个书架上。

c. 作宾语或介词宾语：

We'll have to separate *ours* from *theirs*.　我们得把我们的和他们的分开。

I like *yours* better than *ours*.　我喜欢你(们)的胜过我们自己的。

Her daughter is rather stupid, but both of *yours* are very clever.　她的女儿很愚钝，可你的两个女儿都很聪明。

d. 和 of 连用：

An old friend of mine has just had a child.　我的一位老友刚生了个孩子。

I borrowed *a tie of his*.　我借了他一条领带。

He is *a great admirer of yours*.　他是你的崇拜者。

This girl of mine wrote to say she was coming from Paris today.　我的那个女儿来信说她今天从巴黎来。

That fool of a sister of ours!　我们的那个傻妹妹！

△ yours 常写在信末：

对陌生人可以写 "yours faithfully" 或 "yours truly"，对见到过的人可以写 "yours sincerely"，对朋友可写 "yours" 或 "yours ever"。

5.3   自身代词和相互代词

5.3.1   自身代词

1）自身代词也称**反身代词** (Reflexive Pronouns)，主要有下面这些：

单 数	myself	yourself	himself herself itself
复 数	ourselves	yourselves	themselves

此外，oneself也是自身代词。

2）自身代词主要用作宾语：

John dressed *himself* in the most formal suit. 约翰穿得衣冠楚楚。

They should blame *themselves* for the accident. 出这事应怪他们自己。

This refrigerator defrosts *itself*. 这冰箱是自动除霜的。

I hope you'll enjoy *yourselves*. 希望你们玩得好。

Let me introduce *myself*. 我来介绍一下自己。

To deceive *oneself* is very easy. 骗自己是容易的。

I had a fit of rage — I could hardly control *myself*. 我勃然大怒——简直
    无法控制自己。

He reproached *himself* for his behavior that evening. 他为他那天晚上的表
    现而自责。

She prided *herself* on her cooking. 她为自己的烹调技术感到骄傲。

She busied *herself* (in) tidying up her desk. 她忙着收拾她的写字台。

关于这种结构还可参阅第 13.3.2 节。

3）自身代词也常常用作介词宾语：

She looked at *herself* in the mirror. 她照了照镜子。

Take good care of *yourself*. 好好保重。

He ought to be ashamed of *himself*. 他应当感到惭愧。

The three boys discussed the matter among *themselves*. 那三个小伙子讨
    论了这件事。

I'm annoyed with *myself*. 我生我自己的气。

She was speaking to *herself*. 她在自言自语。

He didn't pay for *himself*. 他自己没付钱。

You must learn to look after *yourself*. 你要学会照顾自己。

4) 自身代词有时用作主语或宾语的同位语:

The president *himself* gave her the medal. 校长亲自给她颁发了奖章。

Mary *herself* opened the door. 玛丽亲自开了门。

I *myself* used to have literary ambitions. 我自己过去也有文学方面的雄心壮志。

The novel *itself* has glaring faults. 小说本身有严重缺陷。

I must begin by telling about the girls *themselves*. 我得先谈谈姑娘们自己的情况。

I liked the diamond *itself* but not the setting. 我喜欢的是钻石本身, 而不是它的底座。

She wanted to see Tom *himself*. 她想见汤姆本人。

有时自身代词有强调作用, 近乎状语:

I'll do it *myself*. 这事我自己来做。

She made the dress *herself*. 这连衣裙是她自己做的。

Henry opened the safe *himself*. 亨利亲自打开了保险柜。

You'd better go there *yourselves*. 你们最好自己到那里去。

5) 自身代词有时还可用作表语 (a), 间或还可用作主语 (b):

a. I haven't been *myself* for weeks. 这几个星期我身体一直欠佳。

Now I'm quite *myself* again. 现在我身体已复原了。

That poor girl was *myself*. 那个可怜的女孩就是我自己。

b. Both my sister and *myself* were anxious about it. 我妹妹和我自己都很为这事着急。

I hope Miss Glenn and *yourself* are keeping well. 我希望格林小姐和你都好。

My brother is as worried as *myself*. 我弟弟和我自己一样发愁。

〔注〕 通常不宜用自身代词作主语, 而要用另一主语, 用自身代词作同位语:
The girl *herself* was to blame for it. 这得怪这女孩自己。

6) 自身代词还可用在一些成语中:

a. among yourselves (themselves, etc) 你们(他们等)相互间:

Don't quarrel *among yourselves*. 你们自己不要相互争吵了。

They were busy arguing *among themselves*. 他们忙着互相争论。

b. between ourselves 咱们私下说说(不可外传):

This is just *between ourselves*. 这是咱们俩私下的悄悄话。

Between ourselves, I think Schmidt's about to resign. 咱们私下说说,我想斯密特即将辞职。

c. by oneself 独自一人,自己(没别人帮助):

Miss Brown was sitting *by herself* on a bench. 布朗小姐独自一人坐在长凳上。

He went out for a short walk *by himself*. 他一个人出去散了散步。

The little girl traveled to London *by herself*. 那小姑娘独自去了伦敦。

d. for oneself 替自己,为自己:

She kept the smallest apple *for herself*. 她把最小的苹果留给了自己。

With the money they could buy food *for themselves*. 用这笔钱他们可以给自己买食物。

You can decide *for yourself*. 你可以自己作出决定。

e. in oneself 本身:

This novel is a history *in itself*. 这本小说本身就是一部历史。

They were good men *in themselves*, but they had to make a living too. 他们本身都是好人,但他们也得谋生。

f. to oneself 供自己用:

She has a small room *to herself*. 她自己有一个小房间。

We want to have some time *to ourselves*. 我们希望有一些供我们自己支配的时间。

5.3.2　相互代词

相互代词只有两个,即:

one another	each other

可表示两个人或几个人之间的相互关系。在句中可以:

1) 用作宾语:

Probably we influence *each other*. 或许我们相互影响。

We've known *each other* for many years. 我们认识许多年了。

The birds fought *each other* over the bread. 鸟儿为了面包互相争斗。

Yes, we can help *one another*. 是的,我们可以互相帮助。

Liz and I have known *one another* for years. 丽丝和我认识多年了。

2) 用作介词宾语：

They struck at *each other*. 他们彼此打斗。

Their rooms were next (to) *each other*. 他们的房间彼此相邻。

The three women looked at *each other*. 三个女人互相望了望。

We don't see much of *each other*. 我们不常见面。

They exchanged news with *one another*. 他们互相交换消息.

You should listen to *one another* a bit more. 你们应多倾听一点彼此的意见。

3) 和 's 一道构成定语：

We enjoyed *each other's* company. 我们喜欢彼此待在一起。

They were holding *each other's* hands. 他们拉着彼此的手。

They often stayed in *one another's* house. 他们常常待在彼此的家里。

We often listen to *one another's* records. 我们常常听彼此的唱片。

有时 each other 还可分开用：

We *each* know what *the other* thinks. 我们都知道彼此的想法。

Each tried to do more than *the other*. 他们争着多干活。

5.4 指示代词

5.4.1 指示代词的基本用法

指示代词有下面四个：

this	that	these	those

在句中可用作：

1) 主语：

Charles, *this* is my wife, Claudia. 查尔斯，这是我妻子克罗狄亚。

These are our children, David and Vicky. 这是我们的孩子大卫和维琪。

This can all wait. 这一切都可以等一等。

Is *this* your first visit to Paris? 这是你第一次到巴黎吗？

Are *these* what you want? 这些是你要的吗？

That isn't what I meant at all. 这完全不是我的意思。

Who's *that* in the garden? —— *That's* my younger brother. 花园里那人是谁？——是我弟弟。

What are *those*?　那些是什么？

That was twenty years ago.　那是二十年前的事了。

△ 常可用 that 代表刚说的事，这时常可译作"这"：

That's where the shoe pinches.　这正是症结所在。

That's why I object to the idea.　这就是我反对这个想法的原因。

That's how the matter stands at present.　这就是目前的情况。

Thank you. *That* will do.　谢谢你，这样就行了。

△ 电话里 this 和 that 可指人：

Who is *this*?　你是哪位？

Was *that* Nancy on the phone?　是南希打电话来吗？

This is Mary.　我是玛丽呀。

2）宾语或介词宾语：

Dad gave me *this*.　这是我爸给我的。

What do you think of *this*?　你觉得这个怎样？

Take *these* to your mother.　把这些带给你母亲。

I want you to promise *that*.　我希望你答应这一点。

I have no doubt about *that*.　我对此没有怀疑。

What? Have you finished all *those* I gave you?　什么？你把我给你的全吃完了？

3）偶尔用作表语：

What I want to stress is *this*.　我想强调的是这一点。

The winning numbers are *these*.　获奖号码是这些。

5.4.2 指示形容词的基本用法

1） 当 this，that 等词用作定语时，有人称为 **指示形容词** (Demonstrative Adjectives)，也有人称为限定词，它们主要用作定语：

This house is (*These* rooms are) for rent.　这所(些)房子(房间)供出租。

This time last year we were in Japan.　去年这时我们在日本。

These two problems are hard.　这两个问题很难。

He went to college *that* autumn.　那年秋天他上了大学。

I put my odds and ends into *that* drawer.　我把杂七杂八的东西都放进了那个抽屉里。

If *those* clouds drift away, we'll have a fine afternoon.　如果那些云彩飘走，

下午天就会好了。

2) 还可和 of 短语连用，表示一定的感情色彩 (厌烦、不满、赞叹等):

I hate *that old bike of yours*. 我讨厌你的那辆破自行车。

I really like *those paintings of your sister's*. 我的确很喜欢你姐姐的那些画。

This daughter of yours is doing fine work at school. 你的这个女儿在学校功课很好。

I like *these poems of Jane's*. 我喜欢简的这些诗。

3) this 可以和某些名词连用，表示 "今天"、"今年" 等:

Are you going out *this evening*? 你今天晚上要出去吗?

She gave me a long distance call *this morning*. 今天早上她给我打了一个长途电话。

How many classes did you go to *this afternoon*? 今天下午你上了几节课?

They are going to college *this autumn*. 他们今年秋天上大学。

He won't go home *this year*. 他今年不回家。

还可用在 **this day week** 这类短语中:

She will be back *this day week*. 她将在一星期后回来。

We've arranged to meet *this day week*. 我们安排好一周后见面。

I saw her *this day week*. 我是一星期前见到她的。

these days 表示 "近来"、"现今":

He was feeling optimistic *these days*. 近来他感到很乐观。

She seldom comes to see me *these days*. 现今她很少来看我。

5.4.3　that 和 those 的特别用法

1) that 可代表前面提到的名词以避免重复:

The wheat crop in 1999 was inferior to *that* of 1995. 1999年的小麦收成比1995年差。

The oil output last year was much higher than *that* of 1990. 去年的石油产量比1990年高得多。

Life today is much better than *that* in the old days. 现在的生活比过去好多了。

His description did not answer to *that* of the thief. 小偷的模样和他所描述的不相符。

2）those 可代表前面提到的复数名词：

His stories are more interesting than *those* I told. 他的故事比我讲的有趣。

My questions are similar to *those* you raised. 我的问题和你提的差不多。

Our performances, of course, can't compare with *those* of professionals.
全我们的演出当然不能和职业演员的相比。

3）that 还可用在某些成语中，如：

a. like that 这样：

Don't hold it *like that* — you'll break it. 不要这样拿，你会把它弄破的。

Do they always dance *like that* in France? 他们在法国都这样跳舞吗？

b. that is (to say) 这就是说：

He's a local administrator, *that is to say*, a civil servant. 他是本地一名行
政人员，也就是说，一名公务员。

I'm on holiday next week. *That is to say*, from Tuesday. 我下星期休假，
确切地说，从星期二开始。

The household was as happy as could be. All, *that is*, except Fiorella. 全家
都非常高兴，只有菲奥列拉除外。

c. that's all 只是，就这些：

"How are you feeling?" "Fine, a bit tired, *that's all*." "你感觉怎样？"
"挺好，只是稍有点累。"

Just don't do it again, *that's all*. 只是以后别再这样做了，就这些。

d. that's (about) it 说对了：

That's it. You've described exactly what I felt about the film. 说对了，你
正好说出了我对这部电影的感受。

"You have no confidence?" "*That's about it*. I'm no good." "你没有信
心？""你说对了，我不行。"

e. that's that 情况就是这样：

He's gone and *that's that*. 他走了，情况就是这样。

Well, *that's that*. No more work until Monday. 情况就是这样，到星期一
才有工作。

f. What's that? 你说什么？

What's that? He refuses to come? 你说什么？他不肯来？

What? *What's that* you say? 什么？你说什么？

5.5　疑问代词和连接代词

5.5.1　疑问代词

疑问代词有下面这些：

| who | whom | whose | what | which |

1）**who** 在句中多用作主语或表语：

Who did this?　这是谁干的？

Who would like to go with us?　谁想和我们一块儿去？

Who are those girls?　——They're Tom's daughters.　那些女孩是谁？

　　——她们是汤姆的女儿。

在口语中也常用作宾语：

Who did you meet at the party?　你在晚会上碰到谁了？

Who did you go with?　你和谁一道去的？

"I'm writing a letter." "*Who* to?"　"我在写信。" "写给谁？"

在笔语或正式文体中不宜这样用。

2）**whom** 在句中用作宾语或介词的宾语：

Whom did you see?　你见到谁了？

Whom are you writing to?　你在给谁写信？

You saw *whom*?　你见到谁了？

在紧跟介词时只能用 whom, 不能用 who：

To *whom* should I write?　我应当给谁写信？

To *whom* did you give the parcel?　你把包裹给谁了？

With *whom* did she come?　她和谁一道来的？

3）**whose** 表示"谁的"，可用作：

a. 定语：

Whose umbrella is this?　这是谁的雨伞？

Whose fault is it?　这得怪谁？

b. 主语：

Whose won the first prize?　谁的获了头奖？

Whose is better, yours or hers?　谁的好一些, 你的还是她的？

c. 表语：

Whose are these?　这些是谁的？

d. 宾语:

Whose are you going to borrow?　你准备借谁的?

4) what 和 **which** 都可在句中用作:

a. 主语:

What's your plan, then?　那么你有什么计划?

What's up?　出了什么事?

Which is your seat?　哪是你的座位?

Which of them came late?　他们谁迟到了?

b. 宾语或介词宾语:

What can we do about it?　这事我们有什么办法?

What's all this about?　这一切都是怎么回事?

Which do you prefer, coffee or tea?　你愿喝咖啡还是茶?

Which of them should I speak to?　我该和他们中的谁谈?

c. 定语:

What color are the curtains?　窗帘是什么颜色的?

What day is today?　今天星期几?

Which way should we go?　我们应往那边走?

At *which* station should I change trains?　我应在哪一站换车?

△ what 还可用作表语:

What's your sister?　你姐姐是干什么的?

5) whoever 和 whatever 是 who 和 what 的强调形式:

Whoever heard of such a thing?　谁听说过这样的事?

Whoever could be phoning so late at night?　这么晚了会是谁来电话?

Whatever do you mean?　你到底是什么意思?

Whatever happened to her?　她到底出了什么事?

5.5.2　连接代词

连接代词与疑问代词同形,引导各种从句,在从句中它们可用作:

1) 主语:

I asked him *who* came into the room.　我问他谁到屋里来了。

No one can tell *what* will happen next.　谁也说不出下一步将发生什么情况。

The twins are so much alike that I never know *which* is which.　那对孪生兄弟长得那么相像,我老弄不清谁是谁。

I can't tell *whose* is better.　我说不上谁的好一些。

2) 宾语 (在口语中可用主格):

I asked him *whom* he saw.　我问他看见谁了。

I don't care *what* he thinks.　我不管他怎么想。

Ask him *which* he wants.　问问他要哪一个。

I don't know *who(m)* you mean.　我不知道你指谁。

3) 介词宾语 (在口语中有时可用 who,但紧接介词之后时只能用 whom):

I wonder *who* he's talking to.　我不知道他在和谁讲话。

I wonder to *whom* he had addressed the letter.　我不知道他把信写给谁。

Remember *what* we're here for.　记住我们来这里要干什么。

She couldn't decide *which* she should listen to.　她不能确定她该听哪一个。

4) 表语:

Do you know *what* that girl's father is?　你知道那女孩的父亲是干什么的吗?

She demanded to know *whose* the child was.　她要求知道这孩子是谁的。

I can't recall *what* his name was.　我记不起他叫什么名字了。

It was so dark that I couldn't tell who was *who*.　天那样黑,我分不清谁是谁。

5) 定语:

I wonder *whose* house that is.　我不知道那是谁的房子。

I asked him *what* clothes I should wear.　我问他我应穿什么衣服。

Let me know *which* train you'll be arriving on.　告诉我你将坐哪趟火车。

连接代词还可引导不定式短语,多作宾语或介词宾语:

We can't decide *whom to invite*.　我们不能决定该邀请谁。

I don't know *who to ask advice from*.　我不知道应当向谁请教。

They exchanged views on the question of *whom to elect*.　他们就选谁的问题交换了意见。

We must decide *what to do with her*.　我们必须决定怎么处置她。

He didn't say anything about *what to do*.　他只字未说该怎么办。

She couldn't decide *which to buy*.　她不能决定该买哪一个。

5.5.3　关系代词型的 what

what 可引导从句,表示"the thing which...",例如:

That's *what I want to know*.　这正是我想知道的事。

What you said was quite right.　你说的话完全正确。

Show me *what you have in your hand*.　把你手上的东西给我看看。

这种 what 引导的从句，相当于"一个名词＋关系从句"：

what you need　你需要的东西

what I want to say　我想说的话

what I don't understand　我所不能理解的

what we have to consider　我们必须考虑的(事)

因此，这种 what 称为"**关系代词型的 what**"(Relative what)，它引导的从句在句中可用作：

1) 主语：

What she saw gave her a little fright.　她看到的情况使她有点惊恐。

What you need is a warm sweater.　你需要的是一件暖和的毛衣。

What I'm afraid of is their taking him to Boston.　我担心的是他们把他带往波士顿。

2) 宾语：

I cannot do *what you asked me to do*.　我不能做你要求我做的事。

She began to criticize *what he had done*.　她开始批评他的所做所为。

I'll do *what I can*.　我将尽力而为。

3) 介词宾语：

He was depressed by *what he had gone through*.　他经历的事使他感到抑郁。

Don't poke your nose into *what doesn't concern you*.　别多管闲事。

The city isn't much different from *what it was ten years ago*.　这座城市和十年前相比没有多大变化。

4) 表语：

I should like to be a teacher. That's *what I want to be*.　我想当老师，这是我的愿望。

Times aren't *what they were*.　时代不同了。

Your mother's health is not *what it ought to be*.　你母亲的健康状况不理想。

5) 插入语：

Then I discovered, *what was news to me*, that his wife was your cousin.　这时我发现了一件新鲜事，他的妻子是你的表妹。

He is an interesting speaker, and, *what's more important*, he knows his subject thoroughly. 他讲话很风趣，更重要的是，他对所讲的话题了解得很透彻。

He went to the meeting and, *what was worse*, insisted on speaking. 他去参加了会议，更糟糕的是，他还坚持要发言。

在从句中 what 有时用作定语：

What little he said on the subject was full of wisdom. 对这问题他的寥寥数语中充满了智慧。

What few friends I have here have been very kind to me. 我这里的少数几个朋友都对我很好。

What education I have is fragmentary, sketchy. 我受的那点教育都是支离破碎的，很肤浅。

I will give you *what help I can*. 我将尽量给你帮忙。

5.5.4 由 ever 构成的连接代词

1) who(m)，what，which 都可以和 ever 构成连接代词，也有人称作连词，可在句中引导状语从句，表示"不管…"：

I'll find the person who did this, *whoever he is*. 我将找出干这事的人，不管他是谁。

Whoever else may object, I mean to do it. 不管还有谁反对，我都将这样做。

Whoever rings, tell him I'm out. 不管谁来电话，都告诉他我不在家。

I'll post that letter *whatever Wilson says*. 不管威尔逊怎么说，我都要把那封信发出去。

Whatever happens, I'm going. 不管发生什么事，我都要走。

Whatever weather it is, we shall start at 9 o'clock. 不管天气怎样，我们都九点出发。

Whichever you choose, the others will be offended. 不管你选谁，其他人总会不高兴。

British foreign policy remains the same, *whichever party is in power*. 不管哪个党执政，英国的外交政策都保持不变。

Whichever road you take, the drive won't be more than an hour. 不管你走哪条路，开车去都不到一小时。

2) 这类代词还可引导名词性从句，表示"任何…的人(或东西)"，在句中用作:

a. 主语:

Whoever is responsible will have to pay for the damage. 凡是责任者都得赔偿损失。

Whoever you invite will be welcome. 凡你邀请的人都在欢迎之列。

Whatever I have is at your service. 我所有的东西任凭你使用。

Whichever you want is yours. 任何东西你想要就归你。

b. 宾语:

They may marry *who(m)ever they desire*. 他们可以娶任何他们想娶的人。

I'll just say *whatever comes into my head*. 我想到什么就说什么。

I said he might have *whichever he liked*. 我说他喜欢哪个就拿哪个。

Take *whichever seat you like*. 你愿坐哪儿就坐哪儿。

c. 介词宾语:

I want to speak to *whoever is in charge*. 我想和随便哪个负责人谈谈。

Talk to me about *whatever is troubling you*. 跟我谈谈任何使你烦心的事。

She might live in *whichever room she liked*. 她愿住哪个房间都可以。

5.6   关系代词

5.6.1   关系代词的作用

关系代词有如下这些:

who	whom	whose	that	which

它们都是用来引导定语从句的。这类代词都起着三重作用，一是代表前面的名词，二是把从句和它所修饰的词连接起来，三是在从句中也担任一个成分，例如:

I met someone *who* said he knew you. 我碰到一个人，他说他认识你。

(who 代表 someone，又引导从句修饰它，同时又在从句中担任主语)

The noise *that* he made woke everybody up. 他弄出的声音把大家都吵醒了。(that 代表 noise，又引导从句修饰它，又在从句中担任 made 的宾语)

I saw something in the paper *which* might interest you.　我在报上看到一点消息，可能会使你感兴趣。（which 代表 something，又引导从句修饰它，又在从句中担任主语）

　　这种代词起着关连作用，把引导的从句和所修饰的词连接起来，因此称作关系代词，它们引导的从句称为 **关系从句** (Relative Clauses)，也称 **定语从句** (Attributive Clauses)。

5.6.2　who, whom 和 whose 的用法

1) who 代表人，在从句中作主语：

The man *who* robbed her has been arrested.　抢她东西的人被捕了。

The girls *who* served in the shop were the owner's daughters.　在商店里接待顾客的那些姑娘是老板的女儿。

The girl *who* spoke is my best friend.　讲话的姑娘是我最好的朋友。

2) whom 也代表人，但在从句中作宾语或介词宾语：

The man *whom* I saw told me to come back today.　我见到的那个人让我今天再来。

The girls *whom* he employs are always complaining about their pay.　他雇用的姑娘们老是抱怨工资太低。

The man with *whom* I was travelling didn't speak English.　和我一道旅行的那人不会讲英语。

在口语中常可用 who 代替，也可省略：

The man *(who)* I saw told me to wait.　我见到的那个人让我等一会儿。

The girl *(who/whom)* I spoke to was a student.　和我讲话的女孩是个学生。

但紧跟介词时只能用 whom：

The man to *whom* I spoke was a foreigner.　我找他讲话的那人是外国人。

The man from *whom* I bought it told me to read the instructions.　卖我货的人让我看一看说明书。

3) whose 表示"某人的"，在从句中作定语：

A mental patient is one *whose* mind is diseased.　精神病人就是脑子有病的人。

I know a boy *whose* father is an acrobat.　我认识一个男孩，他父亲是杂技演员。

That's the boy *whose* mother has just died.　这就是那个刚死了妈的男孩。

The film is about a spy *whose* wife betrays him. 这部电影讲一个间谍,他的妻子出卖了他。

有时可指无生命的东西:

He saw a house *whose* windows were all broken. 他看到一所房子,窗子全都破了。

He showed me a machine *whose* parts are too small to be seen. 他给我展示了一种机器,它的部件都小得无法看到。

I saw a film *whose* name I have forgotten. 我看了一部电影,名字我忘了。

5.6.3 that 和 which 的用法

1) that 可以代表人 (a),也可以代表东西 (b):

a. He *that* would eat the fruit must climb the tree. (谚)想吃果子就得爬树。

Can you think of anyone *that* could look after him? 你能想到什么人能照顾他吗?

The man *that* I spoke to told me to wait. 我找他讲话的人让我等一等。

b. That is the picture *that (which)* caused such a sensation. 这就是那张引起如此轰动的画。

The stairs that lead to the cellar are rather slippery. 通往地窖的楼梯相当滑。

All the apples that fall are eaten by wild boars. 落在地上的苹果都被野猪吃了。

在从句中作宾语时,that 常可省略:

This is the best hotel *(that)* I know. 这是我知道的最好的旅馆。

Who is the man *(that)* you were talking to? 刚才你在和谁讲话?

2) which 只能代表东西或动物,它在从句中可充当:

a. 主语:

She was not in the train *which* arrived just now. 她不在刚到的火车上。

The dog *which* was lost has been found. 丢失的狗找着了。

This is the book *which* was on the table. 这就是原来在桌上的那本书。

b. 宾语:

The car *which (that)* I hired broke down. 我租的汽车坏了。

These are the conditions *which* we have to accept. 这些就是我们必得接受的条件。

His mind was full of ideas *which* he wanted to discuss. 他脑中充满了各种想和别人讨论的想法。

c. 介词宾语:

The day on *which* I saw him was the greatest of my life. 见到他的那天是我一生中最伟大的日子。

That's a formality *which* we have to go through. 这是我们必须履行的手续。

The ladder *which (that)* I was standing on began to slip. 我站的梯子开始滑动。

在作宾语或介词宾语时, which (that) 常可省略:

That's the house (which/that) we built. 这就是我们盖的房子。

This is the book (which/that) you wanted. 这是你要的书。

There are the difficulties (which/that) we got into. 这些就是我们碰到的困难。

但在紧跟介词时, 只能用 which, 不能用 that, 而且不能省略:

Read the passage to *which* I referred in my talk. 读一读我在讲话中提到的那段文字。

The situation in *which* he found himself was very difficult. 他的处境非常困难。

在口语中, 介词和它的宾语分开, 也可以省略:

The situation (that/which) he found himself in was very difficult.

────────────

5.6.4　限制性定语从句和非限制性定语从句

定语从句有两类, 即 **限制性定语从句** (Restrictive Attributive Clause) 和 **非限制性定语从句** (Non-Restrictive Attributive Clause)。

1) 限制性定语从句:

这种从句限制所修饰词的意义, 如把它拿掉, 句子意思即不清楚, 甚至失去意义, 例如:

That's the machine *he designed*. 这就是他设计的机器。(若把he designed 去掉, 句子意思则不清楚)

Madame Curie was a woman *we admired*. 居里夫人是我们崇拜的女性。

（若把 we admired 去掉, 句子就失去意义）

前面举的例子都包含限制性定语从句,在译成汉语时也多译成一个定语,如"我们崇拜的"、"他设计的"。只有在限制性定语从句中，作宾语的关系代词才能省略。

2) 非限制性定语从句：

另有一种定语从句和主句(句子的其他部分)关系不太紧密，对所修饰词的意思没有限制作用，把它拿掉对句子基本上没有影响，句子依然完整。它可以说是一个附加上去的成分，通常都用逗号把它和句子的其他部分分开，译成汉语时常可译成并列句。这种从句只能由 who(m) (a)，whose (b) 或 which (c) 引导：

a. Peter, *who* had been driving all day, suggested stopping at the next town. 彼得开了一天的车，建议在下一个城镇停一停。

I passed the letter to Helen, *who* was sitting beside me. 我把信传给海伦，她就坐在我旁边。

I've invited Mrs Green, *who* lives in the next flat. 我邀请了格林太太，她就住在隔壁。

Peter, *whom* everyone suspected, turned out to be innocent. 彼得受到大家的怀疑，但结果证明他是无辜的。

Mr Black, for *whom* I was working, was very generous. 我给布莱克先生工作，他为人很大方。

David, *whom (who)* I played tennis with on Sundays, was a colleague of mine. 我星期天都和大卫打网球，他是我的一位同事。

b. Anne, *whose* children are at school all day, is trying to get a job. 安妮的孩子们全天上学，她在想法找一份工作。

This is Harry, *whose* class you'll be taking over. 这是哈利，你将接手他的班。

My dog, *whose* temper is very uncertain, often bites judges at dog shows. 我那条狗的脾气捉摸不定，参加狗展时常咬裁判。

c. The 8:30 train, *which* is usually very punctual, was late today. 八点三十分的(火)车通常很准时，但今天晚点了。

My new car, *which* I paid several thousand pounds for, is not running well. 我的那辆新车花了我好几千镑，开起来却不太好。

They drafted two different constitutions, one of *which* was never put in force. 他们草拟了两部不同的宪法，其中一部从未实施过。

5.6.5　which 的特殊用法

1) 在非限制性定语从句中，which 可以代表主句的一部分，甚至全部，而不仅仅限于一个名词或代词：

This I did at nine o'clock, after *which* (=doing it) I sat some time reading the paper.　我九点钟做了这事，之后我就坐着看了一会儿报。

He invited us to dinner, *which* was very kind of him.　他请我们去吃饭，这是他难得的好意。

We had to sleep in our wet clothes, *which* was most uncomfortable.　我们不得不穿着湿衣服睡，这很不舒服。

He said he had never seen her before, *which* was not true.　他说他以前从未见过她，这不是真的。

2) which 有时在从句中作定语：

He advised me to hide behind the door, *which* advice I took at once.　他让我躲在门后，我立即照着做了。

He believes in the abolition of capital punishment, *which* idea I am quite opposed to.　他主张废除死刑，对这种观念我是完全反对的。

She may not be in, in *which* case you could leave her a note.　她可能不在家，如果是那样你可以给她留个条。

He studied computer science, *which* knowledge is very important today.　他学的是电脑，这门知识现在很重要。

在书面语中，有时把这类从句单列成一句：

From *which* he learned a few lessons which were later of value to him.　从中他得到了一些教训，对他后来很有用处。

3) which 还可以和不定式一起用：

Allow me one minute in *which* to change my costume.　给我一点时间去换装。

She had a little money in the bank, with *which* to help her mother.　她在银行存了一点钱，用这钱来帮助她的母亲。

Now he had no pretext on *which* to stay in the house.　现在他没有什么借口再在这家待下去了。

4) which 有时还可以表示"任何一个"，意思和 whichever 差不多：

You may have *which* apple you like.　你想要哪个苹果就拿哪个。

Take *which* dresses you want from my wardrobe.　想要什么衣服就从我的衣柜里拿。

You may *select* which you like. 你可挑选任何你喜欢的。

Use *which* method you prefer. 你愿意用什么方法都行。

关于关系从句，在 22.3.1 — 22.3.2 节中还将作进一步讨论。

5.7 不定代词

5.7.1 两类不定代词

不定代词可分作两类：

1) 由 body，one，thing 构成的合成代词：

somebody	anybody	everybody	nobody
someone	anyone	everyone	no one
something	anything	everything	nothing

2) 兼作代词和限定词的词：

all	another	any	both	each
either	few	little	many	much
neither	none	other	some	

此外还有 every 和 no，只能作限定词 (或称形容词)，不能作代词。

5.7.2 合成不定代词

1) somebody，someone，anybody，anyone:

somebody 和 someone 意思相同，都表示"某人"，但只用于肯定句 (a)，在否定及疑问句中通常用 anybody 或 anyone (b)：

a. *Somebody (someone)* said that you'd been ill. 有人说你病了。

There's *somebody* at the door. 门口有个人。

Somebody (someone) has turned off the light. 有人把灯关了。

Someone had placed a lamp on the table. 有人在桌上放了一盏灯。

I need *somebody* to help me in the work. 我需要人帮我的忙。

She wants *someone* to look after her. 她要人照顾她。

b. Did *anybody* ever hear of such a thing? 谁曾听说过这样的事？

Has *anybody* anything more to say?　还有谁有话要说？

I didn't know *anybody* at the party.　晚会上我谁也不认识。

Is there *anyone (anybody)* here who can speak Japanese?　这儿有会说日语的人吗？

I do not know *anyone* connected with the exhibition.　我不认识与展览会有关系的人。

I hope our delay will not worry *anyone*.　我希望我们的延误不会使什么人着急。

anybody 和 anyone 还可表示"任何人"：

Anybody can tell you how to get there.　谁都能告诉你怎么到那里。

I never discussed it with *anybody*.　我从未和任何人谈论此事。

Anyone can do that.　这事谁都能做。

She felt that she could do it better than *anyone*.　她觉得这事她能比任何人都做得好。

2) everybody 和 everyone 意思相同，表示"人人"、"大家"：

Everybody was glad to see Martin back.　看到马丁回来大家都很高兴。

Everybody's business is nobody's business.　(谚)人人都管等于没人管。

Everyone laughed, me included.　大家都笑了，我也笑了。

The police questioned *everybody (everyone)* in the room.　警察盘问了屋里所有的人。

3) something 表示"某样东西"(a)，在疑问句及否定句中用 anything (b)：

a. *Something* has happened.　出事了。

There was *something* missing.　里面缺了点什么。

She'll be able to do *something* for you.　她将有能力为你做点什么。

I will tell you *something* of my own experience.　我将告诉你一点我自己经历的事。

b. Has *anything* happened?　出什么事了吗？

(Is there) *Anything* I can do?　我能做点什么吗？

We can't decide *anything* now.　现在我们不能决定什么。

I can't do *anything* like that.　我不能做这样的事。

anything 还可用于条件句：

If you want *anything*, you can call me.　你如果需要什么可以叫我。

Hereafter when you need *anything*, I want you to come to me.　从今以后当你需要什么时，希望你来找我。

anything 还可表示"任何东西 (事)":

Anything is better than nothing.　有总比没有好。

I want something to eat, *anything* will do.　我想吃点东西，什么都行。

If it's possible I'd do *anything* for you.　只要可能我愿为你做任何事情。

Take *anything* you fancy.　你喜欢什么就拿什么。

4) everything 表示"一切" (a), nothing 用于否定句 (等于not anything), 表示"没有什么" (b)：

a. How is *everything*?　一切可好？

We're anxious for *everything* to be settled.　我们亟盼一切得到解决。

The strike brought *everything* to a standstill.　罢工使一切都停顿了。

Money isn't *everything*.　金钱不是一切。

b. But *nothing* could make her alter her views.　什么都不能使她改变看法。

He had *nothing* to say against you.　他对你没有什么(不满的)意见。

He knew absolutely *nothing*.　他完全一无所知。

Oh, that's *nothing*.　哦，没什么。

5) nobody 与 no one 意思相同, 表示"没有人"：

Nobody stands on much ceremony with us.　没人跟我们讲客套。

"Who's in the dining-room?" "*Nobody (No one)*." "谁在餐厅里？"
　"没人。"

He said he would marry me or *nobody*.　他说他要娶我, 否则就谁也不娶。

No one dared speak of it.　没人敢谈及此事。

Apart from them, I had *no one* to talk to.　除了他们, 我没有别人可以交谈。

nobody 还可表示"无关紧要的人"：

Why does he give himself such airs; he's a mere *nobody*.　他干吗摆这种架子, 他只是个无足轻重的小人物。

I want to be famous! I'm tired of being a *nobody*.　我要出名! 当无名小卒我都当腻了。

5.7.3　some, any, no 的用法

1) some 和 any 的用法：

some 和 any 都表示"一些", 可以指人或其他可数的东西 (a), 也可代表不可数的东西 (b), 可用作主语、宾语等, some 用于肯定句, any 用于疑问句

及否定句:

    a. *Some* of them can speak Japanese.　他们有些人会说日语。

    Some of his books are very exciting.　他的书有些很激动人心。

    Some still believe he was innocent.　有些人仍然认为他是无辜的。

    Did *any* of your photos come out well?　你的照片洗出来都好吗?

    Do you know *any* of the people?　这些人中有你认识的吗?

    I don't expect to see any of them there.　我估计不会在那里看到他们中的什么人。

    b. I don't need any more money — I've still got *some*.　我不需要再多的钱, 我还有一些。

    He kept *some* and gave the rest away.　他留下一些, 把其余的都给人了。

    I don't think there's *any* left.　我想已不剩什么了。

    Did she give you *any*?　她给你一点了吗?

    Is there *any* left in the fridge?　冰箱里还有吗?

some 间或可用在疑问句中, 这时往往预计有肯定答复:

    Did *some* of you sleep on the floor?　你们中有些人在地板上睡的?

    Can I take *some* of this paper?　这纸我拿点行吗?

any 还可用来表示"任何 (一个) ":

    He was just as hard up as *any* of us.　他和我们中的任何人都一样手头拮据。

    Any is good enough for me.　随便哪个对我来说都是够好的。

    I'll take *any* that you don't want.　你不要的我都要。

    His gift was unknown to *any* (of us) except himself.　他的天赋除了他自己(我们)谁也不知道。

2) some, any, no 作定语的用法:

some, any, no 都可用作定语, some 和 any 都表示"一些", some 用于肯定句, any 用于疑问句及否定句, no 表示"没有", 等于 not any。这些词有些语言学家称为限定词, 也有些人称为形容词, 它们可以修饰可数名词 (a), 也可以修饰不可数名词 (b):

    a. She bought *some* biscuits.　她买了一些饼干。

    Some children learn languages easily.　有些孩子学语言很容易。

    There are scarcely *any* flowers in the garden.　花园里几乎没有花。

    Are there *any* cows in the field?　这牧场里有奶牛吗?

    Did he catch *any* fish?　他捕到鱼了吗?

No man is born wise. (谚)聪明非天生。

b. S*ome* work is pleasant. 有些工作是令人愉快的。

I enjoy *some* music. 我喜欢某些音乐。

Some French wine is quite sweet. 有些法国酒相当甜。

I have hardly *any* spare time. 我几乎没有空余时间。

Have you *any* money on you? 你身上带钱了吗?

I don't think there is *any* petrol in the tank. 我想油箱里没油了。

Martin did *no* reading that night. 马丁那天晚上没看书。

3) some, any, no 的特别用法:

a. some 可用于请求或反问句中:

Could you lend me *some* money? 你能借我一些钱吗?

Would you like *some* tea? 你要不要喝点茶?

Aren't there *some* eggs in the fridge? 冰箱里不是还有些鸡蛋吗?

Didn't you put *some* stamps on the envelopes? 你信封上难道没贴邮票?

b. some 有时和单数可数名词连用,表示"某个"(=certain):

He had a good position in *some* shipping firm. 他在一家船运公司有个好职位。

He's living at *some* place in East Africa. 他住在东非某个地方。

Ask *some* typist to come here. 找一位打字员到这里来。

There must be *some* reason for what he's done. 他这样做总有某种原因。

c. any 可表示"任何(一个)",有时意思较弱,接近于一个不定冠词:

He wanted a job, *any* sort of a job. 他需要一份工作,什么工作都行。

Any time you want me, just send for me. 凡你需要我时就派人来找我。

Any colour will do. 什么颜色都行。

What I have told her isn't *any* secret. 我告诉她的话已不是什么秘密。

If you see *any* (=an) interesting book, please buy it for me. 如果你看到什么有意思的书,请给我买一本。

d. no 可构成否定句,等于 not a:

He is in *no* mood (not in a mood) for jokes. 他没有心情说笑话。

He found that this was *no* light task. 他发现这不是个轻松的工作。

He's *no* fool, he isn't. 他不是傻瓜,他并不傻。

He's *no* friend of mine. 他不是我的朋友。

He's *no* financial expert. 他不是金融专家。

5.7.4 many, much, few, little

1) 这几个词都是表示数量的，都可用作定语 (有人称作限定词，也有人称作形容词)，可构成六个词:

修饰可数名词	many (许多)	few (少数)	a few (几个)
修饰不可数名词	much (很多)	little (很少)	a little (一点儿)

many (用来修饰可数名词) 主要用在疑问句及否定句中 (a)，也可在肯定句中修饰主语等 (b)，还可和 too, so, as 等词一起用 (c):

a. Do you have *many* friends?　你有很多朋友吗？(肯定句多用 a lot of: He has a lot of friends.)

I wonder how *many* people will be at the party.　我不知道将有多少人来参加这个聚会。

Were there *many* pictures by women artists?　女画家的画多吗？

He didn't make *many* mistakes.　他出错并不多。

Not *many* people are interested in the activity.　没多少人对这活动感兴趣。

b. *Many* people do not get enough to eat.　许多人没有足够的东西吃。

Many students supported the plan.　许多学生赞成这项计划。

Rain has been forecast in *many* areas of the country.　预报国内很多地区要下雨。

The financial report had *many* flaws.　财务报告中有许多小毛病。

c. There are *too many* mistakes in this essay.　这篇论文错误太多。

I never saw *so many* swans on the lake.　我从未看见湖上有这么多天鹅。

As many as ten people were found living in a single room.　一间屋里住有十个人之多。

much 也表示"多"，但只能用来修饰不可数名词，主要用于疑问句和否定句 (a)，也可在肯定句中和 too, so 等词连用，或用在句首 (b):

a. Do you take *much* interest in it?　你对此兴趣大吗？(肯定句多用 a lot of: I've *a lot of* interest in it. 我对此很有兴趣。)

We don't have *much* free time.　我们没多少空余时间。

Did you have *much* difficulty in finding the house?　找到那所房子你费了很多周折吗？

I haven't got *much* money on me.　我身上没带多少钱。

How *much* time have you got?　你有多少时间？

b. You've given me too *much* food.　你给我的食物太多了。

So *much* time has been wasted that way.　那样可是浪费了大量时间。

Much money has been spent on it.　这上面花的钱太多了。

间或用在肯定句中(特别是在美国或较正式的文体中):

The news brought us *much* joy.　这消息使我们很高兴。

There is *much* good in him.　他很善良。

I have *much* pleasure in introducing our speaker.　我很高兴介绍我们的演讲者。

few 是 many 的反义词,表示"很少",用来修饰可数名词:

They exchanged *few* words.　他们没交谈几句。

There are *few* men more than six feet tall.　身高超过六英尺的男子很少。

Few people live to be 100.　活到一百岁的人很少。

There are *fewer* cars here today than yesterday.　今天这里的车比昨天少。

little 是 much 的反义词,也表示"很少",但只能用来修饰不可数名词,带有否定意味,意思接近于 no:

They had very *little* money.　他们没几个钱。

There is *little* hope that she will recover.　她痊愈的希望很小。

She had *little* spare time.　她空闲的时间很少。

I had *little* opportunity of seeing the country.　我很少有机会到乡下看看。

a few 表示"有几个",可修饰可数名词,意思接近于 some:

He asked us *a few* questions.　他问了我们几个问题。

This happened *a few* days ago.　这事发生在几天前。

Only *a few* students were awarded scholarships.　只有几个学生获得奖学金。

David had *a few* problems.　大卫有几个问题。

a little 表示"有一点",可修饰不可数名词,意思也接近于 some:

Come in and have *a little* whisky.　进来喝点威士忌。

She had *a little* money, ten pounds or so.　她有一点点钱,十镑左右。

There's only *a little* time left, isn't there?　只剩一丁点时间了,对吧?

Shall I go *a little* way with you?　要不要我陪你走一段路?

2) 这些词还可在句中作主语、宾语等:

many 表示"很多人或东西",代表可数名词:

Not *many* of us will pass the examination.　我们中不会有很多人通过这个考试。

Many of the mistakes were just careless.　错误中有很多是粗心造成的。

Many of the people at the meeting left early.　许多与会者都早早走了。

How *many* do you need?　你需要多少？

much 表示"好多"，可代表不可数的东西:

Much of this information has been inaccurate.　这信息很多都不准确。

Much hangs on his decision.　许多事有赖于他的决定。

I haven't time to do *much*.　我没有时间做很多的事。

I have *much* to talk over with him.　我有很多事要和他谈。

few 是 many 的反义词，表示"很少人或东西"，可代表可数名词:

Few of the players played really well.　没几个球员真正打得好。

Very *few* of the books are easy enough for me.　这些书没几本容易到我能读。

We saw *few* of the sights as we had so little time.　我们只有那么一丁点时间，所看的景点寥寥无几。

I knew *few* of the people there.　那儿的人我认识的很少。

little 是 much 的反义词，表示"很少"，只代表不可数的东西，意思接近于 nothing:

You have done very *little* for us.　你几乎没为我们做什么事。

He had *little* to tell us.　他没什么可告诉我们。

I understood *little* of his speech.　他的报告我几乎都没听懂。

You eat too *little*.　你吃得太少。

a few 有肯定的意思，表示"有几个(一些)"，代表可数的东西:

Only *a few* of the people who applied were suitable.　只有少数几个申请者合适。

I met *a few* of my friends there.　我在那里碰到了我的几个朋友。

She's written lots of books but I've only read *a few* (of them).　她写了很多书，但我只看过几本。

I knew *a few* of the people there.　那儿的人我认识几个.

a little 也有肯定的意思，表示"一点儿"，代表不可数的东西:

Try and eat *a little*.　尽量吃一点吧。

Tell me *a little* about his illness.　告诉我一点他的病情。

If you've got any spare milk, could you give me *a little*?　如果你有多余的牛奶，能否给我一点？

"Is there any butter left?" "Yes, just *a little*."　"黄油还有剩的吗?" "有，就剩一点点。"

5.7.5 all, each, none

1) all 可用作定语 (有人称作限定词)，可修饰可数名词，表示"所有的" (a)，也可修饰不可数名词，表示"一切" (b)，还可与可数名词单数连用，表示"整个" (c)：

a. *All* these girls were anaemic.　这些姑娘都贫血。

　　All my children can swim.　我的孩子都会游泳。

　　She has read *all* these books.　这些书她全看了。

b. *All* hope has gone.　一切希望都破灭了。

　　Not *all* food is good to eat.　并非所有的食物都适宜食用。

　　He has lost *all* his money.　他的钱全都丢了。

c. He spent *all* that year in London.　那一整年他都在伦敦。

　　He worked hard *all* his life.　他一生辛劳。

　　It has been raining *all* day.　雨下了一整天。

all 还可和名词一道用作表语，表示状态：

　　Auntie Ruth was *all sweetness*.　露丝姨妈非常亲切。

　　He was *all tenderness and kindness*.　他非常温柔和蔼。

　　That afternoon it seemed *all disappointment*.　那天下午情况似乎很令人失望。

2) all 也可用作代词，代表可数的东西 (a) 或不可数的东西 (b)，在句中作主语、宾语等：

a. *All* were pale and had dark rings under their eyes.　所有的人都脸色苍白，眼圈发黑。

　　All were sharply criticized.　所有的人都受到严厉的批评。

　　I brought *all* of them.　它们都是我带来的。

　　All of them voted against the plan.　他们都投票反对这项计划。

b. Now *all* was changed.　现在一切都变了。

　　I know that *all* was well with her.　我知道她一切都好。

　　It was she who was the cause of *all*.　这一切都是她造成的。

　　Take *all* of it.　把它全拿走。

all 在句中可用作同位语：

　　The people at the meeting *all* voted against it.　开会的人都投票反对它。

　　My children can *all* swim.　我的孩子们都会游泳。

　　She has read them *all*.　所有这些她全看了。

　　He's pretty sick about it *all*.　他对这一切相当厌烦。

all 后面还可跟一定语修饰它：

All that she lacked was training.　她欠缺的就是训练。

All I desired was leisure for study.　我想得到的只是用于学习的空闲时间。

All I can say is that we are extremely sorry.　我能说的就是我们甚为抱歉。

I have said *all* I intend to say.　我想说的都说了。

You've seen *all* there is to see.　可看的你都看了。

Is that *all* you want to say?　你想说的就是这些?

3) **each** 可作定语，表示"每一个"(这时有人称之为"限定词")：

Each delegation began to state its viewpoints.　各代表团都开始陈述其观点。

He gave *each* child a present.　他给了每个孩子一份礼物。

Each lesson lasts an hour.　每堂课时间为一小时。

Each day passed without any news.　一天天过去，音信杳然。

each 还可用作主语或宾语：

Each of the houses is painted a different color.　每座房子都漆成了不同颜色。

Each went his way.　各走各的路。

A chrysanthemum was presented to *each* of the ladies.　送给每位女士一朵菊花。

He gave two to *each*.　他给了每人两个。

有时还可作主语或宾语的同位语：

They were *each* sentenced to thirty days.　他们各被判处一个月的徒刑。

They went *each* to the room assigned.　他们各自走向所分配的房间。

We had *each* said a few words.　我们每人讲了几句话。

He gave the children a present *each*.　他给了每个孩子一份礼物。

4) **none** 和 no 都是否定词，no 用作定语(前面已经说过)，none 则用作主语 (a)、宾语或介词宾语 (b) 或同位语 (c)：

a. *None* of us would have said such a thing.　我们谁也不会说出这种话。

None of my friends ever come(s) to see me.　我的朋友一个都没来看我。

None of them has (have) replied yet.　他们都还没有回信。

None of these improvements has cost much.　这些改进花费都很少。

b. "Have you brought any books to read?" "No, *none*."　"你带了什么书看?" "没有，一本也没带。"

I like *none* of these pictures. 这些画我都不喜欢。

Some people own several houses, others have *none*. 有些人拥有几处房子，而另外的人则一处也没有。

How many questions are difficult? —— *None*. 难题有几个？ ——一个也没有。

c. We *none* of us live round here. 我们谁也不住在附近。

They have *none* of them fulfilled their tasks. 他们谁也没完成任务。

none 有时可指不可数的东西:

"How much petrol is there in the car?" "*None*!" "车里还有多少油？""一点都没有了!"

He has *none* of his brother's selfishness. 他完全没有他哥哥的那种自私。

He has lost *none* of his charm for her. 他丝毫没失去对她的吸引力。

5.7.6 both, either, neither

这三个词都指两者，both 表示"两者都…"，either 表示"两者中的任何一个"，neither 表示"两者都不":

1) **both** 在句中可用作定语 (这时可说是限定词) (a)，还可用作主语 (b)、宾语 (c) 或同位语 (d):

a. *Both* women were French. 两个妇女都是法国人。

Both (her) children are at college. (她的)两个孩子都在上大学。

He is blind in *both* eyes. 他双眼都失明了。

She held something in *both* (her) hands. 她两只手都拿着东西。

b. He has two brothers; *both* live in Seattle. 他有两个兄弟，都住在西雅图。

Both felt that they ought to do something. 两人都感到应该做点什么。

Both of the women were French. 两个妇女都是法国人。

Both of my parents live in London. 我的父母都住在伦敦。

c. Why not do *both*? 为什么两件事不都做？

I'll borrow *both* of them. 两个我都借。

I like these shirts. I'll take *both* (of them). 我喜欢这衬衫，两件我都要。

I'll do something for *both* of you. 我要为你们两人都做点什么。

d. His parents were *both* dead. 他的父母都不在了。

They have *both* seen the film. 他们俩都看过这部电影。

I shall read them *both*. 两本书我都要看。

We *both* went to their wedding.　我们俩都参加了他们的婚礼。

2) **either** 可用作定语 (这时可说是限定词) (a)、主语 (b) 或宾语 (c)：

a. *Either* proposal will have my support.　两个建议我都支持。

He could write with *either* hand.　他用哪只手写字都行。

Take *either* half; they're exactly the same.　拿哪一半都行，它们完全一样。

You can park on *either* side of the street.　你把车停在街的哪边都行。

b. *Either* (of these) would do.　(这两个)哪个都行。

Either of us is willing to help.　我们两人都愿意帮忙。

Either of the plans is equally good.　两个计划一样好。

She is younger than *either* of us.　她比我们俩都年轻。

c. I did not bring *either* with me.　两个我都没带。

I like *either* of these.　两个中哪一个我都喜欢。

I don't want to owe anything to *either* of you.　我不想欠你们两人中任何一人的情。

You can ask *either* of us for help.　你可以要求我们中随便哪个帮你。

either 还可作定语，表示"两…"：

It is a pleasant road, with trees on *either* side.　这是一条怡人的马路，两边都有树。

There are shops on *either* side of the street.　街道两边都有商店。

There's a staircase at *either* end of the corridor.　走廊的两头都有楼梯。

3) **neither** 可用作定语 (a)、主语 (b)、宾语 (c) 或同位语 (d)：

a. *Neither* man knew the way.　两人都不知道路。

Neither book is satisfactory.　两本书都不令人满意。

Neither statement is true.　两个说法都不真实。

Neither train had a restaurant car.　两列火车都没有餐车。

b. I tried on two dresses, but *neither* fits me.　我试了试两件套裙，哪一件也不合身。

Neither of them knew the way.　他俩谁都不知道路。

Neither of them had a restaurant car.　它们中哪一列都没有餐车。

"Which is your car?"　"*Neither*, mine is being repaired."　"哪辆车是你的?" "都不是，我的车在修。"

c. I've read *neither* of these books.　这两本书我都没看过。

I could answer *neither* of the questions.　两个问题我都答不上来。

She got *neither* of your letters.　你的两封信她都没收到。

"Will you have ice-cream or coca-cola ? " " *Neither*, thank you." "你要冰淇淋还是可口可乐?""谢谢你, 我都不要。"

d. They *neither* of them said anything. 他们谁也没说什么。

I hope that you'll *neither* of you say anything more. 我希望你俩都别再说什么了。

These two books are *neither* of them very good. 这两本书都不太好。

5.7.7　other, another

1) other 可用作定语 (这时可说是限定词), 表示"另外的"、"别的"、"其他的":

Miss Brown and two *other* teachers were there. 布朗小姐和另外两位老师在那里。

Other members may not like the idea. 其他成员可能不赞成这个想法。

Are there any *other* questions? 还有什么别的问题吗?

I'm busy now. Please come some *other* time. 我现在很忙, 请另找时间来。

还可用作主语 (a) 或宾语 (b), 表示"另外那个(的人)"、"别的…"(常可用于复数形式):

a. One of the boys is named Tom, the *other* named David. 一个男孩叫汤姆, 另外那个叫大卫。

Some like chocolate ice-cream, *others* prefer vanilla ice-cream. 有些人喜欢巧克力冰淇淋, 另外的人喜欢香草冰淇淋。

I went swimming while the *others* played tennis. 我去游泳, 另外的人则打网球。

Some people came by car, *others* came on foot. 有的人开车来, 另外的人走着来。

b. Show me some *others*. 另外拿几个给我看看。

These shoes are dirty — I'll have to wear my *others*. 这鞋脏了——我得另穿一双。

I don't like this one. Have you got any *others*? 我不喜欢这个, 你还有别的吗?

He raised one arm and then the *other*. 他举起一只手臂, 然后又举起另一只。

2) another 也可用作定语 (这时可说是限定词), 表示"另一个"(a) 或"又一个"(b):

a. Now she was in *another* difficulty.　现在她碰到了另一个困难。

She's got *another* boyfriend.　她还有一个男朋友。

He's writing *another* novel.　他在写另外一本小说。

He could get *another* girl to do my typing.　他可以找另外一个女孩来帮我打字。

b. She had *another* cup of tea.　她又喝了一杯茶。

Then *another* man rose to speak.　接着又有一个人起来发言。

She's going to have *another* baby.　她又要生孩子了。

In *another* year she'll go to school.　再过一年她就要上学了。

还可和一数词连用:

She'll remain in London for *another* four or five days.　她在伦敦还要逗留四五天。

I've still got *another* three questions to answer.　我还有三道题要答。

In *another* two weeks it'll be finished.　再过两个星期这活就完成了。

We've got *another* 50 kilometres to go.　我们还得往前开五十公里。

3) another 也可用作主语 (a)、宾语 (b)、或表语 (c), 表示"另外一个":

a. We've had many letters like this — *another* of them came today.　我们收到过许多这样的信, 今天又来了一封。

Then *another* put up his hand.　又一个人举手了。

There was a rainbow in the sky, and *another* in his breast.　有一道彩虹在天上, 还有一道在他心里。

b. They've got three children already and they're having *another*.　他们已经有了三个孩子, 很快又将有一个。

If you've already seen that film, we can go and see *another*.　如果这部片子你已看过, 我们可以去看另一部。

I don't like this room — let's ask for *another*.　我不喜欢这个房间——咱们另要一间吧。

c. Is this *another* of your silly jokes?　这是不是你又一个愚蠢的笑话?

Is this *another* of your schemes to make money?　这是不是你赚钱的另一个计划?

Saying is one thing and doing *another*.　说是一回事, 做是另一回事。

5.7.8　one, several

1) **one** 可以用作定语 (也可称为限定词), 表示 "一个":

One flower makes no garland.　(谚)一朵花不能编成花环。

One thing I'm sure of.　有一点我是肯定的。

He can't tell *one* tree from another.　他不会分辨树木。

The journey takes *one* hour.　路上要走一个钟头。

还可以和表示时间的名词连用:

One night there flew over the city a little swallow.　一天夜晚一只小燕子从城市上空飞过。

You'll regret it *one* day.　总有一天你会懊悔的。

One afternoon he went out with Arthus.　一天下午他和阿瑟一起外出。

One morning she was called to the headmaster's office.　一天早上她被叫到校长办公室去了。

有时还可表示 "唯一的":

He's the *one* man who can do it.　他是唯一能做这事的人。

It was her *one* great sorrow.　这是她唯一感到至为伤心的事。

She was the *one* bright ray in his narrow gloomy life.　她是他狭小而阴郁的生活圈子中唯一的一道亮光。

Her *one* fault appeared to be that she was too quiet.　她唯一的缺点似乎是过于沉默寡言。

2) one 可以用作主语 (a)、宾语或介词宾语 (b) 或表语 (c), 表示 "一个 (人)":

a. *One* of the three boys won a scholarship.　三个男生有一个获得奖学金。

Only *one* of them was invited.　他们中只有一个人受到邀请。

There were three coaches and *one* was black.　有三名教练,一个是黑人。

b. The twins are so alike that it's hard to tell *one* from the other.　这对孪生姐妹长得那样相像,很难把一个和另一个区分开来。

It's one for all and all for *one*.　这就是我为人人,人人为我。

Let me have *one*.　给我一个。

c. Perhaps you're *one* of the luckiest ones.　或许你是幸运者中的一个。

She's a quiet *one*.　她是个文静的女子。

还可用来泛指一般人 (a),或用来代替刚提到的一个可数的东西 (b):

a. *One* could see that he was very upset.　我们可以看出他很难过。

How is *one* to interpret his action?　人们该怎样解释他的行为呢?

One has to do one's best.　人总要尽力而为。

One can't work all the time.　你不能总是工作。

b. I haven't got a pen. Can you lend me *one*?　我没带钢笔,你能借我一支吗?

The question was a complicated *one*.　这是一个复杂的问题。

Your plan is a nice *one* on paper.　你的计划在纸上是不错的。

And the big fish continues to devour the little *ones*.　大鱼继续吃小鱼。

还可和一代词或形容词连用:

Which *one* do you mean?　你指哪一个?

I mean this (that) *one*.　我指这(那)一个。

Can you show me a better *one*?　你可否拿一个更好的给我看?

I want larger ones, not small *ones*.　我不要小的,我要大些的。

3) several 可作定语,表示"几个":

Several boys were injured.　有几个小伙子受伤了。

I've read it *several* times.　我看了好几遍。

My friend speaks *several* languages.　我的朋友能讲几种语言。

We received *several* replies to our inquiry.　我们的询问收到了几份回答。

还可作主语 (a) 或宾语 (b):

a. *Several* of us decided to walk home.　我们中有几个人决定步行回家。

Several (of them) were broken.　(它们)有几个破了。

Several of the apples are rotten, and several more have worm holes.　有几个苹果烂了,还有几个有虫眼。

There are *several* here that I don't know.　这儿有几个人我不认识。

b. I already have *several*.　我已经有几个了。

He invited *several* of his friends to the show.　他邀请了几个朋友去观看演出。

We managed to recover *several* of the missing articles.　我们设法找回了几件丢失的东西。

If you are looking for a photo of Alice, you'll find *several* in here.　如果你是在找艾丽丝的照片,这里面你会找到几张。

第6章 数词和量词

6.1 基 数 词

6.1.1 基数词构成法

1) 基数词 (Cardinal Numerals) 指表示数目的词。下面是最基本的基数词，其他数目都由这些基数词构成：

I	II	III	IV
1 one	11 eleven		100
2 two	12 twelve	20 twenty	a hundred
3 three	13 thirteen	30 thirty	1,000
4 four	14 fourteen	40 forty	a thousand
5 five	15 fifteen	50 fifty	1,000,000
6 six	16 sixteen	60 sixty	a million
7 seven	17 seventeen	70 seventy	1,000,000,000
8 eight	18 eighteen	80 eighty	a billion (十亿)
9 nine	19 nineteen	90 ninety	
10 ten			

2) 基数词构成法：

除了上表列出的词外，其他基数词构成的方法如下：

a. 21—99：先说"几十"，再说"几"，中间要加连字号：

    39   thirty-nine   52   fifty-two

    83   eighty-three   91   ninety-one

b. 101—999：先说"几百"，再加 and，再加末尾两位数或末位数：

    375   three hundred and seventy-five

582 five hundred and eighty-two

819 eight hundred and nineteen

902 nine hundred and two

c. 1,000 以上的词:

先从后向前数,每三位数加一个逗号,用这个方法把数目分作若干段,再一段段地念;第一个逗号前的数为 thousand,第二个逗号前的数为 million,第三个逗号前的数为 billion,例如:

4,007	four thousand and seven
8,021	eight thousand and twenty-one
13,849	thirteen thousand, eight hundred and forty-nine
631,562	six hundred and thirty-one thousand, five hundred and sixty-two
54,256,000	fifty-four million, two hundred and fifty-six thousand
970,000,000	nine hundred and seventy million
14,800,000,000	fourteen billion eight hundred million
2,000,000,000,000	two trillion (两万亿)

在这类数词中,hundred, thousand, million, billion 等词都用单数形式。

6.1.2　基数词在句中的作用

1) 基数词在句中主要用作:

a. 定语:

The river is about *eighty* miles long. 这条河大约八十英里长。

Over *4,650,000* workers were involved in the strikes. 有四百六十五万多工人参加了这些罢工。

b. 主语:

There were *millions* of blooms. 有数以百万计的花。

Two of the girls are from California. 姑娘中有两个来自加州。

Three will be enough. 三个就够了。

c. 宾语或介词宾语:

I read *four* of her novels. 我看了她写的四本小说。

"How many workers do they employ?" "Over *two hundred*, I think."

"他们雇佣了多少工人?" "我想有两百多吧。"

The city has a population of *three million*. 这座城市有三百万人口。

d. 表语:

He was a little over *five*. 他才五岁多一点。

Its population is nearly *two million*. 它的人口接近两百万。

I'm *fourteen* and she's *twelve*. 我十四岁,她十二岁。

e. 同位语:

You *two* take these seats. 你们两人坐这里。

Have you got tickets for us *three*? 有我们三个人的票吗?

2) 基数词还可用于复数形式,表示很大的数量:

The boat cost *hundreds* of pounds. 这条船花了几百英镑。

Thousands of people attended the meeting. 数千人参加了这次会议。

Millions (of people) are at risk from the disease. 数以百万计的人受到这种疾病的威胁。

Tens of thousands of buffaloes used to roam the prairie. 草原上过去有数以万计的野牛。

Thousands upon thousands of scallops appear off Long Island in the fall. 秋天长岛附近的海滩上会出现数以万计的扇贝。

They arrived in *twos* and *threes*. 他们三三两两地来了。

3) 某些基数词的复数形式可以用在"in the (one's) —"结构中,表示:

a. 年岁:

He was a thinnish fellow in his *forties*. 他是个偏瘦的人,有四十多岁了。

She is in her early (late) *twenties*. 她现在二十一二(八九)岁。

He died in his *fifties*. 他五十多岁时死了。

b. 年代:

This took place in the *1950's*. 这事发生在(二十世纪)五十年代。

He was working abroad in the *70's*. 七十年代他在国外工作。

4) 一些数学公式的读法如下:

$7 + 4 = 11$　　Seven plus four is eleven.

$12 - 5 = 7$　　Twelve minus five is seven.

$6 \times 8 = 48$　　Six times eight (Six multiplied by eight) is forty-eight.

$24 \div 6 = 4$　　Twenty-four divided by six is four.

$a > b$　　a is more than b.

$a < b$　　a is less than b.

$a \approx b$　　a approximately equals b.

$a \neq b$　　a is not equal to b.

6.2 序 数 词

6.2.1 序数词表示法

1) 序数词 (Ordinal Numerals) 是表示数目顺序的, 和最基础的基数词相对应的序数词如下:

I	II	III
1 **first**	11 eleventh	
2 **second**	12 **twelfth**	20 **twentieth**
3 **third**	13 thirteenth	30 **thirtieth**
4 fourth	14 fourteenth	40 **fortieth**
5 **fifth**	15 fifteenth	50 **fiftieth**
6 sixth	16 sixteenth	60 **sixtieth**
7 seventh	17 seventeenth	70 **seventieth**
8 **eighth**	18 eighteenth	80 **eightieth**
9 **ninth**	19 nineteenth	90 **ninetieth**
10 tenth		

a. 除"第一"、"第二"、"第三"之外, 其他序数词都以在基数词后加词尾 th 构成, 其中有些词(见上表中的黑体部分)在拼法上有少许变化, 如:

fifth   eighth   ninth   twelfth   twentieth 等

b. 两位数的词, 只需把个位数变为序数词:

第二十二   twenty-second   第三十一   thirty-first

第七十八   seventy-eighth   第九十三   ninety-third

c. 三位以上的词, 只把最后的两位数变为序数词:

第一百五十   one hundred and fiftieth

第九百九十九   nine hundred and ninety-ninth

此外, first, second 等词常缩写为 1st, 2nd, 3rd, 20th, 21st 等。

6.2.2 序数词在句中的作用

1) 序数词在句中可用作：

a. 定语 (多和 the 或物主代词一道用)：

We live on the *fifth* floor. 我们住五楼。

Is this your *first* visit to Beijing? 这是你第一次访问北京吗？

Tom is their *second* son. 汤姆是他们的二儿子。

We gave a party to celebrate her *twentieth* birthday. 我们举行晚会来庆祝她二十岁的生日。

There was a ceremony to mark the *hundredth* anniversary of his birth. 为纪念他诞生一百周年举行了一个仪式。

b. 表语：

They were the *first* to taste hardships. 他们吃苦在前。

You are the *second* to make that mistake. 你是第二个犯这种错误的人。

Who was the *third*? 谁是第三名？

c. 主语：

First went to the American team. 美国队获得第一名。

The *first* (one) was no good, the *second* was even worse. 第一个不行，第二个更糟。

The *third* of the month was a holiday. 这月三号是个休假日。

d. 宾语或介词宾语：

I was among the *first* to learn of this. 我是第一批知道这件事的人。

She is arriving on the *second* of June. 她将于六月二日到达。

She got a *third* in biology. 她生物学得了一个丙级分(不及格分)。

2) 序数词的一些其他用法：

a. 序数词还可和 a 连用，表示"再一个"、"又一次"等：

She could not go through that *a second* time. 她不能再次经受那种事。

He's getting married *a third* time. 他将第三次结婚。

A second swan flew down. Then *a third* and *a fourth*. 又一只天鹅飞了下来，接着是第三只，第四只。

b. 表示日期：

May 1st 五月一日   March 8th 三月八日   April 22nd 四月二十二日

c. 用在许多短语中：

I thought that performance *thind-rate*. 我认为那场演出是三流的。

We got four *first-places* in the sports meet. 运动会我们得了四个第一名。

He went *second-class* on the train to New York. 他坐二等车去纽约。

I bought a *second-hand* car. 我买了一辆二手车(旧车)。

3）用基数词表示顺序的办法：

在很多情况下我们可以用基数词表示顺序：

the first part ——→ part one 第一部分

the fifth chapter ——→ chapter five 第五章

the twenty-third section ——→ section twenty-three 第二十三节

the three hundred and fifty-ninth brigade ——→ brigade 359 三五九旅

编号的东西，常避免用序数词，读法也简单化：

第 705 号房间	Room 705 /ˈruːm ˌsevn əʊ ˈfaɪv/
第 254 页	Page 254 /ˈtuː ˈfaɪv ˈfɔː/
第二汽车厂	The No. 2 Auto Plant (No. 读作 /ˈnʌmbə/)
九号车厢	Carriage No. 9
三号及四号卧铺	Berths 3 and 4
第 103 路公共汽车	Bus No. 103
海湾道 7895 号	7895 Bay Road

4）下面数字的读法：

a. 电话号码的读法：

279——1304 /ˈtuː ˈsevn ˈnaɪn ˈwʌn ˈθriː ˈəʊ fɔː/

3321——0073 /ˈdʌbl ˈθriː ˈtuː ˈwʌn, ˈdʌbl ˈzɪərəʊ ˈsevn ˈθriː/

007 号分机 Extension 007 /ˈəʊ ˈəʊ ˈsevn/

b. 年份读法：

2000	the year two thousand
2004	two thousand and four
1949	nineteen forty-nine
1803	eighteen oh three
1600	sixteen hundred
450 B.C.	four fifty B.C. (公元前)
128 A.D.	one twenty-eight A.D. (公元后)

c. 日期读法：

July 22nd	July (the) twenty-second 或 the twenty-second of July
Oct(ober) 1st	October (the) first 或 the first of October

d. 时刻读法：

08：00	eight o'clock 或 eight

09 : 15	nine fifteen 或 a quarter past nine (美：after nine)
02 : 30	two thirty 或 half past two (美：after two)
05 : 45	five forty-five 或 a quarter to six (美：of six)
07 : 00	(oh) seven hundred hours = 7.00 a.m. / 'sevn 'eɪ 'em/
12 : 00	twelve hundred hours = midday / noon
14 : 15	fourteen fifteen = 2.15 p.m. / 'tu: ˌfɪf'ti:n 'pi: 'em/
23 : 05	twenty-three oh five = 11.5 p.m. /ɪ'levn 'faɪv 'pi: 'em/
24 : 00	twenty-four hundred hours = midnight

6.3　分　数　词

6.3.1　分数词

1) 分数词构成法:

分数词 (Fractional Numerals) 由基数词和序数词构成，基数词代表分子，序数词代表分母。除了分子为 1 的情况下，序数词都要用复数形式:

$\frac{1}{4}$	one-fourth	$\frac{5}{9}$	five-ninths
$\frac{2}{3}$	two-thirds	$3\frac{2}{5}$	three and two-fifths
$\frac{7}{12}$	seven-twelfths	$47\frac{3}{8}$	forty-seven and three-eighths

此外还有下面表示法:

$\frac{1}{2}$	a (one) half	$\frac{1}{4}$	a (one) quarter
$\frac{3}{4}$	three-quarters	$2\frac{1}{4}$	two and a quarter
$1\frac{1}{2}$	one and a half	$7\frac{3}{4}$	seven and three quarters

比较复杂的分数读法如下:

| $\frac{23}{9}$ | twenty-three over nine | $\frac{76}{92}$ | seventy-six over ninety-two |

2) 分数在句中的作用:

分数在句中可用作:

a. 主语:

A *quarter* of the population voted for him. 四分之一的人投他的票。

The other *third* of the black population live in poverty. 另外三分之一的黑人生活在贫困之中。

Three-fifths of the computers on display were home-made. 展出的电脑五分之三是国内生产的。

b. 宾语或介词宾语:

Mother divided the cake into *thirds*. 妈妈把蛋糕分成三份。

Give a *quarter* of the pie to each of them. 给他们每人四分之一块馅饼。

They account for *one-seventh* of the population. 他们占人口的七分之一。

c. 表语或同位语:

The crop that year was only *one-third* of the usual amount. 那年的收成只是常年产量的三分之一。

Over twelve million people, about *three-fifths* of the local population are Hans. 有一千二百多万人是汉人,约占当地人口的五分之三。

d. 定语:

It's *one-twentieth* the thickness of a human hair. 它相当于人的头发丝二十分之一那么细。

The mass of an electron is *1/1850* that of a hydrogen atom. 电子的质量只是氢原子质量的 1/1850。

It produces power at *1/8* the cost in a thermal power plant. 它的发电成本只是热电厂成本的八分之一。

e. 状语:

China is *one-sixth* larger than the United States. 中国比美国大六分之一。

This substance reacts *one-tenth* as fast as the other one. 这种物质的反应速度只是另一种物质的十分之一。

6.3.2　小数的读法和用法

1) 小数的读法如下:

6.4 —— six point four

0.8 —— zero (或 naught) point eight

0.05 ——(naught) point naught five 或 zero point zero five

0.726 ——(naught) point seven two six 或 zero point seven two six

12.409 —— twelve point four oh nine

709.06 —— seven hundred and nine point oh six

2) 小数主要用作定语：

Our grain output is now *2.4* times that of 1980. 我们现在的粮食产量是
   1980 年的 2.4 倍。

Its total output value was up *4.7* times. 它的总产值提高了4.7 倍。

Its capacity was *7.3* times as great as in 1985. 它的生产能力是1985年的
   7.3 倍。

6.3.3 百分数的用法

百分数由per cent (美作 percent) 表示，可以在句中作：

1) 主语：

Over *eighty per cent* of all families own a television. 百分之八十以上的
   家庭都有电视机。

What *per cent* of the population can read? 人口中能识文断字的百分比是
   多少？

Ten per cent of the pupils are absent today. 今天有百分之十的学生缺席。

2) 宾语或介词宾语：

They constitute *eight per cent* of the population. 他们占人口的百分之八。

The price of bread has gone up by *40 per cent* in two years. 面包价格两年
   间涨了百分之四十。

The bank charges interest at *12 per cent*. 银行货款利息为百分之十二。

3) 定语：

Leave the waitress a *15 per cent* tip. 给女招待留下百分之十五的小费。

There is a *ten per cent* service charge. 要收百分之十的服务费(小费)。

I paid him *four per cent* interest. 我付给他百分之四的利息。

4) 状语：

I think it's *ninety per cent* probable. 我看这有百分之九十的可能性。

I'm not *a hundred per cent* convinced myself. 我自己也不是百分之百全
   信。

Prices have risen *6 per cent* in the past year. 过去一年里物价上涨了百分
   之六。

偶作表语：

12 is *1 percent* of 1,200.   12 是 1,200 的百分之一。

6.4   量   词

6.4.1   量词范围

量词 (Quantifiers) 不是一种词类，而是许多与数量有关的词和短语，它们包含:

1) 许多与数量有关的代词和限定词，如 some，any，much，many 等。

2) 各种数词，如 two，half，a third，80%等。

3) 名词和 of 构成的表数量的短语，如 a lot of, plenty of 等。

4) 某些与数量有关的形容词，如 enough，whole，half 等。

5) 某些与数量有关的名词，如 feet，miles，years，dozen 等。

6) 某些与数量有关的合成词，如 a five-dollar bill，a 6-page summary 等。

7) 某些与数量有关词组的所有格，如 two months' stay，four weeks' notice 等。

下面将简要地加以处理。

6.4.2   与数量有关的代词和限定词

1) 有很多作定语的代词和限定词，特别是不定代词和相关限定词，可用来表示数量:

How *much* rent do you pay? 你交多少房租?

Few words are best. (谚)少说为妙。

Many hands make light work. (谚)人多好办事。

This might serve *several* purposes. 这也许能达到几个目的。

2) 这类代词也可作主语、宾语等，表示数量:

a. 主语:

Most of the people have fled. 大多数人都逃跑了。

None of us are surprised. 我们谁也不感到吃惊。

Many a little makes a mickle. (谚)集腋成裘。

b. 宾语或介词的宾语:

He ate *a little* before going out. 他外出前吃了一点东西。

I don't know *much* about psychology. 我对心理学不太懂。

A friend to *all* is a friend to none. (谚)滥交者无友。

关于这类词，详见第5.6.5—5.7.7节。

6.4.3   由"名词 + of"构成的量词

1) 这类量词为数很多，它们都加在所修饰词前面：

A lot of people have the same experience.   大量的人有同样的经历。

I have lived here quite *a number of* years.   我在这里住了许多年了。

She had *plenty of* imagination.   她有丰富的想像力。

We need *a sufficient amount of* flour.   我们需要足够量的面粉。

A good many of them are beginners.   他们很多人都是初学者。

He lost *a great quantity of* blood.   他失血很多。

We walked *a couple of* miles.   我们步行了二三英里。

She had *a heap of* trouble.   她有很多麻烦事。

I have *a ton of* work to do before I leave.   我走之前有大量工作要做。

She bears *a load of* anxiety.   她忧心忡忡。

I've *a mass of* things to see to this morning.   今天上午我有很多事要办。

有些这类名词可用复数形式，强调数量之多：

Numbers of people came to the meeting.   与会者人数众多。

We've had *quantities* of rain this summer.   今年夏天下了大量的雨。

I've got *tons* of letters to write.   我有好多好多的信要写。

She bought *lots* of food.   她买了大量的食物。

That man seems to have *heaps* of money.   那个人似乎钱多的不得了。

There are *masses of* people in the hall.   大厅里有好多人。

2) 有些这类量词表示"少量的"：

She is just out to do *a bit of* shopping.   她只是出来买点东西。

He put *a pinch of* salt in his soup.   他在汤里放了一点点盐。

She has *a touch of* cold.   她略微有点感冒。

A dash of vinegar might help the salad.   生菜里加一点醋也许更好吃。

Have *a spot of* tea.   喝一点茶吧。

There's not *a shred of* evidence that he took the money.   没有丝毫证据表明钱是他拿的。

There is *a grain of* truth in his assertion.   他的话有一点真实性。

There was *a trace of* jealousy in her voice.   她的声音里有一丝妒忌情绪。

There is not *a speck of* truth in his claim.   他的话毫无真实之处。

Will you have *a drop of* brandy?　你要不要喝一点点白兰地?

3) 有些这类量词与形状有关:

I need *a ball of* string.　我需要一团线。

He was sucking *a stick of* toffee.　他在吮吸一根棒糖。

The president was surrounded by *a ring of* bodyguards.　总统身边围着一圈保镖。

There is *a strip of* sticky tape round the lid.　盖子周边有一条胶带。

A shaft of sunlight brightened the room.　一道阳光照亮了房间。

Elli brought *a bunch of* flowers.　艾丽带来了一束花。

A thread of light emerged from the keyhole.　从钥匙孔透进一丝亮光。

A goat has *a tuft of* hair on its chin.　山羊下巴上长有一撮胡须。

A wall of fire stood before them.　他们面前有一堵火墙。

There was *a gush of* blood as his wound re-opened.　他的伤口重开时血流如注。

A loud gust of laughter came from the next room.　从隔壁房间传来一阵笑声。

The fountain sent up *a jet of* water.　喷泉喷出一根水柱。

Streams of people were coming out of the railway station.　一股股人流从车站涌出。

She attacked him with *a torrent of* abuse.　她对他一阵谩骂。

A shower of stones greeted him.　石头雨点般地向他砸来。

Clouds of smoke rose from the bombed city.　挨炸的城市升起团团浓烟。

There might still be *a ray of* hope.　可能还有一线希望。

She has *a mountain of* dirty clothes to wash.　她有一大堆脏衣服要洗。

4) 还有不少量词表示一群人(a)或动物(b):

a. *A group of* students asked to see the principal.　有一群学生要见校长。

The discovery was made by *a team of* scientists.　这是由一组科学家发现的。

A gang of workers were repairing the road.　一伙工人在修马路。

You're behaving like *a bunch of* idiots.　你们的举动像一群白痴。

A company of travellers are expected to arrive soon.　一批游客预计不久就要到来。

A troupe of acrobats entertained them.　一群杂技演员为他们作了表演。

We met *a host of* students.　我们碰到了一大群学生。

A strange collection of people attended the party.　一伙稀奇古怪的人参加

了这个聚会。

She's always surrounded by *swarms of* photographers. 她身边总是围着一大群摄影师。

A pack of angry shoppers demanded their money back. 一群生气的顾客要求退钱。

b. *A flock of* sheep blocked the road. 一群绵羊挡住了道路。

The lion was chasing *a herd of* deer. 那头狮子在追逐一群鹿。

A pack of hounds chased the fox. 一群猎犬在追赶狐狸。

We saw *a pride of* lions resting by the stream. 我们看见一群狮子在溪边休息。

A swarm of locusts destroyed the crop. 一大群蝗虫毁坏了庄稼。

Electronic detectors tracked down *schools of* fish. 电子探测器追踪到了鱼群。

A flight of ducks passed overhead. 一群鸭子从头上飞过。

A cloud of mosquitoes came over. 一大群蚊子飞了过来。

5) 还有许多这类量词与容器有关:

a bottle of beer 一瓶啤酒	a box of chocolate 一盒巧克力
a can of soup 一个汤罐头	a bowl of rice 一碗饭
a cup of tea 一杯茶	a basket of fruit 一篮水果
a bucket of water 一桶水	a sack of corn 一袋玉米
a bag of toffees 一袋太妃糖	a crate of bananas 一筐香蕉
a glass of fruit juice 一杯果汁	a mug of milk 一大杯奶
a packet of cigarettes 一包香烟	a pot of jam 一锅果酱
a spoon of sugar 一匙白糖	a tube of toothpaste 一管牙膏
a barrel of oil 一桶石油	a carton of yoghurt 一(纸)盒酸奶
a jar of marmalade 一罐橘子酱	a pack of gum 一小包口香糖
a plate of beef 一盘牛肉	a package of detergent 一包洗涤剂

有些名词后可加词尾 -ful 来表示数量:

a spoonful of vinegar 一勺醋	a basketful of peaches 一筐桃子
a handful of raisins 一把葡萄干	a mouthful of food 一口食物
an armful of flowers 一捧花	a houseful of guests 一屋子客人
a busful of children 一车孩子	a roomful of antiques 一房间的古董

6.4.4　一些与数量有关的词

1) 一些与数量有关的形容词:

有不少形容词与数量有关:

The thesis was about two hundred pages *long*.　这篇论文约有两百页长。

The tree is a hundred feet *tall*.　那棵树有一百英尺高。

The road is 8 metres *wide*.　这条马路有八米宽。

The lake there is eight feet *deep*.　那里的湖有八英尺深。

The river is 30 feet *broad*.　这条河宽三十英尺。

The outer wall is twelve feet *thick*.　外墙厚十二英尺。

The building is over thirty stories *high*.　这座大楼有三十多层高。

2) 一些与数量有关的名词:

a. 有许多单位名称经常和数词连用表示数量:

It weighs over 200 *kilos*.　它重二百多公斤。

The temperature rose ten *degrees*.　气温上升了十度。

There are sixteen ounces in one *pound*.　一英磅有十六英两。

A pint of liquid is about four *cupfuls*.　一品脱约有四杯。

Will two *yards* of dress material be enough?　两码衣料够了吗?

It travels thousands of *miles* per second.　它一秒钟能走几千英里。

b. 也有些名词和 in 连用，表示数量:

The snow is two feet *in depth*.　雪有两尺厚。

He was about five feet *in height*.　他身高约五英尺。

The island is only 4 square kilometres *in area*.　这座岛的面积只有四平方
　　千米。

The river is thirty miles *in length*.　这条河有三十英里长。

The parcel is 2 pounds *in weight*.　这包裹重两磅。

The room is 12 feet in width.　房间宽 12 英尺。

3) 也有一些表示数量的:

a. 合成词:

a ten-dollar bill 十美元的钞票　　　a two-page summary 两页的提纲

a 5-storeyed house 五层楼的房子　　4 per cent interest 百分之四的利息

per-mu yield 亩产量　　　　　　　per capita wage 人均工资

a 44-hour week 每周工作 44 小时　　a four fold increase 四倍的增长

b. 名词所有格:

a week's wage 一周的工资　　　　two weeks' notice 提前两周通知

a day's journey 一天的路程　　　　ten years' experience 十年的经验

an hour's drive 开车一小时　　　　six months' leave 六个月的假期

第7章 动词概说

7.1 动词的种类

7.1.1 动词的种类

动词主要分作下面几类:

- **及物动词** (Transitive Verbs)
- **不及物动词** (Intransitive Verbs)
- **兼作及物动词和不及物动词的动词** (Ergative Verbs)
- **双宾动词** (Ditransive Verbs)
- **成语动词** (Phrasal Verbs)
- **系动词** (Link-Verbs)
- **助动词** 和 **情态动词** (Auxiliary Verbs and Modal Verbs)

7.1.2 及物动词

1) 这类动词通常都跟有宾语,如:

She *committed* a serious error. 她犯了一个严重的错误。

They were busy *making* artificial flowers. 他们在忙着做纸花。

The child *needed* constant attention. 这孩子需要经常照顾。

Where did you *put* the key? 你把钥匙放哪儿了?

这类动词很多,常见的如:

achieve	address	admire	affect	afford	avoid
blame	build	buy	carry	catch	claim
commit	complete	concern	control	convince	correct
cover	create	cut	damage	defy	demand
describe	design	desire	destroy	discover	discuss
display	dread	enjoy	equal	exchange	expect

experience	express	favour	fear	fine	free
get	give	grant	guard	handle	hate
have	heat	hire	include	influence	introduce
issue	justify	lack	like	list	love
lower	maintain	make	mean	mention	need
plant	prefer	prevent	produce	pronounce	protect
provide	raise	receive	recommend	record	release
remove	respect	reveal	risk	shock	spot
support	tease	test	threaten	trust	upset
use	value	want	waste	welcome	

2）有些及物动词以表示人的名词或代词作宾语：

I'll *contact* you as soon as I arrive. 我一到就会和你联系。

Her attitude *surprised* me. 她的态度使我吃惊。

He often *teased* his sister. 他常常逗他的妹妹。

Her words *comforted* the sobbing child. 她的话给了那哭泣的孩子以安慰。

常见的这类动词如：

anger	brief	comfort	contact	frighten	interest
shock	suit	surprise	tease	thank	warn

3）还有些及物动词和一个介词短语或副词连用：

Shakespeare *compared* the world *to* a stage. 莎士比亚把世界比作舞台。

This song *reminded* me *of* my childhood. 这首歌使我想起了童年。

I couldn't *rid* myself *of* this melancholy mood. 我无法摆脱这种忧郁的情绪。

He promised to *treat* us *to* dinner. 他答应请我们吃饭。

常见的这类短语有：

accustom...to	aquaint...with	attribute...to	base...on (upon)
bring...with	cram...into	compare...to	condemn...to
confine...to	convey...to	dedicate...to	deprive...of
direct...to	divide...into	engrave...with	entrust...to
incorporate...into	jot...down	lavish...on	liken...to
mistake...for	owe...to	point...at (to)	present...to (with)

prevent...from	regard...as	remind...of	return...to
rid...of	rob...of	send...to	subject...to
supply...with (to)	treat...to	trust...with	view...as

4）有几个及物动词可以和许多名词一道表示动作，这类动词称为 **虚意动词**（Delexical Verbs），最常见的是下面几个：

have 可以跟：

bath	bathe	celebration	chat	conversation	cry
dance	discussion	dislike	dispute	dream	drink
fear	fight	interview	laugh	lie	look
love	quarrel	read	respect	rest	row(争吵)
run	scene	sleep	smoke	success	swim
talk	try	walk	wash	win	wish

give 可以跟：

account	advice	analysis	answer	approval	beating
blow	chuckle	clean	consent	consideration	cry
dry	gasp	giggle	glance	grin	groan
hint	hug	injection	jump	kick	kiss
knock	laugh	lecture	look	nod	notice
polish	pull	punch	push	reading	report
ring	scream	shock	shout	sigh	sketch
smile	squeeze	start	summary	support	talk
thought	warning	wash	welcome		

take 可以跟：

action	bath	break	care	chance	charge
control	effect	examination	exercise	grip	inspection
lead	lift	look	nap	note	notice
oath	offence	pity	place	power	pride
revenge	risk	seat	shape	sip	stand
step	trip	trouble	turn	vacation	view
vote	walk				

make 可以跟:

advance	answer	apology	appeal	appearance
arrangements	arrest	appointment	attack	attempt
change	choice	comment	comparison	concession
confession	deal	decision	demand	distinction
effort	enquiry	examination	excuse	experiment
explanation	fight	fuss	guess	go
inspection	investigation	love	mention	move
noise	objection	proposal	protest	preparations
progress	promise	purchase	recovery	reference
remark	reply	resolution	sacrifice	scene
search	slip	start	statement	study
success	suggestion	trip	visit	

相关用法的例句可查阅《现代英语用法词典》。

5) 动词 do 可以跟许多名词作宾语，意思随后面的名词而变化:

Go and *do* your hair. 去梳梳头。

Have you *done* your teeth? 你刷牙了吗?

She was *doing* the dishes. 她在洗盘子。

Can you *do* the room now? 你现在能打扫房间了吗?

When are you to *do* the windows? 你什么时候擦窗子?

He found her *doing* the flowers. 他发现她在插花。

Do they *do* science at school? 他们在学校学科学课程吗?

He's learning to *do* sums. 他在学做算术题。

The group is *doing* 'Macbeth'. 这个剧团在演《麦克佩斯》。

We *did* two concerts last week. 上星期我们听了两场音乐会。

Have you *done* the Tower? 你参观伦敦塔了吗?

We *did* Spain in two weeks. 我们在西班牙游览了两周。

He *does* seventy-five on the freeway. 在高速公路上他开车时速为七十五英里。

We *did* the journey in six hours. 路上我们走了六小时。

He *did* ten years for armed robbery. 他因持枪抢劫入狱十年。

The barber will *do* you next. 理发师下一个将给你理。

He *does* his guests well. 他把客人招待得很好。

That shopkeeper *did* me.　那个商店老板骗了我。

He has *done* an excellent article.　他写了一篇精彩的文章。

She *did* some pretty sketches.　她画了几张漂亮的素描。

Jane *did* most of the talking.　大部分时间是简在说话。

Who *does* the cooking?　谁做饭?

She's *doing* her knitting.　她在织毛线。

7.1.3　不及物动词

1) 这类动词都不跟宾语，例如:

I *itch* all over.　我浑身发痒。

She *flushed* and made no answer.　她脸红了，没有回答。

When did it *happen*?　这事什么时候发生的?

He was *shivering* all over.　他浑身发抖。

下面这些动词通常作不及物动词:

ache	appear	arise	belong	blush	collapse
come	cough	crawl	creep	cry	decay
depart	deteriorate	die	dine	disappear	doze
drift	economize	elapse	erupt	evaporate	exist
expire	faint	fall	flourish	flow	gallop
gleam	glide	go	growl	happen	hesitate
howl	itch	kneel	laugh	lie	live
moan	occur	pause	persist	plunge	prosper
quiver	remain	rise	roar	scream	shiver
sigh	sit	slip	smile	snarl	sneeze
snore	soar	sob	sparkle	stink	spring
stroll	subside	sulk	swim	throb	travel
vanish	vibrate	waver	weep	yawn	

2) 有些动词在多数情况下用作vi(不及物动词)，间或用作vt.(及物动词)，这时意思不同:

用作 vi.	用作 vt.
She doesn't *run* fast.　她跑得不快。	She *runs* a store.　她经营一家商店。

They *advanced* 40 miles. 他们推进了 40 英里。

He *advanced* a new theory. 他提出了一个新理论。

The sun is *shining*. 阳光灿烂。

Shine your shoes. 把你的皮鞋擦一擦。

Why are you *crying*? 你为什么哭?

She *cried* herself to sleep. 她哭着哭着睡着了。

还有少数动词通常作 vi.,但可跟同源宾语,如 laugh,smile,sleep,live 等词都如此。(关于这一点可参阅第 13.3.3 节)

3) 还有些动词经常和某个介词连用,如:

The plan *depends on* the weather. 这计划得靠天气决定。

She *objected* to the idea. 她反对这个主意。

Don't *refer to* that matter again. 不要再提此事。

I *care* very little *for* fame now. 我现在对名气不怎么在乎。

常见的这类结构有:

abound in (with)	adhere to	alternate with	amount to
appeal to	aspire for	assent to	associate with
believe in	belong to	bow to	care for
cling to	complain of	conform to	consist of (in)
contend with	contribute to	depend on	dictate to
differentiate between	embark on	emerge from	end with (in)
feed on	flirt with	hint at	hope for
hunger after (for)	improve on	indulge in	insist on
lead to	learn of	listen to	long for
object to	plot against	prevail on	profit by (from)
refer to	relate to	rely on	resort to
result in	shrink from	strive for	suffer from
sympathize with	think of	tire of	trample on
wait for (on)	yearn for		

7.1.4 兼作及物和不及物动词的词

英语中大部分动词都既可作 vt.,也可作 vi.,只能作一种动词而不能作另一种动词的是少数。兼作两种动词的情况很多,大致上有下面这些情况:

1) 用于一个意义时为 vt.,用于另一个意义时为 vi.:

用作 vt.	**用作 vi.**
Happy to *meet* you. 见到你很高兴。	When shall we *meet*? 我们何时碰头？
Mind the dog. 当心有狗。	I'm sure he won't *mind*. 我肯定他不会在意。
She couldn't *stand* the cold. 她受不了严寒。	Don't *stand* in the rain. 别站在雨里。
Don't *move* my things. 别动我的东西。	The train is *moving* now. 火车开动了。
Smoking *hurts* you. 吸烟对你有害。	My head *hurts*. 我头疼。
He *hanged* himself in sorrow. 在悲痛中他悬梁自尽了。	Her portrait *hangs* over the mantel piece. 她的画像挂在壁炉台上方。
They *beat* him unconsccions. 他们把他打得不省人事。	Her heart was *beating* violently. 她的心猛烈地跳动着。
Please *pass* me the salt. 请把盐递给我。	The winter finally *passed*. 冬天终于过去了。

因此，在学某一个具体的动词时，要经常注意它在什么时候用作 vt.，什么时候用作 vi.。

2) 有些动词在意思基本上不变的情况下，有时用作 vt.，有时用作 vi.，例如：

用作 vt.	**用作 vi.**
Can you *help* me? 你能帮我吗？	Every little *helps*. (谚)积少成多。
Tigers *eat* meat. 老虎吃肉。	We *eat* at six. 我们六点吃饭。
She isn't going to *marry* him. 她不准备嫁他。	Don't *marry* in haste. 不要匆忙结婚。
Sing us a *song*, please. 请给我们唱一支歌。	Who's *singing* there? 谁在那儿唱歌？
She *speaks* good English. 她英文讲得很好。	Who is *speaking*? 谁在讲话？
She's *typing* a letter. 她在打一封信。	She's *typing*. 她在打字。
Who *wrote* the poem? 这诗谁写的？	He *writes* very well. 他文笔很好。
She's *studying* medicine. 她在学医。	She *studies* hard. 她学习很用功。

在学每一个英语动词时都要注意在意思大体上不变的情况下是否既可作 vt.，又可作 vi.。

3) 有些动词通常作及物动词，但有时宾语不必讲出（从上下文中可以看出），因此也就成了不及物动词，如：

His father came yesterday. —— Yes, I *know* (it). 他父亲昨天来了。
　　——是的，我知道。

I'm sure she didn't *notice* (it). 我肯定她没注意(此事)。

Oh, yes. Now I *remember* (it). 啊，是的。我想起来了。

"What's his name?" "I *forget* (it)." "他叫什么名字？" "我忘了"。

He aimed at the black spot and *missed* (it). 他瞄准黑点但没击中。

Why didn't you *answer* (me)? 你为什么不回答(我)?

He didn't *understand* (it) very well. 他不很理解。

Who *won* (the game)? 谁赢了(比赛)?

4) 还有些动词可作 vt.，也可作 vi.，后面可跟介词短语：

作 vt.	作 vi.
I'll *fight* you. 我来和你打。	They *fought with* each other. 他们互相斗殴
England is *playing* Australia. 英国对阵澳大利亚。	David *played against* Louise. 大卫和路易斯比赛。
He *wandered* the streets. 他在街上漫步。	They *wandered in* the park. 他们在公园里漫步。
Will you *check* the figures? 你要不要把数字核对一遍？	First *check on* your answers. 先核对一下你的答案。
She's *walking* the street. 她在街上行走。	She *walked along (through)* the street. 她沿着那条街走。
He *ruled* Britain for 60 years. 他统治英国达六十年。	He *ruled over* the empire for a long time. 他长期统治这个帝国。
The whole nation *mourned* his death. 全国哀悼他的逝世。	We *mourn for* our fallen officers and men. 我们为阵亡将士哀伤
Zilla *mocked* him as a country boy. 齐拉嘲笑他是个乡下孩子。	He *mocked at* my pronunciation. 他嘲笑我的发音。

这种现象值得注意。

5) 有些动词，随着主语不同而可用作 vt. 或 vi.，例如：

作 vt.	作 vi.
The continual strain *aged* her. 持续的劳累使她衰老了。	He's *ag(e)ing* fast. 他老得很快。

He *began* a series of experiments. 他开始了一连串的试验。

Boil the potatoes for 20 minutes. 把土豆煮 20 分钟。

Take care not to *break* it. 小心别把它打破了。

When does the play *begin*? 戏什么时候开始？

The water is *boiling*. 水开了。

Brittle things *break* easily. 脆的东西容易破碎。

这类动词很多，常见的如：

age	bake	begin	bend	boil	break
burn	burst	change	close	continue	cook
crack	darken	decrease	disperse	double	drown
dry	empty	end	finish	fly	grow
improve	increase	meet	open	park	roast
rock	rot	run	sail	shake	shatter
show	shrink	shut	slow	sound	spin
split	spread	stand	start	stick	stop
stretch	swing	tear	thicken	turn	widen

7.1.5　双宾动词

1) 有不少动词后面可以跟两个宾语，前面为间接宾语，后面为直接宾语：

主　语	谓　语	间接宾语	直接宾语
They	granted	us	a loan.
I	will lend	you	my typewriter.
We	owed	him	100 dollars.
	Hand	me	the timetable

间接宾语有时可以放到后面去，不过前面要加介词 to，如：

They granted a loan to us.

I'll lend my typewriter to you.

We owed 100 dollars to him.

Hand the timetable to me.

常见的这类动词有:

accord	advance	award	bring	deal	forward
give	grant	band	lease	leave	lend
loan	mail	offer	owe	pass	pay
play	post	read	rent	repay	sell
send	serve	show	sing	take	teach
tell	write				

2）另有一批动词，也可跟两个宾语，但把间接宾语放在后部时，要改为由 for 引导的短语，如:

跟两个宾语	包含 for 引导的短语
Sing us a song, please.	Please sing a song for us.
Father bought me a camera.	Father bought a camera for me.
Fetch me the evening paper.	Fetch the evening paper for me.
Play us some light music.	Play some light music for us.

这类动词常见的有:

book	bring	build	buy	cook	cut
design	fetch	find	fix	get	leave
make	mix	order	paint	pick	play
prepare	reserve	save	set	sing	spare

3）还有少数动词也跟两个宾语，但很少把间接宾语放到句子后面去:

I'll never *forgive* you that lie.　我永远不会原谅你那次撒谎。

I *wish* you good luck.　祝你好运。

I *envy* you your health.　我羡慕你的好身体。

How dare you *ask* me such a question?　你怎么敢问我这样的问题?

She didn't want to *cause* you any inconvenience.　她不想给你造成不便。

The hotel *charged* me ￡15 for a room for the night.　旅馆这一晚收我15镑的房钱。

That suit *cost* me over ￡60.　那套衣服花了我60多英镑。

They *denied* the prisoner all freedom.　他们不给那囚犯任何自由。

I want you to *promise* me one thing.　我要求你答应我一件事。

She can't *refuse* him anything.　她不能拒绝他任何事情。

7.1.6   成语动词

有时两个词或三个词在一起构成一个成语,作用和一个单一动词差不多,称为成语动词。这种动词主要有下面四类:

1) 不及物动词 + 副词:

The war *broke out* in 1939. 战争于 1939 年爆发。

She didn't want to *fall behind* in her studies. 她不愿意学习落后。

How did the accident *come about*? 这事故是怎样发生的?

The wind has *died down* a bit. 风平息了一点。

常见的这类动词有:

back away	back down	back off	boil over	break away
break out	check up	close in	cloud over	come about
come apart	come on	come round	come up	cool off
crop up	cut in	die away	die down	die out
doze off	drag on	drop back	drop by	drop out
ease up	fade away	fall apart	fall behind	fall through
fight back	flare up	fool around	forge ahead	get about
get along	get up	give in	go ahead	go along
go away	go on	go out	go up	grow up
hang together	hit out	hold on	let up	lie back
lie down	look ahead	look back	look in	make off
melt away	move off	move over	own up	pass away
press ahead	press on	push ahead	push on	ring off
run away	run out	rush in	set in	settle down
shop around	sit back	sit down	speak up	stand back
start out	stay on	stay up	step aside	step down
step in	stop by	stop off	stop over	touch down
watch out	wear off			

2) 不及物动词 + 介词:

He could not *account for* his absence from school. 他无法解释他为什么缺课。

I *called on* her this morning. 今早我拜访了她。

I *ran across* her in the library yesterday. 昨天我在图书馆碰到了她。

You'd better wait and *watch for* a better chance. 你最好等等,留心更好

的机会。

常见的这类成语动词有:

abide by	account for	allow for	ask after	bank on
break into	break with	bump into	burst into	call for
call on	care for	come across	come by	come for
come into	come to	come upon	count on	dawn on
deal with	dispose of	draw on	drive at	dwell on
embark on	enter into	fall into	feel for	frown upon
get at	get into	get over	go about	go for
head for	hit on	jump at	keep to	laugh at
leap at	live for	live off	look after	look into
look to	make for	meet with	part with	pick at
plan for	play at	play on	provide for	reason with
reckon on	run across	run into	see to	seize on
set about	stand for	stem from	stick at	take after
trifle with	wait for	wait on	watch for	

有些不及物动词可以跟副词也可以跟介词构成成语动词:

不及物动词 + 副词	**不及物动词 + 介词**
We mustn't *lag behind*. 我们不能落后。	We mustn't *lag behind* others. 我们不能落在别人后面。
They hope to *break through* soon in this research. 他们希望这项研究不久能取得突破。	The allies sought to *break through* the German lines. 盟军设法突破了德军的防线。
We must be *getting off* now. 现在我们得动身了。	Then they *got off* the bus. 随后他们下车了。
Let's all *join in*. 咱们都参加进去。	He *joined in* the march. 他参加了游行。

3) 及物动词 + 副词:

He is trying to *bring about* a reconciliation. 他在努力促成和解。

I'll try to *hurry* him *up*. 我来设法催促他。

The trolley-bus stopped to *put down* three passengers. 电车停下来,让三位乘客下车。

They are going to *knock down* those old houses. 他们要拆掉那些老房子。

这类成语动词很多，常见的有下面这些:

add up	answer back	back up	beat up	blow up
break in	break off	break up	bring about	bring forward
bring in	bring off	bring up	call back	call off
call out	carry off	carry on	carry out	catch up
check in	check out	cheer up	clean out	close down
count out	cover up	cross out	cut down	cut off
cut out	dig up	drag in	drag out	draw up
dress up	drink up	drive out	eat up	fight off
fill up	find out	finish up	fix up	follow up
gather up	get in	get out	give away	give back
give off	give up	hand down	hand in	hand out
hand over	hand round	have on	heat up	help out
hold out	hold up	hunt down	hurry up	hush up
kick out	knock down	knock out	knock over	lay down
lay off	leave behind	leave out	let down	let in
let off	let out	lift up	look out	look up
make out	make up	mix up	note down	open up
order about	pass off	pass over	pass round	pay back
pay off	play down	play up	plug in	point out
pull apart	pull down	put forward	put off	put on
put out	put up	read out	rub out	rule out
run over	rush through	see off	seek out	sell off
send up	set aside	set off	set out	shoot down
show off	show up	sign up	slow down	smooth over
sort out	spread out	stamp out	start off	step up
stick out	sum up	switch off	switch on	take apart
take back	take off	take on	take over	take up
talk over	tear off	tear up	tell apart	think over
thresh out	throw away	throw out	tidy up	tie down
tire out	tone down	track down	try on	try out
turn away	turn back	turn down	turn in	turn on
turn out	turn up	wake up	warm up	wash up
wear out	win back	win over	wind up	work out

也有部分成语动词是由及物动词＋介词构成的，如：

Don't *build on* his promises. 不要信赖他的诺言。

He *talked* me *into* changing my job. 他说服我改换了工作。

They *showed* her *round* the house. 他们带她在屋里到处看了看。

She *set* the children *against* their father. 她让孩子们反对他们的父亲。

4) 动词＋副词＋介词：

还有一部分成语动词由三个词构成，即"动词＋副词＋介词"，介词后跟宾语，如：

I can't *put up with* these noisy people. 我无法忍受这些嘈杂的人。

You might *come up against* a bit of opposition. 你可能会遭到一点反对。

Don't *look down on* this kind of work. 不要看不起这种工作。

I'm *looking forward to* her arrival. 我盼望着她的到来。

这类成语动词常见的有：

be in for	boil down to	brush up on	call out for
catch up with	come down on	come down to	come down with
come in for	come out against	come out in	come out of
come out with	come up against	come up to	come up with
crack down on	cry out against	cry out for	cut back on
date back to	do away with	face up to	fall back on
fall in with	get away with	get down to	get off with
get on to	get on with	get round to	go back on
go in for	go off with	go over to	go through with
grow out of	keep in with	keep on at	keep up with
lead up to	live up to	look down on	look forward to
look out for	look up to	make away with	make off with
make up to	match up to	measure up to	put up with
run away with	run off with	run up against	stick out for
suck up to	take up with	talk down to	tie in with
walk away from	walk away with	walk off with	

5) 包含名词的动词成语：

有些由动词构成的成语包含有一个名词，多数语言学家都不把它们归入成语动词范围之内，但它们的作用和成语动词是差不多的。这类成语可分为以下三类：

a. 动词＋名词:

bear a grudge	break the ice	catch fire
change one's mind	do right (wrong)	face the music
give way	go halves	have one's way
hold one's breath	hold one's tongue	hold water
keep company	keep one's head	keep one's temper
keep one's words	keep silence	lead the way
lose face	lose ground	lose heart
lose one's head	lose one's temper	lose one's way
lose weight	make a fuss	make a hit
make a point	make scene	make haste
make love	make one's way	make sense
make way	play truant	set feet
take a chance	take a risk	take a seat
take steps	take action	take aim
take care	take effect	take heart
take notes	take offence	take office
take place	take root	take sides

b. 动词＋名词＋介词:

attach importance to	catch glimpses of	catch sight of
find fault with	get hold of	get rid of
get wind of	give credit for	give place to
give rise to	give thought to	give voice to
have confidence in	have control of	have design on
have pity on	keep pace with	lay hold of
lose sight of	lose touch with	lose track of
make a mess of	make a note of	make a secret of
make a success of	make allowances for	make demands on
make eye at	make friends with	make fun of
make much of	make room for	pay a visit to
pay attention to	pay tribute to	play a part in
set fire to	set store by	take advantage of
take care of	take control of	take credit for
take delight in	take hold of	take interest in

take liberties with	take note of	take notice of
take leave of	take part in	take pity on
take revenge on	take stock of	

c. 动词＋介词＋名词：

bring to an end	bring to light	bring to power
bring under control	burst into tears	call to mind
call to order	catch by surprise	come into being
come into blossom	come into conflict	come into effect
come into fashion	come into power	come into sight
come to a climax	come to a conclusion	come to a halt (stop)
come to blows	come to fruition	come to grief
come to life	come to light	fall into line
fall to pieces	get in touch	get to work
go to bed (sleep)	go to pieces	go to waste
have in mind	keep in check	keep in mind
leave to chance	put at ease	put in order
put in touch	put into effect (force)	put into practice
put on airs	put on weight	put to bed (sleep)
put to death	put to flight	put to rights
put to shame	put to use	set in motion
set on fire	set to music	stand on ceremony
stand to reason	take by surprise	take in hand
take into account	take into consideration	take to heart

关于成语动词还可参阅第 13.3.4 节及附录 1。

7.1.7　系动词

系动词有下面这些：

appear	be	become	fall	feel	get
go	grow	keep	look	prove	remain
rest	run	seem	smell	sound	stay
taste	turn				

1) be:

这个系动词用得最多，后面可以跟各式各样的表语：

She's *a* good *swimmer*. 她是位游泳好手。(跟名词)

Be quiet! 安静点！(跟形容词)

He *isn't in* at the moment. 他此刻不在家。(跟副词)

He *has been in Germany* for five years. 他在德国住了五年。(跟介词短语)

Who is she? 她是谁？(跟代词)

To know everything *is to know nothing*. 事事皆通，事事稀松。(跟不定式)

Let X *be 10*. 设 X 等于 10。(跟数词)

The flowers in the park *are pleasing*. 公园里的花很怡人。(跟现在分词)

She's *disappointed* with me. 她对我很失望。(跟过去分词)

That's *why I'm against the idea*. 因此我反对这个想法。(跟从句)

He's *twice David's size*. 他的个子比大卫大一倍。(跟词组)

还可用于许多成语中，如 be in, be off, be on, be over, be through, be fond of, be sure of, be tired, be careful of, be mindful of, be keen on, be weary of, be productive of 等。

2) appear:

后面主要跟：

a. 形容词或过去分词：

He *appeared* quite *well*. 他似乎身体很不错。

She *appeared perplexed*. 她显得有些困惑。

b. 跟名词：

It *appears* (to be) *a true story*. 它似乎是一个真实的故事。

He didn't want to *appear a fool*. 他不想显得像一个傻瓜。

c. 跟从句：

It *appeared that he had an unusual taste for music*. 似乎他对音乐有着非凡的鉴赏力。

It *appeared that Harry was taking her to the opera*. 看来哈利准备带她去看歌剧。

3) become:

后面可跟：

a. 形容词：

She had *become quite familiar* with this seaside city. 她对这座海滨城市已非常熟悉。

They *became dizzy* with this momentary "victory". 他们被一时的胜利冲昏了头脑。

b. 过去分词：

She was *becoming annoyed* with me. 她有点儿生我的气。

He *became acquainted* with Balzac. 他和巴尔扎克认识了。

c. 名词：

She talked to me about *becoming a teacher*. 她和我谈起要当老师的事。

But his dream had not *become a reality*. 但他的梦想并未成真。

4) fall:

后面可跟：

a. 形容词 (只限于少数形容词)：

Soon she *fell asleep*. 不久她就睡着了。

He has *fallen ill (sick)*. 他生病了。

还可用于 fall vacant，fall silent 等。

b. 名词：

They didn't want to *fall a victim* to mammonism. 他们不愿成为拜金主义的牺牲品。

I *fell a prey* to evil dreams. 我常常受噩梦的折磨。

5) feel:

这个词有两重意思，一个主要意思是"感觉(如何)"，后面可跟：

a. 形容词 (大量形容词可以和 feel 连用)：

I don't *feel* very *well*. 我感到不大舒服。

I've been *feeling* awfully *bad* about it. 对此我感到很难受。

b. 过去分词：

He *felt troubled and distressed*. 他感到很烦恼痛苦。

I *feel puzzled and upset*. 我感到困惑烦乱。

c. 介词短语：

I *feel at ease* with her. 我和她在一起感到轻松自在。

She no longer *felt in fighting mood*. 她不再感到有旺盛的斗志。

还可表示"摸起来(如何)"：

It *feels rough* on the surface. 它的表面摸上去很粗糙。

Ice *feels cold*. 冰摸起来很凉。

6) get:

后面可以跟：

a. 形容词 (大量形容词可以和 get 连用)：

The whether is *getting* quite *warm*. 天气变得相当暖和。

I hope you won't *get over-tired*. 希望你不要过度劳累。

b. 过去分词：

I *get* more and more *absorbed* in the work here.　我对这里的工作越来越投入了。

Don't *get caught* in the rain.　别让雨淋着。

c. 现在分词：

We'd better *get moving*.　我们最好开始动身。

Then they *got chatting* together.　后来他们在一起聊了起来。

d. 名词：

You're *getting quite a lad* now.　你快长成大小伙子了。

He's *getting a bad influence* on my children.　他在对我的孩子产生坏影响。

e. 介词短语：

It's *getting near dinner-time*.　快到吃饭时间了。

We'll let you know as soon as production *gets under way*.　生产一上轨道我们就通知你。

7) go:

在多数情况下都跟形容词，但只能跟某些形容词，如：

She *went pale* at the news.　听了这消息她脸色发白。

He *went mad (insane)*.　他疯了。

另外还可跟 white, gray, purple, red, hungry, sour, bad, bald, tired, sick, blind, sentimental, wrong, bankrupt, broke, rotten, independent, dead, lame 等。

此外，还可跟：

a. 过去分词：

His complaints *went unnoticed*.　他的抱怨没人理会。

All the men there *go armed*.　那里的男人都带武器。

b. 介词短语：

This *went out of fashion* years go.　这许多年前就已过时了。

He *went off his head*.　他昏了头。

c. 名词：

Her rosy face *went the colour of cream*.　她红红的脸变成乳白色。

Her cheeks *went a very pretty pink*.　她的双颊变成了漂亮的粉红色。

8) grow:

这个词主要跟形容词，如：

The dispute *grew* more *violent*.　争论越来越激烈。

The noise *grew louder*.　声音越来越大。

此外还可跟 cold, hot, calm, old, big, thin, bright, stuffy, angry, rich, restless, uneasy, worse, fat, dark, fierce, serious, loud, intimate, tall 等。

还可跟过去分词：

> You'll *grow used* to it. 对此你会习惯的。
>
> I *grow excited and red-eared, and a little frightened*. 我变得兴奋起来,耳朵也红了，还有点害怕。

偶跟介词短语：

> It has *grown out of fashion*. 它已经不时兴了。
>
> These ideas have *grown out of date*. 这些观念已经陈旧了。

9）keep：

在用作系动词时它后面可以跟：

a. 形容词：

> The whether is *keeping fine*. 天气一直很晴朗。
>
> I hope you are *keeping well*. 我希望你身体(保持)健康。

后面还可以跟 quiet, silent, calm, fit, cool, warm, fine, close, near 等。

b. 副词：

> Danger! *Keep out*! 危险! 切勿靠近!
>
> He *kept apart* from the other students. 他不和别的学生待在一起。

c. 介词短语：

> Please try to *keep out of the way*. 劳驾，请别挡道。
>
> We must *keep in close contact* with the media. 我们必须与新闻媒体保持密切联系。

10）look：

作系动词时表示"看起来…"，后面可以跟：

a. 形容词：

> She *looked nervous and apologetic*. 她显得紧张并有歉意。
>
> The case *looks promising*. 这案子看起来很有希望。

b. 过去分词：

> He *looked startled* when she came in. 她进来时，他显得很吃惊。
>
> She *looked very concerned and troubled*. 她看上去非常忧虑苦恼。

c. 名词：

> Now she *looked a grown-up young women*. 现在她看起来已是一个成年的姑娘了。
>
> He *looks sadness* itself. 他显得很凄伤的样子。

d. 介词短语：

He *looked in splendid health*.   他看上去身体很棒。

The whether doesn't *look like clearing up*.   天看起来不像会放晴。

还可跟副词、数词等：

He *looks* awfully *down*.   他显得很消沉的样子。

She *looked about fourteen*.   她看起来约莫十四岁。

11）prove:

这个词作系动词时表示"事实证明…"，后面可以跟：

a. 形容词：

Treat us well: we shall not *prove ungrateful*.   好好待我们，我们不会忘恩负义的。

The extra room *proved* very *useful*.   这间备用房间证明是很有用的。

b. 名词：

This would *prove an excellent weapon*.   这会证明是极好的武器。

It might *prove the best plan*.   这或可证明是最好的计划。

c. 介词短语：

These books may *prove of use* for you in future.   这些书将来可能证明对你有用。

Her advice *proved of* great value to our test.   她的意见证明对我们的试验很有价值。

12）remain:

这个词有时用作系动词，表示"继续(处于某种状态)"，后面可以跟：

a. 形容词：

For a whole day the enemy *remained inactive*.   一整天敌人都没有动静。

Perhaps he could be induced to *remain silent*.   或许能劝他保持沉默。

b. 过去分词：

She still *remained unconvinced*.   她仍然不相信。

But they *remained unfinished*.   但他们仍然没完成。

c. 现在分词：

She *remained standing* for a good hour.   她站了足有一个钟头。

They *remained listening*.   他们仍然在听着。

d. 名词：

She *remained the same Constance*.   她还是原来的康士坦丝。

Why he did it will *remain a puzzle* forever.   他为什么这样做将永远是个谜。

e. 介词短语:

You can't let the room *remain like this*! 你不能让房间老是这样!

They still *remained at the mercy* of the terrorists. 他们仍然听任恐怖分子的摆布。

13) rest:

这个词只在少数情况下用作系动词:

The affair *rests a mystery*. 这事仍然是个谜。

Rest assured we will do all we can. 请放心，我们会全力以赴。

14) run:

这个词间或用作系动词，表示"变成(什么样子)"，后面主要跟一些形容词:

The rivers were beginning to *run dry*. 河流开始干涸。

My blood *ran cold* with fear. 我吓得毛骨悚然。

还可用在 run high, run low, run wild, run rife, run strong, run small, run loose, run short of, run out of 等词组中。

15) seem:

这是一个常用的系动词，表示"看来"、"似乎"，后面可跟:

a. 形容词:

She *seems happy* to me. 在我看来她似乎很愉快。

It *seems probable* that I'll be sent abroad next year. 看来我明年有可能被派往国外。

b. 分词:

He *seems* rather *agitated*. 他好像相当焦虑不安。

She *seemed lacking* in enthusiasm. 她似乎缺乏热情。

c. 名词:

It *seems* to me (to be) *the best solution*. 在我看来这似乎是最好的解决办法。

She *seemed* an unusually *clever girl*. 她似乎是一个聪明绝顶的姑娘。

d. 介词短语:

He *seemed out of humour*. 他好像情绪不佳。

She *seemed in high spirits*. 她似乎情绪高昂。

16) smell:

作系动词时表示"闻起来…"，多跟形容词:

Roses *smell sweet*. 玫瑰花有香味。

The dinner *smells good*. 饭菜味道很香。

间或跟介词短语:

How *sweet* the music *sounds*!   这音乐听起来多甜美呀!

    The soup *smells of garlic*.   这汤有大蒜味。

    What does the perfume *smell like*?   这种香水是什么味?

17) sound:

作系动词时表示"听起来…",通常后面跟形容词:

    How *sweet* the music *sounds*!   这音乐听起来多甜美呀!

    Don't speak like that. It sounds insincere to me.   别这样讲,在我听来这
       显得不诚恳。

间或跟名词 (a) 或介词短语 (b):

a. Your idea *sounds* (like) a good one.   你的想法听起来不错。

    He *sounded a hard man*.   他听起来像是一个厉害的人。

b. It *sounded like Beethoven*.   这听起来像贝多芬的音乐。

    It almost *sounds like science fiction*.   这听起来几乎像科幻小说。

18) stay:

这个词只在少数情况下用作系动词,意思是"保持 (某种状态)",后面
主要跟形容词:

    He *stayed single* for many years.   许多年他都是单身。

    I'm going to *stay awake* to see the eclipse.   我准备熬夜来观看月蚀。

间或跟介词短语 (a) 或过去分词 (b):

a. They are not likely to *stay in power* after the election.   选举之后他们可能
不会继续执政。

    Father wanted us to *stay out of trouble*.   父亲要我们别惹麻烦。

b. Please *stay seated*.   请不要站起来。

    The police prefer to *stay unarmed*.   警察们宁愿不带枪。

19) taste:

作系动词时意思是"吃(喝)起来…",后面多跟形容词:

    The meat *tastes good*.   这肉味道很好。

    The milk doesn't *taste right* this morning.   今天早上这奶味道不大对。

    This soup *tastes awful*.   这汤味道糟透了。

20) turn:

作系动词时主要表示"变得(成)…",后面可以跟:

a. 形容词:

    He *turned* rather *pink*.   他的脸红了。

    It's *turned* awfully *chilly*. I think it's going to snow.   天变得冷极了,我想
       要下雪了。

b. 名词:

He has *turned traitor (Mahammedan)*.　他成了叛徒(回教徒)。

She *turned botanist*.　她成了植物学家。

7.1.8　助动词和情态动词

1) be, have, do 都可用作助动词:

a. be 可构成进行时态、被动语态和复合谓语:

She *is* writing a novel.　她在写小说。(进行时态)

What have you *been* doing?　你干什么来着?(进行时态)

She *was* given a warm welcome.　她受到热烈欢迎。(被动语态)

The case *is being* investigated.　这案子正在调查。(被动语态)

How *are* you to explain all this?　这一切你怎么解释?(复合谓语)

b. have 可构成完成时态和完成进行时态:

She *'d* (had) been out shopping.　她出去买东西了。(完成时态)

They *have* set up a network of financial advice centers.　他们建立了一个金融咨询中心网。(完成时态)

She *'s* (has) been doing some research work.　她一直在做研究工作。(完成进行时)

That was the letter we *'d* (had) been expecting.　这正是我们在期待的信。(完成进行时)

c. do 可构成疑问句、否定句,用于强调或代表前面动词以避免重复:

When *did* she get there?　她什么时候到的?(疑问句)

He *does*n't know anything about it.　他对此一无所知。(否定句)

Do stay for a couple more days.　务请再待两三天。(强调)

He speaks English better than I *do*.　他英文讲得比我好。(代表前面动词)

2) shall, will, should, would:

这几个词都可用作助动词,但有时有一定的意思,接近一个情态动词:

a. will 主要用来构成将来时态,可用于多个人称 (will not 常可紧缩为 won't /wəʊnt/):

When *will* you be back?　你什么时候回来?

I *'ll* let you know in a day or two.　一两天后我将通知你。

They *won't* let you down.　他们不会让你失望的。

b. shall 主要用在第一人称作主语的问句中，征求对方意见：

Shall I wait for you?　我要不要等你？

Shall we meet again tomorrow?　明天咱们要不要再碰头？

How *shall* I help you?　我该怎么帮助你？

在英国，也有人把它用于第一人称的肯定句或否定句 (在口语中 shall not 可紧缩为 shan't /ʃɑːnt/)：

I *shall* often be coming to Pisa.　我会时常到比萨来。

We *shall* read about it tomorrow.　明天我们就会读到这消息了。

We *shan't* be coming back today.　我们今天不回来了。

c. would 主要用来构成过去将来时态，可用于多个人称：

I knew you *would* agree.　我知道你会同意的。

I asked if he *would* come and join us.　我问他是否愿意来参加我们的活动。

I said that I *would* arrange everything.　我说我会安排一切的。

也可用来提出请求、看法等：

Would you please look over my essay?　可否劳驾看一遍我的文章？

What *would* you like?　你愿意要什么？

I'*d* go there with you.　我愿和你一道去。

还可用在虚拟条件句中：

I *would* do it if I could.　如果我有能力我会这样做的。

If he were in town, he'*d* help.　如果他在城里，他会帮忙的。

d. should 间或还用来构成过去将来时 (但大多数人已改用 would)，用在第一人称后：

We (I) never thought we (I) *should* (would) see you again.　我们以为不会再见到你了。

The weather report said that we *should* have rain.　天气预报说会下雨。

目前更多用来表示"应当"(a) 或用在某些从句中 (b)：

a. You *should* do it for your own good.　为了你自己好，你应当去做。

Why *should* I pay him?　我为什么该付他钱？

b. He wrote, suggesting that we *should* go to Paris.　他来信了，建议我们去巴黎。

It will be better that he *should* be out of France.　他离开法国会好一些。

It is dreadful that they *should* be so miserable.　他们竟然这样悲惨，太可怕了。

We hid it so that he *should* not see it.　我们把它藏了起来以免被他看到。

关于这几个词的详细用法见第 11 章。

3）can, could, may, might, must:

这五个词都是情态动词，它们和一个动词原形构成谓语，各有一定的意思，在各个人称后形式都一样。

a. can 主要表示"能够"、"可以"（它的否定形式 can not 常紧缩为 can't，英国读作 /kɑːnt/，美国读作 /kænt/）：

Who *can* prove it?　谁能证明这一点？

These difficulties, we *can* and must overcome.　这些困难我们能够也必须克服。

I'm like that, you *can't* alter me.　我就是这样，你没法改变我。

We *can* call for you at nine.　我们可以九点钟来叫你。

He *can't* be more than thirty.　他不会超过三十岁。

b. could 可以作 can 的过去式，表示它的多种意思：

He *could* not follow their argument.　他听不明白他们的争论。

He said he *couldn't* come.　他说他不能来。

Mother said we *couldn't* go out at night.　妈妈说晚上我们不能出去。

I thought he *could* be in bed now.　我想这会儿他可能在睡觉。

也可比较婉转地提出请求或看法等：

Could you lend me your car?　你能把车借给我吗？

Yes, his story *could* be true.　对，这个说法可能是真的。

I *could* come earlier, if necessary.　如果必要我可以来早点。

c. may 主要表示"可能"、"或许"：

She *may* come tonight.　她今晚可能来。

He *may* not like the idea.　他可能不赞成这个主意。

They *may* be in the library now.　他们现在或许在图书馆。

也可用在问句中表示"可否"，用在陈述句中表示"可以"：

May I come round in the morning?　——Yes, please do.　我可否早上来？——可以，请来吧。

May he go there with you?　——Yes, he may.　他可以和你一道去那儿吗？——可以。

You *may* come again tomorrow.　你可以明天再来。

d. might 可以作 may 的过去式：

He thought she *might* be in her office.　他想她或许在办公室里。

I was afraid you *might* not be in.　我担心你可能不在家。

He died so that others *might* live.　他牺牲了，以求别人能活下去。

有时可表示现在情况(和 may 一样)，只是口气婉转一些：

Might I have a little more?　我能再多要一点吗？

You *might* just give me half a cup.　你可以给我半杯。

You *might* have some fever.　你可能有点发烧。

e. must 主要表示"必须"、"一定要"，可用于任何时间：

We *must* leave early.　我们必须及早动身。

You *must* finish everything in time.　你一定要及时干完一切。

I *must* be off now.　我得走了。

否定式 must not 常紧缩为 mustn't，读作 /ˈmʌsnt/，表示"一定不要"：

You *mustn't* forget to phone her.　你一定不要忘了给她打电话。

You *mustn't* be late again.　别再迟到了。

在回答包含 must 的问句时，若是肯定回答可用 must，若为否定回答，要用 needn't：

Must we finish everything tonight?　一切都要今晚完成吗？

Yes, you *must*.　是的，必须今晚完成。

No, you *needn't*.　不，不必今晚完成。

此外还有半情态动词(如 dare，need)和相当于情态动词的结构(如 have to，ought to 等)，这些将在第 11 章里详细讨论。

7.2　动词的各种形式

7.2.1　动词的四种主要形式

1) 现在式：就是词典中所给的形式，也可称为动词原形，其他形式都由它派生而来。一般现在时要用现在式：

We *love* peace. 我们热爱和平。

2) 过去式：几乎每个动词都有过去式，表示过去发生的事。一般过去时都由它表示，如：

She *was* (be 的过去式) a worker. Now she is a technician.　她过去是工人，现在是技术员。

3) 过去分词：也是大多数动词都具有的形式，可构成完成时态 (a) 和被动语态 (b)：

a. He has *lived* here for many years. 他在这里住了许多年了。

b. The VCR was *made* in China. 这种录像机是中国制造的。

4) 现在分词：通常由动词原形＋ing 构成，可构成各种进行时态:

We are *learning* grammar. 我们正在学语法。

7.2.2   过去式和过去分词构成法

1) 英语中大部分动词都以加 -ed 词尾的办法构成过去式及过去分词:

现在时(动词原形)	过去式	过去分词
work	worked	worked
appear	appeared	appeared
talk	talked	talked
play	played	played

这类动词称为 **规则动词** (Regular Verbs)。

2) 在加 -ed 词尾时要注意几个问题:

a. 若末尾已有字母e，则只加-d:

live —— lived   please —— pleased   free —— freed

b. 若以"辅音(字母) ＋ y"结尾，先变 y 为 i 再加 -ed:

try —— tried   study —— studied   simplify —— simplified

c. 若是以"一个元音字母＋一个辅音字母"结尾，该音节又重读者，末尾字母要双写，然后再加 -ed:

stop —— stopped   fit —— fitted   chat —— chatted

d. 其他的词都直接加 -ed:

lack —— lacked   open —— opened   repeat —— repeated

3) 另外，还有几点值得注意:

a. 以"一个元音＋l"结尾的词，英国人都把l双写，美国人都不双写:

travel——travelled (英)，traveled (美)

marvel——marvelled (英)，marveled (美)

b. l前若有两个元音，l一概不双写 (英美都如此):

reveal —— revealed   appeal —— appealed

c. 有少数词，尽管末尾音节并不重读，末尾辅音字母在英国仍双写:

worship——worshipped (英)，worshiped (美)

kidnap —— kidnapped (英)，kidnaped (美)

但 program——programmed (英，美)，programed (美国人有时用这种拼法)

d. 以 x 结尾的词，x 不双写：

  mix —— mixed   fix —— fixed

4) 在英语中，在加 -ed 词尾时，末尾字母需双写的词常见的有：

ban	bar	bat	beg	blot	brag	brim	chat
chop	clap	cram	crop	dam	dip	dot	drag
drop	drum	dub	fan	fit	flag	grap	grin
grip	gun	hop	hug	hum	jam	jog	jot
knit	lag	man	mar	mob	mop	mug	nag
net	nip	nod	pad	pat	pen	pin	pit
plan	plod	plug	pop	prop	rip	rob	rot
rub	scan	scar	scrap	skrub	ship	shop	shred
shrug	shun	sin	sip	skid	skim	skin	skip
slam	slap	slip	snap	sob	spot	squat	stap
star	stem	step	stop	strap	strip	stun	sun
swap	tag	tan	tap	thin	throb	tip	top
trap	trim	trip	trot	wag	wrap		
abet	abhor	acquit	admit	allot	commit	compel	confer
control	defer	deter	distil	emit	enrol	equip	excel
expel	incur	instil	occur	omit	outwit	patrol	propel
recap	refer	regret	remit	repel	submit	transmi	handicap

5) 下面的词在加 -ed 时，在英国末尾字母要双写，而在美国却不一定双写：

cancel	dial	equal	hiccup	initial	kidnap
label	level	marvel	model	pedal	pencil
program	quarrel	refuel	revel	rival	shovel
shrivel	total	travel	tunnel	unravel	worship

〔注〕　在加 -ing 词尾时，4) 中所列词情况也一样。

7.2.3　不规则动词

1) 但也有相当多的动词不以加 -ed 的方式构成过去式和过去分词，这类动词称作 **不规则动词** (Irregular Verbs)。这类动词数量有限，却都是非常活跃的词，例如下面这些：

原形　　　过去时　　　过去分词

beat	beat	beaten	become	became	become
begin	began	begun	blow	blew	blown
break	broke	broken	bring	brought	brought
build	built	built	burst	burst	burst
buy	bought	bought	catch	caught	caught
choose	chose	chosen	come	came	come
cost	cost	cost	cut	cut	cut
dig	dug	dug	do	did	done
draw	drew	drawn	eat	ate	eaten
fall	fell	fallen	feel	felt	felt
fight	fought	fought	find	found	found
fly	flew	flown	freeze	froze	frozen
get	got	got	give	gave	given
go	went	gone	grow	grew	grown
have	had	had	hear	heard	heard
hide	hid	hidden	hurt	hurt	hurt
keep	kept	kept	know	knew	known
lay	laid	laid	lead	led	led
leave	left	left	lend	lent	lent
let	let	let	lie	lay	lain
lose	lost	lost	make	made	made
mean	meant	meant /ment/	meet	met	met
pay	paid	paid	put	put	put
read	read	read /red/	ride	rode	ridden
ring	rang	rung	rise	rose	risen
run	ran	run	say	said	said /sed/
see	saw	seen	sell	sold	sold
send	sent	sent	set	set	set
shake	shook	shaken	shine	shone	shone /ʃɒn/
shoot	shot	shot	show	showed	shown
shut	shut	shut	sing	sang	sung
sink	sank	sunk	sit	sat	sat

sleep	slept	slept	speak	spoke	spoken
spend	spent	spent	spin	span	spun
spread	spread	spread	spring	sprang	sprung
stand	stood	stood	steal	stole	stolen
stick	stuck	stuck	strike	struck	struck
sweep	swept	swept	swim	swam	swum
take	took	taken	teach	taught	taught
tear	tore	torn	tell	told	told
think	thought	thought	throw	threw	thrown
understand	understood	understood	wake	woke	woken
wear	wore	worn	weep	wept	wept
win	won	won	write	wrote	written

这些都是最最常用的词，不熟练掌握这些词，学时态就会困难重重。因此学语法的第一步就是把这些常用的不规则动词背熟，要背得烂熟，想到一个词，就能把三个形式都说出来，这是基础的基础。掌握了这些词，就可以适应初期学习的要求，以后还应把书后列出的不规则动词全部学一遍。

2) 有几个动词，在英美有不同的过去式及过去分词形式：

现在式		burn	dream	lean	leap	learn	smell	spell	spill	spoil
过去式及过去分词	英国拼法	burnt burnt	dreamt dreamt /dremt/	leant leant /lent/	leapt leapt /lept/	learnt learnt	smelt smelt	spelt spelt	spilt spilt	spoilt spoilt
	美国拼法	burned burned	dreamed dreamed	leaned leaned	leaped leaped	learned learned	smelled smelled	spelled spelled	spilled spilled	spoiled spoiled

从表中可以看出，在美国英语中这些词都是规则动词。

7.2.4 现在分词

1) 现在分词都是在现在式 (动词原形) 后加 -ing 构成，如：

She is *listening* to classical music on CDs. 她在听激光唱盘上的古典音乐。

Who is *conducting* the orchestra?　谁在指挥管弦乐队？

在多数情况下都直接加 -ing，但有一些特殊情况：

a. 以不读音的 e 结尾的词，去掉 e 再加 -ing：

move —— moving　　　　make —— making　　　write —— writing

但 free —— freeing (ee 读作 /iː/)

b. 以"一个元音字母 ＋ 一个辅音字母"结尾，该音节又重读者，末尾辅音要双写，再加 -ing：

swim —— swimming　beg —— begging　　chat —— chatting

refer —— referring　　begin —— beginning　forget —— forgetting

但 open —— opening (末尾音节不重读)

pack —— packing (末尾有两个辅音字母)

在 7.2.2 节第 4 段中所列词加 -ing 时，末尾辅音字母也要双写。

2) 还有几点值得注意：

a. 以"一个元音字母加 l"结尾的词，在加 -ing 时，l 字母英国人双写，美国人不双写：

travel ——travelling (英)，traveling (美)

patrol——patrolling (英)，patroling (美)

但 reveal —— revealing (英，美) (因末尾音节中有两个元音字母)

b. 下面的词，虽然末尾音节不重读，在英国末尾辅音字母仍双写，不过美国人不双写：

kidnap —— kidnapping (英)，kidnaping (美)

worship —— worshipping (英)，worshiping (美)

但 program 加 -ing 时，m 字母英美都双写：

programming (美国也有人不双写)

c. 下面的词加 -ing 词尾时有特别之处：

die —— dying　　　lie —— lying　　　tie —— tying

hoe —— hoeing　　toe —— toeing　　dye —— dyeing

picnic —— picnicking　panic —— panicking　mimic —— mimicking

age —— ageing 或 aging

7.2.5　-s 词尾的加法

1) 在一般现在时中，主语为第三人称单数时，谓语需加 -s，如：

She *loves* children.　她爱孩子。

This *surprises* us. 这让我们感到吃惊。

这虽然是一个简单的问题，但常常被人忽略。有些人学了几年英语，还养不成第三人称单数后加 -s 的习惯。在日常口语中需加 -s 时很多，因此要特别注意，不要给人以不良印象。

2) 在加 -s 词尾时要注意下面几点：

a. 在一般情况下可直接加 -s (这是多数情况)：

work —— works	like —— likes
come —— comes	feel —— feels

b. 以 ch, sh, s, x, o 结尾的词，需加 -es：

teach —— teaches	fetch —— fetches
wash —— washes	wish —— wishes
guess —— guesses	miss —— misses
fax —— faxes	fix —— fixes
do —— does	go —— goes

c. 以辅音 + y 结尾的词，先变 y 为 i，再加 -es：

cry —— cries	apply —— applies
fry —— fries	reply —— replies

3) -s 词尾的读音和名词复数词尾 -s 的读音一样，有三种情况：

a. 在 /p/, /t/, /k/, /f/ 等清辅音后读 /s/：

stops /stɒps/	keeps /kiːps/
sets /sets/	sits /sɪts/
thanks /θæŋks/	makes /meɪks/
laughs /lɑːfs/	coughs /kɒfs/

b. /s/, /z/, /ʃ/, /tʃ/, /dʒ/ 等音后读 /ɪz/：

misses /ˈmɪsɪz/	relaxes /rɪˈlæksɪz/
amuses /əˈmjuːzɪz/	raises /ˈreɪzɪz/
wishes /ˈwɪʃɪz/	brushes /ˈbrʌʃɪz/
attaches /əˈtætʃɪz/	catches /ˈkætʃɪz/
pledges /ˈpledʒɪz/	

c. 其他情况都读作 /z/：

calls /kɔːlz/	plans /plænz/
gives /gɪvz/	runs /rʌnz/
says /sez/	dies /daɪz/
agrees /əˈgriːz/	allows /əˈlaʊz/
reads /riːdz/	saves /seɪvz/

7.2.6　动词的紧缩形式

1）有很多动词在口语中常有 **紧缩形式** (Contractions)，如：

I'm waiting for him. (= I am waiting for him.)

She's gone home. (= She has gone home.)

He won't be here tonight. (= He will not be here tonight.)

其至在书信等比较随便的文体中也常用这种形式。从头掌握这种形式至关重要。看到这种形式应立即知道它是哪个动词的紧缩形式，听到这种形式也应立即反应过来，知道是什么意思。这也是从头要掌握的基本功。

2）现在将主要的紧缩形式列表说明如下：

原来形式	紧缩形式	例　句
I am	I'm	I'm waiting for the bus.
you are	you're	You're late.
he is	he's	He's busy now.
she is	she's	She's in her office.
it is	it's	It's my job.
we are	we're	We're having a meeting.
they are	they're	They're looking for you .
there is	there's	There's no one in the room.
there are	there're	There're lots of things to do.
here is	here's	Here's the book you want.
that is	that's	That's what I want to know.
I have	I've	I've got your letters.
you have	you've	You've won the game.
he has	he's	He's left already.
she has	she's	She's been there many times.
we have	we've	We've got to be there today.
they have	they've	They've missed the bus.
who has	who's	Who's broken the window?

I had	I'd	I'd never been there before.
I shall/will	I'll	I'll let you know tonight.
you will	you'll	You'll soon get an answer.
he will	he'll	He'll arrive on the 9:30 train.
she will	she'll	She'll come and join us.
we shall/will	we'll	We'll try our best to help you.
they will	they'll	They'll do well in school.
I would	I'd	I'd rather stay at home.
who would	who'd	Who'd like to go with us?

3）否定结构也有紧缩形式:

原来形式	紧缩形式	例　句
I am not	I'm not	I'm not ready yet.
we are not	we aren't	We aren't free. 或 we are not free.
he is not	he isn't	He isn't back yet. 或 He's not back yet.
he was not	he wasn't	He wasn't there.
they were not	they weren't	They weren't happy about it.
I have not	I haven't	I haven't heard about it. 或 I've not...
she has not	she hasn't	She hasn't arrived yet. 或 She's not...
he had not	he hadn't	He hadn't got up yet. 或 He'd not...
I do not	I don't	I don't like the idea.
he does not	he doesn't	He doesn't work hard enough.
she did not	she didn't	She didn't come to the party.
I shall not	I shan't	I shan't go with her. 或 I'll not...
they will not	they won't	They won't stay long. 或 They'll not...
we should not	we shouldn't	We shouldn't miss the lecture. 或 we'd not...
she would not	she wouldn't	She wouldn't accept the offer. 或 she'd not...

you must not	you mustn't	You mustn't do that again.
we can not	we can't	We can't answer the question.
he need not	he needn't	He needn't buy it.
she does not	she doesn't	She doesn't go home alone.
they could not	they couldn't	They couldn't get hold of him.
she might not	she mightn't	She mightn't have time to do it.
we ought not	we oughtn't	We oughtn't to forget this.

7.3　动词的限定形式和非限定形式

7.3.1　动词的限定形式

1）动词在作谓语时要受主语的制约，例如：

a. 它要和主语在"人称"上一致：

I *speak* English. （第一人称）

She *speaks* French. （第三人称）

b. 它在"数"上也要和主语一致：

She *is* a student. （单数）

They *are* students. （复数）

2）它还应表示：

a. 时态 (Tense)：

I *was* ill yesterday. 昨天我病了。（过去时）

I *feel* better today. 我今天好一点了。（现在时）

I'll *be* all right in a couple of days. 过两天我就会好了。（将来时）

b. 语态 (Voice)：

She *wrote* a play. 她写了一个剧本。（主动语态）

The play *was written* by Cao Yu. 这个剧是曹禺写的。（被动语态）

c. 语气 (Mood)：

The children *are* noisy. 孩子们很吵。（陈述语气，说明事实）

Don't be so noisy, children! 孩子们，别这么吵！（祈使语气，提出要求）

I wish they *weren't* so noisy. 但愿他们别这么吵。（虚拟语气，表示愿望）

动词的这些形式都称为 **限定形式** (Finite Forms)，也有人称之为谓语形式，即作谓语时用的形式。有少数动词，如情态动词，不受主语影响，在任何人称后形式都无变化，因此它们被称为 **无变化动词** (Defective Verbs)。动词的限定形式比较复杂，能否掌握是学好英语的关键。

7.3.2 时态

1) 英语中不同时间发生的动作或情况要用不同的形式表示，称为时态。英语中共有十六种时态，它们是：

一般现在时	现在进行时	现在完成时	现在完成进行时
一般过去时	过去进行时	过去完成时	过去完成进行时
一般将来时	将来进行时	将来完成时	将来完成进行时
一般过去将来时	过去将来进行时	过去将来完成时	过去将来完成进行时

2) 各种时态的构成方法大致可归纳如下：

a. 一般现在时用现在式(动词原型)，但在第三人称单数的主语后要加 -s 词尾；

b. 一般过去时用动词的过去式，不分人称，但动词 be 有两个过去式：was 用于第一、三人称单数，其他情况用 were：

　　I *was* (They *were*) excited.

c. 一般将来时，一般由"will + 动词原形"构成，但在有第一人称主语的问句中用"shall + 动词原形"这种形式：

　　I'*ll do* it.

　　Shall I *do* it?

　　Will you *do* it?

d. 一般过去将来时用"would + 动词原形"构成：

　　She hoped the weather *would be* favourable.

e. 各种进行时态都由"be + 现在分词"构成，时间由 be 表现出来：

　　I *am* (You *are* / He *is* / They *are*) *studying*.

　　She *was playing* the piano. They *were playing* football.

　　I (We / She) *will be watching* TV tonight.

　　I thought you *would be waiting* for us.

f. 各种完成时态都由"have + 过去分词"构成，时间由 have 表现出来：

　　She *has* (I *have*) written a novel.

　　He said he *had written* a novel.

They *will have finished* the work by tomorrow.

He said he *would have finished* the work by tomorrow.

g. 各种完成进行时态都由"have been + 现在分词"构成，时间、人称由 have 表现出来：

I *have* (She *has*) *been waiting* for you.

She said she *had been waiting* for you.

I *will have been waiting* for two hours by 9 o'clock.

She told me she *would have been teaching* for 20 years by this summer.

3) 各种时态形式可归纳成下表：

	一般时态	进行时态	完成时态	完成进行时态
现在	write writes	am are }writing is	have }written has	have }been writing has
过去	wrote	was }writing were	had written	had been writing
将来	will write (shall I write)	will be writing	will have written	will have been writing
过去将来	would write	would be writing	would have written	would have been writing

这些时态并不是同样活跃的，最基础的是以下五种时态(这是初学者都得学的)：

一般现在时　现在进行时　一般过去时　一般将来时　现在完成时

其次是以下五种时态，用得也比较多：

过去进行时　　过去完成时　　现在完成进行时　　过去完成进行时
将来进行时

其他时态只是偶然用到。关于各种时态的具体用法，下一章将专门讨论。

4) 否定式的构成：

否定式通常由 { 系动词 be　　助动词　　情态动词 } + not 构成：

主 语	be, 助动词或情态动词 + not	其他部分
She	is not (was not)	in Paris now (then).
She	is not (was not) working	at the moment.
She	does (did) not know	English.
She	has not done	her exercises.
She	will not stay	here long.
She	cannot run	very fast.
She	may not like	the idea.
You	mustn't (needn't/doesn't have to) leave	so soon.

5）疑问式的构成：

一般问句和特殊问句通常都用下面方式构成：

疑问词	动词 be, 助动词或情态动词	主语	其他部分
	Are (Is)	you (he)	a Canadian?
	Were (Was)	you (he)	there then?
	Does (Did)	he	know you (then)?
	Is (Was)	she	waiting?
	Has (Have)	he (you)	got my letter?
Where	are (is)	you (he)	from?
How	are (is)	they (she)	doing?
What time	did	you	arrive?
How long	has	she	been teaching here?
Where	can (must)	I	put it?

在学习时态时要注意各类形式，只有熟练掌握这些形式，才能顺利交谈。

7.3.3　语态

1）英语中有两种语态，一是 **主动语态** (The Active Voice)，一是 **被动语态** (The Passive Voice)，主动语态表示主语的动作，即主语是做这动作的人，如：

　　She wrote a poem.　她写了一首诗。(诗是她写的)

　　She loves the children.　她爱孩子。(孩子是她爱的对象)

大部分的英文句子都是主动语态。用被动语态时表示主语是动作的对象或

结果:

> She is loved by all the children. 她受到所有孩子的爱戴。(她是爱戴的对象)

> The poem was written by a girl. 诗是一个女孩写的。(诗是写出的成品)

被动语态是由"be + 过去分词"构成的，时间由 be 表示出来：

> She *is respected* by everyone. 她受到大家的敬重。(一般现在时)

> He *was born* in 1980. 他于1980年出生。(一般过去时)

> When *will* the book *be published*? 书什么时候出版？(一般将来时)

> The auditorium *has been rebuilt*. 礼堂重建好了。(现在完成时)

> The road *is being widened*. 路正在拓宽。(现在进行时)

2）并不是所有时态都有被动语态，有被动语态的基本上只有八个，在下面表中可以看出主要的被动语态：

	一般时态	进行时态	完成时态
现在	am are }given is	am are }being given is	has }been given have
过去	was }given were	was }being given were	had been given
将来	will }be given shall	×	(will have been done)
过去将来	would }be given (should)	×	(would have been done)

关于语态，在第9章再作详细的讨论。

***

7.3.4 语气

1）按说话意图，动词要用不同形式，称为语气。英语中有三种语气：

a. 陈述语气 (Indicative Mood) ——陈述事实或提出看法或问题：

> She is very busy. 她很忙。(陈述事实)

> She may not agree. 她可能不会同意。(提出看法)

Who's on the phone?　谁打电话来？（提出问题）

b. **祈使语气** (Imperative Mood) —— 表示请求、命令、叮嘱等：

Be seated, please.　请坐。（请求）

Get out!　出去！（命令）

Take care.　保重。（叮嘱）

c. **虚拟语气** (Subjunctive Mood) —— 表示假想情况或主观愿望：

If she *were* here, how nice it *would be*!　她要是在这里就好了。（假设情况）

God *bless* you.　上帝保佑你。（祝愿）

2) 英语中大部分句子都用陈述语气，祈使语气也用得比较多，虚拟语气只在有限的场合下使用。关于虚拟语气的形式和用法，详见第 10 章。

7.3.5　动词的非限定形式

动词除了在句中充当谓语，还可充当许多其他成分。由于它们不受主语制约（即不必和主语在人称、数等方面保持一致），所以被称作动词的**非限定形式**(Non-finite Forms)，也有人称之为非谓语形式。英语中动词有三种非限定形式：

1) **不定式** (The Infinitive)：

一般是在动词原形前加 to，在句中可担任各种成分，例如：

I hope *to see* you soon.　希望不久能见到你。（作宾语）

She has a lot of things *to do*.　她有很多事要做。（作定语）

I've come *to ask* your advice.　我是来找你出主意的。（作状语）

My idea is *to rent* a car.　我的主意是去租一辆车。（作表语）

She *seems to know* everything.　她似乎什么都知道。（构成谓语）

有时前面可以不带 to：

You *had better go* there by plane.　你最好坐飞机去那里。（构成谓语）

Let me *help* you.　让我来帮你。（构成复合宾语）

2) **动名词** (The Gerund)：

有些动词的 -ing 形式可起名词的作用，在句中也可担任许多成分，例如：

Stop *talking* now.　别讲话了。（作宾语）

Thank you for *helping* us.　谢谢你帮助了我们。（作介词宾语）

Smoking is hazardous to your health.　吸烟危害健康。（作主语）

One of my duties is *typing* letters.　我的职责之一是打信件。（作表语）

还可构成合成词：

living-room　客厅　　　　　　　　sleeping-pills　安眠药

singing contest　歌咏比赛　　　　　swimming-pool　游泳池

3) 分词 (The Participle):

分词有两种，一为**现在分词** (The Present Participle)，一为**过去分词** (The Past Participle)，这两种分词除了可构成谓语外，还可用作句中的许多成分，例如：

> The food looks *inviting*.　这菜看起来很诱人。(作表语)
>
> There are two girls *dancing on the lawn*.　有两个女孩在草坪上跳舞。(作定语)
>
> She hurried on, *hoping to catch the bus*.　她着急赶路，希望赶上公共汽车。(作状语)
>
> She seemed *surprised*.　她似乎很惊讶。(作表语)
>
> These are the seats *reserved for you*.　这是给你们留的座位。(作定语)
>
> *Guided by the new theory*, the researchers made a major breakthrough in biology.　在这种新学说的指引下，研究人员取得了生物学方面的重大突破。(作状语)

关于这三种形式的用法，在第 12 章中再作详细的讨论。

第8章 时 态

8.1 一般现在时

8.1.1 一般现在时的基本用法

一般现在时 (The Present Indefinite) 主要表示:

1) 经常发生或反复发生的动作:

He *gets* up at six. 他六点起床。

She *works* eight hours a day. 她每天工作八小时。

Do you often *wash* your hair? 你经常洗头吗?

Thank you. I *don't smoke*. 谢谢你, 我不抽烟。

Do you *go* to work by bus or by bike? 你坐公共汽车上班, 还是骑自行车上班?

2) 现时的情况或状态:

They *live* in the same building, don't they? 他们同住一幢楼, 对吧?

He *is* a law student. 他是学法律的。

She *knows* several languages. 她懂几国语言。

The soup *tastes* good. 这汤味道很好。

They *enjoy* skating. 他们喜欢溜冰。

The trouble *lies* in the socket. 毛病就在插座上。

3) 永恒的真理:

The sun *rises* in the east. 太阳从东边升起。

It *snows* in winter. 冬天下雪。

Metal *expands* when heated. 金属加热后会膨胀。

The river *originates* in a spring in the mountains. 这条河发源于山间的一股泉水。

Hydrogen *is* a light gas. 氢是很轻的气体。

8.1.2　一些常常用于一般现在时的动词

英语中有许多动词表示一种状态，可以称作**静态动词** (Stative Verbs)，常常用于一般现在时，如：

I *love* music.　我喜爱音乐。

What *does* the word mean?　这个词是什么意思？

The book *consists* of five parts.　这书包括五个部分。

I *suppose* they are right.　我想他们是对的。

I *wish* you happiness.　祝你幸福。

That *seems* a good idea.　这似乎是个好主意。

We *owe* everything to you.　一切我们都得归功于你。

Who *owns* this company?　这家公司是谁的？

这类动词常见的有：

admire	adore	appear	be	believe	belong
concern	consist	contain	depend	deserve	desire
despise	detest	dislike	doubt	envy	exist
feel	fit	forget	guess	hate	have
hear	hold	hope	imagine	impress	include
involve	keep	know	lack	like	love
major	matter	mean	need	owe	own
please	possess	prefer	realize	recognize	remember
require	resemble	satisfy	seat	see	seem
smell	sound	suppose	suspect	understand	wish

8.1.3　一些表示短暂动作的动词

有些动词表示极短暂的动作，可称为**短暂动词** (Instantaneous Verbs)，它们也常可用在一般现在时中，例如：

I *declare* Mr. Schiff elected.　我宣布希弗先生当选。

I *advise* that you leave at once.　我劝你们马上离开。

I *suggest* that we have lunch now.　我建议现在就吃午饭。

I *promise* I'll never conceal anything any more.　我答应再也不隐瞒什么。

This, I *admit*, was wrong.　我承认这是不对的。

I flatly *refuse* to do what he says.　我断然拒绝照他的话做。

I *regret* my bad action.　我懊悔我的不良行为。

I *enclose* a check herewith.　随信附上一张支票。

I *send* herewith the catalogue.　现寄上书目。

It's a lovely place.　——I *agree*.　这是个美丽的地方。——我有同感。

Your attitude simply *amazes* me.　你的态度简直使我吃惊。

You *surprise* me.　你吓我一跳。

这类动词一般不宜用于进行时，谈现在情况时，用一般现在时更自然一些。

8.1.4　一般现在时表示现刻动作

在一定的情况下，一般现在时可以表示现刻的动作，例如：

1) 球赛解说：

Hunt *takes* the ball forward quickly. Palmer *comes* across, *tries* to intercept
　　him, but Hunt *slips* past and quickly *pushes* the ball to Smart. Now Smart
　　gathers the ball.　亨特快速向前带球，帕尔默跑过来企图截住他，亨
　　特闪过身，迅速把球传给斯马特，斯马特接住球。

2) 演示说明：

The teacher said, "Watch me. I'm doing a dangerous experiment. Now watch
　　me. I *switch* on the current, and *stand* back..."　教师说，"现在看着我，
　　我做一个危险的实验。注意，我现在接通电流，往后站…"

3) 动作描述或舞台动作描述：

When the curtain rises, Juliet is writing at her desk. Suddenly the window
　　opens and a masked man *enters*.　幕启时，朱丽叶在办公桌旁写东西。
　　突然窗户开了，进来一个蒙面男子。

He *sits* down, *shivers* a little. Clock outside *strikes* twelve.　他坐了下来，微
　　微有些颤抖，外面钟敲了十二点。

还可用来表示一些没有时间性的动作：

1) 剧情介绍：

In *Death on the Nile*, Linet Ridgeway *is* the young and beautiful heiress to
　　an immense fortune, but she has a lot of enemies.　在《泥罗河上的惨案》
　　中，年轻貌美的林奈·里奇韦是一大笔财产的继承人，但她有很多
　　敌人。

How does the story *end*?　故事怎样结局？

The scene of this opera *is set* in Switzerland.　这部歌剧的故事发生在瑞士。

2）讲书面材料的内容：

I've just got a letter from Helen. She *says* she's coming to India next week.　我刚收到海伦的一封信，她说下星期要来印度。

What *does* the notice *say*?　——It *says*, "No parking."　"告示说什么？"　——说"禁止泊车。"

Shakespeare *says*, "Neither a borrower nor a lender be ."　莎士比亚(在书中)说，"既不要向人借钱，也不要借钱给人。"

A notice at the end of the road *warns* people not to go any further.　路尽头有个告示，警告路人不要再往前走。

Chaucer *writes* that love is blind.　乔叟写道，爱情是盲目的。

3）用来指引道路：

"How *do* I *get to* the station?"　"You *go* straight on to the traffic lights, then you *turn* right."　"火车站怎么走？"　"你径往前走，到红绿灯处往右拐。"

4）图片说明：

The Queen *arrives* for the opening of Parliament.　女王出席议会开幕式。

5）用在 here 和 there 后面：

Here *comes* the bus!　公共汽车来了!

There *goes* the bell.　铃响了。

8.1.5　一般现在时表示将来情况

1）在口语中，一般现在时可以表示按规定、计划或时间表要发生的事，通常都有一个表示未来时间的状语：

The plane *takes off* at 9:20 a.m.　飞机早上九点二十分起飞。

Their delegation *arrives* here tomorrow afternoon.　他们的代表团明天下午到达。

I'*m* in my office from two to five this afternoon.　今天下午两点到五点我在办公室。

When *does* the play *begin*?　戏几点开始？

The train *leaves* in five minutes' time.　火车五分钟后离开。

Are you free tonight?　今晚你有空吗？

有时可用这个时态叙述整个计划:

> We *leave* London at 10:00 next Tuesday and *arrive* in Paris at 13:00. We *spend* two hours in Paris and *leave* again at 15:00. We *arrive* in Rome at 19:30, *spend* four hours in Rome. 我们下周二上午十点离开伦敦,下午一点抵达巴黎。在巴黎停留两小时,三点再次出发。晚七点半到达罗马,在罗马待四个小时。

2) 在时间或条件从句中,须用一般现在时表示将来动作:

> If I *see* Nancy I'll ask her. 如果我见到南希我会问她。
>
> I'll discuss this with you when we *meet*. 我们见面时我将和你商讨此事。
>
> I'll tell her after you *leave*. 你走之后我再告诉她。
>
> We'll let you know as soon as you *arrive*. 你一到我们就告诉你。
>
> In case I *forget*, please remind me about it. 万一我忘了,请提醒我。
>
> I won't write unless he *writes* first. 除非他先来信,否则我不会给他写信。

3) 还有一些其他从句中,可以用一般现在时表示将来动作:

> I hope that you *feel* better soon. 我希望不久你能感觉好一点。
>
> Suppose he *doesn't come*, shall we go without him? 假如他不来,我们就自己去吗?
>
> Assuming *it rains* tomorrow, what shall we do? 假定明天下雨,我们该怎么办?
>
> I'll just say whatever *comes* into my head. 我将想到什么就说什么。
>
> Come and stay as long as you *please*. 你来爱待多久就待多久。
>
> I'll get the car fixed no matter how much it *costs*. 不管花多少钱我都得让人把车修好。
>
> Whatever *happens*, I'm going. 不管发生什么情况我都要去。
>
> However long you *argue*, you will never convince him. 不管辩论多久,你永远说服不了他。

8.1.6 一般现在时表示过去动作

1) 有少数动词 (如 say, tell, hear 等) 可以用一般现在时表示过去发生的情况:

> He *says* he can't wait any longer. 他说他不能再等了。
>
> My friends *tell* me that you've been unwell. 我的朋友告诉我你身体欠佳。

I *hear* you want a secretary. 我听说你需要一位秘书。

I *learn* that this boy is in business in Capetown. 我听说这小伙子在开普敦做生意。

I *forget* the man's name. 这人的名字我忘了。

这是因为这类动词发生的时间在说话人的脑中已很模糊,他想表达的是后面谈的情况。

2) 在下面情况下也常用一般现在时表示过去动作:

a. 故事性读物中戏剧性的描绘(用一般现在时可给人以历历在目的印象):

They threatened to shoot, but the marchers could not be stopped. The unarmed workers *press* on and on. 他们威胁着要开枪,却没法挡住游行者,手无寸铁的工人们不断向前逼进。

The crowd *swarms* around the gateway, excitement *grows* as the pop star appears. 人群聚集在大门口,当那位通俗歌星出现时,众人情绪高涨。

这种用法可以称为 **戏剧性的现在时** (Dramatic Present)。

b. 用在报纸标题中:

MASS MURDERER *ESCAPES* 大屠杀凶犯在逃

PEACE TALKS *FAIL* 和谈失败

情节业已发生而用一般现在时,可使标题生动。

c. 用在小说章节的标题中:

VII *Go* to Bristol 第七章 去布里斯托尔途中

〔注〕 have 在表示"有"这个意思时,否定式及疑问式过去在英国多用下面方式构成:

否定式	疑问式
I haven't anything to tell you.	Have you anything to tell me?
He (She) hasn't anything to tell us.	Has he (she) anything to tell us?

但现在,英国人和美国人一样,都借助助动词构成这两种形式:

I don't have anything to tell you.	He (She) doesn't have anything to tell you.
Do you have anything to tell me?	Does he (she) have anything to tell us?

8.2　现在进行时

8.2.1　现在进行时的基本用法

1) 现在进行时 (The Present Continuous Tense) 表示现在正在进行的动作和发生的事:

What *are* you *doing*?　——I'm *reading* a play by Shaw.　你在干什么?
——我在看萧伯纳的一个剧本。

How *are* things *going*?　现在情况怎么样?

Mary *is knitting* and *listening* to the radio.　玛丽在打毛线，听收音机。

It's *snowing* hard.　天正下着大雪。

What *are* they *quarrelling* about?　他们在为什么事争吵?

Why *aren't* you *wearing* a coat? It's so cold.　天这么冷,你怎么没穿大衣?

They're *travelling* in India.　他们在印度旅行。

I'm *waiting* to have a word with you.　我在等着和你说句话。

2) 现在进行时有时表示现阶段正发生的事，此刻动作不一定正在进行:

Hello, Tom, *are* you still *working* in that bank?　嗨，汤姆，你还在那家银行工作吗?

She's *teaching* at a night school.　她在夜校教书。

I'm *writing* a book about ecology.　我在写一本关于生态学的书。

Sorry, you can't take the typewriter away, I'm *using* it.　对不起，你不能把打字机拿走，我在用。

8.2.2　现在进行时和动词的关系

1) 有些动词一般不能用于现在进行时，如第 8.1.2 节中的动词，大部分都不宜用于进行时态，因为它们表示状态和感觉，不能表示正在进行的动作，特别是 know, love, like, belong, detest, hate 这类词。不过有些词有其他意思，有时能用于进行时，试比较下面句子:

表示状态或感觉	**表示动作(可用于进行时)**
She *looks* tired. 她显得很疲倦。	She *is looking* at a bird. 她在看鸟。
The food *smells* nice. 这菜闻着很香。	He's *smelling* the flowers. 他在闻花。

The juice *tastes* good. 果汁味很好。

I'*m tasting* the wine. 我在品尝酒。

It *sounds* a good idea. 这似乎是个好主意。

Why *are* you *sounding* the horn? 你为什么按喇叭？

I *think* you are right. 我想你是对的。

What *are* you *thinking* of? 你在想什么？

Do you *see* that tree? 你看到那棵树吗？

I'*m seeing* Ted off. 我在给特德送行。

It *holds* two gallons. 它能装两加仑。

What *are* you *holding* in your hand? 你手上拿的是什么？

She *has* two sisters. 她有两个姐妹。

She *is having* lunch. 她在吃午饭。

2) 有些表示动作的动词有时转而表示状态，这时就不宜用于进行时态，如：

表示动作	表示状态
He'*s standing* on a chair. 他站在椅子上。	My house *stands* by the river. 我家在江边。
They *are sitting* on the grass. 他们坐在草地上。	The hut *sits* in the forest. 小屋在森林里。
She *is lying* on the beach. 她躺在海滩上。	The town *lies* before us. 这座城就在我们前方。
He'*s fitting* the pieces together. 他在把零件装配起来。	The coat *doesn't fit* me. 这上衣我穿不合适。

3) 有些表示极短暂动作的动词也不宜用于进行时，如 declare, recognize 等(可参阅第 8.1.3 节)。但有些这类词有时用于进行时，表示反复做某动作：

He'*s jumping* up and down. 他在上下蹦跳。

She'*s skipping* rope. 她在跳绳。

The old man *is nodding* his head. 老人频频点头。

They'*re firing* questions at him. 他们向他连连发问。

4) be 在一般情况下不能用于进行时态，但有时却可以这样用来表示一时的表现：

Bob *is being* silly. 鲍勃这样做是在发傻。

You'*re being* very clever today. 今天你聪明起来了。

Am I *being* extravagant? 我这样做是不是太奢侈？

The children *are being* very quiet. I wonder what they're up to. 孩子们现在特别安静，我纳闷他们想干什么。

You're *being* childish. 你这样做太孩子气了。

I'*m* not *being* slow. I'*m being* careful. 我这样并不是动作迟缓, 我只是
  审慎行事。

8.2.3　现在进行时表示将来动作

1) 现在进行时还常可用来表示将来的动作, 特别是在口语中, 这时常有
一个表示未来时间的状语, 多指已计划安排好的事:

I'*m meeting* Peter tonight. He'*s taking* me to the theatre. 今晚我要和彼得
  见面, 他将带我去看戏。

I'*m flying* to Hong Kong tomorrow. 我明天飞香港。

Are you *doing* anything tomorrow afternoon?　——Yes, I'*m playing* tennis
  with Betty. 你明天下午有活动吗?　——有, 我要和贝蒂打网球。

I'*m* not *going* out tonight. I'*m staying* at home. 今晚我不出去, 我要待在
  家里。

When *is* Helen *coming* home? 海伦什么时候回家?

They'*re getting married* next month. 他们下月结婚。

They'*re spending* the summer at Switzerland. 他们准备在瑞士过夏天。

〔注〕　在以事物作主语时多用一般现在时表示按时间安排的活动:
  The train *leaves* at 9:30. 火车九点半开。
  The fashion show *starts* at 7. 时装表演七点开始。
  The programme *begins* at 10. 这个节目十点开始。
  以人为主语时, 多用现在进行时表示计划要做的事:
  Nancy *isn't coming* to the party. 南希不来参加晚会了。

2) 现在进行时也可用在时间和条件从句中表示未来情况:

You can do some reading while you *are waiting* for the train. 你等火车时
  可以看看书。

You must visit Switzerland when you *are travelling* in Europe. 你在欧洲
  旅行时一定要访问瑞士。

If she'*s* still *waiting*, tell her to go home. 如果她还在等, 可以让她回家。

Suppose it'*s* still *raining* tomorrow, shall we go? 假定明天还在下雨, 我
  们要去吗?

3) **be going to** 结构可表示:

a. 准备或打算做某事:

He's *going to buy* a new car. 他准备买一辆新车。

She *is* not *going to be* there tonight. 她今晚不准备到那里。

Is he *going to lecture* in English or in Chinese? 他打算用英语还是用汉语讲课?

He's *going to be* a dentist when he grows up. 他长大了打算当牙医。

What *are* you *going to do* when you get your degree? 你拿了学位后打算干什么?

I'm *going to think* about it. 我要考虑考虑。

b. 即将发生的事或要发生的事:

There's *going to be* a thunderstorm. 雷雨即将来临。

It's *going to be* warm tomorrow. 明天天气会很暖和。

My cousin *is going to have* a baby. 我表姐要生孩子了。

Amy *is going to leave* soon, isn't she? 艾米不久就要走了,是吗?

I'm *going to be* sick. 我要病倒了。

We're all *going to die* some day. 总有一天我们都会死的。

在这种结构后也可跟 go, come 这类词:

Where *are* you *going to go* during the holiday? 假期你准备去哪里?

They're *going to come* with me. 他们准备和我一道去。

8.2.4 现在进行时表示经常性动作

1) 现在进行时还可以用来表示经常性的动作,常和 always, constantly, forever 这类副词连用,表示厌烦、赞美等情绪:

He *is always losing* his keys. 他老是丢钥匙。(不以为然)

I'm *always making* that mistake. 我老犯那个错。(不耐烦)

She's *always working*. 她总是在工作。(赞赏)

You're *always thinking* of others. 你总是想到别人。(赞美)

She's *constantly changing* her mind. 她老是改变主意。(不满)

The baby *is constantly screaming*. 宝宝老是尖叫。(不耐烦)

He's *forever finding* fault with what I do. 他老是找我的茬。(厌烦)

She's *perpetually nagging*. 她老爱唠叨。(厌烦)

2) 这类句子也可用一般现在时,这时只说明事实,用现在进行时则表示某种情绪，试比较下面句子：

用一般现在时(说明事实)	**用现在进行时(表示某种情绪)**
How *do* you *feel* today?	How *are* you *feeling* today?(关切)
We *haul* in lots of fish today.	We're *hauling* in lots of fish today.(欣慰)
She *does fine work* at school.	She's *doing fine work* at school.(赞美)
He often *complains* of his job.	He's *always complaining* of his job.(厌烦)

3) 有些静态动词间或也可用于现在进行时：

I'm *hoping* you'll all come. 我希望你们都来。(表示殷切希望)

I'm *always hearing* strange stories about him. 我老听人讲关于他的奇奇怪怪的事。

Tina *is resembling* her sister more and more. 蒂娜长得越来越像她姐姐。

I'm *forgetting* that I promised to ring him tonight. 我差点忘了我答应过今晚给他打电话。

另外还有少数动词用两种时态意思都差不多：

I *wonder (am wondering)* whether you could give me some advice. 我想知道你可否给我出点主意。

Does your leg *hurt (Is* your leg *hurting)*? 你的腿疼吗？

My left foot *itches (is itching)*. 我的左脚痒。

His bones *ache (are aching)* vaguely. 他的骨头隐隐作痛。

I *write (am writing)* to inform you that your mother is ill. 我来信是要通知你你母亲病了。

I *don't hear (am not hearing)* as well as I used to. 我听力不及从前好了。

Now *do* you *like (are you liking)* your new job? 你觉得你的新工作怎样？

8.2.5 现在进行时的一些特殊用法

现在进行时还有一些特殊用法：

1) 用在戏剧式的描绘中，表示过去的动作：

I'm *driving* along a country road and I'm completely lost. Then I see this old fellow. He's *leaning* against a gate. 我开车顺着一条乡村的道路前行，我已经完全迷路了。这时我看到了这位老人，他倚靠在篱笆门上。

2) 表示暂时的情况：

Her car has broken down. She's *going* to work by bike.　她的小汽车坏了，现在骑自行车上班。

I'm not *hearing* very well these days.　近来我听力不太好。

His house is being renovated. So he's *staying* with us.　他的房子在翻修，因此他暂时在我们家住。

My secretary is ill. Mary's *filling* in for her.　我的秘书病了，玛丽暂时接替她的工作。

3) 用在戏剧性的描述中：

Here's this Scotsman, you see, and he's *walking* through the jungle when he meets a gorilla. And the gorilla's *eating* something. So the Scotsman goes up to the gorilla.　这里，你瞧，是一个苏格兰人。当他在丛林中穿行时碰到一只大猩猩。大猩猩在吃东西，于是这苏格兰人向大猩猩走去。

8.3　一般将来时及将来情况表示法

8.3.1　一般将来时的基本用法

1) **一般将来时** (The Simple Future Tense) 表示将来要发生的事 (在口语中各人称后均用 will，常紧缩为 'll)：

Who *will* be on duty at six?　——I *will*.　六点谁值班？　——我值班。

I *will be* eighteen next week.　下星期我就十八岁了。

We *will know* the result tomorrow.　明天我们就知道结果了。

I'm sure I *won't lose* my way.　我肯定我不会迷路的。

If we can't find the taxi, we *will miss* the plane.　如果找不到出租车，我们就搭不上飞机了。

She'*ll be* here at six.　她六点来。

You'*ll have* time for it.　你会有时间这样做的。

Will you *be* free tonight?　你今晚有空吗？

You *won't be* late.　你不会迟到的。

So she *won't* come?　这么说她不来了？

2) 这个时态常用于下面情况 (都用 will)：

a. 用在 "I think... will" 这类句型中，表示看法：

I think they'*ll succeed*.　我想他们会成功。

I suppose they'*ll buy* the house. 我想他们会把这房买下来。

I'm sure he'*ll come* back. 我肯定他会回来。

Perhaps you'*ll find* him at the hotel. 或许你会在旅馆找到他。

They'*ll* probably *wait* for us. 他们或许会等我们。

b. 也可表示未来习惯性的动作:

Spring *will come* again. 春天还会再来。

Birds *will build* nests. 鸟总要筑巢。

These things *will happen*. 这样的事总是要发生的。

The daffodils *will flower* in spring. 黄水仙春天开花。

c. 提出请求:

Will you *type* this? 你把这打一下好吗?

Will you *tell* her I'll be back at five? 你可否告诉她我五点回来?

If you want help — let me know, *will you*? 如果你需要帮助就告诉我,好吗?

Will you please be quiet? 你们静一点好吗?

Won't you *take* off your coat? 你把外套脱下来好吗?

d. 作出允诺:

I'*ll be* there, I promise you. 我答应你我会去的。

This *won't happen* again, I assure you. 我向你保证,这事不会再发生。

I'*ll be* home in time for supper. 我吃晚饭时回家。

I *won't tell* anybody what you said. 你说的话我不会告诉任何人。

e. 表示同意:

Send off the invitation right today. ——Yes, I *will*. 今天就把请柬发出去。 ——行,没问题。

Don't be late. ——No, I *won't*. 别来晚了。 ——放心吧。

Will you answer him? —— Yes, I *will*. 你来回复他好吗? ——行。

还有 will 的一些其他用法,可参阅第 11.1.5 节。

8.3.2 使用 shall 的一些情况

1) shall 主要用于第一人称后,构成疑问句,询问对方意见:

What time *shall* I *come*? 我什么时候来?

Where *shall* we *go* for our holiday? 我们到哪儿去度假呢?

Shall I *do* the washing-up? 要不要我来洗盘子?

What *shall we* do this weekend?　这个周末咱们干什么？

Let's go, *shall we*?　咱们走吧，好吗？

2) shall 也可用在陈述句中 (但现在口语中这样说的人比较少了，一般多用 will)：

Don't worry. I *shan't (won't) be* late.　别担心，我不会迟到的。

We *shall (will) be* in touch.　我们会保持联系的。

I *shall (will) ensure* that you get a room.　我会保证让你得到一个房间。

We *shall ('ll) have* to hurry.　我们得赶快。

shall 还有一些其他用法，可参阅第 11.1.7 章。

8.3.3　一些表示未来情况的方法

除了一般将来时，还可以下列方式表示将来情况：

1) be going to 结构，表示打算干某事 (a) 或即将发生某事 (b)：

a. I'*m going to play* you a waltz.　我准备给你弹一首华尔兹舞曲。

He *is going to buy* her some flowers.　他打算给她买一些花。

I'*m not going to argue* with you tonight.　今晚我不打算和你争论。

They'*re going to sell* their house.　他们准备把房子卖掉。

b. It'*s going to rain* soon.　快下雨了。

Oh, no! He'*s going to fall*!　糟糕！他要摔下去了！

If the drought continues, there's *going to be a famine*.　如果干旱持续下去，会发生饥荒的。

How pale that girl is! I think she *is going to faint*.　那姑娘脸色这样苍白，我想她要晕倒了。

这个结构有时可和 will 引导的结构换用：

It $\left\{\begin{array}{l}\text{will}\\\text{is going to}\end{array}\right\}$ take a long time to photocopy all the documents.　复印所有这些材料要用很长时间。

I $\left\{\begin{array}{l}\text{won't}\\\text{am not going to}\end{array}\right\}$ tell you my age.　我不打算(想)告诉你我的年龄。

I $\left\{\begin{array}{l}\text{will}\\\text{am going to}\end{array}\right\}$ climb that mountain one day.　有一天我要去爬那座山。

He $\left\{\begin{array}{l}\text{won't}\\\text{isn't going to}\end{array}\right\}$ resign.　他不会(准备)辞职。

另外，在包含条件、时间等从句的句子中，谓语用 will 结构时较多：

He'*ll do* it for you if you ask him to. 如果你提出要求,他会帮你做这件事的。

If I drop the glass it *will break*. 要是我让玻璃杯掉下去, 它会破碎的。

When it gets warmer the snow *will start* to melt. 天暖和一点雪就会开始融化。

I'm putting this letter on top of the pile, so that he'*ll read* it first. 我把信放在这堆东西上面,这样他就会先看它。

在这类从句中常用一般现在时表示将来情况 (见前三句)。

2) 现在进行时 (表示计划或准备要做的事):

My brother *is having* a party tomorrow. 我兄弟明天要开一个晚会。

When *are* you *leaving*? —— At the end of the term. 你什么时候走?——期末走。

I'*m going* to the pictures. Would you like to come? 我要去看电影,你想去吗?

They'*re playing* some folk music first. 他们先要演奏一些民间乐曲。

How *are* you *going* — by train or by plane? 你怎么去——坐火车还是坐飞机?

I'*m taking* the kids to the zoo on Saturday. 我星期六带孩子们去动物园。

What *are* you *doing* tomorrow afternoon? 明天下午你干什么?

He'*s leaving* school in one year's time. 他一年后就要毕业了。

I'*m leaving*. 我要走了。

3) 一般现在时 表示按计划要发生的事, 特别是以事物作主语时 (a), 以人为主语时有时也可以这样用 (b):

a. The new branch *opens* (is opening) next week. 新的分公司下星期开业。

When *does* the main film *begin*? 正片什么时候开始(放映)?

The plane *takes off* in ten minutes. 飞机十分钟后起飞。

Parliament *convenes* next Tuesday. 议会下周二开会。

The train *leaves (arrives)* at 10:45. 火车十点四十五分开(到)。

Tomorrow *is* Sunday. 明天是星期天。

b. The boys *start* school on Monday. 孩子们星期一开始上学。

We *leave* at six and *arrive* in Dublin at ten. 我们六点动身,十点到达都柏林。

They *have* no classes tomorrow. 明天他们没课。

We *get* off at the next stop. 我们下一站下车。

I'*m not* at home tonight. 我今晚不在家。

Are you free tonight? 你今晚有空吗？

此外还可在时间及条件从句中代替一般将来时 (a)，或用在 hope 后的宾语从句中 (b)：

a. Give me a ring before you *leave*. 走之前给我打个电话。

You carry on with the work while I *have* a rest. 我休息时你接着干。

When she *comes*, I'll tell her about it. 她来时我将把这件事告诉她。

If you don't *find* her, just leave her a note. 如果你找不到她，就给她留个条。

b. I hope she *gets* back in time. 我希望她及时回来

We hope you all *have* a good time. 我们希望你们都玩得开心。

We hope you *are* well. 我们希望你身体健康。

4）be + 不定式结构：

be + 不定式也可表示将要发生的动作，可表示安排好的事(a)，也可表示要求做的事 (b)：

a. She *is to be married* next month. 她定于下月结婚。

The expedition *is to start* in a week's time. 探险队将于一周后出发。

The Prime Minister *is to visit* Hungary in May. 首相将于五月访问匈牙利。

Who *is to play* Macbeth? 谁扮演麦克佩斯？

b. You'*re to stay* here till we return. 你得待在这里直到我们回来。

No one *is to leave* this building without their permission. 未经他们允许谁也不准离开这座楼。

He says that we *are to wait* till he comes. 他说我们得等着他回来。

You *are not to smoke* in the office. 你们不得在办公室抽烟。

还有一些其他意思，详见第 13.5.5 节

5）be about to 结构：

表示就要发生的事：

They'*re about to start*. 他们就要出发了。

Quick, jump in! The train *is about to leave*. 快，跳上车，火车就要开了。

Turn off the gas — the soup *is about to boil* over. 把煤气关掉——汤快溢出来了。

I *was* just *about to fall* into a doze when he started up. 我正要打盹时他突然出现了。

6）be due to 构成的谓语：

这种结构表示"定于…"：

Mary *is due to leave* at two o'clock. 玛丽定于两点动身。

They *are due to meet* again tomorrow. 他们定于明天再会面。

She *is due to graduate* next summer. 她明年暑假毕业。

The bridge *is due to be completed* next April. 大桥定于明年四月完工。

8.3.4   将来进行时

1）将来进行时 (The Future Continuous Tense) 表示将来某时将正在进行的动作：

Next Wednesday We'*ll be flying* to Sydney. 下星期三我们将飞往悉尼。

What *will* you *be doing* on Saturday? 星期六你会在干什么？

This time tomorrow we'*ll be sitting* in the cinema and *watching* a film. 明天这时我们会坐在电影院看电影。

On Saturday morning, Bill *will be working* in the garden and Ann *will be shopping*. 星期六早上，比尔会在花园里干活，安会去买东西。

2）这个时态还可表示安排要做的事或预计会发生的事：

He'*ll be taking* his exam next week. 他下星期考试。

He *won't be coming* to the party. 他不会来参加聚会。

I'*ll be seeing* you tomorrow. 我明天会见到你的。

We'*ll be getting* in touch with you. 我们将和你联系。

3）这个时态在口语中用得比较多，有时可以和现在进行时换用：

I $\left\{ \begin{array}{l} \text{am meeting} \\ \text{'ll be meeting} \end{array} \right\}$ her tomorrow evening. 明晚我会和她见面。

When $\left\{ \begin{array}{l} \text{are they} \\ \text{will they be} \end{array} \right\}$ leaving? 他们什么时候动身？

有时也可以和一般将来时换用，两者间有细微的差别，试比较下面句子：

I *won't see* him while I'm in Shanghai. 在上海时我不会去看他。

I *won't be seeing* him while I'm in Shanghai. 在上海时我不会见到他。

Won't you *come* with us? 你不想和我们一道去吗？(邀请)

Won't you *be coming* with us? 你不和我们一道吗？(单纯谈事实)

$\Big\{$ *Will* you please *bring* the TV in here?　请把电视机搬到这里来好吗？
Will you *be bringing* the TV in here?　你准备把电视机搬到这里来吗？

8.3.5　将来完成时和将来完成进行时

1) 将来完成时 (The Future Perfect Tense) 表示将来某时某动作业已完成或某事情业已发生：

By the end of the year I'*ll have saved* £ 1,000.　到年底时我就存了 1,000 英镑了。

Tom *will have had* his exam by 18 December.　汤姆 12 月 18 号就已经考完试了。

By this summer we'*ll have been* here for five years.　到今年夏天我们在这里就满五年了。

The train *will have left* when we get to the station.　我们到车站时火车会已经开了。

2) 将来完成进行时 (The Future Perfect Continuous) 表示在将来某时某个动作已进行多久了：

By the end of the year she'*ll have been acting* for twenty years.　到今年年底她演戏将满二十年。

By this summer he'*ll have been training* horses for ten years.　到今年夏天他干训马工作就满十年了。

In another month's time I'*ll have been studying* here for three years.　再过一个月我在这里学习就满三年了。

On November 1 we'*ll have been living* in this flat for thirty years.　到十一月一号我们在这套房子里就住满三十年了。

8.4　一般过去时和过去进行时

8.4.1　一般过去时的用法

1) 一般过去时 (The Simple Past Tense) 主要表示一个过去发生的动作 (a) 或存在的状态 (b)：

a. I *got to* know her in 1998.　我是 1998 年认识她的。

My grandfather *died* last year.　我祖父是去年去世的。

When *did* this *happen*?　——It *happened* in the Han Dynasty. 这是什么
时候发生的事?　——是汉朝时发生的。

How *did* you *get* the job? 这工作你是怎么得到的?

b. I *didn't know* her at that time. 那时我还不认识她。

They *loved* each other for twenty years. 他们相爱了二十年。

She *suffered* a lot in her childhood. 小时候她受了很多苦。

He *believed* that he *was* right. 他相信自己是对的。

2) was 和 were 的用法:

was 用于第一、三人称单数 (a)，其他情况都用 were (b):

a. She *was* a lawyer. Now she's a senator. 她过去是律师，现在是参议员。

He *was* very busy last Friday. 上星期五他非常忙。

The party *was* a great success. 晚会很成功。

The train *was* ten minutes late. 火车晚点十分钟。

I *wasn't* interested in going. 我没兴趣去。

b. The girls *were* not very happy about it. 姑娘们对此不太高兴。

We *were* both late for the meeting. 我们两人开会都迟到了。

Where *were* you yesterday? 昨天你在哪里?

Most of them *were* fishermen. 他们多数人都是渔民。

Some of us *were* students at that time. 那时我们有些人还是学生。

We *weren't* in town that day. 那天我们不在城里。

3) 前一会儿发生的事也要用过去时表示:

She *was* here a minute ago. 她前一分钟还在这里。

George *came* in just now. 乔治刚才来过的。

Who *told* you this? 这事谁告诉你的?

Did the telephone *ring*? 电话铃响了吗?

也可以表示过去习惯性的动作:

We often *played* badminton together. 我们经常在一起打羽毛球。

Sometimes we heatedly *discussed* these problems. 有时我们热烈地讨论
这些问题。

4) 在叙述性文字(如小说、故事等)中用这个时态时特别多，例如:

Laura *was* born in Bristol. Her parents *came* from Ireland. Laura's father *was*
a customs officer. Unfortunately, he *died* a few years ago. Laura *grew* up
in the suburbs of Bristol. She *started* her education at a local school. When
she *was* 18, she *went* to Bristol University. She *majored* in economics.
While she *was* at university, she *joined* a folk group and *started* singing.

When she *was* 21, she *was married* to Tony Harper. Now they have two children.

5) 在日常谈话中也常会用到它：

Who *said* it?　这话谁说的？

I *didn't know* you *were* here.　我不知道你在这儿。

I *was* glad to get your letter.　我很高兴收到你的来信。

I *thought* they *were* with you.　我以为他们和你在一起哩。

How *did* you *find* your way home?　你怎么找到回家的路的？

已去世者的情况一般用一般过去时表示：

Edison *was* a great inventor.　爱迪生是伟大的发明家。

My grandfather *lived* a very simple life.　我祖父过着简朴的生活。(表示他已不在人间)

〔注〕在口语中，一般过去时有时可用来代替一般现在时，使口气显得更缓和，因而更客气：

> I *wondered* (wonder) if you could do me a favour.　不知你可否帮我一个忙。
>
> I *wanted* (want) to ask if I could borrow your car.　我想问问可否借用你的车。
>
> I *hoped* (hope) you *could* (can) give me some advice.　我希望你能帮我出点主意。
>
> *Did* (Do) you want to see me?　你是想见我吗？
>
> 在家人和熟人间不需用过去时代替现在时。

8.4.2　过去进行时的用法

1) **过去进行时** (The Past Continuous Tense) 主要表示过去某时的一个动作正在进行，过去时间可以由一个状语表示出来：

What *were* you *doing* when I rang you up?　我给你打电话时你在干吗？

I *was having* a bath (at that time).　(那时)我在洗澡。

You *were* then *working* in the post office, weren't you?　那时你在邮局工作，对吧？

I *was writing* a letter when she called.　她来时我正在写信。

I was busy yesterday. I *was preparing* for the exams.　昨天我很忙，我在准备考试。

At that moment, I *wasn't doing* anything.　那会儿我什么也没干。

I *was thinking* of you all those years.　那些年我一直惦记着你。

有时候时间由上下文表示出来：

Jane was in town. She *was doing* some shopping.　简在城里，在买东西。

The bride *was wearing* a pink dress and *carrying* a small bouquet.　新娘穿着粉红色的裙服，手上拿着一小束花。

He *was sitting* alone on the deck.　他一个人坐在甲板上。

Someone *was following* her. She was scared.　有人跟着她，她很害怕。

A small orchestra *was playing*.　一支小型管弦乐队在演奏。

They knew what they *were working* for.　他们知道在为什么而工作。

I didn't know you *were* still *waiting* for me.　我不知道你还在等我。

I asked him to tell me what *was troubling* him.　我让他说出他的烦心事。

这个时态还可以用在状语从句中：

He met the bride while he *was studying* in California.　他是在加州上学时遇到新娘的。

He lost his purse when he *was strolling* across a meadow.　他在草地上散步时把钱包丢了。

I got to know her when I *was working* in a pharmacy.　我在药房工作时认识了她。

While the water *was heating*, I began cooking.　烧水时我开始做饭。

2） 过去进行时可以用来描绘一幅景象，作为描绘的开始：

A fire *was burning* and a cat *was sleeping* in front of it. A girl *was playing* the piano and *singing* softly to herself. Then there was a knock at the door.　炉火烧着，一只猫睡在炉火前。一个女孩在弹钢琴，轻声对自己唱着，这时有人敲门。

She *was sitting* at the window, watching the evening invade the avenue. Suddenly she heard someone calling her from downstairs, and she recognized the voice. She stood up quickly.　她坐在窗前，看着暮色渐渐笼罩大街。突然她听到楼下有人叫她。她听出了这声音，迅速站了起来。

在故事中间也可用这时态来描绘一幅景象：

At last we got to the top of the mountain. White snow covered everything. People *were sitting* in groups of three and four. Some *were lying* on their backs. When they saw us, they were very happy and shouted: "We thought you had lost your way！"最后我们爬上了山顶。白雪覆盖着一切，人们三五成群地坐着，有的人仰面躺着。他们看到我们时非常高兴，高声叫到："我们还以为你们迷路了哩！"

在小说中我们常可看到这样的段落。

8.4.3　过去进行时和一般过去时的比较

1）过去进行时和一般过去时的基本差别是，过去进行时表示一个正在进行的动作，而一般过去时表示一个业已完成的动作。试比较下面的句子：

I *was writing* an essay. 我在写一篇论文。(可能还没写完)

I *wrote* an essay yesterday. 我昨天写了一篇论文。(已写完)

They *were building* a skyscraper. 他们在建一座摩天大楼。(在修建)

They *built* a skyscraper. 他们盖了一座摩天大楼。(已盖好)

She *was knitting* a sweater for Tom. 她在给汤姆织一件毛衣。

She *knitted* a sweater for Tom. 她给汤姆织了一件毛衣。

He *was doing* his homework in the afternoon. 下午他在做作业。

He *did* his homework in the afternoon. 下午他把作业做完了。

2）有些动词本身并不表示动作完成，如 rain, snow, cough, wear, feel, wait, stay, work 等，这时用两种时态意思上差别不大：

It $\begin{cases} \text{snowed} \\ \text{was snowing} \end{cases}$ all night. 下了一整夜的雪。

She $\begin{cases} \text{wore} \\ \text{was wearing} \end{cases}$ a blue coat. 她穿着一件蓝外套。

He $\begin{cases} \text{felt} \\ \text{was feeling} \end{cases}$ a bit uneasy. 他感到有点不自在。

We $\begin{cases} \text{stayed} \\ \text{were staying} \end{cases}$ in a hotel. 我们住在旅馆里。

3）用进行时态时有时有感情色彩，特别是带有 always, forever, constantly 这类状语时，如：

He *was always ringing* me up. 他老是给我打电话。(厌烦)

She *was always working.* 她总是不停地干活。(赞扬)

The old lady *was forever grumbling.* 这老太太老是嘀嘀咕咕。(厌烦)

He *was constantly changing* his mind. 他老是改变主意。(不以为然)

4) 有时用过去进行时表示现在的想法，可以显得客气一点，如：

I *was wondering* whether you could give me some advice. 不知你能否帮
我出点主意。

I *was thinking* maybe he could go by taxi. 我在想或许他可以坐的士去。

I *was hoping* you could reconsider our proposal. 我希望你能再考虑一下
我们的建议。

8.4.4 表示过去某时预计要发生情况的用法

有些结构可以表示过去某时打算要做的事或预计要发生的事，如：

1) 过去进行时 (仅限于 come，go，leave 这类动词，可参阅第 8.2.2 节)：

He was busy packing, for he *was leaving* that night. 他忙着收拾行李，因
为那晚他就要走了。

Mr. Brown *was coming* to dinner. 布朗先生要来吃晚饭。

She told me she *was going* to Boston. 她告诉我她准备去波士顿。

We were very excited as we *were flying* to Europe the next morning. 我们
很激动，因为第二天早晨我们就要飞往欧洲了。

2) was going to:

She said she *was going to come* early. 她说她一早就来。

Judy *was going to meet* me, but she was ill and couldn't come. 朱迪本来
是要来和我会面的，但她生病了没能来。

When I arrived, the train *was just going to start*. 我到时火车正要开出。

3) be about to (表示 "就要"、"即将" 发生某事)：

He *was about to go* out when the phone rang. 他正要出去时电话铃响了。

I *was* just *about to explain* when she interrupted me. 我正要解释，她打断
了我的话。

It was seven o'clock. The show *was about to start*. 七点钟了，演出即将
开始。

4) be due to (表示 "定于")：

He *was due to speak* that night. 他定于那天晚上发言。

Mary *was due to leave* at 2 o'clock. 玛丽定于两点出发。

The conference *was due to start* in 2 weeks' time. 会议定于两周后开始。

She *was due to graduate* in the coming summer. 她将于这个夏天毕业。

8.5　现在完成时和现在完成进行时

8.5.1　现在完成时的基本用法

1) 现在完成时表示一件已发生的事，这事往往与现在情况有联系：

I've *lost* my key. 我的钥匙丢了。(因此无法进屋)

She's *gone* to town. 她进城去了。(现在在城里)

I've *got* a letter from my aunt. 我收到姨母一封信。(因此知道她的近况)

The lift *has broken* down. 电梯坏了。(因此我们得爬楼梯)

Peter *has had* a bad car crash. 彼得出了严重车祸。(可能送医院了)

I've *washed* my car. 我洗过车了。(因此很干净)

He *hasn't come* back yet. 他还没回来。(我们还在等他)

Have you *had* your supper yet? ——Yes, I have. 你吃晚饭了吗?
　　　——吃过了。(不饿了)

2) 常可和 just，already，yet，recently，ever 这类副词连用：

He's **just** *left*. 他刚走。

Has he *phoned* you **yet**? ——No, not yet. 他给你打电话了吗?
　　　——还没有。

Jane *has rung me up* three times this morning **already**. 简今天早上已给我
　　打过三次电话。

The rain *has* **already** *stopped*. 雨已经停了。

Have you **ever** *talked* to him about it? 你曾和他谈过这事吗?

Have you *seen* Lewes **recently**? 你最近见到过路易斯吗?

I *have* **never** *broken* my word. 我从未违背过自己的诺言。

He **still** *hasn't finished* his work. 他的工作还没干完。

There *have been* some changes **lately**. 近来有些变化。

3) 也可和表示从过去某时到现在这段时间的状语连用：

I *haven't seen* him **today**. 今天我没见过他。

How many letters *have* you *received* **this week**? 这星期你收到多少封信?

They *have turned out* over 1,000 cars **this month**. 这个月他们生产了一
　　千多辆汽车。

He *has made* several trips to Paris **this year**. 今年他去过几趟巴黎。

I've *seen* little of her **in the past few years**. 过去几年中我很少见到她。

So far he *has done* very well at school. 到现在为止他在学校表现很好。

Up to now, the work *has been* easy. 到现在为止，这工作还算容易。

4）还常和 for 及 since 引导的状语或与 how long 连用：

I *haven't seen* you **for ages**. 我好久没见到你了。

He *hasn't cleaned* his room **for months**. 他有好几个月没打扫这房间了。

We've *lived* here **for over ten years**. 我们在这里住了十多年了。

I *haven't seen* her **since June**. 六月以来我就没见过她。

He *has worn* glasses **since his childhood**. 他从小就戴眼镜。

Has he *written* **since he left home**? 他离家之后来过信吗？

How long *have* you *known* her? 你认识她多久了？

5）也常常单独使用不需任何状语：

She *has found* a new job. 她找到了一份新工作。

We've *sent* some people to help them. 我们已派了几个人去帮助他们。

We've *put up* thousands of tall buildings. 我们盖起了数以千计的高楼。

Which side *has won*? 哪边赢了？

They *have taken* the injured people to hospital. 他们把伤者送进了医院。

I'm sorry, I've *broken* your cup. 对不起，我把你的杯子打破了。

I wonder if she's *got* well. 我不知道她是否已经痊愈。

Who *has taken* my dictionary away? 谁把我的字典拿走了？

6）这个时态还可表示持续到现在的状态：

How long *has* he *been* ill? 他病了多久了？

The strike *has continued* for several weeks. 罢工已持续了几个星期。

He *has lived* here all his life. 他一辈子都住在这里。

We've *been* good friends since we were children. 我们从小就要好。

They *have loved* each other all these years. 这些年他们一直很恩爱。

I *have* never *believed* those theories. 我从不相信这些理论。

I *have known* them for many years. 我认识他们很多年了。

8.5.2 现在完成时和一般过去时的比较

1）这两个时态都谈已发生的事，主要差别是现在完成时表示的动作与现在有关系，或是对现在有影响，或谈现在以前这一段时间里发生的事，而一般过去时单纯谈过去的事，与现在没有联系。因此**凡是有过去时间状语时，只能用过去时**：

She *was* here **a minute ago**. 一分钟之前她还在这里。

They *gave* it to me **just now**. 这是他们刚才给我的。

When *did* you *come* in?　你什么时候进来的？

I *woke up* **at six**.　我六点醒的。

　　凡是单纯谈过去的事，与现在毫无联系时也多用过去时，试比较下面几组句子：

I'*ve bought* some fruit for you.　我给你买了点水果。(送来这里)
I *bought* the fruit in the supermarket.　这些水果我是在超市买的。

She *has written* some short stories.　她写了一些短篇小说。(说明成就)
She *wrote* the short stories in Shanghai.　这些短篇小说是她在上海写的。

I *have* just *had* my lunch.　我刚吃过午饭。(因此不饿)
I *had* my lunch in a cafeteria.　我是在自助餐厅吃的午饭。

I'*ve learnt* a lot from you.　我向你学到了很多东西。(因此很感谢你)
I *learnt* a lot there.　我在那里学到了很多东西。

2) 有时同一个动作，根据具体情况，可能需用不同的时态，例如：

He'*s been* in the army for two years.　他在部队两年了。(还在部队)
He *was* in the army for two years.　他在部队待过两年。(现已离开)

She'*s done* this all these years.　这些年她都是这样做的。(直到如今)
She *did* this for many years.　她这样做有许多年了。(现在不这样做了)

Tom *has rung* up three times this morning.　今天早上汤姆打来过三个电话。(现在还是早晨)
Tom *rang* up three times this morning.　今天早上汤姆打来过三个电话。(现在是下午)

I *haven't seen* her this afternoon.　今天下午我没见过她。(现仍是下午)
I *didn't see* her this afternoon.　今天下午我没见到她。(现已是晚上)

We'*ve had* little rain this summer.　今年夏天雨水很少。(现仍是夏天)
We *had* little rain in the summer.　夏天雨水很少。(现已不是夏天)

3) 有些动作(显然是过去的动作)，尽管没有时间状语，仍需用过去时：

Did you *know* that he was going to be married?　你知道他要结婚了吗？

I *didn't know* you were in London too.　我不知道你也在伦敦。

When *did* you *get* back?　你什么时候回来的？

I *heard* you were coming to China this autumn.　我听说你今年秋天要到中国来。

Why *did* you *buy* this?　你为什么买这个？

Did you *see* anything interesting at the exhibition?　在展览会上你看到什么有趣的东西吗？

Why *did* you *get* up so early?　你为什么起得这么早?

How *did* you *like* the show?　你觉得演出如何?

这时不宜用现在完成时。

8.5.3　有关现在完成时的几个问题

1) have gone to 和 have been to 的差别:

have gone to 表示"到某地去了",因此人还在那里:

She *has gone to* live abroad.　她到国外居住了。(她现在国外)

The kids *have gone to* the zoo.　孩子们到动物园去了。(他们在动物园)

Where *has* Mary *gone*?　玛丽到哪里去了? (她在哪里?)

have been (to) 表示"到(来)过某地":

Where *have* you *been*?　——I've *been to* the cinema.　你到哪儿去了?
　　——我去看电影了。

Have you ever *been to* Hong Kong?　你到过香港吗?

I've *been to* Europe several times.　我到欧洲去过几次。

Who's *been* here?　谁来过这里? (人已不在)

Has she ever *been* in China?　她到过中国吗?

后面还可跟不定式:

I've *been* to see my grandmother.　我去看我奶奶了。(现已回来)

She's *been* to do some shopping.　她出去买东西了。

2) 由 since 引导的从句中的时态:

由 since 引导的从句一般用过去时(主句谓语用现在完成时):

We've been friends ever since we *met* at school.　自在学校相遇以来,我
　　们一直是朋友。

Much has changed since I *was* there last time.　自我上次到那里之后发生
　　了许多变化。

当表示"有多少时间"时,主句谓语可用一般现在时:

It's two years since I left home.　我离家已经两年了。

How long *is* it since you came here last time?　自你上次来这里之后已经
　　多久了?

在从句中有时可用现在完成时,特别是动词为 be 时:

I have been terribly busy since I've *been* back.　我回来之后一直忙得要命。

She has seldom been out since she *has been* ill.　她生病以来很少出去。

It's some time since I've *wirtten* to her. 有相当时间我没给她写信了。

3）在时间及条件从句中需用现在完成时代替将来完成时：

I'll wirte a preface when I've *finished* the book. 书写完后我将写一篇序。

Don't go away until I *have finished* speaking to your father. 在我和你父亲谈完话之前不要走开。

I'll tell them after you *have left*. 你走后我将告诉他们。

If he *hasn't got up*, don't wake him. 如果他还没起床，不要叫醒他。

Don't rush him unless he's already *got* everything ready. 除非他把一切都准备好了，否则不要催促他。

4）和 time 一道用的情况：

This (It) is the first time I *have seen* a pagoda. 这是我首次看到宝塔。

It is only the second time he's *been* in a palace. 这只是他第二次进皇宫。

That's the third time he's *quarrelled* with her in a week. 这是一星期中他第三次和她吵架。

This is the fourth time she's *been* out with him. 这是她第四次和他一起外出。

在下面句型中也可用现在完成时：

This is the best tea I *have* ever *drunk*. 这是我喝过的最好的茶了。

This is the most interesting book I *have* ever *read*. 这是我看过的最有意思的书。

This is the easiest job I *have* ever *had*. 这是我干过的最容易的工作。

It's the first good meal I've *had* for ages. 这是好久以来我吃过的第一顿好饭。

5）have got 的特殊用法：

have got 在形式上是现在完成时，在意思上却和 have 相同：

Have you *got* (=Do you have) a timetable? 你有时刻表吗?

She *hasn't got* any relations. 她没有什么亲属。

I've *got* only another three minutes. 我只有三分钟了。

What *have* you *got* against me? 你对我有什么意见?

I've *got* a bad headache. 我头疼得很厉害。

I've *got* a cold. 我着凉了。

You've *got* a new dress on. 你穿新衣服了。

I've *got* a few things to see to. 我有几件事要办。

6）have got to 和 have to 意思相同：

have got to 和 have to 意思一样，表示"不得不"：

You've *got to* be careful.　你得当心。

That's what we've *got to* do.　这是我们不得不做的事。

You've *got to* keep this in mind.　你必须把这牢记在心上。

Have you *got to* leave so soon?　你一定要这么早走吗？

在口语中，have 有时可以省略：

We *got to* make ends meet.　我们得收支相抵。

────────

8.5.4　现在完成进行时的用法

1) 现在完成进行时表示一个持续到现在的动作 (这动作可能刚停止，也可能还在进行)：

I've *been waiting* (for) an hour and he still hasn't turned up.　我等了一个钟头，他还没来。

What *have* you *been doing* all these years?　这些年来你一直在干什么？

I'm very tired. I've *been working* all morning.　我很累，我干了一上午了。

I've *been looking* for my dog and still haven't found it.　我一直在找我的狗，还没有找到。

Your fingers are brown. You've *been smoking* too much.　你手指都黄了，你抽烟太多。

Tom *has been digging* in the garden. I've *been helping* him.　汤姆一直在花园里挖土，我在帮他。

2) 这个时态常和 how long, long 这类状语一起用：

How long *have* you *been wearing* glasses?　你戴眼镜有多少年头了？

How long *has* he *been doing* this work?　这工作他干多久了？

Have you *been waiting* long?　你等了很久吗？

This *has been going on* all day long.　这已进行了一整天了。

She's *been expecting* a long distance call all night long.　她等长途电话等了一夜了。

还可以和 since 及 for 引导的状语一起用：

We've *been living* in this city since 1980.　从1980年起我们一直住在这座城市。

They *have been quarrelling* ever since they got married.　自结婚以来他们一直争吵不休。

It *has been raining* for two hours now.　雨已经下了两个小时了。

Her phone *has been ringing* for ten minutes. Why doesn't she answer it? 她的电话铃响了十分钟了，她为什么不接呢？

3) 在不少情况下这动作和现在状态有联系：

I've been shopping all day and I haven't a penny left. 我买了一天的东西，身上一文钱都不剩了。

Her eyes are red. *Has* she *been crying*? 她眼睛红红的，是不是哭来着？

He is out of breath. He's *been running*. 他气喘吁吁，他一直在跑。

Aren't you tired? You've *been standing* for two hours. 你不累吗？你站了两个钟头了。

4) 有时表示动作的重复：

He *hasn't been eating* regularly recently. 近来他吃饭不规律。

He *has been coughing* a lot lately. He ought to give up smoking. 最近他一直咳嗽，他应当戒烟。

I've been using this typewriter for 6 years. 这台打字机我已用了六年。

You've often *been making* mistakes like this. 你老犯这样的错误。

8.5.5 现在完成时和现在完成进行时的比较

1) 这两个时态的主要差别是，现在完成时表示动作业已完成，而完成进行时却不一定如此：

> I've *made* a cake. 我做了一个蛋糕。(已做好)
> I've *been making* a cake. 我一直在做蛋糕。(不一定做好了)

> She's *painted* a picture. 她画了一张画。(已画好)
> She's *been painting* a picture. 她在画一张画。(可能还没画好)

> They've *built* a bridge. 他们建了一座桥。(已建好)
> They've *been building* a bridge. 他们一直在建一座桥。(可能还在建)

> He's *written* a novel. 他写了一部小说。(已完成)
> He's *been writing* a novel. 他在写一部小说。(可能尚未完成)

2) 许多静态动词都只能用于完成时而不能用于完成进行时：

I've known that for a long time. 这事我已知道很久了。

The strike *has lasted* six months. 这次罢工已持续了六个月。

Nobody *has seen* him since last week. 从上周起就没人见到过他。

We've *had* terrible weather for nearly two weeks. 几乎有两星期天气都很恶劣。

They've *owned* the house for many years. 这房子他们已拥有许多年了。

I've always *thought* you're right. 我一向认为你是对的。

但当动词的意思发生转变时也可能用于完成进行时：

I've *been thinking* of doing so for a long time. 我好久以来一直想这样做。

Tom *has been seeing* about a work permit for you. 汤姆一直在设法帮你取得工作许可证。

Which judge *has been hearing* the case? 哪位法官在审这个案子？

She *has been having* a tooth out. 她在拔牙。

The children *have been looking* forward to this holiday for months. 孩子们好几个月来一直盼望着这个节日。

want 这个动词有时可用于完成进行时，表示"一直想"：

You're the very man I've *been wanting* to meet. 你正是我一直想见的人。

3) 有少数动词用两种时态都可以，意思差别不大，如：

They $\begin{Bmatrix} \text{have been working} \\ \text{have worked} \end{Bmatrix}$ very well this term. 这学期他们学习很好。

It $\begin{Bmatrix} \text{has been raining} \\ \text{has rained} \end{Bmatrix}$ for two hours. 下了两小时的雨。

I $\begin{Bmatrix} \text{have been hearing} \\ \text{have heard} \end{Bmatrix}$ from her regularly. 我定期收到她的来信。

We $\begin{Bmatrix} \text{have looked} \\ \text{have been looking} \end{Bmatrix}$ for mushrooms but have not found any. 我们找寻蘑菇但一无所获。

强调时间长度时用完成进行时较好：

I've *been coughing* all night. 我咳了一整夜。(比 I've coughed all night.更强调咳得久)

All the time she's *been sitting* there in silence. 她一直静坐在那里。

All these years we've *been trying* to get in touch with him. 这些年来我们一直在设法和他联系。

He's *been hoping* for a raise in salary all the time. 他一直盼望着加薪。

8.6　过去完成时和过去完成进行时

8.6.1　过去完成时的用法

1) 过去完成时表示过去某时前某事业已发生 (可说是过去的过去):

When I arrived Jane *had* just *left*.　我到时简刚刚离开。

The play *had* already *started* when we got to the theatre.　我们到剧场时戏已经开始了。

Up till then we *had* only *covered* half the distance.　到那时我们才走了一半路程。

She *had rushed* out of the door before I could stop her.　我还没来得及拦阻她已冲出门去了。

By the end of June they *had treated* over 10,000 patients.　到六月底他们已治疗了一万多病人。

Before daybreak they *had* already *wiped* out all the enemy troops.　拂晓前他们已把敌军全部歼灭。

2) 过去时间有时由一时间状语表示出来 (如上例), 但在更多情况下时间都由上下文表示出来:

She found she *had left* her case on the train.　她发现她把箱子遗忘在火车上了。

It was the first time I *had been* in a foreign country.　那是我第一次到国外。

She *had changed* so much I couldn't recognize her.　她变了那么多, 我都认不出她来了。

He *had served* in the army for ten years, last year he retired.　他在部队干了十年, 去年退役了。

He showed me the poems he *had written*.　他让我看他写的诗。

They took us to see the hydroelectric plant they *had built*.　他们带我们去看他们修建的水力发电厂。

He believed that he *had done* the right thing.　他相信他做的事是对的。

I didn't know I *had given* you so much trouble.　我不知道给你添了这么多麻烦。

3) 这个时态还可用在故事中追叙更早时间发生的事:

Tom was 23 when our story begins. His father *had died* five years before.

Since then Tom *had lived* alone. His father *had advised* him not to get married till he was 35, and Tom intended to follow this advice. 我们的故事开始时汤姆二十三岁。他的父亲五年前已经过世。从那时起汤姆一直一个人生活。他父亲曾劝他到三十五岁再结婚，汤姆打算照这个意思做。

Lao Bai was a poor peasant. Back in 1933 he *had come* to settle in Yuan Mao. He *had been* a hard worker and *had cleared* fifty *mu* of land. One year, the rainfall was unfavourable. He began... 老白是一位贫苦的农民，1933年来到元茂村落户。他辛辛苦苦开了五十亩荒地。有一年雨水不调，他开始…

还可描述一幅景像：

Dusk *had fallen*. The moon was shining faintly on the winding road. Silence reigned in the village. 夜色已经降临，淡淡的月光照在蜿蜒的路上，村子里一片宁静。

8.6.2   使用过去完成时的一些常见情况

在下面情况中我们常可使用过去完成时：

1) 用在宾语从句中(特别是在间接引语中)：

He said that he *had been* in China for over ten years. 他说他在中国已经有十多年了。

He told me that he *had known* her since he was a child. 他告诉我他从小就认识她。

I heard that they *had made* an important discovery. 我听说他们有了一个重要发现。

She learned that scientists *had made* a breakthrough in the treatment of that disease. 她了解到科学家在治疗那种疾病方面有了突破。

I was afraid I *had offended* her. 我担心我得罪了她。

2) 用在状语从句中：

When she *had sung* her song she sat down. 她唱完歌后坐了下来。

I found the letter long after he *had gone* away. 他走后好久我才找到那封信。

Before we *had finished* our meal he ordered us back to work. 不等我们吃完饭他就命令我们回去干活。

He refused to go till he *had searched* all the rooms. 他把所有房间搜查了一遍后才离开。

I didn't begin the work until he *had gone*. 直到他走了我才开始这工作。

As soon as he *had done* it, he knew it was a mistake. 他刚一动手就知道做错了。

3) 用在定语从句中：

She showed me the pictures she *had painted*. 她把她画的画拿给我看。

The old oak tree, which *had stood* in the yard for a hundred years, suddenly crashed to the ground. 这棵老橡树在院子里已挺立了一百年，有天突然倒了下来。

Peter, who *had waited* for an hour, was very angry when his sister came up. 彼得等了一个钟头，当看见他妹妹出现时他很生气。

She wore the necklace her mother *had left* her. 她戴着她母亲留给她的项链。

4) 和 time 这个词一道用：

It was the first time I *had made* such a mistake. 这是我首次出这样的错。

It was the second time he *had been* in that house. 这是他第二次进那座房子。

It was the third time she *had been* out with him. 这是她第三次和他外出。

5) 用在 than 或 as 引导的从句中：

We finished the work earlier than we *had expected*. 我们早于预期完成了这项工作。

The concert was more successful than they *had thought*. 音乐会比他们预想的还要成功。

We didn't get along as well as we *had hoped*. 我们相处得没有希望的那样好。

6) 用于 hope, intend, mean, think 等动词表示未实现的愿望：

I *had hoped* to be back last night, but I didn't catch the train. 我本来希望昨晚回来的，但没搭上火车。

I'd *intended* visiting him this weekend but I wasn't able to make it. 我本想这个周末去看望他的，但这次去不成了。

We *had thought* to return early but they wouldn't let us go. 我们本想早回来的，但他们不让我们走。

8.6.3　过去完成进行时的用法

1) 过去完成进行时表示持续到过去某时的一个动作：

He was tired. He *had been working* since dawn.　他很累，天亮起就一直在工作。

It *had been snowing* all night. The ground was covered with thick snow.　下了一夜的雪，地上覆盖着厚厚一层白雪。

They were just back. They *had been skiing* in the mountains.　他们刚回来，他们一直在山里滑雪。

The war *had been going* on for two years until they agreed on a cease-fire.　战争进行了两年直到他们达成了一项停火协议。

She *had been trying* to find a job. She still hadn't found one.　她一直在设法找工作，但仍没找到。

He asked how long I *had been waiting*.　他问我等多久了。

2) 过去完成进行时和现在完成进行时的用法是一致的，只不过是把时间从现在移到了过去：

现在完成进行时	过去完成进行时
I've often *been thinking* of you.	I *had* often *been thinking* of you.
He's *been worrying* about her safety.	He'd *been worrying* about her safety.
Obviously she's *been crying*.	Obviously she'd *been crying*.
All these years he's *been travelling*.	All these years he'd *been travelling*.

3) 过去完成时和过去完成进行时的差别是，前者表示动作业已完成，后者表示动作一直在继续(可能还在进行)：

过去完成时 (动作业已完成)	过去完成进行时 (动作可能还在进行)
He *had painted* the street door.	He *had been painting* the street door.
She *had cleaned* the kitchen.	She *had been cleaning* the kitchen.
They *had repaired* the engine.	They *had been repairing* the engine.
We *had redecorated* the room.	We *had been redecorating* the room.

4) 这个时态常可用在某些从句中：

I didn't know you *had been waiting* for me.　我不知道你一直在等我。

He couldn't guess where she *had been hiding*.　他猜不出她躲在哪里。

Nancy told me she'd *been looking* for me.　南希告诉我她一直在找我。

That was what I *had been trying* to do.　那正是我一直想要做的事。

That was the letter she *had been expecting*.　这正是她一直盼着的信。

8.7　过去将来时态

8.7.1　一般过去将来时的用法

1) 一般过去将来时表示从过去观点看将要发生的事:

It was four o'clock. Soon the sun *would come up*.　这时是四点钟,一会儿太阳就要出来了。

Perhaps she *would be* willing to join us, I thought.　我想或许她会愿意加入到我们中来。

We stopped for a little while. After that we *would go* into town.　我们停留了一会儿,然后我们就将进城。

From their trip to the west, they *would return* in October.　他们西部之行后将于十月回来。

He was sixty-eight. In two years he *would be* seventy.　他六十八了,再过两年就七十了。

2) 这个时态常用在宾语从句中:

I knew you *would agree*. (比较: I know you will agree.)　我知道你会同意的。

I little thought you *would object* to the plan.　我没想到你会反对这计划。

I arose, telling him I *would wait* for him outside.　我站起身,告诉他我将在外面等他。

We expected that you *would stay* here.　我们预料你会住这儿。

I thought the roses *would come out* soon.　我想玫瑰不久就会开花。

She never dreamed the place *would be* so beautiful.　她做梦也没想到这地方会这样美。

还可用于下面这类从句中:

She was confident that she *would find* work.　她自信她会找到工作的。

I was certain that he *would get over* his illness.　我确信他会战胜病魔。

He was sure that he *would succeed*.　他深信他能成功。

It was still a problem whether we *would have* time to do it.　我们是否有时间做这事还是个问题。

8.7.2   过去将来进行时和过去将来完成时

   1）过去将来进行时表示从过去观点看将来某时会正在进行的动作：

I thought Richard *would be looking after* her. 我想里查德会照顾她的。

She didn't know when she *would be seeing* them again. 她不知道她什么
    时候会再见到他们。

I asked him what he *would be doing* that night. 我问他那天晚上他将会干
    什么。

He said he *would be watching* TV that night. 他说那天晚上他将看电视。

   2）这个时态和将来进行时是相似的，只不过是把观点移到过去而已：

将来进行时	过去将来进行时
I'*ll be waiting* for you outside.	He said he'*d be waiting* for me outside.
Tomorrow we'*ll be flying* to Paris.	We'*d be flying* to Paris the next day.
Soon we'*ll be crossing* the border.	Soon we'*d be crossing* the border.
Who *will be looking* after the children while we are away?	Who *would be looking* after the children while we were away?

   3）过去将来完成时表示从过去观点看将来某时前会已发生的事：

I thought you'*d have left* by this time. 我想到这时你会已经走了。

She hoped that they *would have got* everything ready before she got back. 她
    希望在她回来以前他们已把一切都准备好。

He told them he *would have finished* by 8 o'clock. 他告诉他们他八点前
    就会干完。

I guessed that Helen *would have told* her something. 我猜海伦会已告诉她
    一些情况。

   4）过去将来完成进行时用得很少，但用法和将来完成进行时是一致的，
只是把观点移向过去而已：

She said she *would have been teaching* for twenty years by this summer.
    （比较：She will have been teaching for twenty years by this summer.）
    她说到今年暑期她教书就已满二十年了。

They told me that by the end of the year they *would have been working*
    together for thirty years. 他们告诉我到今年年底他们在一起工作就满
    三十年了。

8.7.3 "从过去观点看将来"的一些其他表示法

"从过去观点看将来"还有一些其他表示法：

1）**was (were) going to** —— (过去某时) 准备做某事：

He *was* just *going to go* to bed when there was a knock at the door. 他正准备睡觉时忽然有人敲门。

She *was going to sell* her old car and *buy* a new one. 她打算把旧车卖掉买辆新车。

I thought there *was going to be* a storm soon. 我想就将有一场暴风雨来临。

Was Mary *going to come* with us? 玛丽准备和我们一道去吗？

2）**过去进行时** —— (过去某时) 将要做某事：

He told me he *was leaving* in an hour. 他告诉我他一小时后就要走了。

I asked her whether she *was coming* to the party. 我问她是否要来参加晚会。

I heard they *were getting married* in June. 我听说他们六月结婚。

She said she *wasn't going out* that evening. 她说她那天晚上不外出。

3）**was (were) about to** —— (过去某时) 正要做某事：

We *were about to leave* when a car drove up. 我们正要离开时一辆车开了过来。

He said that he *was* just *about to phone* us. 他说他正要给我们打电话。

I *was about to take* a bath when the telephone rang. 我正要洗澡时电话铃响了。

He *was about to win* the race. Sudderly he stumbled and fell. 他赛跑就要获胜时，突然脚下一绊摔倒了。

4）**was (were) due to** ——定于 (后来某时) 做某事：

The passenger plane *was due to take off* in five minutes. 客机五分钟后将起飞。

The conference *was due to last* five days. 会议将持续五天。

The Cox brothers *were due to graduate* that autumn. 考克斯兄弟将于那年秋天毕业。

He *was due to speak* that night. 他定于那天晚上发言。

5）**was (were) + 不定式** —— (过去某时) 准备将来做某事：

She was to take the 10:30 train, but she got to the station too late. 她本来打算坐十点半的火车，但她到达车站时已经太晚了。

We *were to have* a picnic that afternoon. Suddenly it began to rain. 我们计

划那天下午去野餐，突然天下起雨来。

He was to go hunting after lunch.　午饭后他准备去狩猎。

How *were* they *to cross* the river?　他们该怎样过河呢？

All this I *was to learn* later.　这一切我后来才知道。

6）was (were) + 不定式的完成形式 —— 本来打算做某事：

We *were to have met* in the park, but he didn't turn up.　我们本来要在公园里会面的，但他没有来。

They *were to have been married* that year. Then the war broke out.　他们本来打算那年结婚的，后来战争爆发了。

I *was to have told* you about it, but haven't found time to do so.　我本来想告诉你的，却没腾出空来跟你说。

8.8　时态的呼应

8.8.1　时态的呼应

某些从句(特别是宾语从句)中的动词时态，常受主句谓语时态的制约，如在 I *thought* you *were* free. 这句话中，因受 thought 的影响，从句中的谓语只能用 were free 这个形式。这就称为 **时态的呼应** (The Sequence of Tenses)。如果主句谓语为现在时或将来时，从句中的谓语可以不受影响：

It's reported that they are building a new railway.　据报导他们正在修建一条新铁路。

Has he told you when he is leaving for Kunming?　他告没告诉你他什么时候去昆明？

We are trying to find out who is to take over the job.　我们正设法打听谁将接替这工作。

Will you tell me how you two are getting along?　你可否告诉我你俩相处得怎样？

如果主句谓语为过去时，从句谓语一般要跟着改为相关的过去时。改变的方式如下：

1）一般现在时改为一般过去时：

I was sure he *was* in bed.　(比较：I'm sure he's in bed.)

I didn't know where they *lived*.　(比较：I don't know where they live.)

2) 现在进行时改为过去进行时:

He thought he *was working* for the people. (比较: He thinks he's working for the people.)

I was glad you *were doing* well. (比较: I'm glad you're doing well.)

3) 现在完成时改为过去完成时:

I heard she *had won* a scholarship. (比较: I hear she has won a scholarship.)

I wondered if she *had got* well. (比较: I wonder if she has got well.)

4) 现在完成进行时改为过去完成进行时:

He wanted to know what she *had been doing*. (比较: He wants to know what she has been doing.)

I asked him how long he *had been waiting*. (比较: Ask him how long he's been waiting.)

5) 一般将来时改为一般过去将来时:

I hoped I'*d find* a job soon. (比较: I hope I'll find a job soon.)

He wasn't sure if she'*d accept* the offer. (比较: He isn't sure if she'll accept the offer.)

6) 将来进行时改为过去将来进行时:

I thought she'*d be going* by bus. (比较: I think she'll be going by bus.)

She said she'*d be expecting* us. (比较: She says she'll be expecting us.)

7) 将来完成(进行)时改为过去将来完成(进行)时:

I thought he'*d have gone* to bed now. (比较: I think he'll have gone to bed now.)

I knew she'*d have been teaching* here for 20 years by this summer.

(比较: I know she'll have been teaching for 20 years by this summer.)

8) 一般过去时有时可改为过去完成时:

He said he *had seen* Bob that morning. (比较: I saw Bob this morning.)

如有明确的时间状语，可以保持原来时态:

I knew he *was* born in 1970. (比较: I know he was born in 1970.)

8.8.2 一些特殊情况

1) 在某些情况下，从句谓语不随主句谓语变化，例如:

a. 表示永恒真理时谓语可以不变:

This proved that the earth *is* round. 这证明地球是圆的。

The teacher told us that the Yangtze *originates* in Qinghai.　老师告诉我们
　　说长江发源于青海。

b. 在口语中为了避免误会也可以不变：

She said she'*s leaving* tonight.　她说她今晚走。

Tom said he'*ll do* it.　汤姆说这事他来做。

He told me he *works* in the editorial office.　他告诉我他在编辑部工作。

He told me just now that his wife *is* ill.　他刚才告诉我他妻子病了。

2）有时可变可不变：

如强调现在的情况可以用现在时态：

How did you know I $\left\{\begin{array}{l}\text{am}\\\text{was}\end{array}\right\}$ Max Welson?　你怎么知道我是麦克斯·威尔逊？

I remember you $\left\{\begin{array}{l}\text{are}\\\text{were}\end{array}\right\}$ tall and $\left\{\begin{array}{l}\text{wear}\\\text{wore}\end{array}\right\}$ glasses. 我记得你是高个子戴眼镜。

Did you say you $\left\{\begin{array}{l}\text{have}\\\text{had}\end{array}\right\}$ no interest in it? 你说你对此没有兴趣？

3）can, may, will, shall 可改为 could, might, would, should：

She *can swim* like a fish.　——→ She said that she *could swim* like a fish.

You *may take* it home.　——→ She said I *might take* it home.

We'*ll support* you.　——→ They assured us that they *would support* us.

Shall I *go* with you?　——→ He asked if he *should go* with us.

4）could, might, should, ought, must 都可以不变：

Could I *take* this seat?　——→ I asked if I *could take* that seat.

You *might leave* now.　——→ She said I *might leave* now.

Should I *shut* the door?　——→ I wondered whether I *should shut* the door.

I *oughtn't to do* it.　——→ He said that I *oughtn't to do* it.

I *must leave* right away.　——→ I said I *must leave* right away.

第9章 被动语态

9.1 主动语态与被动语态

9.1.1 主动语态和被动语态

主语和谓语有时是主动关系，即主语是动作的执行者，如：

Everybody *respects* him. 人人都尊敬他。

有时也可以是被动关系，即主语是动作的承受者，如：

He *is respected* by everybody. 他受到大家的尊敬。

第一句的谓语为主动语态，第二句的谓语为被动语态。就句子来说，前一句是主动结构，后一句为被动结构。这里也可看出被动结构句子中的主语是主动结构句子中的宾语：

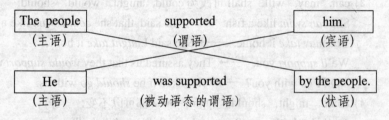

这类句子有些有 by 引导的状语，如：

The supermarket *is run* by a young lady. 这家超市是一位年轻的女士经营的。

The play *was written* by Cao Yu. 这个戏是曹禺写的。

但有些却没有，如：

She *was born* in Hunan Province. 她出生于湖南省。

They *were given* a warm welcome. 他们受到热烈的欢迎。

从这些句子中也可以看出，被动词态由"be + 过去分词"构成，时态由 be 表现出来。

9.1.2　哪些动词可用于被动语态

1) 一般说来及物动词可用于被动语态，因为及物动词有宾语，把宾语变为主语，句子即可改为被动结构：

主动结构	被动结构
Someone *broke* the window.	The window *was broken*.
Judia *painted* a picture.	The picture *was painted* by Judia.
We *keep* the butter in the fridge.	The butter *is kept* in the fridge.
They *killed* two brids last night.	Two brids *were killed* last night.

2) 不及物动词若与介词结合可构成成语动词，这时就可以有宾语，因而也就可以用于被动结构：

主动结构	被动结构
We *are looking into* the case.	The case *is being looked into*.
He *operated on* her yesterday.	She *was operated* on yesterday.
They *discriminated against* him.	He *was discriminated against*.
They *have broken into* his house.	His house *has been broken into*.

3) 由情态动词等构成的谓语也可用于被动结构：

主动结构	被动结构
We *can't do* it in a day.	It *can't be done* in a day.
You *must do* it right now.	It *must be done* right now.
We *should revise* the plan.	The plan *should be revised*.
She *has to finish* the work tonight.	The work *has to be finished* tonight.

4) 非谓语动词，由于不是谓语，不能改为被动语态，但可改为 **被动形式** (Passive Forms)：

主动形式	被动形式
She asked *to see* the manager.	She asked *to be given* a job.
I have nothing *to do*.	There is nothing *to be done*.
She hated *living* alone.	She hated *being treated* like that.
I heard someone *singing* next door.	I heard the song *sung* in Italian.

9.1.3　哪些结构可变为被动结构

除了"主+谓+宾"这种结构可变为被动结构外，还有下面结构可变为被动结构：

1) 主语 + 谓语 + 宾语 + 不定式：

主动结构	被动结构
We *told* the boy to go to bed.	The boy *was told* to go to bed.
They *asked* her to sing a song.	She *was asked* to sing a song.
They *made* him work long hours.	He *was made* to work long hours.
We *saw* him enter the house.	He *was seen* to enter the house.

2) 主语 + 谓语 + 宾语 + 名词作补语：

主动结构	被动结构
They *made* him their leader.	He *was made* their leader.
We *called* her Big Sister.	She *was called* Big Sister.
We *must keep* this a secret.	This *must be kept* a secret.
They *elected* him chairman.	He *was elected* chairman.

3) 主语 + 谓语 + 宾语 + 形容词等作补语：

主动结构	被动结构
She *painted* the walls yellow.	The walls *were painted* yellow.
He *dyed* his hair red.	His hair *was dyed* red.
They *set* her free.	She *was set* free.
We *found* them in high spirits.	They *were found* in high spirits.

4) 主语 + 谓语 + 间接宾语 + 直接宾语（+ 其他部分）：

主动结构	被动结构
They *gave* me something to eat.	I *was given* something to eat.
She *taught* me an English song.	I *was taught* an English song.
He *told* us some stories.	We *were told* some stories.
They *awarded* her a special prize.	She *was awarded* a special prize.

5）主语 + 谓语 + 从句：

主动结构	被动结构
They *said* that she was a saint.	It *was said* that she was a saint.
They *believe* that he has magic power.	It's *believed* that he has magic power.
They *reported* that he had resigned.	It *was reported* that he had resigned.
They *announced* that the contest was to be postponed.	It *was announced* that the contest was to be postponed.

9.2　各个时态的被动语态

9.2.1　一般时态的被动语态

1）一般现在时的被动语态 —— am, are 或 is + 过去分词：

I *am given* a lot of work to do.　他们给了我大量工作。

You *are invited* to give us a talk in English.　邀请您给我们作一个英语讲座。

The three words *are pronounced* in the same way.　这三个单词发音相同。

The boy *is called* Little Tiger.　这男孩叫小虎。

2）一般过去时的被动语态 —— was 或 were + 过去分词：

She *was brought up* by her aunt.　她是她姑姑带大的。

The book *was wirtten* by Dickens.　这本书是狄更斯写的。

Where *were* you *educated*?　你在哪里受的教育?

They *were given* a warm send-off at the airport.　他们在机场受到热烈欢送。

3）一般将来时的被动语态 —— will(shall) be + 过去分词：

When *will* the project *be completed*?　这项工程什么时候完工?

The spacecraft *will be launched* tomorrow.　太空船将于明天发射。

The result *will not be announced* until 6 o'clock.　结果六点钟才会宣布。

Shall I *be allowed* to go with you?　会允许我和你们一道去吗?

4）一般过去将来时的被动语态 —— would be + 过去分词：

I didn't expect that I *would be asked* to speak.　我没料到会被要求发言。

We were afraid we *wouldn't be admitted*.　我们担心会不让我们进去。

We were sure that he *would be punished*.　我们肯定他会受到惩罚。

She little thought she *would be invited*.　她没想到会受到邀请。

9.2.2　进行时态的被动语态

1) 现在进行时的被动语态——am，are 或 is＋being＋过去分词：

I'*m being troubled* by his behaviour.　我正在为他的行为苦恼。

The road *is being repaired*.　道路正在维修。

The case *is being investigated*.　这案子正在调查之中。

They *are being interrogated* by the police.　他们正在被警方盘问。

2) 过去进行时的被动语态——was 或 were＋being＋过去分词：

A new supersonic aircraft *was being designed*.　一种新的超音速飞机正在设计之中。

He *was being looked after* by his sister.　他正由他妹妹照顾着。

These ancient buildings *were being renovated*.　这些古建筑正在翻修。

The troops *were being inspected* by the president.　部队正受总统检阅。

9.2.3　完成时态的被动语态

1) 现在完成时的被动语态——has 或 have＋been＋过去分词：

My brother *has been sent* to work in Tibet.　我弟弟被派去西藏工作了。

Have they *been notified* about it?　这事通知他们了吗？

They'*ve been warned* not to swim there.　他们被告诫不要在那里游泳。

She *hasn't been told* about it yet.　还没告诉她这件事。

2) 过去完成时的被动语态——had＋been＋过去分词：

He told me that the factory *had been closed down*.　他告诉我这家工厂已经倒闭。

I heard she *had* already *been sent* to hospital.　我听说她已被送进医院。

We were glad that she *had been awarded* a gold medal.　我们很高兴她被授予一枚金牌。

I couldn't go to the party because I *hadn't been invited*.　我不能去参加晚会因为我没被邀请。

其他时态或没有被动语态，或极少用被动语态。

9.3　各种结构的被动形式

9.3.1　带情态动词的被动结构

1）由 can，could 构成的被动结构：

This pump *can* also *be operated* by hand.　这种泵也可手动操作。

This *can't be done* in a short time.　这不是短期内能完成的。

How *could* she *be persuaded* to stay?　怎么能劝说她留下？

He thought that expenditure *could be* further *reduced*.　他认为开支还可进一步削减。

△ can，could 后的不定式也可用完成形式：

This *can't have been done* by a human being.　这不可能是人做的事。

Such expenses *could have been avoided*.　这些开支本来是可以避免的。

2）由 may，might 构成的被动结构：

The road *may be* further *widened*.　这条路还可再拓宽一点。

An art school *may (might) be opened* next year.　明年可能开办一所艺术学校。

You *might be asked* to speak at the meeting.　可能会请你在会上发言。

She *might be sent* to work abroad.　她可能被派往国外工作。

△ may, might 后的不定式也可用完成形式：

He *may have been given* wrong information.　可能给了他错误的情报。

They *might have been put* in the wrong place.　它们可能被放错了地方。

3）由 must，mustn't 构成的被动结构：

This *must be considered* carefully.　这事必须仔细考虑。

Glassware *must be handled* with care.　玻璃器皿必须轻拿轻放。

All these factors *mustn't be neglected*.　所有这些因素都不能忽略。

Pupils *mustn't be given* too much homework.　学生作业不能留得太多。

△ must, mustn't 后的不定式也可用完成形式：

The house *must have been broken into* at night.　这房子准是夜里有人强行闯入。

This pagoda *must have been built* in the Ming Dynasty.　这座宝塔一定是明朝建的。

4）由 should 构成的被动语态：

You *should be praised* for what you've done.　你的行为应予表扬。

Should she *be told* about it? 这事应该告诉她吗?

This *should be kept* a secret. 这事应当保密。

Our precious time *shouldn't be wasted* that way. 我们的宝贵时间不应当这样浪费。

△ should 后面的不定式也可用完成形式:

Such people *shouldn't have been invited.* 这样的人本来就不该邀请。

They *should have been* well *treated.* 他们本应受到良好的待遇。

5) needn't 也可用于被动结构:

She *needn't be told* about it. 这事无需告诉她。

The second point *needn't be (needn't have been) mentioned.* 第二点无需提及。

在肯定句及疑问句中要加 to:

They *need to be cautioned.* 他们需要提醒。

Does this *need to be mentioned*? 这一点需要提吗?

9.3.2　一些不定式结构的被动形式

1) **ought to** 的被动结构:

Such behaviour *ought to be criticized.* 这种行为应受到批评。

He *ought to be (have been) given* a chance to try. 应当给他尝试的机会。

This *ought to be done* right away. 这事应当马上去做。

He *ought to have been inoculated.* 他本应先打预防针的。

2) 由 **be going to** 构成的被动结构:

When is the dam *going to be completed*? 水坝什么时候建好?

How many people *are going to be sent* there? 将派多少人去那里?

Two of them *were going to be promoted.* 他们中有两人将要升职。

Her drama *was going to be produced* in July. 她的话剧定于七月份上演。

3) 由 **has (have/had) to** 构成的被动结构:

This *has to be done* promptly. 这事必须赶快办理。

Many problems *have to be discussed* at the meeting. 很多问题得在会上商谈。

This *will (would) have to be handled* with care. 这事得小心处理。

These instructions *had to be carried out* to the letter. 这些指示必须不折不扣地执行。

4）由 "**be + 不定式**" 构成的被动结构：

This book *is to be published* next year. 这本书将于明年出版。

These old buildings *are to be pulled down*. 这些旧楼将要拆掉。

Not a soul *was to be seen*. 一个人影也看不到。

They *were to have been married* that fall, but she fell seriously ill. 他们本来那年秋天结婚，但她得了重病。

5）由 "**be bound (sure) to**" 构成的被动结构：

She *is bound to be convinced*. 她一定会被说服。

They *are (were) bound to be confronted with* all sorts of difficulties. 他们肯定会面临种种困难。

These difficulties *are sure to be overcome*. 这些困难一定会被克服。

These questions *are certain to be given* careful consideration. 这些问题一定会给予认真考虑。

6）由 "**be about (due) to**" 构成的被动结构：

He *was (is) about to be transferred* to another place. 他即将被调往另一地区。

The rally *was (is) due to be held* on Saturday. 大会定于星期六召开。

The work is not *likely to be finished* so soon. 这工作不太可能这么快就完成。

9.3.3　成语动词的被动结构

1）"**及物动词 + 副词**" 的被动结构：

This failure *has been brought about* by your own negligence. 这次失败是你们自己的疏忽造成的。

The proposal *was brought forward* by Senator Douglas. 这个提案是参议员道格拉斯提出的。

His illness *was brought on* by his worries. 他忧虑成疾。

The theory of relativity *was put forward* by Einstein. 相对论是爱因斯坦提出的。

2）"**动词 + 介词**" 的被动结构：

The meeting *was brought to a climax* by her appearance on the stage. 她在台上出现使会议达到了高潮。

The matter *was* soon *brought to his notice*. 这事很快受到他的注意。

The baby *was* closely *looked after* by her. 宝宝受到她细致的照顾。

The plan *was* soon *put into operation*. 这计划不久就实施了。

3）"**动词 + 副词（名词）+ 介词**"的被动结构：

There are some things that *are* not easily *put up with*. 有些事是不容易忍受的。

Lazy people *are looked down on* by everyone. 懒人谁都瞧不起。

His efforts to improve himself *are* constantly *made fun of*. 他自我完善的努力经常遭人取笑。

They're *taken care of* by the factory's nursery. 他们由工厂的幼儿园照顾。

9.3.4 一些特殊结构的被动形式

1）双宾动词的被动结构：

双宾动词有些可用于被动结构，在多数情况下都把间接宾语变为主语，而把直接宾语保留下来，称为 **保留宾语** (Retained Object)：

They *were granted* **permission** to visit the military base. 他们获准参观军事基地。

She *was given* **a warm welcome**. 她受到热烈欢迎。

We *were assigned* **a lot of homework**. 我们被布置了大量的家庭作业。

The best students *are awarded* **scholarships**. 最优秀的学生被颁给了奖学金。

有时也可把直接宾语变为主语，把间接宾语改为to引导的短语：

Excellent rooms *are assigned* to the girls. 上好的房间分给了那些姑娘。

The St. Mungo Prize *was awarded* to Mrs. Rayman. 圣曼戈奖颁给了雷门夫人。

2）带复合宾语动词的被动结构：

You *are requested* to be present at the ceremony. 请您出席这个典礼。

She *was made* a model worker. 她被选为劳模。

Details of the contract *haven't been made* public. 合同的细节尚未公布。

She *was heard singing* in the next room. 有人听见她在隔壁房间唱歌。

3）"**be + 过去分词 + 不定式**"结构：

She *is said to know* five languages. 据说她懂得五种语言。

This *was considered (thought) to be* a great honour. 这被认为是很荣幸的事。

He's *rumoured to have fled* the country.　谣传他已逃离这个国家。

She's *reported to have broken* a world record.　据报导她打破了一项世界纪录。

4) "it + be + 过去分词 + 从句"结构：

It's believed (said) that she has some supernatural powers.　据信(说)她有某些特异功能。

It's rumoured that the girl had eloped with her teacher.　谣传这女孩和她的老师私奔了。

It's reported that they have discovered a new star.　据报导他们发现了一颗新星。

It was feared that they wouldn't be able to defend the town.　大家担心守不住这座城市。

9.4　非谓语动词的被动形式

9.4.1　不定式的被动形式

不定式的被动形式可用作许多成分，如：

1) 用作宾语：

I must ask *to be excused*.　我得请求离开一会儿。

She didn't like *to be treated* as a child.　她不喜把她当作小孩。

He begged *to be forgiven*.　他请求宽恕。

2) 构成复合宾语：

She didn't want her son *to be taken away*.　她不愿意她的儿子被带走。

I'd like this room *to be redecorated*.　我想让这个房间重新装饰一下。

He didn't wish the subject *to be mentioned* in the letter.　他不希望在信里提及这个问题。

3) 用作定语：

There are a lot of things *to be discussed*.　有很多事要讨论。

There was not a soul *to be seen* in the park.　公园里一个人也看不见。

She was invited to a garden party *to be held* that night.　她被邀请参加那天晚上举行的游园会。

4) 用作状语：

She was sent there *to be trained* for the space flight.　她被派到那里接受太空飞行训练。

They were shipped to America *to be sold* as slaves. 他们被运到美洲卖作奴隶。

He shut himself in the room *so as not to be disturbed*. 他把自己关在屋里以免被人打扰。

5) 用作主语：

It's an honour *to be invited* to the ceremony. 受邀参加典礼很是荣耀。

It's a privilege *to be allowed* to study here. 获准在这里学习是难得的荣幸。

What a shame for you three *to be treated* like that! 你们三人受到这样的对待真不像话!

6) 用作表语：

My only wish is *to be allowed* to try my method. 我唯一的愿望就是允许试验我的方法。

His dream was *to be admitted* to a good university. 他的梦想是获准进入一所好大学。

Her ambition was *to be made* a cinema actress. 她的志向是要当一名电影演员。

9.4.2　动名词的被动形式

动名词的被动形式也可担任某些句子成分，如：

1) 作动词宾语或介词宾语：

He hated *being langhed at*. 他讨厌被人嘲笑。

She couldn't bear *being treated like that*. 她不能忍受这样的对待。

He was far from *being satisfied*. 他远未满足。

2) 作主语：

Being offered such a job was sheer good luck. 被给予这样一份工作纯属幸运。

It felt funny *being called Grandmother*. 被人称作奶奶感到怪怪的。

Being killed by sharks was a common occurrence. 以前被鲨鱼咬死是常有的事。

9.4.3　现在分词的被动形式

现在分词有时用于被动形式，如:

1) 构成复合宾语:

I saw *him being carried away* on a stretcher.　我看见他被人用担架抬走。

I watched *the cargo being hoisted* on board.　我看着货物被吊到船上。

One could hear *all kinds of things being discussed* there.　你可以听到那里在谈论的问题五花八门，无所不有。

2) 作定语:

She was not interested in the question *being discussed*.　她对正在讨论的问题没有兴趣。

The building *being erected* is a concert hall.　正在盖的建筑物是一座音乐厅。

This was a campaign *being waged* in the country.　这是国内正在开展的一项运动。

3) 作状语:

Being asked to give a performance, she couldn't very well refuse.　大家要求她表演一个节目，她不好拒绝。

Being protected by a thick wall, they felt quite safe.　有一堵厚墙掩护，他们感到很安全。

Being well looked after, the baby was in perfect health.　有了很好的照顾，宝宝身体非常健康。

9.4.4　过去分词结构

过去分词本身就有被动意思，可以:

1) 和系动词构成谓语:

He nearly *got hit* by a car.　他差点给汽车撞了。

His wound *has become infected*.　他的伤口感染了。

I soon *grew used* to that kind of life.　很快我就习惯那种生活了。

2) 构成复合宾语:

I've just had *a photograph taken*.　我刚刚照了一张相。

Go and get *your hair cut*.　去理一下发。

I don't want *anything said* about this.　我不希望谁谈及此事。

3) 用作状语：

Frustrated, he returned to his homeland.　他沮丧地回到故乡。

They laughed, friendly and *pleased*.　他们友好而高兴地笑了。

Greatly interested, I asked to join them in the game.　我很感兴趣，要求和
　他们一块儿玩。

9.5　在什么情况下用被动结构

9.5.1　使用被动结构的主要情况

　　掌握被动结构的形式很重要，但使用却要慎重。一般说来，没有特殊理由
不宜用被动结构。在多数情况下用主动结构是比较自然的。翻开一页书，你会
发现百分之八九十的句子都用主动结构，只在一定情况下需用被动结构，例
如：

1) 不知道动作的执行者是谁，这时只好用被动结构：

The monastery *was built* in the Middle Ages.　这座寺院建于中世纪。

Three people *were injured*.　三个人受了伤。

The building *was burned down*.　这座建筑完全焚毁了。

The boy *was* nearly *drowned*.　那孩子差点淹死。

When *will* the result *be announced*?　结果什么时候宣布？

The British general election *was held* in October.　英国十月份举行大选。

We *are called on* to take an active part in the movement.　号召我们积极参
　加这项运动。

He *was jailed* for six years.　他被监禁了六年。

2) 不必提到动作的执行者，因此也可用被动结构：

The book *was published* in 2000.　这书是 2000 年出版的。

A peace treaty *was* finally *signed*.　最终签定了一项和约。

The match *had to be cancelled* because of bad weather.　天气不好，比赛
　不得不取消。

The plant *was shut down* for two months.　工厂关闭了两个月。

Rent *has to be paid* in advance.　房租得预交。

Your hand *will be X-rayed*.　你的手要作 X 光透视检查。

Persistent foul play *will be* severely *penalized*.　不断犯规要受到重罚。

This problem *will be dealt with* in the next chapter.　这个问题将在下一章
　中讨论。

3）动作的承受者(或结果)是谈话的中心：

Madame Bovery was written by Flaubert. 《包法利夫人》是福楼拜写的。

Are these goods *made* by machinery? 这些货物是机器生产的吗?

When she was ill her children *were looked after* by neighbours. 她生病时孩子们由邻居照管。

These motions *can be vetoed* by the Governor. 这些动议州长可以否决。

Philip *was depressed* by what he had gone through. 菲利浦因他经历的事而沮丧。

这类句子常有一个 by 引导的短语说明动作的执行者，有时也可没有：

When he arrived home he *was arrested* (by a detective). 他到家时被捕了。

A new public library *is being built* (by our local council). 一座新的公共图书馆正在修建。

The house next door *has been bought* (by someone). 隔壁房子有人买了。

4）动作的执行者很模糊(如指 people，one 等)，故用被动结构也很自然：

It's *suggested* that we put the meeting off. 有人建议会议延期举行。

This sort of advertisement *is seen* everywhere. 这种广告(人们)到处都可以看到。

He *is suspected* of taking bribery. 有人怀疑他受贿。

They *are supposed* to be living in New York. 人们认为他们住在纽约。

The letter *has been opened*! 这信有人拆开了!

He *was believed* to have made an important discovery. 据信他有了重大发现。

It *was rumoured* that he was a spy. 谣传他是个间谍。

It's *alleged* that the hostage is already dead. 有人说人质已经死了。

5）为了措辞上的圆通，常避免说出动作的执行者：

You *are requested* to give us a talk on Japanese culture. 敬请您给我们作一个有关日本文化的讲座。

You *are* cordially *invited* to a dance to be given at the Teachers' Club at 7 p.m. on May Day. 谨订于五一节晚七时于教师俱乐部举行舞会敬请光临。

It *is* generally *considered* rude to stare at people. 盯着看人通常认为是粗鲁无礼的。

It's *hoped* that such things would not happen again. 希望这样的事不再发生。

It's much *to be regretted* that you can't join us in the trip. 你不能参与同行会是很遗憾的。

6) 为了使句子得到更好的安排:

He appeared on the stage and *was* warmly *applauded* by the audience.　他在台上出现, 受到观众的热列鼓掌。(这样用一个主语即可)

The plan *was supported* by those who wish to live on the campus.　这计划受到想在校园住的人的支持。(若为主动结构句子就较难安排)

They *were killed* by a grenade, which exploded under the car.　他们被一颗在汽车下爆炸的手榴弹炸死。

The principle of bottling is very simple. Food *is put* in jars, the jars and their contents *are heated* to a temperature which *is maintained* long enough to ensure that all bacteria, moulds and viruses *are destroyed*.　装瓶的操作很简单。把食物装在瓶内, 把瓶子连同新盛的东西一起加热到某个温度, 将这温度维持足够时间, 以保证所有细菌、霉菌及病毒都被杀死。(这样安排意思清楚, 行文流畅, 把上面任何被动结构改为主动结构都可能造成困难)

9.5.2　一些常常使用被动结构的情况

1) 公告, 通知:

Lying on the floor *is* strictly *prohibited*.　严禁躺在(车厢)地板上。

None of the reference books *are to be taken* out of the reading-room.　参考书不得携出阅览室。

Only fifty kilos *are allowed* for personal baggage.　个人携带物品只限五十公斤。

Applications *must be sent in* by 31st July.　必须于7月31日前提出申请。

2) 新闻报导:

The search for the bank robbers continues. Meanwhile many people *have been questioned* and the owner of the stolen getaway car *has been traced*.　搜索银行劫匪的行动在继续着。与此同时, 许多人受到盘问, 并一直在查找劫匪逃逸所偷汽车的车主。

3) 报纸标题 (动词 be 常被省略):

Congressman *Assassinated*!　国会议员遭到暗杀!

Two Drug Traffickers *Hanged* in Singapore!　两名毒贩在新加坡被绞死!

Five-year-old Boy *Kidnapped*!　五岁男童遭到绑架!

4）科技文章：

The mixture *is placed* in a crucible and *is heated* to a temperature of 300℃. It *is* then *allowed* to cool before it *can be analysed*. 将混合液置于坩锅中，加热至摄氏 300 度，然后令其冷却，随后便可进行分析。

第 10 章 虚拟语气

10.1 语 气

10.1.1 语气

和时态、语态一样，**语气** (Mood) 也是谓语动词的一种形式，表明说话的目的和意图。英语中有四种语气：

- **陈述语气** (The Indicative Mood)
- **疑问语气** (The Interrogative Mood)
- **祈使语气** (The Imperative Mood)
- **虚拟语气** (The Subjunctive Mood)

10.1.2 陈述语气和疑问语气

陈述语气陈述一个事实或提出一个想法：

Ours is a great socialist country. 我们的国家是一个伟大的社会主义国家。(陈述事实)

I hope our country will become strong and prosperous. 我希望我们的国家繁荣富强。(提出想法)

而疑问语气用来提出问题：

Have you ever been to Japan? 你去过日本没有？

What's your nationality? 你是哪国人？

前面章节中谈到的时态、语态形式都属于这两者的范畴。

10.1.3 祈使语气

1) 祈使句中的谓语动词，都用动词原形，称为祈使语气。这种句子可向对方提出请求、邀请，给予忠告、指示、警告，发出命令等：

Come and join us. 来和我们一块儿玩。(邀请)

Hurry up!　赶快!（催促）

Cross the bridge and turn left.　过桥向左拐。（指示）

Remember to give Mary a ring.　记得给玛丽打个电话。（提醒）

Put down your gun!　把枪放下!（命令）

Have one more cup of coffee.　再喝一杯咖啡。（敦促）

Take care!　保重!（叮嘱）

Beware of pickpockets!　小心扒手!（警告）

Please be seated.　请坐下。（请求）

Don't overwork yourself.　不要过于劳累。（劝告）

2) 这种句子的主语一般不说出，但必要时也可说出：

You go on; I'll wait.　你往前走，我等一等。

You get out of the room!　你给我滚出去!

Someone go and fetch a chair.　谁去搬一把椅子来。

You clean the window and you clean the blackboard.　你擦窗子，你擦黑板。

有时加一个呼语，表示是对谁说的：

Be quiet, children.　孩子们，安静点。

Please sign your name here, sir.　先生，请在这里签名。

Fasten your seatbelts, everybody.　请大家系好安全带。

John, (you) listen to me!　约翰，你听我说!

3) let 也可引导祈使句：

Let us stand together in this emergency.　在这紧急时刻让我们站在一起。

Let them go by themselves.　让他们自己去。

Let us not be alarmed by rumours.　咱们不要为谣言惊慌。

Let me out, mother!　让我出去，妈妈!

You're ill. Let me get the doctor.　你病了，我去请医生。

10.1.4　虚拟语气

在表示一种纯然假想的情况或主观愿望时，动词需用一种特殊形式，称为虚拟语气。虚拟语气在形式上大致分为三类：

1) 现在虚拟语气——主要用动词原形：

God *bless* you.　愿上帝保佑你。

It is essential that the ban *be* lifted.　解除禁令至关重要。

She petitioned the king that her father *be* pardoned. 她恳求国王赦免她的
父亲。

2) 过去虚拟语气——和陈述语气的过去式相同，但动词 be 要用 were 形
式：

Imagine your child *played* truant. 设想你的孩子逃学。

She treated me as though I *were (was)* a stranger. 她待我如陌生人。

If only I *were* not so nervous. 我要是不那么紧张就好了。

3) 过去完成形式——和陈述语气中的过去完成时相同：

I wish I *hadn't done* so. 但愿我没这样做。

If I *had seen* her, I would have told her. 如果我见到她，我就会告诉她了。

If only I *had listened* to your advice. 我要是听了你的劝告就好了。

有些情态动词，特别是 should, would, might, could 常用在虚拟语气中。

10.2　虚拟语气在条件句中的用法

10.2.1　虚拟条件句

包含条件从句的句子都是条件句，有些条件句是可能实现的，如：

If I have time I'll come over to see you. 如果我有时间我就来看你。

If we leave now, we can still catch the train. 如果我们现在动身,还可能
赶上火车。

I won't go to the party unless they invite me. 除非他们邀请我,否则我不
会参加这个晚会。

If you are waiting for a bus you'd better join the queue. 如果你是在等车,
你最好排队。

If he has written the letter, I'll post it. 如果他已把信写好，我就去发。

这种条件句称为 **真实条件句** (Sentences of Real Condition)。另有一些条件
句表示纯然假想的情况，称为 **虚拟条件句** (Sentences of Unreal Condition)，在
这类条件句中谓语动词就需要用虚拟语气：

If I *had* enough money, I *would buy* a computer. 如果我有足够的钱，我
将买一台电脑。(但我没有)

If you *had arrived* a little earlier, you *would have seen* her. 你要是早来一
会儿就见到她了。

10.2.2　表示现在和将来情况的虚拟条件句

1) 表示现在或将来情况的虚拟条件句，动词形式可以下表表示：

条件从句中的谓语	主句谓语
相当于过去式的形式	would ＋ 动词原形

这类句子或表示与事实相反的情况或实现可能性不大的情况：

If I *had* a map I *would lend* it to you.　如果我有地图我就借给你。(但我没有)

If you *left* your bicycle outside, someone *would steal* it.　如果你把自行车放在外边，有人会偷的。(当然你不会这样做)

If I *dyed* my hair blue everyone *would laugh* at me.　如果我把头发染成蓝色，谁都会笑我的。(当然我不会干这样的傻事)

If I *lived* near my office, I'*d walk* to work.　如果我住在办公室附近，我就会步行上班。

If I *were* you I'*d plant* some trees round the house.　如果我是你，我会在房子周围种些树。

If Helen *were (was)* here how nice it *would be*!　海伦要是在这里该多好!

在 If I were you 这样的句子中，were 不能改成 was，但在第三人称单数后(如最后一句)用 was 也可以。

2) 在主句中谓语有时也可由 might, could 构成：

If you tried again you *might succeed*.　如果再试一次，你可能会成功。

If I could type, I *might save* a lot of time.　如果我会打字，我可能会节省大量时间。

If I knew her number I *could ring* her up.　我要是知道她的号码我就能给她打电话。

If he had a permit he *could get* a job.　如果他有许可证，他可以找到一份工作。

3) 在条件从句中有时还可以用 "were to ＋ 不定式" (a) 或 "should ＋ 不定式" (b) 这两种形式：

a. If he *were (was)* to resign, who would take his place?　如果他要辞职，谁来接替他?

If I *were to do* the job, I would do it in a different way.　要是我来做这工作，我会是另一种做法。

b. If you *should have* any difficulty in getting the medicine, (you could) ring this number.　如果你找这种药有困难,(你可以)拨打这个电话。

If the toys *should arrive* in a damaged condition, please inform us at once. 如果这些玩具运到时有损坏,请立即通知我们。

在后面这类句子中,主句的谓语有时可用祈使语气(见上例),或用陈述语气:

If I should be free tomorrow, I *will come* to see you.　如果明天我有空我会来看你的。

4) 在某些条件从句(如包括 were 和 should 的从句)中,if 有时可省略,这时语序要改为倒装:

Were I Tom I would refuse.　如果我是汤姆我会拒绝。

Were I in your shoes I would let him know what I thought of him.　如果我处于你的地位,我会让他知道我对他的看法。

Should you *require* anything just give me a ring.　你要是需要什么就给我打个电话。

Should she *be interested*, I'll phone her.　如果她有兴趣,我会给她打电话。

5) 从句有时可用 If it were not for 这种句型,表示"若不是":

If it weren't for your help, we would be in serious trouble.　若不是你帮忙,我们会遇到大麻烦。

Were it not for their loan, our life would be very difficult.　要不是有他们的贷款,我们的生活会很困难。

You wouldn't be anywhere *if it weren't for* Ruth.　要不是露丝你不会有任何成就。

6) 在极少情况下,从句中的谓语可用动词原形,主句中的谓语可用陈述语气:

If any person *be found* guilty, he shall have the right of appeal.　如果有人被判定有罪,他应有上诉权。

If that *be* the official view, it cannot be accepted.　如果这是官方的看法,这是不能接受的。

If any vehicle *be found* parked on these premises, it shall be towed away. 如果发现有车停在此处,它将被拖走。

这是比较大气的说法,口语中很少使用。

10.2.3　表示过去情况的虚拟条件句。

1) 表示过去情况的虚拟条件句动词形式可以下表表示:

条件从句中的谓语	主句谓语 had
相当于过去完成时的形式	would have + 过去分词

这类从句表示一个与事实相反的过去情况 ('d 是 had/would 的紧缩形式):

If I *had known* that you were coming, I *would have met* you at the airport. 如果我知道你要来, 我就会去机场接你了。(但我不知道)

If anything *had happened*, he *would have let* us know. 如果发生了什么情况, 他早就通知我们了。(想必没发生什么事)

She *would have said* more if he *had not walked away*. 如果他没走开, 她还会多说些话的。

If I *had left* sooner, I'*d have caught* the bus. 如果早点动身, 我就赶上巴士了。

If I *had been* Nancy, I *wouldn't have left* him. 我要是南希, 我不会离开他。

What *would* you *have done* if you'*d been* in my position? 如果你处于我的位置你会怎么办?

在主句中, 如果主语是第一人称, 也有人用 should 构成谓语:

I *should (would) have talked* to mother if I *had thought* of it. 如果我想起了那事, 我是会向母亲谈及的。

I *should (would)* never *have done* it if I *hadn't been* so hard up. 如果手头不是那样拮据, 我是不会那样做的。

2) 主句中也可用 could 和 might 构成谓语:

No doubt I *could have earned* something if I *had* really *meant* to. 如果我有心挣点钱, 我肯定能挣到一些的。

If my father *had lived*, he *could have done* all this for me. 如果我父亲活着, 这一切他都会帮我做的。

If I *had been* less cautious, I *might have been* more wise. 如果我少一些谨慎, 也许就会多一些明智。

If we *had found* him earlier we *might have saved* his life. 如果我们早点找到他, 我们或许已把他救活了。

有时还可由 should (应当) 构成:

If he *had received* the present, he *should have thanked* her. 如果他收到了

礼物，他是应当向她道谢的。

If he *had apologized*, you *should have done* so too. 如果他道歉了，你也应当这样做。

3) 从句中也可用 had not been for 来构成谓语，表示"要不是"：

If it *hadn't been for* your timely help, we would have got into serious trouble. 要不是你及时帮助，我们会陷入严重的困境。

If it *hadn't been for* her meticulous care, I wouldn't have got well so soon. 要不是有她精心的照顾，我不会好得这样快。

If it *hadn't been for* Margaret, I might not have understood. 要不是有玛格丽特，我也许不会明白的。

4) if 有时可以省略，但后面部分需改为倒装语序：

Had she been asked, she would have done it. 如果那时请她做，她是会做的。

Had I not seen it with my own eyes, I would not have believed it. 这事要不是我亲眼所见，我都不会相信的。

Had it not been for their support, we couldn't have won the election. 要不是有他们的支持我们不可能赢得选举。

Had Mark been in charge, it wouldn't have happened. 如果是马柯负责，这事就不会发生了。

10.2.4　一些特殊的虚拟条件句

1) 错综时间条件句：

有些条件句主句谓语和从句谓语表示的动作在时间上并不一致，这类句子称为 **错综时间条件句** (Conditional Sentences of Mixed Time)，如：

If the weather *had been* more favourable, the crops *would be growing* still better. 如果前些时候天气好一点，庄稼现在会长得更好。

If he *had received* six more votes, he *would be* our chairman now. 他要是多得六票，现在就是我们的主席了。

If you *had taken* her advice, you *wouldn't be* in such trouble now. 如果你听了她的劝告，你现在就不会有这种麻烦。

If it *hadn't been for* the doctors' care, I *wouldn't be speaking* to you now. 要不是有医生们的照顾，我此时不会在和你说话。

If he *were leaving*, you *would have heard* about it. 如果他真的要走，你

早就听到消息了。

If he *had been trying* hard, her parents *wouldn't be* so worried. 如果她一直
很努力，她的父母也不会这样着急了。

2) 含蓄条件句:

有些句子虽不含条件从句，但意思和条件句差不多，这种句子称为 **含蓄
条件句** (Sentences of Implied Condition)，在这种句子中也可能需用虚拟语气:

I might see her personally, it *would be* better. 我可能亲自去见她，这样
会好一些。

I *would have written* before but I have been ill. 要不是病了，我早给你写
信了。

But for my money that woman *would have persecuted* him. 若不是我花了
钱那女人早就找上他的麻烦了。

I did not press the point as it *would have been* useless. 我没有坚持这一点，
因为坚持也没用。

In the old days she *would have argued*. 要是在过去她早就争论上了。

Such a thing *wouldn't have happened* elsewhere. 这样的事别处是不会发
生的。

Anybody else *would have believed* you. 要换上别人早就信了你的话。

To have told my secret *would have given* me *away*. 讲出了我的秘密就等
于出卖了我。

I wouldn't worry about it. It *wouldn't do* any good. 我不会为此发愁，这
样没好处。

She *would have done* anything to make amends. 她愿做任何事来赔罪。

3) 某些情态动词的使用:

某些情态动词，特别是 should, would, could, might, 在口语中用得很多，
使语气变得客气委婉:

Would you *mind* shutting the window? 劳驾把窗子关上好吗?

Would you *tell* me how to get to the tube? 可否请告诉我怎么去地铁站?

When *would* it *be* convenient for you to begin? 你何时开始比较方便?

Seattle *wouldn't suit* her. 西雅图不会适合她的。

I'*d go* there with you. 我将和你一道去。

I *should be* glad to talk to him. 我愿和他谈谈。

I *should think* you *would be* above anything like that. 我想你不会做出这
样的事来。

I *should find* it very hard to believe. 我会觉得这难以置信。

I *should have preferred* him to do it in a different way. 我倒宁愿他以另一种方式来处理此事。

Could you *lend* me your computer? 你可否把电脑借我用一下？

I *could come* earlier, if necessary. 如有必要我可以早点来。

No one *could be* more generous; he has a heart of gold. 谁也没他慷慨；他有一颗金子般的心。

Might I *ask* for a photograph of Mr. Strakov? 我可否要一张斯特拉可夫先生的照片？

If necessary, you *might shorten* it. 必要的话你可以把它缩短。

I *might have come* to a wrong conclusion. 我也许得出了错误的结论。

这类句子的谓语虽不一定是虚拟语气，却很接近虚拟语气。一是它们在形式上和虚拟条件句中的谓语形式很相近；二是它们不受时态的限制，现在情况可以过去形式表示；三是和一般陈述语气有些差异，更带主观色彩。因此，说它们是虚拟语气或接近虚拟语气也未尝不可。

10.3 虚拟语气在某些从句中的运用

10.3.1 虚拟语气在宾语从句中的运用

在某些动词后的宾语从句中需用虚拟语气：

1) wish 后的宾语从句：

在 wish 后的宾语从句中谓语主要有两种形式 (表示与事实相反的情况)：

a. 用过去式表示现在情况，动词 be 用 were 时较多 (也有人用 was)：

I wish I *knew* what was going to happen. 但愿我知道将要发生什么事。

I wish I *could help* you. 但愿我能帮助你。(但我不能)

I wish I *had* more time. 但愿我有更多的时间。

I wish I *were (was)* young again. 真希望我能再年轻一次。

b. 用相当于过去完成时的形式，表示过去的情况 (常有遗憾的味道)：

I wish (that) I *had listened* to your advice. 我要是听你的劝告就好了。

My father wishes (that) he *had gone* to university. 我父亲很希望自己上过大学。

I wish you *hadn't told* me all this. 但愿你没告诉我这一切。

She wished she *hadn't come*. 她但愿自己没来。

间或用 would 构成谓语:

I wish he *wouldn't go* out every night. 但愿他不要每晚都出去。

I wish you *wouldn't be* so noisy. 但愿你别这么吵。

2) would rather (sooner) 后的宾语从句:

谓语多用相当于过去式的形式,表示现在或将来的情况:

I'd rather you *know* that now, than afterwards. 我宁愿你现在知道而不是
将来知道。

"Do you mind if I smoke here?" "I'd rather you *didn't*." "我在此抽烟你
介意吗?" "我倒是希望你别抽。"

I would rather you *told* me the truth. 我宁愿你给我讲真话。

I'd sooner you *didn't* ask me that question. 我宁愿你别问我那个问题。

谓语用相当于过去式的形式,表示现在或将来的情况:

I'd rather you *hadn't told* me about it. 我倒宁愿你没告诉我这件事。

在 had rather 和 prefer 后的宾语从句中有时也可用虚拟语气:

I had rather you *did* it. 我宁愿你做这事。

She preferred that he *should do* the washing-up in the kitchen. 她宁愿他在
厨房里洗碗碟。

在 suppose 后的宾语从句中也可能包含虚拟语气:

Suppose her father *turned* her out of doors! 设想她父亲把她撵出家门!

Suppose they *did not believe* him what would they do to him? 假如他们不
相信他的话,他们会把他怎么样?

3) suggest, demand, insist, ask 这类动词后的宾语从句:

在这类从句中美国人多用动词原形 (也就是现在虚拟语气):

He **suggested** that a petition *(should) be drawn* up. 他建议起草一份请愿
书。

She **demanded** that I *pay* her immediately. 她要求我立即付款给她。

He **insisted** that Jennie *send* her to dancing school. 他坚持要珍妮送她进
舞蹈学校。

He **asks** that he *be given* an opportunity to explain his case. 他要求给他机
会解释他的情况。

I **advise** that he *go* at once. 我建议他马上就去。

I **propose** that Mr. Parr *be* the chairman. 我提议帕尔先生担任主席。

She **urged** that he *write* and *accept* the post. 她催促他写信去接受这个职
位。

Congress has **voted** that the present law *be maintained*.　国会投票决定维持现行法律。

He **requested** that the Premier *grant* him an interview.　他请求总理接见他。

He **commanded** that we *(should) attack* at once.　他命令我们立即进攻。

The Queen **desires** that you *(should) come* at once.　女王希望你马上来。

I **move** that we *accept* the proposal.　我提议通过这项提案。

He **ordered** that the man *be released*.　他命令释放那人。

I **recommend** that everyone *(should) buy* this dictionary.　我建议这字典每个人买一本。

He **requires** that they *(should) work* all night.　他要求他们通宵工作。

The Senate has **decreed** that such students not *be exempted* from college dues.　参议院规定这样的学生不能免交学费。

They **intended** that the news *(should) be suppressed*.　他们打算封锁这条消息。

She **petitioned** the king that her son *(should) be pardoned*.　她恳求国王宽恕她的儿子。

英国人过去多用"should＋动词原形"作这类从句中的谓语，但现在用原形的人也越来越多了，另外这类句子也可变为被动语态，宾语从句则成了主语从句：

It is suggested that we *make* a special study of the problem.　有人建议我们对这问题作专门研究。

It was intended that you *be* the candidate.　打算让你作候选人。

It was proposed that this matter *be discussed* at the next meeting.　有人提议这问题下次会上再议。

It is requested that a vote *be taken*.　有人提请投票表决。

10.3.2　虚拟语气在主语、表语等从句中的运用

虚拟语气还可在主语、表语及同位语从句中使用，形式和上节第三段谈的句子基本上一样：

1) 虚拟语气在主语从句中的使用：

It is **important** that he *work* hard.　他努力工作是很重要的。

It is **essential** that this mission *not fail*.　这项任务不失败至关重要。

It is **appropriate** that this tax *be abolished*. 废除这项税收是合适的。

It's **imperative** that you *(should) not be seen* here. 你不要在这里露面,这很要紧。

It's **vital** to her health *that* she *take* this medicine. 她吃这药对她的身体非常重要。

另外,在有些这类结构的句子中,主语从句的谓语由"should +动词原形"构成,这时多带有一些情感色彩,可译为"竟然"等 (表示一种不可思议的状况):

It seems so **unfair** that this *should happen* to me. 我身上竟发生这样的事,这似乎很不公平。

I think it is **dreadful** that anyone *should be* so miserable. 有人竟然这样悲惨,我感到太可怕了。

It's **strange** that she *should be* so late. 真奇怪,她竟然来得这样晚。

It is **surprising** that they *should pass* the time like that. 他们竟然这样来打发时间真令人惊讶。

It's **natural** that you *should forget* it. 你忘掉这事是很自然的。

That they *should do* such a wicked thing is **unthinkable**. 他们竟然做这样不道德的事真是不可思议。

2) 用在表语从句中的虚拟语气:

Our **decision** is that the school *remain* closed. 我们的决定是学校暂不开学。

Sophia's **idea** was that they *should lock up* the house. 索菲娅的想法是他们把屋子锁上。

My **suggestion** is that we *take* the 6:00 train. 我的建议是搭六点的火车。

Their **requirement** is that every member *attend* at least one meeting per year. 他们的要求是每个会员每年至少参加一次会议。

3) 用在同位语从句中的虚拟语气:

He made the **suggestion** that they *carry on* their conversation in Japanese. 他建议他们用日语接着交谈。

There have been **demands** that the prime minister *should resign*. 有人要求首相辞职。

They expressed the **wish** that they *be given* more free time. 他们表示希望给他们更多的空闲时间。

The **resolution** that women *be allowed* to join the society was carried. 允许妇女加入该协会的决议通过了。

10.3.3　虚拟语气在状语从句中的运用

在某些状语从句中，谓语有时用虚拟语气，特别是在下面几类状语中：

1) as if, as though 引导的状语从句：

这类状语从句中的谓语形式和一般虚拟语气差不多，表示现在情况时用过去虚拟语气 (a)，表示过去情况时用完成形式 (b)：

a. I have loved you **as if** you *were* my son.　我爱你就像你是我的亲儿子。

　　I remember it vividly **as though** it *were* tonight.　这事我记得很清楚就像发生在今晚似的。

　　He behaves **as if** he *owned* the place.　他表现得像是这地方的主人。

　　He talks **as though** he *knew* where she was.　他谈起来仿佛他知道她在哪儿似的。

b. He talks (talked) about Rome **as though** he *had been* there himself.　他谈起罗马就仿佛他到过那里似的。

　　Fancy you sitting there **as if** nothing *had happened*.　瞧你坐在那里好像什么事也没发生似的。

　　He looks (looked) **as though** he *had known* Millie for years.　他看上去就像他认识米丽好多年了。

在 look, seem, taste, smell 后，as if 引导的从句中可以用陈述语气：

　　It **looks** as if they are in a terrible hurry.　看起来他们好像忙得要命。

　　It **seems** as if we shall have to walk.　看上去我们得步行了。

　　The meat **tastes** as if it has gone bad.　这肉吃起来好像已经坏了。

　　The milk **smells** as if it is sour.　这奶闻起来好像酸掉了。

as if (though) 还可引导表语从句：

　　It isn't **as if** *you were going away for good*.　又不是你一去不复返了。

　　It is not **as though** *we were poor*.　我们又不是穷人家。

　　You look **as if** *you didn't care*.　你看上去好像不在乎的样子。

2) 有些让步从句中也可能用虚拟语气，特别是某些句型，其中有些用现在虚拟语气 (a)，有些用 may, might, would 构成谓语 (b)：

a. Though he *be* the President himself, he shall hear us.　即使他是总统本人，他也得听我们讲话。

　　Whether she *be* right or wrong, we will support her.　不管她是对还是错，我们都会支持她.

　　Whatever *be* the reasons for his action, we cannot tolerate such disloyalty.　不管他这样做的原因何在，我们都不能容忍这种不忠诚的行为。

b. *Be* that as it *may*, we have nothing to lose. 即使如此,我们也不损失什么。

Come what *may*, we will go ahead with our plan. 不管发生什么情况,我们也要推行这个计划。

Poor though you *might be*, you cannot live all your life on charity. 尽管你穷,你也不能一辈子靠救济过日子。

Try as I *would*, I cannot prevail upon him to follow my advice. 不管想什么办法,我都不能劝说他按我的意见行事。

这些句子 (特别是第一类) 的从句谓语也可用陈述语气:

Though he is the President himself...

Whether she is right or wrong...

上面的 b 类句子可以看作是一种句型。

3) 有些目的从句也可用虚拟语气作谓语 (主要是用动词原形):

They removed the prisoner in order that he *not disturb* the proceedings any further. 他们把犯人带走以免他继续干扰诉讼进程。

The President must reject the proposal, lest it *cause* strife and violence. 总统必须拒绝这个提议,以免引起冲突和暴力。

Earth mounds were being hastily erected lest an attack *(should) be launched* that night. 正在匆忙地垒起土堆,以防那晚(敌人)会发起袭击。

但这种用法已日渐减少,现在多用 would, should, could, might 等构成谓语 (属于陈述语气范畴):

He left early in order that the children *would not be* alone in the house. 他早早动身以免孩子们单独待在家里。

I lent him £50 so that he *might go* for a holiday. 我借给他五十英镑以便他能去度假。

I hired a boat so that I *could go* fishing. 我租了一条船以便能出去钓鱼。

He hurried on, lest she *should meet* him again. 他匆忙往前走,以免她再碰到他。

4) 在 "be + 形容词" 这种结构后的从句,有时用 should + 动词原形构成谓语:

I'm surprised that you *should press* the suggestion. 我很奇怪你怎么会坚持你的建议。

He was amazed that some countries *should express* indignation at it. 他很惊讶有些国家竟对此感到愤怒。

They're especially anxious that you *should come*. 他们特别期盼你能来。

They were insistent that we *be ready*.　他们坚持要我们做好准备。

但这类结构后的从句用陈述语气的时候可能更多一些。

10.4　虚拟语气的一些其他用法

10.4.1　虚拟语气在祝愿语中的用法

在一些表示祝愿的话语中仍可找到虚拟语气(多用动词原形):

God *be praised*!　愿上帝受到赞美!

God *save* all living beings!　愿上帝拯救众生!

Heaven *forbid* that I should ever say nasty things about you.　我要是说你坏话上天不容。

God *damn* it!　该死的!

Long *live* peace!　和平万岁!

So *be* it.　就这样吧。

Please God, there hasn't been an accident.　谢天谢地，没有出事。

So *help* me God.　上天作证!

Far *be* it from me to spoil the fun.　我才不愿意扫别人的兴哩。

Curse this fog!　这讨厌的雾!

有些祝愿的话用 may 开始:

May you *enjoy* many years of health and happiness.　祝您健康长寿美满幸福。

May God *bless* you!　愿上帝保佑你!

May there never *be* another world war.　愿永远不再有世界大战。

10.4.2　It's (high) time 后的定语从句中的虚拟语气

1) 在 It's time 后的定语从句中谓语要用虚拟语气(多用过去虚拟语气):

It's time we *went*.　我们该走了。

It's time we *were leaving*.　我们该动身了。

It's time we *ordered* dinner.　现在该点菜了。

I think it's time they *were taught* a lesson.　我想现在是给他们一次教训的时候了。

2）在 It's high time 后情况也如此：

It's high time you *bought* a new car. 你该买辆新车了。

It's high time that you *made up* your mind. 该是你下决心的时候了。

It's high time you *got* a job and *settled down*. 你该找个工作安定下来了。

10.4.3　在某些句型中使用的虚拟语气

在少数句型中谓语需用虚拟语气：

1）由 that 引导的句子 (表示愿望或沮丧情绪)：

Oh that the rain *would stop*!　但愿雨能停下来！

Oh, that I *were* with her now!　但愿我现在和她在一起！

That I *should be accused of* murder!　我竟然被控谋杀！

That he *should act* so rudely toward you!　他竟然对你这样无礼！

2）由 would that 引导的句子 (表示"但愿…")：

Would (that) he *were* gone!　但愿他已走掉！

Would that we *had seen* her before she died.　如果在她临终前我们去看她一面就好了。

Would that he *could have listened to* his father.　他要是能听了他父亲的话就好了。

3）由 to think 引导的句子 (表示"没想到…")：

To think that I *trusted* him!　没想到我竟然信任了他！

To think he *knew* about it all the time!　没想到这事他一直都知道！

To think that she *should have died* such a tragic death.　没想到她竟会死得这样惨。

10.4.4　某些成(短)语中包含的虚拟语气

某些成(短)语本身就包含虚拟语气：

1）as it were (were 就是虚拟语气) —— 通常插在句子中间，表示"姑且这么说"：

He is, *as it were*, a walking dictionary.　他可说是一部活字典。

He is my best friend, my second self *as it were*.　他是我最好的朋友，可说是我第二个自己。

The English, the Scots and the Welsh are all, *as it were*, members of the same family. 英格兰人、苏格兰人和威尔士人都可说是一家人。

2) would have thought —— 本身也是虚拟语气，表示"会想到"、"会以为"等：

Who *would have thought* to see you here! 谁会想到在这里见到你!

Who *would have thought* it was going to break like that? 谁会想到它会这样碎掉?

You *would have thought* they would do more to help us. 你原本会以为他们会更多地帮助我们的。

3) if need be —— 表示"如果必要"：

I can earn my own living *if need be*. 如有必要,我可以自己赚钱维持生活。

I'll fight you *if need be* to the High Court. 必要的话我可以和你一直打到高等法院。

If need be, I can do extra work at the weekend. 倘有必要,我可以在周末加些班。

第11章 助动词和情态动词

11.1 助动词

11.1.1 英语中的助动词

英语中常用作助动词的有三组词：

1) be, am, are, is, was, were, been, being

2) have, has, had, having

3) do, does, did

另外还有 shall, will, should, would 虽然也是助动词，却有时有情态动词的作用，可说是介乎助动词和情态动词之间的词，它们的作用和 can, may, must 有很多相近之处。为了方便，也把它们放在本章中讨论。

11.1.2 be 的用法

1) be 作助动词，主要用来构成：

a. 各种进行时态：

I'm seeing a friend off. 我在给一位朋友送行。

We're trying to get in touch with her. 我们正在设法和她取得联系。

She's working as an air-hostess. 她在当空姐。

He was groping in the dark, so to speak. 他可说还在黑暗中摸索。

What were you doing when I called? 我打电话时你在干什么？

Come on time. We'll be expecting you. 准时来，我们会等着你。

What have you been doing all these years? 这些年来你一直在干什么？

b. 各种被动语态：

Smoking is not allowed in this building. 本大楼内禁止吸烟。

You are requested to give a performance. 请你表演一个节目。

I'm being shown round the city. 有人正带我在城里逛。

He was penalized for a foul. 他因犯规而受罚。

Hundreds of soldiers *were killed* or *wounded* in the battle. 这次战役伤亡了数百士兵。

The trip *has been cancelled*. 这次远足取消了。

c. 各种被动形式：

He hates *being interrupted*. 他不愿受人打扰。

She was afraid of *being seen* by her father. 她怕被她父亲看见。

He was there *being trained* as an astronaut. 他在那里被培训为宇航员。

Such problems have *to be handled* with care. 这类问题得谨慎处理。

He asked *to be sent* to work in the northwest. 他请求派他去西北工作。

2) be 用作其他类动词：

a. 用作系动词：

He *is (was)* an atheist. 他是个无神论者。

Remember your father's directions and *be* a good girl. 记住你爸爸的话做个好姑娘。

Be always on your guard. (你)要时刻保持警惕。

He *had (has) been* in Beijing for five years. 他在北京待了五年。

She *wasn't* in when I called. 我打电话时她不在家。

b. 作不及物动词 (表示发生某事或存在某种情况)：

"How long ago *was* it?" "Oh, not many minutes." "这是多久以前的事？" "啊，就几分钟前的。"

The party will *be* in a week. 晚会一周后举行。

When is the wedding to *be*? 婚礼什么时候举行？

When a thing has to *be*, it had better *be* quickly. 凡事赶早不赶晚。

What will *be*, will *be*. (谚)该发生的事总要发生。

I'm sorry, sir, the meeting's already *been*. 对不起，先生，会已经开过了。

Could it *be* that they had no place to go? 是不是他们没地方可去？

3) be + 不定式结构：

这种结构可表示：

a. 打算做某事或计划好要做的事 (意思接近于 be going to)：

I *am (was) to play* Juliet. 我将扮演朱丽叶。

I *am to edit* a volume of Irish Fairy Tales. 我打算编一本爱尔兰童话。

The President *is to make* a statement tomorrow. 总统明天将发表声明。

The expedition *is (was) to start* in a week's time. 考察队将于一周后起程。

不定式可用完成形式，表示"本来打算"：

She *was to have got married* last month. 她本来准备上月结婚的。

I *was to have seen* him yesteday, but he didn't come.　昨天我本来是要见到他的，但他没来。

The mayor *was to have laid* the foundation stone but he was taken ill last night.　市长原本要来主持奠基典礼的，但昨晚病了。

b. 该做某事 (接近于 should，must，ought to，have to 等)：

Suppose he comes here, what *am I to tell* him?　假如他到这里来，我该对他讲什么？

You *are not to smoke* in the room.　你不得在这房间里抽烟。

You *are not to open* the box.　你不能打开这个箱子。

c. 能做某事 (接近于 can，may)：

How *am I to pay* such a debt?　这笔债我怎么还得起？

Not a sound *was to be heard*.　听不到一丁点声音。

We Chinese people *are not to be bullied*.　我们中国人是不好欺侮的。

d. 将来必然要发生的事：

The worst *is still to come*.　更糟糕的事还在后头。

They said goodbye, little knowing they *were* never *to meet* again.　他们互相告别，不知道彼此将再也不会见面了。

This I *was* only *to learn* later.　这一点我只是以后才知道。

11.1.3　have 的用法

1) have 作助动词，主要用来构成：

a. 完成时态和完成进行时态：

I'*ve seen* this film before.　我以前看过这部电影。

She'*s been* in Hong Kong for six months.　她在香港待了六个月。

They *had* already *told* me the news.　这消息他们已告诉我了。

She'*ll have arrived* in Shen Zhen by 6 o'clock.　六点时她将已到达深圳。

What *has* she *been doing* since?　此后她一直在干什么？

Have you *been waiting* long?　你等好久了吗？

I was afraid he *would have gone* to bed by then.　我担心那时他会已经上床睡觉了。

b. 完成形式：

He ought *to have arrived* by now.　现在他应当已经到了。

I'm pleased *to have made* your acquaintance.　认识了你我很高兴。

I regretted *having been* so rude to him.　我懊悔对他那样粗鲁无礼。

Don't be angry with me for *not having written*. 没给你写信请别生我的气。

Having lived there for ten years, she was reluctant to leave. 她在那里住了十年,因而不愿意离开。

Not having got an answer, he was rather worried. 由于没得到回音,他很着急。

2)have 作及物动词的用法:

have 是一个非常活跃的及物动词,可以:

a. 表示所有关系:

Bad news *has* wings. (谚)坏消息传得快。

Mr Green *had* living with him a nephew and a niece. 格林先生有一个侄儿和一个侄女和他住在一起。

The house *has* five rooms. 这屋子有五个房间。

I *have* an impression that he's been improving. 我有感觉他在改进。

常有较灵活的译法:

She *has* blue eyes. 她的眼睛是蓝颜色。

He *has* a good temper. 他脾气很好。

She *had* a happy childhood. 她童年很幸福。

If his car is not out, he'll let us *have* it. 如果他的车在家,他会借给我们的。

b. 和许多名词连用表示动作:

have a long walk 作长时间散步	have a chat (with) (和…)聊天
have a look at 瞧(某物)	have a drink of water 喝一杯水
have a wash 洗一洗	have a swim 游一会儿泳
have a rest 休息一会儿	have a read 看一会儿书
have a good lie 好好躺一会儿	have a quarrel (with) (和…)吵一架
have a win in a competition 比赛获胜	have a smoke 抽一支烟
	have an accident 出事
have a fight 打了一架	have a bath 洗个澡
have a dream 做了一个梦	have a love (of) 很喜欢(某物)
have respect (for) 很尊敬(某人)	have a wish (to) 愿意(做某事)
have a dislike (of) 不喜欢	have a good laugh 畅笑了一阵子
have a try 试一试	have a fear (of) 害怕(某物)
have a conversation (with) (和…)谈话	have a discussion 讨论
	have a success 很成功
have an X-ray 去透视	have a scene 争吵

c. 表示"吃"、"喝"、"患(病)"等:

They are *having fish* for supper. 他们晚饭吃鱼。

Then *have* some *coffee*. 那么就喝点咖啡。

Will you *have a cigarette*? 要不要抽根烟?

Everybody here *has the influenza*. 这里人人都患流感。

She *has the measles*. 她出麻疹了。

Do you often *have colds*? 你常常感冒吗?

Which *injection* did you *have*? 你打的什么针?

My sister has just *had a child*. 我姐姐刚生了孩子。

I never *had* any *education*. 我从未上过学。

3) 构成某些句型:

a. **have + 名(代)词 + (不带 to 的)不定式** —— 让某人做某事:

I'm going to *have her live* with me. 我准备让她和我一起住。

I'll be proud to *have you read* it. 我将自豪地让你读它。

I won't *have him cheat* me. 我不能让他欺骗我。

b. **have + 名(代)词 + 过去分词** —— 让(别人)做某事或遭遇某事:

She's *having her eyes tested*. 她在请人验光。

He's *having them repaired*. 他正请人修理它们。

Pa's *had his hands burned*. 爸的手给烫了。

The pilot *had his plane hijacked*. 飞行员的飞机遭到劫持。

c. **have + 名(代)词 + 现在分词** —— 让某人做某事,让某事发生:

He tried to *have her talking*, but no use. 他设法让她讲话,但没有用。

She soon *had us* all *laughing*. 她很快让我们都笑了起来。

We can't *have that sort of thing happening*. 我们不能允许这种事发生。

d. **have (got) to** 不得不:

I *had to* walk very fast to overtake you. 我得走很快才能赶上你。

One of them *will have to go*. 他们中间得去一个人。

These last two days I *have had to* take a rest. 最近这两天我不得不休息了一下。

We *may have to* cancel the plan. 我们可能不得不取消这项计划。

It'*ll have to* be done all over again. 这事将不得不重新做一遍。

I'*ve got to* be off now. 我现在得走了。

We'*ve got to* be careful about these things. 这些事我们得小心。

e. **have got (= have):**

She *hasn't got* a bank account. 她没有银行户头。

I've got a fellow coming to see me tomorrow. 明天有个人来看我。

I've got one or two things to see to. 我有一两件事要办理。

What's that got to do with you? 那和你有什么关系?

It was acute pneumonia that she had got. 她患的是急性肺炎。

11.1.4   do 的用法

1) do 作助动词的用法:

作为助动词, do 可以用来:

a. 构成疑问句和否定句:

Does he work here? 他在这里工作吗?

I didn't see him at the meeting. 开会时我没见到他。

He lives here, doesn't he? 他在这里住, 对吧?

I don't care what she thinks. 她怎么想我不在意。

Didn't she sing well? 她唱得真好!

b. 加在动词前表示强调:

I did see her at the party. 晚会上我的确见过她。

Do come with us. 务请和我们一块儿去。

I do hope you'll come to China again. 我真希望你将再次来中国。

Please! Do be quiet a moment! 求求你们! 请安静一会儿!

She does sing well! 她确实唱得好!

c. 用来表示刚提到过的动作, 以避免重复:

Tom talks too much. ——Yes, he does. 汤姆话太多。 ——是的。

He lives here but I don't. 他住在这里而我不是。

She doesn't drive but I do. 她不会开车, 但我会。

He didn't see you, did he? 他没看到你, 对吧?

Do you smoke? ——No, I don't. 你抽烟吗? ——不抽。

2) do 作及物动词的用法:

作及物动词时主要有下面用法:

a. 和一个名(代)词连用, 表示"做(某事)":

What are you doing? 你在干什么?

Has he done his homework? 他作业做完了吗?

I'm doing some research on the subject. 我在就这问题做些研究。

I have a number of things to do this morning. 今天早上我有很多事要做。

They want to do business with us. 他们想和我们做生意。

She *did* her lessons in the afternoon.　她下午做功课了。

可用于被动结构:

What's *to be done*?　该怎么办?

Easier said than *done*.　(谚)说易行难。

b. 和动名词连用:

He *does some writing* in his spare time.　他有空时写些东西。

She *did lots of acting* when she was at university.　她在大学时演过很多戏。

She is *doing the ironing (cooking)*.　她在烫衣服(做饭)。

I *did some reading* before I went to bed.　睡觉前我看了一会儿书。

Maria *did most of the talking*.　大部份时间都是玛丽亚在说话。

You should *do more thinking*.　你应作更多的思考。

We can *do some sightseeing* here.　在这里我们可以观光游览。

She's gone out to *do some shopping*.　她出去买东西了。

c. 和一些表示物件的名词连用，表示"梳"、"刷"等:

Can you *do* the rooms now?　你现在能打扫房间吗?

When is he coming to *do* the windows?　他什么时候来擦窗子?

Go and *do* your hair.　去梳梳头。

Have you *done* your teeth?　你刷牙了吗?

We *did* two concerts last week.　上星期我们听了两场音乐会。

He *did* 200 miles a day.　他一天开(车)两百英里。

We *did* the journey in six hours.　我们跑这一趟花了六小时。

You should have seen him *do* Hamlet.　你真该看看他扮演哈姆雷特。

3) do 作不及物动词的用法:

a. 表示工作、学习等方面的情况:

How do you *do*?　你好！

He's *doing* well at school.　他在学校学习良好。

He *did* poorly in the examination.　他考得很差。

She is *doing* nicely.　她过得很好。

The patient is *doing* well.　病人康复情况良好。

Everything in the garden is *doing* well.　花园里的花木长势都很好。

b. 表示"行"、"够了"、"合适"、"可以"等:

I've got some muslin here, will it *do*?　我有一些细棉纱,能用吗?

Will £5 *do*?　五英镑够吗?

This place would *do* for a gymnasium.　这地方可以作体育馆。

That jacket won't *do* for skiing.　这件夹克衫不适合滑雪。

This hotel won't *do*.　这家旅馆不行。

That piece of material would *do* to make a dress for you.　这块料子适合给你做件连衣裙。

―――――――――――

11.1.5　will 的用法

1）用于将来时态(各种人称后都可以用)：

I *will* give you a definite answer tomorrow.　明天我将给你个明确回答。

We *will* never again be separated.　我们再也不会被分开。

Will you be taking your leave in South Africa?　你准备在南非度假吗？

By this time next year she *will* have taken her university degree.　明年这时她将已获得大学学位。

It looks as if he *won't* be in time for the train.　看来他好像赶不上火车了。

2）用于疑问句表示请求：

Will you tell her that I'm Mrs Pater?　你可否告诉她我是佩特夫人？

Will you have a little soup?　你要不要喝点汤？

Bring me the papers, *will* you?　把报纸拿给我好吗？

Will you please sit down, everybody?　请大家坐好。

Won't you take off your overcoat?　你要不要把大衣脱掉？

3）用于各个人称，表示：

a. 愿意，肯：

I *will* have nothing to do with this matter.　我不愿和这事扯上关系。

I meant to reason with you, but you *won't* reason.　我是想和你讲道理,但你不听劝。

She *won't* so much as look at David.　她连看大卫一眼都不肯。

Go where you *will*.　你想去哪里就去哪里。

If you *will* allow me, I will see you home.　如你允许,我愿意送你回家。

b. 决心，承诺：

I *won't* have anything said against her.　我绝不让谁说她的坏话。

I *won't* give her a divorce.　我不会同意和她离婚。

I *won't* let her down in any way.　我绝不会做任何对不起她的事。

I *won't* do it any more, I promise you.　我答应你我再也不会这样做。

c. 习惯，倾向：

She *will* sit there for hours, waiting for her son to come home.　她常常在那里一坐几个小时等候儿子回家。

Some animals *will* not mate in captivity.　有些动物关起来就不交配。

These things *will* happen.　这样的事总是要发生的。

Boys *will* be boys.　男孩终究是男孩。

d. 命令，叮嘱：

You *will* report to the headquarters right today.　你今天就去总部报到。

You *will* not go out today: you'll stay in and work.　你今天不准出去，你
　得留在家里干活。

You *will* stay here till you are relieved.　放你走你才能走。

No one *will* leave the examination room before 12 o'clock.　十二点前谁也
　不得离开考场。

e. 表示猜测：

The man with the umbrella *will* be the Prime Minister.　打雨伞的人想必是
　首相。

I knew his father, Professor Pile — you'*ll* have heard of him.　我认识他父
　亲派尔教授，想必你听说过他的。

That *will* be the postman at the door.　门口想必是邮差。

11.1.6　would 的用法

1) 作助动词的用法：

a. 用来构成过去将来时态(各人称后均可以用)：

He knew he *would* be late.　他知道他要迟到了。

I said I'*d* be glad to see him.　我说我会很高兴见到他。

I thought she *would* be looking after you.　我想她会照顾你的。

I guessed he'*d* have told you everything.　我猜他会把一切都告诉你了。

From her trip to Paris, she *would* return on Monday morning.　巴黎之行后
　她会于星期一早上回来。

He asked if I *would* go in.　他问我是否要进去。

b. 用来婉转地提出请求、问题、看法等：

Would you kindly send me his address?　劳驾可否把他的地址寄给我？

Would you help us, please?　劳驾可否帮帮我们？

Let's fix a day. *Would* Saturday night suit you?　咱们来定个日子，星期六
　晚上合适吗？

How do you think she *would* feel?　你想她会有什么感受？

I'm sure he *wouldn't* mind your going.　我肯定他不会介意你去。

I think that *would* be the most convenient time for us. 我想这对我们是最合适的时间。

I'*d* go there with you. 我愿意和你一道去。

2) 用于虚拟语气:

a. 用于虚拟条件句:

If we were men, we *would be doing* something now. 如果我们是男人,我们现在会采取一些行动。

He *would be* delighted if you went to see him. 你要是去看他,他会很高兴的。

I *would have done* more, if I'd had the time. 如果我有时间我就会做得更多些。

If I had seen the advertisement, I *would have applied* for the job. 如果我看到了广告,我早就申请这份工作了。

They *would* never *have met* if she hadn't gone to Emma's party. 要是她没去参加爱玛的晚会,他们就决不会相遇的。

b. 用于含蓄条件句:

She'*d be* stupid not to accept. 她不接受是愚蠢的。

Hurry up! It *would be* a pity to miss the beginning of the play. 赶快,要是看不到戏的开头就太遗憾了。

In the old days she *would have argued*. 要是在过去,她早就争论上了。

I *would have taken* a firm stand. (如果是我)我会采取坚定的立场。

Legalizing this *drug would have* disastrous consequences. 使这种毒品(售卖)合法化会产生灾难性的后果。

c. 用于其他情况:

I wish the sun *would come out*. 但愿太阳会出来。

She burned the letters so that her husband *would* never *read* them. 她把信烧掉,这样她丈夫就永远不会看见了。

He wishes (that) she *would leave* him. 他希望她会离开他。

She worried for fear that her child *would be hurt*. 她很担心唯恐孩子受到伤害。

3) (用于过去情况) 表示"愿意"、"肯"、"会"等(也可说是 will 的过去形式):

She just *wouldn't do* what I asked her. 她就是不肯答应我的要求。

She *would not go* to the dentist even though she was in considerable pain. 尽管牙疼得厉害,她仍不愿意去看牙医。

He *would* never *enter* this hateful house again. 他再也不想走进这间讨厌
　　的房子了。

They had to do that whether they *would* or not. 不管愿不愿意,他们都得
　　这样做。

She *would* never *permit* anything of that sort. 她绝不会允许出这种事。

可用在虚拟条件句的从句中:

I should be obliged if you *wouldn't George* me. 如果你能不叫我乔治我会
　　很感激。

I would be glad if you *would give* me an account of it. 如果你愿意谈谈这
　　事的经过,我会很高兴。

4) 过去的习惯性动作或倾向:

When he was young he *would* often *walk* in these woods. 他年轻时常常在
　　这些树林里散步。

When my parents were away, my grandmother *would look after* me. 我父
　　母不在家时,总是我奶奶照顾我。

He'*d* always *be* the first to offer to help. 他总是第一个主动帮忙的人。

Now and then a blackbird *would call*. 画眉不时会鸣叫两声。

The wound *would not heal*. 伤口老不愈合。

My car *wouldn't start* this morning. 我的车今天早上开不起来了。

5) 表示猜测:

I'*d say* she's about 40. 我猜她有四十岁左右。

I *would imagine* the journey will take about an hour. 我猜测这段路程可
　　能需要一个钟头。

The person you mentioned *would be* her father. 你提到的那个人想必是
　　她父亲。

I thought you *would have come back*. 我想你可能已回来了。

6) 用在一些结构中:

Where *would* you *like* to sit? 你想坐在哪儿?

I'*d be* only too glad to help. 我很高兴帮忙。

I'*d hate* to leave you. 我真不愿意离开你们。

I'*d love* a coffee. 我想喝一杯咖啡。

I'*d prefer* to go by plane. 我愿坐飞机去。

I'*d rather* have the blue one. 我愿意要蓝的。

I'*d sooner* go home. 我宁愿回家去。

11.1.7 shall 的用法

1) 作助动词的用法:

a. 主要用于第一人称,构成疑问句以征求对方意见:

What time *shall* I come? 我什么时候来?

Where *shall* we go for our holiday? 我们到哪里去度假?

Let's look at it again, *shall* we? 我们再瞧瞧,好吗?

Shall I turn on the light? 要不要我把灯打开?

b. 在英国也可用于肯定句和否定句中(现在用 will 的人可能更多一些),构成将来时态:

I *shall* be very happy to see him again. 我会很高兴再次见到他。

We *shan't* be arriving until ten o'clock. 我们要到十点钟才到。

I *shall* have been working here for ten years by the end of this year. 到今年年底我在这里就已工作十年了。

I *shall* often be coming to Pisa. 我会常到比萨来的。

We *shall* have finished with this tomorrow. 明天这事就会干完了。

2) 在英国可用在比较文气的语言中,表示"规定"、"许诺"、"命令"等:

Candidates *shall* remain in their seats until all the papers have been collected. 收卷前考生须留在各自的座位上。(规定)

In the rules, it says that a player *shall* be sent off for using bad language. 有明确规定球员出言不逊应罚出场。(规定)

If you really want a pony, you *shall* have one. 如果你确实想要小马,我就给你一匹。

I *shall* write to you at the end of the month. 月底我会给你写信。(许诺)

She *shall* not stay under my roof. 她不得留在我家中。(命令)

11.1.8 should 的用法

1) 作助动词的用法:

在英国 should 可用于第一人称,构成过去将来时态(在口语中用 would 更多一些):

I *should (would)* be most grateful if you could do it for me. 如果你能帮我做这事我会非常感激。

I said I *should* be glad to help. 我说我将乐于帮忙。

I never thought I *should (would)* see you again. 我以为我再见不到你了。

We hoped we *should* have confidence in each other again.　我们希望我们重新彼此信任。

2）作情态动词 —— 表示"应该(当)"(接近于 ought to)：

She considered how she *should* answer.　她考虑应当怎样作答。

The police *should* do something about it.　警方对此应想些办法。

You *should* try that new restaurant.　你该去试试那家新餐馆。

He really *shouldn't* work so hard.　他的确不应当工作这样劳累。

Should I try again?　我是不是该再试一次？

You *shouldn't* drink and drive.　你不应当酒后开车。

后面的不定式可用完成等形式：

We *should* have checked the time before we left.　我们本应先核对一下时间再动身的。

You *shouldn't* have trusted him so readily.　你不应当这样轻易信赖他。

You *shouldn't* be reading a novel. You *should* be reading a textbook.　此刻你不应当在看小说，而应当在看课本。

You *should* have been helping Tom.　你应当在帮助汤姆。

3）用在某些句子中使口气显得更婉转(仅用于第一人称)：

I *should like* to phone my lawyer.　我想给我律师打个电话。

We *should be* grateful for your help.　我们将很感谢你的帮助。

There are a lot of things I *should have liked* to ask you.　有好多事我本想问你的。

I *should have preferred* him to do it in a different way.　我倒是愿意他以别种方式来做此事。

I *should be* glad to talk to you.　我将高兴和你谈谈。

4）用在某些宾语从句中构成谓语(美国常用动词原形)：

She advised that we *should keep* the gate locked.　她劝我们把大门锁上。

They agreed the roof *should be repaired*.　他们同意房顶要维修一下。

He arranged that I *should go* abroad.　他安排我出国。

They asked that relief work *should be given* priority.　他们要求优先处理救济事务。

He commanded that the army *should advance*.　他命令部队向前推进。

She determined that he *should study* music.　她决定他学音乐。

He ordered that the goods *should be sent* by air.　他命令将货物空运。

They stipulated that the best materials *should be used*.　他们规定要使用最好的材料。

The chairman proposed that they *should stop* the meeting. 主席提议休会。

I suggested that she *should wear* a jacket. 我建议她穿一件夹克。

5) 用在某些主语从句中构成谓语 (美国常用动词原形):

It is advisable that everyone *should have* a map. 每人都带一张地图是明智的。

It is better that he *should hear* from you. 他从你这儿知道更好一些。

It is essential that he *should be prepared* for this. 让他对此有准备至关重要。

It is only right that she *should have* a share. 她分得一份是对的。

It is his suggestion that I *should come round* to you. 我来找你是他的建议。

It was necessary that he *should work* hard. 他用功是必要的。

6) 有时 should 可用在某些从句甚至主句中，带有感情色彩 (可译为"竟然"等):

It's queer that you *should be* so different from Jane. 你和简竟然这样不同真是奇怪。

It does seem silly that I *should have to* learn this. 我竟然不得不学这个确实显得很傻。

It strikes me as odd that he *should ask* you about it. 我感到奇怪他竟向你问及此事。

I find it quite astonishing that he *should be* so rude to you. 我感到惊讶他对你竟然如此粗鲁无礼。

I can't think why she *should have done* such a thing. 我不明白她为什么竟然做出这样的事。

I don't know why you *should think* I did it. 我不明白你怎么竟然认为是我干的。

Why *should* he *have asked* you such a question? 他怎么竟然会问你这样的问题？

How *should* I *know*? 我怎么会知道？

7) 用在虚拟条件句中:

a. (在英国) 用在主句中的第一人称后 (这时用 would 的人较多):

If I was asked to work on Sunday I *should resign*. 如果要我星期六工作我就辞职。

I *should have helped* her if she had asked me. 要是她提出来，我本来会帮她的。

I *should not have laughed* if I had thought you were serious. 如果我认为

你是认真的，我就不会笑了。

We *shouldn't have succeeded* without your help.　要不是你帮忙，我们本不会成功。

b. 用在条件从句中 (主句谓语可用虚拟语气、祈使语气或陈述语气):

I should be most happy to go with you if I *should not be* in the way.　如果不妨碍什么，我会很高兴和你们一道去。

I could persuade her to make room for you *should* it *be* necessary.　如果有必要，我可以说服她给你腾地方。

If the pain *should return*, take another of these pills.　万一还疼，就再吃一片这个药。

If you *should be passing*, do come and see us.　万一你从这儿过，务请来看看我们。

Should I *be* free tomorrow, I will come.　如果明天有空我就来。

I don't think it will happen, but if it *should*, what shall we do?　我想这事不会发生，但万一发生，我们怎么办?

8) 用在某些由 in case, so that, lest 等引导的状语从句中:

Here is a shilling in case you *should need* it.　给你一先令以备需要。

I'll keep a seat for you in case you *should change* your mind.　我给你留个座位以备你改变主意。

She hid it under the pillow so that he *should not see* it.　她把它藏在枕头下面以防他看到。

He wore a mask so that no one *should recognize* him.　他戴了一个面罩以免有人认出他。

He was terrified lest he *should slip* on the icy rocks.　他很害怕，唯恐在结冰的岩石上滑倒。

She began to be worried lest he *should have met* with some accident.　她开始着急，担心他会出事。

9) 用来表示猜测:

It's 4:30. They *should be* in New York by now.　现在是四点半，他们应该到达纽约了。

He *should have arrived* by now.　他现在想必已经到了。

I *should imagine* it will take about three hours.　我推测这大约需要三个小时。

I *should say* she's over forty.　我猜她有四十多岁了。

11.2　情态动词

11.2.1　can 的用法

can 表示现在或将来的情况，主要表示：

1) 能力 (即能做某事)：

Can you *ride* a bicycle?　你能骑自行车吗？

She *can run* very fast.　她能跑得很快。

Who *can answer* this question?　谁能回答这个问题？

I *can't pay* you today. *Can* you *wait* till tomorrow?　我今天不能给你钱，你能等到明天吗？

I *can't promise* anything, but I'll do what I *can*.　我不能许诺什么，但我将尽力而为。

be able to 可以表示同样意思，并还可明确表示未来时间，甚至用于完成时态：

Our baby *will be able to walk* in a few weeks.　我们的宝宝几周后就能走路了。

Since his accident he *hasn't been able to walk* properly.　出事之后他一直未能正常走路。

2) 可能性 (可以、可能做某事)：

Can you *help* me with the box?　你能帮我抬这箱子吗？

We *can eat* in a restaurant.　我们可以在餐馆吃饭。

I *can call* you tomorrow.　我可以明天给你打电话。

I'm afraid I *can't go* with you.　恐怕我没法和你一道去。

3) 有时会 (不经常如此)：

You *can be* very annoying.　有时你会让人生气。

He *can be* very tactless sometimes.　他有时讲话很笨拙。

Scotland *can be* very cold.　苏格兰有时很冷。

It *can be* quite windy on the hills.　山上有时风很大。

Wasp stings *can be* very painful.　黄蜂蜇人有时很疼。

4) (用于否定句及疑问句) 可能：

That *can't be* Mary — she's in hospital.　那不可能是玛丽，她在住院。

Surely you *can't be* hungry. You've only just had lunch.　你肯定不会饿的，你刚刚吃过午饭。

There's someone outside — who *can* it *be*?　外边有人，这能是谁呢？

Can he still *be* alive after all these years?　过了这么多年他还活着吗?

后面有时跟不定式的完成形式或进行式:

He *can't have taken* it upstairs.　他不可能把它拿上楼了。

She *can't be telling* the truth.　她讲的不可能是真话。

What *can* she *be doing* at this time?　此时她会在干什么呢?

5) 表示"允许(做某事)"(和 may 的意思差不多, 在日常口语中 can 用得更多):

You *can* (may) *park* here.　你可以把车停在这里。

You *can* (may) *take* the book home.　你可以把这书带回家。

They *can phone* the police.　他们可以给警察打电话。

This sort of thing *can't go on*!　这种事情不能继续下去了。

You *can't smoke* here.　你不能在这里抽烟。

11.2.2　could 的用法

could 主要有下面用法:

1) 作为 can 的过去式, 表示过去情况:

a. 表示能力:

When I was young I *could climb* any tree in the forest.　小时候森林里的树我都能爬上去。

I *could drive* a car before I left school.　我中学毕业前就会开车。

He read the message but *couldn't understand* it.　他看了电报但没看懂。

I *could see* her through the window.　从窗口我可以看见她。

She *couldn't answer* the teacher's question.　她回答不上老师的问题。

这时也可用 was (were) able to, 甚至用过去完成形式:

I *was able to see* her through the window.　从窗口我可以看见她。

He said he had lost his passport and *hadn't been able to leave* the country.　他说他的护照丢了, 不能离境。

b. 表示可能性:

It was so dark we *could see* nothing.　天那样黑, 我们什么也看不见。

He said he *couldn't come*.　他说他不能来。

I thought I *could smell* something burning.　我想我可以闻到糊味。

He *could be* pretty naughty when he was a child.　他小时候有时很淘气。

2）用来代替 can，说明现在情况：

a. 婉转地提出请求、想法、建议等：

Could (Can) you send me an application form?　你可否寄我一张申请表？

Could you *show* me the way?　你可否告诉我怎样去？

Couldn't you *come* a little earlier?　你不能稍微早一点来？

I *could get* you a copy.　我可以帮你找一份。

I *could do* it now if you like.　如果你愿意我现在就可以做。

You *could be* right, I suppose.　我想你可能是对的。

We *could write* a letter to the director.　我们可以给主管写一封信。

You *could have* a nursery here.　你可以在这里办一个托儿所。

b. 用于疑问及否定句表示惊异、不相信等：

Could this *be* true?　这能是真的吗？

How *could* you *be* so careless?　你怎么能这样粗心大意？

后面的不定式常可用完成形式或进行式：

I *couldn't have left* it on the bus.　我不可能把它丢在公共汽车上。

They *couldn't have left* so soon.　他们不可能这么早就走了。

Could he still *be working* at this late hour?　这么晚了他还在工作吗？

Could you *have been waiting* so long?　你竟然等了这么久吗？

3）用于虚拟条件句：

You *could get* into university if you applied.　如申请的话，你能进大学。

If you tried you *could do* that work.　如果你试试你可以干这工作。

I *could have earned* something if I had meant to.　如果我真有心这样做，我是可以挣些钱的。

Even if he had been there, he *couldn't have helped* you.　即使他在那里，他也帮不了你的忙。

Why didn't you apply for the job? You *could have got* it.　你为什么没申请这份工作？你是可以得到它的。

4）could + 不定式的完成形式，可用来谈过去情况：

a. 表示"那时(不)可能"：

The money has disappeared! Who *could have taken* it?　钱不见了，是谁拿了呢？

Tom *could have taken* it; he was here alone yesterday.　可能是汤姆拿了，昨天他一人在此。

Don't worry— they *could have* just *forgotten* to phone.　别着急，可能他们只是忘了打电话。

She *could not have been* more than six then. 那时她不可能超过六岁。

b. 表示"本来可以"或"差点就":

He *could have sent* a message. 他本来可以捎个口信来的。

I *could have lent* you the money. Why didn't you ask me? 我本来可以借这笔钱给你的，你怎么没向我借？

The accident *could have been prevented*. 这事故本来是可以防止的。

I *could have died* laughing. 我差点笑死了。

c. 提出婉转的批评:

You *could have been* more considerate. 你本可考虑得更周到些。

You *could have started* a little earlier. 你本可稍早一点动身的。

They *could have let* me know they were going to be late. 他们本可提早通知我他们将要晚点。

You *could have told* me beforehand. 你本可事先告诉我的。

11.2.3   may 的用法

may 主要有下面几种用法:

1) 用来提出问题，问可不可以:

 May I *use* your phone? 我能用一下你的电话吗？

May I *come in*? 我可以进来吗？

"*May* I *leave* this with you?" "Yes, you may." "我可以把东西放你这儿吗？" "可以。"

I *may leave* now, *mayn't* I? 我现在可以走了，对吧？

May I *come* round in the afternoon? ——Yes, please do. 我下午来好吗？ ——行，好的。

2) 用于陈述句，表示"可以"或"不可以":

You *may* only *borrow* books for two weeks. 书你只能借两个星期。

You *may come* if you wish. 如果你愿意你可以来。

Passengers *may cross* by the footbridge. 行人过街可走天桥。

You *may not take* photographs in the museum. 博物馆内不得拍照。

Dogs *may not be taken* into these carriages. 不得携狗进入这些车厢。

3) 表示"可能":

Anna *may know* Tom's address. 安娜可能知道汤姆的地址。

Jim *may emigrate*. 吉姆可能要移居国外。

He *may have gone* abroad. 他可能出国了。

They *may be waiting* at the station. 他们可能正等在车站。

I *may be going* to Europe next year. 我明年或许去欧洲。

4) 用在某些状语从句中:

Speak clearly so that they *may understand* you. 讲清楚些以便他们能听明白。

However frightened you *may be* yourself, you must remain calm. 不管你自己多么害怕,你必须保持镇静。

However much she *may desire* it, she can't express her sympathetic feelings. 她无法表达她的同情心,不管她多么想这样做。

Try as he may, he will not pass the examination. 不管多努力,他都无法通过考试。

Shut the window for fear (that) it *may rain*. 把窗子关上,以防下雨。

He's decided to get a college education, *come what may*. 不管发生什么情况,他都决定要上大学。

5) 表示祝愿:

May you *be* happy! 祝你幸福!

May God *be* with you. 愿上帝与你同在。

Long *may* she *live* to enjoy her good fortune! 祝她长寿好运!

6) 用于某些成语中:

a. may as well 不妨:

You *may as well bring* me a chocolate too. 你不妨也给我带一块巧克力来。

If that's the case, I *may as well try*. 如果情况是这样,我不妨一试。

b. may...but 或许…但是:

They *may* be good reports, *but* they seem to lack facts. 这些报告或许写得不错,但似乎缺乏事实。

Oxford *may* have changed a lot in recent years, *but* it's still a beautiful city. 牛津近年来可能改变很多,但它仍是一座美丽的城市。

c. may well... 很可能…:

His appearance has changed so much that you *may well* not recognize him. 他的外貌变了很多,你可能都认不出他了。

The team *may well* have won the football match, but I don't know because I wasn't there. 那支球队很可能赢得了足球赛,但我不知道,因为我没去。

11.2.4 might 的用法

might 主要有下面这些用法:

1) 用作 may 的过去式:

a. 表示"可以":

I asked if I *might go* home half an hour earlier today. 我问我是否可以提早半小时回家。

He asked if he *might use* the phone. 他问是否可以用一下电话。

He suggested one or two books which they *might buy*. 他推荐了一两本他们可以买的书。

I thought you *might stay* with us. 我想你可以住我们这儿。

b. 表示"可能"(或许会):

He said he *might be* late. 他说他可能晚到。

She told me that she *might go* to Hawaii this winter. 她告诉我她今年冬天可能去夏威夷。

I guessed he *might come* tomorrow. 我猜他可能明天来。

c. 用在某些状语从句中:

I did this so that I *might have* time to prepare my manuscript. 我这样做以便我有时间把稿子准备好。

She was not allowed to go to bed, lest she *might be needed*. 没让她去睡觉以防不时之需。

I lent him ￡50 in order that he *might go* for a holiday. 我借给他五十英镑,以便他能去度假。

Marina made up her mind that, *come what might*, she would stay there. 玛丽娜下了决心,不管发生什么情况,她都留在那里。

Try as she might, she could not persuade her friends to go. 不管她怎样想办法,都不能说动她的朋友们去。

2) 用来代替 may,谈现在的情况,口气比 may 更婉转些:

a. 表示"可以"(用 may 时更多一些):

Might (May) I have a little brandy? 可否给我一点白兰地?

In that case you *might bring* your father to live with us. 如果那样你可以把你父亲接来和我们一道住。

You *might* just *call at* the chemist on the way home. 在回家路上你可以到药房去一下。

Might I *use* your phone (*say* something)? 我能用一下你的电话吗(我能说几句话吗)?

b. 表示"可能"、"或许":

He *might tell* his wife.　他可能会告诉他妻子。

She *might not believe* your story.　她可能不会相信你的说法。

He *might have gone* home.　他或许回家了。

Eva *might not have seen* him yesterday.　昨天夏娃可能没见到他。

She *might* still *be waiting* there.　她可能还在那里等。

We *might be going* to Spain on holiday this year.　今年我们或许会去西班牙度假。

She *might have been taken ill* quite suddenly.　她或许是突然生病了。

3) 用于虚拟条件句:

If I had known the film was about Wales, I *might have gone* to see it.　要是我知道这部影片是关于威尔士的，我可能就去看了。

The pills *might have helped* him, if he'd taken them regularly.　如果这些药片他定时吃，可能对他是有效的。

If you invited him, he *might come*.　如果你邀请他，他可能会来。

If you didn't mind, we *might go* there.　如果你不介意，我们可能去那里。

It was really very dangerous. You *might have injured* him.　真的是很悬，你会让他受伤的。

4) 表示轻微的埋怨或批评:

They *might* at least *have phoned* if they're not coming.　要是他们不来了，至少可以打个电话来嘛。

You *might tell* me if you're going to be late.　如果你要晚到，你可以告诉我一声。

Honestly, you *might have told* me!　说真的，你本可告诉我一声的。

5) 用于 **might as well** (意思和 may as well 差不多)，表示"不妨…":

We *might* (may) *as well* go together.　我们不妨一块儿去。

You *might as well* phone the customer service department about it.　你不妨给客户服务部打个电话谈谈这事。

Shall we walk?　——We *might as well*.　咱们步行去吗？　——不妨走走吧。

11.2.5　must 的用法

must 主要有下面用法:

1) 表示"必须"、"一定要"、"得…"(多指现在或将来情况):

You *must cut down* on smoking.　你必须少抽些烟。

Passengers *must cross* the line by the footbridge. 旅客必须由天桥穿越铁路。

I *must remember* to go to the bank today. 我今天一定要记住去银行。

"*Must* we *finish* the exercise today?" "Yes, you must. (No, you don't have to.)" "我们今天必须做完这项练习吗?" "是的, 必须做完 (不, 不必做完)。"

I'm afraid I *must be going*. 我看我得走了。

The work *must be finished* by the end of the week. 这工作周末必须完成。

△ 否定形式表示"不得"、"一定不要":

You *mustn't take* photographs in here. It's forbidden. 此处不得拍照, 这是禁止的。

Cars *must not park* in front of the entrance. 大门前不得停车。

We *mustn't be* late, must we? 我们不得迟到, 对吧?

You *mustn't drive* without a license. 你不得无照驾车。

△ 表示过去情况用 had to 更清楚一些, 虽然 must 也可以表示过去情况:

I *had to go* to see the dentist. 我得去看牙医。

When *did* you *have to leave*? 你什么时候得动身?

She asked him if she *must (had to) work* overtime. 她问他她是否一定要加班。

2) 表示推想, 可译作"一定"、"准是"等:

You *must be* hungry. Have something to eat. 你一定饿了, 吃点东西吧。

They *must be* twins. 他们一定是双胞胎。

The police are stopping all cars. They *must be looking for* the escaped prisoner. 警察让所有的车都停下来, 他们准是在搜寻逃犯。

There's a lot of noise from next door. They *must be having* a party. 隔壁那屋很嘈杂, 他们准是在开晚会。

I can't find my cheque book. I *must have left* it at home. 我找不到我的支票本, 准是留在家里了。

We *must have read* the same report. 我们一定是看了同一份报告。

You *must have been thinking of* something. 你准是在想什么心事。

3) 表示"应当(做某事)" (和 should, ought 的意思差不多):

You really *must see* that film. It's wonderful. 你真应该去看这部电影, 非常精彩。

You *must see* what the authorities have to say. 你应当去了解一下当局怎么说。

We *must think of* this matter very seriously. 我们应当认认真真地考虑此事。

You *must recognize* that we can't allow such behaviour. 你应当明白我们不容许这种行为。

11.2.6 ought 的用法

ought 总是和 to 一道用，表示：

1) 应该，应当(意思接近于 should)：

I *ought to write* to him today. 我今天应当给他写信。

You *ought to read* this book. It's marvellous! 这本书你应当看看，真是好极了。

What *ought* I *to say* to him? 我该对他说什么呢？

You *ought to visit* your parents more often. 你应当更多地探望你的父母。

You *oughtn't to make* private phone calls in work time. 在工作时间你不应该打私人电话。

I knew I *ought to write* to her. 我知道我应当给她写信。

Ought I *to write* to say thank you? 我是不是该写信去致谢？

△ 后面的不定式可用完成、进行或被动形式：

They *ought to have stopped* at the traffic lights. 在红绿灯前他们本应停车。

You *ought to have come* to the meeting. 你是应该来开会的。

We *ought to be leaving* now. 我们现在该走了。

He *oughtn't to have been driving* so fast. 他是不应当把车开这么快的。

He *ought to be isolated*. 他应当被隔离。

Something *ought to be done* about it. 对此应当想些办法。

2) 表示揣测：

She *ought to pass* her test. 她应当能通过测试。

He *ought to be there (to have arrived)* by now. 他现在应该已经到了。

The water *ought to have boiled* by now. 现在水应该开了。

We *ought to be hearing* from Wendy soon. 我们不久就应可以收到温迪的信。

11.3 一些半情态动词的用法

11.3.1 need 的用法

1) 作情态动词的用法:

a. 用于否定结构中,表示"不必":

You *needn't make* two copies. One will do. 你不必写两份,一份就行。

They *needn't send* me a receipt. 他们不必寄我收条。

You *needn't come* to the meeting if you're too busy. 如果你太忙就不必来开会了。

We *needn't have* packed our thick clothes. The weather was really warm. 我们本来不需要带厚衣服的。天气确实很暖和。

She *needn't have come* in person — a letter would have been enough. 她其实不必亲自来的,写封信就够了。

She *need not have been punished* so severely. 她本来不必受这么严厉的惩罚。

△ 可用在宾语从句中,即使主语动词是过去式,仍可用 need:

He said (says) I *needn't pay* till the 31st. 他说我到 31 日才需要付款。

They said he *needn't* send a deposit. 他们说他无需寄定金来。

b. 用在带有否定意思的句子中:

I *need hardly tell* you that the job is dangerous. 我用不着告诉你这工作是危险的。

I *scarcely need say* how much I enjoyed the holiday. 我简直不用说我假期过得多愉快。

Nobody *need be* afraid of catching the disease. 谁都不必害怕染上这种疾病。

I *don't believe* you *need* worry. 我认为你不必忧虑。

I *don't think* you *need* take it too seriously. 我想你对此不必太较真。

c. 可构成疑问句:

Need I *tell* Tom? 我需要告诉汤姆吗?

Need he *do* it at once? 他有必要马上这样做吗?

Need we *come* tomorrow? —— No, you needn't (Yes, you must). 我们要来吗? ——不必来(你们得来)。

Why *need* you *go* today? 你为什么今天就得走?

Need you *have paid* so much?　你需要支付那么多钱吗?

也可用在表示疑问的从句中:

I *asked* him whether he *need* go.　我问他是否必须得去。

I *wonder* if I *need* bring my mosquito-net.　不知我是否需要带上蚊帐。

I *do not see* why we *need* discuss it further.　我看不出我们还有什么谈下
　去的必要。

〔注〕在少数肯定句中,也有用 need 作情态动词的,例如:

I'll help you any time, you *only need ask*.　我随时可以帮你,你只需
　说一声。

If she wants anything, she *need only ask*.　如果想要什么,她只需说
　一声就行。

Here you *need give* way to her.　在这一点上你需要向她让步。

---

2) 作及物动词的用法:

作为及物动词, need 表示"需要",后面可以跟:

a. 名词或代词:

All living things *need* water.　一切生物都需要水。

I *need* a new film for my camera.　我需要一个新(照相)胶卷。

Do you *need* any help?　你需要什么帮助吗?

What we *need* is some proof.　我们需要的是证明。

Don't go — I may *need* you.　别走了,我可能会需要你。

b. 不定式:

I *need* to ask some advice.　我需要求教。

Do we *need* to buy tickets in advance?　我们需要预先购票吗?

I *need* to get some sleep.　我需要睡一会儿。

All you *need* to do is (to) fill in this form.　你只需要填一下这张表。

The instruments *needed* to be sterilized.　这些器械需要消毒。

c. 动名词:

His hair *needed* cutting.　他的头发该理了。

This jumper *needs* washing (to be washed).　这件套衫需要洗了。

The garden doesn't *need* watering — it rained last night.　花园无需浇水,
　昨晚下雨了。

d. 复合宾语:

He *needed* his eyes tested.　他需要请人验光。

I *need* my coat mended. 我的上衣需要补一补。

I *need* you over to help me with the children. 我需要你过来帮我照料孩子。

We need you to work for us. 我们需要你帮我们工作。

11.3.2 dare 的用法

1) 作情态动词的用法：

作情态动词时，dare 表示"敢…"，这时没有人称形式，但有过去式 dared，主要用于：

a. 否定句（有时借助助动词，这时不定式可带 to 也可不带 to）：

I *daren't ask* her to marry me. 我不敢求她嫁给我。

The government *dared not increase* taxes again this year. 今年政府不敢再加税了。

They *dared not move*. 他们不敢动。

She *dare not say* what she thinks. 她不敢说出她的想法。

He *doesn't dare (to) say* anything. 他什么都不敢说。

They were so frightened that they *didn't dare go* into the room. 他们怕得不敢进屋。

They *didn't dare (to) disobey*. 他们不敢不服从。

△ 也可用在带有否定意思的句子中：

I *daren't have done* it yesterday, but I think I dare now. 昨天我没敢这样做，但我想今天我敢。

No one dared speak of it. 没人敢谈及此事。

He *never dared stay* long. 他从不敢多待。

We *hardly dared (to) breathe* as somebody walked past the door. 有人从门口过时，我们几乎都不敢喘气了。

I *scarcely dare think of* it. 这事我简直不敢想。

b. 疑问句及条件从句（有时也可借助助动词）：

Dare you *interrupt* him? 你敢打断他的话吗？

How *dare* you *speak* to me like that! 你怎么敢对我这样讲话！

How *dare* he *take* my bicycle without even asking! 他怎么敢不问一声就把我的自行车拿走！

I wonder if she *dared come* home. 不知道她敢不敢回家。

Do you *dare tell* him? 你敢告诉他吗？

If you *dare speak* to me like that again, you will be sorry.　要是你再敢这样对我说话，你就会后悔的。

Jump if you *dare*!　你要是敢就跳！

c. 用于 I dare say，don't you dare 引导的句子中：

I dare say you're right.　我认为你是对的。

I dare say you are British.　我看你是英国人。

You're tired, *I dare say*.　我想你是累了。

Don't you dare tell my parents about this!　你敢告诉我父母这件事！

Don't you dare touch that vase.　不准碰那花瓶。

"I'm going to tell your father about the drugs."　"*Don't you dare!*"　"我要把毒品的事告诉你爸。"　"你敢！"

2) 作及物动词的用法：

作及物动词时可以表示：

a. 敢(做某事) (可用于多类句子)：

He *dared* to walk the tightrope without a net.　他敢不用安全网来踩钢丝。

He *dares* to accuse me of dishonesty.　他竟敢说我不老实。

I did not *dare* to complain.　我不敢抱怨。

I sat at the back, never *daring* to speak.　我坐在后面，从不敢说话。

Do you *dare* to suggest that I'm capable of such an act?　你敢说我能做出这样的事？

b. 敢于面对 (尝试)：

He will *dare* any danger.　他敢于面对任何危险。

He *dared* the anger of her family.　他敢于面对家人的愤怒。

The *actress* dared a new way of playing that famous character.　这位女演员敢尝试以新的方式扮演那个名人。

c. 向…挑战，要某人做一件危险的事：

Can you jump off the wall? Go on, I *dare* you!　你能从墙上跳下来吗？来，我要你跳！

Somebody *dared* me to jump off the bridge into the river.　有人问我敢不敢从桥上跳到河里去。

I *dared* them to debate with me about it.　我问他们敢不敢和我辩论这个问题。

11.3.3　be able to 的用法

1） be able to 可以跟一动词，意思和 can 差不多，有时两者可以换用：

I'm not able to (can't) answer your question.　我回答不了你的问题。

Are you *able to* (Can you) type?　你会打字吗?

When he was young he *was able to* (could) climb any tree.　小时候他什么树都爬得上去。

He *wasn't able to* (couldn't) understand that sentence.　他不懂那句话。

但 be able to 可用于更多时态，有时不能用 can 代替：

I *shan't be able to* come to your wedding.　我将不能来参加你的婚礼。

Since his accident he *hasn't been able to* leave the house.　他出事以来一直不能出门。

She said she had lost her passport and *hadn't been able to* leave the country.　她说她护照丢了，一直无法出境。

She wasn't sure whether she *would be able to* get back that week.　她不能肯定那个星期能否赶回来。

2） be able to 还可和某些情态动词或系动词连用：

I *ought to be able to* get in touch with him.　我应当可以和他取得联系。

He *might be able to* find a good hotel.　他或许能找到一家好旅馆。

She *should be able to* offer you some good advice.　她应当可以给你出点好主意。

He *seemed able to* put complicated thought in simple words.　他似乎能把复杂的思想用简单的话语说出来。

3） 还可用于非谓语动词中：

I should like *to be able to* read the book in the original.　我希望能阅读这本书的原文。

He much regretted not *being able to* come to your wedding.　他很遗憾没能来参加你们的婚礼。

She grasped my hand, not *being able to* say anything.　她抓住我的手,什么也说不出来。

11.3.4　have to 的用法

1） have to 的意思接近 must，但 must 强调说话人的意愿：

We must remember this.　我们必须记住这一点。

You must take good care of her. 你要好好照顾她。

而 have to 表示客观上的必要性，常可译为"(不)得(不)"，否定形式表示"不必"：

You *have to have* a visa to go to another country. 你到别国去得有签证。

She *has to go* to the bank this afternoon. 今天下午她得去银行。

We *have to be* careful in such matters. 处理这类事我们得小心。

He *has to do* a lot of reading. 他得看很多书。

△ 这种结构的疑问式和否定式都借助 do 构成：

Do you *have to* leave so soon? 你这么快就得走吗？

Does she *have to* go with you? 她得和你一起去吗？

What *do* I *have to* do to get a licence? 我要怎样才能取得驾驶执照？

You *don't have to* get up so early. 你不必起这么早。

She *doesn't (didn't) have to* answer all those questions. 她不必回答所有那些问题。

△ 还可用于多种时态：

I missed the bus and *had to* walk home. 我没赶上巴士，只好走着回家。

We'*ll have to* help him as much as we can. 我们将不得不尽力帮助他。

First I'*d have to* get my father's consent. 首先我必须取得我爸的同意。

These last few days I'*ve had to* take a rest. 最近这几天我不得不休息了一下。

If it hadn't been for your help, I *would have had to* leave. 要不是你帮忙，我就得离开这里了。

2) 这种结构可用于被动语态：

All kinds of difficulties *have to be overcome*. 有种种困难需要克服。

A lot of letters *had to be answered*. 有大量的信要回。

The whole thing *will have to be done* all over again. 整件事将不得不重做一遍。

还可和 may，might 连用：

We *may have to* cancel the plan. 我们可能不得不取消这项计划。

They *might have to* ask her permission to do this. 他们要这样做可能得请求她的许可。

3) have got to 和 have to 意思差不多：

I'*ve got to be* off now. 我现在得走了。

We'*ve got to send* her to hospital. 我们不得不送她进医院。

Has he *got to get* himself involved in this affair? 他有必要卷入此事吗？

She *has got to be operated on*.　她得动手术。

11.3.5　had better (best) 的用法

1) had better 也接近一个情态动词，后面总跟动词原形，表示"最好…"
(had 常可紧缩为 'd):

We'*d better go* before it gets dark.　我们最好趁天没黑就走。

You'*d better take* a nap after lunch.　午饭后你最好小睡一会儿。

Hadn't we *better* take an umbrella?　我们是不是带把雨伞比较好？

You'*d better* not *talk* like that.　你最好别这样讲话。

What *had* we *better do*?　我们最好怎么办？

后面有时可跟不定式的进行式，表示立即做某事:

I think I'*d better be going*.　我想我最好还是马上走。

We'*d better be getting* our clothes ready.　我们最好马上把衣服准备好。

had 有时可以省略:

You *better stop* arguing.　你们最好别争论了。

Better not wait for them.　最好别等他们了。

2) had best 的用法和 had better 差不多:

We *had best* have his opinion first.　我们最好先听听他的意见。

I *had best* be going now.　我最好现在就走。

第 12 章　非谓语动词

12.1　不定式的用法

12.1.1　概说

1) 不定式有两种，即带 to 的不定式 (a) 和不带 to 的不定式 (b)：

a. I've come *to seek* your advice.　我是来向你求教的。

b. What you said made me *think*.　你的话使我深思。

不带 to 的不定式和动词原形相同，有人称作**光秃不定式** (Bare Infinitive)，不过在大多数情况下不定式都带 to。

2) 不定式在句中可充当许多成分：

a. 构成谓语：

He *seems to be in good health*.　他似乎身体很好。

b. 作主语：

To know everything is to know nothing.　事事皆懂，无一精通。

c. 作宾语：

I hope *to be back* in a couple of days.　我希望两三天就回来。

d. 构成复合宾语：

She wanted *this meeting to be a successful one*.　她希望这次会议成功。

e. 作定语：

Do you have anything *to say*?　你有什么话要说吗？

f. 作状语：

I was delighted *to receive your letter*.　我很高兴接到你的来信。

g. 作表语：

My duty is *to get you away, to save you*.　我的职责是帮你逃走，是要救你。

3) 不定式毕竟还是动词，因而也具有动词的某些特点，如：

a. 可以有自己的宾语：

They asked to see *my passport*.　他们要求查验我的护照。

b. 可以有自己的状语：

She told me to go *home*.　她要我回家。

不定式和它后面的宾语或 (和) 状语构成不定式短语 (下面谈到不定式时也都包含了不定式短语)。

4) 不定式有一些不同形式：

	主动形式	被动形式
一般式	to do	to be done
完成式	to have done	to have been done
进行式	to be doing	—
完成进行式	to have been doing	—

5) 不定式虽然不能有自己的主语，但在意思上仍有履行这动作的人或物，称为 **逻辑主语** (Logical Subject)。下面句中的黑体词就是不定式的逻辑主语：

She taught **me** *to read*.　她教我认字。(我认字)

I'll be glad *to help you*.　我将乐于帮助你。(我将帮助你)

当不定式和它的逻辑主语有被动关系 (即动作被它做) 时，不定式就需要用被动形式：

She was sent there *to be trained* as an astronaut.　她被派到那里接受宇航员的训练。

不定式前面有时有一个由介词 for 引导的短语，来表示它的逻辑主语：

The simplest thing is *for him* to resign.　最简单的办法就是他辞职。

12.1.2　不定式构成谓语

不定式构成谓语有下面几种方式：

1) 不带 to 的不定式和某些助动词构成谓语：

Will you please *call* back again in a little while?　请过一会儿再打电话来好吗？

Shall I *help* you?　要不要我帮你？

Would you *like* me to interpret for you?　要不要我来给你当翻译？

I'*ll be* back right away.　我马上就回来。

He *won't tell* me his address.　他不肯告诉我他的地址。

I *should think* so. 我想是这样的。

2) 不带 to 的不定式和情态动词构成谓语:

We *must keep* this in mind. 我们必须记住这一点。

How *can* we *convince* him? 我们怎样才能使他相信?

She *might not like* the idea. 她可能不赞成这个想法。

We *needn't wait* for him. 我们不必等他了。

How *dare* you *call* me a liar? 你怎么竟敢说我是撒谎者?

We'*d better wait* and *see*. 我们最好等着瞧。

3) 不定式和某些动词构成谓语:

How *are* you *going to solve* the problem? 你准备怎样解决这个问题?

What time *is* the plane *to take off*? 飞机什么时候起飞?

You *ought to be prepared* for the worst. 你必须准备应付最坏的情况。

We *have (got) to be cautious*. 我们必须慎重行事。

I'm sorry I *haven't been able to do* much. 抱歉我没能多帮忙。

We *used to work* in the same department. 我们过去在一个部门工作。

She *happened to live* in the same area. 她碰巧住在同一个地区。

How *did* you *get to know* all this? 这一切你是怎么知道的?

He *seemed to be doing* all right. 他似乎情况不错。

You *appear to have travelled* a lot. 你好像走过很多地方。

4) 不定式和某些形容词构成复合谓语:

The plan *is bound to succeed*. 这计划一定会成功。

Madame *is sure to be right*. 夫人肯定是对的。

He *is certain to return*. 他一定会回来。

He *is* much more *likely to be in Spain*. 他更可能在西班牙。

He *is unlikely to arrive* before 1:00 p.m. 他下午一点前到达的可能性不大。

He *was apt to become excited*. 他很容易激动。

The talk *is due to start* on Monday. 会谈定于星期一开始。

5) 不定式和某些被动结构构成复合谓语:

He *is said to have been in China* many times. 据说他曾多次到过中国。

Another spaceship *is believed to have landed* on Mars. 据信又有一艘宇宙飞船在火星上着陆了。

This *was thought to be impossible*. 过去这被认为是不可能的。

His situation *was considered to be dangerous*. 他的处境被认为是很危险的。

He *is known to be a great artist.* 大家都知道他是一位伟大的画家。

You *are not supposed to know* that. 你不应当知道此事。

The situation there *is reported to be deteriorating.* 据报导那里的形势正在恶化。

You *are expected to speak* at the meeting. 大家期待你在会上发言。

12.1.3 不定式作主语

不定式可以作主语，如:

To compromise appears advisable. 妥协似乎是明智的。

To lean out of the window is dangerous. 把头伸出窗外是危险的。

To stop the work now seems impossible. 现在把这工作停下来似乎已不可能。

To ignore this might have serious consequences. 忽略这一点可能会有严重后果。

To err is human, *to forgive*, divine. (谚)犯错误人皆难免, 宽恕才难能可贵。

但在更多情况下都用 it 作先行主语, 而把不定式这个真正主语放到句子后部去, 这样可使主语不至显得太长, 避免头重脚轻的现象。常见的这类句子有下面几种:

1) It + be + 形容词 + 不定式 (斜体部分为真正的主语):

It's hard (difficult) *to say which is better.* 很难说哪个更好。

It's foolish (silly) *to act like that.* 这样做是愚蠢的。

Is it easy *to learn a foreign language*? 学外语容易吗?

It is not necessary *to do all these exercises.* 没有必要做所有这些练习。

It's impossible *to finish the job in one day.* 一天完成这项工作是不可能的。

It's so good (nice) *to talk to you.* 和你谈话真好。

It isn't right *to waste so much money on it.* 在这上面白花这么多钱是不对的。

It is essential (important) *to know all the facts.* 掌握所有事实至关重要。

It's still possible *to catch the train.* 还有可能赶上火车。

It's advisable *to revise the plan.* 修改计划是明智的。

It is wrong *to steal.* 偷窃是错误的。

2) It + be + 名词 + 不定式:

It's an honour *to meet you.* 见到你很荣幸。

It's our duty *to obey the law.* 遵守法律是我们的责任。

I think **it's a pity** *to waste so much money.* 我想浪费这么多钱是很遗憾的。

It's my privilege *to serve you.* 为你服务是我难得的机会。

It was great fun *to have a picnic there.* 在那里野餐很有意思。

It's a good habit *to eat slowly.* 细嚼慢咽是好习惯。

It's a shame *to deceive your friends.* 骗你自己的朋友是很可耻的。

It's a great pleasure *to work with you.* 和你们一起工作非常愉快。

It's my wish *to do something for the public.* 为公众做些事是我的愿望。

3) It + 动词 (宾语) + 不定式:

It cost a lot of money *to build this museum.* 盖这座博物馆花了很多钱。

How long does it take *to fly across the Pacific Ocean?* 飞渡太平洋要多少时间?

It requires patience *to be a teacher.* 当老师要有耐心。

It amused me *to hear these jokes.* 听到这些笑话我很开心。

It would take ages *to really master a language.* 要真正掌握一种语言需要花很长时间。

It amazed me *to hear that you were leaving.* 听说你要走了我很惊讶。

It takes two *to make a quarrel.* (谚)吵架要有两个人。

It made us very angry *to hear him talk like that.* 听他这样讲话让我们很生气。

It feels good *to be out here for a while.* 出来在这待一会儿是挺惬意的。

What harm can it do *to give advice?* 给人出主意有什么不好?

4) It + be + 介词短语 + 不定式:

It's against my principles *to collaborate with them.* 和他们合作违我的原则。

It's beyond me *to explain these.* 要解释这些我力所不及。

It's not within my power *to change his view.* 要改变他的观点非我所能。

It would be beneath him *to accept such a job.* 接受这份工作会有失他的身份。

It is just like you *to be always ready to help a friend.* 随时准备帮助朋友正是你的本色。

12.1.4 不定式作宾语

1) 不定式作宾语时特别多，许多动词都可跟这种宾语：

He **agreed** to pay $ 4,000 for the car. 他同意出四千美元买这辆车。

They **failed** to fulfil the plan. 他们没能完成计划。

We **managed** to put the fire out. 我们终于把火扑灭了。

They are **preparing** to build a freeway between the two cities. 他们正准备在两座城市之间建一条高速公路。

She **preferred** to stay behind. 她宁愿留下。

The soldiers **refused** to surrender. 士兵们拒不投降。

She **volunteered** to go and work in the northwest. 她志愿到西北地区工作。

We can't **afford** to stay at a five-star hotel. 我们住不起五星级酒店。

Don't **bother (trouble)** to answer the letter personally. 不必费事亲自回信。

You must **learn** to look after yourself. 你必须学着照顾自己。

常见的这类动词有：

afford	agree	aim	arrange	ask	attempt
bear	begin	bother	care	choose	claim
consent	continue	dare	decide	decline	demand
deserve	desire	determine	endeavour	expect	fail
forget	guarantee	hate	help	hesitate	hope
intend	learn	like	long	love	manage
mean	need	neglect	offer	plan	pledge
prefer	prepare	pretend	promise	prove	refuse
remember	resolve	scorn	seek	strive	swear
threaten	trouble	try	undertake	volunteer	vote
vow	wait	want	wish		

2) 不定式有时和一连接代 (副) 词一道构成宾语：

He **discovered** how to open the safe. 他发现了开保险箱的方法。

I'll **ask him** how to operate the machine. 我来问他怎样开这机器。

She **showed** me which button to press. 她教我按哪个按钮。

She **couldn't think** what to say. 她想不出该说什么。

He **taught me** how to swim. 他教我怎样游泳。

Have you **decided** what to do next? 下一步干什么你决定了吗？

You must **learn** how to be patient. 你必须学会怎样保持耐心。

We have to **find out** *where to buy food cheaply.* 我们得打听一下哪里能买到便宜食品。

Do you **remember** *which way to get there?* 你记得到那里怎样走吗？

I **forgot** *how to say it in English.* 我忘了这话英语怎么说了。

He **didn't know** *whether to laugh or to cry.* 他感到啼笑皆非。

She **wondered** *whether to turn left or right.* 她不知道该向左拐还是向右拐。

3) 间或还可用这种结构作介词宾语：

He wrote a book **on** *how to protect the environment.* 他写了一本关于环保的书。

They were worried **about** *how to find the necessary equipment.* 他们为如何找到所需设备而发愁。

Then there is the problem **of** *what courses to offer.* 接着就是开些什么课程的问题。

We also had a discussion **about** *what investments to make.* 我们还讨论了应作哪些投资。

4) 偶尔可使用一个先行词 it 作形式上的宾语，而把不定式转放到句子后部去：

I have long had **it** in mind *to answer your letter.* 好久以来我一直想回你的信。

She took **it** on herself *to apologize to me.* 她亲自来向我道歉。

12.1.5　用不定式构成复合宾语

1) 许多动词可跟一个由"名词（代词）＋不定式"构成的复合宾语：

I **asked** *George to convey my best wishes to his mother.* 我请乔治向他母亲问好。

My boss **told** *me to type out two letters.* 我的老板让我打两封信。

He **likes (wants)** *the students to eat well.* 他愿意学生们吃得好。

He **begged** *her to forgive him.* 他恳求她宽恕他。

I **expected** *him to arrive on Saturday.* 我估计他星期六到达。

She **encouraged** *me to try again.* 她鼓励我再试一次。

They **forbade** *her to leave the country.* 他们禁止她出境。

They **persuaded** *him to give up smoking.* 他们劝他戒了烟。

They are **training** *these dogs to sniff out drugs.* 他们在训练这些犬嗅出

毒品。

These glasses **enable** *me to see better.* 这副眼镜能使我看得清楚一些。

Please **remind** *me to post this letter.* 请提醒我发这封信。

常见的这类动词有:

advise	allow	ask	beg	bribe	cause
challenge	command	compel	convince	direct	enable
encourage	expect	forbid	force	induce	instruct
invite	oblige	order	permit	persuade	press
recommend	remind	request	require	teach	tell
tempt	train	urge	want	warn	

2) 有些动词可跟带有 to be 的复合宾语,如:

I **consider** *him to be the best candidate.* 我认为他是最佳候选人。

I **supposed** *him to be away from home.* 我想他不在家。

They **believed** *these principles to be universally true.* 他们认为这些原则
　　是普遍适用的。

They **declared** *it to be a province of Morocco.* 他们宣布这是摩洛哥的一
　　个省。

We **discovered** *him to be quite untrustworthy.* 我们发现他很不可信赖。

He **felt** *that to be the highest praise.* 他感到这是最高的赞美。

She **found** *the Chinese people to be happy and cheerful.* 她发现中国人非
　　常幸福愉快。

He **judged** *them to be the best work he had yet done.* 他认为它们是他迄
　　今写的最好作品。

I **know** *him to be a liar.* 我知道他是个爱说谎的人。

We have **shown** *the story to be false.* 我们已表明这种说法是不真实的。

这类动词后的不定式有时可以是完成形式或进行形式,此时的不定式不
是 be:

His record **shows** *him to have worked hard at school.* 他的成绩单表明他
　　上学时很勤奋。

I **considered** *him to have acted disgracefully.* 我认为他的表现很可耻。

I **judge** *them to have finished.* 我估计他们已经干完了。

They **knew** *the man to have been a spy.* 他们知道那人过去当过间谍。

They **believed** *him to be hiding somewhere*.　他们认为他躲在什么地方。

3) 跟复合宾语的动词有时可用于被动结构,这时可说形成一种复合谓语:

She *was told to wait at the door*.　他们让她在门口等着。

You *are not expected to work such long hours*.　并不指望你工作这么长时间。

This vase *is estimated to be 2,000 years old*.　这花瓶估计已有两千年的历史。

He *is known to be honest*.　大家知道他是诚实的。

He *was thought to be a great novelist*.　他被认为是一位伟大的小说家。

He *was asked to testify in Congress*.　他被请到国会作证。

He *was warned not to go there*.　有人警告他不要去那里。

They *were forced to pay heavy taxes*.　他们被迫交纳重税。

She *was forbidden to stay out after midnight*.　禁止她午夜后在外逗留。

They *were not allowed to form secret societies*.　不允许他们秘密结社。

这类结构中的不定式可用完成式或进行式:

He *was known to have worked for the French*.　大家知道他曾给法国人干过事。

They *are believed to have found a cure for cancer*.　据信他们发现了一种治疗癌症的方法。

He *was rumoured to have married a widow*.　谣传他和一个寡妇结了婚。

He *is said to have won another gold medal*.　据说他又获得一枚金牌。

The allied forces *were reported to be pushing towards Berlin*.　据报导盟军正在向柏林推进。

They *were thought to be hiding in the woods*.　人们认为他们躲在树林里。

He *is supposed to be washing the car*.　此刻他应当在洗车。

She *is believed to be living in Tokyo*.　据信她现在住在东京。

4) 有些动词可跟由不带 to 的不定式构成的复合宾语:

Did you **see** *anyone enter the house*?　你看见什么人进屋了吗?

I **heard** *her lock the door*.　我听见她锁门了。

She won't **let** *me do it*.　她不让我做这事。

He **made** *me move the car*.　他让我把车移动一下。

We **watched** *the children skip rope*.　我们看孩子们跳绳。

Did you **notice** *a man come in*?　你注意到有个人进来吗?

I won't **have** *him cheat me like that*.　我不会让他这样骗我。

I **felt** *something crawl(ing) up my arm*.　我感到有东西顺着我手臂往上

爬。

但这类句子变为被动结构时，不定式前要加to:

A child *was seen to enter the building*. 有人看见一个孩子进了大楼。

She *was* often *heard to sing this song*. 人们常常听见她唱这首歌。

He *was* often *made to recite poems in class*. 老师经常让他在课堂上背诵诗句。

在 listen to 和 look at 后面也可跟这种结构:

He **listened to** *us retell stories*. 他听我们复述故事。

Look at *the girls dance*! 瞧那些女孩子跳舞!

在 help 后的不定式可加to，也可不加to (美国人不加to时较多)，但被动结构中要加to:

I'll help you *(to) push the cart*. 我来帮你推车。

You'll be helped *to fulfil the task*. 有人将帮助你完成这项任务。

5) 有些"动词 + 介词"结构后也可跟由不定式构成的复合宾语:

He **shouted to** *me to come over*. 他喊我过去。

She **appealed to** *women to participate in the struggle*. 她呼吁妇女参加这一斗争。

The teacher **called on** *me to answer this question*. 老师叫我回答这个问题。

He **pleaded with** *her to go back*. 他恳求她回去。

She **longed for** *him to ask her out*. 她希望他邀她外出。

I am **counting on** *you to help me through*. 我指望你帮我度过难关。

He **relied on** *his subordinate to prepare the report*. 他依靠他的下属来准备这份报告。

I **depend on** *you to do it*. 我指靠你来办这事。

We hope to **prevail upon** *her to attend the concert*. 我们希望劝动她来听音乐会。

She wouldn't **care for** *the man to be her husband*. 她不愿意那个男人当她的丈夫。

He **waited for** *it to be light*. 她等着天亮。

6) 某些动词后可跟先行词it，借此把构成复合宾语的不定式放在后部:

I **find it easy** *to get on with Jim*. 我发现和吉姆相处很容易。

He **thought it best** *to be on his guard*. 他认为最好小心提防。

The judge **deemed it inadvisable** *to hear the appeal*. 法官认为听取这个上诉不明智。

All this **made it hard** *for her to make a decision*.　这一切使她难于作出决定。

He didn't **feel it necessary** *to mention this to her*.　他感到没有必要向她提及此事。

She **regarded it as important** *to win the competition*.　她认为赢得这场比赛很重要。

Do you **think it worthwhile** *to visit him*?　你认为拜访他值得吗?

We don't **consider it possible** *to set back the clock of history*.　我们认为要使历史的时针倒转是不可能的。

We **consider it our duty** *to safeguard world peace*.　我们认为保卫世界和平是我们的职责。

He **made it a rule** *to walk two miles a day*.　他规定自己每天走两英里路。

12.1.6　不定式作定语

1) 不定式常可用来修饰一样东西:

We have a lot of things *to do today*.　今天我们有很多事要做。

Do you have any suggestions *to offer*?　你有什么建议要提吗?

I've got two letters *to write tonight*.　今晚我有两封信要写。

He made a device *to make the door shut by itself*.　他制作了一个让门自动关闭的装置。

Would you like something *to drink*?　你想喝点什么吗?

It's a difficult question *to answer*.　这是个难以回答的问题。

Please give me a book *to read*.　请给我一本书看。

I'll find you something *to eat*.　我来给你找点东西吃。

I want a machine *to answer the phone*.　我要一台电话答录机。

This is not the right attitude *to take*.　这不是应当采取的正确态度。

It seems to be the only thing *to do*.　这似乎是唯一可做的事。

We were looking for somewhere *to live*.　我们在找一个地方住。

I need a case *to keep my compact discs*.　我需要一个盒子装我的激光唱盘。

There is plenty *to do here*.　这儿有很多事要做。

不定式有时需用被动形式:

There are a lot of things *to be done*.　有很多事要做。

He is dead. There's nothing *to be done now*.　他人已死了,无法可想了。

Where are the things *to be taken to her*? 要带给她的东西在哪里？

On which page is the question *to be answered*? 要回答的问题在哪一页？

Are you going to the banquet *to be given at the consulate*? 你准备参加领事馆举行的宴会吗？

2）不定式还可用来修饰人：

He was the first guest *to arrive*. 他是第一个到达的客人。

He was the second man *to hear the news*. 他是第二个听到这消息的人。

She was the only one *to survive the crash*. 她是这次空难中唯一的幸存者。

I want someone *to talk to*. 我想找个人交谈。

Miss Brown was the next person *to rise to speak*. 布朗小姐是下一个起来发言的人。

He is not a man *to bow before difficulties*. 他不是一个向困难低头的人。

You're the right person *to do this job*. 你是做这工作的合适人选。

We need twenty more people *to work in the boat*. 我们还需要二十个人在船上工作。

You're the only person *to complain*. 你是唯一一抱怨的人。

He was a brave man *to do what he did*. 他是个勇者才有这样的作为。

不定式有时需用被动形式：

She was the first person *to be awarded this prize*. 她是第一个获得这奖项的人。

He was the second man *to be killed this way*. 他是第二个这样被杀害的人。

She will be a suitable person *to be given this job*. 她是适合给予这项工作的人。

He was the only foreigner *to be given such an honour*. 他是唯一被授予这项荣誉的外国人。

3）在不少名词后可用不定式作定语：

It's **time** *to go to bed*. 该睡觉了。

There's no **reason** *to doubt his word*. 没有理由怀疑他的话。

I haven't had a **chance** *to think yet*. 我还没有机会思考。

They have now an **opportunity** *to air their views*. 现在他们有机会发表各自的看法了。

To scare a bird is not the **way** *to catch it*. (谚)吓唬鸟儿不是捕鸟的法子。

There is no **need** *to worry at all*. 根本用不着担心。

His **efforts** *to get her back were vain*. 他争取她回来的努力都白费了。

Jane expressed a **wish** *to earn her own living*. 简表示愿意自谋生计。

He has a **tendency** *to forget things*.　他容易忘事。

I have a **right** *to know*.　我有权知道。

He has a burning **ambition** *to become famous*.　他一心想成名。

4) 有些名词的同根词常跟不定式，因而它也常跟不定式作定语：

I don't trust his **promise** *to come for a visit*.　我不相信他来访的诺言。

（比较：He **promised** to come for a visit.）

He said he had no **plans** *to increase taxes*.　他说他没有要增税的计划。

（比较：He didn't **plan** to increase taxes.）

He made an **attempt** *to stand up*.　他试图站起来。

（比较：He **attempted** to stand up.）

Their **offer** *to assist in the work* was not taken seriously.　他们提出协助这项工作并未受到认真对待。

（比较：They **offered** to assist in the work.）

His **decision** *to resign* was welcomed by the Opposition.　他辞职的决定受到反对党的欢迎。

（比较：He **decided** to resign.）

She persisted in her **refusal** *to go home*.　她坚持不肯回家。

（比较：She **refused** to go home.）

His **failure** *to answer questions* made the police suspicious.　他答不出问题使警察产生怀疑。

（比较：He **failed** to answer questions.）

His **ability** *to get on with people* is his chief asset.　他能和人相处是他主要的优点。

（比较：He is **able** to get on with people.）

Her **anxiety** *to succeed* led her to work hard.　她迫切想成功,这促使她努力工作。

（比较：She was **anxious** to succeed.）

I was surprised at his **eagerness** *to return*.　他急切想回去使我感到惊讶。

（比较：He was **eager** to return.）

In February they announced their **willingness** *to send delegates to the conference*.　二月里他们宣布愿意派代表参加会议。

（比较：They were **willing** to send delegates to the conference.）

They showed a surprising **readiness** *to accept the proposal*.　他们表示乐意接受这个建议,这一举动令人吃惊。

（比较：They were **ready** to accept the proposal.）

5) 有时一个不定式 (短语) 的作用接近于一个定语从句 (大多表示要发生的事):

> That will be the right procedure **to follow** (=you should follow).　这将是应遵循的正当程序。
>
> Soup, and then steak *to follow*, please.　请先上汤, 然后上牛排。
>
> She was quiet for days *to come*.　此后许多天她都沉默无语。
>
> That would be a rash step *to take*.　那可能是一个鲁莽的举动。
>
> They were invited to the dance *to take place after the wedding*.　他们被邀参加婚礼后的舞会。
>
> Are you going to the banquet *to be held on Friday at the embassy*?　你要去参加星期五在大使馆举行的宴会吗?

另外, 不定式还可以和关系代词 which 连用作定语:

> She must have time *in which to pack*.　她必须有时间收拾行李。
>
> They would raise some money *with which to buy medicines*.　他们将筹集一些钱购买药品。
>
> He also had a revolver *with which to defend himself*.　他还有一把防身用的左轮手枪。
>
> He only had long nights *in which to study*.　他只有漫漫长夜可用来学习。

在个别名词后可用不定式作同位语 (说明前面这个词的内容):

> Then came the order *to evacuate the city*.　接着传来撤出城市的命令。
>
> They had received instructions *to watch him*.　他们接到指示要监视他。

12.1.7　不定式作状语

不定式作状语的时候很多, 主要有下面这几种情况:

1) 用于 "be +形容词+不定式式" 这种结构:

a. be +表示情绪的形容词+不定式:

> She was **eager** *to see her friends*.　她急于见到她的朋友们。
>
> I am **afraid** *to tell her*.　我很害怕告诉她。
>
> I was **sorry** *to hear that you were ill*.　听说你病了我很难过。
>
> Helen was **pleased** *to see him*.　海伦见到他很高兴。
>
> I'm **proud** *to be a Chinese*.　我为自己是个中国人而骄傲。
>
> She was **surprised** *to see George walk in*.　她惊讶地看到乔治走进来。
>
> He was very **disappointed** *to hear it*.　听了这话他感到很失望。

I'm **ashamed** *to have to trouble you.*　我很惭愧不得不麻烦你。

She was **keen** *to go.*　她非常想去。

I shall be **glad** *to help you find a new job.*　我将乐于帮你找一份新工作。

b. be＋表示状态的形容词＋不定式：

I'm not **ready** *to go back to work yet.*　我还不准备回去上班。

Gray was **prepared** *to leave the country.*　格蕾已准备好出境。

He was **determined** *to teach them a lesson.*　他决心给他们一个教训。

She was **careful** *to make no observation.*　她很谨慎，不作任何评论。

He was **quick** *to offer his counter-proposal.*　他迅速提出反建议。

He was **curious** *to know what was happening in the office.*　他好奇地想知道办公室里发生的事。

She's not **fit** *to live by herself.*　她不适合一个人住。

She was **free** *to go where she liked.*　她想去哪里就可以去哪里。

He was **lucky** *to find such a good job.*　他很幸运找到这样好的工作。

c. be＋表示品质等的形容词＋不定式：

He was **brave** *to act like that.*　他这样做很勇敢。

You were **right** *to do what you did.*　你这样做是对的。

I was **wrong** *to speak to her about it.*　我和她谈及此事是错误的。

You were **foolish** *to act like that.*　你这样做很愚蠢。

He was **generous** *to give you so much money.*　他很大方，给你这么多钱。

She's **interesting** *to talk to.*　和她谈话很有意思。

He was **amusing** *to be with.*　和他在一起很有趣。

Rosa will be **easy** *to deal with.*　罗莎会很容易对付。

She was **hard (difficult)** *to convince.*　她很难说服。

这类句子有时可以表示"物"的名词作主语：

The fruit is not **fit** *to eat.*　这种果子不宜食用。

Its seeds are particularly **good** *to eat.*　它结的籽特别好吃。

Polyester is **easy** *to iron.*　涤纶很容易熨烫。

Do you think the water is **safe** *to drink*?　你认为这水喝起来安全吗？

The question is **difficult** *to answer.*　这问题很难回答。

2) 不定式可用作状语，表示目的 (a)、原因 (b)、结果 (c) 等：

a. A friend of mine came *to see me* last night.　昨晚有个朋友来看我。

A gentleman stopped *to talk to me.*　一位先生停下来和我谈话。

We slept together *to keep warm.*　我们睡在一起以保持暖和。

To do good work, one must have the proper tools.　要干出像样的活得有合

适的工具。

As if to remind him, the church clock struck eleven. 仿佛是要提醒他,教堂的钟敲了十一点。

b. I rejoice *to hear that you are well again*. 听说你痊愈了我很高兴。

She shuddered *to think of those days*. 想到那些岁月她不寒而栗。

We jumped with joy *to hear it*. 听到这消息我们都高兴得跳了起来。

To hear him talk in that manner, you would think he's a foreigner. 听他这样讲话你会以为他是外国人。

c. What have I said *to make you so angry*? 我说了什么话使你这样生气?

The curtains parted, *to reveal a market scene*. 帷幕拉开,露出一个集市的场景。

He left, *never to return*. 他走了,再也没回来。

She lived *to be 100*. 她活到了一百岁。

3) 在许多句型中可用不定式作状语:

He was **so** careless **as to** leave his car unlocked. 他如此粗心大意,车门都没锁就走了。

Would you be **so** good **as to** forward my letters to me? 劳驾把我的信转给我好吗?

Go in quietly **so as not to** wake the baby. 悄悄进去,别把宝宝吵醒。

He had sacrificed so much **in order to** avoid pain. 他牺牲这么大为的是避免痛苦。

His behavior is **such as to** make his friends angry. 他这样的行为惹恼了他的朋友们。

Would you be good **enough to** close the door? 可否劳驾关门?

She isn't old **enough to** travel by herself. 她年纪尚小,不能独自去旅行。

You are **too** young **to** understand. 你太年轻不能理解。

It was **too** late **to** do anything now. 现在做什么都已为时太晚。

4) 有些不定式可用来修饰整个句子,因而可以称作 **句子状语**(Sentence Adverbial):

To be honest, I just don't like him. 说实话,我就是不喜欢他。

To be fair (to him), he wasn't entirely to blame. 说良心话,不能全怪他。

To tell you the truth, I've never met him. 说真的,我从来没见过他。

To be frank, you're a bad driver, 坦率地说,你开车技术不行。

To cut a long story short, we said, "No!" 长话短说,我们回绝了。

He's a nice person, **to be sure**. 毫无疑问,他是一个好人。

To put it in another way, she was sweet-tempered. 换句话说,她脾气非常好。

To begin with, it's too cold. Besides, we've no money. 首先,天太冷,再者我们也没有钱。

12.1.8　不定式作表语

1) 不定式有时可用作表语,说明主语的具体内容:

Her **ambition** was *to be a film star*. 她的志向是当电影明星。

Our **aim** is *to make the students' speech comprehensible*. 我们的目标是让学生讲的话能被人听懂。

Mary's **task** is *to set the table*. 玛丽的任务是摆桌子。

His **goal** is *to be a scientist*. 他的目标是当科学家。

My only **wish** is *to do something for the public*. 我唯一的愿望是为公众做些事。

The first **step** will be *to get a job in some office*. 第一步就是找一份办公室的工作。

The **purpose** of this meeting is *to elect a new captain*. 这次会议的目的是选一名新队长。

Your **mistake** was *to sign that letter*. 你的错误是签署了那封信。

2) 不定式作表语还可表示其他东西(如目的等):

This wall is *to keep people out of the garden*. 这堵墙为的是不让人到花园里来。

The thing now is *to get ahead*. 当务之急是要取得进展。

The problem was *to find the right people for the job*. 问题是要找到合适的人来干这工作。

The point is *to win at any cost*. 要紧的是不惜一切代价取得胜利。

The important thing is *not to wrong any person*. 重要的是不要冤枉任何人。

All you have to do is *to listen*. 你只要听着就行了。

My plan was *to go from Cornwall to Glasgow*. 我的计划是从康沃尔到格拉斯哥。

12.1.9　不定式的完成形式、进行形式和被动形式

1）不定式的完成形式：

当不定式表示的动作在谓语所表示情况之前发生，就需要用完成形式：

a. I happened *to have been there once*.　我碰巧到过那里一次。

She seemed *to have lost her patience*.　她似乎已失去耐心。

You are supposed (ought) *to have heard of it*.　你应该已听说此事。

b. What a mistake it is *to have come here*!　来了这里是个多大的错呀！

It would have been amusing *to have joined them*.　参加了他们的活动会很有意思的。

It was my intention *to have stopped there*.　在那里停下来是我本来的意图。

c. They claimed *to have shot down five planes*.　他们声称打下了五架敌机。

She pretended *not to have seen him*.　她假装没看见他。

I remember *to have told you about it*.　我记得告诉过你这件事。

d. I am sorry *to have given you so much trouble*.　对不起给了你这么多麻烦。

He was pleased *to have made your acquaintance*.　他很高兴认识了你。

He felt ashamed *to have done such a thing*.　他做了这样的事感到很惭愧。

e. He was known *to have worked for the International Olympic Committee*.　大家知道他曾为国际奥委会工作过。

They are believed *to have discussed the problem*.　据信他们曾讨论过这个问题。

She is rumoured *to have eloped with a priest*.　谣传她和一个牧师私奔了。

这类不定式可以在句中构成谓语(a)，充当主语(b)、宾语(c)、状语(d)，还可构成另一类复合谓语，即复合宾语的被动结构(e)。

2）不定式的进行形式：

当不定式表示一个正在进行的动作时需用进行形式：

a. He seemed *to be dreaming*.　他似乎在做梦。

She happened *to be travelling in that area*.　她恰好在这个地区旅游。

You ought *to be reviewing your lessons now*.　你现在应当在复习功课。

b. It's strange *to be sleeping in this house again*.　真奇怪又要在这屋子里睡觉了。

It's a delightful experience *to be touring the lake district*.　在湖区旅游是一段愉快的经历。

What a shame (it is) *to be wasting your time like that*.　把你的时间这样浪费掉真不好意思。

c. The man pretended *to be weaving*.　那人假装在织布。

I really hope *to be working with you*. 我的确希望和你们在一起工作。

I hate *to be quarrelling with her*. 我不愿意和她吵架。

d. I was pleased *to be talking with them*. 我很高兴和他们在一起谈话。

Are you glad *to be going home*? 你高兴回家吗?

She was happy *to be earning her own living*. 她很高兴能自食其力。

e. He is believed *to be living in Mexico*. 据信他住在墨西哥。

Thousands were reported *to be working in concentration camps*. 据报导那时有数以千计的人在集中营干活。

He is thought *to be hiding* in the woods. 人们认为他躲藏在林子里。

间或不定式也可用于完成进行形式:

He appears *to have been waiting a long time*. 他似乎已等了好长时间。

He pretended *to have been studying*. 他假装一直在学习。

She is said *to have been doing this work for twenty years*. 据说她干这工作已二十年了。

3) 不定式的被动形式:

不定式有时需用被动形式:

a. She *ought to be praised* for her heroic deeds. 她的英勇行为应受赞扬。

The parcel *has to be sent* by air mail. 这个包裹得寄航空。

The election *was due to be held* in November. 选举定于十一月举行。

b. It's an honour *to be awarded* a scholarship. 被颁给奖学金是一种荣耀。

It's just my luck *to be caught* in the storm. 碰上暴风雨我真倒霉。

It was his good fortune *not to have been injured*. 他很幸运没受伤。

c. She asked *to be given an opportunity* to try her method. 她要求给她机会试验她的方法。

They wanted *to be better treated*. 他们希望受到更好的对待。

He hates *to be flattered*. 他讨厌受人恭维。

d. These are the major problems *to be discussed* at the meeting. 这些是会上要讨论的主要问题。

Are you going to the conference *to be held* in June? 你要去参加六月举行的大会吗?

She was the first one *to be asked to speak*. 她是第一个被邀请发言的人。

e. She went to the hospital *to be inoculated*. 她到医院去打预防针。

She left the city, *never to be seen again*. 她离开了这座城市,再也没人见到过她。

He was sent abroad *to be educated*. 他被派去国外受教育。

这种不定式可构成谓语 (a)，也可用作主语 (b)、宾语 (c)、定语 (d) 或状语 (e)。关于这问题还可参阅第 9.4.1 节。

───────

12.1.10　不定式的逻辑主语

1) 每个不定式可以有其逻辑主语，它可能是句子的主语或宾语，如：

I had a lot of letters *to write*.　(I 是 to write 的逻辑主语)

I'll give **you** something *to read*.　(you 是 to read 的逻辑主语)

当句中没有适当的词可作不定式逻辑主语时，可以借助一个由 for 引导的短语来表示它的逻辑主语：

Here are some books **for you** *to read* on the way.　这儿有几本书给你在路上看。

2) 这种短语在句中可以和不定式一道起作用，如：

a. 作主语：

It won't be easy **for you** *to find a new job*.　你想找新工作不会很容易。

It isn't right **for people** *to marry for money*.　人们为金钱结婚是不对的。

For an old man *to run fast* is dangerous.　老年人快跑是危险的。

b. 作定语：

It's time **for you** *to reconsider your decision*.　现在是你重新考虑你的决定的时候了。

There's no reason **for us** *to doubt his words*.　我们没有理由怀疑他的话。

It's a good opportunity **for us** *to exchange our experience*.　这是我们交流经验的好机会。

c. 作状语：

He stood aside **for her** *to pass*.　他站到一边让她过去。

Please do send **for Mummy** *to come too*.　请一定派人把妈妈也叫来。

Her circumstances had never been good enough **for her hopes** *to be realized*.　她的境况从来没有好到使她的希望成为现实。

d. 作表语：

The simplest thing is **for him** *to resign at once*.　最简单的办法是他马上辞职。

What I want is **for you** *to talk to Lanny*.　我希望的是你和兰尼谈一谈。

It's **for you** *to decide* what we should do next.　得由你来决定我们下一步该做什么。

3) 在少数情况下可用 of 引导的短语，表示不定式的逻辑主语：

It was kind **of you** (You were kind) *to help us*.　难得你好心帮助我们。

It was silly **of you** (You are silly) *to trust such a man*.　你太愚蠢竟然信赖这样一个人。

It was selfish **of him** *not to do anything for the orphans*.　他很自私不愿为孤儿们做任何事。

It was generous **of you** *to contribute so much money*.　你很大方捐出这么多钱。

It's unfair **of him** *to say such things about her*.　他说她这样的话是不公道的。

It was annoying **of him** *to damage my car*.　他损坏了我的车让人生气。

只有那些作表语的形容词能修饰人时，才能在不定式前用 of 引导的短语，否则还是应当用 for 引导的短语来表示不定式的逻辑主语。

12.1.11　关于不定式结构的一些问题

1) 不定式的省略：

为了避免重复，有时不定式中的主要动词可以省略，只剩下 to：

Would you like to come with us?　——　Yes, I'd **love to**.　你愿意和我们一道去吗?　——愿意。

Did you get a ticket?　——　No, I **tried to**, but there weren't any left.　你买到票了吗?　——没有，我去买过，但都卖光了。

Do you often play bridge?　——　I **used to**, but not now.　你经常打桥牌吗?　——过去常打，但现在不打了。

Have you cleaned the windows?　——　No, but I'm just **going to**.　你擦窗子了吗?　——没有，不过我正要去擦。

I wanted to get in touch with her but **wasn't able to**.　我想和她联系，但没能联系上。

You can go if you **want to**.　你如果想去可以去。

You don't know her? You **ought to**.　你不认识她? 你该认识她的。

Will you join me in a walk?　——　I'd **be glad** to.　你愿意和我一道去散散步吗?　——好呀。

在个别情况下 to 可保留，也可一道省略：

He says he will come as soon as he has got a chance (**to**).　他说他一有机会

就来。

They won't encourage you to do it even if you have the time **(to)**.　他们不会鼓励你这样做，即使你有时间(这样做)。

She may go if she likes **(to)**.　她如果想去可以去。

在用不定式作表语时，to 有时也可省略，如：

All I did was **(to)** press the button.　我只是按了一下电钮。

What you have to do is **(to)** fill in the questionaire.　你所要做的是把问卷填好。

在 used to，be going to，mean to，ought to，try to，plan to 等结构后，当不定式省略时，to 通常是保留的。

2）并列的不定式：

当有两个或更多不定式并列使用时，通常只在第一个不定式前加 to，在后面的不定式前 to 常省略：

We ought *to read more* and *have more practice*.　我们应多读多练习。

She told us *to stay at home* and *wait till she came back*.　她让我们留在家里等她回来。

I'd like *to stay with you, help you* and *learn from you*.　我愿意留在你身边，帮助你并向你学习。

但如果二者有对比关系，每个不定式前都应带 to：

To try and fail is better than *not to try at all*.　尝试而失败也比不尝试好。

He hasn't decided whether *to quit* or *to stay*.　他还没决定是去还是留。

To go or *not to go*, it's a question.　去还是不去是一个问题。

3）分裂不定式：

有时 to 和后面的动词间可插入一个副词：

They have started a drive *to **further** improve* the miners' working conditions.　他们开始作一番努力来进一步改善矿工们的工作条件。

He was too ill *to **really** carry out his duty*.　他病得太重，不能切实履行他的职责。

He likes *to **half** close his eyes*.　他喜欢半闭着眼睛。

Mother asks you *to **kindly** come over* to see us tonight.　妈妈请你今晚劳驾到我们家来一趟。

这称为 **分裂不定式** (Split Infinitive)，这种用法在口语中最好避免。如可能，可以把副词放后面去，如 to completely cover the floor 可改为 to cover the floor completely，to unduly alarm people 可改为 to alarm people unduly。

4) 在个别情况下，可用不定式构成或引导一个句子：

a. 不带 to 的不定式：

Why bother? 干吗费这个事？

Why worry about such trifles? 干吗为这些小事烦心？

Why not wait for a couple more days? 干吗不再等上一两天？

Why not do it right now? 干吗不现在就干？

b. 带 to 的不定式：

To think he would come to anything like that! 没想到他竟是这样的下场！

And *to think* that I trusted him! 没想到我竟然信任了他！

To think of his not knowing anything about it! 没想到他对此竟一无所知！

12.2 动名词的用法

12.2.1 动名词概说

动词的 -ing 形式在起名词作用时，称为动名词，动名词在句中可以：

1) 用作主语：

Dancing bored him. 跳舞使他厌烦。

2) 用作表语：

Her hobby is *collecting stamps*. 她的爱好是集邮。

3) 用作宾语：

Please stop *talking*. 请不要说话了。

4) 用作介词宾语：

He was arrested for *smuggling*. 他因走私而被捕。

5) 构成合成词：

Who won the *singing* contest? 歌咏比赛谁赢了？

还可用在下面这类句子中：

No smoking. 禁止吸烟。　　　　No loitering. 不许在此逗留。

No spitting. 禁止吐痰。　　　　No parking. 禁止泊车。

作为动词，它也有几种形式：

	主动形式	被动形式
一般式	doing	being done
完成式	having done	having been done

它也可以有它的宾语 (a) 或状语 (b):

a. He was fond of playing *tennis*. 他喜欢打网球。

b. She is thinking of going home *this summer*. 她想今年夏天回家。

它还可以用一个代词或名词所有格表示其逻辑上的主语:

He disliked *her* working late. 他不喜欢她工作到很晚。

用名词所有格显得比较文气,在口语中常把 's 省略掉:

I don't remember *my mother's* talking about it. (较文气的说法)

I don't remember *my mother* talking about it. (较口语化的说法)

有些动名词已变得接近名词或已变成名词,它们可有复数形式 (a),前面可加冠词 (b),甚至有定语修饰 (c):

a. Dickens often gave *readings* of his works. 狄更斯常常朗读自己的作品。

b. Who did *the cooking*? 谁做的饭?

c. I always enjoy *a little light reading*. 我一向喜欢读点轻松的东西。

这些可称为**名词化动名词** (Verbal Nouns)。有些以 -ing 结尾的词已完全变成名词:

He could not analyze his *feelings*. 他没法分析自己的感情。

Take good care of your *belongings*. 注意保管好你的东西。

12.2.2   动名词作主语和表语

1) 动名词可用作主语:

Reading French is easier than speaking it. 阅读法文比讲法语容易。

Talking to him is talking to a wall. 和他说话等于对牛弹琴。

Finding work is difficult these days. 现今找工作不容易。

Smoking may cause cancer. 吸烟会致癌。

Walking is my sole exercise. 散步是我唯一的运动。

To her, *windsurfing* is too dangerous. 在她看来冲浪太危险。

Growing roses is her hobby. 种玫瑰是她的爱好。

Gambling is forbidden in our country. 我国禁止赌博。

Sailing a boat is great fun. 驾驶帆船很有意思。

Talking mends no holes. (谚)空谈无济于事。

2) 有时可用先行词 it 作主语,而把动名词主语放到句子后部去,作表语的可以是形容词 (a),也可以是名词 (b):

a. It's **nice** *seeing you again*. 再次见到你太好了。

It's **hopeless** *arguing about it*. 争辩这事没有用。

Is it **worthwhile** *quarrelling with her*? 和她吵架值得吗?

It was **pleasant** and **comfortable** *sitting there*. 坐在那里惬意舒适。

It was **tiring** *driving from morning till night*. 从早到晚开车很累人。

b. It's **a wonder** *meeting you here*. 在这里碰到你真是奇迹。

It's **no good** *coming before that*. 在那之前来没有用。

It's **no use** *asking me*. I don't know any more than you do. 问我没用,我知道的不比你多。

It's been **a lot of fun** *staying here*. 住在这里很有意思。

It was **a waste of time** *reading that book*. 看那本书是浪费时间。

3) "There is + no" 后可以用动名词作主语,表示"没法…":

There was *no knowing* what he could do. 他能做什么很难说。

There was *no telling* when this might happen again. 没法预料这样的事什么时候会再发生。

He's selfish, there's *no denying* it. 他很自私,这是不可否认的。

There was *no arguing* with her. 没法和她争论。

There was *no mistaking* in his intention. 他的意图不可能看错。

4) 动名词还可用作表语:

Her hobby is *painting*. 她的爱好是绘画。

Their pastime is *going to movies*. 他们的消遣是看电影。

Her favorite sport is *skiing*. 她最喜欢的运动是滑雪。

One of her duties is *keeping the department files*. 她的任务之一是管理部门的档案。

His favorite occupation is *fishing*. 他最喜欢的活动是钓鱼。

Their major amusement is *raising pigeons*. 他们的主要消遣是养鸽子。

Her job was *tending the sheep*. 她的工作是放羊。

Seeing is *believing*. (谚)眼见为实。

12.2.3　动名词作宾语

1) 有许多动词可用动名词作宾语:

I **suggested** *bringing the meeting to an end*. 我建议结束会议。

He **admitted** *taking the money*. 他承认钱是他拿的。

Do you **enjoy** *teaching*? 你喜欢教书吗?

Avoid *over-eating*. 要避免暴食。

Fancy *meeting you*! 真想不到在这里碰到你!

I **couldn't help** *laughing*. 我禁不住笑了起来。

He **considered** *going to see Paul in person*. 他考虑亲自去见保罗。

I **detest** *looking at snakes*. 我讨厌看蛇。

I **dread** *going to big parties*. 我害怕参加大型晚会。

He **loves** *playing the piano*. 他爱弹钢琴。

I **like** *travelling very much*. 我非常喜欢旅行。

I **hate** *lying and cheating*. 我讨厌撒谎欺骗。

It has **stopped** *raining*. 雨已经停了。

I **finished** *reading the book* last night. 这书我昨晚看完了。

He **kept** *complaining*. 他不停地抱怨。

I couldn't **risk** *missing the train*. 我不能冒搭不上火车的危险。

They're **practising** *singing the new song*. 他们在练习唱新歌。

He **denied** *making any statement* to that effect. 他否认作过这种内容的声明。

So you **prefer** *living abroad*? 这样说你更愿意住在国外?

He **proposed** *founding a school there*. 他建议在那里建一所学校。

I **advised** *taking a different approach*. 我建议采取另一种处理办法。

She **continued** *watching me*. 她继续瞧着我。

He **loathed** *travelling by air*. 他讨厌坐飞机。

Would you **mind** *moving your car*? 劳驾把车挪一下行吗?

To raise wages **means** *increasing purchasing power*. 增加工资意味着提高购买力。

He didn't **recall** *saying it*. 他不记得说过这话。

Do you **recollect** *meeting her*? 你还记得见过她吗?

He never can **resist** *making a joke*. 他总是禁不住要说笑话。

The garden **needs** *watering*. 花园需要浇水。

Your coat **wants** *brushing*. 你的大衣需要刷一下。

2) 许多成语动词也可以用动名词作宾语:

He has **given up** *playing football*. 他现在不踢足球了。

They will **put off** *doing it until next year*. 他们将推迟到明年再做此事。

Even then she **carried on** *talking*. 即使在那时,她还继续谈话。

Prices **keep on** *increasing*. 物价不断上涨。

Ned **left off** *talking about the firm*. 奈德不再谈公司的事。

She waved to me and **went on** *sketching*. 她向我挥挥手,又接着画素描。

He **burst out** *crying* like a child.　他像小孩一样突然哭了起来。

She decided to **cut out** *smoking*.　她决定戒烟。

在 (be) worth 后也可跟动名词作宾语：

His suggestion is **worth** *considering*.　他的建议值得考虑。

It's **worth** *making an effort*.　这值得作一番努力。

That's **worth** *watching*, isn't it?　那值得一看，对吧？

New York is a city **worth** *visiting*.　纽约是一座值得一看的城市。

3）有些动词后可以用动名词作宾语，也可以用不定式作宾语，有时两者意思不同，如：

I **remember** *telling* you about it.　我记得曾告诉过你这件事。

Remember *to tell* him about it.　记得告诉他这件事。

We've always **regretted** *selling* the farm.　我们一直懊悔把农场卖掉。

I **regret** *to tell* you that my father is ill.　我遗憾地告诉你我父亲病了。

I'll never **forget** *hearing* Chaliapin singing in that opera.　我永远不会忘记听查里亚平在那部歌剧中的演唱。

He **forgot** *to bring* his umbrella.　他忘了带雨伞。

Try *doing* more exercises; you'll soon lose weight.　多做些运动试试，你的体重很快就会减轻。

I'll **try** *to improve*.　我将设法改进。

She couldn't **help** *feeling* depressed.　她禁不住感到沮丧。

All this **helped** *(to) raise* farm yields.　这一切帮助提高了农业产量。

Your hair **wants** *cutting*.　你的头发需要理了。

Somebody **wants** *to see* you.　有人想见你。

The pants **need** *pressing*.　这条裤子需要熨烫。

I don't think you **need** *to worry* about it.　我想你不必为此发愁。

4）有时两种结构只有细微的差别，例如在 like, love, prefer, hate, dread 等动词之后，动名词多表示一般情况，不定式多表示即将发生的事：

Do you **like** *reading*?　你喜欢看书吗？

I should **like** *to hear* others' views.　我愿意听听别人的意见。

She **loves** *working* in the garden.　她喜欢在花园里干活。

She said she'd **love** *to come* sometime.　她说以后有一天她会愿意来的。

I **hate** *asking* favors.　我不愿意求人帮忙。

He would **hate** *to disappoint* you.　他不愿意让你失望。

Oh, I **prefer** *being* alone.　啊，我宁愿一个人待着。

We **preferred** *to walk* there.　我们宁愿步行到那里。

⎰ She **dreads** *seeing* them. 她害怕见到他们。
⎱ I **dread** *to think* what may happen. 我害怕去想会发生什么情况。

有时两者可以换用，意思上没有差别:

He hated *thinking (to think)* about it. 他不愿想这件事。

She loves *having (to have)* lots of young men round her. 她喜欢周围有许多青年男子。

I like *reading (to read)* detective stories. 我喜欢看侦探小说。

She prefers *living (to live)* among the office workers. 她宁愿生活在上班族中间。

5) 在 begin，start，intend，continue 和 cease 后跟动名词或不定式都可以，有时意思上没什么差别，例如:

It has started *raining (to rain)*. 开始下雨了。

The band began *playing (to play)*. 乐队开始演奏。

He intended *coming (to come)* back soon. 他打算不久就回来。

She continued *working (to work)* as if nothing had happened. 她继续干活，好像什么也没发生似的。

They ceased *talking (to talk)* and I began reading. 他们停止了交谈，我开始看书。

有时有点细微的差别，在 begin，start 和 cease 后，不定式多表示情况发生变化 (a)，而动名词表示有意识地开始或停止 (a):

a. Suddenly it *started to rain*. 天突然下起雨来。

Philip *began to cry*. 菲利浦哭了起来。

The matter has *ceased to be a mystery* to us. 这事对我们不再是个谜。

b. Then the little girl *started singing*. 这时那小姑娘开始唱歌。

We *began making preparations* for the trip. 我们开始做旅行的准备。

The factory has *ceased making bicycles*. 该厂已停止生产自行车。

在以 -ing 结尾的动词后不宜再用动名词，以避免 -ing 的重复:

He was beginning to miss her. 他开始惦记她。

It's starting to rain. 天开始下起雨来。

〔注〕stop 后面有时跟不定式，但它并不是宾语而是状语，用于说明 stop 的目的:

He stopped to talk to us. 他停下来和我们说话。

(比较: He stopped talking to us. 他停止和我们交谈。)

12.2.4   动名词作介词的宾语

1) 有许多由介词构成的成语动词后可以跟动名词作宾语：

She **insisted on** *writing at once*. 她坚持马上就写。

Why do you **persist in** *writing such things*? 你为什么老要写这样的东西？

Robbie couldn't **keep from** *laughing*. 罗比禁不住笑了起来。

They **objected to** *leaving the motel*. 他们反对离开这家汽车旅馆。

He **thought of** *writing to her*. 他考虑给她写信。

The young man **dreamed of** *becoming a surgeon*. 这个小伙子一心想成为一名外科医生。

I've always **believed in** *being broad-minded*. 我一向主张宽宏大量。

The plant must **aim at** *increasing production*. 工厂必须努力增加生产。

Andrew **set about** *writing his report*. 安德鲁着手写他的报告。

I don't **feel like** *going to the movie*. 我不想去看电影。

She **succeeded in** *making a most favourable impression*. 她成功地给人留下非常好的印象。

Please **refrain from** *smoking* during the performance. 演出时请勿吸烟。

Goodness **consists in** *being honest*. 善良主要在于诚实。

He never **complained about** *working overtime*. 他从不抱怨加班加点。

He was so poor that he **resorted to** *stealing*. 他穷得只能去偷。

She was **looking forward to** *leaving the hospital wards*. 她盼望离开医院病房。

2) 还有不少 "be + 形容词 + 介词" 的结构后也常可用动名词作宾语：

Are you **interested in** *going with us*? 你有兴趣跟我们一道去吗？

I **was afraid of** *making them uneasy*. 我怕使他们感到不安。

He **was fond of** *speaking French*. 他很喜欢讲法语。

She **is** awfully **good at** *looking after people*. 她很会照顾人。

He **wasn't keen on** *buying a car*. 他并不急着想买车。

I **was angry about** *missing the film*. 没看上这部片子我很生气。

He **was excited at** *hearing the news*. 听了这消息他很激动。

We **were surprised at** *finding the house empty*. 发现房子里空无一人我们感到惊讶。

Who **is responsible for** *locking up the school*? 谁负责给学校锁门？

I'm **tired of** *thinking about it*. 想这事我已经想烦了。

He **was not accustomed to** *associating with such people*. 他不习惯于和这类人来往。

He **is** quite **capable of** *neglecting his duty*.　他很有可能失职。

I'm **used to** *dealing with matters of this sort*.　处理这种事我已经习惯了。

I'm **sick of** *hearing you talk like that*.　我烦听你这样说话。

I'm **fed up with** *talking to you*.　和你谈话我都谈烦了。

3) 在"及物动词＋宾语＋介词"这类结构后，也常可跟动名词作宾语：

They **accused him of** *playing his radio too loudly*.　他们指责他收音机开得太响。

He **charged them with** *receiving stolen goods*.　他指控他们收受赃物。

They **suspected him of** *being the thief*.　他们怀疑他偷盗。

Thank you for *doing this job for us*.　谢谢你帮我们做了这件事。

Excuse me for *not answering your letter earlier*.　请原谅我没早一些给你回信。

Forgive (Pardon) me for *interrupting you*.　请原谅我打断你的话。

That did not **prevent him from** *doing so*.　这并没有阻止他那样做。

Keep that child from *yelling*.　别让那孩子大喊大叫。

Nothing would **stop me from** *achieving my ambition*.　什么也不能阻止我实现我的抱负。

He **dedicated his life to** *fighting corruption*.　他毕生致力于和腐败作斗争。

Mother Teresa **devoted herself to** *caring for the poor*.　特丽莎嬷嬷献身于照顾穷人。

在 How about 后也常用动名词作宾语：

How about *coming with us to the club*?　和我们一道去俱乐部如何？

How about *putting the sofa closer to the window*?　把长沙发放得靠窗子近点怎么样？

4) 许多介词可以跟动名词构成状语：

Bass waited a little while **before** *making up his mind*.　巴斯稍等了一会才拿定主意。

After *standing in the queue for an hour*, we got two tickets.　站了一小时的队，我们买了两张票。

And, **in** *doing so*, he fell into contradictions.　在这样做时，他陷入了矛盾之中。

On *reaching the city*, he called up Lester.　一到达这座城市，他就给莱斯特打了电话。

I don't blame you **for** *being cautious*.　你小心谨慎我不怪你。

What has he done **besides** *reading the paper*? 除了看报他还干了什么？

Thereis nothing to gain **by** *waiting*. 坐等不会有收获。

Without *waiting for any reply*, he left the room. 他不等回答就离开了房间。

He had not bought a new suit **since** *coming to Oxford*. 来牛津之后他没买过一套新衣服。

She dissuaded me **from** *doing it*. 她劝我不要做那事。

5) 还有一些由介词构成的短语，后面可跟动名词作宾语：

Instead of *going to New York*, we got off at Boston. 我们没去纽约,而是在波斯顿下了车。

Guests can relax in the lounge **prior to** *entering the theatre*. 客人在进入剧场之前可以在休息厅放松一下。

He was afraid to speak **for fear of** *making errors*. 他怕出错而不敢讲话。

He is studying **with a view to** *going to university*. 他在学习,准备上大学。

I called **in the hope of** *finding her at home*. 我去拜访是想在她家找到她。

6) 有些介词可以和动名词构成定语：

He is good at the art *of making friends*. 他甚谙交友之道。

I admired his skill *at driving*. 我佩服他开车的技术。

He had the chance (opportunity) *of visiting Beijing*. 他有机会访问北京。

It's a device *for opening bottles*. 这是一种开瓶装置。

He invented a new process *of dyeing*. 他发明了一种染色新工艺。

She doesn't have much experience *in dealing with children*. 在对待孩子方面她经验不多。

She couldn't invent a reason *for not going*. 她编造不出不去的理由。

What's the advantage of *using nuclear power*? 利用核能有什么好处？

He advocated a new method *of teaching English*. 他倡导一种教英语的新方法。

I have no objection *to sending him abroad*. 我不反对派他出国。

I had no intention *of defending myself*. 我无心为自己辩护。

To whom do I have the honour *of speaking*? 我有幸和哪一位讲话？

I do not like her way *of talking*. 我不喜欢她的讲话方式。

间或介词也可和动词一道构成表语：

I'm *for doing nothing* till the police arrive. 我主张在警察到来之前不要采取任何行动。

I'm *in the habit of reading the newspaper at breakfast*. 我习惯于吃早饭

时看报。

Father was *against selling the property*. 父亲反对出售这份产业。

Talking to him was *like playing on an exquisite violin*. 和他谈话就像弹奏一把美妙的提琴。

12.2.5 动名词的被动形式和完成形式

1) 动名词有时需用被动形式，可作动词的宾语 (a) 或介词的宾语 (b)：

a. He **hates** *being interrupted*. 他不愿意被人打断。

He narrowly **escaped** *being run over*. 他差点被车压了。

I **appreciate** *being given this opportunity*. 我很感谢给了我这个机会。

I **remembered** *being taken to Paris as a small child*. 我记得小时候曾被带到巴黎。

Grace **resented** *being called a baby*. 格雷斯讨厌别人叫他小宝宝。

He just **missed** *being caught*. 他差点没被抓住。

She **disliked** *being spoken to like that*. 她不喜欢别人对她这样讲话。

We **cannot help** *being touched by their zeal*. 我们禁不住被他们的热情所打动。

b. I **object to** *being spoken to like that*. 我反对别人对我这样讲话。

He hoped to get out **without** *being seen*. 他希望不被人看见溜出来。

All laws have to be submitted to Parliament for ratification **before** *being put into force*. 所有法律在实施前均需提交议会批准。

He ran away **for fear of** *being hurt*. 他跑掉了，唯恐受到伤害。

Who can **prevent** their plans **from** *being carried out*? 谁能阻止他们那些计划的实现？

She **is far from** *being pleased about it*. 对此她很不满意。

I'm not **used to** *being treated like this*. 我不习惯受这种款待。

She openly **talked of** *having been let down*. 她公开谈到被人涮了。

间或也可用作主语：

It felt funny **being called Grandma**. 被人称作奶奶感到怪怪的。

Being lost can be a terrifying experience. 迷路有时会很害怕。

2) 动名词有时需要完成形式，可作动词的宾语 (a) 或介词的宾语 (b)：

a. He **denied** *having been there*. 他不承认到过那里。

I could not **recall** *having heard anyone say that before*. 我不记得以前听

人说过这话。

I don't **recollect** *having seen him before*.　我不记得以前见过他。

I **regretted** *having left Montreal*.　我后悔离开了蒙特利尔。

He **reported** *having* met *only a cyclist*.　他报告说只碰到一个骑车的人。

She **admits** *having seen us*.　她承认见到了我们。

I don't **remember** *having heard you say that*.　我不记得听你说过这话。

b. He **accused** me **of** *having broken my word*.　他指责我不守信用。

　We **congratulated** him **on** *having passed the examination*.　我们祝贺他通
　　过了考试。

　He **was ashamed of** *having failed to pass the test*.　测试没通过他感到羞
　　愧。

　Don't **be angry with me for** *not having written* to you.　我没给你写信,请
　　别生气。

　After *having had some practice*, he decided to try again.　经过一番练习,
　　他决定再试一次。

　The safe showed no signs **of** *having been touched*.　保险柜没有被人动过
　　的痕迹。

12.2.6　动名词的逻辑主语

动名词的逻辑主语多用一个物主代词或名词所有格表示,可用在:

a. 主语前:

　Your coming to help is a great encouragement to me.　你们来帮忙对我是
　　很大的鼓舞。

　Her going off in such a hurry is very risky.　她这样匆忙离去很危险。

　Jane's not having received proper training was to her disadvantage.　简没
　　受过适当训练对她是不利的。

　Your denying everything will get you nowhere.　你否认一切不会对你有好
　　处。

　It has been a great honour *your coming to visit* us.　你来看我们真是不胜
　　荣幸。

　It seems so strange *your going like this*.　你这样去显得很奇怪。

b. 宾语前:

　I hate *your going away*.　我不愿意你走掉。

Forgive *my (me) ringing you up so early*. 原谅我这么早给你打电话。

You can't prevent *his (him) spending his own money*. 你不能阻止他花自己的钱。

I appreciate *your giving me so much of your time*. 感谢你为我花了这么多时间。

I don't remember *my mother's complaining about it*. 我不记得我母亲抱怨过这事。

She suggested *his sending it to Tagore*. 她建议他把它寄给泰戈尔。

Excuse *my opening your letter by mistake*. 请原谅我误拆了你的信。

I can still recall *your saying to me* that you were going to be a lawyer. 我还记得你曾对我说过你想当律师。

c. 介词宾语前：

I strongly object to *your saying that*. 我强烈反对你说这话。

I'm fed up with *your grumbling*! 你唧唧咕咕我都听烦了！

I'm not surprised at *your misunderstanding me*. 我并不为你误会我而感到奇怪。

I never dreamt of *its hurting you*. 我绝没想到它会伤你的心。

I have made no objection to *his doing it*. 我对他这样做没表示过反对。

There was no chance of *his getting scholarships*. 他没有机会得奖学金。

Since *my coming to London* I have not been well. 自从来到伦敦，我身体一直不舒服。

They're looking forward to *Mary's coming*. 他们都盼着玛丽来。

在口语中，有时用名词或人称代词宾格表示动名词的逻辑主语：

He didn't mind *Flora (her) leaving home*. 他不介意弗洛拉(她)离开家。

I don't remember *my mother complaining about it*. 我不记得我母亲曾抱怨此事。

I can't understand *him (his) leaving his wife*. 我不懂他为什么离开他的妻子。

He resented *me (my) being promoted before him*. 他怨恨我比他早升职。

12.2.7　动名词构成的合成名词

1) 许多合成名词由"动名词 + 名词"构成：

swimming pool 游泳池　　　　　　　　swimming suit 游泳衣

boxing competition 拳击比赛	speaking contest 演讲比赛
sleeping bag 睡袋	sleeping pill 安眠药片
writing desk 写字台	writing paper 信纸
diving suit 潜水衣	diving board 跳板
watering can 洒水壶	filling station 加油站
drawing board 绘图板	drawing pin 图钉
washing machine 洗衣机	washing powder 洗衣粉
fishing pole (美)钓鱼竿	fishing line 钓鱼线
drinking water 饮用水	drinking fountain 饮水台
waiting room 候车(诊)室	waiting list 候选人名单
parking lot (space) 停车场(位)	parking meter 停车计时器
checking account 活期账户	banking system 银行系统
sewing machine 缝纫机	printing-press 印刷机
hearing aid 助听器	operating table 手术台

2) 还有一类合成词由"形容词(名词)＋动名词"构成：

deep-ploughing 深耕	close-planting 密植
physical training 体育(锻炼)	job-hunting 找工作
weight lifting 举重	sight seeing 观光
window-shopping 逛商店(只看不买)	tap dancing 踢跶舞
air conditioning 空调	shadow boxing 打拳
zebra crossing 斑马纹人行横道	data processing 数据处理
food poisoning 食物中毒	family planning 计划生育
water-skiing 滑水	house-warming 乔迁酒宴
fire fighting 消防	ice-skating 滑冰
money grabbing 不择手段地捞钱	roller skating 溜旱冰

〔注〕有些动名词已成为名词，有些为不可数名词：

boating 划船	bowling 打保龄球	yachting 乘坐游艇
surfing 冲浪	dancing 跳舞	mountaineering 登山

有些为可数名词：

painting 画	saying 俗话	warning 警告
meaning 意思	ending 结局	feeling 感觉

有些甚至经常以复数形式出现：

findings 调查结果	savings 积蓄	surroundings 环境
sufferings 苦难	earnings 挣的钱	belongings 财物

12.3 现在分词的用法

12.3.1 现在分词概说

动词的 -ing 形式，除了作动名词外，还可以起其他作用，称为现在分词，它在句中可用来：

1) 构成谓语（主要是构成各种进行时态）：

They *are doing* some pattern practice. 他们在做句型练习。

She *is seeing* a friend off. 她在给一个朋友送行。

I'*ll be waiting* for you at the entrance. 我将在大门口等你。

They *have been designing* a new jet plane. 他们一直在设计一种新型喷气机。

2) 构成不定式的进行形式：

He seems *to be worrying* about something. 他似乎在为什么事发愁。

Walter happened *to be working* in the next room. 沃尔特碰巧在隔壁屋里干活。

They're said *to be making* an important experiment. 据说他们在进行一项重要试验。

I don't want you *to be wasting* your time like this. 我不希望你这样浪费时间。

3) 作表语：

The situation is quite *encouraging*. 形势很令人鼓舞。

4) 作定语：

He found her a *charming* girl. 他发现她是位迷人的姑娘。

5) 构成复合宾语：

I watched *the children flying kites*. 我看孩子们放风筝。

6) 作状语：

We spent all day *looking for you*. 我们花了一整天找你。

作为动词，它也可有自己的宾语 (a) 或状语 (b)，以构成现在分词短语：

a. He stood there for two hours watching *the game*. 他在那里站了两个钟头看比赛。

b. I saw her speaking *to a neighbour*. 我看见她和一位邻居讲话。

间或还可跟表语：

Feeling *tired*, I went to bed. 我感到很累就睡觉了。

现在分词可有下面这些形式：

	主动形式	被动形式
一般形式	doing	being done
完成形式	having done	having been done

12.3.2　现在分词作表语

1) 现在分词常可用作表语，特别是那些表示情绪的词：

The dirty street is *disgusting*.　那条肮脏的街道令人厌恶。

It's *amazing* that you should know that!　你竟然连这都知道，真令人惊奇!

The report is most *alarming*.　这份报告很令人惊恐。

He was very *amusing*.　他很有趣。

This interruption is very *annoying*.　这样的打断很让人恼火。

It's *astonishing* to me that he should be absent.　他竟然缺席，这使我感到吃惊。

The plight of the starving natives is *appalling*.　土著居民挨饿的境况简直可怕。

The book was rather *boring*.　那本书相当枯燥乏味。

The day was so *charming*.　天气真是好极了。

Some foreign press reports are quite *confusing*.　某些外国新闻报道很令人迷惑不解。

To us all this was peculiarly *distressing*.　对我们来说这一切都特别令人苦恼。

This was very *disappointing*.　这很令人失望。

The test results have been very *discouraging*.　测试结果很让人沮丧。

The sight had not been *encouraging*.　那景象并不令人鼓舞。

It is *frightening* even to think of the horrors of nuclear war.　即便是想象一下核战争的恐怖都令人毛骨悚然。

Skiing is more *exciting* than skating.　滑雪比溜冰更刺激。

She was very *pleasing* in her appearance.　她的外貌很招人喜欢。

It's all very *puzzling*.　这事整个令人困惑。

His concern for his mother is most *touching*.　他对母亲的关爱很感人。

It was *thrilling* to listen to the story of his adventures.　听他的冒险故事很激动人心。

2）一些表示状态、品质的现在分词也可用作表语：

The photograph is *missing*.　那张照片不见了。

She is always very *obliging*.　她总是乐于助人。

The reason he gave was not very *convincing*.　他给的理由不太有说服力。

These developments were rather *disturbing*.　这些发展情况相当令人不安。

The article was *misleading*, and the newspaper has apologized.　这篇文章具有误导性，报纸已经道歉了。

In a way, teaching *is rewarding*.　从某种意义上说，教书是有回报的。

The tea smells *inviting* and tastes fresh.　这茶香气诱人，味道清新。

The breeze was cool and *refreshing*.　这阵微风很凉爽提神。

That cake looks *tempting*.　那块蛋糕很诱人。

Is the matter *pressing*?　这事很紧迫吗？

The wheat crop looks *promising*.　小麦收成看来不错。

The difference was most *striking*.　差别很明显。

这样用的现在分词很多都已成了形容词。

12.3.3　现在分词作定语

1）上节提到的这类现在分词几乎都可以用作定语，修饰一个名词：

Mary is an *appalling* cook.　玛丽做饭很糟糕。

Those relations of his are *boring* people.　他那些亲属是些讨人嫌的人。

The experiment was an *amazing* success.　那项试验是一个惊人的成功。

That is the least *convincing* excuse you could offer.　那是你能提出的最没有说服力的理由。

It was an *astonishing* performance.　这是一场令人惊讶的演出。

That's a *frightening* thought.　这是一个可怕的想法。

There is a page *missing* from this book.　这本书缺了一页。

He's a *promising* new painter.　他是一位很有希望的新画家。

That must have been a *terrifying* experience.　那准是一段可怕的经历。

I found nothing *amusing* in the streets.　我在街上没发现什么趣事。

I found him a *charming* person.　我发现他是一个讨人喜欢的人。

I have had rather a *depressing* time. 我有过一段相当压抑的时期。

Acid rain has a *devastating* effect on the environment. 酸雨对环境有破坏性的影响。

It was a *distressing* situation for them. 对他们来说这是个痛苦的局面。

I have long thought of it as the most *enchanting* village in the area. 我长久以来都认为它是这地区最迷人的村庄。

It's the most *exciting* news. 这是最激动人心的消息。

He's a most *interesting* man. 他是个非常有趣的人。

What a *shocking* waste of time! 这样浪费时间真令人震惊!

It was a *thrilling* development. 这是令人激动的发展。

I've had a *tiring* day. 我累了一天。

2) 还有一些不及物动词的现在分词,不能用作表语,却可用作定语:

the *ailing* economy 不景气的经济

dwindling profits 日益减少的利润

growing doubts 越来越大的怀疑

the *existing* conditions 现有条件

the *remaining* days 剩下的岁月

a *shining* example 光辉的榜样

developing countries 发展中国家

a *falling* star 流星

living things 有生命的东西

the *rising* generation 在成长的一代

a *booming* town 日渐繁荣的城市

increasing demand 日益增长的需求

diminishing returns 日益减少的效益

the *prevailing* fashion 盛行的时装

lasting peace 持久的和平

the *leading* newspapers 主要报纸

the *ruling* class 统治阶级

the *ageing* population 日益老化的人口

the *reigning* champion 当前的冠军

a *resounding* victory 辉煌的胜利

3) 这类定语和构成合成词的动名词是有区别的。现在分词往往表示所修饰名词的动作,而动名词表示目的、用途等。试比较下面内容:

用现在分词作定语	由动名词构成的合成词
flying sauces (=a sauce that flies) 飞碟	*flying* suit (a suit one wears when flying) 飞行服
sleeping beauty 睡美人	*sleeping*-pills 安眠药片
the *waiting* crowd 等候的人群	the *waiting* room 候机(车)室
a *walking* dictionary 活字典	a *walking* stick 手杖
running water 自来水	*running* track 跑道
the *working* personnel 员工	*working* conditions 工作条件
a *living* language 活的语言	*living* standard 生活水平

4) 现在分词还可构成合成形容词作定语:

long-lasting effects 长远的影响	*long-standing* policy 传统政策
close-fitting clothes 紧身服	a *man-eating* beast 吃人的野兽
a *good-looking* girl 漂亮姑娘	a *hard-working* teacher 勤奋的教师
far-reaching designs 远大的计划	*never-ending* work 没完没了的工作
a *time-consuming* job 费时的工作	an *easy-going* man 好说话的人
a *record-breaking* jump 破纪录的一跳	an *epoch-making* event 划时代的事件
earth-shattering news 震撼世界的新闻	*labor-saving* device 节省劳力的装置
oil-bearing crops 油料作物	*fine-sounding* words 动听的言辞

5) 现在分词(短语)还可用在名词后作定语,作用接近一个定语从句:

a. Here is a leaflet *giving (=that gives) full particulars of the plan*. 这里有一份介绍这计划全部细节的宣传单。

This village is made up of 490 families *belonging (=who belonged) to five nationalities*. 村子里有四百九十户人家,分属五个民族。

China stretches across a vast area *covering (=which covers) the cold, temperate and tropical zones*. 中国幅员辽阔,包括寒带、温带和热带。

We are brothers *sharing (=who share) weal and woe*. 我们是患难与共的兄弟。

They plan to build a highway *leading (=which lead) into the mountains*. 他们计划修一条公路通往山区。

b. Who is the woman *talking (=who is talking) to Jim*? 和吉姆交谈的女人是谁?

There were 220 children *studying (=who were studying) in the art school*. 有二百二十个孩子在这所艺术学校学习。

There are a few boys *swimming (=who are swimming) in the stream*. 有几个男孩在小溪里游水。

There is a car *waiting (=which was waiting) outside*. 有一辆小汽车在外边等着。

The girl *sitting (=who was sitting) next to me was my cousin*. 坐在我旁边的姑娘是我表妹。

There is a bus *coming (=which is coming) up*. 一辆公共汽车正开过来。

He was woken up by a bell *ringing (=which was ringing)*. 他被铃声惊醒。

在把分词短语改为定语从句时,从句谓语可以是一个一般时态的动词 (a),

也可以是一个进行时态的动词(b)，这从上面的例句中可以看出。

12.3.4   现在分词构成复合结构

1) 现在分词可在某些动词后面构成复合宾语：

I **see** *him passing my house every day.*   我看见他天天从我房前走过。

Did you **hear** *the clock striking*?   你听见钟敲响吗？

I **smelt** *something burning.*   我闻到有东西烧糊了。

He **watched** *them rehearsing the play.*   他看他们排戏。

She **caught** *them stealing her apples.*   她撞见他们偷她的苹果。

I **found** *a man standing at the door.*   我发现门口站着一个人。

I could **feel** *the wind blowing on my face.*   我能感到风迎面吹来。

She **noticed** *him carrying a bag.*   她注意到他提着一个包。

He **kept** *them working all day.*   他让他们整天干活。

She soon **had** *them all laughing.*   她很快就让他们都笑了。

My clumsy mistake **set** *all the girls giggling.*   我愚蠢的错误使姑娘们都咯咯地笑了。

His letter **left** *me feeling pretty humble.*   他的信使我感到自己很卑微。

This news **started** *me thinking.*   这消息使我深思。

在 listen to 和 look at 后也可跟这种复合宾语：

I **listened to** *the band playing in the park.*   我听乐队在公园里演奏。

Just **look at** *the rain pouring down*!   瞧这倾盆大雨！

在某些动词后，复合宾语可由现在分词或不带 to 的不定式构成，表示动作正在进行时用现在分词，表示动作完成时用不定式，试比较下面句子：

> He saw her *working* in the garden. (She was working in the garden.)   他看见她在花园里干活。
>
> He saw her *enter* the room. (She entered the room.)   他看见她走进屋子。

> I heard a bell *ringing*. (The bell was ringing.)   我听见铃在响。
>
> I heard someone *knock* at the door. (He knocked at the door.)   我听见有人敲门。

> She felt her heart *beating* fast. (It was beating fast.)   她感到心跳很快。
>
> She felt someone *touch* her shoulder. (He touched her shoulder.)   她感到有人碰了碰她的肩膀。

有时两者都可以用:

I saw the train $\begin{Bmatrix} coming \\ come \end{Bmatrix}$ into the station.　我看见火车进站。

Did you notice him $\begin{Bmatrix} leaving \\ leave \end{Bmatrix}$ the house?　你注意到他离开这房子吗?

2) 上述结构很多可变为被动形式,这时句中可说包含了一个复合谓语:

He *was found lying on the floor*.　有人发现他躺在地上。

She *was* often *heard humming this song*.　人们常听见她哼这首歌。

He *was seen sitting in a cafe*.　有人看见他坐在一家咖啡馆里。

I *have been kept waiting for over an hour*.　让我等了一个多钟头。

The man *was caught selling drugs*.　那人卖毒品时被当场抓住。

The papers *were left lying around*.　文件散落了一地。

3) 有些介词后有时也可以跟包含现在分词的复合宾语:

This is a picture of *an old woman kneeling in a temple*.　这张画画的是一位老太太在庙里跪拜。

He was like *an old tree blossoming again*.　他就像古树又开了花。

The story is about *several boys hunting for treasure in the mountains*.　这故事讲的是几个男孩去深山寻宝。

The day was bright, with *a fresh breeze blowing*.　天气晴朗,不时吹来阵阵清风。

I can't move about in the city without *everybody knowing*.　在这座城市我的行踪无法不让大家知道。

4) 下面这类“名(代)词 + 现在分词”结构也可说是一种复合宾语:

I can't imagine *Grandma riding a motor-bike*.　我想象不出奶奶骑摩托车的样子。

I can't stop *him talking to the press*.　我无法阻止他和新闻界谈话。

I remember *him (my father) telling me about it*.　我记得他(我父亲)曾告知我此事。

Excuse *me not having come earlier*.　原谅我没早一点来。

He objected to *people working for such low wages*.　他反对人们为这么低的工资干活。

He insisted upon *a second message being sent*.　他坚持再发一份电报。

I should ask you instead of *you asking me*.　是我该问你而不是你问我。

12.3.5　现在分词作状语

1) 在某些动词 (a) 或复合谓语 (b) 后可用现在分词 (短语) 作状语:

a. He **spent** a lot of money *modernizing the house*.　他花了很多钱,把房子搞得很新潮。

We **wasted** a whole afternoon *trying to repair the car*.　我们试着修车浪费了整个下午。

She's **going** *shopping this afternoon*.　她今天下午要去购物。

The boy **came** *running into the house*.　男孩跑进屋来。

He **rode away** *whistling*.　他吹着口哨骑车走了。

Sophia **sat** *waiting* on the sofa in the sitting-room.　索菲娅坐在客厅沙发上等着。

I **stood** *watching her*, not knowing what to do.　我站着看着她,不知如何是好。

She was **lying** in bed *crying*.　她躺在床上哭。

He pretends to **busy** himself *writing*.　他假装忙着写东西。

Some **left** the hall *still weeping*.　有些人离开大厅时还在哭泣。

The manager **approached** us *smiling*.　经理笑着走近我们。

He **ran** out of the house *shouting*.　他喊叫着跑了出来。

b. The girls **are busy** *making artificial flowers*.　姑娘们在忙着做纸花。

She **was in the kitchen** *preparing supper*.　她在厨房做晚饭。

Many vehicles there **are idle** *awaiting repairs*.　许多车辆停在那里等候修理。

Over 20,000 people **were there** *watching the football match*.　有两万多人在那里观看足球赛。

Thousands of people **were gathered** at the airport *cheering the visiting president*.　数以千计的人聚集在机场向来访的总统欢呼。

The students **were assembled** in the school hall *celebrating the occasion*.　小学生们聚集在礼堂里庆祝这个日子。

Have you **been around** *seeing places*?　你去附近参观了什么地方没有?

2) 在不少情况下,现在分词 (短语) 可表示一个同时发生的次要的 (或者说伴随的) 动作,这时常有一个逗号把它和句子的主要部分分开,分词短语可以放在句首 (a),也可放在后部 (b),间或插在中间 (c):

a. *Opening the drawer*, he took out a box.　他打开抽屉,拿出一个盒子。

Taking off our shoes, we crept along the passage.　我们脱下鞋沿通道慢慢潜行。

Following Tom, they started to climb.　他们跟着汤姆开始往上爬。

Taking a key out of his pocket, he opened the door.　他从口袋里掏出钥匙开了门。

Travelling by jeep, we visited a number of cities.　我们坐吉普车旅行,参观了许多城市。

b. She went out, *slamming the door*.　她走了出去,砰的一声把门关上。

He fired, *wounding one of the bandits*.　他开枪打伤了一个匪徒。

Mary walked round the town, *looking at the sights*.　玛丽在城里转悠观景。

Please fill in this form, *giving your name, address, etc.*　请把这份表填一下,写下你的姓名、住址等。

I got home, *feeling very tired*.　我到了家,感觉非常疲劳。

c. Those youngsters, *shouldering spades and hoes*, left merrily for the fields.　那些年轻人扛着铁锹和锄头,高高兴兴下地去。

An old peasant, *bringing his own food*, volunteered as guide for us.　一位老农自带干粮要给我们当向导。

一般说来,现在分词表示的是句子主语的动作,换句话说,句子主语也是分词的逻辑主语。

3) 分词短语有时表示原因,相当于一个表示原因的状语从句,可以放在前面 (a)、后面 (b) 或中间 (c):

a. *Being a student* (=As he was a student), he was naturally interested in museums.　由于他是学生,他自然对博物馆很感兴趣。

Not knowing her address (=As we didn't know...), we couldn't get in touch with her.　因为我们不知道她的地址,没法和她联系。

Seeing nobody at home, she decided to leave them a note.　因为没见有人在家,她决定给他们留一个条。

Calling early, I found him at home.　因为去得早,我在他家找到了他。

b. They sent us an open letter, *hoping to get our support*.　他们寄给我们一封公开信,希望得到我们的支持。

They went on with their struggle, *thinking theirs was a just cause*.　他们继续斗争,认为他们的事业是正义的。

He never went out in daylight, *fearing that the police would recognize him*.　他白天从不出去,害怕警察会认出他来。

c. Many of us, *being so excited*, could not go to sleep that night.　那一晚上,我们中有很多人激动得都没睡着。

The doctor, *not wishing to alarm her*, didn't tell her how serious her condition was. 医生不想让她惊慌，没告诉她病情有多么严重。

4) 分词短语还可表示时间，相当于一个时间状语从句，这有三种情况：

a. 表示一个动作一发生，另一个动作则随即发生（相当于 when 引导的从句）：

Turning around (=When she turned around), she saw an ambulance driving up. 她转过身，看见一辆救护车开了过来。

Hearing the news (=When they heard the news), they all jumped with joy. 听到这消息，他们都高兴得跳起来。

Arriving at the worksite, he found them busy laying bricks. 到达工地时，他看见他们在忙着砌砖。

Returning home, he began writing a melody for it. 回到家里，他开始给它谱曲。

b. 表示在做某事的过程中，发生某事或做某事，这时前面仍保留连词 when 和 while：

They got engaged *when travelling in Europe*. 他们在欧洲旅行时订了婚。

We wear plimsolls *when doing physical exercises at school*. 我们在学校运动时都穿帆布球鞋。

Don't mention this *while talking to him*. 和他谈话时别提这事。

She got to know them *while attending a conference in Beijing*. 她在北京开会时认识了他们。

c. 表示上述情况时有也不带连词 when 或 while：

Coming (=While he was coming) down the mountain, he met Tom on the way. 他在下山路上碰到了汤姆。

Jim hurt his arm *(while) playing tennis*. 吉姆打网球时手臂受了伤。

The man slipped and fell *(when) getting off the bus*. 那人下车时一滑摔倒了。

Reading my newspaper, I heard the doorbell ring. 看报纸时我听见门铃响了。

〔注〕有时由动名词和介词构成的短语中，介词会省略，这短语也可看作是分词短语：

I'm fortunate *(in) having you with me*. 我很幸运有你和我在一起。

There's no point *(in) telling her about it*. 告诉她这事毫无意义。

Are you through *(with) asking questions*? 你问题问完了没有？

What's the use *(of) worrying*? 着急有什么用？

5）分词短语偶尔也可表示结果：

Her husband died in 1960, *leaving her with 5 children.* 她丈夫死于 1960 年，给她留下了五个孩子。

They opened fire, *killing one of our patrolmen.* 他们开枪打死了我们一个巡逻兵。

The snow lasted a week, *resulting in a serious traffic confusion in the whole area.* 雪下了一星期，造成整个地区严重的交通混乱。

有些表示状态或条件的从句，可以省略一些词，只剩下现在分词和连词一道构成状语：

He turned round from time to time *as if (he was) searching for someone.* 他不时转身望望，仿佛在找什么人似的。

She paused for a while *as though (she was) waiting for a reply.* 她停了一会儿，好像在等候回答。

If (you're) travelling north, you must change at Leeds. 如果是向北走，你得在利兹换车。

Unless (you are) paying by credit card, please pay in cash. 除非你用信用卡付款，否则请付现金。

12.3.6　关于现在分词短语结构的几个问题

1）现在分词的完成形式：

现在分词有时需用完成形式，说明它表示的动作在主要谓语表示的动作之前发生，这类短语或是作时间状语 (a)，或是作原因状语 (b)：

a. *Having found a hotel,* they began to look for a restaurant. 找到旅馆之后，他们就开始找餐馆。

Having reviewed his lessons, he went to bed. 他复习完功课就睡觉了。

Having got our tickets, we drove to the airport to board the plane. 买到机票之后，我们就开车到机场登机。

Having sent the children to school, she got ready to go to work. 送孩子们上学之后，她就准备去上班。

b. *Having been ill for two weeks,* she felt rather weak. 由于病了两周，她感到身体很虚弱。

Having lived there for some time, she knew the place quite well. 她在那里住过一段时间，因此对那地方很熟悉。

Having invited so many people, we had to prepare sufficient food.　既然请了那么多人，我们就得准备足够的食物。

Not having got an answer, I decided to write him another letter.　由于没收到回音，我决定再给他写一封信。

2）独立结构:

有时现在分词可以有自己的逻辑主语，称之为 **独立结构** (Absolute Construction):

The day being fine (=As the day was fine), we decided to go swimming.　由于天气晴朗，我们决定去游泳。

It being a holiday (=As it was a holiday), all the shops were shut.　由于这天是假日，所有商店都关门了。

We're playing golf this afternoon — *weather permitting (=if the weather permits)*.　要是天气允许，我们今天下午去打高尔夫球。

We explored the caves, *Peter acting as guide*.　由彼得当向导，我们探察了那些洞穴。

There being ice on the road, I told the driver to slow down.　路上有冰，我让司机开慢点。

3）现在分词构成句子状语:

现在分词一般表示句子主语的动作，但作句子状语 (说明说话人的看法) 时，则情况不是这样:

Strictly speaking, that school is not very old.　严格地说，那所学校不算很古老。

Broadly speaking, adjectives are words that qualify nouns.　广义地说，形容词是修饰名词的词。

I think, *personally speaking*, it's a good idea.　就我个人来说，我认为这是个好主意。

Judging by his testimonials, I think he will suit the post.　从他的推荐信看，我认为他适合这项工作。

He leads a very active life, *considering his age*.　考虑到他的年纪，他的生活是很活跃的。

Supposing he can't come, who will do the work?　假如他来不了，谁来干这活?

这类状语也可称为 **独立成分** (Independent Element)。

12.4 过去分词的用法

12.4.1 过去分词概说

过去分词在句中可以:

1) 构成谓语:

a. 和 have 一道构成完成时态或非谓语动词的完成形式:

I *haven't been* out much recently. 我最近没太出门。

I knew you *had been* busy. 我知道你一直很忙。

I'm sorry *not to have given* you enough help. 对不起没给你足够的帮助。

Having read the instructions, she snatched up the fire extinguisher. 看完说明书之后, 她抓起了灭火器。

b. 和 be 一道构成被动语态或非谓语动词的被动形式:

The letter *has been opened*! 信被人拆开了!

The children *were* well *looked after*. 孩子们受到很好的照顾。

He ought to *have been told* about it. 这事早该告诉他的。

He was said *to have been arrested*. 据说他被捕了。

2) 用作表语:

I am awfully *worried*. Daddy is ill. 我很着急, 我爸爸病了。

3) 用作定语:

She had a *worried* look on her face. 她满面愁容。

4) 构成复合宾语:

She wanted *the work finished* by Friday. 她要求这工作星期五前完成。

5) 作状语:

Aroused by the crash, he leapt to his feet. 他被撞击声惊醒, 一跃站起身来。

过去分词只有一种形式, 在大多数情况下都有被动的意思。

12.4.2 过去分词作表语

1) 过去分词作表语的时候很多 (其中有很多已变成形容词):

He was *amazed* and *enchanted* at the sight. 看到这景象他感到惊异着迷。

She was *annoyed* at your saying that. 你这样讲她很不高兴。

We were so *bored* that we couldn't help yawning. 我们厌烦得要命, 禁不住打起了呵欠。

She felt *confused*, even *frightened*. 她感到困惑不解，甚至很惊恐。

I'm *convinced* that what you said is quite right. 我相信你说的话很对。

They were very *pleased* with the girl. 他们很喜欢这姑娘。

His clothes were *covered* with dust. 他的衣服上尽是尘土。

I'm *disappointed* with you. 我对你很失望。

He was *astonished* to see his father. 他看到他父亲时很吃惊。

I'm afraid I'm slightly *drunk*. 可能我有一点醉了。

Personally, I'm extremely *satisfied*. 就我个人来说我感到极为满意。

I was *touched* by his sincerity. 他的诚恳使我很感动。

We were *delighted* to receive your letter. 收到你的信我们很高兴。

They were *thrilled (excited)* at the suggestion. 听了这建议他们非常激动。

He is not *interested* in research. 他对研究工作没兴趣。

We are all *involved*, whether you like it or not. 不管你愿不愿意，我们都已卷了进去。

I'm *obliged* to you for all you've done for us. 我很感激你为我们所做的一切。

How long have you been *married*? 你结婚多久了？

The couple were *devoted* to each other. 这对夫妻十分恩爱。

2）这种结构和被动语态是有差别的，"be＋表语"结构表示一种状态，而被动语态表示一个动作，试比较下面句子：

be＋表语结构（表示状态）	被动结构（表示动作）
The shop is closed now. 商店已关门。	It's usually closed at 8 o'clock. 它通常8点关门。
The window is broken. 窗子破了。	It was broken by Tim. 是蒂姆打破的。
The town is surrounded by hills. 该城四面环山。	Soon they were surrounded by bandits. 不久他们被匪徒包围了。
He was (is) wounded in the leg. 他腿受了伤。	They were wounded during the battle. 他们在战斗中受了伤。
The room is (was) deserted. 房间里空无一人。	She has been deserted by her husband. 她被丈夫遗弃了。
The new railway is not completed yet. 新的铁路还没建成。	It'll be completed next spring. 它将于明年春天建成。

"be＋表语"结构都包含 be 或其他系动词加过去分词，而被动结构必须与其相应的主动结构在时态上一致。例如右边例句的主动结构（Tim broke the window. / Her husband has deserted her. / They will complete the railway.) 和它们在时态上是一致的。

> 〔注〕有些带 -ed 结尾的词，并不是过去分词，而是由名词变化而来的形容词：
>
> I'm *ashamed* of myself for it. 为此我自感羞愧。
>
> As an artist, she is quite *gifted*. 作为画家，她很有天赋。
>
> I'm *indebted* to you for your help. 我很感谢你对我的帮助。

12.4.3 过去分词作定语

1) 有很多过去分词可用作定语，特别是表示情绪的词：

Mr. Knight gave a *satisfied* smile. 奈特先生满意地笑了笑。

She threw me a quick, *frightened* glance. 她迅速而惊恐地看了我一眼。

The *worried* look deepened upon her face. 她脸上的愁容加重了。

She had a *pleased* look on her face. 她脸上现出高兴的神情。

Martin's *confused* sorrows turned to optimism. 马丁烦乱的悲哀情绪转而变成了乐观情绪。

His *embarrassed* manner increased her doubt. 他尴尬的态度增加了她的怀疑。

He didn't noticed the *surprised (astonished)* look on her face. 他没有注意到她脸上惊讶的表情。

She could hear his *agitated* voice. 她可以听到他激动的声音。

His face wore a *puzzled* expression. 他脸上有一种困惑的表情。

2) 还有许多其它的过去分词可用作定语：

printed matter 印刷品	a written report 书面报告
guided missile 导弹	armed forces 武装力量
cooked food 熟食	boiled water 开(过的)水
frozen food 冷冻食品	canned food 罐头食品
smoked fish 熏鱼	fried eggs 煎鸡蛋
condensed milk 炼乳	dried fruit 果干
finished products 成品	classified document 机密文件
required courses 必修课	united front 统一战线
animated cartoons 动画片	furnished rooms 有家具的房间
a forced smile 勉强的笑容	mixed feelings 混杂的情绪

3) 还有许多由过去分词构成合成形容词:

air-conditioned rooms 有空调的房间

a simply-furnished apartment 一套陈设简单的房间

half-finished products 半成品

a hand-operated pump 手摇泵

a well-dressed woman 穿着讲究的女子

hand-made goods 手工制品

closed-circuit TV 闭路电视

a cautiously-worded statement 措辞谨慎的声明

strongly motivated students 学习动力很强的学生

4) 绝大多数过去分词都有被动的意思,有少部分过去分词却不然,而带有完成的意思:

the risen sun (=the sun that has just risen) 初升的太阳

an exploded bomb (=a bomb that has exploded) 爆炸了的炸弹

faded flowers 萎谢的花

vanished jewels 消失了的珠宝

returned students 归国留学生

a retired professor 退休的教授

escaped prisoners 逃犯

departed friends 离去的朋友

fallen leaves 落叶

abdicated emperor 退位的皇帝

his deceased wife 他的亡妻

new arrived visitors 新到的客人

swollen eyes 肿胀的眼睛

a dated map 过时的地图

〔注〕有些以 -ed 结尾的词,并不是过去分词,而是由名词变来的形容词:

armoured cars 装甲车

a bearded man 留络腮胡须的人

a detailed account 详细的叙述

a gifted boy 有天赋的孩子

flowered curtains 印花窗帘

concerted effort 同心协力

skilled workers 熟练工人

salaried class 工薪阶层

有些合成形容词也是由"名词 + ed"构成的:

absend-minded 心不在焉的

cold-blooded 冷血的

good-natured 天性善良的

kind-hearted 心地善良的

one-sided 片面的

open-minded 心胸开阔的

short-sighted 近视的

muddle-headed 糊里糊涂的

5) 有些过去分词短语跟在所修饰词后面,作用接近于一个定语从句:

What's the language *spoken (=that is spoken) in that country*? 那个国家讲的是什么语言?

Is there anything *planned for tonight*? 今晚有什么活动吗?

They're problems *left over by history*. 它们是历史遗留下来的问题。

Suddenly there appeared a young woman *dressed in green*. 突然出现一个穿绿衣服的青年女子。

This is something *unheard of in history*. 这时史无前例的事。

In the end the program *offered by Wilson was adopted*. 最后威尔逊提出的计划通过了。

The conference *suggested by the Czar* was held in Hague. 沙皇建议的会议在海牙召开了。

The play *put on by the teachers* was a big success. 老师们表演的戏很成功。

6) 间或跟在名词后的可能是一个单一的过去分词，而不是短语：

They didn't allow us to make the alterations *suggested*. 他们不允许我们根据建议进行修改。

The experience *gained* will be of great value to us. 取得的经验对我们将有重大价值。

The designers decided to change the materials *used*. 设计者决定改变所用的材料。

The man *concerned* was her husband. 有关者即是她的丈夫。

Is there anybody *injured*? 有人受伤了吗？

Do you know the number of books *ordered*? 你知道订购的书有多少？

She liked all the courses *offered*. 她对所开的课程都很喜欢。

How much time is there *left*? 还剩下多少时间？

7) 作定语的过去分词常指已经完成的动作，若要表示现在正在进行的动作，要用过去分词的进行形式，也就是现在分词的被动形式：

We must keep a secret of the things *being discussed (=which are being discussed)* here. 我们必须对在此讨论的问题保密。

What do you think of the summit meeting *being held* in Vienna? 你对正在维也纳召开的峰会有什么看法？

I knew nothing about the experiment *being conducted there*. 我对在那里进行的试验一无所知。

12.4.4 过去分词构成复合宾语

1) 在某些动词后可用过去分词构成复合宾语：

We'll **get** her X-rayed. 我们要给她透视。

I've recently **had** *my appendix removed*.　我最近把盲肠割了。

Have you ever **heard** *a song sung in Japanese*?　你听过用日语唱的歌吗?

Rarely had I **seen** *him so worked-up*.　我很少见他这样激动过。

He **watched** *the bed carried out of the door*.　他看着床被搬出屋去。

We all **wished** *the problem settled*.　我们都希望这问题得到解决。

She didn't **want** *her daughter taken out after dark*.　她不希望天黑后女儿被带出门。

He **felt** *a great weight taken off his mind*.　他感到心头如释重负。

Keep *your mouth shut* and *your eyes open*.　(谚)少说多看。

The scents **made** *her drunk*.　这些气味使她陶醉。

How would you **like** *your hair cut*?　你喜欢把头发剪成什么式样?

He **found** *the house deserted*.　他发现房子里空无一人。

At 4:30 p.m. the chairman **declared** *the session closed*.　下午四点半主席宣布闭会。

He **acknowledged** *himself defeated*.　他承认自己被打败了。

We do **consider** *ourselves justified in doing so*.　我们的确认为我们这样做是有道理的。

2) 介词 with 后有时也可以跟这类复合宾语:

He sat **with** *his arms clasped round his knees*.　他双手抱膝坐着。

All afternoon he worked **with** *the door locked*.　整个下午他都锁着门在家工作。

That year ended **with** *nothing settled*.　那一年什么事也没解决就结束了。

12.4.5　过去分词作状语

1) 过去分词有时可用作状语,修饰谓语(多放在句首,也可放在后面或插在中间):

Seen from the hill, the city looks magnificent.　从山上看这座城市非常壮观。

Convinced that they were trying to poison her, she refused to eat anything.　她认为他们想毒害她,便拒绝吃任何东西。

Weakened by successive storms, the bridge was no longer safe.　连续的暴雨使桥身受损,这座桥已不再安全。

A bit frightened, I handed it to her.　我略带惊恐地把它递给了她。

Greatly interested, I asked how he played these new works.　大感兴趣之下，我问他是如何演奏这些新作的。

Given good health, I hope to finish the work this year.　如果身体好，我希望今年完成这工作。

She entered, *accompanied by her mother*.　她由她母亲陪着走进来。

They came in, *followed by their wives*.　他们走了进来，妻子们跟随在后。

He soon felt asleep, *exhausted by the journey*.　由于旅途劳顿，他很快就睡着了。

Henry, *terribly embarrassed*, blushed too.　亨利十分尴尬，脸也红了。

Mr. Cooper, *deeply moved*, thanked him again and again.　库柏先生深为感动，一再向他表示感谢。

Tom, *horrified at what he had done*, could at first say nothing.　汤姆对他做的事感到恐惧，一时说不出话来。

2）有时一个单独的过去分词也可用作状语：

Depressed, he went to see his elder sister.　情绪低沉时他就去看他的姐姐。

Frustrated, he went back to his hometown.　他灰心丧气地回到家乡。

"She's right," he said, *pleased*.　他高兴地说，"她是对的。"

He turned away *disappointed*.　他失望地走开了。

Shelley, *astonished*, urged her to explain.　雪莱很是吃惊，忙催她解释。

3）过去分词有时和连词一起用：

I went on talking, *though continually interrupted by George*.　我继续讲我的，尽管不断被乔治打断。

They would never do this *unless compelled*.　除非受到强迫，否则他们决不会做这样的事。

He will come *if asked*.　若受到邀请，他会来的。

When treated with kindness, he was very amiable.　当别人善待他时，他是非常和蔼可亲的。

He started *as if awakened from a dream*.　他吓了一跳，仿佛从梦中惊醒似的。

Whenever asked about it, he could hardly hold back his emotions.　每当有人问及此事，他就难以控制自己的感情。

4）在少数情况下，过去分词可引导一个句子状语：

Judged by ordinary standards, he was reliable.　用普通标准来判断，他是可靠的。

Granted the exceptions, Tony agreed that all English women are haughty.　如

果允许有例外的话，托尼同意英国女人都是很高傲的。

Given good weather, our ship will reach Bombay on Monday evening.　如
　果天气好，我们的船星期一晚上可到达孟买。

Provided (that) there is no opposition, we shall hold the meeting there.　如
　果没有人反对，我们将在那里开会。

分词前有时还有一个逻辑上的主语：

Everybody, *myself excepted*, said no.　除我之外，所有的人都不赞成。

They'll send you the book for $ 2.75, *postage included*.　你若寄去2.75美
　元，他们就会寄你这本书，邮资在内。

Everything considered, his plan seems better.　从各方面考虑，他的计划
　似乎好一些。

第 13 章　动词句型

13.1　概　说

13.1.1　英语的基本句型

1) 语言是千变万化的，要掌握语言，必须掌握语言的核心。动词句型可说是语言的核心，是骨干。纲举则目张。因此要对英语有比较全面的了解，应当抓住 **英语动词句型** (English Verb Patterns)。掌握好这些基本句型，就可为灵活运用语言打下基础。

2) 英语有五种基本句型：

(1) 主语＋不及物动词：

　　Everybody smiled.　大家都笑了。

(2) 主语＋及物动词＋宾语：

　　He knows everything.　他什么都知道。

(3) 主语＋双宾动词＋间接宾语＋直接宾语：

　　I showed him my passport.　我把护照拿给他看。

(4) 主语＋系动词＋表语 (补语)：

　　The boy looks healthy.　那男孩看来身体很好。

(5) 主语＋及物动词＋宾语＋宾语补语：

　　What made you angry?　什么使你生气?

祈使句的主语一般都省略掉。

13.1.2　动词、动词短语和成语动词

1) 担任谓语的可以是一个单一的动词：

　　Who *knows*?　谁知道?

　　Water *flows*.　水会流。

2) 也可以是一个 **动词短语** (Verbal Phrase)：

　　I *have been reading* (a novel).　我一直在看书(小说)。

Have you *got* any carbon paper?　你有复写纸吗？

Where *are* you *going to stay*?　你准备住哪儿？

3) 也可以是**成语动词** (Phrasal Verb)：

Jane's *looking after* the children.　简在看孩子。

He *turned down* the proposal.　他拒绝了这项建议。

The match *has been called off*.　比赛被取消了。

因此谈到动词时就有这三种可能性。

13.1.3　每个成分都可有多种表示法

句子的成分常有多种表示法，例如宾语就可以有多种形式：

1) 名词或代词：

Love me, love *my dog*.　(谚)爱屋及乌。

Look at *the bird (it)*.　瞧那只鸟(它)。

2) 数词：

I want *two*.　我要两个。

3) 动名词：

She loves *window-shopping*.　她喜欢逛商店。

4) 不定式：

I hope *to see you again*.　我希望再次见到你。

5) 复合结构：

I wish *you happy*.　我希望你幸福。

His words made *her weep*.　他的话使她哭了。

6) 从句：

I suppose *you're right*.　我想你是对的。

(Do you) See *what I mean*?　懂我的意思吗？

7) 连词 + 不定式：

I'll show you *how to do it*.　我将教你怎样做。

其他成分如表语、宾语的补语也有多种形式，因此实际动词句型不止五个，而是四十多个。

13.1.4　修饰语

1) 许多名词和代词常有不少修饰语，称为定语。可担任定语的有：

a. 数词：

Five people were injured.　五个人受了伤。

b. 代词：

He must marry her, there is *no other* alternative.　他必须和她结婚,别无选择。

c. 形容词 (包括合成形容词)：

Your nephew is a *nice little* boy.　你的侄子是个好小孩。

He is an *out-and-out* conservative.　他是个十足的保守派。

d. 名词或名词所有格：

He majors in *computer* science.　他是学电脑的。

We're studying *Robert Burns'(s)* poems.　我们在学罗伯特·彭斯的诗。

e. 介介短语：

My love *for you* is deeper than the sea.　我对你的爱比海深。

f. 不定式：

There is no need *to worry* at all.　根本没有必要发愁。

g. 分词和动名词：

What are the issues *facing the workers today*?　今天工人们面临的是些什么问题?

They're making a study of the farming methods *used* in *developed* countries.　他们正在研究发达国家使用的耕作方法。

h. 副词：

Is there anything *on* after supper?　晚饭后有什么活动吗?

The *then* headmaster ordered these books.　这些书是那时的校长定购的。

i. 从句：

I'll do all *I can* to help you.　我将竭尽所能来帮助你。

2) 动词也有修饰语, 称为状语, 也可以由许多成分担任：

a. 副词：

Your sister dances *beautifully*.　你妹妹舞跳得很优美。

b. 介词短语：

A mother loves a baby *from the bottom of her heart*.　母亲打心眼里爱自己的婴儿。

c. 不定式：

I'm sorry *to bother you with all this*.　对不起用这些事来麻烦你。

d. 分词：

Romeo, *believing that Juliet was dead*, decided to kill himself.　罗密欧以

为朱丽叶死了，决定自杀。

Stunned by the blow, Peter fell to the ground.　受到重重的一击，彼得倒在地上。

e. 形容词：

She gave him the overcoat, *anxious to be of service*.　她把大衣给他，急着要帮他点忙。

f. 词组 (成语)：

He thought about it *day and night*.　他日夜想着这事。

g. 复合结构 (独立结构)：

The weather being so nice, we didn't want to stay indoors.　天气那么好，我们不想待在家里。

h. 从句：

I'll find her *wherever she may be*.　不管她在哪里我都要找到她。

i. 名词：

She is feeling *miles* better today.　她今天感觉好多了。

正因为有这些修饰语，英语就变得丰富多彩。如果说动词句型是躯干，修饰语就是枝叶，基本句型是骨架，各类修饰语就是血肉。这两者是相辅相成的，片面强调一方面对语言学习都是不利的，在初学阶段掌握基本句型至关重要。脑中有一个全图，有明确的结构概念，添枝加叶就不难了。按这样的规律安排句子，句子就可以比较平稳地站起来，然后再充实血肉，就相对比较容易了。

13.2　第一类句型——主语 + 不及物动词

13.2.1　主语 + 不及物动词 (1)

The sun *is rising*.　太阳正在升起。

Tim *is sleeping*.　蒂姆在睡觉。

It's *snowing*.　天在下雪。

The train *is arriving*.　火车就要到站了。

We *waited* and *waited*.　我们等了又等。

"Are you going?" "That *depends*."　"你要去吗？" "那得看情况。"

The blind *do not see*.　盲人看不见东西。

Can you *read*?　你识字吗？

May I *go*?　我可以去吗？

It *doesn't pay*. 这不值得。

Will £ 5 *do*? 五英镑够吗?

I'*ll try*. 我试试看。

13.2.2   主语 + 不及物动词 + 状语 (2)

Did you *sleep well*? 你睡得好吗?

Don't *drive so fast*. 车别开这么快。

She *is studying hard at the university*. 她在大学学习很用功。

They *sat together* very *quietly*. 他们静静地坐在一起。

She *swims like a fish*. 她游起来像条鱼。

He *danced for joy*. 他高兴得跳起舞来。

She *often dreams*. 她常常做梦。

The man *then walked off*. 那人随后走了。

She *is trembling all over*. 她浑身发抖。

You *go first* and I *will follow behind*. 你先走,我跟着。

Her lecture *lasted an hour*. 她的讲座持续了一个小时。

The temperature *fell ten degrees*. 气温下降了十度。

13.2.3   主语 + 不及物动词 + 副词(构成成语动词) (3)

The economic crisis *broke out* first in the United States. 那场经济危机首先在美国爆发。

The meeting *broke up* in great confusion. 会议在一片混乱中散了。

The engine *broke down*. 发动机坏了。

The bomb *blew up*. 炸弹爆炸了。

How did the accident *come about*? 事故是怎样发生的?

Her temperature *came down* in the morning. 早上她的体温下降了。

The concert *came off* well. 音乐会开得很成功。

The baby *is coming on* well. 宝宝长得很健康。

Sales *have been dropping off* badly. 销售量大大下降。

If you don't like the idea, *drop off*. 如果你不喜欢这个主意,可以退出。

The scheme *fell through*. 计划失败了。

13.2.4　主语 + 不及物动词(有被动意思) (4)

The door *blew* open.　门被风吹开了。

Cheese *cuts* easily.　干酪很好切。

Protein *digests* slowly.　蛋白质消化很慢。

The door *locks* automatically.　这门会自动锁上。

She *photographs* well.　她很上相。

Is the book *selling* well?　这书好销吗?

The window *won't shut*.　窗子关不上了。

Silk *stains* easily.　丝绸染色很容易。

Does this cloth *wash* well?　这布耐洗吗?

Her eyes *filled* with tears.　她的眼睛充满泪水。

Where *is* the new film *showing*?　新片在那里上映?

The vegetables *are cooking*.　蔬菜正在炖。

13.3　第二类句型——主语 + 及物动词 + 宾语

13.3.1　主语 + 及物动词 + 名词(代词) (5)

1)"主 + 谓 + 宾"可能是英语中最常见的句型,在多数情况下宾语由名词或代词表示:

Do you *know these people (them)*?　你认识这些人(他们)吗?

I*'ll have vanilla ice-cream*.　我要香草冰淇淋。

The orchestra *played the National Anthem*.　管弦乐队演奏了国歌。

He *loved poetry*.　他喜欢诗。

Have you *ordered your meal*?　你点饭菜了吗?

We *took the early flight to Brussels*.　我们乘早班飞机去布鲁塞尔。

What did he *say*?　他怎么说?

Silence *means consent*.　(谚)沉默意味着同意。

Shall I *call a taxi*?　我要不要叫一辆出租车?

He *left school* in 1998.　他 1998 年从学校毕业。

They *found a cure* for cancer.　他们找到了一个治疗癌症的方法。

Wilhelm Roentgen *discovered X rays*.　威廉·容特根发现了 X 光。

2) 有些动词和名词构成一种 **习惯用语**(Idiom),有特别的意思:

Don't *catch cold*.　别感冒了。

This theory doesn't *hold water*. 这种理论站不住脚。

Make haste, or we shall be late. 快点，否则我们要迟到了。

At the end of the week George *took leave*. 周末时乔治告辞离去。

This sentence doesn't *make sense*. 这句子毫无意义。

She's always *making a fuss*. 她老是大惊小怪。

We'll *make room* for you in the back of the car. 我们将在车后部为你腾地方。

She's always *making trouble* for her friends. 她老给朋友们制造麻烦。

The storm *played havoc* with the orchard. 暴风雨给果园造成了巨大损害。

Other airlines also *followed suit*. 别的航空公司也照着做了。

Take care! The ice is thin. 当心！冰很薄。

When will the drug *take effect*? 这药什么时候开始起作用？

He always *takes pains* with his work. 他工作一向尽心尽力。

The action of the play *takes place* in ancient Rome. 这出戏的故事发生在古罗马。

The idea *took root* in his mind. 这想法在他脑中扎了根。

He always *takes offence* at any kind of criticism. 听到任何批评意见他都会生气。

13.3.2　主语 + 及物动词 + 自身代词 (6)

1) 有大量动词可以用自身代词作宾语：

I can't *express myself* in English. 我不会用英语表达自己的思想。

He *reproached himself* for his rudeness. 他为自己的无礼而自责。

Now I'll *introduce myself*. 现在我来自我介绍一下。

He often *contradicts himself*. 他常常自相矛盾。

She *saw herself* in the mirror. 她在镜子里看到了自己。

I can *support myself*. 我能自己养活自己。

Don't *deceive yourself*. 不要自己骗自己。

She *killed herself* by jumping into the well. 她跳井自杀了。

I *asked myself* several questions. 我问了自己几个问题。

They *blamed themselves* for the accident. 他们为事故而自责。

This refrigerator *defrosts itself*. 这台冰箱能自动除霜。

有些成语动词后也可跟自身代词：

> *Look after yourself.* 照顾好自己。
>
> *Take care of yourselves.* 自己保重。

2) "动词 + 自身代词" 可构成固定词组：

Don't *overwork yourself.* 别让自己太劳累。

Are you *enjoying yourselves*? 你们玩得好吗？

She *prided herself* on her financial success. 她为她经济上的成就而感到自豪。

She *busied herself* tidying up her desk. 她忙着整理她的书桌。

Why did you *absent yourself* (from school) yesterday? 你昨天为什么缺席(课)?

They *seated themselves* on the bench. 他们在长凳上坐了下来。

Help yourself to a beer. 请喝杯啤酒。

He *excused himself* from the meeting. 他请求不参加会议。

You must *behave yourself* at the party. 在晚会上你要规矩一点。

Pull yourself together and try and eat something. 打起精神来，多少吃点东西。

Don't *strain yourself* talking, dear. 亲爱的，别说得太累。

He *distinguished himself* in the examination. 他在考试中表现出色。

3) 有些动词后可跟自身代词，也可以不跟：

> Go and *wash yourself*, Tom. 汤姆，去洗一洗。
>
> I must *wash* before dinner. 吃饭前我得洗一洗。

> The kid is still too young to *dress itself*. 孩子还太小，不能自己穿衣。
>
> Get up and *dress* quickly. 起来，快穿好衣服。

> Tim rose and *hid himself* in the little study. 蒂姆起身躲在小书房里。
>
> Where is he *hiding*? 他躲在哪里？

> We *engage ourselves* to fulfil our obligations. 我们保证尽职尽责。
>
> He had *engaged* to finish it by May. 他曾保证在五月前办完此事。

13.3.3　主语 + 动词 + 同源宾语 (7)

有些动词通常为不及物动词，都可用一个与之同源的名词构成宾语，这种宾语称为 **同源宾语** (Cognate Object)：

Alice *laughed a* scornful *laugh.* 爱丽丝鄙夷地笑了笑。

He could *sleep* the peaceful *sleep* of the young.　他可以睡得像年轻人那样平静。

He *smiled a* strange *smile*.　他古怪地笑了笑。

As he slept, he *dreamed a dream*.　他睡觉时做了一个梦。

She closed her eyes and *wished a wish*.　她闭上眼睛许了一个愿。

She *lived a* long happy *life* and *died a* natural *death*.　她一生幸福长寿,寿终正寝。

They were to *dance the Rose-dance* together.　他们将在一起跳玫瑰舞。

He *said his say* and then sat down.　他说完他的话然后坐下。

13.3.4　主语 + 成语动词 + 宾语

成语动词大体上有下面六类:

1) 及物动词 + 副词 (8):

He *handed in* his resignation this morning.　他今天上午递交了辞呈。

Cross out those two sentences.　把那两句划掉。

They *brought forward* a new scheme of taxation.　他们提出了一个新的征税计划。

You could only *bring about* her misery.　你只会给她带来痛苦。

Overwork brought on insomnia.　过度劳累造成失眠。

He had *carried out* our instructions to the letter.　他不折不扣地执行了我们的指示。

She has *put aside* a good sum of money.　她存了一大笔钱。

All the chestnut trees have *put forth* blossoms.　所有的栗树都开花了。

Who *put forward* such a view?　谁提出了这样的观点?

We can *put off* the meeting.　我们可以推迟开会。

副词有时可放到宾语后面去:

I'm not *putting* my meaning *across* very well.　我没把我的意思讲清楚。

We can *put it off* one more week.　我们可以把它再推迟一星期。

I'll *put* the particulars *down* in my notebook.　我将把详细情况记在笔记本上。

Put your coat *on*.　把外套穿上。

Take your shoes *off*, please.　请把鞋脱掉。

I'll *think it over*.　我要好好想一想。

这类句子也可用于被动结构:

The rebellion *was put down* with extreme brutality. 这次叛乱被极其残酷地镇压下去了。

The meeting *has been put off*. 会议被推迟了。

Another supermarket *has been put up* near our house. 我们家附近又建了一座超级市场。

A guerilla warfare *was carried on* successfully there. 在那里游击战进行得很成功。

2) 不及物动词 + 介词 (9):

We must *abide by* the rules of the game. 我们必须遵守游戏规则。

The Yellowstone Park *abounds in* wild animals. 黄石公园有大量的野生动物。

They will not *agree to* that arrangement. 他们不会同意那样的安排。

I *called upon* Mrs. Froster this evening. 今晚我去拜访了佛罗斯特夫人。

She's been *looking after* the luggage. 她一直在照看行李。

He was *looking for* summer employment. 他在找暑期工作。

We'll *look into* this matter together. 我们一道来调查这件事。

He *came on* an old friend in thelibrary. 他在图书馆碰到一位老朋友。

I don't *object to* the idea. 我不反对这个意见。

Her suggestion *met with* opposition. 她的建议遭到反对。

He *thought of* his boyhood. 他想起了他的童年。

Light *consists of* waves. 光由光波构成。

个别这种成语动词也可用于被动结构:

The baby *was looked after* by her little sister. 宝宝由她的小姐姐照看。

Many difficulties and setbacks *will be met with*. 会碰到很多困难挫折。

3) 不及物动词 + 介词 + 名词 (10):

Thus the first workers' league *came into being*. 就这样第一个工人联盟诞生了。

Their hydrangeas were *coming into flower*. 他们的绣球花正在绽放。

The treaty will *come into force* next month. 条约下月生效。

The spring term had *come to an end*. 春季学期结束了。

The old building was *falling into pieces*. 那座老楼要崩塌了。

He *rose to his feet* to reply to the speech of welcome. 他站起身答谢欢迎词。

Stand at attention! 立正!

Don't *stand on ceremony*. 不要客气。

Soon he *went to sleep*. 不一会儿他就睡着了。

She *went to pieces* when she heard her daughter was in the hospital. 听说
    女儿住院，她精神崩溃了。

Don't *fall into bad habits*. 不要养成坏习惯。

在这类结构中虽然介词后有宾语，但整个成语却接近于一个不及物动词，
后面没有句子宾语，为了方便列在这里，放在 13.2.3 节后也可以。

4）不及物动词 + 副词 + 介词 (11)：

We shouldn't *look down on* this work. 我们不应当看不起这种工作。

The children were eagerly *looking forward to* the party. 孩子们都急切盼
    望着这个晚会。

Look out for snakes. 当心蛇。

The window *looks out on* the flower-beds. 窗子面对着花坛。

He will *carry on with* his plan. 他将继续推行他的计划。

We must *catch up with* them. 我们必须赶上他们。

The teacher *came down on* me for talking in class. 因为我在课堂上讲话
    老师批评了我。

Many Congressmen *came (cried) out against* the bill. 许多国会议员表示
    反对这项法案。

This town *dates back to* Roman times. 这座城市罗马时代就有了。

They have *done away with* this barbarous custom. 他们破除了这个野蛮
    的习俗。

We must *face up to* our difficulties. 我们必须勇敢地面对困难。

He doesn't *feel up to* the job. 他感觉不能胜任这项工作。

这类成语动词有时可用于被动结构：

They *are looked down on* by everyone. 谁都瞧不起他们。

The day had *been looked forward to* for a month. 这个日子大家已盼望了
    一个月了。

These privileges must *be done away with*. 这些特权应当废除。

The truth *has to be faced up to*. 必须正视事实。

5）及物动词 + 名词 + 介词 (12)：

Pay attention to your grammar. 注意你的语法。

I'll *take care of* it. 我来料理此事。

A bad workman *finds fault with* his tools. 拙匠常怪工具差。

We've *lost touch with* him. 我们和他失去了联系。

Suddenly he *caught sight of* Mary.　突然他瞧见了玛丽。

The depression *gave rise to* wide spread unemployment.　经济萧条引起了广泛的失业。

The book soon *found favour with* the American public.　这书很快受到美国公众的欢迎。

The naughty boy *takes* great *delight in* pulling the dog's tail.　那调皮男孩喜欢拉狗尾巴。

She always *takes* particular *notice of* me.　她总是特别注意我。

He *made friends with* the other boys.　他和其他男孩子交了朋友。

Then he *gave place to* a younger man.　后来他把位置让给了一个较年轻的人。

He *made* no *reference to* Peter.　他没有提到彼得。

这类成语动词也可用于被动结构：

The matter has never been paid attention to (No attention has ever been paid to this matter).　这问题从来没被注意过。

No reference was made by anyone to the past.　没有任何人提到过去。

Preparations are being made for the sports meet.　运动会的准备工作正在进行。

She's well taken care of.　她受到很好的照顾。

6）及物动词＋自身代词＋介词 (13)：

Finally he *avenged himself on* the enemy.　最后他向敌人报了仇。

He had to *accustom himself to* the cold weather here.　他得让自己习惯于这里的寒冷天气。

Help yourself to some more meat (vegetable).　再吃点肉(蔬菜)吧。

He *applied himself to* the task before him.　他致力于眼前的工作。

He *availed himself of* the opportunity to speak to her.　他利用这机会和她说话。

She *abandoned herself to* despair.　她陷入绝望之中。

She *dedicated herself to* conserving our natural resources.　她致力于保护我们的自然资源。

He *devoted himself to* helping the poor.　他献身于帮助穷人的工作。

She has to *familiarize herself with* the use of the new tool.　她得让自己熟悉新工具的用法。

I must *accommodate myself to* your plan.　我必须使自己适应你的计划。

They no longer *troubled themselves about* him.　他们不再为他烦心了。

You must *reconcile yourself to* a life of hardship and poverty. 你必须让自己安于一种艰难困苦的生活。

13.3.5　主语 + 及物动词 + 不定式（作宾语）

1） 有大量及物动词可以跟不定式作宾语 (14):

Someone is **asking** *to see you.* 有人要求见你。

We can't **afford** *to pay such a price.* 我们出不起这样高的价钱。

I can't **bear** *to see you like this.* 我不忍看你这个样子。

I didn't **expect** *to find you here.* 我没想到在这里看见你。

He **decided** *to move to Chicago.* 他决定搬到芝加哥去。

They **demanded** *to see my passport.* 他们要求验看我的护照。

She **longed** *to be back in England.* 她渴望回英国。

She **hated** *to lose her temper.* 她不愿发脾气。

He **offered** *to lend me some books.* 他主动提出借我几本书。

He **promised** *to see her home.* 他答应送她回家。

You must **try** *to improve.* 你必须设法改进。

I don't **wish** *to leave my mother.* 我不愿意离开我母亲。

关于这种结构可参阅第 12.1.4 节。

2） 有些动词后可用连接副词（代词）和不定式一道构成宾语 (15):

You must *learn when to give advice* and *when to be silent.* 你得学会什么时候出主意什么时候沉默。

He *explained how to use the parachute.* 他讲解了如何使用降落伞。

Ask him where to go. 问他该往哪里走。

I don't *know who to ask advice from.* 我不知道该向谁请教。

I must *think what to do.* 我必须考虑怎么办。

He was *wondering whether to follow her or to go upstairs.* 他不知道该跟她走还是该上楼。

He *forgot which way to go.* 他忘了该走哪条路。

I *discovered how to start the machine.* 我弄懂了该怎样启动这台机器。

13.3.6　主语 + 及物动词 + 动名词（作宾语）(16)

Would you *mind waiting a few minutes*? 可否劳驾等几分钟？

Why have they *delayed opening the new school*? 他们为什么推迟开办这所新学校?

I can't *imagine lying like this*, I would go crazy. 我不能想象这样躺着,我会发疯的。

I don't *recommend buying that dictionary*. 我不建议买那本字典。

I *prefer standing*. 我宁愿站着。

I *propose resting for half an hour*. 我建议休息半小时。

Do you *like reading novels*? 你喜欢看小说吗?

She could not *help feeling depressed*. 她禁不住感到抑郁。

关于这种结构可参阅第 12.2.3 节。

13.3.7 主语 + 及物动词 + that 引导的从句(作宾语)(17)

1) 有大量动词可以跟 that 引导的从句作宾语(that 有时可省略):

I **guess** *we'll leave now*. 我想我们得走了。

Andrew **heard** *that they were shortly leaving for South Africa*. 安德鲁听说他们不久要去南非。

I **hope** *that I have said nothing to pain you*. 我希望我没说什么使你难过的话。

They **proved** *that the earth was round*. 他们证明地球是圆的。

I **learn** *that he is in business in Boston*. 听说他在波士顿做生意。

I **felt** *I had little energy left*. 我感觉一点力气都没有了。

We have to **admit** *that he's a highly competent man*. 我们得承认他是一个非常称职的人。

She **never doubted** *that she was right*. 她从未怀疑过她是对的。

He **estimated** *that the vase was 3,000 years old*. 他估计这花瓶已存在三千年了。

He **claimed** *that he saw the accident*. 他声称他目睹了这次车祸。

关于哪些动词后可跟这种成分作宾语,可参阅第 21.4.1 节。

2) 在某些动词后,从句中谓语(在美国)要用动词原形,在英国多用 "should + 动词原形" 构成谓语(用动词原形的人也不少):

I **suggest** *that we (should) leave early for the airport*. 我建议我们早点动身去机场。

She **insisted** *that I (should) be present*. 她坚持要我出席。

They **demanded** *that the right to vote (should) be given to every adult.* 他们要求给予每个成年人以选举权。

I'd **recommend** *(that) you see a solicitor.* 我建议你去找律师。

He **proposed** *that we go into the city to see her.* 他建议我们进城去找她。

He **requested** *that they free the hostages.* 他请求他们释放人质。

The situation **requires** *that I (should) be there.* 形势要求我待在那里。

Mrs. Godwin **urged** *that he see her.* 戈德温夫人敦促他去见她。

He **asked** *that the message be given to Madame immediately.* 他要求把这电报立即送给夫人。

I **ordered (commanded)** *that we (should) attack at once.* 我命令我们立即发起进攻。

〔注〕有时可用先行词 it 作形式上的宾语，而把宾语移到句子后部去：

I take **it** *you have been out.* 我想你是外出了。

I have **it** on my conscience *that I offended you.* 我得罪了你，心里一直感到不安。

Legend has **it** *that Wu Song was buried at Hangzhou.* 传说武松埋葬在杭州。

13.3.8　主语 + 及物动词 + 连接副(代)词引导的宾语从句 (18)

1) 有不少动词后面可跟连接副(代)词引导的宾语从句：

I didn't **know** *where they had gone.* 我不知道他们到哪里去了。

This **shows** *how much she sympathized with him.* 这说明她多么同情他。

Do you **see** *now why I did it*? 你现在明白我为什么这样做了吗？

He **asked** *when we would be in London.* 他问我们什么时候到伦敦。

I don't **care** *what they say.* 我不在乎他们说什么。

You can **discuss** *which is his best poem.* 你们可以讨论哪是他最好的诗。

I don't **remember** *when that happened.* 我不记得这事是什么时候发生的。

He just **said** *how he looked at it.* 他只是说了他对这事的看法。

She **described** *how all this had happened.* 她描述了这一切是怎样发生的。

Can you **tell** *which is which*? 你能分辨它们吗？

2) 也有些动词后可以跟由连词 whether 或 if 引导的从句：

I **wonder** *whether (if) you could give me some advice.* 不知你可否给我出点主意。

She **asked** *if (whether) she might call and see me.* 她问她可否来看我。

I'll **see** *whether I can find time to do it.* 我会留意是否能挤出时间做这事。

I don't **know** *whether you like these patterns.* 我不知道你是否喜欢这些图案。

I'll **find out** *if she's interested in going.* 我会搞清楚她是否有兴趣去。

3) 有些宾语从句由关系代词型的 what 及 whatever 这类词引导 (19)：

I'll tell you *what I hear.* 我将告诉你我听到的事。

They criticized *what he had done.* 他们批评了他做的事。

I'll do *what I can.* 我将尽力而为。

He could not express *what he felt.* 他无法表述内心的感受。

You can eat *whatever you like.* 你可以吃你喜欢的任何东西。

Whatever he does, he does well. 他无论做什么都做得很好。

He can marry *whomever he chooses.* 他愿意和谁结婚就可以和谁结婚。

Buy *whichever is cheapest.* 买最便宜的。

13.4　第三类句型——主语 + 双宾动词 + 间接宾语 + 直接宾语

13.4.1　主语 + 双宾动词 + 名词或代词 + 名词 (20)

这类句型主要有三种：

1) 某些动词引导的间接宾语可改为 to 引导的短语：

She **gave** *me her telephone number* (gave a job to John). 她给了我她的电话号码(派给约翰一件工作)。

He **handed** *me the letter* (the letter to me). 他把信递给了我。

Please **throw** *me the key* (the key to me). 请把钥匙扔给我。

They **awarded** *her a special scholarship.* 他们颁发给她一份特别奖学金。

They never **denied** *us assistance.* 他们从不拒绝给我们帮助。

He **assigned** *the students a few books to read.* 他指定了几本书给学生读。

Can you **lend** *us your car?* 你能把车借给我们吗？

I **owed** *him $ 50.*　我欠他五十美元。

Please **fax** *us your plans.*　请把你们的计划传真给我们。

I'll **phone** *her the news* (the news to her).　我将打电话告诉她这消息。

2) 某些动词引起间接宾语可改为由 for 引导的短语:

She **sang** *us a folk song* (a folk song for us).　她为我们唱了一首民歌。

I'll **make** *you some fresh tea.*　我去给你沏一点新茶。

She'll **find** *you a situation.*　她将给你找一份工作。

He **bought** *himself a new suit.*　他给自己买了一套新衣服。

He **ordered** *them some children's books.*　他为他们订购了一些儿童读物。

Can you **play** *me some light music?*　你能否给我放一点轻音乐?

Please **choose** *me a good one.*　请给我选一个好的。

That will **save** *us a lot of trouble.*　这会给我们省去许多麻烦。

Could you **fetch** *me the evening paper?*　你能否给我把晚报拿来?

She **cooked** *us a delicious meal.*　她给我们做了一顿可口的饭菜。

3) 有些动词后的间接宾语不能改为 to 或 for 引导的短语:

She **flung** *him a scornful look* (a scornful look at him).　她鄙夷地看了他一眼。

She still **bore** *him a grudge* (a grudge against him).　她仍对他怀有怨恨。

I **envy** *you your good luck.*　我羡慕你的好运。

They **fined** *her $ 200.*　他们罚了她两百美金。

Careless driving **cost** *him his life.*　开车马虎使他赔了性命。

She **kissed** *her mother goodbye.*　她吻别她的母亲。

I'll stay and **keep** *you company.*　我将留下来给你作伴。

I **mean** *you no harm.*　我对你没有恶意。

They **forgave** *him his crimes.*　他们宽恕了他的罪行。

The teacher **set** *us a difficult problem.*　老师给我们出了一道难题。

13.4.2　主语 + 双宾动词 + 名词或代词 + 从句

1) 这类句子中的从句多数由 that 引导 (that 有时省略) (21):

Tell him *I'm out.*　告诉他我不在家。

I'll call Betty and **remind** her *that we are meeting at 8.*　我将给贝蒂打电话, 提醒她我们八点钟碰头。

Our teacher **notified** us *that there would be a test on Monday.*　老师通知我

们星期一有测验。

She **informed** me *that she was to send for it the next day*. 她通知我她将在第二天派人来取它。

He **assured** the passengers *that there was no danger*. 他向乘客保证没有危险。

I **promise** you *I'll never conceal anything any more*. 我答应你我决不会再隐瞒什么。

He instantly **convinced** himself *that it was so*. 他立即让自己相信情况就是如此。

She **wrote** Tom *that she was coming to Paris*. 她写信给汤姆说她要到巴黎来。

I have **warned** him *that it is not allowed*. 我警告过他这是不允许的。

She **persuaded** them *that she had done right*. 她使他们相信她做得对。

2）也有些从句由连接副词（代词）或连词 whether (if) 引导 (22)：

Can you **inform** me *where Miss Green lives*? 你可否告诉我格林小姐住在哪里？

I can't **tell** you *how pleased I am* to be here tonight. 我无法告诉你我今晚在这里多高兴。

She **asked** me *what time it was*. 她问我什么时间。

Write me *how you got through*. 写信告诉我你怎样通过考试的。

Show me *where your leg hurts*. 告诉我你的腿哪儿疼。

He **taught** us *why we should love our country*. 他教导我们为什么要热爱祖国。

Please **advise** me *whether (if) I ought to go with them*. 请告诉我是否应当和他们一道去。

3）有时从句也可由关系代词型的 what 或 whatever 引导 (23)：

Show me *what you bought*. 把你买的东西给我看看。

I'll **tell** you *what I read in today's paper*. 我来告诉你我在今天报上看到的消息。

Give me *what books you have on the subject*. 把你有关这问题的书全都给我。

Tell me *whatever you know about it*. 把你知道的一切都告诉我。

13.5 第四类句型——主语 + 系动词 + 表语

13.5.1 主语 + 系动词 + 形容词 (24)

这是最常见的句型之一，共有下面几种情况：

1) 有些系动词表示处于某种状态：

"*How* are you?" "I'm *fine*." "你好么？" "我挺好。"

She **felt** *a bit dizzy*. 她感到有点头晕。

You're not **looking** *very well*. 你气色不太好。

The dish **smells** *good*. 这盘菜闻起来不错。

The medicine **tastes** *awful*. 这药难吃极了。

The report **sounds** *true*. 这报道听起来是真实的。

He **seemed** *quite normal*. 他显得很正常。

She **appeared** *calm*. 她看上去很镇静。

2) 有些系动词表示状态的改变或证明如何：

Gradually he **became** *silent*. 慢慢地他安静了下来。

When she saw this, she **turned** *red*. 看到这她脸红了。

The weather is **getting** *quite warm*. 天气变得相当暖和。

The sea is **growing** *calm*. 大海变得平静起来。

She **went** *pale* at the news. 听见这消息，她脸色变得苍白。

Things will **come** *right* in the end. 情况最后会变好的。

When he saw this, his blood **ran** *cold*. 看到这情景，他不寒而栗。

He has **fallen** *ill*. 他生病了。

His advice **proved** *sound*. 他的告诫证明是对的。

3) 有些系动词表示状态的继续：

She **remained** *comparatively calm*. 她保持相对镇静。

They **stayed** *awake* to see the eclipse. 他们熬夜来看月蚀。

Jennie, alone, **kept** *silent*. 只有珍妮保持沉默。

His temper **continued** *very uncertain*. 他的脾气仍然喜怒无常。

This law **holds** *good*. 这项法律依然有效。

4) 有些系动词后面可跟现在分词 (a) 或过去分词 (b) (其中很多已变成形容词)：

a. This food **looks** *inviting*. 这食物看上去令人垂涎。

Those chocolates **smell** *tempting*. 那些巧克力闻起来很诱人。

The results of the explosion **were** *appalling*. 爆炸的结果很可怕。

She **remained** *standing* for a good hour. 她足足站了一个钟头。

His theory **sounds** *convincing*. 他的理论听起来很有说服力。

She **seemed** *lacking* in enthusiasm. 她似乎缺乏热情。

b. She always **seems** *pleased*, happy and *contented*. 她总是显得开心、幸福和满足。

He **felt** *troubled* and *distressed*. 他感到很烦恼痛苦。

She didn't **look** *convinced*. 她显得不太信服。

He nearly **got** *hit* by that car. 他差点被那辆车撞了。

After a time I **grew** *dissatisfied* with the work. 过了一段时间我对这工作感到不满起来。

The boundary question **remained** *unsolved*. 边界问题仍然没有解决。

关于这种用法可参阅第 12.3.2 节和 12.4.2 节。

5) 在个别不及物动词后也可跟一形容词作表语:

The prisoner **broke** *free*. 囚犯越狱出逃。

The soldiers have **returned** *safe and sound*. 士兵们平安无事地回来了。

The morning **dawned** *bright*. 这天早晨天亮时天气晴朗。

Many talented people **died** *young*. 许多有才华的人年纪轻轻就夭亡了。

She **sat** *motionless* with horror. 她吓得一动不动呆坐在那里。

The rent **falls** *due* today. 房租今天该交了。

I **stand** *prepared* to dispute it. 我准备好对它提出质疑。

Ten others **lay** *wounded* there. 另外十个人受了伤躺在那里。

He **played** *dead*. 他躺下装死。

这类表语接近于一个状语。

13.5.2 主语 + 系动词 + 名词(代词)(25)

1) 有许多系动词后面可跟名词(代词)作表语:

That girl **was** *my fiancée (me)*. 那女孩是我的未婚妻(我)。

His dream has at last **become** *a reality*. 他的梦想终于成为现实。

He used to be a teacher till he **turned** *writer*. 他过去是教师后来成了作家。

He stood there and **felt** *a stranger*. 他站在那里,觉得自己像个陌生人。

We can **remain** *friends*. 我们可以继续做朋友。

She **looks** *a grown-up young woman* now. 现在她看起来像个大姑娘了。

The affair **rests** *a mystery*. 这件事一直是个谜。

He **appeared** *a fool*. 他看上去像个傻瓜。

It **seems** *to me a very marvellous book*. 这在我看来是一本很出色的书。

It **sounds** *a good idea*. 这听起来是个好主意。

He **fell** *(a) victim to her charms*. 他成了她媚力的俘虏。

2) 有少数其他动词后面也可跟名词作表语:

He **died** *a martyr* at his post. 他殉职了。

I still **stand** *your friend*. 我仍然是你的朋友。

From these debates the Prime Minister **emerged** *victor*. 在这些辩论中首相获胜。

They **parted** *the best of friends*. 他们分手时是最要好的朋友。

Don't **act** *the fool*. 别发傻了。

She often **played** *the great lady*. (玩耍时)她经常假扮贵妇人。

3) 有些名词可作表语,意思接近于形容词:

He was *all attention (sweetness)*. 他聚精会神(非常和蔼可亲)。

She was *all tears (smiles)*. 她泪流满面(满面笑容)。

He is *skin and bones*. 他骨瘦如柴。

All this is *no use*. 这一切都没用。

They are *the same size (age)*. 它们大小相同(他们年龄相同)。

I am not *fool enough* to believe that. 我没傻到相信这个。

What colour is your shirt? 你的衬衫什么颜色?

What nationality is this man? 这人是哪国人?

13.5.3 主语 + 系动词 + 副词 (26)

1) 动词 be 可跟许多副词作表语:

Is Helen *in*? 海伦在家吗?

I have been *out* for a walk. 我出去散步了。

But I've got to be *off* now. 不过现在我得走了。

I'll see if he is *around*. 我会留意他在不在附近。

If he's not here, he's *about* somewhere. 如果他不在这儿,那就在附近什么地方。

She had been *away* on a long trip.　她出远门去了。

All right, I'll be *down* immediately.　好的，我马上就下楼来。

The television was still *on*.　电视还开着。

Summer is *over* — it is autumn.　夏天已经过去——现在是秋天了。

When will you be *through* (with your work)?　你什么时候(事情)可以干完？

He was *up* all night with a sick child.　他照顾生病的孩子一夜没睡。

When will you be *back*?　你什么时候回来？

2) 还有少数其他系动词也可以这样用：

I *feel down* today.　我今天心情不佳。

He *looks* awfully *down*.　他看来情绪很低落。

You'd better *keep away* from that chap.　你最好离那个家伙远点。

I don't *feel up* to the long journey.　我感到身体不适，不能胜任这次长途旅行。

13.5.4　主语 + 系动词 + 介词短语 (27)

1) 大部分介词都可引导短语作表语：

I want to consult you. It's *about my boy*.　我来向你请教，是关于我儿子的事。

The bus stop is just *across the road*.　公共汽车站就在马路对面。

You know *what* you are *after*.　你知道你在寻求什么。

It's *against your conscience*, but you still want to do it.　这是违背你良心的，但你还是想这样做。

Paris is *among the largest cities* in the world.　巴黎是全世界最大的城市之一。

I was *at a loss* what to say.　我不知道说什么好。

The darkest hour is *before the dawn*.　黎明之前最黑暗。

They are fully *behind his welfare policy*.　他们完全支持他的福利政策。

She was *beside herself with joy*.　她高兴得要命。

The temperature is *between 80° and 90°*.　气温在八九十度之间。

To do this was quite *beyond my power*.　这样的事我远远做不到。

Whom is that book *by*?　这本书是谁写的？

She was *for abandoning the project*.　她主张放弃这项工程。

This music is *from one of Mozart's operas*.　这段音乐取自莫扎特的一部歌剧。

These mobile phones are *in great demand*.　这种手机需求量很大。

I had only been *inside their house* once.　我只进过他们家一次。

She is *like a narcissus* trembling in the wind.　她像一株在风中颤动的水仙花。

Cork Street was *near Bond Street*.　考克街在邦得街附近。

He was *of an excitable temperature*.　他是一种好激动的性格。

She is *off smoking*.　她戒烟了。

He is *out of work* at present.　他眼下失业了。

The workers were *on strike*.　工人们在罢工。

They had been *through a lot of hardships*.　他们受过很多苦。

Have you ever been *to Beijing*?　你到过北京吗?

All the children were *under seven*.　所有这些孩子都不到七岁。

Anna was *with child* again now.　安娜现在又怀孕了。

The task is not *within my powers*.　这项任务非我能力所及。

His face was *without expression*.　他脸上毫无表情。

2) 一些其他系动词也可跟这种表语:

They **remained** *in sad poverty*.　他们仍过着凄楚贫困的日子。

He **seemed** *on the watch* to control himself.　他似乎很注意控制自己。

Keep *off the grass*.　请勿践踏草地。

He **looked** *in splendid health*.　他看起来身体很棒。

It has **grown** *out of date*.　这已变得过时了。

They **ran** *out of petrol*.　他们的汽油用完了。

I wish I could **get** *out of debt*.　但愿我能偿清债务。

3) 这类结构后可能还跟另一个介词短语:

He is *in charge of* the trade union work.　他负责工会工作。

He is *in command of* the First Division.　他指挥第一师。

These ballads are *of special interest to* us.　对这些歌谣我们特别感兴趣。

His actions are not *in keeping with* his promises.　他的行为与他的诺言不相符。

We are always *on the lookout for* new business opportunities.　我们一直在寻找新的商机。

The students are *in favour of* reform.　学生们赞同改革。

This book may be *of use to* you.　这本书可能对你有用。

We were completely *at a loss for* an answer.　我们全然不知该如何回答。

He was *on the point of* leaving when the phone rang.　他正要走时电话铃响了。

We must get *in touch with* her.　我们必须和她取得联系。

Soon he fell *in love with* her.　不久他爱上了她。

He seemed *out of touch with* the outside world.　他似乎和外界失去了联系。

13.5.5　主语＋系动词＋不定式 (28)

1) 有时可用不定式作表语:

His plan is *to keep the affair secret*.　他的计划是将此事保密。

Their aim was *to modernize their agriculture*.　他们的目标是实现农业现代化。

Your job is *to make sure* that the work is finished on time.　你的任务是保证按时完成这项工作。

My duty is *to get you away*, *to save you*.　我的职责是带你离开，把你救出来。

His purpose was *to become a surgeon*.　他的目标是当一名外科医生。

Their goal was *to eradicate malaria*.　他们的目标是消灭疟疾。

The main objective of this policy is *to reduce unemployment*.　这一政策的主要目的是减少失业。

My ambition is *to become a pilot*.　我的志愿是当一名飞行员。

My only wish is *to do what's best for you*.　我唯一的愿望是为你做到最好。

The problem was *to find the right place quickly*.　问题是要迅速找到合适的地点。

My advice to you is *to speak the truth*.　我对你的忠告是讲真话。

The only thing now is *to take a taxi*.　目前唯一的办法是叫一辆出租车。

2) 不定式有时需用被动形式:

These books are *to be read* for pleasure.　这些书是供看着玩的。

Surely she was *to be trusted*.　她无疑是值得信赖的。

This house is *to be let*.　这所房子供出租。

13.5.6 主语 + 系动词 + 动名词 (29)

1）系动词 be 后面有时跟动名词作表语：

Her hobby is *collecting stamps*. 她的爱好是集邮。

His occupation was *teaching*. 他的职业是教书。

My job is *repairing cars*. 我的工作是修车。

Her main interest is *playing tennis*. 她的主要兴趣是打网球。

My favourite sport is *swimming*. 我最喜欢的运动是游泳。

Our problem is *not having sufficient fund*. 我们的问题是资金不足。

His weakness is *not having enough confidence in himself*. 他的弱点是自信心不足。

Their favourite pastime is *playing chess*. 他们最喜欢的消遣是下棋。

2）有时主语和表语都是动名词：

Buying such a white elephant *is* simply *wasting money*. 买这样大而无用的东西简直就是浪费金钱。

Talking to him *is talking to a wall*. 和他谈话是白费劲。

Doing that *would be playing with fire*. 那样做等于玩火。

13.5.7 主语 + 系动词 + 从句

1）最常见的这类表语是 that 引导的从句 (that 有时省略) (30)：

Their first idea was *that he had hidden it*. 他们首先想到的是他把它藏起来了。

My opinion is *that the plan won't work*. 我的意见是这个计划行不通。

His view is *that it's better not to increase investments*. 他的看法是最好别增加投资。

The fact is, *I never liked him*. 事实是我从来没喜欢过他。

His only fault is *that he lacks ambition*. 他唯一的缺点是缺乏雄心壮志。

The reason for my lateness is *that I missed my bus*. 我迟到的原因是没赶上公共汽车。

The only trouble is *the plan won't work*. 唯一的问题是这计划行不通。

What surprised me was *that he spoke English so well*. 使我吃惊的是他英语讲得这么好。

2）有些作表语的从句由连接代词 (副词) 引导 (31)：

The question is *what you want to do*. 问题是你想干什么。

The problem is *who can be put in charge of the job*. 问题是谁能来负责此事。

What I want to know is *how we can solve the fuel problem*. 我想知道的是我们怎样才能解决燃料问题。

That's *where we differ*. 这就是我们的分歧所在。

That's *how I look at it*. 这就是我的看法。

That's *why I came round*. 这就是我来的原因。

The coat is *where you left it*. 大衣还在你原来放的地方。

April is *when the lilacs bloom*. 四月是丁香花开的季节。

3）从句有的由关系代词型的 what 引导 (32)：

That's *what I wish to do*. 这就是我想做的事。

That's *what I'm here for*. 我来的目的就是这个。

Power is *what they are after*. 他们所追求的就是权力。

Times aren't *what they were*. 时代不同了。

13.5.8 主语＋系动词＋形容词＋介词短语 (33)

1）这种结构是非常多的，"be＋形容词＋介词"已成为习惯用语，有时相当于一个及物动词：

She **was afraid of** (=feared) snakes. 她怕蛇。

We **are short of** (=lack) funds. 我们缺乏资金。

She **is fond of** this country. 她喜欢这个国家。

I **was frightened of** rats then. 那时候我很怕老鼠。

He **was very conscious of** his shortcomings. 他很清楚自己的缺点。

She **was delighted with** the boat. 她非常喜欢那条小船。

We **are very pleased with** our new house. 我们很喜欢自己的新屋。

I have always **been interested in** Chinese history. 我一向对中国历史很有兴趣。

I'm rather **proud of** this place. 为这地方我感到相当骄傲。

I'm **tired of** living abroad. 我在国外居住已经厌倦了。

I **was sick of** lying in bed. 我已经在床上躺烦了。

She **was disappointed with** him (at the outcome of the talks). 她对他(谈判结果)感到失望。

We **were confident of** his ability (**in** the future). 我们对他的能力(未来)有信心。

He **was worried about** you. 他为你担心。

I'm **ignorant of** mathematics (what happened). 我对数学(发生的事)一无所知。

He's well **qualified for** the job. 他完全有条件做这工作。

I'm not **equal to** the position. 我不胜任这职位。

I don't believe he **is capable of** winning it. 我不相信他能获胜。

I'm **surprised (amazed) at** his attitude. 我对他的态度感到惊讶。

These plans **are subject to** their approval. 这些计划有待他们批准。

2) 一些其他系动词也可用于这类结构:

She **looked astonished at** the news. 听到这消息她显得很吃惊。

I've **got (become) used to** a vegetarian diet (hard work). 我已习惯于吃素食(干苦活)。

He **feels confident of** passing the examination. 他有信心通过考试。

I've **grown accustomed to** traveling. 我已经习惯于旅行了。

They **seem delighted with** the result. 他们似乎对结果很满意。

We're **running short of** funds. 我们的资金不多了。

She **remained ignorant of** what had happened. 她对发生的事仍然一无所知。

He **proved quite equal to** the task. 他证明完全胜任这项工作。

Your exam results **fell short of** our expectations. 你的考试成绩没达到我们的期望。

13.5.9　主语 + 系动词 + 形容词 + 不定式 (34)

I'm **glad** *to have the opportarity of talking to you.* 我很高兴有机会和你交谈。

I was very **sorry** *to hear* that you were ill. 听说你病了我很难过。

I'm **happy** *to meet you.* 我很高兴见到你。

I'm **anxious** *to visit your country.* 我亟盼访问贵国。

She was **eager** *to see her people.* 她急于见到她的家人。

He was **keen** *to visit China.* 他很想访问中国。

He's always **ready** *to help people.* 他总是乐于助人。

We're **proud** *to be Chinese citizens.* 作为中国公民我们感到骄傲。

They're all **willing** *to help.* 他们都愿意帮忙。

I'm **inclined** *to think she's right.* 我倾向于认为她是对的。

We are **determined** *to follow his example*.　我们决心仿效他的榜样。

They are **prepared** *to make concessions*.　他们准备作出让步。

She was **afraid** *to tell you*.　她害怕告诉你。

He was **reluctant** *to go with them*.　他不愿意和他们一道走。

Glass is **liable** *to break*.　玻璃很容易破碎。

He is **content** *to live a simple life*.　他甘愿过简朴的生活。

13.5.10　主语 + 系动词 + 形容词 + 从句

1) 这类结构用 that 引导的从句时较多 (that 有时省略) (35)：

I'm **afraid** *there is some sort of misunderstanding*.　恐怕有误会的地方。

I'm awfully **sorry** *that this has occurred*.　发生了这样的事我非常抱歉。

I'm **glad** *you have come*.　我很高兴你来了。

I'm **sure** *he meant well*.　我肯定他是好意。

I am **certain (positive)** *that he had seen me*.　我肯定他看见了我。

He's **confident** *that he will pass the exam*.　他有信心能通过考试。

I'm **convinced** *that he knew the truth*.　我相信他知道事实真相。

You must be **aware** *that what you are doing is illegal*.　你一定知道你的行为是非法的。

He was **delighted** *that we were successful in our experiment*.　他很高兴我们的试验成功了。

I'm **disappointed** *that you cannot come*.　你不能来我很失望。

I'm **surprised (astonished)** *he didn't come*.　他没来我很吃惊。

He was **thankful** *that the journey was over*.　旅行结束了他很欣慰。

They were **hopeful** *that they will win the championship*.　他们对夺冠抱有希望。

He suddenly became **conscious** *that someone was looking at him*.　他突然意识到有人在看他。

The team feels **proud** *that it has won every match this year*.　该队为今年比赛获得全胜而感到骄傲。

I'm **irritated** *that he is so stubborn*.　他那样固执真让我生气。

2) 有时从句由连接代 (副) 词引导 (36)：

We're not **clear** yet *what they're up to*.　我们还不清楚他们想干什么。

I was not **sure** *what I ought to do*.　我不能肯定我该做什么。

He's **doubtful** *whether he can afford it.* 他怀疑他能否付得起这笔钱。

She was not **aware** (of) *how much her husband earned.* 她不清楚她丈夫挣多少钱。

I am not **certain** *who he is.* 我不能肯定他是谁。

I'm **worried** (about) *how the money was spent.* 我烦恼的是这钱是怎么花掉的。

They were **uncertain** *whether they could find time to do it.* 他们不能肯定是否能找到时间做这事。

I'm **undecided** *whether to go to France or Italy for my holidays.* 我还没决定是去法国还是去意大利度假。

13.6 第五类句型——主语 + 及物动词 + 复合宾语

13.6.1 主语 + 及物动词 + 宾语 + 形容词(作补语) (37)

1) 这类句子很多，最常用的跟复合宾语的动词大致有下面这些(见黑体部分)：

He **found** *his new job rather boring.* 他发现他的新工作相当乏味。

Sit down and **make** *yourself comfortable.* 坐下来，不要拘束。

He **got** *his clothes wet.* 他把衣服弄湿了。

She **painted** *the walls light blue.* 她把墙漆成了淡蓝色。

Good food **keeps** *you healthy.* 良好的饮食使人健康。

I **thought** *her so nice and sincere.* 我认为她为人很好，很诚恳。

I **felt** *myself unworthy of the praise.* 我感到自己不配受这样的赞扬。

Do you **consider** *him trustworthy?* 你认为他值得信赖吗？

She **dyed** *her hair brown.* 她把头发染成了棕色。

Finally they **set** *him free.* 最后他们释放了他。

The accused man **declared** *himself innocent.* 被告宣称自己是无辜的。

They didn't **believe** *such a thing possible.* 他们认为这样的事不可能。

I **like** *my tea very hot (strong).* 我喜欢喝热(浓)茶。

She **pushed** *the door open.* 她把门推开了。

He **beat** *her black and blue.* 他打得她青一块紫一块。

The noise was **driving** *him mad (crazy).* 这声音使他受不了。

Facts have **proved** *these worries groundless.* 事实证明这些忧虑是没有根据的。

I **wish** *you well*.　我希望你身体健康。

He **counted** *himself fortunate to have such an opportunity*.　他认为自己有
　　这样的机会很幸运。

They may **hold** *you responsible for the consequence*.　他们可能要你对后
　　果负责。

2) 有时可用 it 作形式上的宾语，而把真正的宾语放后面去，构成复合宾
语的可以是不定式 (a) 或是从句 (b)：

a. I **felt** *it necessary* to make everything clear.　我感到有必要说清楚一切。

They **judged** *it better* to put the meeting off.　他们认为把会议延期更好一
　　些。

I don't **think** *it possible* to finish everything in one week.　我认为一周内
　　完成一切不可能。

He **found** *it difficult* to satisfy their needs.　他发现要满足他们的需要不容
　　易。

She **deemed** *it unwise* to quit now.　她认为现在离职不明智。

b. Germany **made** *it clear* that she would support OPEC.　德国表明它要支持
　　石油输出国组织。

I **think** *it best* that you should stay with us.　我想最好你和我们一起住。

They **kept** *it quiet* that he was dead.　他们未对外公开他死亡的消息。

I **think** *it likely* that we will get a certain amount of money.　我想我们很可
　　能会得到一笔钱。

13.6.2　主语 + 及物动词 + 宾语 + 名词（作补语）(38)

1) 这种结构也相当多：

They **called** *their daughter Mary*.　他们给女儿取名叫玛丽。

They **named** *the city Leningrad*.　他们把这座城市命名为列宁格勒。

We **elected** *Smith our chairman*.　我们选史密斯为主席。

All work and no play **makes** *Jack a dull boy*.　(谚)只工作不玩耍,聪明小
　　孩也变傻。

They **appointed** *him chairman of the committee*.　他们任命他为主任委员。

The President **nominated** *him Ambassador to China*.　总统任命他为驻华
　　大使。

We all **consider** *the book a masterpiece*.　我们都认为这本书是一杰作。

The doctor **thought** *that a good sign.* 医生认为这是一个好现象。

They **kept** *their marriage a secret.* 他们对结婚保密。

Shelley **counted** *this experience a part of his education.* 雪莱把这段经历看作是他经受的一段教育。

They **christened** *the ship the Queen Mary.* 他们把这艘船命名为玛丽皇后号。

The King **dubbed** *him a knight.* 国王授予他骑士称号。

We all **voted** *the trip a great success.* 我们一致认为这次旅行很成功。

I now **pronounce** *you man and wife.* 我现在宣布你们为夫妇。

The people **acclaimed** *him King.* 人民拥戴他为国王。

The judge **declared** *the contest a tie.* 裁判宣布这次比赛不分胜负。

2）这类动词后也可用先行词it作形式上的宾语，而把真正的宾语放到句子后部去：

He **felt** *it his duty* to mention this to her. 他感到有责任向她提及此事。

He **made** *it a rule* to go jogging every morning. 他规定自己每天早上慢跑锻炼。

We **thought** *it our duty* to help them. 我们认为有责任帮助他们。

I **consider** *it a privilege* to work in your country. 我认为在贵国工作很是荣幸。

I **shall always count** *it an honour* to have known you. 认识了你我将永远感到荣幸。

I **felt** *it a terrible thing* that my mother should have to toil so endlessly. 我母亲要没完没了地干苦活我感到太可怕了。

3）这类句子也常可用于被动结构（后面部分可说是复合谓语）：

This *is called numerical control.* 这被称为数码控制。

The book *is entitled "Pilgrim's Progress".* 这本书书名是《天路历程》。

He *was voted a model worker.* 他被公认为劳动模范。

The play *may be termed a tragi-comedy.* 这个戏可以称为悲喜剧。

She *was christened Janet.* 她洗礼时被命名为珍妮特。

She *was nicknamed "Little Rabbit".* 她的绰号叫"小白兔"。

13.6.3 主语 + 及物动词 + 宾语 + 介词短语(作补语) (39)

1）这类句子中的介词短语为宾语的补语，和宾语一起构成复合宾语，不少动词后可跟这类结构：

> I **found** *her in better spirits* when we met again. 再次见面时我发现她情绪好些了。
>
> They **kept** *him in custody.* 他们把他拘留了。
>
> He **put** *his books in order.* 他把他的书整理好了。
>
> The news of his safe arrival **set** *my mind at rest.* 他平安到达的消息使我放宽了心。
>
> The strike **left** *the railway system in confusion.* 罢工使铁路系统陷于一片混乱。
>
> They all **held** *him in great esteem (contempt).* 他们都很尊敬(鄙视)他。
>
> This **placed** *her in a very difficult position.* 这使她处境很困难。
>
> They always **consider** *themselves in the right.* 他们总认为自己是对的。
>
> They soon **got** *the fire under control.* 他们很快把火势控制住了。
>
> He **wished** *himself out of the affair.* 他真希望自己未参与此事。
>
> This will **bring** *us all into harmony.* 这会使我们都和睦起来。
>
> She **cried** *herself to sleep at last.* 她哭着哭着最后睡着了。
>
> They **declared** *themselves for (against) the plan.* 他们宣布支持(反对)这项计划。
>
> She tried to **talk** *her husband out of going.* 她试图劝说丈夫不要去。
>
> We'll be glad to **help** *them over their difficulties.* 我们将乐意帮助他们克服困难。

2) 这类句子也可用于被动结构，下面斜体部分可说是复合谓语：

> The thief *was found in possession* of a large quantity of stolen property. 这小偷被发现藏有大量赃物。
>
> He *was kept in custody* for two days. 他被拘留了两天。
>
> She *was* soon *set at liberty.* 他不久被释放了。
>
> The treaty *is* still *considered in force.* 这条约仍被视为有效。
>
> Those regulations *will be put into force* next week. 这些规定下周开始生效。
>
> I *was left without a ray of hope.* 我处于毫无希望的境地。
>
> The fire *was* soon *got under control.* 火势不久就控制住了。
>
> It *was taken for granted* that they would come and join us. 大家理所当然地认为他们会来参加我们的活动。

13.6.4 主语＋及物动词＋宾语＋副词(作补语) (40)

1) 有些动词后可跟带副词的复合宾语:

I'm **having** *some friends over* for bridge tomorrow. 明天我有些朋友来打桥牌。

We went to her house but **found** *her out*. 我们到他家去,但发现她不在家。

She **wished** *herself home*. 她希望自己在家就好了。

Don't **leave** *me behind*. 别把我留下。

It's my own act. Why do you **bring** *my mother in*? 这是我自己干的,干吗把我妈扯进来?

Get *me home* at once. 快让我回家。

Congress **voted** *the bill down*. 国会否决了这项法案。

She has **slept** *her headache off*. 她一觉把头疼睡好了。

I didn't **expect** *you back so soon*. 我没料到你这么快回来。

Why don't you **turn** *the TV on*? 你为什么不开电视?

He is sure to **help** *us through*. 他一定会帮助我们渡过难关。

They **declared** *the war over*. 他们宣布战争结束。

By citing more examples, he **drove** *his points home*. 他举出更多的例子阐明了自己的论点。

I won't **let** *him down* in any way. 我不会做任何对不起他的事。

Please **count** *me in (out)* on the project. 请让我参加(别让我参加)这个项目。

2) 这种结构有时也可用于被动形式,斜体部分可说是复合谓语:

My bag *has been left behind*. 我的包忘拿了。

The suggestion *was voted down*. 这项建议被否决了。

The war *was declared over*. 战争被宣布结束。

This point *should be driven home*. 这一点应当讲清楚。

Why *are* these lights *left on*? 这些灯为什么没关?

He *was* often *asked round* to play cards with us. 他常被请来和我们打牌。

13.6.5 主语＋及物动词＋宾语＋不定式(作补语) (41)

1) 有大量动词可跟这种复合结构:

What do you **advise** *me to do*? 你建议我怎么做?

You should **get** *them to help you*.　你应当请他们来帮你。

Don't **allow** *yourself to indulge in false hopes*.　别让自己沉迷于幻想。

We **requested** *him to put a stop to such activities*.　我们请求他终止这种活动。

At the meeting they **invited** *me to speak*.　在会上他们邀请我发言。

He **liked** *a boy to be conscientious in his work*.　他喜欢男孩子工作认真。

My heart **compelled** *me to come*.　我的勇气驱使我来。

Circumstances **forced** *them to adopt this policy*.　环境迫使他们采取这一政策。

Ill health **obliged** *him to retire at an early age*.　身体不好迫使他早早退休了。

I **wish** *you to be happy*.　我希望你快乐。

I **hated** *this to have happened*.　我不愿意发生这种事。

I should **prefer** *him to do it in a different way*.　我倒愿意他以另一种方式做这事。

He **instructed** *me to come to work earlier*.　他嘱咐我早点上班。

Permit *me to explain*.　请允许我解释一下。

Remind *me to write that letter*, will you?　提醒我写这封信，好吗?

He **ordered (commanded)** *the soldiers to retreat*.　他命令士兵们往后撤。

They **warned** *us not to swim in that river*.　他们警告我们不要在那条河里游泳。

He **urged** *me to join their company*.　他催促我加入他们的公司。

Heating a copper bar will **cause** *it to expand*.　加热铜条会使其膨胀。

She could not **bring** *herself to tell him about Vesta*.　她无法让自己把维斯塔的事告诉他。

关于这类结构可参阅第 12.1.5 节。

2) 在某些动词后，这类不定式只限于用 to be 这种形式 (a)，但可用其他动词不定式的完成形式或进行形式 (b)：

a. We **thought** *him to be an honest man*.　我们认为他是老实人。

Do you **consider** *that to be important*?　你认为这重要吗?

Suppose (Imagine) *this grain of sand to be the universe*.　设想这粒沙子就是宇宙。

She **found** *this to be true* in all the cities she visited.　她发现她访问的城市都是这种情况。

They **believed** *Aziz to be innocent*.　他们相信阿齐斯是无辜的。

They **suspected** *her to be my sister.* 他们疑心她是我妹妹。

I **understand** *him to be willing to help.* 我听说他愿意帮忙。

He **proved** *himself to be a coward.* 他证实自己是一个懦夫。

We all **felt** *the plan to be unwise.* 我们都觉得这计划不明智。

b. He **believed** *them to have discussed the problem.* 他相信他们讨论过这个问题。

She **suspected** *me to have done it.* 她怀疑这事是我干的。

I **judged** *them to have finished.* 我估计他们已经干完了。

They **suspected** *him to be dying.* 他们怀疑他命已垂危。

He **believed** *her to be telling the truth.* 他相信她讲的是真话。

They **thought** *him to be hiding in the woods.* 他们认为他躲在树林里。

He **considered** *the situation there to be deteriorating.* 他认为那里的局势正在恶化。

3） 这类句子也常可用于被动结构，这时句子可说包含了一个复合谓语：

They *were not allowed to see* him. 他们未获准去看他。

I *was asked to go* with them. 他们请我和他们一道去。

Nelson *was instructed to sail* for Naples. 纳尔逊接到指示向那不勒斯航行。

She *was obliged to abandon* the idea. 她被迫放弃这个想法。

He *was cautioned to speak* as little as possible. 有人告诫他尽量少说话。

She *was discovered to be quite trustworthy.* 他们发现她很值得信赖。

Passengers *were requested to fasten* their seatbelts. 请乘客们系好安全带。

He *was forced (obliged) to postpone* his visit. 他被迫推迟他的访问。

4） 个别成语动词后也可跟这类复合宾语：

He **called on** *Jack to answer the difficult question.* 他叫杰克回答这个难题。

We'll **prevail upon** *her to attend the concert.* 我们将劝说她去听这个音乐会。

I'm **counting on** *you to support us.* 我指望你支持我们。

I **longed for** *her to come and join us.* 我盼望她来参加我们的活动。

He **motioned to** *them to sit down.* 他做手势让他们坐下。

We are **waiting for** *the rain to stop.* 我们在等雨停下来。

We **depend on** *you to do it.* 我们依靠你来完成这事。

He **pleaded with** *me to go back.* 他恳求我回去。

13.6.6　主语＋及物动词＋宾语＋不带 to 的不定式(作补语)（42）

1) 有些动词后面的复合宾语中包含一个不带 to 的不定式:

What **makes** *you tremble* so? 什么让你抖成这样?

We can't **let** *this go on*. 我们不能让这事继续下去。

I'm going to **have** *her live with us soon*. 我准备不久让她和我们一起住。

I **saw** *Martin's face go pale*. 我看见马丁的脸变得苍白。

We had never **heard** *her sing like that before*. 我们以前从未听她这样唱过歌。

Did you **notice** *him come in*? 你有没有注意到他进来?

I **watched** *her go off* with amazement. 我惊异地瞧着她走掉了。

Suddenly we **felt** *the atmosphere grow tense*. 突然我们感到气氛变得紧张起来。

在 help 后的不定式可带 to, 也可不带 to (美国人不加 to 时比较多):

I will **help** *her (to) solve* the problem. 我将帮助她解决这个问题。

2) 在被动结构中不定式一概带有 to:

He *was made to recite* the whole poem. 他们让他把整首诗都背出来。

He *was seen to fall*. 有人看见他跌倒。

She *was* often *heard to sing* this song. 人们常听见她唱这首歌。

13.6.7　主语＋及物动词＋宾语＋现在分词(作补语)（43）

1) 有些动词后面可跟带现在分词的复合结构:

He **found** *Helen knitting there*. 他看见海伦在那里织毛线。

I **saw** *her chatting with Nancy*. 我看见她在和南希聊天。

She could **hear** *the rain pattering against the windows*. 她能听到雨敲打着窗子。

He **noticed** *a crowd of people shouting and cheering*. 他注意到一群人在喊叫欢呼。

I could **smell** *trouble coming*. 我能感觉到麻烦即将来临。

He **felt** *Jamie watching him*. 他感觉到杰米在注视他。

She had **kept** *him waiting twenty minutes on this occasion*. 这次她让他等了二十分钟。

They **watched** *the sun setting behind the trees*. 他们瞧着太阳在树林后缓缓下沉。

They walked off and **left** *me sitting there*.　他们走了，只剩我坐在那里。

The lecturer soon **got** *us thinking*.　讲课的人很快就让我们思考起来。

The cries **brought** *the neighbours running*.　喊叫声使邻居们纷纷跑来。

I should like to **catch** *them saying a word against me*!　别让我抓住他们说我一句坏话！

Can you **imagine** *me doing such a thing*?　你能想像我做这样的事吗？

I can't **understand** *you keeping a thing like this to yourself*.　我不能理解你怎么把这样一件事瞒着别人。

He doesn't **like** *people praising him*.　他不喜欢听人赞扬他。

This news **started** *me thinking*.　这消息使我深思。

I **hate** *you being unhappy*.　我不愿意你不快乐。

I **remember** *him*, as a child, *playing the piano beautifully*.　我记得他小时候弹一手好钢琴。

在 listen to 和 look at 后面也可跟这种复合宾语：

Sometimes she would **listen to** *him playing the saxophone*.　有时她会听他吹奏萨克斯管。

She **looked at** *him waiting there*.　她瞧着他等在那里。

2）这类句子有时也可用于被动结构：

Voices *were heard calling for help*.　听见有人呼救。

She *was seen speaking to a policeman*.　有人见她在和一位警察说话。

He *was kept working all day*.　他整天被逼着干活。

She *was found jogging* in the park.　有人看见她在公园里跑步。

They *were caught trespassing* on private land.　有人撞见他们进入私人地界。

Only one of its walls *was left standing*.　它只剩一堵墙还立在那里。

关于这类结构可参阅第 12.3.4 节。

13.6.8　主语＋及物动词＋宾语＋过去分词(作补语)（44）

1）有些动词可跟带过去分词的复合宾语：

I have **heard** *it said that he is a miser*.　我听人说他是个吝啬鬼。

I have **seen** *that method applied by many people*.　我曾见过很多人使用这种方法。

He **watched** *the piano carried upstairs*.　他看着钢琴被搬上楼去。

They **found** *themselves stranded at the airport*.　他们发现自己被困在飞机场了。

You have to **get** *a photograph taken*.　你得去照一张像。

Father's **had** *his hands burned*.　爸把手烫了。

I **noticed** *his car parked outside*.　我注意到他的车停在外面。

We **want** *the work finished by Friday*.　我们希望这工作周五之前完成。

We **wished** *the problem settled outside the court*.　我们希望这问题在庭外解决。

You must **make** *yourself respected*.　你必须使自己受到尊重。

He **kept** *his eyes shut* and stayed where he was.　他一直闭着眼睛坐在原处。

She **left** *the ironing undone* and went bowling.　她衣服没熨完就去打保龄球了。

He **felt** *himself compelled to take this action*.　他感到自己被迫采取这个行动。

Everyone **considered** *it greatly improved*.　大家都认为它大有改进。

The convention **declared** *itself dissolved*.　会议宣布解散。

2) 其中有少数可用于被动结构：

Jones *was found shot* in the head.　琼斯被发现头部中了弹。

My patient *can't be left unattended*.　不能让我的病人没人照顾。

They *are considered underpaid*.　大家认为他们工资偏低。

You *will be kept informed* of what's going on here.　将让你随时了解这儿发生的情况。

关于这类结构可参阅第 12.4.4 节。

第 14 章　形容词

14.1　形容词的类型

14.1.1　形容词的类型

形容词大体上可以分为下面几类:

- **品质形容词** (Qualitative Adjectives)
- **类属形容词** (Classifying Adjectives)
- **颜色形容词** (Colour Adjectives)
- **强调形容词** (Emphasizing Adjectives)
- **-ing 形容词** (-ing Adjectives)
- **-ed 形容词** (-ed Adjectives)
- **合成形容词** (Compound Adjectives)

有些语法学家把作定语的代词都称作为形容词 (具体可参阅 *A Practical English Grammar* 第三章),美国词典也多把它们标作形容词 (如 this, some 都标作形容词),有些英国语法学家则把它们称为限定词。关于这一问题可参阅第 5.1.3 节。

14.1.2　品质形容词

英语中大量形容词属于这一类,它们表示人或物的品质,如:

He's the *happiest* man on earth.　他是世界上最快乐的人。

She looks very *healthy*.　她看起来身体很好。

The play was *boring*.　那出戏很枯燥乏味。

It was a *lovely quiet* beach.　这是一片美丽而宁静的海滩。

He is a *humourous* magician.　他是位富于幽默感的魔术师。

You have an *honest* face.　你有一张诚实的脸。

这类形容词常见的有：

active	angry	anxious	attractive	bad	beautiful
big	brief	bright	broad	busy	calm
careful	cheap	clean	clear	cold	comfortable
common	complex	cool	curious	dangerous	dark
dear	deep	different	difficult	dirty	dry
easy	effective	efficient	expensive	fair	familiar
famous	fast	fat	fine	firm	flat
frank	free	fresh	funny	good	great
happy	hard	heavy	high	hot	important
joyful	kind	large	late	light	likely
long	loose	loud	lovely	low	lucky
narrow	nervous	new	nice	obvious	odd
old	pale	patient	plain	pleasant	poor
popular	powerful	pretty	proud	quick	quiet
rare	reasonable	rich	rough	sad	safe
sensible	serious	sharp	short	sick	significant
silly	simple	slow	small	soft	special
strange	strong	stupid	successful	suitable	sure
sweet	tall	terrible	thick	thin	tight
tiny	useful	violent	warm	weak	wet
wide	wild	young			

这类形容词一般都能用于比较级，如 bigger, simpler, younger。

14.1.3　类属形容词

这类形容词表示属于哪一类，如：

In that case they would receive *financial* aid from the state. 如果出现那种情况，他们将获得国家的财政援助。

We must learn to use our *cultural* heritage. 我们应学会利用我们的文化遗产。

These subjects reflect our *daily* lives. 这些题材反映我们的日常生活。

This medicine is for *external* use only. 此药仅供外用(不能内服)。

常见的这类形容词有:

absolute	agricultural	alternative	annual	apparent
available	basic	central	chemical	civil
commercial	communist	conservative	cultural	daily
democratic	direct	domestic	double	due
east	eastern	economic	educational	electric
empty	external	female	financial	foreign
free	full	general	golden	historical
human	ideal	independent	industrial	inevitable
intellectual	internal	international	legal	local
magic	male	medical	mental	military
modern	moral	national	natural	negative
north	northern	nuclear	official	open
original	personal	physical	political	positive
possible	potential	private	professional	proper
public	raw	ready	real	religious
revolutionary	right	royal	rural	scientific
separate	sexual	single	social	solid
south	southern	standard	straight	sufficient
theoretical	traditional	urban	west	western
wooden	wrong			

这类形容词一般都不能用于比较级。

14.1.4 颜色形容词

有少数表示颜色的形容词,如:

His face went *purple* with rage. 他的脸气得发青(紫)。

He's got *scarlet* fever. 他患了猩红热。

She had on a *blue* coat. 她穿了一件蓝色的外套。

Carrots are *orange*. 胡萝卜是橘红色的。

这类形容词主要有:

black	blue	brown	cream	crimson	green
grey	orange	pink	purple	red	scarlet
violet	white	yellow			

这类词前面还可加 light, pale, dark, deep, bright 等词，如:

light brown hair 淡褐色的头发　　a pale green dress 淡绿色的裙服
a deep blue skirt 深蓝色的裙子　　a dark grey suit 深灰色的套服

后面还可加 -ish 这样的词尾:

yellowish teeth 微黄的牙齿　　　reddish hair 略带红色的头发
a greenish-yellow tinge 黄中带　　eyes of bluish green 绿中带蓝的
绿的颜色　　　　　　　　　　　眼睛

14.1.5　强调形容词

有些形容词起强调作用，如:

He was a *total* stranger to me.　他对我来说完全是个陌生人。
It's an *utter* mystery.　这完全是个谜。
That's *sheer* nonsense.　这纯粹是胡说八道。
I have *perfect* trust in his judgement.　我绝对信任他的判断力。

常见的这类形容词有:

absolute	complete	entire	outright	perfect	positive
pure	real	sheer	total	true	utter

14.1.6　-ing 形容词

1) 有大量现在分词正在或已经变为形容词，如:

It was a tiring journey.　这是一趟累人的旅行。(The journey tired me.)
This is a convincing argument.　这是个有说服力的论据。(It convinces us.)
She is pleasing in her appearance.　她的模样很喜人。(She pleases us.)
It has a satisfying ending.　它的结局令人满意。(It satisfies us.)

这类形容词多由及物动词变来，常见的这类形容词有：

alarming	amazing	amusing	annoying	appalling
astonishing	bewildering	boring	challenging	charming
confusing	convincing	demanding	depressing	devastating
disappointing	disgusting	distressing	disturbing	embarrassing
enchanting	encouraging	exciting	frightening	humiliating
infuriating	inspiring	interesting	intimidating	misleading
mocking	overwhelming	pleasing	refreshing	relaxing
rewarding	satisfying	shocking	startling	surprising
tempting	terrifying	threatening	thrilling	tiring

这类形容词有很多也是品质形容词，有时可用于最高级(如most amazing, most disappointing)。

2) 还有一些 -ing 形容词和不及物动词有关，如：

We hope to lessen the *existing* tension.　我们希望缓解目前的紧张局势。

(比较：Obstacles to agreement still *exist*. 达成协议的障碍仍然存在。)

I have been fighting the *prevailing* decadence for years.　多年来我一直在和盛行的颓废现象作斗争。

(比较：Truth will *prevail*. 真理将占上风。)

Rising crime has driven many families out of downtown areas.　上升的犯罪率迫使许多家庭迁离市区。

(比较：Prices continued to *rise*. 物价继续上涨。)

He's is one of the greatest *living* composers.　他是当今最伟大的作曲家之一。

(比较：The birds *live* only on this island. 这种鸟只生活在该岛上。)

常见的这类形容词有：

ageing	ailing	bleeding	booming	bursting
decreasing	diminishing	dwindling	dying	existing
increasing	living	prevailing	recurring	reigning
remaining	resounding	rising	ruling	

这类形容词只能作定语，不能用于比较级。

3）还有一些 -ing 形容词并不与动词有关，如：

neighbouring cities 邻近的城市	a cunning trick 狡猾的计谋
an impending disaster 即将来临的灾难	an enterprising woman 有事业心的女子
a balding man 头发日稀的人	an appetizing smell 引起食欲的香味

还有少数 -ing 形容词，包含一个副词：

the outgoing mail 准备寄出的邮件	the forthcoming election 即将到来的选举
outlying areas 偏远地区	an overbearing manner 傲慢的态度
an ongoing debate 在进行的辩论	the incoming president 新选的总统
an oncoming car 在开来的汽车	an outstanding writer 杰出的作家

14.1.7　-ed 形容词

1）大多数 -ed 形容词都与及物动词有关，是由它们的过去分词变过来的，一般有被动意义，多数为品质形容词，如：

She looked *embarrassed*.　她好像很尴尬。

These people are from *distressed* areas.　这些人来自贫苦地区。

She had *confused* feelings about him.　她对他有一种混杂的感情。

I could hear his *agitated* voice.　我可以听到他激动的声音。

I felt *depressed*.　我感到很沮丧。

常见的这类形容词有：

agitated	alarmed	amazed	amused	appalled
astonished	bored	confused	contented	delighted
depressed	deprived	disappointed	disgusted	disillusioned
distressed	embarrassed	excited	frightened	interested
pleased	puzzled	satisfied	shocked	surprised
tired	troubled	worried		

2）有些 -ed 形容词可说是类属形容词，也由动词的过去分词变来，但不能用于比较级，如：

You have to pass the *required* examination to become a doctor.　你需要通过规定的考试才能成为医生。

It was only a small cut, but it became *infected*. 这只是一个小口子,但已被感染了。

She is a *trained* nurse. 她是一个受过训练的护士。

He has very *fixed* ideas of how a wife should behave. 他对一个妻子应怎样处事有着很固执的看法。

常见的这类形容词有:

abandoned	armed	boiled	broken	canned
classified	closed	cooked	divided	dried
established	fixed	furnished	haunted	hidden
improved	infected	integrated	known	licensed
loaded	paid	painted	processed	reduced
required	torn	trained	united	wasted

3) 有少数 -ed 形容词,不是由动词,而是由名词变来的:

a principled stand 原则立场   skilled workers 技术工人

salaried class 工薪阶层   armoured vehicles 装甲车

a gifted pianist 有天赋的钢琴家   winged insects 有翅膀的昆虫

a flowered headscarf 印花头巾   barbed wire 铁丝网

还有少数 -ed 形容词,和动词和名词都没有关系:

beloved leaders 受爱戴的领导   concerted effort 协同努力

his deceased aunt 他死去的姨   assorted sweets 杂拌糖(果)

sophisticated equipment 尖端设备   rugged country 崎岖不平的田野

4) 有些 -ed 形容词包含有副词:

a well-equipped army 一支装备精良的部队   strongly-motivated students 学习动力强的学生

simply-furnished rooms 陈设简单的房间   a well-known musician 著名的音乐家

a cautiously-worded statement 一篇措辞谨慎的声明   smartly-dressed ladies 穿着漂亮的女士们

a tall, powerfully-built man 身材高大魁梧的男子   highly-developed industry 高度发展的工业

14.1.8　合成形容词

1) 合成形容词在英语中是比较普遍的，最常见的有下面几类：

a. 形容词＋名词＋ed：

good-natured 天性善良的　　　　soft-hearted 心肠很软的

sweet-tempered 脾气很好的　　　　narrow-minded 心地狭窄的

b. 副词＋过去分词：

low-paid 工资很低的　　　　well-bred 很有教养的

far-fetched 牵强附会的　　　　poorly-written 写得很差的

c. 形容词＋现在分词：

fine-sounding 动听的　　　　nice-looking 漂亮的

easy-going 好说话的　　　　sweet-tasting 有甜味的

d. 副词＋现在分词

hard-working 勤劳的　　　　far-reaching 深远的

low-lying 低洼的　　　　long-standing 长期存在的

e. 名词＋现在分词：

time-consuming 费时间的　　　　labor-saving 节省劳动力的

heart-breaking 令人心碎的　　　　trouble-making 捣乱的

f. 形容词＋名词：

present-day (life) 当代的(生活)　　　　white-collar (staff) 白领(员工)

full-time (staff) 全时工作(员工)　　　　high-class (restaurant) 高级(餐馆)

2) 还有一些其他类型的合成形容词，如：

a tree-lined avenue 林荫大道 (名词＋过去分词)

duty-free shops 免税商店 (名词＋形容词)

a two-piece suit 两件套的西服 (数词＋名词)

cast-off shoes 丢弃的鞋 (过去分词＋副词)

all-out attempt 全力以赴的努力 (副词＋副词)

take-home pay (扣税等后的)实得工资 (动词＋副词)

3) 还有一些三个或更多词构成的合成形容词，如：

wait-and-see policy 观望政策　　　　heart-to-heart talk 推心置腹的谈话

wall-to-wall carpet 满铺地毯　　　　well-to-do families 富裕家庭

the day-to-day administration 日　　　　an out-of-date driving license 过期
　常行政工作　　　　　　　　　　　　　驾照

a life-and-death struggle 生死斗　　　　state-of-the-art technology 尖端科
　争　　　　　　　　　　　　　　　　　技

an out-of-the-way place 偏僻之地

14.2　形容词在句中的作用

14.2.1　形容词的主要作用

形容词在句中主要可用作:

1) 定语:

It supplies us with *up-to-the-minute financial* information.　它向我们提供最新的财经消息。

What a *fine* day!　多好的天气!

He is a *self-made* man.　他是个自学成才的人。

2) 表语:

The scene was *horrifying*.　这景象很恐怖。

I am getting *bored* and *homesick*.　我感到有些厌烦想家。

His comments were *well-meant*.　他说这些话都是出于好心。

3) 宾语的补语(构成合成宾语):

Praise made good men *better* and bad men *worse*.　(谚)赞扬使好人更好,坏人更坏。

I find this hot weather very *trying*.　我感到这种炎热天气很难受。

Do you think it *necessary*?　你认为这有必要吗?

4) 状语:

She was back, *eager* to see her friends.　她回来了,亟想见她的朋友们。

She gave him the overcoat, *anxious* to be of service.　她把大衣拿给他,亟愿为他服务。

He arrived home, *hungry and tired*.　他又饿又累地回到家里。

14.2.2　作表语的形容词

1) 有一些形容词,特别是以 a- 开头的形容词,一般在句中只用作表语,如:

He's a bit *afraid* (of her).　他有点害怕(她)。

They were *unable* to help.　他们没法帮忙。

Several students were *ill*.　好几个学生病了。

In a little while he fell *asleep*.　不一会儿他就睡着了。

常见的这种形容词有:

afraid	alive	alone	ashamed	asleep	aware
content	due	fond	glad	ill	likely
ready	sorry	sure	unable	unlikely	well

2) 有些形容词在用作表语时,后面常跟一个由 to 引导的短语:

She is *allergic to* pollen.　她对花粉过敏。

Her office is *adjacent to* mine.　她的办公室和我的紧挨着。

We are *immune to* smallpox as a result of vaccination.　由于种了牛痘我们对天花有免疫力。

Smoking is *injurious to* the lungs.　抽烟对肺有害。

常见的这类形容词有:

accustomed	adjacent	allergic	attributable	attuned
averse	close	conducive	devoted	immune
prone	proportional	proportionate	reconciled	related
resigned	resistant	similar	subject	used

3) 有些形容词作表语时后面跟 of 引导的短语:

He was not *aware of* her presence.　他不知道她在场。

She was already *desirous of* fame.　她已经在渴望出名了。

The meeting wasn't *productive of* any important decisions.　会议没作出任何重要的决定。

Fever may be *indicative of* an infection.　发烧说明可能有炎症。

常见的这类形容词有:

aware	bereft	capable	characteristic	desirous
devoid	fond	full	illustrative	incapable
indicative	mindful	reminiscent	representative	

4) 还有不少形容词可用作表语,后面可跟其他介词:

He is not *lacking in* intelligence.　他的智力并不差。

She was also *connected with* the government.　她也和政府有联系。

The government is *responsible for* the nation's welfare.　政府负责国家的福利。

I'll never be *dependent on* anyone again. 我将决不再依靠任何人。

常见的这类形容词如:

answerable for (to)	compatible with	connected with (to)
dependent on (upon)	filled with	immune from (to)
intent on (upon)	lacking in	parallel with (to)
reliant on (upon)		

5) 有些作表语的形容词后常跟不定式 (a) 或由 that 引导的从句 (b):

a. He was *doomed to fail*. 他注定要失败。

He is *liable to shout* when angry. 他生气时常大声吼叫。

He is physically *fit to be* an astronaut. 他的身体适合当宇航员。

b. She was *confident that she would find work*. 她有信心能找到工作。

I'm *surprised I didn't see the trick*. 我很奇怪这花招我竟没有看出来。

I'm so *happy that you could visit us*. 我真高兴你能来看望我们。

关于这两类结构可参阅第 13.5.8 和 13.5.9 节。

14.2.3　作定语的某些形容词

1) 大部分形容词都可作定语, 也可作表语, 但有一部分形容词只能作定语, 不能作表语:

a. 许多类属形容词只能作定语, 如:

atomic	bridal	cardiac	countless	cubic
digital	east	eastern	eventual	existing
federal	indoor	institutional	introductory	judicial
lone	maximum	nationwide	neighbouring	north
northern	occasional	orchestral	outdoor	phonetic
remedial	reproductive	south	southern	supplementary
underlying	west	western	woolen	

b. 也有少数品质形容词只能用作定语, 如:

belated	checkered	commanding	fateful	flagrant	scant
thankless	unenviable				

强调形容词总用作定语，颜色形容词在多数情况下都用作定语。

2）有些形容词通常用作表语，但在个别情况下都可用作定语，如：

sure: It's a *sure* thing they'll come.　他们肯定会来。

glad: Where were you when you received the *glad* news?　你得到这喜讯时人在哪里？

sorry: His triumph seemed a *sorry* one.　他的胜利似乎价值不大。

fond: She has *fond* hopes of becoming a movie star.　她有当电影明星的幻想。

ill: Let's disregard any *ill* comments that are aimed at us.　咱们不要理会任何针对我们的恶意评论。

ready: A kind man gives *ready* help to children.　善良的人随时乐于帮助孩子。

14.2.4　形容词的其他用法

1）很多形容词可用作宾语的补语，关于这种结构可参阅第13.5.10节，特别是能作表语的形容词一般都可用来构成复合宾语：

ill: I found her *ill* with influenza.　我发现她得了流感。

ready: Have your tickets *ready*.　大家把车票准备好。

alive: Let's keep the fish *alive*.　咱们要让鱼活着。

alone: We should leave her *alone* for a moment.　我们应当让她一个人待一会儿。

well: I hope to see you *well* soon.　希望早日看到你痊愈。

unable: I found myself *unable* to answer the question.　我发现自己回答不了那问题。

2）形容词作状语时也不少，在很多情况可引导一个短语：

Overjoyed, she dashed out of the house.　狂喜之下她冲出屋去。

Curious, we looked around for other guests.　由于好奇，我们向四周张望看有什么别的客人。

She grasped my hands, *unable to say anything*.　她抓住我的双手，说不出话来。

He's come back to his hometown *full of grand resolutions*.　他满怀壮志回到家乡。

He emerged from the accident *unharmed*.　在这次事故中他毫发无损。

Anxious for a quick decision, the chairman called for a vote. 因急于作出一个快速决定，主席要求投票表决。

They like living in a village, *free of crowds and noise*. 他们喜欢住在村子里，远离人群和喧嚣。

3）形容词间或也可用作同位语，放在所修饰的词后面：

He read all kinds of books, *ancient and modern, Chinese and foreign*. 他读了很多书，古今中外都有。

People, *old and young*, look to the streets to watch the parade. 老老少少的人们都走上街头看游行。

The current fair, *the biggest* in its history, is being held in Guangzhou. 目前的这届交易会是有史以来规模最大的，正在广州举行。

I found Jim, *unconscious*, a few hours later. 几个小时后我发现了吉姆，他已不省人事。

14.3　形容词的位置

14.3.1　形容词作定语时的位置

1）作定语时的通常位置：

作定语的形容词通常放在所修饰词前面，如果有几个形容词，大体上按下列顺序排列：

冠词	品质形容词	颜色形容词	类别形容词	所修饰的词	
a	little	white	wooden	house	一幢白色的小木屋
a	pretty	black	lacy	dress	一件漂亮的带花边的黑裙服
a	beautiful	crimson	velvet	robe	一件漂亮的深红色丝绒睡袍
a	small	yellow	wooden	table	一张黄色的小木桌
the		black	triangular	fin	三角形的黑鳍

有时也按下面顺序:

冠词	品 质	大小／年岁	颜色	国家	分 词	所修饰词	
a	beautiful	old	red	French	handmade	cupboard	一个漂亮的法国老式手工制作的红柜子
an	elegant			French		clock	一座典雅的法国钟
a	handy	little			home-made	calculator	一个方便小巧的国产计算器

2）个别形容词常放在所修饰词后面:

Japan *proper* excludes the outlying islands.　日本本土不包括外围岛屿。

I had an interview with the ambassador *designate*.　我采访了即将赴任的大使。

Their leader was the devil *incarnate*.　他们的头目是魔鬼的化身。

特别是在一些固定词组中，形容词通常放在所修饰词后面:

the Poet Laureate 桂冠诗人　　　　　heir apparent 当然继承人

court martial 军事法庭　　　　　　　sum total 总额

governor general (英)总督　　　　　　Asia Minor 小亚细亚

postmaster general 邮政部长　　　　　Attorney General (美)司法部长，

president *elect* 当选总统　　　　　　　(英)总检察长

3）有些形容词可以放在名词前面，也可放在名词后面，意思有时不同，例如:

There were many old men *present*.　有许多老年人在场。

What's your *present* feeling?　你现在是什么感觉?

The city *proper* is half the size of the metropolitan area.　市区只占这个大都市面积的一半。

You must learn the *proper* way to behave.　你必须学习正确的处世之道。

He is concerned about the problems *involved*.　他很关心所牵涉的问题。

He could not fully understand *involved* scholarly lectures.　他不完全明白那些复杂的学术报告。

He urged all *concerned* to participate in the seminar.　他敦促全部有关人员参加研讨会。

She looked up with a *concerned* air.　她用关心的神情抬头看了看。

有些放在所修饰词的前面或后面意思相同:

> Is there a doctor *available*? 找得到医生吗?
>
> We must set every *available* man to work. 我们必须让所有能找到的人都干起来。

> We must help them in every way *possible*. 我们必须以一切可能的方式帮助他们。
>
> There is more than one *possible* explanation. 有不止一种可能的解释。

> He is the most suitable person *imaginable*. 他是能想到的最合适人选。
>
> He had had the worst *imaginable* day. 他度过了再糟糕不过的一天。

> There was something *missing*. 有东西不见了。
>
> We started off in search of the *missing* child. 我们动身去找丢失的孩子。

4) 修饰 nothing，something 这类合成代词的形容词通常放在它们后面:

I was looking for something *cheaper*. 我在找便宜一点的东西。

Has anything *special* happened? 发生了什么特别的事吗?

There is nothing *wrong* with his heart. 他的心脏没有问题。

14.3.2　形容词作其他成分时的位置

1) 形容词作表语时都跟在系动词后面:

Two of them remained *single*. 他们中有两人一直是单身。

Presently she grew *calmer*. 不久她平静了一些。

有时前面可插入其他词(如状语等):

He became *quite* cheerful. 他变得很快活。

He seemed *to me quite* normal. 在我看来他似乎很正常。

2) 作宾语补语时一般紧跟宾语:

This delay has made me *late*. 这一耽搁使我迟到了。

This kept me *busy*. 这使我很忙。

有时前面可插入其他成分 (如状语):

It'll make me *so* happy if you'll accept it. 如果你愿意收下它的话会使我非常高兴。

I've never seen her *quite* so sure of herself. 我从未见她这样自信过。

3) 作状语时可放在句子前面 (a)，也可放在句子后部 (b)，间或插在主语后面 (c):

a. *Greatly interested*, I asked how he played the new instrument. 我带着极大的兴趣问他这新乐器怎么弹。

Enthusiastic, they are quite cooperative.　他们有热情，很愿意合作。

b. She hurried up the steps, *nervous and pale*.　她匆忙走上台阶，神情紧张，脸色苍白。

He came round *greatly concerned*.　他很关切地走了过来。

c. Mrs. Carey, *much concerned*, insisted on sending him to hospital.　卡利夫人很关心，坚持要送他去医院。

The girl, *amazed at the sight*, didn't know what to say.　那姑娘看到这景象后很惊讶，不知道说什么好。

有些形容词有时用在动词后面，表示状态：

Many poets died *young*.　许多诗人英年早逝。

I drink the milk *hot*.　我喝热牛奶。

4) 作同位语的形容词通常紧跟在名词后面：

The middle-aged man is a newly elected team leader, *able, open and sincere*.　那位中年男子是新选出的队长，能干、开朗、为人诚恳。

I met Sallie, *angry at me as always*.　我见到了萨莉，还是像往常那样生我的气。

这类同位语有时放在句首，特别是当主语很短时：

Conscientious and eager, she took down everything he said.　她很认真热情，把他说的话都记下了。

Cheerful, efficient and warm-hearted, they do everything to make your journey comfortable.　他们乐观、能干、热情，总是想方设法使你旅途舒适愉快。

5) 作句子状语 (或称独立成分) 的形容词，多放在句子前头：

Strange to say, no one was hurt.　说也奇怪，没有人受伤。

More important still, I didn't want to worry Maxim.　更重要的是，我不想让马克西姆担心。

He may be late. *Worse still*, he may not come at all.　他可能会迟到，更糟糕的是，他可能压根儿就不来了。

14.4　形容词的比较级别

14.4.1　形容词比较级和最高级的构成法

1) 形容词有些有两种形式，即 **比较级** (The Comparative Degree)，表示"比较…"和 **最高级** (The Superlative Degree)，表示"最…"，与之相对的形容

词本身称为 **原级** (The Positive Degree)，例如：

原级	比较级	最高级
high 高	higher 较高的	highest 最高的
warm 暖和	warmer 较暖和	warmest 最暖和
cold 冷	colder 较冷的	coldest 最冷的
short 短	shorter 较短的	shortest 最短的

这三种形式总起来称为形容词的 **比较级别** (Degrees of Comparison)。

2）单音节词及少数双音节词都以在后面加词尾 -er, -est 的方式构成比较级，构成的方式如下：

情　况	加　法	例　词		
一般情况	直接加词尾	small	smaller	smallest
以 e 结尾的词	加 -r, 及 -st	brave	braver	bravest
以"辅音+y"结尾的词	变y为i，再加词尾	busy	busier	busiest
		happy	happier	happiest
以一个辅音字母结尾的词	将该辅音字母双写，再加词尾	hot	hotter	hottest
		big	bigger	biggest

除以 y 结尾的双音节词外，以 -ow, -er, -te 等结尾的双音节词，也可用加词尾的方法构成比较级和最高级，如：

原级	比较级	最高级
narrow	narrower	narrowest
clever	cleverer	cleverest
simple	simpler	simplest
polite	politer	politest
common	commoner	commonest
quiet	quieter	quietest

3）其他双音节词及多音节词都以在前面加more和most的方式构成比较级和最高级：

原级	比较级	最高级
careful	more careful	most careful
active	more active	most active
likely	more likely	most likely
difficult	more difficult	most difficult
beautiful	more beautiful	most beautiful
effective	more effective	most effective

有少数单音节词，如 pleased，glad，tired，fond 等，也可以这种方法构成比较级和最高级：

原级	比较级	最高级
pleased	more pleased	most pleased
glad	more glad	most glad

4) less 和 least 也可用来构成比较级和最高级，表示"较／最不…"：

原级	比较级	最高级
careful	less careful	least careful
selfish	less selfish	least selfish
dangerous	less dangerous	least dangerous
necessary	less necessary	least necessary

14.4.2 不规则的比较级和最高级形式

1) 有些形容词有不规则的比较级和最高级形式：

原级	比较级	最高级
good, well	better	best
bad	worse	worst
much, many	more	most
little	less	least
far	farther, further	farthest, furthest
old	older, elder	oldest, eldest

2) 这些不规则形式的意思可表示如下：

better:

Two heads are *better* than one. （谚）两人智慧胜一人。

This is a *better* example. 这是一个较好的例子。

The child is *better* today. 今天孩子的情况好些了。

best:

The *best* mirror is an old friend. (谚)老友是宝镜。

East, west, home's *best*. 东跑西跑还是家里最好。

worse:

His behaviour is *worse* than ever before. 他的表现比过去更糟。

Her cold was growing *worse*. 她的感冒更厉害了。

worst:

The *worst* part of the journey was over. 旅途中最糟糕的一段路程过去了。

This is the *worst* accident for years. 这是多年以来最严重的事故。

more:

He went abroad to gain *more* experience. 他出国去学习更多的经验。

We won't have any *more* discussion about it. 这事我们不再讨论了。

most:

Least talk, *most* work. 少说话，多干活。

The busiest men have the *most* leisure. (谚)最忙的人闲暇最多。

less:

I have *less* strength than he has. 我的力气比他小。

More haste, *less* speed. (谚)欲速则不达。

least:

He didn't have the *least* desire to go to bed. 他一点都不想睡觉。

There isn't the *least* wind today. 今天一点风都没有。

3）older 和 elder 意思不尽相同，**older** 表示年纪较大的，**oldest** 表示年纪最大的：

John is *older* than Tom. 约翰比汤姆年纪大。

He is the *oldest* student in our class. 他是我们班年龄最大的学生。

elder 和 **eldest** 主要用来表示兄弟姐妹或子女的长幼关系：

He's my *elder* brother. 他是我哥哥。

Sarah is the *elder* of the two. 两人中萨拉是姐姐。

This is her *elder* daughter. 这是她较大的女儿。

Their *eldest* son died in infancy. 他们的大儿子在襁褓中就死了。

Her *eldest* child is at university. 她的大孩子上大学了。

He has three sons, and his *eldest* has just started school. 他有三个儿子，老大刚上学。

4) farther 和 further 的意思不尽相同:

father: Manchester is *farther* from London than Oxford is. 曼彻斯特
(较远)   离伦敦比牛津远。

farthest: Which of the cities is the *farthest* from us? 这些城市哪座离
(最远的)   我们最远?

further: It was a few miles *further*. 它要远几英里。
(更远)

There is a cottage on the *further* side of the hill. 小山的那一
边有一座农舍。

(进一步的) They made *further* arrangements. 他们作了进一步的安排。

(更多的) Have you any *further* questions to ask? 你还有更多的问题
要问吗?

furthest: It is the *furthest* point west in England. 这是英格兰最靠西
(更远的)   的地方。

14.4.3   形容词比较级的用法

1) 形容词的比较级可以单独使用:

Are you feeling *better* today? 你今天感觉好点了吗?

Be *more careful* next time. 下次小心点。

It was *quieter* outside. 外面安静点了。

He feels *more content* now. 他现在比较满意了。

It couldn't be *easier*. 不能再容易了。

This car's *more expensive*. 这辆车比较贵。

She hoped to get a *better* job. 她希望得到一份更好的工作。

Further supplies will soon be available. 不久将会有更多的供应品。

Further discussion wouldn't be necessary. 没有必要作进一步讨论。

Who is *taller* (*more suitable*)? 谁高(更合适)一点?

We must do more with *less* money. 我们要少花钱多办事。

Which book is *better* (*less difficult*)? 哪本书好一些(不难一些)?

I'll try to make *fewer* mistakes in future. 以后我要少犯错误。

2) 也可以和 than 一起用, 表示两者相比, than 后可以跟:

a. 名词或代词(若为人称代词, 在口语中多用宾格):

He is **older than** me. 他年龄比我大。

Tokyo is **bigger than** New York. 东京比纽约大。

He made **fewer** mistakes **than** *you* (do). 他出的错比你少。

She has **more** time **than** *me* (I do). 她的时间比我多。

There are **more** boys **than** *girls* in our class. 我们班男生比女生多。

b. 动名词:

Skiing is **more exciting than** *skating*. 滑雪比溜冰更刺激。

This is **more interesting than** *sitting in an office*. 这比坐办公室有意思。

Nothing is **more unpleasant than** *finding insects in your bath*. 什么也不
   如在浴缸里发现虫子更令人不快。

Travelling by train is **more comfortable than** *travelling by bus*. 坐火车旅
   行比坐公共汽车旅行舒服。

Shopping at a supermarket is **cheaper than** *going to the local shops*. 在超
   市购物比在邻近商店购物便宜。

c. 从句:

I am **happier than** *I have ever been*. 我现在比过去任何时候都快活。

I was a **better** singer **than** *he was*. 我唱歌比他好。

He is **stronger than** *I expected*. 他比我预料的更健壮。

It was more **expensive than** *I thought*. 它比我想的要贵些。

We produce 25 percent **more steel than** *we did five years ago*. 我们的钢
   产量比五年前增加了百分之二十五。

d. 状语 (包括副词、介词短语等):

She felt **worse than** *usual*. 她感到比平时更难受。

It's even **colder than** *yesterday*. 今天比昨天还冷。

He is **busier than** *ever*. 他比过去更忙了。

She is in **better** health **than** *last year*. 她身体比去年好了。

It takes **less** time to go there by plane **than** *by train*. 坐飞机到那里比坐火
   车快。

e. 跟其他成分 (如动词、形容词等):

Better cut the shoe **than** *pinch the foot*. 把鞋铰开也比夹脚好。

It's **easier** to do it yourself **than** *(to) explain it* to her. 你自己干比给她解
   释更容易。

It's **better** to be prepared **than** *unprepared*. 有准备比没准备好。

She was **more surprised than** *angry*. 她吃惊甚于生气。

He was **more lucky than** *clever*. 他是运气好,而不是聪明。

14.4.4　形容词比较级的修饰语

1）形容词比较级前可加 much，a lot，far，a bit，a little，slightly 之类表示程度的状语：

He's feeling *a lot better* today.　他感到今天好多了。

You have *far more* imagination than I have.　你的想像力比我丰富多了。

She is *a little bit better* now.　她现在稍稍好一点了。

It's *slightly warmer* today.　今天稍暖和一点。

Now I feel *a great deal more confident*.　现在我感到信心强多了。

You look *much happier* than you did yesterday.　你比昨天显得高兴多了。

She's actually *a good deal older* than she looks.　她的实际年龄比她看上去要大得多。

2）也可在比较级前加 any，no，some，even，still 这类词：

Do you feel *any better* today?　你今天感觉好一点了吗？

She was *no older* than Zilla.　她并不比齐拉大。

You must go and get *some more* milk.　你得再去弄些牛奶来。

This book is *even more useful* than that.　这本书甚至比那本书更有用。

He is fat, but his brother is *still fatter*.　他很胖，但他哥哥更胖。

When she heard the news, she became *all the more depressed*.　听到这消息，她变得更加沮丧了。

3）比较级前还可加其他表示数量的词：

Shall I get *a couple more* chairs?　我要不要再搬两把椅子来？

Where can I get *a few more* computers?　我从哪里还能再弄几台电脑来？

He had not *so very many more* years to live.　他已没有多少年好活了。

My sister is *ten years younger* than me.　我妹妹比我小十岁。

You're *a head taller* than Jane.　你比简高一个头。

It was *one-fourth cheaper* than the market price.　它比市场价格低四分之一。

Cotton output was *20 per cent higher* than in the previous year.　棉花产量比前一年高百分之二十。

14.4.5　形容词比较级的特殊用法

形容词比较级有些特殊用法，例如：

1）"**more...than**" 有时可以把两种品质加以比较，表示"更多…而不是"：

I was *more* annoyed *than* worried when he didn't come home.　他没回家时

我更多的是生气而不是担心。

This is *more* a war movie *than* a western. 这应当说是战争片而不是西部片。

To them, music is *more* a way of life *than* just an interest. 对他们来说,音乐是一种生活方式而不仅仅是一种爱好。

2) **more and more** 这类结构可表示 "越来越":

Secretly she became *more and more indignant*. 她内心感到越来越气愤。

The story gets *more and more exciting*. 故事变得越来越激动人心。

Your English is getting *better and better*. 你的英语越来越好了。

Holiday flights are getting *less and less expensive*. 节假日的机票越来越便宜了。

3) **the more...the more** 可表示 "越是…越…":

The more learned a man is, *the more modest* he usually is. 一个人越有学问,往往越谦虚。

The more difficult the questions are, *the less likely* I am to be able to answer them. 问题越难,我能回答的可能性越小。

The warmer the weather, *the better* I feel. 天气越暖和我感觉越舒服。

4) **more than** 常用在数词前,表示 "超过…"、"…多":

He can't be *more than* thirty. 他不可能超过三十岁。

More than 800 people attended the concert. 八百多人出席了音乐会。

They enrolled *more than* 500 new students. 他们招收了五百多新生。

She has been away for *more than* a year. 她离开已一年多了。

5) **less than** 常表示 "不到…",或(美) "不太":

In *less than* a week, the MS was ready. 不到一周稿子就准备好了。

I bought it for *less than* a dollar. 我买它花了还不到一美元。

We were busy and *less than* delighted to have company that day. 那天我们很忙,不太想接待客人。

The boys were *less than* happy about having a party. 男生们并不太高兴开晚会。

6) **no less than** 表示 "多达"、"不少于":

He won *no less than* £ 500. 他赢了不少于五百英镑。

Its population is *no less than* two million. 它的人口多达两百万。

No less than 1,000 people came. 至少来了有一千人。

There were *no less than* three officials waiting there. 至少有三名官员在那里等候。

7) more or less 表示"基本上"、"大体上"或"大约":

The work is *more or less* finished. 这项工作基本上完成了。

The answers were *more or less* right. 这些回答大体上是正确的。

It's an hour's journey, *more or less*. 这段路程大约需要一个小时。

It's a mile, *more or less*, from here to the station. 从这里到火车站大约有一英里。

14.4.6　as...as 和 not so...as 结构

1) as...as 可表示"和…一样…"(注意形容词要用原级):

Some of their states are *as big as* France. 他们有些州的面积有法国那样大。

He considered her opinion *as valuable as* ours. 他认为她的意见和我们的一样有价值。

He is *as energetic as* a young man. 他像年轻人一样充满活力。

She was *as busy as* before. 她还是和过去一样忙。

They were *as firm as* we could expect. 他们像我们所期待的那样坚定。

英语中有大量这样的成语:

as brave as a lion 十分勇敢;无畏	as bright as day 亮如白昼
as busy as a bee 忙碌	as cheerful as a lark 兴高采烈
as cold as ice 非常冷;无反应的	as cunning as a fox 狡诈
as fat as a pig 体胖如猪	as fierce as a tiger 凶猛如虎
as firm as a rock 坚如磐石	as graceful as a swan 举止端庄
as innocent as a dove 非常天真的	as greedy as a wolf 贪得无厌
as loud as thunder 声如雷鸣	as light as a feather 轻如鸿毛
as proud as a peacock 非常高傲	as obstinate as a mule 像骡子一样固执
as quiet as a mouse 娴静	
as round as an apple 滚圆的	as quick as lightning 迅如闪电
as silly as a goose 蠢如呆鹅	as red as a cherry 脸色绯红
as sour as vinegar 味道很酸的	as sharp as a needle 非常敏锐
as straight as an arrow 快捷的	as slippery as an eel 滑头的
as strong as a horse 非常健壮	as stupid as a donkey 笨极了
as sweet as honey 非常甜的	as tame as a cat 非常听话
as timid as a hare 胆小如鼠	as ugly as a toad 特别丑陋
as watchful as a hawk 警惕监视着	as white as snow 洁白如雪

2) 在否定句中可用 not as... (a) 或 not so... (b) 表示"不像…那样":

a. Manslaughter is *not as (so) bad as murder*. 过失杀人没有谋杀那么严重。

The food was*n't as good as* yesterday. 今天的饭菜没有昨天的好。

Your coffee is *not as (so) good as* the coffee my mother makes. 你煮的咖啡没我妈煮的好。

The hotel was *not as good as* they expected. 旅馆没有他们预期的那样好。

b. It is*n't so cold as* yesterday. 今天没有昨天那么冷。

He is *not so handsome as* his brother. 他不像他哥哥那样英俊。

I'm *not so experienced as* you think. 我没有你想的那样有经验。

The situation is *not so bad as* had been painted. 形势没有描绘的那样糟。

3) 在 as...as 结构中也可以插入修饰语:

Petrol is *twice as expensive as* it was a few years ago. 汽油比前几年贵了一倍。

Their house is about *three times as big as* ours. 他们的房子比我们的房子约大两倍。

My command of English is *not half so (as) good as* yours. 我的英文学得还不及你一半好。

There the tuberculosis rate is *10 times as high as* in North Carolina. 那里的肺结核发病率是北卡罗来纳州的十倍。

14.4.7 形容词最高级的用法

1) 形容词最高级的主要用法:

形容词最高级主要表示"最…",前面一般带定冠词 the:

This is *the oldest theatre* in London. 这是伦敦最古老的剧院。

It was *the quickest route* from Rome to Milan. 这是从罗马到米兰最快捷的路线。

Jim is *the tallest* of the three. 吉姆是三人中最高的。

This book is *the most interesting one*. 这本书是最有意思的一本。

Which is *the longest river* in China? 哪条河流是中国最长的?

She has *the worst task* of us all. 我们所有人中她的任务最艰巨。

有时后面有一从句修饰:

This is *the best beer* (that) I've ever drunk. 这是我喝过的最好的啤酒。

That was *the worst film* (that) he had ever seen. 那是他看过的最糟糕的电影。

He is *the kindest man* (that) I 've ever met.　他是我碰到过的最善良的人。

That's *the most ridiculous story* I've ever heard.　这是我听过的最荒唐的故事。

It was *the most expensive hotel* we had ever stayed in.　这是我们住过的最贵的饭店。

That was *the most tasty meal* I've ever had.　那是我吃过的最可口的饭菜。

2) 最高级形容词也可单独使用，后面不跟表示比较的范围的修饰语：

Her *oldest daughter* is eleven years old.　她的大女儿十一岁。

Who is the *tallest*, Julia, Mary or Helen?　谁最高，是朱丽亚、玛丽还是海伦？

No one dared to raise *the least objection*.　没人敢提丁点反对意见。

Which is *the nearest river*?　哪一条是最近的河流？

Who picked *the most apples*?　谁摘的苹果最多？

Now we come to *the most important thing*.　现在我们来谈最重要的事。

The smallest ones live in trees.　最小的生活在树上。

3) 最高级形容词前面有时可有一个状语 (a)，有时有一个定语修饰 (b)：

a. It was **by far** *the best* hospital I had ever seen.　这是我见过的最最好的医院。

It was of *the* **very** *highest* quality.　它的质量是最最高的。

That is **much** *the worst* stretch of motorway in this area.　那是这个地区最最糟糕的一段公路。

This is **quite far** *the most expensive* bicycle in the shop.　这是这家商店最最贵的自行车。

b. It's Japan's **third** *largest* city.　它是日本的第三大城市。

Hainan is China's **second** *largest* island.　海南是中国第二大岛。

He is *the most suitable* person **imaginable**.　他是能想到的最合适人选。

We will finish the work in *the shortest* **possible** time.　我们将在尽可能短的时间内完成这项工作。

14.4.8　形容词最高级的特殊用法

1) 形容词最高级可用作表语，这时定冠词 the 可以省略：

I think her plan is *best*.　我认为她的计划最好。

Cotton blankets are generally *cheapest*.　棉毛毯一般最便宜。

We are *busiest* on Mondays. 我们星期一最忙。

Her argument is *most convincing*. 她的论点最有说服力。

2）形容词最高级前可以加 a 或不加冠词来表示"非常…"：

It is *a most joyful occasion*. 这是一个非常快乐的日子。

That was *a most extraordinary thing*. 这是一件很特别的事。

She is *a most mysterious person*. 她是个非常神秘的人。

He has been *most kind* to me. 他对我非常好。

We were all *most anxious* to go home. 我们都很想回家。

I should be *most happy* to help you. 我会非常高兴帮助你。

3）形容词最高级还可和 at 构成短语作表语，表示"处于最…的状态"：

The peony was *at its brightest*. 牡丹花正在盛开。

She was *at her happiest* in her home in the country. 她在乡下家里时最高兴。

I knew she was *at her worst*. 我知道她这时情绪最糟。

She is never *at her best* in the presence of her mother. 在她妈跟前她的表现从来不是最好的。

4）形容词最高级还可和 at 构成许多短语作状语：

He is, *at best*, a second-rate novelist. 他充其量也就是个二流小说家。

I may not be good, but *at least* let me have a try. 我可能不算好，但至少让我试试。

He had been gone 15 minutes *at the most*. 他离开顶多才一刻钟。

I can't go to London till May 5th *at the earliest*. 我最早也要到五月五日才能去伦敦。

I'll be with you *at latest* by ten. 我最迟十点钟就来陪你。

14.5   名词化的形容词

14.5.1 "the + 形容词" 可以表示一类人

1）the 可以和某些形容词一道表示一类人：

The poor get poorer; *the rich* get richer. 穷人更穷，富人更富。

The well-to-do had their cares also. 富裕的人也有他们的烦恼。

She was always good with *the unfortunate*. 她一向善待不幸的人。

They poisoned the minds of *the young*. 它们毒害青年人的头脑。

Forture favors *the brave*. (谚)命运青睐勇者。

He had a natural sympathy for *the down-trodden*. 他对被践踏者怀有天生的同情心。

Take care of *the wounded* and *the dying*. 救死扶伤。

The old and *the young* should be able to live together. 老年人和青年人应该能过到一起。

They are building a school for *the deaf* and *the dumb*. 他们正在盖一所聋哑学校。

He always sided with *the oppressed* and *the exploited*. 他总是站在被压迫和被剥削者一边。

The very wise avoid such temptation. 真正明智的人总是避开这种诱惑。

The injured were immediately taken to hospital. 伤者被立即送往医院。

The sick (*elderly*) must be cared for. 病人(老年人)应受照顾。

These provide shelters for *the homeless*. 这些为无家可归的人提供了栖身之处。

The living are more important to us than *the dead*. 对我们而言,生者比死者更重要。

2) the 也可和某些表示国家民族的形容词一道表示"某国(民族)的人":

The English have a wonderful sense of humour. 英国人幽默感很强。

The French like to eat well. 法国人喜欢吃得好。

the Chinese 中国人　　　　　　　the Japanese 日本人

the Swiss 瑞士人　　　　　　　　the Spanish 西班牙人

the Welsh 威尔士人　　　　　　　the Dutch 荷兰人

从上例可以看出这样用的主要是一些以 sh,ch,se,ss结尾的词。

这种结构间或指一个人,如: the accused (被告), the deceased (死者)。

14.5.2 　"the + 形容词"可表示一些事物或品质

the 可加在某些形容词前表示一些事物或品质:

This was nothing out of *the ordinary*. 这并没有什么异乎寻常之处。

They would have to bow to *the inevitable*. 他们将不得不向无可避免的事(命运)低头。

He expected me to do *the impossible*. 他期待我做办不到的事。

The difficult we do at once. *The impossible* takes a little longer. 困难的事

我们马上就做, 不可能的事需要稍长一些时间。

We must be ready to cope with *the unexpected*. 我们必须准备应付预料不到的问题。

Let X be *the unknown* in this equation. 设X为这个方程式中的未知数。

Do you believe in *the supernatural*? 你相信有神奇古怪的事吗?

He is fond of writing about *the unusual*. 他喜欢写些古怪的题材。

She admires *the mystical*. 她喜欢神秘的东西。

We have to take *the rough* along with *the smooth* in life. 生活中好事坏事都得承受。

This policy is a mixture of *the old* and *the new*. 这项政策是新旧混合的产物。

14.5.3 包含名词化形容词的词组

1) 有不少词组中包含名词化形容词:

The killer remained *at large* for weeks. 那杀手好几周都逍遥法外。

Things were going *from bad to worse* between them. 他们之间的关系日益恶化。

I can't say *for sure*. 我说不准。

I know *for certain* that he has a car. 我确实知道他有一辆车。

He will leave the city *for good*. 他将永远离开这座城市。

He cuts my hairs *for free*. 他免费给我理发。

The National Broadcasting Company is called NBC *for short*. 国家广播公司简称 NBC。

They are neighbours, *for better for worse*. 好歹他们是街坊。

I told him the story *in full*. 我给他讲了全部的故事。

The weather in Florida is warm *in general*. 佛罗里达的气候总的来说是暖和的。

In brief, Sophia was no longer a stranger. 简而言之,索菲娅已不再是陌生人了。

In short, they were happy together. 总之,他们在一起很快活。

She waited *in vain*, however. 然而,她白等了。

2) 有不少形容词最高级有时可以名词化:

We're not going to Japan. *At least* not for the present. 我们不准备去日本,至少目前不准备去。

My book will be out in a day or two, a week *at most*. 我的书一两天后就出版, 至多一星期就出版。

You ought to hear *at the latest* by Friday. 最迟到周五你就会听到消息。

At the very most, she can't be more than eighteen. 她最多也就十八岁。

He thought that *at worst* he could get a scolding. 他想他最多只会挨一顿说。

At best we can do only half as much as last year. 最多我们只能完成去年工作量的一半。

She took leave of the party *in the liveliest of spirits*. 她兴高采烈地告别了晚会。

They were too poor to rent even *the cheapest of houses*. 他们穷到连最便宜的房子都租不起。

It was one of *the most interesting of these discoveries*. 这是这些发现中最有意思的一个。

〔注〕有不少形容词已变成名词:

That music is popular with the *young*. 那种音乐年轻人很欢迎。

After the storm comes a *calm*. (谚)风暴之后是宁静。

She had a bad headache and needed *quiet*. 她头疼得厉害需要安静。

It's much better in the *cool*. 在荫凉地就好多了。

I got my *medical* on Thursday. 星期四我体检了。

Of course it won't hurt you, *silly*. 当然你不会疼的, 傻瓜。

第15章 副词

15.1 副词的类型

15.1.1 副词的类型

副词大体上可分为下面几类:

- **时间副词** (Adverbs of Time)
- **地点副词** (Adverbs of Place)
- **方式副词** (Adverbs of Manner)
- **程度副词** (Adverbs of Degree)
- **强调副词** (Emphasing Adverbs)
- **疑问副词** (Interrogative Adverbs)
- **连接副词** (Conjunctive Adverbs)
- **关系副词** (Relative Adverbs)
- **句子副词** (Sentence Adverbs)

15.1.2 时间副词

时间副词有三类:

1) 表示发生时间的副词:

It's beginning to rain *now*! 现在开始下雨了!

I haven't seen her *recently*. 最近我没见到她。

Will you be free *tonight*? 你今晚有空吗?

See you *later*. 回头见。

常见的这类副词有:

ago	before	just now	last night	lately	later (on)
now	recently	so far	then	today	tomorrow
tonight	yesterday				

2) 表示频繁程度的副词，也称 **频度副词** (Adverbs of Frequency)：

She is *constantly* changing her mind. 她老是改变主意。

We do meet now and then, but not *regularly*. 我们确实偶尔也见面，但不经常见面。

Lester *rarely (seldom)* left his room. 莱斯特很少离开他的房间。

He goes to see her *continually*. 他频繁地去看她。

这类副词常见的有：

always	constantly	continually	continuously	ever
frequently	generally	hardly ever	much	never
normally	occasionally	often	periodically	rarely
regularly	repeatedly	seldom	sometimes	usually

3) 还有一些其他表示时间的副词：

I'll be back *presently (shortly)*. 我一会儿就回来。

What decision did you *finally* arrive at? 你们最后作出了什么决定？

Nancy was up *early*. 南希很早就起来了。

He has *just* had an operation. 他刚动过手术。

常见的这类副词有：

already	early	finally	first	immediately
just	late	long	presently	right away
shortly	since	soon	yet	

15.1.3　地点副词

1) 有不少表示地点的副词：

She is studying *abroad*. 她在国外留学。

If he is not here, he's about *somewhere*. 如果他不在这儿，那就在附近什么地方。

They moved *downtown*. 他们搬到城里去了。

Then I went *upstairs* to bed. 然后我就上楼睡觉了。

常见的这类副词有：

abroad	ahead	anywhere	ashore	away
close (by)	downstairs	downtown	eastward	elsewhere
everywhere	halfway	here	home	indoors
nearby	nextdoor	northward	nowhere	offshore
outdoors	overhead	overseas	somewhere	southward
there	underground	upstairs	uptown	westward

2) 还有一些部分与介词同形的副词，有人称它们为 **副词小品词** (Adverb Particles)。这些副词与介词同形，跟宾语的为介词，否则是副词：

用作介词	用作副词
The Dead Sea is *below* see level. 死海在海平面之下。	I could see the river down *below*. 我可以看到下方的那条河。
Don't stand so *near* the train. 不要站得离火车这么近。	He lives quite *near*. 他住得很近。
A cat climbed *up* the tree. 猫爬上了树。	Stand *up*! 起立!
He jumped *off* the horse. 他从马上跳了下来。	The bird flew *off*. 鸟儿飞走了。

这类副词主要有：

aboard	about	above	across	along	around
behind	below	beneath	beyond	down	in
inside	near	off	on	out	outside
over	past	round	throughout	underneath	up

3) 还有一些地点副词表示地区范围等：

We have no shops *locally*. 我们在本地区没有商店。

Fortunately the news was not yet spread *widely*. 所幸这消息还没有四处传开。

Eight million people *globally* are infected with the virus. 全世界有八百万人染上了这种病毒。

The theory has been *universally* accepted. 这个理论已被普遍接受。

常见的这类副词有：

globally	internationally	locally	nationally
nationwide	universally	widely	worldwide

此外，以 where 构成的副词也是地点副词：

Let's go *anywhere* where it's quiet. 咱们去一个安静的地方吧。

Where did you go? ——*Nowhere*. 你去哪儿了？ ——哪儿也没去。

If she doesn't like it here, she can go *elsewhere*. 如果她不喜欢这里，她可以去别的地方。

It's the same *everywhere*. 到处都一样。

I seemed to have met you *somewhere*. 我似乎在哪儿见过你。

15.1.4 方式副词

英语中有大量方式副词，说明行为方式(回答 how 的问题)：

She *gently* refused to accept the gifts. 她委婉地拒绝接受那些礼物。

These countries were *ruthlessly* invaded. 这些国家受到残暴的侵略。

They hoped to see the problem settled *peacefully*. 他们希望看到这问题和平解决。

How *beautifully* your wife dances. 你夫人舞跳得真优美。

下面是一些常见的这类副词：

abruptly	accurately	awkwardly	badly	beautifully
brightly	brilliantly	briskly	carefully	carelessly
casually	clearly	closely	clumsily	comfortably
consistently	conveniently	correctly	dangerously	delicately
differently	distinctly	dramatically	effectively	efficiently
evenly	explicitly	faintly	faithfully	fiercely
finely	firmly	fluently	formally	frankly
freely	gently	gracefully	hastily	heavily
honestly	hurriedly	intently	meticulously	neatly
nicely	oddly	patiently	peacefully	peculiarly
perfectly	plainly	pleasantly	politely	poorly
professionally	properly	quietly	rapidly	readily

roughly	ruthlessly	securely	sensibly	sharply
silently	simply	smoothly	softly	splendidly
steadily	strangely	subtly	superbly	swiftly
systematically	tenderly	thoroughly	thoughtfully	tightly
truthfully	urgently	vaguely	vigorously	violently
vividly	voluntarily	warmly	willingly	wonderfully

2）还有相当多的副词，表示某些情绪：

This I *gladly* accepted.　这东西我高兴地接受了。

He shook hands *eagerly* with Sherlock Holmes.　他热切地与福尔摩斯握手。

She smiled *gratefully*.　她感激地笑了笑。

He looked at her *sadly*.　他凄然地看了看她。

下面是一些常见的这类副词；

angrily	anxiously	bitterly	boldly	calmly
cheerfully	confidently	desperately	early	excitedly
furiously	gladly	gloomily	gratefully	happily
helplessly	hopefully	hopelessly	impatiently	miserably
nervously	passionately	proudly	reluctantly	sadly
shyly	sincerely	uncomfortably	uneasily	wearily

3）还有一些以 -ly 结尾的副词，表示动作发生的情况：

The process was controlled *automatically*.　生产工序是自动控制的。

They trafficked in smuggled goods *openly*.　他们公开地贩卖走私货。

He left the town *secretly*.　他悄然离开了这座城市。

I only met her *accidentally*.　我只是偶然碰见她的。

常见的这类副词有：

accidentally	artificially	automatically	collectively	deliberately
directly	duly	illegally	independently	indirectly
individually	innocently	instinctively	involuntarily	jointly
legally	logically	mechanically	naturally	officially
openly	overtly	personally	politically	privately
publicly	scientifically	secretly	specially	symbolically

4) 大部分方式副词都由形容词加 -ly 构成，但有少数不带 -ly 词尾：

I had to work all *alone*.　我得独自一人工作。

Do you buy *wholesale* or *retail*?　你是批发还是零售？

She was to fly *solo* the next day.　第二天她将作单人飞行。

He spoke *impromptu*.　他即席讲了话。

15.1.5　程度副词和强调副词

1) 程度副词可修饰动词，表示"到某种程度"：

I'm *extremely* disappointed in him.　我对他极其失望。

He loved his mother *dearly*.　他深爱他的母亲。

I *strongly* object to your saying that.　我强烈反对你这样说话。

Is she *badly* hurt?　她伤得重吗？

常见的这类副词有：

absolutlety	adequately	almost	altogether	amazingly
awfully	badly	completely	considerably	dearly
deeply	drastically	dreadfully	enormously	entirely
exceedingly	excessively	extensively	extremely	fairly
fully	greatly	half	highly	immensely
incredibly	intensely	largely	moderately	nearly
partly	perfectly	poorly	practically	pretty
profoundly	purely	quite	rather	really
reasonably	remarkably	significantly	simply	slightly
somewhat	soundly	strongly	sufficiently	supremely
surprisingly	terribly	totally	tremendously	truly
utterly	very	virtually	well	wonderfully

这类副词除修饰动词外，还可修饰形容词 (a) 或另一副词 (b)：

a. fairly simple　相当简单　　　　　rather difficult　相当难

awfully sorry　非常抱歉　　　　　perfectly clear　十分清楚

highly confidential　高度机密的　　quite correct　完全正确

utterly unreasonable　极不合理　　truly grateful　确实很感激

b. fairly smoothly　相当顺利地　　　wonderfully well　好极了

know full(y) well　完全清楚　　　work quite hard　工作相当努力

run pretty fast　跑得相当快　　　　speak exceedingly well　讲得极好

act quite right　做得完全对　　　　do it very quickly　干得很快

2) 强调副词和程度副词很相近，有些就是程度副词。它们主要对所修饰的动词(a)、形容词(b)加以强调：

a. I *quite* agree.　我完全同意。

He knew *absolutely* nothing.　他是毫无所知的。

Your attitude *simply* amazes me.　你的态度简直使我吃惊。

b. You're *entirely* wrong.　你完全错了。

She's *perfectly* correct.　她完全正确。

The food is *just* wonderful.　这饭菜简直好极了。

这类副词主要有：

absolutely	completely	entirely	just	outright
perfectly	positively	purely	quite	really
simply	totally	truly	utterly	

3) much 是一个特殊的程度副词，它可以：

a. 修饰动词 (特别是用在否定句中)：

She didn't talk *much*.　她不怎么说话。

I don't *much* like the idea.　我不太喜欢这个想法。

Thank you very *much*.　非常感谢你。

Do you go to the cinema *much*?　你常去看电影吗？

b. 修饰形容词等：

I'm *much* obliged to you for telling me.　非常感谢你告诉了我。

I'm not *much* good at singing.　我唱歌不太好。

I'm very *much* afraid that she won't come.　我很担心她不来。

Much to my surprise she forgot our meeting.　令我很吃惊的是她把我们的约会忘了。

c. 和形容词或副词的比较级或最高级连用：

You sing *much* better than me.　你比我唱得好多了。

Their house is *much* nicer than ours.　他们的房子比我们的好多了。

That was *much* the best meal I've had for a long time.　这是好久以来我吃过的最最好的一顿饭了。

d. 和 how, so, too 等词连用：

How much do you like him?　你喜欢他到什么程度？

He would *so much* like to go.　他会很想去的。

She is *much too* busy to see visitors.　她实在太忙,不能会客。

15.1.6　疑问副词、连接副词和关系副词

1)疑问副词:

疑问副词用来引导特殊问句:

how:

How is your grandmother's rheumatism?　你奶奶的风湿病怎样了?

How long ago was it?　这是多久以前的事?

How do we get to the town center from here?　我们从这里怎么到市中心?

where:

Where did you study medicine?　你在哪儿学医的?

Where does she come from?　她是哪儿人?

Where does this affect us?　这对我们有什么影响?

when:

When can you come?　你什么时候能来?

When did you hear about it?　你什么时候听说这事的?

When is the contract effective from?　合同什么时候开始生效?

why:

Why was she so late?　她为什么来得这样晚?

Why didn't you come by plane?　你为什么没坐飞机来?

Why not go by taxi?　为什么不坐出租车去?

2)连接副词:

连接副词意思和词形都和疑问副词一样,但都引导从句或与不定式连用:

how:

That's *how* I look at it.　这是我的看法。(引导表语从句)

Tell me *how* you're getting on.　告诉我你进展如何。(引导宾语从句)

How all this happened was a mystery.　这一切怎么发生的是个谜。(引导主语从句)

Do you know *how* to start this machine?　你知道这台机器怎样启动吗?
　(引导不定式短语)

where:

I don't know *where* he lives.　我不知道他住在哪儿。(引导宾语从句)

It's none of your business *where* I stay. 我住哪儿不干你的事。(引导主语从句)

I can't decide *where* to go for my holidays. 我不能决定去哪里度假。(引导不定式短语)

when:

Tell me *when* you'll be ready. 告诉我你什么时候准备好。(引导宾语从句)

When she'll be back depends on the weather. 她什么时候回来得看天气。(引导主语从句)

Tell me *when* to use this construction. 告诉我什么时候用这种结构。(引导不定式短语)

why:

That's *why* I came round. 这就是我来的原因。(引导表语从句)

Why he did it will remain a puzzle forever. 他为什么这样做将永远是个谜。(引导主语从句)

I'll tell you *why* you have to study grammar. 我将告诉你为什么要学语法。(引导宾语从句)

3) 关系副词:

关系副词用来引导关系从句:

where:

We then moved to Paris, *where* we lived for 6 years. 此后我们搬到巴黎, 在那里住了六年。

This's the hotel *where* we stayed last summer. 这就是我们去年夏天住的旅馆。

There's one point *where* I'd like your advice. 有一点我想征求你的意见。

when:

There came a day *when* the rain fell in torrents. 有一天下起了倾盆大雨。

At the time *when* I saw him, he was well. 我见到他那时,他身体还不错。

I'll never forget his surprise *when* we told him. 我永远不会忘记我们告诉他时他的惊讶表情。

why:

The reason *why* he came is not very convincing. 他来的理由不太有说服力。

That is the reason *why* I came so early. 这就是我来得这样早的原因。

Can you tell me the reason *why* you are so unhappy? 你能告诉我你这样

不高兴的原因吗?

关于这类关系从句请参阅第 22.3.1 — 22.3.3 节。

15.1.7　句子副词

1) 有些副词并不修饰动词，而是修饰整个句子，表示说话人的看法:

Frankly I'm afraid your mother will be a little disappointed.　坦率地说，我担心你妈会有点失望。

Evidently he was sensitive on this topic.　显然他对这个话题很敏感。

Luckily, she was in when I called.　幸好我去时她在家。

I can't come, *unfortunately*.　真不巧，我来不了。

Hopefully we'll win.　但愿我们能赢。

Honestly, I don't know.　真的，我不知道。

Interestingly, consumer spending has increased.　说也有趣，消费额增加了。

Surprisingly, she has married again.　令人惊讶的是，她又结婚了。

Seriously now, you ought to take more care of your health.　说真的，你应当多注意身体。

常见的这类副词有:

absurdly	admittedly	anyway	astonishingly	coincidently
curiously	fortunately	happily	incredibly	interestingly
ironically	luckily	miraculously	mysteriously	naturally
oddly	of course	paradoxically	please	sadly
significantly	strangely	surprisingly	unbelievably	understandably
unexpectedly	unhappily			

2) 有少数副词可以和 enough 连用，起同样的作用:

I thought it would rain, and *sure enough* it did.　我想天会下雨，结果果然如此。

Oddly enough I had no doubt that he would be glad to see me.　说也奇怪，我毫不怀疑他会高兴见我。

Curiously enough he had never seen the little girl.　说也奇怪，他从未见过这个小姑娘。

He's lived in France for years, but *strangely enough* he can't speak a word of

French.　他在法国住了好多年，但说也奇怪他一句法语都不会讲。

Interestingly enough, this proportion has not increased.　说也有趣，这个比例并未增加。

Funnily enough, I met her only yesterday.　说来真怪，我昨天还碰到她的。

Surprisingly enough, even petty larceny has seldom occurred.　说来也怪，连小偷小摸都很少发生。

15.1.8　一些其他类型的副词

除了以上这些类型的副词外，还有一些其他类型的副词，例如：

1) 表示方向的副词：

Let's go *inside*.　咱们到里面去。

Take two steps *forward*.　向前两步走。

He looked *backwards*.　他回头看了看。

Walk three blocks and then turn *left*.　走三个路段后往左拐。

Leaving the city, we headed *north*.　出城后我们向北走。

He walked a little *further on*.　他又往前走了一点。

2) 使与上文连接更紧的副词：

The rain was heavy — *consequently* the land was flooded.　雨下得很大，因此土地被淹了。

They *therefore* removed him from his position.　他们因此把他免职了。

She asked me to go, *so* I went.　她要我去，所以我就去了。

He was different, *however*, from the others.　不过他和别人不同。

Nevertheless, she decided to act.　尽管如此，她决定采取行动。

Jack ran for a doctor; *meanwhile* we stayed with the patient.　杰克忙跑去请医生，在此期间我们守护着病人。

Besides, I want you to promise me one thing.　此外我还要你答应我一件事。

3) 表示"方面"的副词：

They suffered *economically* as a result of that policy.　由于那项政策，他们在经济上受了损失。

Financially we are doing quite well.　在经济方面我们情况良好。

It's *politically* short-sighted not to recognize this.　不认识这一点在政治上是短视的。

I feel *morally* obliged to help them.　我在道义上有责任帮助他们。

Theoretically you are right, but things may not work like that in fact.　在理论上你是对的，但事实上情况可能不会这样。

She was far beneath him *socially*.　她的社会地位远比他低。

15.2　副词在句中的作用

15.2.1　副词作状语

1）副词最主要的作用是作状语，可修饰动词 (a)，也可修饰动词的非谓语形式 (b)：

a. She welcomed us *warmly*.　她热情地欢迎我们。

He'll be here *directly*.　他一会就到这里来。

He behaved very *coolly* in this dangerous situation.　在这险境中他表现得很冷静。

They spoke very *highly* of him.　他们对他评价很高。

Have you seen her *lately*?　你最近见到她了吗？

He was *justly* punished.　他受到了应得的惩处。

b. Her little girls are always *prettily* dressed.　她的小女孩们总是打扮得漂漂亮亮的。

She promised to see me *home*.　她答应送我回家。

Excuse me for coming *back*.　原谅我又回来了。

Having failed *twice*, he didn't want to try again.　失败两次后他不想再试了。

He seemed *much* agitated.　他似乎很不安。

Greatly disappointed, she went home.　大失所望之下，她回家去了。

2）也可修饰形容词 (a) 或副词 (b)：

a. We were *terribly* lucky to find you here.　我们很幸运在这里找到了你。

He is *slightly* lame.　他腿稍稍有点瘸。

I'm *quite* happy here.　我在这里很高兴。

It was a *pretty* poor imitation.　这是一件很粗劣的复制品。

b. *Pretty* soon the lilacs would be in bloom.　丁香花很快就要开了。

The summer passed *too* quickly.　夏天过得太快了。

He didn't work hard *enough*.　他不够用功。

Can you explain it *more* simply?　你能解释得更简单些吗？

3) 还可修饰整个句子:

Naturally, she's attached to the place. 当然她很喜欢这个地方。

Sure I will come. 肯定我会来。

Normally we go to bed at ten. 通常我们十点上床睡觉。

Ironically, he became ill on the day of his marriage. 具有讽刺意味的是，他结婚那天病倒了。

Miraculously, no one was killed. 真是奇迹，竟没有人丧生。

Hopefully, we'll meet again on Thursday. 希望咱们星期四再见面。

15.2.2   副词作表语

1) 大部分副词小品词(即与介词同形的副词)都可用作表语:

Mary was *down* with a slight fever. 玛丽有点发烧。

The light is still *on*. 电灯还亮着。

I'll be *along* in a minute. 我一会儿就来。

Are the children *back* yet? 孩子们回来了吗？

He'll be *round* this afternoon. 他今天下午就来。

Are you *through* (with your work)? 你干完了吗？

Is Staley *about*? 斯坦利在附近吗？

He hid the jewels when nobody was *by*. 他趁没人时把首饰藏了起来。

The storm was *over* before the morning. 天亮前暴风雨停了。

He isn't *up* yet? 他还没起床？

Her office is just *above*. 她的办公室就在上面。

His leave is *up* tomorrow. 他的假期明天结束。

We're *behind* in our plan. 我们落在计划后面了。

I must be *off* now. 我得走了。

2) 另外一些副词也有这样用的:

Communications were *back* to normal at noon. 午时通讯恢复正常。

I shall be *home* around five o'clock. 我将在五点左右到家。

I haven't been *away* from home before. 我以前从未离开过家。

The holidays will soon be *here*. 假期很快就要来临。

The bedrooms are *upstairs*. 卧室在楼上。

Have you been *abroad* before? 你以前出过国吗？

It's just *there* — under your book. 它就在那儿，在你的书下面。

15.2.3 副词的其他用法

副词还有一些其他用法，如：

1) 作定语：

Please forward my letters to the *above* address. 请把我的信转到上面的地址。

Write your name in the place *below*. 把你的名字写在下面空格中。

We had to get off and take the bus *behind*. 我们只得下车，换乘后面的巴士。

The buildings *around* were badly damaged. 周围的建筑物都受到了严重的损坏。

There is a good show *on* at the Calladium. 在卡来登剧院有一场精彩的演出。

Take the *up* escalator. 坐往上去的电梯。

Tickets are cheaper during the *off* season. 淡季机票便宜一些。

I hope you'll enjoy your stay *here*. 希望你在这儿住得愉快。

2) 作宾语的补语 (一起构成复合宾语)：

I'm pleased to see you *back*. 看到你回来我很高兴。

I asked her *in* (over to my house). 我请她进来(到我家来)。

Keep your coat *on* if you feel cold. 如果你觉得冷可以穿着大衣。

I'm having a tooth *out* tomorrow. 我明天要拔一颗牙。

He'll never let you *down*; he's reliable. 他很可靠，决不会拆你的台。

I want it *back* right now, plus the interest. 我要你现在就还，外加利息。

Could you put me *through* to the manager? 能帮我接通经理的电话吗？

She doesn't know how to put her ideas *across*. 她不知道该怎样讲清楚自己的意思。

3) 还可构成成语动词：

We *leave off* work at five o'clock. 我们五点钟下班。

Some flowers *give off* their richest fragrance at night. 有些花夜间散发出最浓郁的香味。

The roses will *come out* next week. 玫瑰下星期就要开花了。

The actors were *making up* when we arrived. 我们到达时演员正在上装。

Some try to *get on* by making up to the boss. 一些人设法拍老板马屁来往上爬。

He will carry these aims *through to the end*. 他将把这些目标贯彻到底。

关于成语动词请参阅第 13.3.4 节。

15.3　副词的比较级和最高级

15.3.1　副词的比较级和最高级形式

1) 副词和形容词一样，也有比较级和最高级形式。但单音节词和少数双音节词可以加词尾的方法构成比较级和最高级 (a)，双音节词和多音节词大多以加 more 和 most 的方法构成比较级和最高级 (b)：

	原级	比较级	最高级
a.	hard	harder	hardest
	fast	faster	fastest
	late	later	latest
	early	earlier	earliest
b.	quickly	more quickly	most quickly
	strongly	more strongly	most strongly
	carefully	more carefully	most carefully
	efficiently	more efficiently	most efficiently

副词的比较级和最高级也有不规则的形式：

原级	比较级	最高级
well	better	best
badly	worse	worst
little	less	least
much	more	most
far	farther, further	farthest, furthest

15.3.2　副词比较级的用法

1) 单独使用：

Try to do *better* next time.　下次争取干好一点。

I had seen the film only a few days *earlier*.　我是几天前才看的这部电影。

He'll come back *sooner* or *later*.　他迟早会回来的。

Please speak more *slowly*.　请讲慢一点。

I determined not to travel *farther* that night.　我决定那天晚上不再往前走

了。

Let's talk *more* another time.　改天我们再多聊聊。

Can't you stay *longer*?　你不能再多呆一会吗?

She did not argue *further* about it.　她没进一步争论此事。

He should speak *less* and listen *more*.　他应当少说多听。

She was determined to work *harder* in future.　她决心以后更用功一些。

2) 和 than 一起使用:

He swims *better than* I do.　他游泳游得比我好。

He works *less than* he used to.　他工作的时间比过去少了。

Can you do (any) *better than* that?　你能不能干得好一些?

We went *farther than* we meant to.　我们比原来打算的走得更远了些。

He behaved even *worse than* he did before.　他的表现比过去还差。

Gray loathed him *more than* ever.　格雷比过去更讨厌他了。

He arrived *earlier than* usual.　他到得比平时早。

I go there *more frequently than* she does.　我去那里比她勤。

Perhaps they like you *better than* me.　或许他们喜欢你胜过喜欢我。

He studied the subject *further than* I do.　这问题他研究得比我深入。

3) 比较级前有时可有状语修饰:

You must work *much faster*.　你必须大大加快干活的速度。

He walked *no further*.　他没再往前走。

She could dance *even more gracefully* than a dancer.　她能比舞蹈演员跳得还美。

Helen came late, but her sister came *still later*.　海伦来晚了,而她妹妹来得更晚。

They walked *three miles farther (on)*.　他们往前又走了三英里。

China is *a little further south* than the U.S.　中国比美国稍微靠南一点。

We reached the destination *two days earlier* than the others.　我们比别人早两天到达目的地。

She works *a lot harder* than before.　她工作比过去努力多了。

You speak English *far more fluently* than the others.　你讲英语比其他人流利得多。

Can you come over *a bit more quickly*?　你能稍稍快一点来吗?

15.3.3 as...as 和 not so...as 结构

这两个结构也可结合副词使用:

1) as...as 可用在肯定句中,表示"像…一样",后面的副词要用原级:

She can run *as fast as* a deer. 她能跑得像鹿一样快。

They work *as hard as* you do. 他们工作像你一样努力。

You can stay there *as long as* you want. 在那儿你爱待多久都行。

I hate him *as much as* you do. 我像你一样恨他。

You know all this *as well as* I do. 这一切你和我一样了解。

I'll be round *as quick as* I can. 我将尽快过来。

She sings *as sweetly as* a nightingale. 她唱歌像夜莺一样甜美。

She loved me *as much as* her own child. 她待我像亲生孩子。

2) 在否定句中,as...as 和 so...as 都可以用:

I don't go there *as much as* I used. 我现在到那里不像过去那么多了。

I didn't do *as (so) well as* I should. 我做得不如我应做的那么好。

I don't think he can speak English *as well as* an Englishman. 我认为他英文讲得没有英国人好。

I can't jump *so (as) high as* Bill. 我跳高不如比尔。

I don't like it *so (as) well as* your other works. 我喜欢它不及你的其他作品。

He doesn't snore *so (as) loudly as* you do. 他打呼噜没你厉害。

3) 这种句子中也可以有一个表示程度的状语:

I don't speak *half as (so) well* as you. 我讲得不及你一半好。

She can read *twice as fast as* he does. 她的阅读速度比他快一倍。

The substance reacts *three times as fast as* the other one. 这种物质的反应速度是另一种物质的三倍。

15.3.4 **副词最高级的用法**

副词最高级可修饰动词,前面多数不带定冠词 the:

I shall give a prize to the pupil who reads *best*. 我将给朗读最好的学生发一份奖品。

He laughs *best* who laughs last. (谚)谁笑在最后谁笑得最好。

Of the four of us, I sang (the) *worst*. 我们四人中我唱得最差。

Of these sports, I like rowing *most*. 这些运动中我最喜欢划船。

Of all your CDs, I like that one *least*. 你所有的激光唱盘中,我最不喜欢那一张。

He went (the) *farthest* of the explorers. 这些探险家中他走得最远。

He likes painting *best* of all. 他最喜欢绘画。

Who arrived (the) *earliest* of all? 谁到得最早?

During the famine, the poor people suffered (the) *worst*. 在饥荒期间,穷人受苦最深。

The burden fell *most heavily* on these people. 这些人的负担最沉重。

She behaved *most generously*. 她表现得最大方。

15.3.5 副词比较级和最高级的一些特殊用法

副词比较级和最高级还可用在一些特别结构或短语中:

1) **more and more** 越来越…:

It rained *more and more* heavily. 雨下得越来越大了。

Indeed, she liked him *more and more*. 的确她越来越喜欢他了。

Now we see it *more and more* clearly. 现在我们对这看得越来越清楚了。

He played the piano *better and better*. 他钢琴弹得越来越好了。

She went *farther and farther* away. 她越走越远了。

Easter is drawing *nearer and nearer*. 复活节越来越近了。

2) **the more...the more** 越…,越…:

The more I work, *the more* I accomplish. 我干得越多,完成得就越多。

The more I thought, *the more extraordinary* did it appear. 我越想,这事就越显得离奇。

The better I knew him, *the more* I liked him. 我对他了解越深就越喜欢他。

The more we are together, *the merrier* we will be. 我们越多在一起就越高兴。

3) **had better** 最好:

We'*d better* not disturb him. 我们最好不要打扰他。

What *had* we *better* do? 我们最好怎么办?

I think I'*d better* be going. 我想我最好还是走。

(Had) better not wait for them. 最好别等他们了。

4) **know better than (to) do something** 懂得不宜做某事:

You ought to *know better than* to go out without an overcoat on such a cold day. 你应当懂得这样冷的天不穿大衣出去可不行。

You ought to *know better than* stay away from school. 你该知道不应当逃学。

He *knew better than* to mention this to her. 他知道不宜向她提及此事。

5) **think better (of)** 改变主意，决定不这样做：

He was going to leave school, but later he *thought better of* it. 他打算退学，但后来改变了主意。

He used to be a radical and has *thought better of* it. 他以前是个激进分子，后来改变了看法。

He was going to answer me back, but he *thought better of* it. 他本想和我顶嘴的，但没有这样做。

6) **had best** 最好：

I *had best* fax them our plans. 我最好把我们的计划传真给他们。

I *had best* have your opinions first. 我最好先听听你的意见。

We *had best* get home before midnight. 我们最好午夜以前到家。

15.4　副词的位置

15.4.1　一般副词的位置

1) 多数副词都放在所修饰动词后面(a) 或句末(宾语或状语后面) (b)：

a. It's raining *hard*. 雨下得很大。

They lived *happily ever after*. 从此他们过上了幸福的生活。

She moved about *gracefully*. 她优雅地走来走去。

He speaks (behaves) *naturally*. 他讲话(举止)很自然。

b. He gave her the money *reluctantly*. 他不情愿地把钱给了她。

He looked at me *suspiciously*. 他用怀疑的目光看着我。

She doesn't work here *now*. 她现在不在这里工作了。

I'll come and see you *tomorrow*. 我明天来看你。

2) 有时放在主语和动词之间，这时有三种情况：

a. 宾语较长时，副词常常提前 (以免副词离动词太远)：

He *carefully* picked up all the bits of broken glass. 他仔细地把碎玻璃都捡了起来。

He *angrily* denied that he had stolen the documents. 他气愤地否认窃取了文件。

They *secretly* decided to leave the town. 他们秘密决定离开这座城市。

The firemen *bravely* went into the burning house. 消防队员勇敢地冲进熊熊燃烧的房子。

b. 有些说明性格或智力的副词，常可放在动词前面：

I *foolishly* forgot my passport. 我愚蠢地忘了带护照。

He *generously* paid for us all. 他大方地替大家付了钱。

He *kindly* waited for me. 他好心地等候我们。

They *warmly* welcomed us at the door. 他们在门口热烈欢迎我们。

c. 有些副词，如 suddenly，soon，nearly，surely，almost，just，still，really 等，常可以放在动词前面：

I *almost* forgot about the whole thing. 我几乎把整个这件事给忘了。

She *suddenly* fell ill. 她突然病了。

He *nearly* died of starvation. 他差点饿死。

I *still* don't understand. 我还是不懂。

3）有些副词常放在助动词和主要动词之间 (a) 或主语和表语之间 (b)：

a. I'm *still* waiting for an answer. 我还在等待答复。

I've *just* returned from Shanghai. 我刚从上海回来。

She's *already* gone home. 她已经回家了。

b. The meeting is *just* over. 会刚结束。

She was *still* weak after her long illness. 她久病之后身子还很虚弱。

Then she was *already* out of his mind. 这时他已不想她了。

4）有些副词为了强调可放在句首：

Indoors it was nice and warm. 室内非常暖和舒服。

Recently I haven't been feeling very well. 最近我感到身子不太舒服。

Indeed the note has disappointed me. 的确这条子使我很失望。

Really, it needs watering. 真的它该浇水了。

Apparently, he knew the town well. 显然他很熟悉这座城市。

15.4.2 频度副词的位置

1）频度副词通常放在下面三个位置：

a. 放在动词前面：

They *sometimes* stay up all night. 他们有时彻夜不眠。

She *never* saw him again. 她再也没见到他。

He *seldom* watches TV. 他很少看电视。

I *usually* go to bed at eleven. 我通常十一点睡觉。

b. 放在助动词后面(主要动词前面):

He can *never* understand that.　他永远理解不了这一点。

I have *often* thought of you.　我常常想到你。

Have you *ever* ridden a camel?　你骑过骆驼吗?

Does she *often* come to see you?　她常来看你吗?

c. 如句子里有系动词 be,则通常放在 be 后面:

He's *always* at home in the evening.　他晚上总在家。

She's *often* late.　她常常迟到。

He's *seldom* out of pain.　他很少有不疼的时候。

His thoughts were *frequently* on her.　他经常想到她。

2) 频度副词有时可放在其他位置:

a. 为了强调可放在句首:

Always, we went on foot.　我们总是步行去。

Occasionally he came to see us.　偶尔他来看望我们。

Often I didn't see her until the evening.　常常我要到晚上才看到她。

Generally she remained in on weekdays.　一般周日她都待在家里。

Sometimes we're busy and *sometimes* we're not.　我们有时很忙,有时不忙。

b. 有时为了强调,可放在情态动词、助动词及动词 be 前面:

We *usually* don't get up until nine on Sundays.　星期天我们通常九点才起床。

He *never* would go to a doctor, he didn't believe in them.　他从不去看医生,他不相信他们。

She *hardly* ever has met him.　她几乎从未见过他。

I *never* can remember telephone numbers.　我从来记不住电话号码。

He *always* is late when we've an important meeting.　我们有重要会议时,他总是迟到。

c. 间或也可放在句末:

I have endless occupation *always*.　我总是有做不完的事。

I don't see her *often*.　我不常见她。

He comes over to see us *sometimes*.　他有时过来看望我们。

Lester came only *occasionally*.　莱斯特只是偶尔来。

I should certainly visit her *frequently* to cheer her up.　我确实应当经常去看她,让她高兴起来。

15.4.3　某些类副词的位置

1）疑问副词、连接副词和关系副词通常都在句子或从句的开头：

How are things going?　情况如何？

That's *how* I look at it.　这就是我的看法。

The first thing is to find out *where* she is.　首先得打听她在哪儿。

We have reached a point *where* a change is needed.　我们到了必须改一改的地步。

Here are the reasons *why* we do it.　这些就是我们这样做的原因。

2）句子副词一般放在句首：

Maybe he would come round yet.　或许他会回心转意。

Actually, she had altered much less than I.　实际上她的变化比我小。

Fortunately, he found the money he'd lost.　幸好他找到了丢失的钱。

Surely you'll stay for dinner.　你一定留下吃晚饭。

有时也可放在其他位置，如：

She *actually* expected me to do it for her.　她实际上是指望我替她干。

There has *evidently* been some mistake.　显然哪儿出了岔子。

You must know Bulla, *surely*!　你肯定认识波拉, 没错的！

3）程度副词都放在所修饰的词前面：

I'm *awfully* sorry for what has happened.　发生了这事我非常抱歉。

We are getting along *fairly* well.　我们相处得相当好。

She was *extremely* friendly.　她极为友好。

I wasn't *much* surprised.　我并不太吃惊。

4）有些副词位置很灵活，如 only 和 even，可放在与它们意思最密切的词之前：

only:

Only he knows some English.　只有他懂些英语。

He can *only* read. He can't speak.　他只会看, 不会说。

She speaks *only* French.　她只会讲法语。

I'll stay *only* for two days.　我只能待两天。

There were *only* five girls in our class.　我们班上只有五个女生。

even:

Even my father doesn't know this word.　连我父亲都不认识这个词。

She *even* helped us to do our housework.　她甚至帮助我们做家务。

Even at night he seldom relaxed.　即使在晚上他也很少休息。

It was cold *even* in August.　即使在八月这儿也很冷。

He was afraid to take *even* a drink of water.　他连一口水都不敢喝。

He looked happy, *even* gay.　他显得高兴，甚至很快活。

第16章 介 词

16.1 介词分类

16.1.1 介词按结构的分类

从结构上看，介词可以分为下面几类：

1）简单介词 (Simple Prepositions)：

about	above	across	after	against	along
amid(st)	around	as	at	before	behind
below	beneath	beside	besides	between	beyond
but	by	despite	down	during	except
for	from	in	like	minus	near
of	off	on	opposite	over	past
per	plus	round	since	than	through
till	to	toward(s)	under	underneath	unlike
until	up	via	with	worth	

2）合成介词 (Compound Prepositions)：

alongside	inside	into	onto	out of
outside	throughout	upon	within	without

3）带 -ing 词尾的介词 (-ing Prepositions)：

barring	concerning	considering	excepting	excluding
failing	following	including	pending	regarding

4）成语介词 (Phrasal Prepositions):

according to	ahead of	along with	apart from
as for	as from	as regards	as to
because of	but for	by means of	due to
except for	in accordance with	in front of	in place of
in spite of	instead of	in view of	near to
next to	on account of	on behalf of	owing to
prior to	together with	up to	in regard to

以上成语都起着与介词同样的作用，因此许多语法学家把它们称作成语介词。

16.1.2   介词按意思的分类

从意思上考虑，介词可分为下面三类：

1）引导时间短语的介词：

at (5 o'clock)	on (Saturday)	in (autumn)
during (the summer)	before (dawn)	after (that)
over (the years)	from (now on)	following (his speech)
by (that time)	till (Saturday)	until (10 o'clock)
towards (midnight)	for (two weeks)	throughout (the day)
upon (arrival)	since (then)	pending (his return)
all through (the night)	prior to (her marriage)	

2）引导地点短语的介词：

in (Beijing)	at (the airport)	across (the river)
to (town)	down (the river)	under (the tree)
near (the park)	between (two trees)	over (our heads)
from (the city)	into (the water)	through (the door)
onto (the stage)	off (the wall)	outside (the house)
out of (the room)	inside (the building)	within (the area)
beside (the river)	behind (the house)	below (the surface)
among (the mountains)	beyond (the hill)	against (the wall)

around (the lake)	before (the children)	up (the hill)
ahead of (us)	via (Hong Kong)	in front of (us)
under (the table)	along (the street)	past (the house)
opposite (the cinema)	above (the clouds)	next to (me)

3）引导其他短语的介词：

by (train)	with (a knife)	about (a topic)
except (her)	like (a child)	of (the city)
according to (plan)	instead of (him)	without (friends)
in (detail)	due to (the storm)	because of (it)
along with (her)	as for (me)	in spite of (that)
on account of (it)	owing to (rain)	on behalf of (us)
against (the enemy)	apart from (that)	for (someone)
failing (that)	plus (experience)	including (myself)
in regard to (this matter)	with regard to (his plan)	

16.2　介词短语在句子中的作用

16.2.1　介词短语

　　介词不能单独担任一个成分，必须构成介词短语来担任一个成分。能和介词构成短语的有下面这些：

　　1）名词：

　　Who's knocking at *the door*?　谁在敲门？

　　I put the calculator into *my pocket*.　我把计算器放到口袋里。

　　2）代词：

　　I'm looking for *something (her)*.　我在找东西(她)。

　　You're always thinking of *others*.　你总是为别人着想。

　　3）动名词：

　　Are you interested in *going with us*?　你有兴趣和我们一道去吗？

　　I strongly object to *your saying that*.　我坚决反对你这样说话。

　　4）由连接代（副）词或关系代词型 what 引导的从句：

　　He thought over *what he had better do*.　他想了想他最好怎么办。

　　She was grateful to him for *what he had done*.　她为他所做的事而感激他。

5）由连接代 (副) 词引导的不定式短语：

She gave a talk on *how to fight the disease*. 她作了一个报告,讲如何同这种疾病作斗争。

The discussion centered on *how to increase production*. 讨论围绕着如何增产而进行。

6）另一个介词：

I saw her from *across the street*. 我从街对面看到她。

We never play bridge until *after dinner*. 我们只在晚饭后打桥牌。

7）副词或形容词：

I heard someone calling me from *below*. 我听见有人在下面叫我。

My English is far from *perfect*. 我的英语远不是完美的。

8）复合结构：

I had no objection to *Dinny marrying him*. 我不反对丁妮和他结婚。

The policy of *land to the tillers* was finally put into effect. 最后实行了耕者有其田的政策。

在个别情况下，介词后面还可跟 where 和 that 引导的从句 (a)，甚至跟带 to 或不带 to 的不定式 (b)：

a. The car stopped only a few inches from *where I stood*. 汽车在离我站的地方仅几英寸处停了下来。

He is a good student except *that he is occasionally careless*. 他是一个好学生，只是有时粗心大意。

b. I had no alternative but *to walk out*. 我别无他法只好走出去。

She can do everything except *cook*. 她什么都会，就是不会做饭。

介词后的宾语可称为为 **介词宾语** (Prepositional Object)。

16.2.2 介词短语作状语

1）介词短语作状语时最多，主要修饰谓语：

I arrived *at the concert hall in good time*. 我及时到达了音乐厅。

At first he opposed the marriage, but *in the end* he gave his consent. 起先他反对这门亲事，但最后同意了。

He has been here *since Monday*. 从星期一起，他一直在这里。

Bake it *for two hours*. 把它烘烤两小时。

They flew (cycled) *from Paris to Rome*. 他们乘飞机(骑自行车)从巴黎到罗马。

We have friends *all over the world*.　我们的朋友遍天下。

2) "be＋形容词"这种结构也常跟介词短语：

She *is afraid of* dogs.　她怕狗。

We *were eager for* news.　我们急于得到消息。

I'*m* not so *bad at* bridge.　我打桥牌还不错。

She *is used to* a vegetarian diet.　她习惯于吃素食。

He *is familiar with* the district.　他对这个地区很熟悉。

I'*m sorry about* the air tickets.　机票的事我很抱歉。

3) 还可用介词短语修饰非谓语动词：

I asked to speak *to the dean*.　我要求和院长说话。

I'm sorry to have trodden *on your foot*.　对不起踩了你的脚。

Thank you for doing this *for us*.　谢谢你帮我们做了这事。

There was a bird perching *on the television aerial*.　有只鸟停在电视天线上。

Have you read any plays written *by Ibsen*?　你读过易卜生写的剧本吗？

Around the city were mountains covered *by snow*.　该城周围是白雪覆盖的群山。

16.2.3　介词短语作定语

1) 在不少情况下也可用介词短语作定语：

She seems to know the solution *to the problem*.　她似乎知道这问题的解决方法。

Here is a cheque *for $ 30*.　这是一张三十美元的支票。

What are the major differences *between British English and American English*?　英国英语和美国英语有什么主要差别？

The house *opposite ours* was burnt down last week.　我们家对面的房子上星期烧毁了。

They lived in a flat *above the shop*.　他们住在那家商店上面的一套公寓里。

The man *next to Bill* was talking to him in Spanish.　比尔旁边的那个人在用西班牙语说话。

2) 有些介词常可引导短语作定语：

of:

a child of six　六岁的孩子　　　　　a pupil of English　学英语的学生

a boy of middle height 中等身材的男孩

a lady of character 有个性的女子

a professor of phonetics 语音学教授

a congress of unity 团结的大会

a man of immense capacity 能力很强的人

men of easy temper 脾气好的男子

an hour of danger 危险时刻

a gentleman about sixty years 年约六十的一位先生

fishes of many sizes 大大小小的鱼

an act of friendship 友好的行动

a member of great importance 要员

things of great value 很有价值之物

a house of red bricks 红色砖房

with:

a child with dark eyes 黑眼珠的孩子

a boy with red hair 红头发的男孩

a girl with a pigtail 梳辫子的姑娘

a man with a gun 带枪的人

a widow with 3 children 有三个孩子的寡妇

a man with a moustache 留着小胡子的男人

a clerk with glasses 戴眼镜的职员

a jacket with a hood 带帽兜的夹克

a man with suitcase 提着箱子的人

a house with a garden 带花园之房

in:

the girl in blue 穿蓝衣裳的姑娘

a man in his 40s 四十多岁的男子

a boy in khaki shorts 穿咔叽短裤的男孩

a report in preparation 正在撰写的报告

a mistake in tactics 战术错误

an exam in math 数学考试

a Ph D in economics 经济学博士

a novel in translation 翻译小说

a request in reason 合理的请求

a policeman in disguise 便衣警察

to:

an answer to a puzzle 谜底

a reply to his letter 给他的复信

damage to the house 对房子的损害

devotion to parents 对父母的热爱

his fidelity to his wife 他对妻子的忠诚

her contribution to science 她对科学的贡献

her attachment to her mother 她对母亲的依恋

an introduction to botany 植物学概论

the key to this lock 这把锁的钥匙

secretary to a doctor 医生的秘书

for:

a war for profits 利润战

a medicine for colds 感冒药

a machine for making boxes 制盒机

enthusiasm for music 对音乐的热情

a thirst for knowledge 求知欲

a change for the better 好转

a passion for sports 对体育的热爱

room for improvement 改进的余地

sympathy for orphans 对孤儿的同情

his hunger for power 他的权利欲

about:

doubts about his ability 对他能力的
怀疑

illusions about wealth 对财富的幻
想

my opinion about it 我对它的看法

an agreement about trade 贸易协定

a dispute about where to go 关于到
哪里去的争论

news about their progress 他们进展
的消息

information about Paris 关于巴黎的
情况

a debate about the question 关于这
问题的辩论

my idea about friendship 我对友谊
的看法

16.2.4　介词短语作表语或作宾语的补语

1) 介词短语用作表语时也很多，几乎大部分常用介词都可这样用：

The museum is just *across the street*. 博物馆就在街对面。

He knows *what* she is *after*. 他知道她追求的是什么。

What's the article *about*? 这篇文章是讲什么的?

I assumed that she was *above reproach*. 我认为她不应受到责备。

It was *against the law*. 这是违法的。

He was *among the first to arrive*. 他是首批到达的。

He didn't feel *at ease*. 他感到心神不宁。

The workers are *behind them* and that's their strength. 工人们支持他们，
这就是他们的力量所在。

My position in the firm was *below his*. 我在公司的职位比他低。

It is *by one of our most celebrated painters*. 它是我们最著名画家之一的
作品。

"It's *for you*." He handed it to me. 他把它递给我说，"这是给你的。"

This music is *from Mozart's operas*. 这音乐选自莫扎特的歌剧。

The poor girl was *in tears*. 可怜的女孩泪流满面。

His opinion was *near my own*. 他的看法和我自己的看法差不多。

We are *like brothers and sisters*. 我们就像兄弟姐妹。

Jack is *of the same opinion*.　杰克也持同样的看法。

She's *off smoking*.　她已戒烟了。

They're always *on the lookout for new investment opportunities*.　他们总在寻找投资机会。

The post office is just *round the corner*.　邮局就在拐角处。

They have been *through too much*.　他们受的苦太多了。

It's not *within my power*.　这超出了我的能力。

His face was *without expression*.　他脸上毫无表情。

It's *worth trying*, isn't it?　这值得一试，对吧？

2）许多介词可构成短语作表语：

at:

He's *at* odds with his wife.　他和妻子不合。

She's *at* her worst.　她情绪糟透了。

The flower was *at* its brightest.　花开得正艳。

She was *at* the end of her resources.　她智竭计穷。

He was *at* his meal.　他在吃饭。

They were *at* school together.　他们是同学。

Business was *at* a standstill.　业务停顿了下来。

Bus services were *at* a halt.　公共汽车停驶了。

Summer is *at* its height.　正值盛夏。

She was *at* her happiest here.　她在这里最高兴。

He was *at* a disadvantage.　他处于不利地位。

She was *at* a loss.　她不知所措。

The country was *at* war.　该国在打仗。

He's *at* his work now.　他此刻正在工作。

beyond:

The road is *beyond that hill*.　公路在山那边。

The explanation is *beyond me*.　这解释我不懂。

This is *beyond my means*.　这超过了我的财力。

The rumour's *beyond belief*.　这谣言不可信。

The scene is *beyond description*.　那景色无法形容。

Good advice's *beyond price*.　有益的忠告是无价之宝。

He's *beyond my control*.　他是我控制不了的。

The results were *beyond dispute*.　结果不容争议。

Our stand is *beyond reproach*.　我们的立场是无可厚非的。

He is *beyond redemption*.　他已不可救药了。

in:

He's still *in danger*. 他仍在危险期。

She's *in good health*. 她身体很好。

His mind's *in confusion*. 他脑子很乱。

The letter was *in French*. 信是用法语写的。

Congress is *in session*. 国会在开会。

He's heavily *in debt*. 他负债累累。

She was *in despair*. 她绝望了。

I'm *in earnest*. 我是认真的。

All was *in ruins*. 成了一片废墟。

The room is *in disorder*. 房间很乱。

The roses are *in bloom*. 玫瑰开花了。

The Labor Party was *in power*. 工党当政。

They were *in flight*. 他们在逃窜。

He's *in good spirits*. 他情绪很好。

I'm *in doubt* about it. 我对此有怀疑。

You're *in the right*. 你是对的。

of:

She's *of middle height*. 她中等身材。

He is *of a different way of thinking*. 他是另一种思路。

It's *of no value*. 这毫无价值。

The gown was *of red velvet*. 这袍子是红色丝绒的。

She's *of peculiar disposition*. 她性格很特别。

He is *of feeble will*. 他意志薄弱。

Is it *of any use* to you? 这对你有用吗？

But it was *of no avail*. 但这没有用。

It won't be *of real benefit* to her. 它对她没有真正的好处。

He was *of an excitable temperament*. 他是好激动的性格。

on:

He was always *on the move*. 他总是东奔西跑。

He is *on guard*. 他在站岗。

Crimes are *on the rise*. 犯罪率在上升。

He's always *on the go*. 他总是忙忙碌碌。

Who's *on the phone*? 谁来电话？

She's *on diet*. 她在节食。

He's *on night duty*. 他值夜班。

She is *on tour* in Europe. 她在欧洲旅行。

They're *on holiday*. 他们在度假。

She was *on piece-work*. 她在做计件工作。

The dockers are *on strike*. 码头工人在罢工。

Is he *on board* yet? 他上船了吗？

He was *on his round*. 他在查病房。

The show is *on the air*. 演出在转播。

out of:

He's *out of work*. 他失业了。

I'm a bit *out of sorts*. 我有点不舒服。

He's *out of breath*. 他气喘吁吁。

He is *out of humor*. 他情绪不佳。

She must be *out of her senses*. 她准是发疯了。

She was soon *out of patience*. 她很快就失去了耐心。

We're *out of touch* with her. 我们和她失去了联系。

Rest was out *of the question*. 休息根本谈不上。

The grocer was *out of coffee*. 杂货店咖啡卖完了。

She's a bit *out of practice*. 她有点荒疏了。

Pears are *out of season*. 梨下市了。

We're *out of flour*. 我们没面粉了。

The car is *out of repair*. 车坏了。

I am *out of element*. 我不适应环境。

We are *out of food*. 我们已断粮。

The book is *out of print*. 书已绝版。

under:

He's *under forty*. 他不到四十。

The road is *under repair*. 路在维修。

It's *under examination*. 这问题正在审查。

The fort was *under attack*. 要塞正受到攻击。

It is *under review*. 这事在审核。

He's *under a strain*. 他很累。

The matter is *under consideration*. 这事正在考虑。

The bridge is *under construction*. 桥正在修建。

He was *under an anaesthetic*. 他处于麻醉状态。

I'm a bit *under the weather*. 我感到有点不适。

He was *under fire*. 他受到批评

He was *under age*. 他还未成年。

The land is *under water*. 土地被淹了。

You're *under arrest*. 你被捕了。

3) 介词短语有时可作宾语的补语 (一道构成复合宾语):

We found her *in better spirits* that evening. 那天晚上我们发现她情绪好些了。

They found the boy already *in the hands of a doctor*. 他们发现那男孩已有医生照顾。

They kept the man *in custody*. 他们把这人拘留了。

He always considers himself *in the right*. 他总认为自己是对的。

He thought it *beneath him* to do such a thing. 他认为这种事不屑一做。

I saw George *at work*. 我看见乔治在干活。

We could hear the children *at play* outside. 我们可以听见孩子们在外面玩耍。

A cold kept him *in bed* for three days. 感冒使他卧床三天。

16.3 由介词构成的成语动词和介词成语

16.3.1 由介词构成的成语动词

由介词构成的成语动词主要有两类：

1）动词 + 介词：

agree with 同意(某人意见)	agree to 同意(某种安排等)
answer for 对…负责	appear for 为…出庭
ask for 要求得到(见某人等)	bank on 依靠
bear with 容忍	break with 和…断绝关系
burst into (tears) 突然(哭起来)	call for 来找(某人)，要求，需要
come across 碰到	come by 得到
count on 指望	enter for 参与(比赛等)
fly into (a rage) 勃然(大怒)	get into 碰到(困难等)
get over 克服,(病)愈	get about 干(活)，履行(职责等)
go after 追求	go into 调查
hang on 取决于	head for 向…前进
hit on 想起(某主意)	jump at 立即接受
keep at 继续(干某事)	keep from 避免(做某事)
live on 靠…生活	look after 照顾，照看
look for 找寻	look into 调查
make after 追赶	pass for 冒充(某人)
press for 要求	run across (into) 碰到
run into 碰到(困难)	run through 用完
see about 负责处理	see through 看破
stand by 支持	stand for 主张
stand on (ceremony) 客气	stick to 坚持
touch on 提到(某问题)	wait on 招待

2）动词 + 副词 + 介词：

back on to 背后是	boil down to 归结是
break out into 出(疹子)	brush up on 复习
come across with 讲出来	come down on 斥责
come in for 受到(批评)	come out against 表示反对
come out with 推出(产品等)	come up against 碰到
come up to 达到(水平)	come up with 提出(建议等)

cry out against 大声疾呼地反对   do away with 废除
face up to 面对   fall back on 转而依靠
fall behind with 迟迟未交(房租)   feel up to 感到想(做某事)
get away with (犯罪)不受惩罚   get down to 开始认真考虑
get on for 快到(某时)   get on with 继续进行(某事)
give on to 面对(花园等)   go back on (说了话)不遵守
go in for 从事(某项活动)   go off with 和…私奔
go through with 把…进行到底   keep up with 跟上(发展)
live up to 达到(期望)   look down on 看不起
look forward to 盼望   look out for 当心
look up to 敬重(某人)   make up for 弥补
make up to 拍…马屁   put up with 忍受
run out of 用完   run up against 碰到
stand out against 坚决反对   stand out for 坚决要求
stand up to 面对(危险等)   stick out for 坚持要求

关于成语动词可参阅 7.1.6 和 13.3.4 节及附录 1。

16.3.2　介词成语

1) 除了成语动词，英语中还有大量成语由介词构成，单是一些常用介词就可构成大量成语：

at:

at a stretch 一连，连续地   at a time 一次，每次
at all costs 不惜一切代价   at all events 不管怎样
at all hazards 不顾一切危险   at any rate 不管怎样
at ease 稍息，安心   at fault 有错误
at first 最初，开始时   at first sight 一见(钟情)
at hand 不远，快到   at heart 在内心
at home 在家，随便   at large 逍遥法外，未被关注
at last 最后   at least 至少
at leisure 从容不迫地   at length 最后，详细地
at liberty 自由，有权(做某事)   at the moment 此刻
at most 至多   at once 立即，同时
at one blow (stroke) 一下子   at one's fingertips 非常熟悉

at one's service 听候吩咐

at one's wit's end 计穷，没有办法

at peace (war) 处于和平(战争)状态

at play (work) 在玩耍(工作)

at present 现在，目前

at random 随意地，胡乱地

at sea 茫然，不知所措

at the earliest (latest) 至早(迟)

at the outset 从——开头

at the risk of 冒…的危险

at the same time (与此)同时

at the start 一开头

at the time 此刻，这时

at the top of one's voice 高声地

at times 有时候

at will 任意地

by:

by accident 偶然

by air 航空

by all means 想一切办法

by any chance 碰巧，恰好

by birth 出身…

by bus (plane, etc.) 坐巴士(飞机等)

by chance 偶然

by cheque 用支票

by credit card 用信用卡

by choice 出于自愿

by daylight 在大白天

by day (night) 白天(夜间)

by far 最(修饰最高级)

by dint of 通过(下功夫)

by force 靠武力

by fits and starts 干一干停一停

by leaps and bounds 飞跃地

by hook or by crook 想一切办法

by mistake 错误地，误把…

by means of 借助

by post 邮(寄)

by no means 绝不，一点也不

by turns 轮流

by stages (degrees) 分阶段地(一步步地)

by surprise 突然，出其不意

by virtue of 由于(某些优越处)

by the way 顺便说一句

in:

in a nutshell 概括地说，总之

in a row 一连

in a sense 从某种意义上说

in accordance with 按照，根据

in addition (to) 此外(除…之外)

in advance 事前

in all 总共

in any case (event) 不管怎样，反正

in brief 简而言之

in case 要是，如果

in case of 在…情况下

in comparison 比较起来

in danger 处于危险中

in debt 负债

in demand 有需求

in depth 深入地

in detail 详细地

in doubt (对…)有怀疑

in fact 实际上

in full 全部地，全文地

in general 一般说来

in love 在恋爱

in one's opinion 在(某人)看来

in order to (that) 以便，为了

in part(s) 部分地

in practice 实际上

in regard to 关于

in short 总之

in spite of 尽管

in that 在…方面，因为

in the dark 蒙在鼓里，不知情

in the end 最后

in (the) face of 在…面前

in the long run 从长远来说

in the mean time 与此同时，在此期间

in the nick of time 正好及时

in vain 白白地，没有结果

in ink (pencil) 用钢笔(铅笔)写

in no time 很快(就…)

in order (disorder) 井井有条(很乱)

in other words 换句话说

in person 亲自

in public (private) 公开(私下)地

in return 回过来，作为报答

in so far as 就…来说

in terms of 就…来说

in the course of 在…过程中

in the day time 在白天

in the event of 如果发生(某事)

in the least 一点(也不)

in the main 一般来说

in the middle of 在…中间

in time 及时地，经过一段时间

in turn 轮流

in view of 考虑到…

on:

on account of 由于

on average 平均

on board 在船(飞机)上

on condition 在…条件下

on the decline 在衰退中

on demand 在要求支付时

on duty 值班

on foot 步行

on hand 在身边

on no account 绝不

on one's mind 在想某事

on purpose 故意地

on strike 罢工，罢课

on the mend 在痊愈(改善)中

on the point of 正要(做某事)

on approval 允许退货

on behalf of 代表(某人)

on business 出差，办事

on credit 赊购

on the decrease 在减少中

on display 展出

on fire 着火

on guard 有警惕，值班

on holiday 在休假

on one's chest 有心事

on one's own 独立地

on sale 在出售

on the contrary 相反

on the (tele) phone 在接(打)电话

on the run 东跑西颠，正在逃窜

on the spot 就地

on the way 在路上

on top of 在…上面

out of:

out of action 失灵

out of control 失去控制

out of date 过时

out of element 格格不入

out of favor 失宠

out of hand 失去控制

out of keeping (with) 和…不协调

out of one's mind 不想(某事)

out of pain 没有疼痛

out of place 格格不入, 不合适

out of print 不再印行

out of season 下市了

out of service 退役, 不再使用

out of sight 看不见

out of step 不合拍

out of sympathy 不同情

out of the ordinary 不同寻常

out of touch (with) 和…失去联系

out of use 不再使用

on the spur of the moment 即兴

on time 准时

on trial 正在受审

out of breath 气喘吁吁

out of danger 脱(离危)险

out of doors 在户外

out of fashion 不时新

out of focus 对焦不准

out of humor 情绪不佳

out of luck 倒霉, 运气不佳

out of order 坏了

out of patience 失去耐心

out of practice 荒疏

out of reach 无法得到(拿到)

out of senses 头脑不正常

out of shape 变形

out of sorts 身子不舒服

out of stock 售罄

out of temper 发脾气

out of the question 不可能

out of tune 走调

out of work 失业

2) 有些介词夹在名词之间构成成语:

day after day 日复一日地

one after another 一个接一个地

little by little 一点一点地

step by step 一步步地

arm in arm 手挽手地

hand in glove 互相勾结

head above water (生意)能维持

day to day 日常的

day before yesterday 前天

heart in one's mouth 提心吊胆

year after year 年复一年地

one by one 一个接一个

side by side 并肩

face to face 面对面

hand in hand 手牵手地

hand over fist 大量赚(赔)钱

head over heels 倒栽葱

day by day 一天一天地

day after tomorrow 后天

heart-to-heart 互相交心的

3）还有一些成语包含两个介词：

from beginning to end 从头至尾　　from bad to worse 越来越糟

from time to time 不时地　　　　　from head to foot 从头到脚，浑身

from morning to night 从早到晚　　from start to finish 从头至尾

from door to door 挨门挨户地　　　from top to bottom 整个地，彻底

from place to place 到各地　　　　from hand to mouth 勉强糊口

from generation to generation 一　　from cover to cover （书）全部地，
代一代地　　　　　　　　　　　　　从头到尾

4）此外，"be＋形容词＋介词"也是一类成语：

be found of 喜欢　　　　　　　　be full of 充满

be interested in 对…有兴趣　　　　be keen on 热衷于

be confident in 对…有信心　　　　be short of 缺乏

be sick of 厌恶　　　　　　　　　be proud of 对…感到骄傲

be loyal to 对…忠诚　　　　　　　be ashamed of 为…感到羞耻

be worried about 为…担心　　　　be allergic to 对…过敏

be satisfied with 对…感到满意　　　be aware of 意识到

be busy with 忙于(某事)　　　　　be different from 和…不同

be sympathetic with 对…同情　　　be capable of 能干某事

be famous for 因…而出名　　　　　be curious about 对…好奇

关于各介词短语和成语动词的用法可参阅《现代英语用法辞典》(外研社
出版)。

第17章 连 词

17.1 概 说

17.1.1 连词的作用

连词是一种虚词，不能担任一个句子成分，但可以起连接的作用，即连接词与词或句与句，例如：

We may be leaving today *or* tomorrow. 我们可能今天或是明天走。(连接词与词)

Now I must go *or* I shall be late for the party. 我现在得走,否则晚会我就要迟到了。(连接句与句)

连词数量有限，却很重要，许多从句由它引导，单是 that 这个连词就可引导许多类从句，如：

That she should have ignored the realistic world was natural. 她忽视现实世界是很自然的。(引导主语从句)

He phoned me *that* he wanted to see me. 他给我打电话说要见我。(引导宾语从句)

Your fault is *that* you're too careless. 你的毛病是过于粗心。(引导表语从句)

He came to the decision *that* he must act at once. 他决定必须马上行动。(引导同位语从句)

I am hopeful *that* he will come. 我希望他能来。(引导状语从句)

Bring it closer *that* I may see better. 拿近点让我看得清楚些。

还可把句子联系得更紧密，使句子更紧凑：

Honey is sweet, *but* the bee stings. 蜂蜜很甜,但蜜蜂会蜇人。

The manager was sick *so* I went in his place. 经理生病了,因此我代他去了。

17.1.2 连词的种类

连词有两类:

1) 从属连词 (Subordinating Conjunctions):

这类连词都引导从句。随着从句作用不同,它们又可分为几类:

从句种类	主要从属连词
时间从句 (Time Clauses)	when while as before after until till whenever
条件从句 (Conditional Clauses)	if unless supposing provided(ing) suppose
目的从句 (Purpose Clauses)	in order that so that so that lest
结果从句 (Result Clauses)	so...that such...that so that so
原因从句 (Reason Clauses)	because as since
让步从句 (Concessive Clauses)	although though even though (if) while
方式从句 (Clauses of Manner)	as like the way as if as though
地点从句 (Place Clauses)	where wherever
比较从句 (Clauses of Comparison)	than as

此外还有 that,whether 等从属连词可引导名词从句,在句中担任主语、宾语等。

2) 并列连词 (Coordinating Conjunctions):

并列连词连接两个互不依从的词、短语或分句:

Slow *but* sure. 要慢而稳。(连接单词)

She'll be back *either* this week *or* next week. 她将在这周或下周回来。(连接短语)

I went *and* she went also. 我去了,她也去了。(连接分句)

并列连词有下面几类:

表示意思转折的连词	but yet however nevertheless
表示因果关系的连词	for so therefore hence
其他并列连词	and or either...or neither...nor not only...but also both...and as well as

17.2　从属连词

17.2.1　引导时间状语从句的连词

这类连词主要有：

when:

Don't get excited *when* you talk.　讲话时别激动。

When he got up he felt dizzy.　他站起身时感到头晕。

When he comes I'll tell him about it.　他来时我将把这事告诉他。

We were going to the zoo *when* we met her.　我们去动物园时碰到了她。

We wear plimsolls *when* doing physical exercises.　我们体育锻炼时穿帆布球鞋。

He gave good practical advice *when* asked.　向他请教时他总出一些切实可行的好主意。

Often she would weep *when* alone.　她一人独处时常常哭泣。

while:

We must strike *while* the iron is hot.　我们要趁热打铁。

While she ate she grew more restless.　她一边吃一边变得更加忐忑不安。

While the discussion was going on Peter came in.　讨论正进行时彼得走了进来。

While I was having dinner Ann was packing.　我吃饭时安在收拾行李。

While doing so, we decided to sell the boat.　在这样做时，我们决定把船卖掉。

He had an accident *while* on his way here.　在来这里的路上他出了车祸。

as:

As he spoke two men came up.　在他讲话时两个人走了过来。

As she was leaving, Mr White saw her.　她正要走时怀特先生看见了她。

He smiled *as* he passed.　他经过时笑了笑。

As she sang tears ran down her cheeks.　她唱歌时眼泪簌簌而下。

Even *as* a boy he was hopeless at maths.　他小时候数学就很差。

before:

Look *before* you leap.　(谚)三思而后行。

It will be five years *before* we meet again.　要五年后咱们才能再相见。

It wasn't long *before* he told us about it.　不久他就把这事告诉我们了。

I slipped out *before* the lecture started.　不等讲座开始我就溜了出来。

Just *before* I left London I sent him a telegraph.　就在离开伦敦前我给他发了一份电报。

after:

I arrived *after* he had left.　在他走后我到了。

After he had said a few words, I took his floor.　他讲了几句话之后我开始发言。

Soon *after* we returned, the child vomited.　我们回来不久孩子就吐了。

I'll tell them *after* you have left.　你走后我再告诉他们。

until, till:

We danced and danced *until* they all joined in.　我们不停地跳舞直到他们都参加进来。

Go away *until* I have finished speaking to your father.　离开一下, 直到我和你父亲谈完。

It was not *until* I saw her next morning that I felt happy.　直到第二天早上见到她我才感到高兴。

I'll take no steps *until* you arrive.　你来之前我不会采取什么行动。

I propose waiting *till* the police get here.　我建议等警察来了再说。

He determined to stay *till (until)* the year was up.　他决心住满一年。

since:

How long is it *since* you came to London?　你到伦敦有多久了?

He has never been to see me *since* I have been ill.　我生病以来他从未来过我。

Since Marie had left, Martha had married.　玛丽走后, 玛莎结婚了。

It was years *since* I had seen her.　我有好多年没见到她了。

whenever:

You can borrow my car *whenever* you want.　你随时可以借我的车。

I go and visit him *whenever* I'm in town.　我每次进城都去看他。

Whenever he stayed home he went to bed early.　每当待在家里, 他早早就睡觉了。

Whenever anyone was ill he installed himself as sick-nurse.　谁要是病了, 他就充当护士。

Whenever possible, they play outside.　一有机会他们就到外面玩耍。

2) 还有一些其他类型的时间状语从句, 例如:

Next time you come in, please close the door.　下次你进来请把门关上。

Did he tell you anything important *the last time* he saw you?　上次他见到你时告诉你什么重要的事吗？

Now (that) you're well again you can travel.　既然你身体又好了，可以出去旅行。

Once you have learned Spanish you will find Italian easy.　一旦你学了西班牙语你就会觉得意大利语很容易了。

Immediately she entered, his eyes lit up.　她一进来，他的眼睛就亮了起来。

She'll come over *as soon as* I've settled down.　我一定居下来她就会来。

No sooner had she arrived *than* she began to complain.　她刚一到就开始抱怨。

The moment he spoke I recognized his voice.　他一说话我就听出了他的声音。

Hardly had we got out *when* it began to snow.　我们刚出门天就开始下雪了。

Scarcely had I come in *when* the phone rang.　我刚一进门电话就响了。

这些句子中的某些词(组)起着连词的作用(如as soon as, no sooner...than, the moment ..., hardly...)，有的词甚至已变为连词(如immediately, now, now that)。

17.2.2　引导条件状语从句的连词

1) 条件状语从句主要由 if, unless, supposing (suppose) 引导：

if:

I must leave *if* that's the case.　如果情况如此我就得走了。

What would Diana think of him *if* he failed?　如果他失败，戴安娜会对他怎么想？

If she said so, she's a liar.　如果她这样讲了，她就是撒谎。

If true, this will cause us a lot of trouble.　如果是真的，这会给我们造成很多麻烦。

If necessary, ring me at home.　必要的话往我家里打电话。

He will come *if* asked.　如果邀请的话他是会来的。

If convenient, I'll be with you next Tuesday.　如方便的话，我将于下星期二和你见面。

unless:

I won't write *unless* he writes first. 我不写信, 除非他先给我写。

Unless I'm mistaken, I've seen that man before. 除非我记错了, 那人我以前见过。

I'll go there tomorrow *unless* it rains. 除非下雨, 否则我明天去那里。

He'd never do this *unless* compelled. 除非被迫, 否则他决不会这样做。

Unless redeemed, it'll be for sale. 除非有人赎回, 否则它将出售。

supposing:

Supposing that he asks you, will you go? 假定他请你去, 你会去吗?

Supposing his plan goes wrong, what will we do then? 如果他的计划出了问题, 我们怎么办?

Supposing (that) you're wrong, what will you do then? 假如你错了你怎么办?

suppose:

Suppose she finds out, what shall we do then? 假如她发现了, 我们怎么办?

Suppose you lost your job tomorrow, what would you do? 假定你明天失业, 你怎么办?

provided:

I will agree to go *provided (providing)* (that) my expenses are paid. 如果有人给我掏路费我将同意去。

She agreed to go and work there *provided* that her family could go with her. 如果她家人能随她同行, 她同意去那里工作。

providing:

I'll dry the dishes, *providing* that you do the washing-up. 如果你刷盘子, 我就把它们擦干。

2) 条件状语从句还有其他形式:

You will always have a home *as long as* I have anything. 只要我有家产, 你就永远会有一个家。

I don't mind your knowing anything *as long as* it goes no further. 你知道什么我都不介意, 只要你不告诉别人。

In case he arrives before I get back, please ask him to wait. 如果我还没回来他就到了, 请让他等一等。

They'll stand by you *even if* you don't succeed. 即使你不成功他们也会支持你。

Were I Tom I would refuse. 如果我是汤姆, 我会拒绝。

Should you require anything, just let me know. 如果你需要什么, 告诉我

就行。

Had I thought of it, I'd have talked to mother.　如果我想过这事，我早就
和妈讲了。

此外，as long as, so long as, in case, even if 都起连词作用。

17.2.3　引导目的状语从句的连词

引导目的状语从句的连词主要有下面这些：

in order that:

He left early *in order that* his children would not be alone in the house.　他
早早动身，以免孩子们单独待在家里。

I locked the door *in order that* we might continue our discussion undisturbed.
我把门锁上，以便我们能不受干扰继续讨论。

I lent him ￡50 *in order (so) that* he might go for a holiday.　我借给他50
英镑，使他能去度假。

so that:

Ask her to hurry up with the letters *so that* I can sign them.　让她快点把信
打好，以便我能签字。

Please interpret this Chinese woman's remarks *so that* I can understand them.
请翻译一下这个中国妇女的话以便我能听懂。

He looked down *so that* she should not see his eyes.　他低下头以免她看见
他的眼睛。

so:

Can't you fix it somehow *so* you could stay longer?　难道你不能作某种安
排以便能多待些日子？

Check carefully, *so* any mistakes could be caught.　仔细检查，以便找出所
有的错误。

I'll give him a map *so* he won't get lost.　我会给他一张地图免得他迷路。

that:

She did it *that* he might go free.　她这样做以便他能获得自由。

I am anxious to get it done *that* I may be back in Ireland.　我急于完成此事
以便我能返回爱尔兰。

I tell you this *that* you may not shrink from the responsibility.　我告诉你这
个以便你不会回避责任。

lest:

He hurried on, *lest* she should meet him again.　他赶紧往前走,唯恐她再碰到他。

He was very cautious *lest* he should be discovered by his wife.　他小心翼翼,唯恐被他妻子发现。

He hid the money *lest* it should be stolen.　他把钱藏起来唯恐被人偷去。

还有一些其他这类从句:

She worried *for fear that* her son would be hurt.　她很担心怕儿子受到伤害。

She didn't dare to call me *for fear* they might hear us.　她不敢叫我,唯恐他们会听到我们的声音。

Take warm clothes *in case* the weather is cold.　带上厚衣服以防天冷。

I'll stay in the hotel *in case* there is news of Harry.　我将待在旅馆里以防有哈里的消息。

这里的 for fear (that), in case 都起连词的作用。

17.2.4　引导结果状语从句的连词

1) 结果状语从句主要由 so...that 和 such...that 引导:

so...that:

He was *so* young *that* you must excuse him.　他那样年轻, 你得原谅他。

Bill pitched *so* well *that* everyone cheered him.　比尔球投得那么好,大家都为他欢呼。

He was *so* fat *that* he couldn't get through the door.　他胖得连门都过不去了。

So absorbed was he *that* she didn't dare to make a sound.　他那么聚精会神,致使她都不敢弄出一丁点声音。

such...that:

Jim made *such* a noise *that* his sister told him to be quiet.　吉姆吵成那样,他姐姐让他安静点。

He shut the window with *such* force *that* the glass broke.　他关窗时那样使劲,连玻璃都震碎了。

They had *such* a fierce dog *that* no one dared to go near their house.　他们的狗那样凶,谁也不敢走近他们家。

that 有时可省略,特别是在口语中:

They were *so* tired they could do nothing but yawn.　他们疲倦得一个劲儿打呵欠。

There was *such* a draught, it's no wonder he caught a cold.　过堂风这样厉害，难怪他感冒了。

2) so that 也可引导结果状语从句，表示"因此"：

One of her lungs is affected *so that* she has to rest.　她有一叶肺受到感染，因此得休息。

It fell under my desk, *so that* I couldn't see it.　它掉在我书桌下面，因此我看不见它。

so 也可引导这类从句：

It was dark *so* I couldn't see very well.　天很黑因此我看不太清楚。

She felt very tired so she went to bed early.　她感到很累，因此早早就睡觉了。

so 和 that 之间有时可稍稍停顿：

His heart beat so *that* he could hardly breathe.　他的心跳得这样厉害，他都快喘不过气来了。

Explain it so *that* a 10-year-old boy could understand it.　要讲解得让十岁的孩子都能听懂。

17.2.5　引导原因状语从句的连词

1) 引导原因状语从句的连词主要有 because，as，since：

because:

Because it was wet he took a taxi.　由于下雨他叫了一辆出租车。

He was worried *because* he hadn't had any letter from her.　他很担忧因为他没收到过她一封信。

Why aren't you coming with us?　——*Because* I have got a bad headache.　你为什么不和我们一块去？　——因为我头很疼。

as:

As David had a passion for walking, we started off on foot.　由于大卫喜欢走路，我们就步行出发了。

We don't go there much now, *as* we are going away so soon.　我们现在不常去那儿，因为我们不久就要离开了。

As you're sorry, I'll forgive you.　既然你悔悟了，我就原谅你。

since:

Since they've obviously forgotten to phone me, I'll have to telephone them.
由于他们显然忘了给我打电话，只好由我来打给他们。

Since you can't answer my questions, I'll have to ask someone else. 既然你回答不了我的问题，我只好问别人。

He was not prepared for the question, *since* he had not made up his mind. 对这问题他没有思想准备，因为他还没拿定主意。

2) 还有一些表示原因的状语从句由 seeing (that)，considering (that) 或 now that 等引导：

Seeing that he's been ill all week, he's unlikely to come. 鉴于他已病了一个星期，他来的可能性不大。

We could have a joint party, *seeing* your birthday is the same day as mine. 由于你我的生日在同一天，我们可以办一个联合晚会。

Considering he has only just started, he knows quite a lot about it. 考虑到他刚刚开始，对此他算是知道得很多了。

Considering you've only been studying for a year, you speak English very well. 考虑到你学英语才一年，你英语讲得算是很好的。

Now that you have the chance you had better avail yourself of it. 既然你有了机会，你最好利用起来。

Please don't try to back out *now that* everything has been arranged. 现在一切都安排好了，请不要打退堂鼓。

Now you're here, you may make yourself useful. 你已经来了，不妨帮帮忙。

seeing，considering，now that 都可以看作连词。

3) 许多用在形容词后的 that 从句也起原因状语的作用 (that 有时可省略)：

She was glad *that she had controlled herself.* 她很高兴控制住了自己。

He felt ashamed *that he had done so little.* 他为自己做得这么少而感到惭愧。

I am awfully sorry *that this has happened.* 发生了这事我非常遗憾。

I'm very pleased *you've decided to come.* 你决定来我很高兴。

I'm disappointed *that they cannot come.* 他们不能来我很失望。

I am surprised *I didn't see that before.* 我很吃惊我以前没看到这一点。

17.2.6　引导让步状语从句的连词

引导让步状语从句的连词主要有下面这些:

although:

Although (Though) everyone played well, we lost the game.　尽管每个人都打得不错，我们却输了比赛。

He said they were married, *although* I'm sure they aren't.　他说他们结婚了，不过我肯定他们没有。

I didn't know that then, *although* I learned it later.　那时我并不知道这事，尽管后来我知道了。

He's very lovable *although* not at all tidy.　他很可爱，虽说一点都不整洁。

though:

Though times were changed, Bossily was still Bossily.　尽管时代变了，柏斯莱还是柏斯莱。

Though he was going to Edinburgh, he was in no hurry.　虽说就要去爱丁堡，他却并不慌忙。

It is right for us to go, *though* I left all for Gerry to decide.　我们去是对的，不过我还是让格里来决定一切。

Though not large, the room was light and airy.　房间虽然不大，采光和通风却很好。

The girl, *though* plain, had a kind *face.*　这姑娘虽然相貌平庸，却有一张善良的脸。

even though:

He's an honest man *even though* I have opposed him.　尽管我曾反对过他，他还是一个诚实的人。

She still loved him *even though* he had treated her so badly.　她仍然爱他，尽管他待她那么不好。

even if:

I wouldn't do it, *even if* you paid me a thousand pounds.　即使你付我一千英镑，我也不干。

I'm going to expose him *even if* he's brother of mine.　尽管他是我的兄弟，我也要揭露他。

while:

While they are my neighbors, I don't know them well.　虽然他们是我的邻居，我对他们却不太了解。

While I understand what you say, I can't agree with you.　尽管我理解你的

话，却不能同意你的意见。

2) 下面句子中的从句也是让步状语从句:

Clever though she was, she couldn't conceal her eagerness for praise. 她虽然聪明，却无法掩饰她亟想获得赞扬。

Intelligent as she was, she had not much in sight. 她虽然聪明，却没有多少洞察力。

Try as he would, he could not get her out of his mind. 尽管他努力这样做，却不能把她忘怀。

She was unable to make much progress, *hard as she tried*. 不管她多努力都不能取得多大进步。

However long you argue you will never convince her. 不管争辩多久你都不能说服她。

However cold it is, he always goes swimming. 不管天多冷他都去游泳。

He swore that, *come what may*, he would never let her know what he was doing for her sake. 他发誓，不管发生什么情况，他绝不让她知道他在为她做的事。

Marija made up her mind, *come what might*, she would stay there. 玛丽亚下定决心，不管发生什么情况她都要留在那里。

The moon is a moon still, *whether it shines or not*. (谚)不管亮不亮，月亮终归是月亮。

Whether we go or whether we stay, the result is the same. 不管我们是去还是留，结果都一样。

Granted that he has enough money to buy the house, it doesn't mean he's going to do so. 即使说他有足够的钱买这栋房子，这也不意味着他就要去买。

17.2.7　引导方式状语从句的连词

1) 引导方式状语从句的连词主要有as, like, as if, as though, however:

as:

You ought to do *as* I tell you. 你应当照我说的做。

When in Rome, do *as* the Romans do. (谚)入乡随俗。

Shelley, *as* we had seen, had met her through his uncle. 正如已证实的那样，雪莱是通过他叔叔认识她的。

As expected, the afforestation movement rapidly spread. 正如所预料的那

样,造林运动迅速展开了。

like:

She can't draw *like* her sister can.　她不能像她姐姐那样画画。

Do it *like* I tell you.　照我告诉你的那样做。

She behaves *like* she owns the place.　她表现得就像这儿的主人似的。

It looks *like* I'll be late today.　看起来我今天要迟到了。

as if:

She looked a bit queer, *as if* she knew something.　她显得有点怪,仿佛她知道什么情况似的。

I remember the whole thing *as if* it happened yesterday.　整个这件事我都记得,就像发生在昨天似的。

He paused *as if* expecting her to speak.　他停了停,像是在期待她说话。

He glanced about *as if* in search of something.　他四处看了看,仿佛在找什么似的。

as though:

We felt *as though* we had witnessed the whole thing.　我们感到像亲眼目睹了整件事情似的。

I remember it vividly *as though* it were tonight.　这件事我记得清清楚楚,就像是今晚发生似的。

He shivered *as though* with cold.　他颤抖了一下,好象受了寒气似的。

When she had finished she waited *as though* for a reply.　她讲完之后等了等,像是在等候回答。

however:

Arrange your hours *however* you like.　你的时间你可以随意安排。

You may use it *however* you like.　你可以随意使用它。

In one's own home one can act *however* he wishes.　在自己家里你愿干什么就干什么。

2) the way 也常可引导方式状语从句:

He doesn't speak *the way* I do.　他不像我这样说话。

I was never allowed to do things *the way* I wanted to do them.　他们从不让我按自己的意愿行事。

17.2.8 引导地点状语从句的连词

1) 引导地点状语从句的连词有 where, wherever, everywhere:

where:

> I'll drive you *where* you're going.　你到哪儿我都可以开车送你去。
>
> Please keep sitting *where* you are.　请仍坐在原处。
>
> I'm quite comfortable *where* I am.　我在哪里都行。
>
> Put in an article *where* necessary.　在必要的地方填入冠词。

wherever:

> *Wherever* he goes, there's always a spy hanging about.　不管他到哪里,总有一个密探跟着。
>
> *Wherever* he is he'll be thinking of you.　不管他在哪里,他总会想着你。
>
> We'll go *wherever* you say.　你说到哪里我们就到哪里。
>
> Avoid structure of this kind *wherever* possible.　要尽可能避免这种结构。

everywhere:

> *Everywhere* they appeared there were ovations.　他们所到之处都有人欢呼。
>
> *Everywhere* he went, he was introduced as the current United States champion.　不管他到哪里, 人们都介绍他是当前的美国冠军。
>
> You see it *everywhere* you look.　不管从哪儿看你都能看见它。

2) no matter where 也可引导地点状语:

> *No matter where* you now are in writing, you can improve with practice.　不管目前在写作上你处于什么水平,练习都能帮你提高。
>
> Keep your mobile phone with you *no matter where* you are.　不管在哪里你都要带着手机。

17.2.9　引导比较状语从句的连词

1) 引导比较状语从句的连词是 than 和 as:

than:

> You sing better *than* I do.　你的歌唱得比我好。
>
> There were more casualties *than* was reported.　伤亡人数比报导的多。
>
> It was more expensive *than* I thought.　它比我想的要贵。
>
> They work harder *than* we do.　他们比我们勤奋。

as:

> You know *as* much about that *as* I do.　对这事你了解得和我一样多。
>
> I haven't done *as* much *as* I should have liked.　我做的没有我希望的那么多。

They're *as* firm *as* one could expect.　他们像我们期望的那样坚定。

Martin was *as* impatient *as* he was stubborn.　马丁既急躁又固执。

That's not *so* simple *as* it sounds.　那事并不像听起来那么简单。

2）这类从句常有词省略，只剩下单词或词组：

They are wiser *than* us.　他们比我们明智。

It is even colder *than* yesterday.　今天比昨天还冷。

He was more lucky *than* clever.　他不是聪明，而是走运。

Hard beds are healthier *than* soft ones.　硬床比软床更有益于健康。

This is more amusing *than* sitting in an office.　这比坐在办公室里有意思。

He was almost *as* well off *as* myself.　他差不多和我自己一样富裕。

She doesn't work *as* hard *as* you.　她没有你那样勤奋。

He can run *as* fast *as* 20 miles an hour.　他快跑能达到一小时二十英里的速度。

Those trees can be *as* big *as* 20 feet across.　那些树可以大到直径二十英尺。

17.2.10　引导其他从句的连词

1）引导主语从句和宾语从句的连词有 that 和 whether，if 可以引导宾语从句：

that:

She always complains *that* he is down on her.　她老是抱怨他看不起她。

I'll prove to the world *that* he was right.　我要向全世界证明他是对的。

That you're coming to China is the best news I have heard this long time.　你要到中国来是这么长时间以来我听到的最好消息。

It's natural *that* they should have different views.　他们有不同看法是很自然的。

whether:

I don't know *whether* you like flowers.　我不知道你喜不喜欢花。

I'll see *whether* I can induce him to accept it.　我要看看我能否劝说他接受这东西。

Whether it will do us harm or good remains to be seen.　它会对我们有害还是有益还需看一看。

It was uncertain *whether* my playmates would come (or not).　我的玩伴们是否会来还不肯定。

if:

> I wonder *if* it's large enough.　不知这够不够大。
>
> He asked *if* I would show him the way.　他问我可否给他带路。

2）that 和 whether 还可引导表语从句或同位语从句：

that:

> The fact is *that* he doesn't really try.　事实是他没有真正去努力。
>
> The reason was *(that)* he was afraid.　原因是他害怕。
>
> He came to the decision *that* he must act at once.　他决定必须立即行动。
>
> I have a feeling *that* our team is going to win.　我觉得我们队会获胜。

whether:

> His first question was *whether* Holmes had arrived yet.　他的第一个问题是福尔摩斯是否来了。
>
> The point is *whether* we ought to recommend him.　问题是我们是否应当推荐他。
>
> They raised the question *whether* we ought to call in a specialist.　他们提出了是否应请专家来的问题。

3）that 和 whether 还可以用在形容词之后：

> It's doubtful *whether* we'll be able to come.　我们是否能来还是个疑问。
>
> Secretly he was pleased *that* Jennie should have this fine chance.　他暗中高兴珍妮有这个好机会。
>
> I am certain *that* I posted the letter.　我肯定这信我发了。
>
> He wasn't sure *whether* he ought to laugh or cry.　他啼笑皆非。

4）除了连词外，连接代（副）词也可引导主语从句、宾语从句等。关于这类句子可参阅第 5.5.2 和第 15.1.6 节。另外，关系代（副）词可引导宾语从句，关于这类句子可参阅第 5.6.1 —5.6.5 及第 15.1.6 节，以及后面的 22.3.1 —22.3.2 节。

17.3　并列连词

17.3.1　并列连词 and 和 or

1）and 和 or 是用得最多的并列连词，可以连接：

a. 两个并列的动词：

> We were singing *and* dancing all evening.　整个晚上我们都在唱歌跳舞。

He started to shout *and* swear. 他开始又喊又骂。

You can walk up *or* take the cable car. 你可以走上去,也可坐缆车上去。

He never smokes *or* drinks. 他从不抽烟喝酒。

b. 名词、形容词等:

Father *and* son went to New York by a morning train. 父子两人坐早上的火车去了纽约。

She was sweet *and* amiable. 她甜美和蔼。

Read it slowly *and* clearly. 念慢一点,清楚一点。

Would you like fish *or* beef? 你要鱼还是牛肉?

It's now *or* never, shall we chance it? 机不可失, 时不再来。咱们要不要碰碰运气?

c. 两个并列的分句 (句子):

I said it *and* I meant it. 我说话算话。

He had plenty of money *and* he spent it freely. 他很有钱,花起来很随便。

Do you want a bath at once, *or* shall I have mine first? 你想马上洗澡,还是我先洗?

Do you want to leave now *or* would you rather set off later? 你想现在就走,还是愿意晚点出发?

2) and 可连接两个分句, 表示 "只要…就":

Utter one word, *and* you are a dead man! 说一句话就要你的命!

Go straight on *and* you'll see a church. 一直往前走你会看到一座教堂。

Give him an inch *and* he will take a mile. 他会得寸进尺。

3) or 可连接分句, 表示 "否则":

He had to have a job *or* (he would) go hungry. 他得有一份工作,否则就要挨饿。

Have a care what you say *or* you may regret it. 说话要当心,否则你会后悔。

Don't drive so fast *or* you'll have an accident. 别开这么快,不然你会出车祸。

17.3.2 表示意思转折的连词

表示意思转折的连词主要有 but, yet:

1) but 主要连接两个并列的分句:

All this he did, *but* it had no effect at all. 这一切他都做了, 但一点都不

起作用。

James hasn't got a car, *but* his sister has. 詹姆斯没有小汽车,但他姐姐有。

She's been learning Italian for six years, *but* she doesn't speak it very well. 她学意大利语有六年了,但还是讲得不太好。

I'd love to come *but* I can't make it till 8 o'clock. 我愿意来,不过要到八点才行。

有时也可连接两个并列的成分:

The weather will be sunny *but* cold. 天气会晴朗但很冷。

The fox may grow grey, *but* never good. (谚)狐狸会变老,却不会变好。

He no longer felt despondent, *but* happy and hopeful. 他不再沮丧,而是开心并充满希望。

He is not a novelist, *but* a dramatist. 他不是小说家,而是剧作家。

They see the trees, *but* not the forest. 他们只见树木不见森林。

间或还可引导状语:

He tried to save it, *but* in vain. 他努力想救活它,但没有用。

He glanced about, *but* seeing only the empty room. 他向四周张望,但只看见那个空房间。

2) yet 主要连接两个分句:

Though the sore be healed, *yet* a scar may remain. (谚)创痛虽愈,伤痕犹在。

Jane said she was ill, *yet* I saw her in the street just now. 简说她病了,但刚才在街上我曾看到她。

They are ugly and expensive, *yet* people buy them. 它们又丑又贵,但人们还是要买。

有时连接两个形容词:

It is strange, *yet* true. 这很奇怪,却是真的。

The judge was stern, *yet* completely fair. 这法官很严厉,但绝对公正。

有时还可与 and 和 but 一起用:

I offered him still more, *and yet* he wasn't satisfied. 我又给了他一些,但他仍然不满意。

She's a funny girl, *but yet* you can't help liking her. 她是个奇怪的姑娘,但你禁不住会喜欢她。

3) however, nevertheless, still 等为副词,但可起连接作用,表示意思的转折:

however:

His first response was to say no. Later, *however*, he changed his mind. 他的第一反应是不行, 但后来他改变了主意。

Sales are poor this month. There may, *however*, be an increase before Christmas. 这个月销量很差, 但圣诞节前可能会增加。

I'll offer it to Tom. *However*, he may not want it. 我将把它送给汤姆, 不过他可能不会要。

nevertheless:

They hadn't trained hard, *nevertheless* (but) they won. 他们并没有努力训练, 但还是打赢了

He's charming; *nevertheless*, I don't trust him. 他很迷人, 但我不太信任他。

He was angry, *nevertheless* (however) he listened to me. 他很生气, 不过他还是听了我的话。

still:

You did wrong. *Still*, I'm ready to forgive you. 你做错了事, 不过我愿意原谅你。

It's raining; *still* I'd like to go. 天在下雨, 但我还是想去。

He is naughty, (but) *still* you cannot help liking him. 他很调皮, 但你还是禁不住会喜欢他。

all the same:

Nobody wishes you harm, (but) they down you *all the same*. 没有人有心伤害你, 但他们还是看不起你。

She is naughty, *all* (just) *the same* we have to laugh at her jokes. 她很调皮, 但对她的恶作剧我们还是要发笑。

I am sure she'll say yes, but I should ask her permission first *all the same*. 我肯定她会答应的, 但我还是应该先征求她的同意。

17.3.3　表示因果关系的连词

1) for 可表示 "因为", 但引导的不是从句, 而是分句, 对前面情况加以解释, 常用逗号把它和前面的分句分开, 这在书面语中比较多见 (口语中多用 because, as, since 等):

The days were short, *for* it was now December. 白天很短, 因为现在已经是十二月。

He took the food eagerly, *for* he had eaten nothing since dawn. 他吃得很香,因为自天亮起他就没吃东西。

The children soon lost their way, *for* they had never been in the forest before. 孩子们很快迷了路,因为他们从未进过这座森林。

它还可以表示为什么有前面的看法 (此时不能用 because, as, since):

It must have rained in the night *for* when I woke the next morning I saw the grass wet. 夜里准是下了雨,因为我早上我醒来看见草地是湿的。

She must have gone out early, *for* she had not shown up at breakfast. 她肯定一早出去了,因为她没来吃早饭。

2) so 表示结果,可译为"因此"、"所以":

Nobody seemed about, *so* I went in. 附近似乎没人,因此我走了进去。

The play began at eight, *so* they must dine at seven. 戏八点开始,所以他们得七点吃饭。

She felt very tired *so* she went to bed early. 她感到很疲倦,于是早早就睡觉了。

Our cases were heavy, *so* we took a taxi. 我们的箱子很重,因此我们坐了出租车。

3) therefore 为副词,也表示同样的意思,但比较文气一点,可以放在分句前:

There is fog at Heathrow; *therefore* the plane has been diverted. 希思罗机场有雾,因此飞机改到别的机场降落。

It rained; *therefore* the game was called off. 天下雨了,比赛因此取消。

也可插在句子中间:

He's out of the country and *therefore* unable to attend the meeting. 他在国外,因此不能参加会议。

He had finished the Times, there was *therefore* nothing to do. 他已看完泰晤士报,因此没事可干了。

He had gone; she *therefore* gave the money to me. 他走了,于是她把钱给了我。

4) hence 也是副词,也表示类似意思,多用在说理性文章中,且多用在分句或句子开头:

My mother is by herself; *hence* I must go home now. 我妈一个人在家,因此我得回去了。

Microwaves have got cheaper and *hence* more people can afford it. 微波炉便宜些了,因此更多的人买得起了。

Hence he was annoyed by many unwelcome attentions.　因此许多不受欢迎的殷勤举动惹得他不高兴。

有时后面只跟一个动词：

The town was built on the side of a hill, *hence* the name Hillside.　这座城市建在山腰，因此称作山腰城。

I fell off my bike yesterday — *hence* the bruises.　我昨天从自行车上摔下来了，因此身上摔青了。

17.3.4　其他并列连词

1) 其他并列连词有下面这些，多连接两个并列的成分：

either...or:

Either Tim *or* his brother has to shovel the snow.　要么是蒂姆要么是他弟弟得去铲雪。

She's *either* French *or* Spanish.　她不是法国人就是西班牙人。

I left it *either* on the table *or* in the drawer.　我把它不是放在桌上就是放在抽屉里了。

You can *either* write *or* phone to order a copy.　你可寄信或打电话去定购一本。

It was *either* pink, red *or* orange.　它或是粉红色、红色，或是橘红色。

Either you must improve your work *or* I shall dismiss you.　要么你得改进工作，要么我就辞退你。

neither...nor:

He can *neither* read *nor* write.　他既不能读又不能写。

They have *neither* natural gas *nor* running water.　他们既没有天然气又没有自来水。

He was *neither* clever *nor* stupid.　他既不聪明也不笨。

Paul came just at the right time, *neither* too early *nor* too late.　保罗来得正是时候，既不太早也不太晚。

Neither your mother *nor* I have any other thought but what is best for you.　不管是你妈妈还是我，除了一切为你好没有别的想法。

both...and:

You've given *both* your uncle *and* myself a lot of trouble.　你给你姑父和我都添了很多麻烦。

Sophia was *both* glad *and* sorry to see her.　索菲娅看到她既高兴又难过。

I decided to play safe *both* for own sake *and* the job's.　为我自己,也为了
工作,我决定谨慎行事。

He *both* speaks *and* writes Swahili.　他既能说又能写斯瓦希里语。

as well as:

John can speak Chinese *as well as* French.　约翰能讲汉语及法语。

We shall travel by night *as well as* by day.　我们将日夜兼程。

The conflict spread everywhere, into villages, *as well as* into the cities.　冲
突到处蔓延,蔓延到了农村,也蔓延到了城市。

It is a political *as well as* an economic question.　这是一个政治问题,也
是一个经济问题。

2) **not only...but aslo** 也连接两个并列成分:

He *not only* did the shopping *but* he *also* cook the meal.　他不仅买东西,而
且还做饭。

The cuts will affect *not only* this school *but also* other schools in this area.　削
减经费不仅影响这所学校,而且影响区内的其他学校。

Not only was my mother unhappy, *but* Marian, *too*.　不仅我母亲很痛苦,
玛丽安也很痛苦。

Not only did he speak more correctly, *but* he spoke more easily.　他不光讲
得更正确,也讲得更不费劲了。

第18章 感叹词

18.1 概 说

18.1.1 感叹词的作用

感叹词是表示说话时的情绪的,它不构成句子的一个成分,却和后面句子在意思上有关连,后面句子常常表明这种情绪的性质或原因等:

> Oh, what a fine day! 呵, 多好的天气!

> Oh, good, here's the bus. 啊, 好了, 公共汽车来了。

在感叹的情绪较强时,后面多跟一个感叹号,如果不强,后面通常跟一个逗号:

> Oh! How you frightened me! 啊, 你把我吓了一跳!

> Oh, is that so? 啊, 是这样吗?

感叹词一般都搁在句子前面, 间或也可能插在句子中间:

> That little sister of his, oh, is such a dear! 他那个小妹妹, 嗬, 真逗人喜欢!

这类词常不易译为确切的汉语,同一感叹词在不同上下文中表示的情绪不尽相同,译成的汉语也就不同。有时表示的感情很细致,在汉语中常不易找出确切的译法。这时只能从上下文中去琢磨,找出近似的汉语译出。

18.1.2 常见的感叹词

常见的感叹词有下面这些:

ah	aha	blast	bother	bravo	damn
good gracious		good heavens		good lord	goodness me
gosh	hurrah	oh	oh dear	ouch	ow
ugh	I never	well	what	why	wow

日常招呼语 hello 和 hi，hey 也是感叹词。有些感叹词 (如 alas) 现已不多用了。

18.2   一些常用感叹词的用法

18.2.1 oh, ah, well 的用法

平时用得最多的是 oh，ah，well 这几个词：

1) oh 可用来表示惊奇、恐慌、痛苦、懊恼、高兴等：

"I'm a teacher." "*Oh*? Where?" "我是教师。" "是吗? 在哪里教书?" (惊奇)

"*Oh* no!" she cried as she began to read the letter. "啊不可能!" 她开始看信时惊叫道。(惊恐)

Oh, how terrible! 啊，多可怕! (恐慌)

Oh, aren't these flowers gorgeous! 哇，这些花真漂亮! (赞叹)

She got the job? *Oh* great! 她找到工作了? 那太好了! (高兴)

Oh, what a pity! 啊，真遗憾! (遗憾)

Oh, please don't ask me any more. 啊，请不要再问我了。(恳求)

在回答问题时，或在呼语前，有时加 oh，并无特别意思：

"What time are you going into town?" "*Oh*, I haven't decided yet." "你什么时候进城?" "嗯，我还没决定。"

Oh yes, I will. 是的，我会的。

Oh Pam, can you come over here for a minute? 啊，帕姆，你能过来一会吗?

Oh, Simon, take this letter to the post, would you? 啊，西蒙，把这封信发掉好吗?

2) ah 表示惊奇、恐惧、高兴、痛苦、恳求、松一口气等：

Ah, there you are. 好了，你来了。(高兴)

Ah, good, here is the bus. 好了，公共汽车来了。(高兴)

Ah, what a lovely baby! 呀，多可爱的宝宝! (赞美)

Ah, how pitiful! 啊，真可怜! (怜悯)

Ah, that's inexcusable. 啊，这是不能原谅的。(气愤)

Ah, I've never heard of such things before. 嚯，我可从未听说过这样的事! (惊奇)

3) well 表示欣慰、惊奇、犹疑、无奈等：

Well, here we are at last!　好了，我们终于到了！（欣慰）

Well, who would have thought of it?　嗨，谁会想到呀？（惊奇）

Well, what shall we do next?　嗯，我们下一步怎么办？（犹疑）

Well, that's the only thing I can do now.　哎，目前只好这样。（无奈）

Well, thank goodness you've arrived.　谢天谢地你到了。（欣慰）

Well, well — I would never have guessed it.　嗯，真是意想不到。（惊异）

还可用来表示同意、犹疑、思考、等待回答、结束谈话等：

Well, you may be right.　嗯，你可能是对的。

Very well then, I'll accept the offer.　很好嘛，我将接受这个提议。

"Do you want to come?" "*Well*, I'm not sure."　"你想来吗？""嗯，我不能肯定。"

I think it happened, *well*, towards the end of last summer.　我想，嗯，这是去年夏末发生的。

Well, are you going to tell us or not?　嗨，你到底打不打算告诉我们？

Well, I'd better be going now.　好了，我最好走吧。

18.2.2　一些表示感叹的词组

1) 一些女性用得较多表示感叹的词组——oh dear，dear me，(good) gracious，(my) goodness 等，表示惊异、不耐烦、难过等，这与汉语中的"天哪"有点相近：

Oh dear! Why should you be so stubborn?　天哪！你怎么这样固执？

Dear me, I didn't know you were so sharp-tongued.　嗨，不知道你的嘴竟然这样厉害。

My goodness! How could you work so fast!　我的天，你怎么干得这么快！

Goodness what a big cake!　(我的)天哪，这么大的蛋糕！

Gracious, what an ugly house.　天呀，这房子真难看！

Good gracious! (Goodness gracious!) Is that the time?　天呀,已经是这个时候啦?

Gracious me! What have you done to your hair?　我的天,你把头发弄成什么样子了?

2) 一些男性用得较多的表示感叹的词组—— oh Lord，Good Heavens，Heavens，Good lord 等，也表示惊异、不高兴等情绪：

Good lord, it's you!　我的老天，原来是你！

Oh Lord, what shall we do now?　天啦，我们现在怎么办？

O Lord, can a cabbage grow that big?　啊天哪，白菜能长这么大？

Good Heavens! It'll get into the papers.　天哪，这会登到报上去的。

Heavens, what a cold room!　吓，这房间真冷！

18.2.3　另一些较常用的感叹词

1) 用来打招呼的感叹词:

Hallow, John! How are you?　嗨，约翰！你好呀？

Hullo. It's nice to meet you.　嗨，见到你很高兴。

Hello, is Mrs. Brown there?　喂，布朗夫人在吗？

Hello, who's speaking, please?　喂，你是哪一位？

Hello, hello, hello, what's going on here?　喂，喂，喂，出什么事了？

Hi, there, Mr. Smith, good to see you.　嗨，史密斯先生，见到你很高兴。

"*Hi*, Uncle Herald," Thomas said.　"嗨，海拉德叔叔，"汤姆斯说。

Hi, Alice. This is Fred.　喂，艾丽斯，我是弗雷德。

Hey, come and look at this!　嘿，过来瞧瞧！

Hey, can I ask you a question?　嘿，我能问你一个问题吗？

2) 表示疼痛痛苦等的感叹词:

Ow! That hurts.　啊，疼。

Ow! Don't do that!　噢，不要这样做。

Ouch, you're hurting me!　啊，你把我弄疼了！

Ouch! That hurt!　噢，疼！

Alas! It was not so easy as all that.　唉！可惜情况不那么简单。

But, alas, this was most unwise.　唉，这是非常不明智的。

Alas! My lover has forsaken me.　唉，我的恋人把我甩了。

3) why 也可用作感叹词，表示惊奇或不足为奇，可译为"这简单"、"你这都不知道"等:

Why, what a bruise you have got!　怎么搞的，你身上青了这么大一块！

Why! Why! The cage is empty!　怎么搞的！笼子空了！

Why, Jane, it's you!　啊，简，原来是你！

Why, it's easy — a child could do it.　嗨，这容易，小孩都能干。

"How should we answer the question?"　"*Why*, that's simple enough."

　"这问题怎样回答？"　"嗨，这简单极了！"

Why! You are ahead of time too.　怎么，你也提前完成了！

Why, man, she's after your money.　这都不知道, 伙计, 她是想你的钱。

"What's twice two?" "*Why*, four." "二乘二是多少?" "这还不知道, 是四。"

18.2.4　一些次要的感叹词

1) aha /ɑːˈhɑː/　表示得意:

Aha, so that's where she hides her money!　哈哈, 原来她把钱藏在这儿。

Aha! So you planned at this, did you?　哈哈, 这都是你策划的, 是吧?

Aha! Here at last, is the answer to the question that has baffled scholars.　哈, 终于找到这个把许多学者难倒的问题的答案了。

2) bother /ˈbɒðə/　表示不高兴、不耐烦等:

Oh *bother*! I forgot to phone Jane.　糟糕! 我忘了给简打电话了。

Oh *bother*! I've left my money at home.　倒霉! 我把钱留在家里了。

Bother the flies!　讨厌的苍蝇!

3) bravo /brɑːˈvəʊ/　表示喝彩:

Bravo! Encore!　好! 再来一个!

Bravo! Well played!　好! 弹得好!

4) hurrah /huˈrɑː/, **hurray** /huˈreɪ/　表示赞许:

Hurrah for the weekend!　周末万岁!

Hurray!　好极了!

5) hush /hʌʃ/　表示"别出声"、"小声点":

Hush! Someone's coming.　别出声, 有人来了。

Hush, or you'll wake the baby.　小声点, 要不会把宝宝吵醒。

6) damn /dæm/　为诅咒语, 表示"该死":

Damn this computer — what's the matter with it?　这台该死的电脑, 怎么回事?

Damn! I've forgotten the key.　该死! 忘带钥匙了。

7) blast /blɑːst, blæst/　表示不高兴:

Blast! I've burnt the toast again.　倒霉! 面包又烤糊了。

Blast this useless car.　该死, 这没用的车。

8) bah /bɑː/　表示厌恶、鄙视:

Bah! That's stupid.　哼! 这真愚蠢。

Bath! Did he imagine I would accept that?　咄! 难道他以为我会接受?

9) whew /hjuː/　表示惊异、慰藉等:

Whew, that man has some temper!　瞧，那人还有点脾气！

Whew! That was a lucky escape!　唉！总算幸运地逃出来了！

10) **wow** /waʊ/ 表示赞佩、羡慕：

Wow! You look terrific!　噢！你看起来漂亮极了！

Wow! Look at that car!　吓！瞧那辆车！

11) **mm** /m/ 表示赞许、犹疑等：

Mm, lovely cake.　嗯，蛋糕真漂亮。

Mm? I'm sorry, I wasn't listening.　什么？对不起，我没听。

12) **ugh** /ɜː, ʌg/ 表示厌恶、恐惧等：

Ugh! How can you eat that stuff?　咄，你怎么吃这样的东西？

Ugh! This medicine tastes awful!　这药难吃极了！

13) **gosh** /gɒʃ, gɑːʃ/ 表示惊异：

Gosh, it's cold.　嗨，真冷。

Gosh, is that the time?　到时候了吗？

14) **ooh** /uː/ 表示赞许、惊讶等：

"Look what I've bought." "*Ooh*!"　"瞧我买什么了。" "哦！"

"Red? *Ooh* how nice."　"红的？啊，真好。"

第 19 章 主 语

19.1 主语表示法

19.1.1 主语表示法

主语可以用下面这些成分表示:

1) 名词:

Another *rocket* is going to be launched next week. 下周将发射一枚新的火箭。

Are there other *universes* outside our own? 我们的宇宙之外还有别的宇宙吗?

2) 代词:

Who's on the phone? 谁来电话?

Nobody knows the answer. 没人知道答案是什么。

3) 数词:

Two-thirds of them are college students. 他们中间三分之二是大学生。

First went to the Chinese team. 第一名由中国队获得。

4) 动名词:

Reading French is easier than speaking it. 阅读法语比讲法语容易。

There's no *knowing* how long he'll be away. 没法知道他将离开多久。

5) 不定式:

To compromise appears advisable. 妥协可能是明智的。

It is an offence *to drop litter in the street*. 在街上乱扔杂物是犯禁的。

6) 词组:

To each according to his work is a socialist principle. 按劳分配是社会主义的一个原则。

"*Safety First*" is our slogan. "安全第一"是我们的口号。

7) 从句:

What she saw gave her a little fright. 她看到的情况使她有点吃惊。

Why he did it will remain a puzzle forever.   他为什么这样做将永远是个谜。

8) 名词化的其他词类：

A is the first letter of the English alphabet.   A 是英语字母的第一个。

The well-to-do had their cares also.   富裕的人也有他们的烦恼。

在口语中有时还可能用副词、介词短语作主语：

Slowly is exactly how he speaks.   他说话就是慢吞吞的。

Out on the lake will be all right.   到湖上玩玩倒不错。

Between 8 and 9 will suit me.   8 点到 9 点之间对我合适。

19.1.2   动名词作主语

1) 动名词可直接作主语：

Dancing bored him.   跳舞使他厌烦。

Putting in a new window will involve cutting away part of the roof.   安一个新窗户得拆掉一部分房顶。

Keeping hens is her hobby.   养鸡是她的爱好。

Thus *rowing* is a sport.   因此划船是一种运动。

Going to the movies is a popular pastime.   看电影是一种大众化的消遣。

Being lost can be a terrifying experience.   迷路有时是很可怕的。

Slow cooking make tougher meat tender.   慢火可以把较老的肉炖烂。

Not being punctual makes him unreliable.   不准时使他变得不可靠。

2) 有时，动名词前可以有一代词或名词所有格表示其逻辑上的主语：

Their coming to help was a great encouragement to us.   他们来支援对我们是很大的鼓舞。

Mary's grumbling annoyed him.   玛丽的嘟嘟囔囔使他厌烦。

Rose's going won't be of much help.   罗丝去不会有多大帮助。

有时还可名词化，前面带有冠词：

The reading of the will took place in the lawyer's office.   遗嘱是在律师事务所宣读的。

A ringing of bells marks the end of the old year.   一阵钟声标志着旧年的结束。

3) 有时可用先行词 it 作形式主语，而把作主语的动名词放到后面去：

It's no use *asking me*.   问我没用。

Is *it* any good *trying*?   试一试有好处吗？

It doesn't matter *throwing that away*.　把它扔掉没有关系。

It's a waste of time *your talking to him*.　　你和他谈是白费时间。

关于用动名词、不定式和从句作主语可参阅下面多节。

19.2　用 it 作主语的句子

19.2.1　用 it 作人称代词 (Personal Pronoun)

1) it 最基本的用法是作人称代词，主要代表刚提到的东西以避免重复：

Did the black snake frighten you?　—— Yes, *it* did.　那条黑蛇吓着你了吗?　——是的。

Look at that car. *It*'s going much too fast.　瞧那辆车，开得实在太快了。

"Where's my coat?"　"*It*'s in the cupboard."　"我的大衣在哪里?"　"在衣柜里."

"Where is your car?"　"*It*'s in the garage."　"你的车在哪里?"　"在车库里。"

2) 也可代表抽象的事物：

The government has become very unpopular since *it* introduced the new tax.　该政府自开征新税后就变得很不得人心。

It was a great surprise to me when he did a thing like that.　他做这样的事我大为吃惊。

"I've broken the mirror."　"*It* can't be helped."　"我把镜子打破了。"　"这是没法帮忙的事。"

It's all my fault.　这都怪我。

3) 也可以指动物或未知性别的婴儿：

"Is this your dog?"　"No, *it* isn't."　"这是你的狗吗?"　"不是的。"

Her new baby is tiny. *It* only weighs 2 kilos.　她的新生婴儿很小,只有两公斤重。

What a beautiful baby — is *it* a boy?　多漂亮的宝宝,是男孩吗?

4) 还可代表一个彼此都知其何所指的东西：

Does *it* itch much?　痒得厉害吗?

Where does *it* hurt?　哪儿疼?

It's meingitis.　这是脑膜炎。

19.2.2 非人称代词 it

it 有时并不指具体东西，而指天气、时间、环境等，称为**非人称代词** it (Impersonal it)，可以：

1）指天气：

It's raining (snowing). 在下雨(雪)。

It's frosty (a lovely day). 今天霜冻(天气晴朗)。

It's a fine night (full moon tonight). 这是个晴朗的夜晚(今晚是满月)。

It's sunny (a bit windy). 现在阳光灿烂(微微有点风)。

It was pouring with rain. 这时下着倾盆大雨。

It was very cold (quite warm) at the weekend. 周末天气很冷(很暖和)。

2）指时间：

It's Tuesday today. 今天是星期二。

It's nearly half past eight. 快八点半了。

It's the third of June. 今天是六月三日。

It was twilight (midnight) when they came out of the hall. 他们从大厅出来已是黄昏时分(午夜)。

"What time is *it*?" "*It*'s ten to eleven." "现在是什么时候?" "是十点五十。"

It's five years since I saw you last. 从上次见到你以来已经五年了。

It's our wedding anniversary. 这是我们结婚周年纪念日。

3）指环境：

It gets very crowded here in the summer. 夏天这儿很拥挤。

It's lovely here. 这儿环境很优美。

It's quiet (very noising) here. 这儿很安静(吵)。

They're sure to see you. *It*'s bright moonlight. 他们肯定能看到你,月亮这么亮。

It's nice down there. 在那儿很好。

It's getting so dark. 天这么黑了。

4）指距离：

How far is *it* to Kunming? 到昆明有多远?

It's two miles to the beach. 到海滨有两英里。

It's 112 miles form London to Birmingham. 从伦敦到伯明翰有 112 英里。

It's half an hour's walk to the city library. 去市图书馆走路只要半小时。

It's only twenty minutes' drive to our university. 到我们大学乘车只要二

十分钟。

How far is *it* from your home to your office? 从你家到办公室有多远?

It's about a night journey to this place by train. 到这地方差不多要坐一晚上的火车。

19.2.3 用于强调的 it

1) it 可用来对句子的某一成分加以强调,例如 Nancy saw your sister in Tokyo last week. 可改为许多强调结构:

It was Nancy *who* saw your sister in Tokyo last week. (强调主语)

It was your sister *whom* Nancy saw in Tokyo last week. (强调宾语)

It was in Tokyo *that* Nancy saw your sister last week. (强调状语)

It was last week *that* Nancy saw your sister in Tokyo. (强调状语)

从这些句子可以看出这类句子的结构是:

it + 动词 be + 强调部分 + who(m) 或 that + 其他部分

这类句子可称为 **分裂句**(Cleft Sentence), 这种结构称为 **分裂结构**(Cleft Structure)。

2) 在强调主语时,可用 who(间或用 that) 引导后面部分:

It was Peter *who* lent us the money. 是彼得借钱给我们的。

It was you *who* had been wrong. 错的是你。

Was *it* you *who* (that) broke the window? 打破窗子的是你吗?

Who was *it that* called the meeting? 召集会议的是谁?

若主语是物不是人,则需用 that:

But here *it*'s my word *that* counts. 但在这里是我说了算。

3) 在强调宾语或介词宾语时,若是人,则关系代词用 whom, 间或用 that (a);若是物,则需用 that (b):

a. *It*'s Tom *whom* you should ask. 你应当问的是汤姆。

It was Jim in *whom* she still had her faith. 她信任的仍然是吉姆。

It was Peter with *whom* I first came in contact. 我最初接触的是彼得。

It was the president *that* (whom) Jean shot yesterday. 昨天吉恩枪杀的是总统。

It's me *that* he blamed. 他责怪的是我。

It's pilots *that* we need, not ground staff. 我们需要的是飞行员,不是地勤人员。

b. *It*'s money *that* they want. 他们要的是钱。

It's Spain *that* they're going to, not Portugal.　他们准备去的是西班牙，不是葡萄牙。

It was a key *that* I found there.　我在那里找到的是一把钥匙。

4） 在强调状语时后面多用 that：

It was on Monday night *that* all this happened.　这一切是在星期一夜里发生的。

It's today *that* he's going.　他是今天走。

It was here *that* he chiefly differed from an Englishman.　他和英国人的主要不同就在这里。

Why is *it that* you object to the idea?　你为什么反对这个意见？

5） 在口语中，who，that 这类关系代词有时省略：

I think *it* was Goethe said this.　我想这话是歌德说的。

It was Philip drove Miss Sophia yesterday, wasn't it?　昨天是菲力普给索菲娅小姐开车，对吧？

It was you I thought of all the time.　我一直惦念的是你。

It was then I heard Phuong's steps.　就在这时我听到了冯的脚步声。

What is *it* you want me to do?　你要我做的是什么？

Was *it* in 1980 this happened?　这事是 1980 年发生的吗？

6） 有些否定句也可改成这种强调结构：

> I didn't hear from her until last summer.
> It wasn't until last summer that I heard from her.
> 　直到去年夏天我才接到她的信。

> I didn't do all this for myself.
> It wasn't for myself that I did all this.
> 　我做这一切并非都是为我自己。

> I did not have an opportunity of seeing her again for several years.
> It wasn't for several years that I had an opportunity of seeing her again.
> 　好几年我都没有机会再见到她。

问句也可变成这种结构：

> Who called him "comrade"?
> Who was it that called him "comrade"?
> 　谁把他称作"同志"的？

> Why does everyone think I'm narrow-minded?
> Why is it that everyone thinks I'm narrow-minded?
> 　为什么大家都认为我很小气？

> How did you forget to lock the door?
> How was it that you forgot to lock the door?
> 你怎么忘了锁门？

19.2.4　先行主语 it

1) it 可以用作先行词，作为句子形式上的主语，而把真正的主语移到句子后部去。这可使句子变得更平稳，不致主语太长，显得头重脚轻。这种 it 称为 **先行主语** (Preparatory Subject)。可移到句子后部去的主语最常见的是不定式。句子谓语可有下面几种类型：

a.　be + 形容词 + 不定式：

It is easy to criticize others.　批评别人是容易的。（比较：　To criticize others is easy.）

It's better to be early.　早去好一点。（比较：To be early is better.）

It's absurd to be afraid.　害怕是荒谬的。

It's nice not to be dependent on them.　不依靠他们是好的。

b.　be + 名词 + 不定式：

It was his duty to take care of the orphans.　照顾孤儿是他的职责。

It's a privilege to visit your country.　访问贵国是一大荣幸。

It would be a pity to miss this opportunity.　错过这个机会是可惜的。

It was not my habit to ask people for things.　我没有向人索取东西的习惯。

c.　be + 介词短语 + 不定式：

It was against my principle to do that.　做这样的事有悖我的原则。

It's beyond me to say why.　我无法说明原因。

It's not within my power to help them.　我没有力量帮助他们。

It's unlike him to be late; he's usually on time.　迟到在他来说是不正常的，他一向很准时。

d.　及物动词 + 宾语 + 不定式：

It cost 100 dollars to repair the car.　修车花了一百美元。

It gave me great pleasure to watch them.　观察它们给了我很大的乐趣。

It takes two to make a quarrel.　（谚）吵架要有两个人。

It makes me sick to think about it.　想到那事就让我恶心。

不定式前有时可有 for 引导的短语，表示其逻辑上的主语：

What time would it be most convenient *for me* to call again?　什么时候我再来最方便？

It's getting harder every day *for a poor man* to get a living. 穷人维持生计日益困难。

关于不定式作主语可参阅第 12.1.3 节。

2) 用 it 作先行主语，代表动名词时也不少，这类句子用 "be＋名词" 作谓语时最多 (a)，也可以 "be＋形容词" (b) 或其他结构 (c) 作谓语：

a. *It's no use* studying for an exam at the last minute. 临时抱佛脚来应考是没用的。

It's no good standing here in the cold. Let's go home. 在这寒风中站着没好处，咱们回去吧。

It isn't much fun staying at home by yourself. 一个人待在家里没意思。

It's a waste of time talking to him. 和他谈话是白费时间。

b. *Is it worthwhile* quarrelling with him? 和他吵值得吗？

It's hopeless trying to convince her. 想说服她是没有希望的。

It's terribly tiring working like this. 这样干非常累。

It's pleasant sitting here. 在这里坐着很愉快。

c. *It doesn't matter* waiting a few more days. 再等几天没有关系。

It doesn't make any difference my being there. 我是否在那里无所谓。

It felt funny being dressed like a boy. 打扮成男孩感觉怪怪的。

关于这类句子可参阅第 12.2.2 节，关于用先行主语 it 代表从句将在下面第 19.3.2 节再谈。

19.2.5　it 的其他用法

1) it 还可表示 "是谁 (在某处或做某事)"：

"Who is that (*it*)？" "*It's* me." （在电话上）"你是哪位？" "是我。"

Is that Tom over there? ——No, *it's* Peter. 是汤姆在那里吗？ ——不是的，是彼得。

It's your Mum on the phone. 是你妈来电话。

"Who is that？" "*It's* the postman." "是谁呀？" "是邮差。"

"What's that noise？" "*It's* only the dog." "这声音是怎么回事？" "是狗。"

"Why, *it's* you！" she cried. "啊，原来是你！" 她叫道。

Her face lighted when she saw who *it* was. 看到是谁时她的脸开朗起来。

Nothing has happened. *It's* only the wind shaking the house. 什么也没发生，只是风刮得房子晃动。

2) 还可以用来泛指某件事:

It says here there was a big fire in SoHo.　听说梭荷中心有一场火灾。

Isn't *it* awful!　真糟糕!

It's a shame, isn't *it*?　这很遗憾,是吧?

It doesn't matter.　没关系。

It's getting very competitive in the car industry.　汽车业竞争越来越激烈了。

So you're going to be married this time. When is *it*?　这么说这次你要结婚了,什么时候结?

It's my turn.　该轮到我了。

19.3　主语从句

19.3.1　三种类型的主语从句

主语从句有三种类型:

1) 由 that 引导的主语从句:

That he hasn't phoned is odd.　他没来电话是很奇怪的。

It's certain *that prices will go up*.　物价要上涨是肯定的。

2) 由连接代(副)词引导的主语从句:

Why he left wasn't important.　他为什么走并不重要。

It was uncertain *whether he would come or not*.　他来不来还不肯定。

3) 由关系代词型 what 或 whatever 引导的从句:

What I want is a canvas travelling bag.　我要的是一个帆布旅行袋。

Whatever she did was right.　她做的一切都是对的。

19.3.2　由 that 引导的主语从句

1) 这是用得最多的一种主语从句,但把这种主语从句放在句首是很少的,只有为了强调或谓语较长时才作这样的安排:

That prices will go up is certain.　物价要上涨是肯定的。

That she is still alive is a consolation.　她还活着是令人感到宽慰的。

That she became an artist may have been due to her father's influence.　她成为画家可能是受她父亲的影响。

That she was chosen made a tremendous stir in her village.　她被选中在她

村子里引起很大轰动。

绝大部分主语从句都借助先行主语放到句子后部去。

2）带先行主语的句子主要有下面几类：

a. it + be + 形容词 + that 从句：

It is natural that they should have different views. 他们有不同观点是很
　　自然的。

It was quite plain that she didn't want to come. 很明显她不想来。

It is imperative that we leave at once. 我们必须马上离开。

It's strange that he knows nothing about it. 很奇怪他对此竟一无所知。

b. it + be + 名词 + that 从句：

It's a shame (that) you're sick. 真遗憾你病了。

It's a pity (that) he can't swim. 真遗憾他不会游泳。

It's a wonder that he is still alive. 他还活着真是奇迹。

It was a fearful disappointment to your mother that you didn't come
　　yesterday. 你昨天没来让你母亲大失所望。

c. it + 动词（+ 宾语或状语）+ that 从句：

It happened that she wasn't in that day. 碰巧那天她不在家。

It never occurred to me that perhaps she was lying. 我从未想到或许她
　　是在说谎。

It seems that you're right. 似乎你是对的。

It struck me that we ought to make a new plan. 我忽然想起我们应制订一
　　个新计划。

d. it + 动词的被动语态 + that 从句：

It's said that there has been an earthquake in India. 据说印度发生了地震。

It was rumoured that he was suffering from a stone in the kidney. 谣传说
　　他患有肾结石。

It's reported that the enemy troops have crossed the border. 据报导敌军
　　已越过边界。

It is estimated that 25 million school lunches are sold each day. 据估计每
　　天要出售两千五百万份学校午餐。

e. it + 动词 be + that 从句：

It may be that you'll prove yourself the most suitable man. 或许你会证明
　　自己是最合适的人选。

Is it that the gentleman is not your uncle? 是否那位先生并不是你的叔叔？

No, no, *it couldn't be* that they were interested in him. 不，不，他们不可

能对他有兴趣。

在口语中 that 有时可以省略：

It was clear his words pleased her.　显然他的话使她很高兴。

It's not our fault this has happened.　发生这事不是我们的错。

It strikes me Kent is a nice lad.　我感到肯特是个好小伙子。

19.3.3　由连接代（副）词引导的主语从句

1）这类从句还不少，可放在句首：

When he'll be back depends much on the weather.　他什么时候回来很大程度上取决于天气。

How it was done was a mystery.　这是怎样做的是一个谜。

Who is to be sent there hasn't been decided.　派谁去还没有决定。

Whether we'll succeed remains to be seen.　我们能否成功还要拭目以待。

也可借助先行主语 it 把从句放到句子后部去：

It hasn't been announced *who are the winners*.　谁获胜还没有宣布。

It was clear enough *what he meant*.　他的意思很清楚。

It's no business of yours *where I spend my summer*.　我在哪儿过夏天不干你的事。

It's doubtful *whether we'll be able to come*.　我们是否能来还是个疑问。

虽然两种结构都能用，但带 it 的结构还是用得多一些。

2）用 it 作先行主语时后面也有四类结构：

a. it + be + 形容词 + 从句：

It was not clear to me why he behaved like that.　我不太清楚他为什么会这样做。

It's uncertain whether the game will be held.　球赛是否举行还不确定。

It's doubtful whether the payment is legal.　这样付款是否合法是一个疑问。

It is amazing that he should have said nothing about the murder.　对这起谋杀案他竟然只字未提真令人惊讶。

b. it + be + 名词 + 从句：

It was a mystery how the burglars got in.　小偷怎么进去的是一个谜。

It's a puzzle how life began.　生命如何开始的是一个谜。

It was a question whether he should get married.　他是否应结婚还是个问题。

It is a marvel why he works so hard. 他为什么这样拼命干活令人惊异。

c. it + 动词 (+ 宾语或状语) + 从句:

It doesn't matter much where we live. 我们在哪儿住都没多大关系。

It makes no difference whether we go by train or by boat. 我们坐火车去还是坐船去都无所谓。

It struck her how considerate he was. 她深感他考虑得多么周到。

It became a matter of doubt whether he had really done it. 他是否真做了这事变得可疑起来。

d. it + 动词的被动语态 + 从句:

It is not yet settled whether I am going to America. 我是否去美国还没决定。

Is it known where he went? 有人知道他去哪里了吗?

It is not decided who will edit it. 还没决定谁来对它进行编辑。

It is being considered whether she should be promoted. 正在考虑她是否应当升职。

19.3.4 由关系代词型 what 引导的主语从句

1) 关系代词型 what 也常可引导从句作主语:

What you said is perfectly true. 你说的完全是实情。

What will be, will be. (谚)该发生的事总会发生。

What is over is over. 过去的事就过去了。

What follows is the narrative of his experiences. 下面是他对自己经历的叙述。

What I'm afraid of is their taking her to Paris. 我担心的是他们把她带往巴黎。

What he saw made him tremble. 他看到的情况使他发抖。

What hurt my feelings was the judge's comment. 伤害我感情的是评审员的评语。

What you should do is to choose a company to invest in. 你该做的是选一家公司投资。

2) whatever,whoever 这类词也可以引导主语从句:

Whatever she did was right. 她做的一切都是对的。

I didn't think *whatever they say* amounts to much. 我不认为他们说的话有多大价值。

Whatever she says goes.　一切她说了算。

Whoever comes will be welcome.　谁来都欢迎。

Whoever wants to go may sign up here.　谁想去可以在这里签名。

Whoever gets the job will have lots of work to do.　谁要是得到这份工作，就会有很多活要干。

Whichever (of you) comes in first will receive a prize.　不管(你们)谁第一个到都可以得到一份奖品。

Whichever you want is yours.　你要哪一个，哪一个就归你。

19.4　there 引导的句子

19.4.1　there 引导的句子

1) there 引导的是一种特殊的句子，there 放在句首好似主语，但真正的主语在后面，表示"有…"：

There is a rainbow in the sky.　天上有一道彩虹。

这里的 there 不同于一般的副词 there，它读作 /ðə/，而平常的副词则读作 /ðeə/。

there 常和后面的动词 be 或助动词构成紧缩形式，仿佛它是主语似的：

There's no problem.　没问题。

There's a car coming.　有一辆车开过来了。

There's been a gentleman here asking to see you.　这儿有位先生要见你。

Sooner or later there'll be a big row.　迟早会大吵一场。

在构成问句时，there 也起主语的作用，但真正的主语在后面：

Are there many parks in the city?　城里公园多吗？

Is there a car-park nearby?　附近有停车场吗？

How many new words are there in the text?　这篇课文有多少生词？

2) 通常动词和主语保持一致：

There's a television in the sitting-room.　客厅里有一台电视机。

There're six chairs round the table.　桌子周围有六把椅子。

There're a number of swans on the lake.　湖上有许多天鹅。

如果有两个或更多主语时，动词一般和最近的一个保持一致：

There was a sofa and two armchairs.　有一张长沙发和两张小沙发。

There is a boy and two girls dancing on the meadow.　草坪上有一个男孩和两个女孩在跳舞。

有时也可和所有主语保持一致:

> There were one or two chaps there. 那儿有一两个人。
>
> In addition to her, there were Mr. and Mrs. Delby. 除了她,还有戴尔比夫妇。

──────────

19.4.2　there + 动词 be

1) there 引导的句子大部分都以 be 作谓语动词,可用于各种时态:

> Where *there's* a will, *there is* a way. (谚)有志者事竟成。
>
> *There was* little change in him. 他没有什么变化。
>
> *There has been* no rain today. 今天没下雨。
>
> *There'll be* a concert in the park tonight. 今晚公园里有一场音乐会。

可有各种灵活的译法,表示发生某事,这时不宜译作"有":

> There was thunder in the air. 天上在打雷。
>
> Then there would be a plebiscite. 然后将举行公民投票。
>
> I hope there will be a change in the weather. 我希望天气能变一变。
>
> There was no wind that night. 那天夜里没刮风。

2) 在主语后面有时有修饰语:

> There're ten people *coming to dinner*. 有十个人来吃晚饭。
>
> There're a lot of difficulties *facing us*. 我们面前有很多困难。
>
> There were many things *to be done*. 有许多事情需要做。
>
> What was there *to be afraid of*? 有什么可害怕的?
>
> There are dozens of reasons *why I must leave*. 我有种种必须离职的理由。

3) there 可和 to be 或 being 一道用:

> You wouldn't want *there to be* another world war. 你不会希望再发生一次世界大战吧。
>
> Is it possible for *there to be* any more trouble? 还可能有更多的麻烦吗?
>
> Would you like *there to be* a meeting to discuss the problem? 你希望开一次会来讨论这个问题吗?
>
> I expect *there to be* no argument about this. 我预计对这一点不会有争议。
>
> I shall prefer *there to be* no discussion of such things. 我倒愿意大家别谈这些事。
>
> *There being* nothing else to do, we went home. 由于没别的事要做,我们就回家了。

──────────

19.4.3　there + **复合谓语**

1) there 后面可跟由情态动词和 be 构成的复合谓语：

There may be another demonstration tonight.　今晚可能又有一次示威游行。

There must be something wrong with it.　里面准有问题。

There could be no doubt that he was the best novelist alive.　毫无疑问，他是在世的最优秀的小说家。

There might still *be* hope.　可能还有希望。

There ought to be a comma here.　这儿应当有一个逗号。

There shouldn't be any doubt about it.　对此不应有什么怀疑。

2) 谓语也可能是由不定式构成的复合谓语：

Is there going to be any activity tonight?　今晚有什么活动吗？

There used to be a cinema here.　过去这儿有一家电影院。

There's sure to be a restaurant around.　附近一定有餐馆。

There are bound to be controversial questions.　准会有些有争议的问题。

There seems to be something the matter with her.　她似乎有些问题。

There appeared to be a war between his heart and his mind.　他的情感和理智之间似乎有一场斗争。

19.4.4　there + **不及物动词**

1) there 后面有时可跟别的动词 (通常为不及物动词)：

Once upon a time, *there lived* a fisherman on the island.　很久以前，岛上住着一位渔夫。

There followed a flood of indignation in the newspapers.　随后报纸发出一片愤怒的声音。

There came a knock at the door.　有人敲门。

In 1859, *there came about* a war between the two countries.　1859 年两国间发生了一场战争。

There remained just fifty dollars.　只剩五十美元了。

Hence *there has arisen* the agrarian question.　因此产生了土地问题。

2) 有时状语放在前头 (a) 或插在主语和谓语之间 (b)：

a. *At the top of the hill there stands* an old temple.　山顶上有一座古庙。

In recent years, there has been produced more food than the country needs.

最近几年生产的粮食超过了国家的需要。

In the distance there was heard again the lowing of the cattle.　远处又传来牛叫声。

b. One night *there flew over the city* a little swallow.　有天夜里，一只小燕子从城市上空掠过。

There sprang from the audience a cry of indignation.　听众中突然发出一阵愤怒的吼声。

第20章 谓 语

20.1 谓语的类型

20.1.1 谓语及谓语类型

1) 谓语有广义与狭义之分。广义的谓语指主语之外，包括动词在内的部分，主语可说是句子的主题，谓语指关于主语的情况：

主 语	谓 语（广义）
Beijing	is the capital of the country. 北京是中国的首都。
China	trades with many different countries. 中国和很多国家开展贸易。

狭义的谓语主要指动词，不包括宾语和状语，我们这里讨论的谓语是狭义的谓语。

2) 谓语不等同于动词，却包含动词在内，有些谓语只包含一个动词：

Time *flies*! 光阴似箭!

He *works* in a bank. 他在一家银行工作。

但在很多情况下谓语包含几个词：

She *doesn't like* the idea. 她不赞成这个想法。

I'*ll take care of* the expenses. 费用由我负担。

3) 谓语主要有两类：

● 简单谓语 (Simple Predicate)

● 复合谓语 (Compound Predicate)

20.1.2 简单谓语

1) 凡是由一个动词构成的，不管是什么时态、语态、语气，都属于简单谓语：

She'*ll be leaving* for Hong Kong on April 3rd. 她将于四月三日去香港。

He *has been designing* a new plane model.　他一直在设计一种新的飞机型号。

The space shuttle *will be launched* at 5 p.m.　太空梭将于下午五点发射。

I suggest that the game *be cancelled*.　我建议取消这次比赛。

2）大量成语动词可用作谓语，尽管它们由两个或更多的词构成，仍然是简单谓语：

Dick *fell for* baseball when he was a little boy.　狄克很小就爱上了棒球。

I *shall have* it *out* with him later.　以后我将和他谈清楚。

Ned *left off* talking about the firm.　奈德停止谈论公司的事。

I wish you *wouldn't look down on* this kind of work.　希望你别看不起这种工作。

The windows of our bedroom *looked out upon* the lawns.　我们卧室的窗户面对着草坪。

Share prices *have picked up* recently.　最近股票上涨了。

在第 13.2.3 及 13.3.4 节可以看到大量由成语动词构成的谓语。

20.2　复合谓语

20.2.1　第一类复合谓语

1）这类复合谓语都由两部分构成。有些由"情态动词 + 动词原形"构成：

Can you *explain* this sentence?　你能解释这个句子吗？

She *may be bringing* some friends home.　她可能会带几个朋友来家。

I *might have come to* a wrong conclusion.　我可能得出了一个错误的结论。

He *must have arrived* by air.　他准是坐飞机来的。

Of course she *mustn't leave* us.　当然她不能离开我们。

We *should have* confidence in each other.　我们应当对彼此有信心。

You *needn't have mentioned* it.　你本来不必提到此事的。

No one *dared speak of* it.　没人敢谈及这事。

2）另一些则由不定式和另外的词构成：

I *oughtn't to go on* living this way.　我不应当继续这样生活下去。

We *used to swim* every day when young.　我们小时候天天都游泳。

She *isn't going to make* any concessions.　她不准备作任何让步。

First I'*d have to get* my father's consent.　首先我得征求我父亲的同意。

We *have got to be careful* in such matters.　这种事我们都得小心。

Vesta *happened to be playing* in one corner of the room.　维斯塔恰好在房间的一角玩耍。

I *seemed to have caught* a cold.　我似乎感冒了。

He *is said to have translated* many books into English.　据说他把许多书译成了英文。

They *are not likely to succeed*.　他们成功的希望不大。

3) 许多带复合宾语的句子改为被动结构后，里面都可说包含了一个复合谓语：

They *were made to work* long hours.　他们被迫长时间工作。

He *was forced to make* concessions.　他被迫作出让步。

We're expected to fulfil the task ahead of time.　他们期待我们提前完成任务。

She *was* often *heard to sing* that song.　人们常听见她唱这支歌。

He *was seen to go out* with her.　有人看见他和她一道出去了。

He *was found lying* on the floor.　有人发现他躺在地上。

She *was been kept waiting* for two hours.　有人让她等了两个小时。

He *was known to have taken* money from the Germans.　据传他拿过德国人的钱。

20.2.2　第二类复合谓语

1) 第二类复合谓语主要由"系动词＋表语"构成：

The prospects *looked excellent*.　前景看来极好。

It *sounds a good idea*.　这听起来是个好主意。

I'*m keeping in very good health*.　我身体一直很好。

Roses *smell sweet*.　玫瑰花有香味。

She *is growing restless*.　她变得忐忑不安起来。

He *remained standing* for nearly an hour.　他差不多站了一个钟头。

She *seemed embarrassed*.　她显得很尴尬的样子。

He *appeared perplexed*.　他显得困惑不解。

His hair *turned grey* in a few weeks.　他的头发几星期内就变灰白了。

The prediction *came true*.　这个预言应验了。

Please *stay seated*.　请不要站起来。

He *felt troubled and distressed*.　他感到很烦恼痛苦。

关于这类句子可参阅第 13.5.1 — 13.5.7 节。

2） 有些动词（如 wear，flush，lie 等不及物动词）有时也可跟一个表语，与它构成复合谓语：

He *flushed crimson* with anger.　他气得满脸通红。

The carpet *is wearing thin*.　地毯磨得很薄了。

He *blushed crimson* with embarrassment when she kissed him.　她吻他时他窘得满脸通红。

The snow *lay thick* on the ground.　地上铺着厚厚一层雪。

One of the tigers *broke loose (free)*.　有一头老虎跑出来了。

His promises *rang false* to me.　他的诺言在我听来很虚假。

有时一个不及物动词后跟着一个形容词或名词，说明主语的状态，作用接近于表语，这类结构也可说是一种复合谓语：

She *sat silent* in the corner.　她静静地坐在角落里。

The day *dawned misty and overcast*.　这天天亮时雾气很重，乌云密布。

They *parted the best of friends*.　他们分手时是最要好的朋友。

He *died a rich man (a millionaire)*.　他死时成了富翁（百万富翁）。

有些语法家把这种结构称为 **双重谓语** (Double Predicate)，意思是它们把两个谓语揉和在一起，成为一个谓语。

3） 另外，某些带形容词或名词的复合宾语，在变为被动结构时，也可形成复合谓语：

The walls *were painted light green*.　墙被漆成了淡绿色。

She *was found injured* at the foot of a cliff.　她被发现受了伤躺在一座山崖下。

None of these actions *are considered likely*.　这些行动被认为采取的可能性不大。

He *might be called a truthful boy*.　他或许称得上是一个诚实的孩子。

He *was thought to be a spy*.　他被认为是一名间谍。

He *was made president* of the society.　他被任命为该协会主席。

20.3　表　语

20.3.1　表语表示法

表语亦称 **补语** (Complement)，可由下面这些成分表示：

1） 名词：

He proved *a trustworthy friend*.　结果证明他是一个可靠的朋友。

You're looking *a different person*.　你看起来像是换了一个人。

2）代词：

Seventy-four! You don't look *it*.　七十四啦! 你看起来可不像。

It's *something* to be home again without an accident.　能再次平安到家真不简单。

3）数词：

My daughter is *sixteen* next month.　我女儿下月十六岁。

Gordon Johncock was *third*.　戈登·约翰科克是第三名。

4）形容词：

He has gone *mad (blind)*.　他疯了(眼睛瞎了)。

She looked quite *cheerful* (a little *tired*).　她看上去挺高兴(有点累)。

5）分词：

My teacher is both gentle and *encouraging* towards me.　我的老师既对我很温和又督促我学习。

Where is Shakespeare *buried*?　莎士比亚埋葬在哪里?

6）动名词：

My aunt's hobby is *growing roses*.　我姑姑的爱好是种玫瑰花。

His first job had been *selling home computers*.　他的第一份工作是销售家用电脑。

7）不定式：

An alternative plan might be *for you to go to Lyon*.　另一个计划可能是让你到里昂去。

All you have to do is *to press this button*.　你只需按一下这个电钮。

8）副词：

I'm *off* to Europe on Monday.　我星期一动身去欧洲。

Sales are *down*.　销售量下降了。

9）介词短语：

The Conservatives were once more *in power*.　保守党再次当政。

His show is *on the air* at six o'clock.　他的节目六点钟播放。

10）词组：

They are *twice the size of chickens*.　它们有鸡的两倍大。

That would be *a great weight off my mind*.　这会了却我一大心事。

11）从句：

That's *where we differ*.　这就是我们的分歧所在。

Money is *what they are after*.　他们追逐的是金钱。

关于各种表语的表示法可参阅第13.5.1—13.5.6节。关于现在分词和过去分词作表语的用法可参阅第 12.3.2 及 12.4.2 节。

20.3.2　表语从句

表语从句有三类:

1) 由 that 引导的表语从句 (that 有时省略):

The fact is *(that) she never liked him*.　事实是她从未喜欢过他。

Their first idea was *that he had hidden it*.　他们的第一个想法是他把它藏起来了。

The reason Hollywood was a good place for making movies was *that the sun shines there every day*.　好莱坞是拍电影的好地方，原因是那里天天有太阳。

His only fault is *that he lacks ambition*.　他唯一的缺点是缺乏雄心壮志。

My point is *that you may have to face the problem*.　我的看法是你也许得面对这个问题。

The trouble was *they couldn't agree among themselves*.　问题是他们内部意见都不能统一。

2) 由连接代 (副) 词引导的表语从句:

That's *how matters stand*.　情况就是如此。

That's not *what I meant*.　这不是我的意思。

That was *why he spoke French so funnily*.　这就是他法语讲得这样滑稽的原因。

That's *where the battle took place*.　这就是那次战役发生的地方。

His first question was *whether Holmes had arrived yet*.　他第一个问题是福尔摩斯到了没有。

The question is *who's responsible for what has happened*.　问题是发生了这事该谁负责。

3) 由关系代词型的 what 引导的从句:

I want to be a teacher. That's *what I want to be*.　我想当教师,这是我的志愿。

Times aren't *what they were*.　时代不同了。

Your mother's health is not *what it used to be*.　你母亲的身体已大不如前了。

That's *what we are here for*.　这就是我们来这里的目的。

That's not *what she is after*.　这不是她追求的东西。

She's no longer *what she used to be*.　她已不是过去的她了。

关于这类句子可参阅第13.5.7节。

20.4　主语和谓语的一致

20.4.1　主语和谓语应在数上一致

1) 主语和谓语必须在数上一致，即复数主语须用复数谓语，单数主语须用单数谓语，不受修饰语的影响：

The results of the research *are* to be published soon.　研究成果不久将发表。

The theory advanced by these scientists *is* quite convincing.　这些科学家提出的理论相当有说服力。

What *are* his *views* on this subject?　他对这问题持什么观点？

The suggestion put forward by the girls *has been accepted*.　姑娘们提的建议被接受了。

2) 如果主语是一个抽象概念，一般都用单数谓语：

Smoking cigarettes *is* hazardous to your health.　吸烟危害健康。

Training astronauts *is* not an easy task.　训练宇航员不是一件容易的工作。

That she should oppose these ideas *is* quite natural.　她反对这些意见是很自然的。

"Senior citizens" *means* people over sixty.　"年长公民"指六十岁以上的人。

3) 当主语是 and 连接的两个名词时，在指一样东西时用单数谓语，若指两样东西，则需用复数谓语：

Iron and steel industry plays an important role in our national economy.　钢铁工业在国民经济中起着重要作用。

The food and textile industry depend mainly on agriculture for raw material.　食品工业和纺织工业主要依靠农业提供原料。

To try and fail is better than not to try at all.　尝试而失败也比不尝试好。

To mean to do something and to actually do it are two different things.　打算做某事和真正去做完全是两回事。

4) 如果主语是单数，尽管后面跟有 with, together with, as well as, except 这类词引导的短语，谓语仍用单数形式，因为这种短语多为修饰语：

An iron and steel works, *with several satellite factories*, is being built in that city. 在那个城市正在修建一座钢铁厂和几家卫星工厂。

John, *together with his wife*, was at the party. 约翰和他的妻子参加了晚会。

Lily *as well as Helen* was in mourning. 莉莉和海伦都在带孝。

Everybody *except Tim* speaks some Chinese. 除了蒂姆每人都能讲点汉语。

No one *but myself* knows anything about it. 除了我没有人知道此事。

─────────────

20.4.2 某些代词作主语时的谓语

1) each 和 some，any，no，every 构成的代词作主语时，谓语都用单数形式：

Two boys entered. *Each was* carrying a suitcase. 两个小伙子进来了，每人提着一个箱子。

Somebody wants to see you, sir. 有人要见你，先生。

Is there anything I can do for you? 我能帮你做什么吗？

There's really *nothing* to be said. 真的没什么话可说。

Everybody was glad to see her back. 看见她回来大家都很高兴。

2) both，some，many，few，all (of them) 后的谓语多用复数形式：

Both (of them) *are* English. 两个都是英国人。

Many are for going by plane. 许多人都赞成坐飞机去。

Some (of them) *are* still out of work. (我们)有些人依然失业。

Few of my friends *like* Sheila. 我的朋友中没什么人喜欢希拉。

All present *are* against the idea. 所有在场的人都反对这个主意。

代表不可数东西的代词则跟单数谓语：

So *all is* going well. 因此一切都进展顺利。

Every little helps. (谚)点点滴滴都有用。

Some of the milk *has* gone sour. 有部分牛奶酸掉了。

3) 有些代词可跟单数谓语，也可跟复数谓语，根据意思来决定：

Who has borrowed my pen? 谁借走了我的钢笔？
Who are those girls? 那些姑娘是谁？

Which is my seat? 哪是我的座位？
Which are our seats? 哪些是我们的座位？

None of us has ever been to Japan. 我们谁也没去过日本。
None of the passengers are aware of the danger. 旅客们谁也没有意识到危险。

Neither of the books is of any use to me.　两本书哪一本对我都没用。

Neither are suitable for a newspaper.　两篇都不适合登报。

在个别情况下用单复数谓语都可以:

Is (Are) there any left?　还剩一些(几个)吗?

Neither of the days is (are) suitable.　两个日子都不合适。

None of the telephones is (are) working.　没有一部电话是好的。

20.4.3　一些集体名词作主语的情况

1) 有些集体名词都指复数的人或动物，后面都用复数谓语;

The police *are* going to question him.　警察将审讯他。

The media *are* covering the presidential election thoroughly.　传媒在详细报导总统选举。

Cattle *are* allowed to graze on the village common.　牛群被允许到村子的公有草地上放牧。

Most bacteria *grow* best in slightly acid medium.　多数细菌在微酸性的介质中生长最好。

2) 有些集体名词可跟单数谓语，也可跟复数谓语，视作整体时跟单数谓语，着重于所包含的成员时，则可跟复数谓语:

My family *was* very poor.　我家那时很穷。

Your family *are* quite well, I hope.　我希望你家里人都很好。

There *was* a large audience at the concert.　音乐会听众甚多。

The audience *are* dressed in a variety of ways.　观众有各式各样的打扮。

The committee *is* to deal with the matter.　委员会将处理此事。

The committee *quarrel* as to who its next chairman should be.　委员们就谁应出任下一届主席而争论不休。

The team *is* the best in the league.　这个队是联赛中最强的一队。

The team *are* driving to the game in their own cars.　队员们都自己开车去参加球赛。

有些集体名词后面的谓语用单数或复数都可以:

The enemy is (are) retreating.　敌军正在后撤。

The school's teaching staff is (are) excellent.　这所学校教师素质很好。

The jury is (are) about to announce the winner.　裁判团即将宣布优胜者名单。

The data is (are) correct.　这些数据是正确的。

3）有些集体名词通常跟单数谓语：

The Opposition *was* quick to reply to the charge. 反对党迅速对指控作出反应。

The entire community *is* behind the appeal. 整个社区都支持这项呼吁。

The local press there *is* full of lies. 那里的地方报刊充满谎言。

The play's cast *was* given a standing ovation. 剧组演员受到观众起立鼓掌。

20.4.4 某些名词作主语时的情况

1）有些名词，随着意思的不同，有时跟单数谓语，有时跟复数谓语：

Half of his work *is* to design programmes. 他一半的工作是程序设计。

Half of them *go* to private schools. 他们中有一半人上私立学校。

Two thirds of the earth's surface *is* covered with water. 地球表面的三分之二被水覆盖。

Two thirds of Chad's exports *were* cotton. 乍得三分之二的出口商品是棉花。

A large proportion of the state *is* desert. 该国很大一部分地区是沙漠。

A high proportion of Americans *go* to college. 相当比例的美国人都上大学。

There *was* a considerable variety of opinions. 不同意见相当之多。

A good variety of flowers *were* on show there. 那里展出了各式各样的花。

Statistics *is* a branch of mathematics. 统计学是数学的一个分支。

These statistics *show* that exports are still low. 这些统计数字表示出口额仍然很低。

Youth *is* time for action. 青年时期是活跃的时期。

The youth of today *are* very fond of dancing. 今天的青年人很爱跳舞。

2）有些单复同形的名词要根据意思决定谓语的形式：

All means *have* been tried. 各种手段都试过了。

One means *is* still to be tried. 还有一种手段尚待一试。

This species of rose *is* very rare. 这个品种的玫瑰很罕见。

There *are* thousands of species of butterflies. 蝴蝶有成千上万种。

The steel works *is* closed for the holidays. 这家钢铁厂节假日不开工。

The works *have* closed since January. 这些工厂一月份起就关闭了。

Her offspring *is* like her in every respect. 她的孩子各方面都像她。

Her offspring *are* all in bed by now. 她的孩子们现在都睡觉了。

3）一些以 -s 结尾的单数名词，后面谓语也都作单数：

Phonetics *is* a required subject in our department. 语音学是我们系的一门必修课。

Billiards *is* becoming more and more popular. 打台球越来越流行。

Measles *is* a contagious disease. 麻疹是一种传染病。

A crossroad *is* a place where two roads meet and cross. 十字路口是两条路交叉的地方。

Mathematics *is* a subject studied nearly in every school. 数学是几乎每个学校都学的课程。

也有些以 -s 结尾的词后面可跟单数或复数谓语：

Mumps *are (is)* fairly rare in adults. 成年人患腮腺炎的相当少。

Mathematics *is (are)* well taught in our school. 我们学校数学教得很好。

Their headquarters *are (is)* in New York. 他们的总部在纽约。

第21章 宾 语

21.1 概 说

21.1.1 宾语的种类

宾语有下面几类:

1) **直接宾语** —— 绝大多数及物动词都跟有直接宾语，成语动词有些也跟有宾语，表示动作的对象、承受者或后果:

We love our *motherland*. 我们热爱祖国。(动作对象)

They robbed a *bank*. 他们抢劫了一家银行。(动作承受者)

Then he composed a *symphony*. 此后他谱写了一首交响曲。(动作结果)

Who put forward the *suggestion*? 这建议是谁提出的?

2) **间接宾语** —— 双宾动词后可跟两个宾语，一个是直接宾语，一个是间接宾语，间接宾语表示动作是向某人或为某人做的:

主语	谓语	间接宾语	直接宾语
Auntie	gave	me	a toy car.
My wife	sends	you	her greeting.
I	will play	you	some light music.
He	bought	himself	a new tie.

关于间接宾语可参阅第 13.4.1 节。

3) **复合宾语** —— 是由两部分构成的宾语，后面部分可称为宾语的补语:

主语	谓语	复合宾语
They	asked	him to speak at the meeting.
She	saw	a girl waving to her.
My kids	never heard	the song sung in Italian.
They	elected	him vice-president.

关于这类宾语可参阅第 13.6.1 — 13.6.8 节。

21.1.2　宾语表示法

宾语可以由下面这些成分表示：

1）名词：

May I see your *passport*?　我能看看你的护照吗？

Fasten your *seatbelts*, please.　请系好安全带。

2）代词：

Do you have *anything* to declare?　你有什么东西申报吗？

Give me *some*.　给我一点。

3）数词：

Let me have *one* or *two*.　给我一两个。

They laid off *one-third* of the workers.　他们暂时解雇了三分之一工人。

4）名词化的形容词：

Success goes to *the determined*.　(谚)有志者事竟成。

Respect *the old* and cherish *the young*.　敬老爱幼。

5）动名词：

Stop *acting like a child*.　别像小孩一样。

Has it left off *raining*?　雨停了吗？

6）不定式：

He tried *not to offend her*.　他设法不得罪她。

They asked *to see his ID card*.　他们要求验看他的身份证。

7）复合结构

I find *this weather very trying*.　我发现这种天气很难受。

He had *his passport visaed* for South Korea.　他在护照上盖了去韩国的签证。

8）从句

I'll see *that you get a good seat*.　我一定设法让你有一个好座位。

I don't understand *what you mean*.　我不懂你的意思。

关于不定式和动名词作宾语可参阅第 12.1.4，12.2.3，13.3.5 及 13.3.6 节。

21.2　复合宾语

21.2.1　复合宾语的类型

复合宾语主要有下面几种类型：

1) 名词 (代词)＋形容词

The pot calls *the kettle black*. (谚)五十步笑百步。

I've never known (seen) *you so cheerful*. 我从未看见你这样高兴过。

2) 名词(代词)＋名词

He nominated *Coy Ambassador to France*. 他任命科伊为驻法大使。

Don't be formal. Call *me Jim*. 别太拘礼，叫我吉姆好了。

3) 名词 (代词)＋不定式

Tell *them to hurry up*. 让他们赶快。

What made *you think so*? 什么使你这样想的?

4) 名词 (代词)＋分词

I heard *a nightingale singing in the wood*. 我听见一只夜莺在林中歌唱。

You must have *your lungs X-rayed*. 你必须把肺部透视一下。

5) 名词 (代词)＋介词短语或副词

I found *him in excellent spirits*. 我发现他情绪好极了。

I'm pleased to see *you back*. 看到你回来了,我很高兴。

21.2.2　第一类复合宾语——名词(代词)＋形容词

这类复合宾语比较普通,不少动词可以跟这种宾语:

Have I *made myself clear*? 我的意思讲清楚了吗?

That *kept her warm*. 这使她身子很暖和。

The accused man *declared himself innocent*. 被告宣称自己是无辜的。

He *shouted himself hoarse*. 他把声音都喊哑了。

Then he will *hold you responsible* for it. 那样他就会要你来对它负责。

常见的这类动词有:

account	beat	believe	call	confess	consider
count	declare	drive	dye	feel	find
get	have	hold	imagine	keep	knock
leave	like	make	paint	pronounce	prove
push	render	send	set	shout	slam
sleep	stain	suppose	sweep	think	turn
want	wish				

关于这种结构可参阅第 13.6.1 节。

21.2.3 第二类复合宾语——名词(代词)+ 名词

跟这类复合宾语的动词也不少，如：

I *find her a very sensible woman*.　我发现她是个很有头脑的女子。

They *considered Paris the heart of France*.　他们认为巴黎是法国的心脏。

She *counted herself a fortunate wife*.　她认为自己是个幸运的妻子。

They *dubbed him a traitor*.　他们叫他叛徒。

He *entitled the book Crime and Punishment*.　他给这书题名为《罪与罚》。

常见的这类动词有：

acclaim	appoint	brand	call	christen	consider
count	declare	dub	elect	entitle	fancy
imagine	judge	label	make	name	nominate
pronounce	suppose	term	think	vote	

关于这种结构可参阅第 13.6.2. 节。

21.2.4 第三类复合宾语——名词(代词)+ 不定式

1) 跟这类复合结构的动词很多：

He strongly *advised her not to do so*.　他使劲劝她不要这样做。

She *asked me to get in touch with him*.　她要我和他联系。

He *instructed Sophia to remain where she was*.　他嘱咐索菲娅留在原处。

Permit me to introduce myself.　请允许我介绍一下自己。

They *urge me to write a play for children*.　他们催我写一个儿童剧。

You know I *wish you to be happy*, don't you?　你知道我是愿意你幸福的，是吧？

常见的这类动词有：

advise	allow	ask	bear	beckon	beg
bribe	bring	cause	challenge	command	commission
condemn	compel	dare	defy	enable	encourage
expect	force	get	hate	help	inspire
instruct	intend	invite	know	like	oblige
order	permit	persuade	prefer	press	prompt
provoke	recommend	remind	request	require	sign
stimulate	teach	tell	train	urge	want
warn	wish				

2) 在某些动词后, 这类不定式只限于动词 be (a), 但其他动词的完成式和进行式有时也可以用 (b):

a. They *considered him to be a selfish man.* 他们认为他是个自私的人。

They *believed these principles to be universally true.* 他们相信这些原则是放之四海而皆准的。

I *know this to be a fact.* 我知道这是事实。

All the neighbours *supposed her to be a widow.* 所有邻居都以为她是寡妇。

We *discovered her to be a good cook.* 我们发现她很会做饭。

We have *shown the story to be false.* 我们已表明这个报导是虚假的。

b. I *consider him to have acted disgracefully.* 我认为他的行为很可耻。

I *believe her to have done right.* 我相信她做得对。

They *know the man to have been a spy.* 他们知道这人当过间谍。

They *suppose man to have descended from animals.* 他们认为人是由动物进化而来的。

They *suspected him to be dying.* 他们猜想他已命在旦夕。

We *thought him to be hiding in the woods.* 我们以为他躲在树林里。

3) 有少数动词后面的复合宾语包含一个不带 to 的不定式:

What *makes you think so?* 什么使你这样想?

Don't forget to *have him come.* 别忘了让他来。

Delighted to *hear you say that.* 很高兴听你这样说。

For an instant I *saw his face go pale.* 一时间我看见他脸色变得苍白。

I *watched him get into his jacket.* 我瞧着他穿上上衣。

They *felt the atmosphere grow tense.* 他们感到气氛变得紧张起来。

4) 个别成语动词后也可以跟这类复合宾语:

He *called on* Tom to answer the question. 他叫汤姆回答这个问题。

I am *counting on* you to help me through. 我指望你帮助我度过难关。

She *motioned to* me to be silent. 她对我做手势要我别说话。

He *pleaded with* me to go back. 他恳求我回去。

They *prevailed upon* me to remain a little longer. 他们劝我再稍微多待一会儿。

We are *waiting for* the rain to stop. 我们在等雨停下来。

关于由不定式构成的复合宾语可参阅第 13.6.5 和 13.6.6 节。

21.2.5　第四类复合宾语——名词(代词)＋分词

1) 有不少动词后面可跟由现在分词构成的复合宾语：

The teacher *caught a boy cheating*.　老师发现一个男生(考试)作弊。

I could *feel the wind blowing on my face*.　我能感觉到风吹着我的脸。

I tried to *keep things going* by a little teaching.　我设法教点书来维持生活。

His question has *set me thinking*.　他的问题让我深思。

They *left me sitting alone there*.　他们丢下我一个人坐在那里。

They *watched the sun setting behind the trees*.　他们瞧着太阳在树后徐徐西沉。

能跟这种复合宾语的动词常见的有：

bring	catch	discover	fancy	feel	find
get	hate	have	hear	imagine	keep
leave	like	listen to	look at	notice	observe
remember	see	set	smell	start	stop
understand	watch				

2) 也有不少复合宾语由过去分词构成：

You should *make your views known*.　你应当让人了解你的看法。

You'll have to *get that tooth filled*.　你得把那颗牙(请医生)补一补。

She's *having her eyes tested*.　她正在验光。

Rarely had I *seen him so worked-up*.　我很少见他这样激动过。

We *want the work finished* by Saturday.　我们希望这工作在星期六以前完成。

He *felt himself powerfully attracted* by the idea.　他感到自己受到这想法的强烈吸引。

跟这类复合宾语的动词常见的有下面这些：

acknowledge	consider	declare	feel	find	get
have	hear	keep	leave	make	notice
order	see	want	watch	wish	

关于包含分词的复合结构可参阅第 13.6.7 和 13.6.8 节。

21.2.6　第五类复合宾语——名词(代词)+介词短语或副词

这类复合宾语由介词短语 (a) 或副词 (b) 构成:

a. *Make yourselves at home*, everybody.　大家请随便一点。

They *found her* already *in the hands of a doctor*.　他们发现她已有医生照顾。

He *held the others in contempt*.　他对别人都看不起。

Please *ask her into the dinner-room*.　请让她到餐厅来。

His jokes *set the whole room in uproar*.　他的笑话引起哄堂大笑。

I know you'll be able to *help me out of the difficulty*.　我知道你能帮助我克服困难。

b. We went to her house but *found her out*.　我们去她家,但发现她外出了。

You'd better *ask her round* here.　你最好请她到这里来。

We're *having some friends in* tonight.　今晚我们要请些朋友来家里。

We must *help forward every project* we can.　我们必须尽力帮助促进每一个计划。

Let's *turn the TV on (off)*.　咱们把电视机打开(关上)。

He knew how to *put his ideas across*.　他知道怎样把他的意思讲清楚。

能跟这种复合宾语的结构比较少。关于这种结构可参阅第 13.6.3 和 13.6.4 节。

21.3　用 it 作宾语

21.3.1　人称代词 it 作宾语

1) 人称代词 it 常可以用作宾语,代表刚提到的一样东西:

Have you got my express mail?　——Yes, I've got *it*.　收到我的快件了吗?　——收到了。

Where is my bike?　——Pam is riding *it*.　我的自行车在哪儿?　——帕姆在骑。

Where is the car key?　——I put *it* in your drawer.　我的车钥匙在哪儿?　——我放在你抽屉里了。

You can't eat your cake and have *it*.　(谚)蛋糕吃了就没有了。

也可以代表一个婴儿:

How about the baby?　——I'll take care of *it*.　宝宝怎么办?　——我来照看。

2) 也可表示刚提到的一件事:

If I can help, I'll do *it*. 如果我能帮忙，我一定会这样做。

If he doesn't come, I can't help *it*. 如果他不来我也没有办法。

You promised to support us. You've got to do *it*. 你答应支持我们的，你就应当这样做。

I want to go to the dance. ——Your father won't like *it*. 我想去参加舞会。——你父亲不会赞成的。

If I have improved in any way, I owe *it* all to you. 如果说我有什么改进，那都得归功于你。

You have saved my life. I shall never forget *it*. 你救过我的命,我永远不会忘记。

21.3.2 先行词 it 作宾语

it 也可用作先行宾语,借助它把真正的宾语放到句子后部去,特别是用在一些复合宾语中。it 可以:

1) 代表不定式:

She found *it difficult to convince him*. 她感到很难让他相信。

He thought *it best to be cautious*. 他认为最好小心行事。

I'd think *it well worthwhile to go*. 我认为去是很值得的。

He felt *it his duty to take good care of them*. 他感到好好照顾他们是他的责任。

He made it *a rule to do an hour's work in the garden every day*. 他给自己规定每天在花园里干一小时的活。

2) 代表 that 引导的从句 (that 有时省略):

I took *it for granted (that) you would be coming*. 我想当然地认为你会来的。

Depend upon *it, we shall win the war*. 放心吧,我们会打赢这场战争的。

I take *it from your silence that you don't want to go*. 从你的沉默中我猜想你不想去。

You can put *it that it was arranged before*. 你可以说这是以前安排的。

I have *it on my conscience that I haven't done my duty*. 我良心不安,感到没尽到我的责任。

He doesn't want *it to be known that he's going away*. 他不想让人知道他准备离开。

间或代表连接代(副)词引导的从句或动名词:

> He hasn't made *it* clear *when he is coming back.* 他没有说明他什么时候回来。

> They haven't made *it* known *where the meeting is to take place.* 他们没宣布会议在哪里开。

> I think *it* very unwise *going on like this.* 我认为这样进行下去很不明智。

21.3.3　一些意义不明确的 it

有些作宾语的 it，并不指具体的东西，意思很含糊，甚至没有意思:

> The last train's gone. We'll have to *foot it.* 最后一班火车已经开了,我们得步行了。

> He escaped, and *tramped it* home, working at odd jobs. 他逃了出来,沿路打零工,像流浪汉似的回到家里。

> He likes to *lord it over* the union staff. 他喜欢对工会下属发号施令。

> You may have to *rough it* a bit if you come to stay. 如果你来住,你可能要过点苦日子。

> *Leg it* to the nearest telephone. 跑到最近的电话亭去打。

> I shall *have it out* with him later. 以后我要和他谈清楚。

> He *has it over* me that he's been to Egypt and I haven't. 他比我强的是他去过埃及而我没去过。

> *Hang it all*, we can't wait all day for them. 见鬼,我们不能一整天都等着他们。

> I'm feeling rather *off it* today. 我今天感到不大舒服。

> We'll make *a day of it.* 我们要玩一整天。

21.4　宾语从句

21.4.1　由 that 引导的宾语从句

1) 有大量动词可以跟由 that 引导的宾语从句 (有时 that 可省略):

> I *know* she was against us. 我知道她反对我们。

> I *felt* that she had a strong will. 我感到她有坚强的意志。

> We *suspected* that it was a trick to get our money. 我们疑心这是骗我们钱的圈套。

Who can *guarantee* that he'll keep his word?　谁能保证他会遵守诺言？

She suddenly *revealed* that she was not married.　她突然透露出她并没有结婚。

He *wrote* me that his wife was not well.　他给我写信说他妻子身体欠佳。

常见的能跟 that 从句的动词有：

acknowledge	add	admit	advise	agree	allege
announce	answer	assure	boast	believe	claim
command	comment	complain	confess	confirm	decide
demand	deny	determine	direct	discover	(not)doubt
dream	estimate	expect	explain	fear	feel
find	forget	guarantee	guess	hear	hint
hope	imagine	inform	insist	intend	know
learn	maintain	mean	move	order	predict
prefer	promise	propose	prove	provide	read
realize	recommend	remember	reply	report	request
require	reveal	say	see	sense	shout
show	suggest	suppose	suspect	swear	tell
think	urge	vote	wish	write	

其中有些词后面的连词 that 常可省略，如 believe, suppose, presume, think; 在 say, see, know, hear, propose, understand 和 be told 后，that 可用可不用，但在笔语中不宜省略。

2）有时可用 it 作先行宾语，而把从句放到句子后部去：

You can depend upon *it, I shall be there.*　你放心，我会去那里的。

I feel *it a terrible thing that my mother should have to toil so endlessly.*　我母亲只好这样没完没了地吃苦受累，我感到太可怕了。

I take *it they have left for home.*　我猜想他们已经回家了。

Why don't you bring *it to his attention that you're too ill to go on working?*　你为什么不让他注意到你病得厉害不能继续工作？

I've heard *it said that you've won a scholarship.*　我听说你获得了一项奖学金。

She has seen to *it that all the children are well taken care of.*　她已设法让所有孩子都得到很好的照顾。

关于这类结构可参阅第 13.3.7 和 13.4.2 节。

21.4.2　由连接代（副）词引导的从句

1）也有不少动词可跟连接代词或副词引导的从句：

She was curious to know *where we had been*.　她很想知道我们去了哪里。

Write me *how you got home*.　写信告诉我你怎么到家的。

She inquired *why he had not thought of that before*.　她问他为什么以前没想到这一点。

Only you can decide *who is the best choice*.　只有你能决定谁是最佳人选。

I wonder *what you call these flowers*.　我想知道你把这些花叫作什么。

常见的这类动词有：

agree	ask	calculate	care	decide	describe
discover	discuss	enquire	exclaim	explain	express
find out	forget	guess	hear	imagine	inquire
know	learn	realize	recollect	remember	report
reveal	say	see	show	suggest	tell
think	understand	watch	wonder		

2）whether 和 if 也常可用来引导宾语从句：

I don't know *whether you like flowers*.　不知道你是否喜欢花。

I'll see *whether I can help you*.　我会留意我是否能帮助你。

I wonder *whether you would mind doing me a favour*.　不知你是否介意帮我一个忙。

She didn't say *if her aunt was still with them*.　她没说她姨母是否还跟他们在一起。

I asked her *if I might call and see her*.　我问她我是否可以去看她。

I'm wondering *if you would care to spend the evening with us*.　不知你愿不愿意和我一起共度今宵。

关于这些结构可参阅第 13.3.8 节。

21.4.3　由关系代词型 what 引导的从句

1）关系代词型 what 引导的从句也常可用作宾语：

Show me *what you've bought*.　把你买的东西给我看看。

She began to criticize *what I had done*.　她开始批评我做的事。

We cannot do *what you ask of us*.　我们不能做你要求我们做的事。

As a friend of yours, I want to tell you *what I hear*.　作为你的朋友,我想把听到的事告诉你。

He could not express *what he felt*.　他无法表达内心的感受。

Have you got *what you wanted*?　你要的东西得到了吗?

甚至用作介词的宾语(其他从句这样用时是比较少的):

Don't poke your nose into *what doesn't concern you*.　别多管闲事。

Can you give us a description of *what has happened*?　你能否描述一下发生的事情?

Who is responsible for *what has happened*?　发生的事谁负责?

She was shocked by *what she had seen*.　她看到的情况使她震惊。

They were not affected by *what he said*.　他的话对他们并无影响。

He was indifferent to *what others were doing*.　他对别人在做些什么漠不关心。

2) whatever 这类词也可引导宾语从句:

I will do *whatever you wish*.　我将做你想要我做的任何事。

I'll just say *whatever comes into my head*.　我想到什么就说什么。

Please talk to me about *whatever is troubling you*.　请给我谈谈任何使你烦心的事。

I always succeed in *whatever I try*.　我干什么都很成功。

"*Whatever you want* you shall have," said the Fairy.　仙女说,"你要什么就会得到什么。"

She would tell him *whatever news she got*.　她会把她听到的任何消息告诉他。

You should read whatever book your teacher recommended.　你应该阅读老师推荐的任何书籍。

3) whichever, whomever 也可引导宾语从句:

Buy *whichever is cheapest*.　买最便宜的。

I said he might have *whichever he liked*.　我说他喜欢哪个就拿哪个。

Take *whichever seat you like*.　你想坐哪儿就坐哪儿。

They can vote *in whichever district they choose*.　他们可以随意选择在哪个区投票。

Give it to *whomever you like*.　你愿意把它给谁就给谁。

She can marry *whoever she chooses*.　她想和谁结婚就可以和谁结婚。

21.5　直接引语和间接引语

21.5.1　直接引语

1) 在引用别人的原话时，被引用的句子称为 **直接引语** (Direct Speech):

"*I never eat meat*," he explained.　　"我从不吃肉，" 他解释说。

"What's the matter?" "*Nothing*," she answered.　"什么事?"　"没事，" 她答道。

He said, "*I have lost my wallet*."　他说，"我的皮夹子丢了。"

在用直接引语时，引语前后要加引号，引导引语的动词称为 **引用动词** (Reporting Verbs)。除 say，ask，answer，reply 之外，还有许多其他引用动词:

"Listen," she *whispered*.　"听着，"她低声说。

"Who is it?" Wilson *shouted*.　"是谁?"威尔逊嚷到。

"Look out!" she *screamed*.　"小心！"她叫到。

"I'm leaving at once," he *told* me.　他告诉我，"我马上要走了。"

"It won't cost much," she *assured* me.　她向我保证，"这花不了多少钱。"

"But it will take longer," Jim *objected*.　吉姆反对说，"但这样花的时间就要长一些。"

2) 引用动词多数放在后面，有时放在前面(见上例)，间或插在引语中间:

"Darling," Max *said* to her, "don't say it's impossible."　"亲爱的，"麦克斯对他说，"不要说这是不可能的。"

"Sit up," he *commanded*, "and hold out your hands."　"坐直了，"他命令道，"伸出手来。"

"I presume," he *commented*, "that she will learn how to do it in time." "我想，"他评论说，"慢慢她会学会怎么做的。"

"I do hope," *said* Mary, "they haven't forgotten all about it."　"我真希望，"玛丽说，"他们没把这事全忘掉。"

3) 在把引用动词放在后面时，有时主语和动词位置可以颠倒 (特别是主语较长时):

"We wish we didn't have to take exams," *said the children*. "要是我们不用考试就好了，"孩子们说。

"Bill wants to go alone," *said Lily*, "but I'd rather he went with a group." "比尔想一个人去，"莉莉说，"但我宁愿他带一组人去。"

"I shall be 20 tomorrow," *said Peter*.　彼得说，"明天我二十岁。"

"The children had better go to bed early，" *said Tom*.　"孩子们最好早点去睡觉，"汤姆说。

如果主语较短，放在前面更好一些：

"What's the meaning of that?" *he asked*.　"这是什么意思?"他问道。

"No, thank you," *she replied*.　"不用了，谢谢你。"她回答道。

"Here you are at last!" *she exclaimed (exclaimed Jack's mother)*.　"你终于到了！"她(杰克的母亲)叫道。

21.5.2　间接引语

1) 当用自己的话报导别人的话时，被报导的部分称为 **间接引语** (Indirect Speech)，这种结构称为 **引语结构** (Report Structure)：

Kitty said *she could wait another day*.　凯蒂说她可以再等一天。

Tom replied *that he was going by plane*.　汤姆回答说他将坐飞机去。

这时被引语部分常常是引用动词的宾语。除了 say，reply 这几个词以外，还有许多动词可引导间接引语：

I *felt* I had little energy left.　我感到没剩多少力气了。

I *guess* they've already got home.　我猜他们已经到家了。

She *complained* that the exam was too hard.　她抱怨说考题太难了。

He *explained* that the buses were not running.　他解释说公共汽车停驶了。

I *objected* that he was too young for the position.　我反对说他年纪太小不能担任这个职务。

I *protected* that I had no view of that sort.　我分辩说我没有那种看法。

在多数情况下，引语都由连词 that 引导，但在 say，tell 等词后(在口语中)可以省略：

He said (that) he had lost the wallet.　他说他的钱包丢了。

Tell him I am out.　告诉他我不在家。

2) 把直接引语变成间接引语时，要根据意思改变人称：

"I've already taken **your** son to the nursery," Jane said.
Jane said **she** had already taken **my** son to the nursery.

"I bought these pearls for **my** mother," Joe said.
Joe said he had bought the pearls for **his** mother.

She said to me, "**You** speak English better than **me**."
She told me that **I** spoke English better than **her**.

"**I**'ll come to help **you** whenever **you** need my help," he answered her.

He answered her that **he** would come to help **her** whenever she needed **his** help.

3）同时要根据时态呼应的原则把时态加以调整（关于这一点可参阅第 8.8.1 节）：

She said, "I **need** a calculator." （一般现在时）

She said that she **needed** a calculator. （一般过去时）

Nancy said, "I'**ll call** again later." （一般将来时）

Nancy said that she'**d call again** later. （一般过去将来时）

Jim said, "I'**m expecting** a long distance call." （现在进行时）

Jim said that he **was expecting** a long distance call. （过去进行时）

Paul said, "Our team **has won** the match." （现在完成时）

Paul said that their team **had won** the match. （过去完成时）

He said, "I'**ve been waiting** here for an hour." （现在完成进行时）

He said that he'**d been waiting** there for an hour. （过去完成进行时）

She said, "I'**ll be using** the car myself on the 12th." （将来进行时）

She said she'**d be using** the cat herself on the 12th. （过去将来进行时）

He said, "I **took** it home with me." （一般过去时）

He said that he **had taken** it home with him. （过去完成时）

如一般过去时有表示具体时间的状语，也可以不变：

She said, "I **was born** in 1995." （一般过去时）

She said (that) she **was born** in 1995. （仍用一般过去时）

4）指示代词、地点及时间状语等也需要作必要的变动：

He said, "She **is coming this week**."

He said that she **was coming that week**.

He said, "I saw her **the day before yesterday**."

He said he'd seen her **two days before**.

She said, "I'**ll come here** again **tonight**."

She said (that) she **would go there** again **that night**.

He said, "I **arrived yesterday morning**."

He said (that) he **had arrived the morning before**.

She said, "My husband'**ll be back tomorrow evening (next week)**."

She said (that) her husband'**d be back the following evening (week)**.

He said, "This **happened two years (days) ago**."

He said (that) that **had happened two years (days) before**.

He said, "I'm starting **the day after tomorrow**."
He said he was starting **in two days' time**.

这类改变大致可以下表表示：

	在直接引语中	在间接引语中
指示代词	this (place)	that (place)
	these (places)	those (places)
时间状语	now	then
	Today, tonight	that day, that night
	this week (month, etc.)	that week (month, etc.)
	yesterday	the day before
	the day before yesterday	two days before
	last week (month, etc.)	the previous week (month, etc.)
	2 days (a year, etc.) ago	2 days (a year, etc.) before (earlier)
	tomorrow	the next (following) day
	the day after tomorrow	in two days' time
	next week (month, etc.)	the next (following) week (month, etc.)
地点副词	here	there
动词	come, bring	go, take

不过改变时不必过于机械，要根据实际情况灵活掌握，如果说话的地点没有改变，或是当天说的话，有时状语就不必变了。例如：

She said (today) she'd call back again tonight.

She said (just now) she had got back yesterday.

She said (this morning) she was leaving tomorrow afternoon.

He said (yesterday) he was leaving today.

5） 在下面情况下动词形式不作改变：

a. 虚拟语气：

"If I *had* the instruction manual, I *should* (*would*) *know* what to do," said Tom.
Tom said that if he *had* the instruction manual he *would know what to do*.

"If my children *were* older I *would emigrate*," he said.

He said that if his children *were* older he *would emigrate*.

"We wish we *didn't have to take exams*," said the children.

The children said (that) they wished they *didn't have to take exams*.

"It's time we *began planning our holidays*," she said.

She said that it was time they *begin planning their holidays*.

b. 某些情态动词:

"I *would like* to see it," she said.

She said she *would like* to see it.

He said, "Helen *might ring* today."

He said that Helen *might ring* that day.

He said, "We *should (ought to) have* more time for recreation."

He said that they *should (ought to) have* more time for recreation.

"The children *had better go* to bed early," said Nancy.

Nancy said that the children *had better go* to bed early.

"We *used to work* in the same department," Paul said.

Paul said that they *used to work* in the same department.

"I *could do* it tomorrow," Peter said.

Peter said that he *could do* it the next day.

c. 过去进行时 (有时不变):

She said, "When I saw them they *were playing* tennis."

She said that when she saw them they *were playing* tennis.

He said, "We often met when we *were living* in Paris."

He said that they often met when they *were living* in Paris.

6) 除了用 say 以外，还可以用各种动词作引用动词:

"I've just heard the news."	He **told me** he'd just heard the news.
"It won't cost much."	He **answered** me it wouldn't cost much.
"I did it."	He **admitted** that he had done it.
"He was rude to me."	She **complained** he'd been rude to her.
"You are late."	He **whispered** that I was late.
"I can speak six languages."	He **boasted** he could speak six languages.
"I won't tell anyone."	He **promised** he wouldn't tell anyone.

21.5.3　间接问句

1) 直接问句可以变为间接问句，如：

He said, "Where is she going?"

He asked where she was going.

从这里可以看出间接问句前无需加连词，连接代 (副) 词就起连接作用了。间接问句除连接代 (副) 词提前外，其他部分都用自然语序，同时后面不再加问号，而用句号：

直接问句	**间接问句**
Who lives next door?	He asked who lived next door.
What happened?	He asked what had happened.
When is the next train?	She asked when the next train was.
Where are you going?	She asked me where I was going.
Who do you want to see?	He asked me whom I wanted to see.
How do you like the tea?	She asked me how I liked the tea.
Why don't you go by air?	She asked him why he didn't go by air.

2) 一般问句、选择问句和反意问句变成间接问句之时，前面可用 if 或 whether：

直接问句	**间接问句**
Do you know her?	He asked me if (whether) I know her.
Did you see the accident?	He asked me if I had seen the accident.
Do you want to go by train or by plane?	He asked me whether (if) I wanted to go by train or by plane.
Are you leaving today or tomorrow?	She asked whether (if) I was leaving that day or the following day.
You like the city, don't you?	She asked whether (if) I liked the city.

3) 有时直接问句也可以变为不定式(结构)或其他结构：

Shall I bring you some tea?	He **offered** to bring me some tea.
Will you stand still?	He **told** me to stand still.
Will (Would) you file the letters?	He **asked** me to file the letters.
Would you like to come for a drink?	He **invited** me round for a drink.
Shall we meet at the theater?	He **suggested** meeting at the theatre.

21.5.4   如何引用祈使句和感叹句

1）在引用祈使句时，多使用一个不定式，前面谓语根据语气来决定：

Lie down, Tom.	He **told** Tom to lie down.
Don't swim in that river.	He **warned** us not to swim in that river.
Go away!	He **ordered** them to go away.
Do give us more time, please.	He **begged** me to give them more time.
Show us your passport.	They **asked** her to show them her passport.
Please sit down.	She **invited** me to sit down.
Please don't take any risks!	She **begged** (**implored**) him not to take any risks.
Don't forget to post that letter.	He **reminded** me to post that letter.
Go on, apply for the job.	He **urged** me to apply for that job.
See a neurologist.	He **advised** me to see a neurologist.
Stay where you are.	He **commanded** us to stay where we were.

2）有时可使用一个从句：

Let's break into small groups.	Someone suggested that we should break into small groups.
Don't open the letter.	He said I wasn't to open the letter.
Meet me at the station.	He says we are to meet him at the station.
Don't drive so fast.	He told me that I shouldn't drive so fast.
Let them go to their consul.	She said they should go to their consul.
Lift the ban.	He commanded that the ban be lifted.
Release that man at once.	He ordered the man be released at once.

3）感叹句一般不宜改为间接引语，用直接引语更能传神。偶尔也有改为间接引语的：

⌠ "What a dreadful idea!" he said.
⌡ He exclaimed that it was a dreadful idea.

⌠ "Good!" he exclaimed.
⌡ He gave an exclamation of pleasure.

⌠ "Ugh!" she exclaimed, and turned the programme off.
⌡ With an exclamation of disgust she turned the programme off.

⌠ He said, "Good luck!"
⌡ He wished me (good) luck.

"Congratulations!" she said.

She congratulated me.

"Liar!" he said.

He called me a liar.

"What a lovely garden!" he said.

He remarked with admiration that it was such a lovely garden.

"Oh, dear! I have torn my shirt!" he exclaimed.

He exclaimed in exasperation that he had torn his shirt.

第22章　定　语

22.1　定语表示法

22.1.1　定语表示法

定语可以用下面这些成分表示：

1) 形容词：

It's a *fine (windy, rainy, warm)* day. 这是一个晴朗(刮风、下雨、暖和)的日子。

He's a *sensible (kind, selfish, cruel)* man. 他是一个有头脑(善良、自私、残酷)的人。

2) 代词 (和限定词)：

Whose child is it? 这是谁的孩子？

Help yourself to *some (more)* fish. (再)吃一点鱼。

3) 数词：

There are *twenty* students in our class. 我们班上有二十名学生。

Is it your *first* visit to Japan? 你是第一次到日本？

4) 名词或名词所有格：

She is a *college* graduate. 她是大学毕业生。

What's your *government's* attitude towards the problem? 你们政府对此态度如何？

5) 分词 (短语)：

These are the roads *leading to the beach*. 这些是通往海滨的路。

He disapproved of the *proposed* conference. 他不赞成提议召开的会议。

6) 不定式 (短语)：

She was quiet for days *to come*. 在以后的好些天中她都沉默寡言。

I've something important *to discuss with you*. 我有一件重要的事情要和你商谈。

7) 介词短语：

He is absorbed in his work *on bacteria*.　他专心于他的细菌研究。

Who is that girl *with a pigtail*?　那个梳辫子的女孩是谁?

8) 副词：

I have nothing special *on* tonight.　今晚我没有什么特别活动。

On my way *home*, I continued angry with Betty.　在回家的路上我继续生贝蒂的气。

9) 词组或合成词：

Is anything *the matter* with you?　你出什么事了?

He is an *easy-going* man.　他是一个好说话的人。

10) 从句：

Is there anything *I can do for you*?　有什么事我可以帮你做吗?

She's a girl *everyone likes*.　她是个人人都喜欢的姑娘。

22.1.2　用分词作定语

1) 现在分词作定语的时候不少，有些现在分词已变成形容词：

The town's water comes from the *surrounding* hills.　该城市的用水来自周围的群山。

She did well under *trying* conditions.　她在困难条件下干得很不错。

There were *growing* doubts about the victory statement.　对这胜利的声明越来越多的人表示怀疑。

That's a *convincing* argument.　这是一个有说服力的论点。

It's a rather *boring* book.　这是本相当枯燥乏味的书。

We had a most *stimulating* conversation.　我们有过一次令人兴奋的交谈。

It was a very *touching* story.　那是个非常动人的故事。

There is another *pressing* matter which we ought to take up.　还有一件我们该办的要紧事。

2) 在不少情况下，现在分词跟在所修饰的词之后，其作用相当于一个定语从句：

There is a lady *asking to see you*.　有一位女士要求见你。

The girl *sitting by my side* is my cousin.　坐在我旁边的是我表妹。

It's a room on the second floor, *looking on the street*.　它是三楼上一个临街的房间。

Jane joined the line of people *waiting for the bus*. 简加入到那排候车者之中。

Here is a map *showing you how to get there*. 这儿有一张地图,告诉你怎样去那里。

There are two hundred children *studying here*. 有两百个孩子在这里学习。

The old lady *waving to us* is my aunt. 向我们挥手的老太太是我姨母。

Those of you *wishing to join us* please stay for a few minutes. 你们中间想参加我们活动的人请留几分钟。

3) 过去分词也常用作定语,有些已变成形容词:

The *excited* children were opening their Christmas presents. 兴奋的孩子们正在打开他们的圣诞礼物。

The *worried* look deepened on her face. 她脸上的愁容加深了。

We have a very *crowded* schedule. 我们的日程很紧。

He passed the *required* examination and became a doctor. 他通过了规定的考试成了医生。

Her father is a *retired* general. 她父亲是一位退休将军。

The *escaped* convict has been captured. 逃犯被抓获了。

It was a *cautiously worded* statement. 这是个措辞谨慎的声明。

It was a *beautifully furnished* bedroom. 这是一间陈设漂亮的卧室。

4) 过去分词也可引导短语作定语,放在所修饰词后面,相当于一个定语从句:

That summer we launched a rocket *designed by ourselves*. 那年夏天我们发射了一枚我们自行设计的火箭。

What did you think of the play *put on by the students*? 学生们演的戏你觉得怎样?

They showed a French feature film *dubbed into English*. 他们放映了一部有英语配音的法国故事片。

I seconded the motion *made by Gray*. 我赞同格雷提出的动议。

He turned over in his mind the idea *presented by Dad*. 他考虑了一下爸提出的想法。

He joined an organization *headed by Lord Berry*. 他加入了一个以贝里勋爵为首的组织。

She is a nurse *trained by ourselves*. 她是我们自己培养的护士。

The tiny seed *planted ten years before* had flowered. 十年前种的一小颗种子最后开花了。

关于分词作定语可参阅第 12.3.3 和 12.4.3 节。

22.1.3　用不定式作定语

1) 在一定的句型中可用不定式作定语：

I have tons of letters *to answer*.　我有大量的信要回。

There is nothing *to be done now*.　现在已无法可想了。

I'll go and get something *to drink*.　我去找点饮料。

The teacher assigned us some books *to read*.　老师指定了几本书要我们阅读。

She needed someone *to take care of her bab*y.　她需要一个人帮她看孩子。

They were the first *to bear hardships*, the last *to enjoy comforts*.　他们吃苦在前，享乐在后。

She is not a girl *to act rashly*.　她不是一个卤莽行事的姑娘。

He is a nice man *to work with*.　他是个好共事的人。

2) 在某些名词后常可用不定式作定语：

Has he the **ability** to do the work?　他有能力干这工作吗？

His **anxiety** to go was obvious.　他亟于想去是很明显的。

Their **attempt** to hurt her failed.　他们伤害她的企图失败了。

His **decision** to resign was welcomed by the Opposition.　他辞职的决定受到反对党的欢迎。

I haven't had **chance** to think yet.　我还没有时间考虑。

I had not the **courage** to tell you.　我没有勇气告诉你。

You have no **right** to do such a thing!　你没有权利这样做！

常见的能跟不定式作定语的名词有：

ability	ambition	anxiety	attempt	campaign
chance	courage	decision	determination	drive
eagerness	effort	failure	inclination	intention
movement	need	opportunity	plan	promise
reason	right	struggle	time	way
wish				

3) 不定式有时也可代替一个定语从句：

Perhaps in years *to come* we'll meet again.　也许在未来的岁月中我们还

会再见面。

In the lectures *to follow*, she talked of her trip to Peru. 在后来的讲座中，她谈到了她的秘鲁之行。

She made a list of things *to be taken on the way*. 她开了一张要带在路上用的物品清单。

These are the two trainee teachers *to be sent to work there*. 这是将派到那里工作的两位实习教师。

We are invited to a party *to be held in our club next Friday*. 我们被邀请参加下周五在俱乐部开的晚会。

She had little time left *in which to make the necessary preparations*. 她没剩多少时间来做必要的准备。

关于不定式作定语的问题可参阅第 12.1.6 节。

22.1.4　介词短语和副词作定语

1）介词短语作定语的时候不少，如：

The streets *about the castle* are full of places *of historic interest*. 城堡附近的街道到处是名胜古迹 。

The plan *for the year* was fulfilled ahead of schedule. 今年的计划已提前完成。

One might call it a mistake *in tactics*. 我们也许可以称其为战术上的错误。

She began to give us her views *on the costumes*. 她开始告知我们她对那些服装的看法。

He is not worthy to talk to a man *like you*. 他不配和你这样的人谈话。

She is a woman *of even temper*. 她是个性情温和的女人。

No rose *without a thorn*. (谚)没有不带刺的玫瑰。

2）某些名词后常跟介词短语作定语：

She has a great **fear** *of snakes*. 她非常怕蛇。

He shows an **absence** *of initiative*. 他表现出缺乏主动性。

I was impressed by her **anxiety** *for knowledge*. 她对知识的渴望给我留下了深刻的印象。

Loyalty *to his moral convictions* was his dominating passion. 对道德信念的忠诚是他的主导感情。

He showed great **jealousy** *of their success*. 对他们的成功他显得很是嫉

炉。

He had lost his **interest** *in politics*.　他失去了对政治的兴趣。

She could not bear the thought of **separation** *from her children*.　想到要和
孩子们分开她就难以忍受。

3) 副词作定语的时候也不少：

The clouds *above* began to get thicker.　上方的云朵开始密集起来。

From the hill top we could see the plains *below*.　从山顶上我们可以看到
下面的平原。

He tried to write poetry in his *off* hours.　在空闲时他试着写诗。

Have you anything *on* this evening?　你今晚有什么活动吗？

She went to see them on her evenings *out*.　凡她晚上外出总去看他们。

Take the *up* escalator.　坐往上的电梯。

The *then* headmaster ordered these textbooks.　那时的校长订了这些教材。

I called on Richard on my way *back*.　在回途中我看望了理查德。

22.2　名词和名词词组作定语

22.2.1　名词作定语

1) 名词经常可用作定语，有些已成为固定搭配，甚至构成合成词：

information desk 问讯处	service counter 服务台
cat food 猫食	fish pond 鱼塘
music hall 音乐厅	art circles 艺术界
piano concerto 钢琴协奏曲	violin solo 小提琴独奏
football match 足球赛	tennis player 网球手
news bulletin 新闻简报	press conference 记者招待会
test paper 考卷	book report 读书报告
liver trouble 肝炎	lung cancer 肺癌
kidney stone 肾结石	heart attack 心脏病发作
bank account 银行户头	credit card 信用卡
contact lens 隐形眼镜	life insurance 人寿保险
blood pressure 血压	case history 病历
birth control 生育控制	family planning 计划生育
health centre 医疗中心	emergency room 急诊室
income tax 所得税	import duty 进口税

brain drain 人才外流

greenhouse effect 温室效应

feature film 故事片

science fiction 科幻小说

food poisoning 食物中毒

cotton wool 药棉

space station 太空站

space shuttle 航天飞机

air conditioner 空调器

air-conditioning 空调(设备)

aircraft carrier 航空母舰

arms race 军备竞赛

mineral water 矿泉水

nail varnish 指甲油

welfare state 福利国家

generation gap 代沟

2) 还可用合成名词作定语：

a long-distance call 长途电话

first-class tickets 头等舱机票

a deep-sea diver 深海潜水员

a full-page ad 整版广告

one-way traffic 单向交通

two-way traffic 双向交通

first-page news 头版新闻

second-hand shop 旧货商店

a part-time job 兼职工作

full-time staff 全职工作人员

third-world countries 第三世界国家

last-minute arrangement 最后一分钟的安排

day-to-day teaching 日常教学

a life-and-death struggle 生死斗争

one-parent families 单亲家庭

first-rate surgeon 一流的外科医生

a five-star hotel 五星级饭店

nuclear-power program 核能计划

关于名词作定语可参阅第 3.5.2 节。

22.2.2 由名词和 of 构成的定语

1) 由名词和 of 构成的定语非常多，而且非常有用：

a bottle of orange juice 一瓶橘汁

a cup of coffee 一杯咖啡

a glass of milk 一杯牛奶

a carton of yoghurt 一盒酸奶

a packet of cigarette 一包香烟

a tin of sardines 一听沙丁鱼

a pound of sugar 一磅白糖

a liter of beer 一公升啤酒

a bar of chocolate 一大块巧克力

a loaf of bread 一大块面包

a slice of meat 一片肉

a portion of pudding 一份布丁

a roll of paper 一卷纸

a yard of velvet 一码丝绒

an ounce of gold 一盎司金子

a spoonful of medicine 一匙药

a pair of glasses 一副眼镜

a pair of pants 一条裤子

a game of chess 一盘棋

a game of volleyball 一场排球赛

a fit of anger 一阵怒气

a bit of advice 一点忠告

a set of books 一套书	a series of problems 一系列问题
a ray of hope 一线希望	a shower of criticism 一阵批评
an expanse of water 一片水域	a stretch of land 一片土地
a crowd of people 一群人	a gang of thieves 一伙小偷
a pack of wolves 一群狼	a pride of lions 一群狮子
a school of fish 一大群鱼	a herd of cattle 一群牛
a string of pearls 一串珍珠	a bouquet of flowers 一束花
a bunch of grapes 一串葡萄	a clump of trees 一丛树

2) 也有些这类定语由复数名词构成:

lots of people 很多人	tons of fruit 大量的水果
rows of houses 一排排的房子	heaps of books 大量的书
miles of swamps 大片的沼泽地	quantities of food 大量的食物
masses of work 大量的工作	torrents of rain 倾盆大雨
numbers of tourists 大批游客	gusts of wind 一阵阵的风
groups of children 一群群的孩子	columns of smoke 一缕缕的烟

关于这类定语可参考第 6.4.3 节。

22.3 定语从句

22.3.1 限制性定语从句

1) 大多数定语从句对所修饰词的意思加以限制, 表示"…的人 (或东西)", 称为 **限制性定语从句** (Defining Attributive Clauses), 如:

The man *who robbed him* has been arrested. 抢劫他的人被逮捕了。

The girl *whom I saw* told me to come back today. 我见到的那个姑娘叫我今天再来。

That's the best hotel *(that) I know*. 这是我所知道的最好的旅馆。

These are the books *(which) you ordered*. 这些是你订购的书。

2) 这类从句多由关系代词 (a) 或关系副词 (b) 引导:

a. Everyone *who (that) knew him* liked him. 认识他的人都喜欢他。

The friend *with whom I was traveling* spoke French. 和我一道旅行的那位朋友能讲法语。

The film is about a spy *whose wife betrays him*. 这电影是讲一个间谍, 他的妻子出卖了他。

The car *which (that) I hired* broke down. 我租的汽车坏了。

b. At the time *when I saw him*, he was quite strong. 　以前我看到他的时候，他身体挺壮实的。

This is the village *where I was born*. 　这是我出生的村子。

These are the reasons *why we do it*. 　这些就是我们这样做的理由。

3) 在限制性定语从句中，当关系代词在从句中作宾语时，在绝大多数情况下都可以省略，特别是在口语中，在被修饰的词为 all，everything 等词时尤其如此：

Have you got the postcard *(which) I sent you*? 　我寄给你的明信片收到了吗？

These are the things *(that) you need*. 　这些就是你要的东西。

Have you got everything *you need*? 　你需要的东西都有了吗？

Anything *I can do* for you? 　我能帮你做什么吗？

All *you have to do* is to fill out this form. 　你只需要填这张表就行了。

That's the only thing *we can do now*. 　这是我们现在唯一能做的事。

You can take any room *you like*. 　你随便要哪间房都行。

4) 有些表示时间的定语从句并不由 when 引导，特别是在某些句型中：

Every time *the telephone rings*, he gets nervous. 　电话铃一响他就紧张。

This was the first time *I had serious trouble with my boss*. 　这是我第一次和老板发生严重纠纷。

Come any time *you like*. 　你随便什么时候来都行。

In the ten days *I was there* I gained four pounds in weight. 　在那里的十天中我体重增加了四磅。

But help never stopped coming from the day *she fell ill*. 　从她生病的那天起就不断有人来帮忙。

She made me feel at home the moment *I arrived*. 　我刚到达她就给我宾至如归的感觉。

Throughout the period *I was in London*, it rained heavily. 　我在伦敦期间一直下着大雨。

where 间或也可省略：

This's the place *(where) we met yesterday*. 　这是我们昨天碰头的地方。

在 way 后也可跟一定语从句，不需关系代词或副词：

That's the way *I look at it*. 　这就是我对这事的看法。

They can't help seeing things in the way *they do*. 　他们不由自主地以这种方式看事情。

I did not like the way *he eyed me*. 　我不喜欢他瞪着眼睛瞧我的样子。

〔注〕在口语中甚至在从句中作主语的关系代词间或也能省略:

There's a strange man *(that) lives in that small village.* 有一个怪人住在那个小村子里。

There's something *(that) keeps worrying me.* 有件事总使我发愁。

There's a table *stands in the corner near the window.* 挨着窗子的角落里有一张桌子。

22.3.2　非限制性定语从句

1) 非限制性定语从句 (Non-defining Attributive Clauses) 对所修饰的词没有限制词义的作用,而只是补充一些说明,通常都有一个逗号把它和句子的其他部分分开,在译成中文时,这个从句多译成一个并列句。限制性定语从句拿掉以后,句子意思常发生变化,甚至不能成立,而非限制性定语从句拿掉以后对剩下部分没有太大的影响:

Peter, *who had been driving all day*, suggested stopping at the next town.　彼得开了一天的车,提议在下一座城市停下来。

Paul, *whom everyone suspected*, turned out to be innocent.　大家都怀疑保罗,后来证明他是无辜的。

Mr. Smith, *for whom I was working*, was very generous about overtime payments.　史密斯先生是我的老板,他付超时工资很大方。

This is George, *whose class you will be taking*.　这是乔治,你将接手教他的班。

The 9:30 train, *which is usually very punctual*, was late today.　9点30分的火车通常都很准时,今天却误点了。

This house, *for which he paid $ 150, 000*, is now worth $ 300,000.　这所房子他买时花了十五万美元,现在值三十万美元了。

They went to the Royal Theatre, *where they saw Ibsen's Peer Gent*.　我们去了皇家剧院,在那里我们看了易卜生的《彼尔·英特》。

Sunday is a holiday, *when people do not go to work*.　星期天是假日,这一天人们不上班。

应注意的是,在这类从句中不能使用关系代词 that 和关系副词 why,也不能省略任何关系副词,这类从句主要出现在书面语中。

2) 在非限制性定语从句中 which 和 whom 常可和 of 或其他介词连用:

It now has 20,000 hectares of land, *more than two-thirds of which* are under cultivation. 现在它拥有两万公顷土地, 其中三分之二已经耕种。

The buses, *most of which* were already full, were surrounded by an angry crowd. 公共汽车大部分都已满载, 周围是一大群愤怒的人。

I picked up the apples, *some of which* are badly bruised. 我拾起了那些苹果, 其中有些碰损很严重。

It had drafted two constitutions, *one of which* was never put in force. 它草拟了两份宪法, 其中一份从未实施过。

This morning some Port wine arrived, *for which* I know I have to thank you. 今天早上送来了一些波尔图红葡萄酒, 对此我知道我得感谢你。

She had eight children, *three of whom* lived to grow up. 她生了八个孩子, 其中三个长大成人了。

Her sons, *both of whom* work abroad, ring her up every week. 她的两个儿子都在国外工作, 每周都给她打电话。

I met the fruit-pickers, *several of whom* were college students. 我碰到那些摘水果的人, 其中有几个是大学生。

3) which 有时不代表一个名词, 而代表前面句子的全部或部分意思:

They rely on themselves, *which* is much better. 他们依靠自己, 这样好得多。

He invited us to dinner, *which* was very kind of him. 他请我们吃饭, 这是他的好意。

He has to work on Sundays, *which* he doesn't like. 他星期天得工作, 这是他不喜欢的。

He changed his mind, *which* made me very angry. 他改变了主意, 这使我很生气。

He drank beer, *which* made him fat. 他喝啤酒, 这使他发胖。

When deeply absorbed in work, *which* he often was, he would forget all about eating or sleeping. 他常常聚精会神地工作, 这时他会废寝忘食。

She was very patient towards the children, *which* her husband seldom was. 她对孩子们很耐心, 她丈夫却很少这样。

4) which 在从句中有时作定语:

I called him by the wrong name, for *which mistake* I should apologize. 我把他的名字叫错了, 对此错误我应当道歉。

He is studying economics, *which knowledge* is very important today. 他在

学经济学, 这种知识今天很重要

Tom spent four years in college, during *which time* he learned French. 汤姆在大学待了四年, 在此期间他学了法语。

I may have to go into hospital, in *which case* I won't be going on holiday. 我可能得住院, 如果那样我就不去度假了。

关于定语从句还可参阅第5.6.1—5.6.5节和第15.1.6节。

〔注〕在书面语中, whose 有时指某样东西:

His house, *whose* windows were all broken, was a depressing sight.
他的房子, 窗户都破了, 让人看了感到沮丧。

The car, *whose* handbrake wasn't very reliable, began to slide backwards. 这辆车的手刹车不太牢靠, 开始向后滑动。

It was an island, *whose* name I have forgotten. 它是一座岛屿, 名字我忘了。

22.3.3　一些其他的定语从句

1) as 也可以用作关系代词, 可引导定语从句, 主要和 such 连用:

We have *such* grapes *as* you never saw. 我们有你从未见过的葡萄。

They felt *such* heat in the jungle *as* they had never felt before. 在丛林中他们感受到了从未感受过的炎热。

He returned with *such* provisions *as* were needed. 他回来时带来了所需的用品。

Such money *as* he earned was spent on spirits and tobacco. 他挣的那点钱都花在烟酒上了。

such 和 as 有时连在一起:

We hoped to give you a chance *such as* nobody else ever had. 我们希望给你一个别人从未有过的机会。

There was a look of fear in his eyes, *such as* people have when they are suddenly awakened. 他眼中透出一种人们突然被叫醒时露出的惊恐情绪。

as 还可以单独引导定语从句:

Sophia was not unconscious, *as* could be judged from her eyes. 索非娅并未失去知觉, 这从她的眼神中可以看出来。

He was a foreigner, *as* I knew from his accent.　他是个外国人,我从他的口音中可以听出来。

He is a teacher, *as* is clear from his manner.　他是一位教师,这从他的举止上可以看得很清楚。

As was expected, he performed the task with success.　正像预料的,他成功地完成了任务。

2) but 也可用作关系代词来引导定语从句,意思接近于 that (who)...not (这种用法已经有些陈旧):

There is no tree *but* bears some fruit.　(谚)没有不结果实的树。

There are very few *but* admire his talents.　很少有人不佩服他的才华。

Surely there isn't a mother *but* faces this problem.　可以肯定,凡是母亲都面临着这个问题。

3) whereby, wherein, whereupon 也可引导定语从句:

They've set a plan *whereby* (=by which) you can spread the cost over a period. 他们定出了一个办法,照此你可以分期付款。

We need to devise a system *whereby* people can liaise with each other.　我们需要设计一种系统,通过它人们可以互相联络。

He gazed once more around the room, *wherein* (=in which) were assembled his entire family.　他再次注目于屋内各处,那里聚集了他全家。

I told her she looked fat, *whereupon* (=upon which) she threw the entire contents of a saucepan at me and burst into tears.　我告诉她她看上去胖了,听了这话她把平底锅里的东西都向我泼来,然后便放声大哭。

这种用法仅限于书面语,而且有些陈旧。

22.4　同位语

22.4.1　用名词、代词或数词作同位语

1) 在名词后常可跟另一名词作它的同位语,说明它指谁:

She is my niece *Maria*.　她是我的侄女玛丽亚。

同位语有两种:

a. 限制性同位语 —— 它和前面的名词 (代词) 关系比较紧密,中间没有逗号把它们分开:

My aunt *Lena* is staying with me.　我的姨母丽娜和我们住在一起。

He wrote a biography of the Russian writer *Tolstoy*.　他写了一部俄国作家托尔斯泰的传记。

You *girls* are much more active than us *boys*.　你们女生比我们男生活跃多了。

b. 非限制性同位语 —— 它和前面名词的关系比较松散，中间通常有一个逗号把它们分开(表示略有停顿)：

This is Professor Baker, *head of our department*.　这是我们的系主任贝克教授。

They are staying at Beidaihe, *a summer resort in Northern China*.　他们现在北戴河，它是华北的一个避暑胜地。

We completed the project in six months, *half the usual time*.　我们用六个月时间完成了这项工程，这只是平常时间的一半。

We have everything we need: *land, funds and technology*.　我们拥有所需的一切：土地、资金和技术。

Qinghai, *the largest inland body of salt water in China*, lies 3,198 meters above sea-level.　我国最大的内陆咸水湖青海湖海拔 3,198 米。

One, *Haisipi Island*, has an area of 0.46 sq. km. and the other, *Bird Island*, measures 0.11 sq. km.　一个叫海西皮岛，面积0.46平方公里，另一个叫鸟岛，面积 0.11 平方公里。

多数的同位语属于后一类。

2) 有些同位语是代词(a)或是数词(b)：

a. We're *both* from (*both* came from) the north.　我们俩都是北方人。

The theory *itself* is all right.　这理论本身没有问题。

We *each* put forward a proposal.　我们每人提出了一个建议。

They *none* of them said anything.　他们谁也没有说什么。

She seemed different from us *all*.　她似乎和我们大家都不同。

b. Is there room for us *two*?　有我们两人的位置吗?

You *three* sit here.　你们三人坐这里。

Another example is John Brown Senior, now *66*, who has been here for 40 years.　另外一个例子是老约翰·布朗，现在六十六岁，在这里已经四十年了。

Some 485 million people, *about two-fifths of our population*, live in this immense area.　约有四亿八千五百万人，占我们人口的五分之二，居住在这片辽阔的地区。

22.4.2   用形容词或词组作同位语

1) 有些同位语可以是形容词:

People, *old and young*, came out to greet the distinguished visitors. 老老少
    少都出来迎接贵宾。

Middle-aged, tall and thin, he looked the typical Shanxi farmer. 他是中年
    人, 瘦高个儿, 看上去是一个典型的山西农民。

2) 有些同位语结构复杂一些, 带有一个副词或代词:

Xiao Yan, *normally a timid girl*, argued heatedly with them about it. 小燕
    平常是一个腼腆的姑娘, 现在也和他们热烈地辩论此事。

It has several waiting rooms, *all airy and filled with chairs and sofas*. 它有
    几间候车室, 通风很好, 摆满了椅子和长沙发 。

Two phosphate mines, *one in Hubei and the other in Guizhou*, are being
    speedily built. 两座磷矿, 一在湖北, 一在贵州, 正在加速建设。

These methods, *systematically summarized*, are now being popularized in
    the whole country. 这些方法经过系统总结, 正在全国推广。

这类同位语也可以提前, 特别是主语比较短时, 来给它以突出的位置:

A peasant by birth, Liu Qiang is straightforward in character. 刘强是农民
    出身, 是个直性子。

A skilful hand at improving tools, Xiao Hu helped to make a new type of
    cutter. 小胡是改革工具的能手, 他帮助制作了一种新型刀具。

Formerly a worker himself, he is now an engineer. 他过去是工人, 现在
    是工程师了。

3) 有些同位语结构更复杂一点, 由 for example, including 等引导:

They visit eight cities, *for example, London and Paris*. 他们访问了八座城
    市, 如伦敦和巴黎。

New Zealand possesses rich mineral deposits, *including gold*. 新西兰拥有
    丰富的矿藏, 包括黄金。

The children like the animals, *particularly the panda*. 孩子们很喜欢那些
    动物, 特别是熊猫。

I like all the kids, *especially Lester*. 我喜欢所有的孩子, 特别是莱斯特。

I'm pleased with only one boy, *namely George*. 我只喜欢一个男孩子, 那
    就是乔治。

He is a cutter — *that is to say, a man who sells knives and sharp tooles*. 他
    是一位刀具匠, 也就是说, 一个出售各种刀和锋利工具的人。

22.4.3　同位语从句

1) 有很多名词后可以跟 that 引导的从句，说明其内容，可称为**同位语从句** (Appositive Clauses):

There was no **doubt** *that he was a fine scholar*.　毫无疑问，他是位优秀的学者。

He was conscious of the **fact** *that she did not approve of what he was doing*.　他意识到她不赞成他在做的事。

We received a **message** *that he would be absent*.　我们收到了他将缺席的消息。

We have **proof** *that this man committed the crime*.　我们有证据说明是这个人犯的罪。

I've expressed the **opinion** *that she can act*.　我表明了她能演戏的看法。

I have good **hopes** *they will give you a visa at Locarno*.　我抱有很大希望，他们会在洛迦诺发给你签证。

I had the **impression** *that she chose her words with care*.　我有印象，她选词很小心。

He presented **evidence** *that his thesis was based on original research*.　他提交证据表明，他的论文是根据原先的研究写成的。

I had no **idea** *that your husband was opposed to my visit*.　我不知道你丈夫反对我来访。

He came to see her in the **belief** *that he will be welcome*.　他来看她，相信他会受到欢迎。

He had the **feeling** *that he would not see her again*.　他感觉他再也见不到她了。

I've come to the **conclusion** *that it won't be wise to do so*.　我得出结论这样做是不明智的。

There is a **rumour** *that you have resigned*.　有谣言说你辞职了。

The **report** *that he was going to resign* was false.　他将辞职的传闻是假的。

There is some **possibility** *(that) he may be late*.　他有可能晚到。

I give my **guarantee** *that he will support the idea*.　我(向你)保证他会支持这个想法。

Tears filled her eyes at the **thought** *that she might never see him again*.　想到她可能再也见不到他，她眼中充满了泪水。

They received **assurance** *that the Union would stand by them*.　他们得到保证工会将支持他们。

2） 同位语从句有时和前面的名词分开：

The **rumour** spread *that a new school would be built here*. 谣传这里要盖
　　一所新学校。

The **news** got about *that he had won a car in the lottery*. 消息传开说他彩
　　票中奖赢得了一辆汽车。

The **story** goes *that he often beats his wife*. 传说他经常打老婆。

The **order** soon came *that all civilians must evacuate the village*. 不久传
　　来命令，所有村民必须撤离村庄。

Report has it *that five people were killed in the accident*. 据传这次事故中
　　死了五个人。

The **thought** came to him *that maybe the enemy had fled the city*. 他突然
　　想到敌人可能已逃离这座城市。

3） 在少数情况下可用连接副(代)词引导的从句作同位语：

You have no idea *how worried I was*. 你不知道我多发愁。

I have no idea *why she left*. 我不知道她为什么走了。

He had no idea *what a remarkable woman Maggie is*. 他不知道玛吉是个
　　多么出色的女人。

There is some doubt (as to) *whether John will come on time*. 对约翰是否
　　会准时到有一些怀疑。

第23章 状 语

23.1 状语表示法

23.1.1 状语表示法

状语可以由以下成分表示:

1) 副词:

He *secretly* decided to leave the town. 他私下决定离开这座城市。

We'll raise the money *somehow*. 我们将以某种方式筹集这笔钱。

2) 介词短语:

He traveled *in the desert for six months*. 他在沙漠里走了六个月。

We have friends *all over the world*. 我们的朋友遍天下。

3) 不定式(短语):

I went there *to see my grandmother*. 我到那里去看我奶奶。

The suitcase is too heavy *to be carried by a child*. 箱子太重小孩拿不动。

4) 分词(短语):

Being a poor teacher, he can't afford to buy a car. 他是一位穷教师,买不起汽车。

Compared to her affection, nothing else had any worth. 和她的感情相比,别的东西都没有什么价值。

5) 形容词:

He said nothing but sat *silent* smoking. 他没说话,只静坐在那里抽烟。

Fresh from the oven, rolls are delicious. 刚出炉的小面包很好吃。

6) 词组:

I shall stay *another five months*. 我将再待五个月。

First thing in the morning we swept the courtyard for the landlord. 每天早上我们的第一件事就是给房东扫院子。

7) 复合结构:

It being a holiday, the library isn't open. 这天是假日,图书馆不开门。

They will send you the book for $ 2.50, *postage included*.　他们将把书寄给你，书价2.50美元，邮资在内。

8）从句：

Next time you come in, please close the door.　下次你进来时请关好门。

However often I try, I can't find the answer.　不管尝试多少次，我都找不到答案。

间或可以用名词作状语：

We've been sitting *hours* waiting for you.　我们坐了好几个钟头等你。

She's feeling *miles* better today.　她今天感到好多了。

—————————————

23.1.2　不定式（短语）作状语

1）不定式常可作状语来表示目的(a)、结果(b)、程度(c)、原因(d) 等：

a. We can send a car over *to fetch you*.　我们可以派车去接你。

She had suffered so much *to bring up the children*.　她受了很多苦来把孩子带大。

The test questions are kept secret, *so as to prevent cheating*.　考题都保密以防止作弊。

b. Who could be so mean *as to do a thing* like that?　谁会这样缺德做出这样的事？

He hurried to the place *only to find the house empty*.　他赶到那里只发现房子里空无一人。

She left home, *never to return again*.　她离开了家，再也没有回来。

c. It was too late *to do anything now*.　现在做什么都已为时太晚。

You're far too clever *to have done that*.　你很聪明，不会做出这种事的。

We are fortunate enough *to get an empty car*.　我们很幸运，找到了一辆空车。

d. I rejoice *to see you here*.　在这里见到你很高兴。

She shuddered *to think of it*.　想到这事她不寒而栗。

What has happened *to make you so sad*?　出了什么事让你这样伤心？

2）在许多作表语的形容词后可跟不定式(短语)作状语(多表示原因)：

I'm sorry *to have given you so much trouble*.　对不起给你添了这么多麻烦。

I'm surprised *to hear you say that*.　听到你这样讲我很吃惊。

Be careful *not to break anything.* 小心点别打破什么东西。

I was wrong *to tell her about it.* 我把这事告诉她是错误的。

有很多形容词后面可跟不定式，常见的有：

able	afraid	angry	anxious	apt
ashamed	bound	careful	certain	clever
considerate	content	cruel	curious	delighted
destined	determined	disappointed	due	eager
easy	fit	fortunate	free	frightened
glad	good	grieved	happy	impatient
inconsiderate	keen	kind	likely	lucky
naughty	pained	prepared	proud	prompt
quick	ready	reluctant	right	rude
shocked	slow	sorry	sure	surprised
thoughtless	unable	unfortunate	unlikely	unwilling
unwise	willing	wise	worthy	wrong

3) 不定式(短语)还可以用来修饰整个句子，可称为**句子状语** (Sentence Adverbials)：

To be frank, your English is not flawless. 坦率地说，你的英语不是完美无暇的。

To be honest, I don't quite agree with you. 说老实话，我不完全同意你的意见。

We must go cautiously, *to be sure*. 的确，我们得谨慎行事。

The dog is, *so to speak*, a member of the family. 狗可以说是家庭的一个成员。

To tell you the truth, I hate to do it. 说真的，我不愿这样做。

To make a long story short, they began to study the problem in earnest. 长话短说，他们开始认真研究这个问题。

You are wrong about the facts *to begin with*. 首先你把事实都弄错了。

To put it mildly, she's just a bit inquisitive. 说得轻一点，她就是有点爱打听。

To be fair, he wasn't entirely to blame for that. 说句公道话，这不能全怪他。

This is inconsistency, *to say the least*. 说得再轻些，这也是前后矛盾。

关于不定式作状语的情况可参阅 12.1.7 节和 13.5.9 节。

23.2　副词作状语

23.2.1　副词作状语

1）副词的主要作用就是作状语，特别是以 -ly 结尾的副词，它们可以修饰动词 (a)，也可以修饰形容词、副词等 (b)：

a. He looked at me *suspiciously*.　他用怀疑的眼光看着我。

He *angrily* denied that he had stolen the document.　他气愤地否认他偷了文件。

She *kindly* waited for me.　她好心等候我。

He behaved *badly*.　他表现很差。

b. You're *entirely* wrong.　你完全错了。

Perhaps you're *partly* right.　或许你有一部分是对的。

He behaved *extremely* badly.　他表现极差。

They were getting along *fairly* well.　他们相处得相当好。

2）还有相当多副词不以 -ly 结尾，它们可以修饰动词 (a)，也可以修饰形容词或副词 (b)：

a. I've seen that man *somewhere*.　我在什么地方见过那个人。

She speaks French *well*.　她法语讲得好。

Round and round flew the plane.　飞机不断盘旋着。

She is living *abroad*.　她现在国外居住。

b. You've done *quite* well.　你干得挺好。

I have been *rather* unwell this week.　这星期我感到相当不舒服。

The bag isn't big *enough*.　这袋子不够大。

Pretty soon the lilacs would be in bloom.　很快丁香就要开花了。

23.2.2　句子副词

有一些副词可以修饰整个句子，说明说话人的态度，称为**句子副词** (Sentence Adverbs)：

Honestly, I think you're a little prejudiced.　说真的，我感觉你有点偏见。

Luckily, she were in when I called.　幸好我去时她在家。

Curiously enough, he had never seen the little girl.　说也奇怪，他从未见过那小女孩。

Most likely, he's gone to bed.　很可能他已经睡了。

What he says is true, *possibly*.　他的话可能是真的。

常见的这类副词如:

actually	apparently	briefly	certainly	clearly
curiously	evidently	fortunately	frankly	happily
honestly	inevitably	luckily	maybe	most likely
naturally	of course	perhaps	possibly	strangely
surely	surprisingly	typically		

23.2.3　起连词作用的副词

还有许多副词可起连词的作用,使句子与上下文连系更紧密,从而使句子更流畅:

She went to a party and *therefore* did not study her lesson.　她去参加了晚会,因此没复习功课。

The cost of materials rose sharply last year. *Accordingly*, this increase was passed on to the consumer in higher prices.　去年原料价格猛涨,因此,这一成本的增加以提价的方式转嫁到了消费者头上。

There were no news; *nevertheless* she went on hoping.　没有消息,尽管如此,她还继续期待着。

Bicycling is good exercise; *moreover*, it doesn't pollute the air.　骑自行车是很好的运动,而且不会污染空气。

这类副词常见的如:

accordingly	besides	consequently	first	furthermore
hence	however	lastly	moreover	nevertheless
otherwise	secondly	so	then	therefore
thirdly	thus			

23.2.4　一些特别的副词

1) 不少副词与形容词同形:

I bought it *cheap*.　我买得很便宜。(比较: It's very cheap.)

I *clean* forget about it. 这事我完全忘了。(比较: Is it clean?)

Come *close*. 走近些。(比较: He's close to my house.)

He doesn't play *fair*. 他不能公平行事。(比较: It's a fair comment.)

下面这些常用词都既可作副词又可作形容词:

cheap	clean	clear	close	daily	dead
dear	direct	downstairs	early	easy	extra
fair	far	farther	fast	fine	firm
first	free	further	high	home	hourly
inside	kindly	last	late	long	loud
low	monthly	outside	overseas	past	quick
quiet	right	sharp	slow	straight	sure
thick	thin	through	tight	weekly	well
wide	worse	wrong	yearly		

2) 有许多对同根的副词,一个带 -ly 词尾,一个不带,意思不尽相同:

带 -ly 词尾的副词

I'm *deeply* impressed. 我印象很深。

I'll come *directly*. 我马上就来。

He's *easily* hurt. 他容易生气。

She *flatly* refused. 她干脆地拒绝了。

They talked *freely*. 他们随意地交谈。

He was *fully* recovered. 他完全恢复了。

I *hardly* ever go out. 我很少出门。

It's *highly* confidential. 这极其机密。

He was treated *justly*. 他受到公正对待。

Lastly, I wish you a good journey. 最后,我祝你旅途愉快。

I haven't been well *lately*. 我近来身体不太舒服。

It was *nearly* midnight. 快到午夜了。

How *prettily* she sings! 她唱得真美!

不带 -ly 词尾的副词

I went *deep* into the woods. 我深入到树林中。

Go *direct* home. 直接回家。

Go *easy* with her. 对她要慢慢来。

Lie down *flat*. 平着躺下。

Don't let the dog run *free*. 别让狗随便乱跑。

You know it *full* well. 这一点你完全清楚。

Hit the ball *hard*. 使劲击球。

The eagle flies *high*. 鹰飞得很高。

He's *just* a child. 他还只是个孩子。

When did you see her *last*? 你上次见到她是什么时候?

I went to bed *late*. 我睡得很晚。

He lives quite *near*. 他住得很近。

It rained *pretty* hard. 雨相当大。

关于副词作状语还可参阅 15.2.1 节。

23.3 介词短语和相关副词作状语

23.3.1 介词短语作状语

介词短语作状语的时候最多，可以表示：

1) 时间：

She was born *in 1990*. 她是 1990 年出生的。

A reception was held *on New Year's Eve*. 除夕晚上开了一个招待会。

He swims every day *during the summer*. 夏天他每天都游泳。

She stayed with me *throughout my illness*. 在我生病期间她都陪着我。

2) 地点：

We sat down *on the grass*. 我们在草地上坐下。

English is being spoken *all over the world*. 全世界都讲英语。

She had pains *in her back* all the time. 她一直背疼。

I live *at 403, Brook Street*. 我住在布鲁克街 403 号。

3) 方式：

I'm going there *by plane (bus, taxi)*. 我准备坐飞机(巴士、出租车)去。

He stared at me *in astonishment*. 他惊异地凝视着我。

She faced it *with calmness*. 她镇静地面对它。

He looked at me *without expression*. 他毫无表情地看着我。

4) 原因：

I am so sorry *for what I said to you*. 我为我对你说的话而抱歉。

Her sister had died *of cancer*. 她姐姐因癌症而死。

She is now, *owing to ill health*, not so active in class. 由于身体不好，她在课堂上不那么活跃。

He's angry *on that account*. 为此他很生气

5) 其他：

She was pleased *with the result*. 她对结果感到满意。

In my opinion, the scheme is unsound. 照我看，这计划不够稳妥。

I think you are prejudiced *against Jack*. 我想你对杰克有偏见。

He quarreled *with everyone*. 他和谁都吵架。

23.3.2   be + 形容词 + 介词短语

1) 这种结构非常普遍，许多形容词可以跟介词短语作状语：

He **was fond of** history. 他很喜欢历史。

She **was** very **keen on** art. 她酷爱艺术。

He **was afraid of** nothing. 他什么也不怕。

She **was frightened of** the police. 她害怕警察。

He's not **interested in** research. 他对研究工作没兴趣。

She **was annoyed with** me. 她生我的气。

He **was angry with** me (**at** what I said). 他生我的气(对我的话生气)。

I'm **ashamed of** what I did. 我为我的行为感到羞愧。

Of course she's **proud of** what you've done. 她自然为你的行为感到骄傲。

He **was amazed at** her attitude. 他对她的态度感到惊讶。

I'm **bored with** the subject. 对这问题我已感到厌烦。

What **are** you **busy about**? 你在忙什么？

She **is** very **glad (happy) about** her new job. 她为她的新工作而高兴。

He **was delighted with** the child (**at** the news). 他很喜欢这孩子(听了这消息很高兴)。

He **was sorry about** her departure. 他为她的离去感到难过。

She **was good at** looking after people. 她善于照顾人。

We **are** fully **aware of** the gravity of the situation. 我们完全意识到形势的严峻。

He **was** completely **absorbed in** his work. 他专心致志于他的工作。

He **is full of** good ideas (hope and happiness). 他好主意很多(充满希望和喜悦)。

She **is jealous of** you. 她嫉妒你。

They **were pleased with** the girl (their new house). 他们很喜欢这女孩(他们的新房子)。

I'm very **satisfied with** you (the present situation). 我对你(目前形势)很满意。

He **was eager for** success. 他渴望成功。

She **was excited about** it (**at** hearing this). 对此(听了这消息)她很兴奋。

You should **be content with** what you have. 你应该满足于你已有的东西。

Lily has **been anxious for** your return. 莉莉一直盼望你回来。

Be careful of what you are doing (**with** your work). 要小心做事(你的工作)。

He's **careless about** his appearance (money matters). 他对自己的外表(金钱的事)漫不经心。

I'm quite **certain (sure) of** it. 我对此是有把握的。

She's **used (accustomed) to** doing this work. 她习惯于做这种工作。

The driver **is responsible for** the accident. 发生这事故开车的人有责任。

She **is liable to** colds (disease). 她容易感冒(生病)。

He's quite **capable of** neglecting his duties. 他完全有可能玩忽职守。

I'm most **grateful to** you. 我对你非常感激。

He **was faithful to** his principles. 他忠于他的原则。

2) 有时句子主语可以是一样东西或事物：

Your system **is different from** ours. 你们的制度和我们的不同。

France **is famous for** its wines. 法国因其葡萄酒而出名。

Wheat **is similar to** barley. 小麦和大麦相像。

Is the book **suitable for** publication? 这书适合出版吗?

Vegetables **are good for** you. 蔬菜对你有好处。

It's **ready for** use immediately. 它马上就可使用。

His death **was due to** negligence. 他的死是疏忽造成的。

The shipyard **is capable of** producing nuclear submarines. 这家造船厂能生产核潜艇。

No one's life **is entirely free from** troubles. 没有哪个人的一生完全没有麻烦事。

This **was contrary to** her usual habits. 这和她通常的习惯是相反的。

Her eyes **were full of** tears. 她眼中充满泪水。

The room **was** almost **bare of** furniture. 这房间几乎没有家具。

The age **was productive of** men of genius. 那个时代天才辈出。

His argument **is devoid of** logic. 他的论证毫无逻辑性。

The streets **were empty of** traffic at night. 夜里街上没有车辆。

23.3.3   用副词小品词作状语

与介词同形的副词称为 **副词小品词** (Adverb Particles)，它们多数都可用作状语：

I'm used to going **about** alone. 我习惯于独来独往。

Stars glittered **above**.　星星在天空闪烁。

He came **across** slowly.　他慢步走了过来。

He whistled softly as he walked **along**.　他一面走，一面轻轻地吹着口哨。

There was a clear stream running **alongside**.　旁边流淌着一条清澈的小溪。

He looked **around** but could see nobody.　他四处张望，但看不见任何人。

He had never been in love **before**.　他从未谈过恋爱。

Look **behind**.　往后瞧。

The rose-garden lay **below**.　玫瑰园在下方。

Marx did not merely see the surface but penetrated **beneath**.　马克思不仅看到表面，而且深入其里。

Besides, I want you to promise me one thing.　此外，我要你答应我一件事。

We visited the Art Gallery in the morning and an exhibition later, with a hurried lunch **between**.　我们上午先参观了美术馆，后来看展览会，中间匆匆吃了一顿饭。

Kate came several times to the front door, but not **beyond**.　凯特曾几次来到大门口，但没有出大门。

Mr. Brown came **by** and saw us.　布朗先生从一旁走过，看见了我们。

The little girl has fallen **down**.　小女孩跌倒了。

A taxi came along and I got **in**.　一辆出租车开过来，我坐了上去。

Stay **inside** till the rain stops.　留在家里，直到雨停了再出去。

The bird flew **off**.　鸟飞走了。

We went **on** down the road.　我们沿着马路往前走。

Let's sleep **out** (in the garden).　咱们在外边(花园里)睡。

He heard a step **outside**.　他听见外面有脚步声。

Some wild geese have just flown **over**.　几只大雁刚从上方飞过。

He walked **past** without noticing me.　他从一旁走过，却没看见我。

Shall I show you **round**?　我要不要带你到处看看？

What have you been doing **since**?　在那以后你一直在干什么？

They wouldn't let us **through**.　他们不让我们过去。

They followed a sound policy **throughout**.　他们一直奉行一项正确的政策。

The swimmer surfaced and went **under** again.　那游泳者浮上水面又潜入

水下。

But he wasn't hard, **underneath** he was kind. 但他并不厉害，内心里他很善良。

He got **up** and looked out of the window. 他站起身向窗外张望。

The curtains were white **without** and green **within**. 窗帘外面是白的，里面是绿的。

23.4 形容词及分词(短语)作状语

23.4.1 形容词作状语

1) 形容词有时也可用作状语，常和句子的谓语用逗号隔开：

She went back to Boston, **eager** to see her children. 她回到波斯顿，急于见她的孩子。

He rushed over, **anxious** to help. 他跑了过来，亟想帮忙。

The boy nodded, **pale and scared**. 男孩点了点头，脸色苍白，十分惊恐。

The company laughed, **friendly and pleased**. 这伙人笑了，友好而高兴。

Greatly instrested, I asked him how to operate the machine. 我很感兴趣，问他这机器怎样操作。

Greatly disappointed, he decided to leave the place. 他大失所望，决定离开这个地方。

Helpless, I decided to give up the job. 我无可奈何，决定辞去这份工作。

Modest and unassuming, he soon put everybody at ease. 他谦逊没有架子，很快使大家感到无拘无束。

2) 有时和动词一起用，中间不加逗号：

He **stood helpless**, not knowing what to do. 他无可奈何地站着，不知如何是好。

He **sat motionless**. 他一动不动地坐着。

Barbary **lay still and happy**. 巴巴里静静地躺着，感到很高兴。

The hunter fired and the tiger **fell dead**. 猎人开枪，老虎倒地死了。

All men are **born equal**. 所有的人生而平等。

Don't throw that plastic bag away, it may **come in handy**. 别把那塑料袋扔掉，它可能会有用处的。

He **flushed crimson** with indignation. 他气得满脸通红。

He offered to supply him with another clock **free of charge**. 他答应免费
  给他另一台钟。

3) 有些形容词和宾语有较密切的关系(这些形容词介乎状语和宾语补语之
间):

She **pushed** the door **open**. 她把门推开。

He **pulled** his belt **tight**. 他勒紧裤带。

They **eat** the fish **raw**. 这种鱼他们生吃。

We **drink** it **hot**. 我们喝热的。

They **beat** him **uncurious**. 他们把他打得失去知觉。

He **knocked** her **senseless**. 他把她打得不省人事。

This noise is **driving** me **mad (crazy)**. 这嘈杂的声音吵得我快疯了。

23.4.2   现在分词(短语)作状语

1) 现在分词(短语)也常可用作状语,通常有逗号把它和主谓语分开,可
以表示伴随情况 (a)、原因 (b)、时间 (c) 等:

a. *Opening* the drawer, he took out a revolver. 他打开抽屉,拿出一把左轮
  手枪。

  Taking off our shoes, we crept cautiously along the passage. 脱掉了鞋,我
  们小心翼翼地沿着通道爬行。

  He lay still, *staring blankly at the ceiling*. 他静静地躺着,茫然地望着天
  花板。

  She went out of the room, *taking the flowers with her*. 她带着那些花走出
  屋去。

  Lena shook her head, *smiling*. 丽娜笑着摇了摇头。

b. *Fearing* that the police would recognize him, he never went out in daylight.
  由于怕被警察认出,他白天从不出去。

  Being poor himself, he couldn't help us. 他自己就很穷,没有力量帮助
  我们。

  Not knowing her address, we couldn't get in touch with her. 由于不知道
  她的地址,我们无法和她联系。

  Feeling rather tired, she went to bed. 由于感到相当疲劳,她就睡觉了。

c. *Hearing* the news, they decided to act. 听到这消息,他们决定采取行动。

  Seeing this, she became rather worried. 看到这情况,她很有些发愁。

Arriving there, he made up his mind to go in.　到达那里后，他决定进去。

Walking through the park, we saw a fine flower show.　我们从公园穿过时看到一个漂亮的花卉展。

2）分词有时用完成形式 (a)，有时有自己的逻辑主语 (b)：

a. *Having been there once*, he knew the place fairly well.　由于去过那里一次，他很熟悉这地方。

Not having received instructions, he didn't know what to do.　由于没收到指示，他不知道该怎么办。

Having divorced twice, she didn't want to marry again.　由于离过两次婚，她不想再结婚。

I didn't feel terribly shocked, *having expected all this*.　这情况我早已料到，因此我并不觉得过于震惊。

b. *The day being fine*, we decided to have a picnic by the lake.　天气很好，我们决定到湖边野餐。

There being nothing else to discuss, he declared the meeting closed.　由于没有别的事要讨论，他宣布闭会。

Her sister being dead, she brought up her nephew.　她姐姐死了，她把她的外甥带大。

Weather permitting, we'll go on a tour of the lake district next week.　如果天气允许，我们下星期将去游览湖区。

以上结构主要用在书面语中。

3）有些分词常和某些动词连用，中间不带逗号：

She was always ready to *go skating (swimming, fishing)*.　她向来爱去溜冰（游泳、钓鱼）。

He *came running* in from the yard.　他从院子里跑了进来。

I have *spent* all day *looking for you*.　我花了一整天时间找你。

I *wasted* a whole afternoon *trying to convince her*.　我白费了一整个下午设法劝说她。

They *were busy making artificial flowers*.　他们忙着做纸花。

I *lay tossing* half the night.　我翻来覆去半夜没睡着。

He *sat at his desk working*.　他坐在办公桌前工作。

I *had a difficult time persuading him*.　我费了很大劲才说服他。

这类句子口语中也常出现。

关于现在分词作状语的用法可参阅第 12.3.5 节。

23.4.3　过去分词(短语)作状语

1) 用过去分词作状语的时候也不少，可表示伴随情况(a)、原因(b)、时间(c)等：

a. He entered, *accompanied by his secretary*.　他由秘书陪着走了进来。

Aroused by the crash, he leapt to his feet.　被轰然的响声惊醒,他一跃站了起来。

A woman came in, *followed by her daughter*.　一个妇女走了进来,后面跟着她的女儿。

"Of course," said Rose, *astonished*.　罗丝惊讶地说,"当然。"

Seated in the car, the president waved to the crowd.　总统坐在车上向人群挥手。

b. *Moved by his speech*, many people volunteered to help in the work.　受他讲话的感动,许多人自愿参加这项工作。

Tom, *horrified at what he had seen*, could not say anything.　汤姆对看到的情况感到惊恐,什么话也说不出来。

Having been warned about the bandits, she left her valuables at home.　由于有人警告她有盗匪,她把贵重物品都留在家里。

c. *Driven beyond endurance*, he ran away from the plantation.　他忍无可忍,逃出了种植园。

Surprised at my reaction, she tried to console me.　我的反应使她吃惊,她设法安慰我。

Taken in time, the medicine will be quite effective.　如果及时服用,这药是相当有效的。

Looked at politically, it is an important question.　从政治上看,这是一个重要的问题。

2) 有些动词可以跟过去分词作状语，中间并不加逗号：

Ten others *lay wounded there*.　另外十个人受伤躺在那里。

He decided to *lie hidden* for a few days longer.　他决定再躲藏几天。

The valley *lay spread out* before us.　河谷展现在我们面前。

The thought *lay buried* in her heart.　这想法一直埋藏在她心中。

The girls *stood grouped together* at one end of the room.　姑娘们聚在一起,站在房间的一头。

I *stand prepared* to dispute it.　我准备对此提出异议。

关于过去分词作状语可参阅第 12.4.5 节。

23.5 状语从句

23.5.1 时间状语从句

1) 英语中有大量的 **时间状语从句** (Adverbial Clauses of Time)，多由连词引导 (关于这类连词可参阅第 17.2.1 节)：

When she pressed the button the lift stopped. 她一按电钮电梯就停住了。

As the sun rose, the fog dispersed. 太阳升起时雾消散了。

While the discussion was going on, George came in. 讨论正在进行时乔治进来了。

All things are difficult *before they are easy*. (谚)凡事总是先难后易。

I found the letter *long after he had gone away*. 他走了好久之后我才发现那封信。

I will return the book *as soon as I have read it*. 书一看完我就还回来。

I have had another baby *since I saw you last*. 自上次见到你之后我又有了一个宝宝。

On and on he went, *till (until) he reached the outskirts of the wood*. 他走了又走，直到走到林子边。

Come and talk to me *whenever you feel lonely*. 凡你感到寂寞时就来和我说说话。

Once you've finished, go to bed. 你一干完就去睡觉。

Now (that) you mention it, I do remember the incident. 有你这么一提，我的确想起了这事。

2) 还有一些时间状语不由连词引导：

He came *directly I called*. 我一叫他就来了。

You ought to come and see us *next time you are home*. 下次回家你要来看我们。

She demands sweets *every time she sees me*. 她每次见到我都要糖吃。

He felt a thrill *the moment he got into the theatre*. 他一走进剧场就感到十分激动。

I left *immediately the clock struck twelve*. 钟一敲十二点我就动身了。

He had *no sooner* reached the door *than he came back*. 他刚到门口又走了回来。

He had *hardly* arrived *when it began to snow*. 他刚一到就开始下雪了。

23.5.2　条件状语从句

1) 条件状语从句 (Adverbial Clauses of Condition) 主要由 if 或 unless 引导:

If I had been less cautious, I might have been more wise.　要是我不那么谨慎, 也许我还明智一点。

If I were you, I'd go to night school.　我要是你, 我会去上夜校。

We can't exercise our influence *unless we have an organ*.　除非我们有一份刊物, 否则我们不能发挥我们的影响力。

They have a meeting every Friday, *unless there is nothing to discuss*.　他们每星期五开一次会, 除非没有事情可商谈。

2) 条件状语从句还可以由其他连词或起连词作用的短语引导:

Supposing (that) you are wrong, what will you do?　假定你是错的, 你怎么办?

Suppose you had a million pounds, how would you spend it?　设想你有一百万英镑, 你会怎么花呢?

You may go out *providing you do your homework first*.　如果你先把作业做了, 那就可以出去玩。

She may come with us *provided (that) she arrives in time*.　如果她及时到达, 她可以和我们一道去。

I'm going to expose him *even if he is a relative of mine*.　即使他是我的亲戚, 我也要揭发他。

In case the house burns down, we'll get the insurance money.　如果房子烧毁, 我们会领到保险金。

You can go out, *as long as you promise to be back before 11 o'clock*.　只要你答应十一点钟前回来, 你可以出去。

You may borrow the book, *on condition that you don't lend it to anyone else*.　你可以借这本书, 条件是别把它借给别人。

Granted that he's not brilliant, he is at least competent and works hard.　就算他不够出色, 他至少称职, 而且工作努力。

I show everything on my face, *whether I'm angry or pleased*.　不管是生气还是高兴, 我什么都表现在脸上。

3) 由 if 引导的条件状语从句, 有时可把 if 省略, 而把从句的语序倒装:

Were it not for their assistance, we would be in serious difficulty.　如果不是他们帮忙, 我们会陷入严重的困境。

Had we made adequate preparations, we might have succeeded.　如果我们做了充分的准备, 我们或许就成功了。

Should she call, what would you tell her? 万一她来电话, 你怎么对她说?

Had it not been for the reservoir, we'd never have been able to beat the drought. 要不是有水库, 我们绝不可能战胜这次旱灾。

23.5.3 目的状语从句和结果状语从句

1) 目的状语从句 (Adverbial Clauses of Purpose) 主要由 that, so that, lest, for fear that, in case 等引导:

My father has bought me a bicycle *so (in order) that* I can get to school quickly. 我爸给我买了辆自行车, 以便我能快速赶到学校。

They spoke in whispers *lest they should be heard*. 他们低声说话, 以防被人听见。

Shut the window *for fear that it may rain*. 把窗子关上以防下雨。

I shall stay in the hotel all day *in case there is news of Henry*. 我将一整天待在旅馆里以防有享利的消息。

I'll show you *so you can see how it's done*. 我将做给你看以便你知道怎样做。

We have *so* arranged matters *that one of us is always on duty*. 我们作了这样的安排, 以便我们总有一个人在值班。

2) 结果状语从句 (Adverbial Clauses of Result) 主要由 so that, so...that, such...that, that 等引导:

So many people came to the concert *that some couldn't get in*. 那么多人来听音乐会, 以致有些人没法进来。

She's so ill *(that) she can't get out of bed*. 她病得很重, 都下不了床了。

It was such a cold night *that we stayed at home*. 那是一个非常寒冷的夜晚, 我们都待在家里。

What was the matter with the fellow *that he looked so happy*? 那人怎么回事, 看起来这样高兴?

The situation is such *that agreement is unlikely*. 局势是这样, 达成协议的可能性不大。

There was such a draught, *it is no wonder he caught a cold*. 过堂风这样厉害, 难怪他感冒了。

He is such a marvellous joker *(that) you can't help laughing*. 他的笑话讲得那样出色, 你会禁不住哈哈大笑的。

I'm so busy, *I have no time to write a letter*. 我忙极了, 没时间写信。

3) otherwise，or else 或 else 也可引导从句，表示后果：

She had intellect, *otherwise I would have scorned her*. 她很聪明,否则我
　　早就瞧不起她了。

Run *or else you'll be late*. 快跑，否则你就会迟到了。

Drink this, *else you will be sick*. 把这喝掉，否则你会生病。

关于这两类从句，可参阅 17.2.3 和 17.2.4 节。

23.5.4　原因状语从句

1) **原因状语从句** (Adverbial Clauses of Reason) 主要由 because, as, since, in case 等引导：

I did it *because I was angry*. 我这样做是因为我生气。

As she had a passion for walking, we started off on foot. 由于她酷爱走路，
　　我们就步行出发了。

As you make your bed, so you must lie on it. 你是自作自受。

Since they've forgotten to phone me, I'll have to phone them. 既然他们忘
　　了给我打电话，我就得给他们打了。

Since I haven't got her address, I can't write to her. 由于没有她的地址，
　　我没法给她写信。

She ought to come down *just in case anything happened*. 她应当下来,以
　　防发生什么情况。

Seeing he refused to help us, there's no reason why we should now help him.
　　既然他以前拒绝帮助我们，我们现在也没有理由去帮助他。

Considering he's only just started, he knows quite a lot about it. 鉴于他才
　　刚刚开始，他对此已懂得相当多了。

2) 某些 "be + 形容词" 结构后的从句也说明原因：

I'm **glad** *(that) he's feeling better*. 我很高兴他感觉好点了。

I'm awfully **sorry** *that this has occurred*. 发生了这事我非常抱歉。

You should **feel** very **proud** *that you have been chosen*. 你被选上了,你
　　应该感到很骄傲。

He's **annoyed** *that nobody believes him*. 他很生气没人相信他。

They **are** very **disappointed** *that she can't stay longer*. 他们很失望她不
　　能再待久些。

I'm **surprised** *he didn't come*. 他没来，我感到吃惊。

He **was** **ashamed** *that he had lied*. 他很羞愧，他撒谎了。

I **was delighted** *that you were successful*. 你成功了我很高兴。

关于这类从句可参阅第 13.5.10 和 17.2.5 节。

23.5.5　让步状语从句

1) **让步状语从句** (Adverbial Clauses of Concession) 主要由 although，though，while，whereas 等连词引导，表示"虽然"、"尽管"这类意思：

Although she was tired, she stayed up to watch the late night film on television.　虽然她很累，她还是熬夜看电视上的午夜电影。

Though he had very little money, he always managed to dress smartly.　虽说他没几个钱，却总是穿得时髦潇洒。

She still loved him *even though he had treated her so badly*.　尽管他待她那样差，她还是爱他。

I wouldn't do it, *even if you paid me a thousand pounds*.　即使你付我一千英镑，我也不干这事。

Some praised him, *whereas others condemned him*.　有些人赞扬他，而另一些人却谴责他。

2) 还有一些其他类型的让步状语从句：

You won't be heard, *however loudly you shout*.　不管你喊得多响，没人会听见你的声音。

Wherever he is he will be thinking of you.　不管在那里，他都会想着你。

Whoever you are, you can't pass this way.　不管你是谁，都不能从这里通过。

So don't lose heart, *whatever you do*.　因此不管你干什么，都不要气馁。

She was going to be a singer *no matter what difficulties she met*.　她决心成为一名歌手，不管遇到什么困难。

You can't go in *no matter who you are*.　不管你是谁，都不能进去。

He had to get the car *no matter how much it cost*.　不管花多少钱，他都要买这辆车。

I'll do it *whether you like it or not*.　这事我得干，不管你喜不喜欢。

Much as I would like to come, I can't.　虽说我很想来，但我来不了。

Try as I would, I couldn't prevail upon him to change his mind.　不管费多大劲，我都无法劝说他改变注意。

Poor as he was, he was honest.　他虽然贫穷却很诚实。

He was unable to make much progress, *hard as he tried*.　尽管他作了努力，

却不能取得多大进步。

Exhausted though she was, there was no hope of her being able to sleep. 尽管疲惫不堪，她却毫无能够入睡的希望。

Come what may, he would never let her down. 不管发生什么情况，他绝不会做对不起她的事。

关于这类从句可参阅第 17.2.6 节。

23.5.6　方式状语从句

1) **方式状语从句** (Adverbial Clauses of Manner) 主要由 as，like，as if，as though 等引导：

I did *as he asked*. 我照他要求的那样做了。

Robbie didn't feel *as she did*. 罗比没有她那种感觉。

Do it *like he does*. 照他那样做。

She looked a bit queer, *as if she knew something*. 她看起来有点怪，仿佛她知道什么似的。

She closed her eyes *as though she too were tired*. 她闭上眼睛，就像她也累了似的。

2) 这类状语间或也不用连词引导：

They didn't do it *the way we do now*. 他们以前的做法和我们现在不一样。

You can travel *how you please*. 你愿意怎么旅行都行。

Arrange the hours *however you like*. 你怎么安排时间都行。

She's behaving *the same way her elder sister used to*. 她的表现和她姐姐过去的表现一样。

关于这类从句可参阅第 17.2.7 节。

23.5.7　地点状语从句

1) **地点状语从句** (Adverbial Clauses of Place) 主要由 where，wherever 和 anywhere 引导：

Cross the stream *where it is shallowest*. (谚)在最浅的地方过河。

Where I live there are plenty of sheep. 我住的地方(绵)羊很多。

We'll go *wherever you say*. 你说到哪儿我们就到哪儿。

You can go *anywhere you want*.　你想去哪里就可以去哪里。

Everywhere they appeared there were ovations.　不管他们在哪里出现，人们都热烈鼓掌。

2) where 引导的从句，除了表示地方外，还可以表示处境等，可有各种灵活译法：

He signed to Janey to stay *where she was*.　他给简妮打手势，让她待在原处。

It's your fault that she is *where she is*.　她今天这样是你的错。

Where others are weak, he is strong.　别人的弱点正是他的优势。

Where bees are, there is honey.　有蜂就有蜜。

关于这类从句可以参阅第 17.2.8 节。

23.5.8　比较状语从句

比较状语从句 (Adverbial Clauses of Comparison) 主要由 than 或 as 引导：

He earns less *than his wife (does)*.　他挣的钱比他妻子少。

She knows more *than I did at her age*.　她知道的东西比我在她这年龄时知道的要多。

It was more expensive *than I thought*.　它比我想的要贵。

He is *as* tall *as his father*.　他和他父亲一般高。

Manslaughter is not *as* (so) bad *as murder*.　过失杀人罪没有谋杀罪那样严重。

I haven't done *as* much *as I should have liked*.　我做的没有我希望的那么好。

关于这类从句可参阅 14.4.1 — 14.4.4，14.4.6，15.3.2 及 17.2.9 节。

第24章 语 序

24.1 自然语序与倒装语序

24.1.1 自然语序

1）英语大多数句子中主语在前谓语在后，和汉语一样，称为**自然语序**
(Natural Order)，如：

We must prevent the pollution of the environment. 我们必须防止环境污染。（主语＋谓语＋宾语）

We are taking measures to improve our environment. 我们正在采取措施以改善我们的环境。（主语＋谓语＋宾语＋状语）

陈述句绝大部分为自然语序。

2）疑问句中有一小部分 (主要是特殊问句中以疑问词作主语或修饰主语的句子)用自然语序：

Who put forward the proposal? 这建议是谁提出的？

What caused his illness? 他的病是什么引起的？

How many students are leaving school this year? 今年多少学生毕业？

What problem are worrying you? 什么问题使你烦恼？

3）有些陈述句子改为问句，或是期待对方同意自己的意见(a)，或是表示惊异、怀疑等情绪(b)，这时仍用自然语序(但用升调)：

a. You work here? 你在这里工作？

She is your sister? 她是你妹妹？

She is not back yet? 她还没回来？

b. He has broken another world record? 他又打破了一项世界纪录？

Her father has passed away? 她父亲过世了？

You know nothing about it? 你对这毫不知情？

4）感叹句多数也是自然语序：

What nonsense you talk! 你说什么胡话！

How gracefully they danced! 他们跳得多优美！

24.1.2　倒装语序

1）如果谓语提到主语前面，则句子为 **倒装语序** (Inverted Order)，有时整个谓语提前，称为 **全部倒装** (Full Inversion)，如：

Down fell half a dozen apples.　忽然掉下五六只苹果来。

There comes the bus!　公共汽车来了！

有时只有部分谓语提前，称为 **部分倒装** (Partial Inversion)，如：

How are you doing?　你情况怎样？

Why didn't you come?　你为什么没来？

2）疑问句大部分都用倒装语序，不管是一般问句 (a)、特殊问句 (b)、选择问句 (c) 还是反意问句 (d)：

a. Are you going home for Christmas?　你回家过圣诞节吗？

Do you have many friends here?　你在这儿朋友多吗？

b. Where can I park the car?　我能在什么地方泊车？

How much do you need?　你需要多少？

c. Is she an undergraduate or a postgraduate?　她是本科生还是研究生？

Are we going to meet here or at the airport?　我们在这里碰头还是在机场碰头？

d. It's a nice day, isn't it?　今天天气很好，是吧？

You don't smoke, do you?　你不抽烟，是吧？

只有上节提到的某些问句用自然语序。

24.2　一些常见的倒装句

24.2.1　一些倒装句型

1）由引导词 there 引导的句子：

There's an outdoor concert tonight in the park.　今晚公园里有一个露天音乐会。

Have there been any fresh developments of the project?　这项计划有什么新的进展吗？

In 1859 there came a war between the two countries.　1859年两国间发生了一场战争。

In the distance there was heard the lowing of the cattle.　远处可听到牛叫声。

关于这类句子可参阅第 19.4.1 — 19.4.4 节。

2) 由 there，here，now，then 等副词引导的句子：

There come the rest of the party. 剩下的人都来了。

There's the bell. 铃响了。

Here is the address of your hotel. 这儿是你旅馆的地址。

Here are my replies to your questions. 这儿是我对你问题的回答。

Here comes a bus. 来了一辆公共汽车。

Now comes your turn. 现在轮到你了。

Then came the day of his examination. 这时他考试的日子到了。

Then opens an epoch of social revolution. 这时开始了一个社会革命的时代。

3) 由 so，neither，nor 引导的句子：

He's a teacher and *so is his wife*. 他是位教师，他妻子也是。

"I've been to New York." "*So have I*." "我去纽约了。" "我也是。"

I like singing and *so does Helen*. 我喜欢唱歌，海伦也喜欢。

I don't eat meat and *neither does Tom*. 我不吃肉，汤姆也不吃肉。

James didn't attend the meeting and *neither did Jane*. 詹姆斯没去开会，简也没去。

"I haven't seen that film." "*Neither (Nor) have I*." "我没看过那部电影。" "我也没有。"

"I don't like football." "*Nor do I*." "我不喜欢足球。" "我也是。"

"I couldn't afford to stay there." "*Nor could I*." "我住不起那里。" "我也住不起。"

Nor will I deny that. 我也不会否认这一点。

24.2.2　一些状语从句中的倒装语序

1) 有些由 if 引导的条件状语从句 (主要是包含有 were，had，should 的从句)，可以把 if 省略，把上述动词放到主语前面去：

Weren't it for their assistance, we wouldn't be able to do so well. 若不是有他们帮助，我们不会干得这样好。

Had we got there earlier, we would have caught the train. 要是我们到得早一点，我们就赶上火车了。

Should Mary call, say that I'll be back in an hour. 如果玛丽来电话，就说我一个小时后回来。

Were I Tom, I would refuse. 如果我是汤姆，我会拒绝。

Should you require anything, just give me a call. 如果你需要什么,给我打个电话就行。

Had he known that, he would have told you. 他要是知道这事,他早就告诉你了。

这是比较文气的说法,口语中仍以用 if 比较自然。

2) 有些让步状语从句中有时也有倒装的情况(主要是把表语或部分谓语提前):

Clever though he was, he couldn't conceal his eagerness for praise. 虽说他很聪明,却不能掩饰他亟于获得赞扬的神情。

Strange though it may seem, the tallest boy is the youngest. 尽管说来奇怪,最高的男孩却是最年少的。

Try as I would, I couldn't make her change her mind. 不管多努力,我都没法让她改变主意。

Try as he might, he couldn't open the box. 不管他想什么办法,都没法把那箱子打开。

Talented as he is, he is not yet ready to turn professional. 尽管他有天赋,他还没有拿定主意当职业演员。

Search as they would, they could find no one in the woods. 尽管他们努力搜寻,在林子中都找不到一个人。

24.2.3 某些副词或状语引导的倒装句

1) 某些有否定意思的副词,若放在句首,句子常用倒装语序:

Never *would he know* what she had suffered. 他绝不会知道她受过的苦。

Never before *has such a high standard been achieved.* 以前从未达到过这样高的标准。

Seldom *have I seen such brutality.* 我很少见过这样残忍的行为。

Little *does he care* whether we live or die. 他丝毫不在乎我们的死活。

Nowhere *could I find him*. 我哪儿都找不到他。

Scarcely *was she out of sight* when he came. 她刚走掉他就来了。

Hardly *had he arrived* when she started complaining. 他刚到她就开始诉苦。

Only then *could the work be seriously begun.* 只有那时这工作才能真正开始。

Not only *did he work faster*, he worked better also. 他不仅干得更快,也

干得更好。

Not once *has he failed to fulfil his task.* 他没有一次不完成任务的。

Rarely *does the temperature go above ninety here.* 这里的温度很少达到九十度。

2）有个别其他副词放在句首时，有时也有这个现象：

Often *would she (she would) weep* when alone. 她一个人时常常哭泣。

Well *do I remember the days* when we were at school together. 我清楚地记得我们一起读书时的情景。

Bitterly *did he repent* that decision. 他深深地悔恨那个决定。

Gladly *would I give my life* to save the child! 我愿牺牲自己来救那孩子!

Brightly *shone the moon* that night. 那天晚上月亮特别亮。

这类句子多出现在书面语中，在日常口语中这样说时较少。

3）有些短语（特别是介词短语）移到句首时也可能引导倒装语序：

On no account *must we give up* this attempt. 我们绝不能放弃这个努力。

Under no circumstances *must we relax* our vigilance. 在任何情况下我们都不能放松警惕。

In no circumstances *could we agree* to such a principle. 在任何情况下我们都不能同意这样一个原则。

In vain *did he try* to open the locked door. 他设法打开那扇锁着的门但没成功。

Only in this way *can our honour be saved*! 只有这样才能保住我们的荣誉!

Not until yesterday *did I learn* anything about it. 直到昨天我才对这件事有所了解。

At no point south of the river *did the enemy advance* more than a mile. 在江的南边任何地方敌人推进都不到一英里。

So bright *was the moon* that the flowers were bright as by day. 月亮是那样亮，花都像在白天那样艳丽。

24.2.4　一些谓语前移的情况

1）有些句子没有宾语而主语又比较长，有时可把状语提前，而把主语放到谓语后面去：

Before him **lay** miles of undulating moorland. 他面前是一片高低起伏的荒原。

After the banquet **came** a firework display in the garden.　宴会后花园里燃放了烟火。

On the table **stood** two glasses and an empty brandy bottle.　桌上有两个玻璃杯和一只白兰地空酒瓶。

On every side **stretched** fields of luxuriant green wheat.　四周都是葱笼的麦田。

From the distance **came** occasional shots.　从远处传来零星的枪声。

To the list **may be added** the following names.　名单上还可以加上以下这些名字。

In the distance **could be seen** the purple mountains.　远处可以看见紫色的群山。

2) 为了使描绘显得更生动，有些与介词同形的副词可以移到句首，而把主语放到谓语后面去：

Up *went* the arrow into the air.　飕的一声箭射上了天。

She rang the bell. **In** *came* a girl she had not seen before.　她按铃,进来一个她从未见过的姑娘。

Following the roar, **out** *rushed* a tiger from the bushes.　一声吼叫，草丛中呼地冲出一只老虎。

Out *sprang* the cuckoo.　布谷鸟蹦了出来。

Down *flew* the eagle to seize the chicken.　老鹰飞下来抓小鸡。

24.2.5　分词和表语移到句首的情况

1) 进行时态中的分词有时可移到句首，来对这动作加以强调：

Lying on the floor was a boy aged about seventeen.　躺在地板上的是一个约十七岁的男孩。

Standing beside the table was an interpreter.　站在桌旁的是一位翻译。

Hanging from the rafters were strings of onions.　椽子上挂着一串串洋葱。

Running across it is a stream named Peach Brook.　穿过这里有条小溪,叫作桃花溪。

Watching the performances were mostly foreign tourists.　观看演出的大多是一些外国游客。

2) 以过去分词作表语的句子，过去分词有时也可以提前，把主语放到后面去：

The most widely distributed is the Hui people.　分布最广的是回族。

Seated on the ground are a group of young people. 坐在地上的是一伙年
   轻人。

Hidden underground is a wealth of gold, silver, lead and zinc. 地下埋藏着
   大量的金、银、铅和锌。

Pictured here is a wooden tub used for gathering water-chestnuts. 这里画
   的是一个采菱用的木盆。

Scattered like stars in the deep mountains are numerous reservoirs and
   ponds. 在深山里有无数星罗棋布的水库和蓄水池。

3) 作表语的介词短语有时也可以提前：

On the other side is northern Xinjiang. 在另一边是北疆。

Among its products are farm machines and mining equipment. 它的产品
   中有农业机械和采矿设备。

Next to it is another restaurant where we can have Chinese food. 它隔壁是
   另一家餐馆，在那里可以吃中餐。

Around the lake are a huge number of farms. 湖四周有为数众多的农场。

Near the southern end of the village was a large pear orchard. 靠近村子南
   头有一座大梨园。

4) 其他表语也可提前：

Higher up were forests of white birches. 再往上去是一片片白桦林。

Nearby are houses built by the peasants themselves. 附近是农民自己盖的
   房子。

Worst of all is the humiliations he suffered. 最不堪的是他经受的许多屈
   辱。

Below is a restaurant. 楼下是一家餐厅。

Southwest of the reservoir were 2,000 *mu* of sandy wasteland. 水库西南有
   两千亩沙荒地。

24.2.6 其他倒装句

1) 还有一些其他类型的倒装句，如表示祝愿的句子：

Long live world peace! 世界和平万岁！

May you *have* a long and happy life. 祝你幸福长寿。

2) 又如在间接引语后的插入语中，主语有时可放在谓语后面：

"I do hope," *said Nancy*, "they haven't all forgotten about it." 南希说，
   "我真希望他们没把这事完全忘掉。"

"You've eaten so much!" *cried Frank*.　弗兰克叫道，"你吃了这么多!"

"You're late," *whispered Jack*.　"你迟到了，"杰克低声说。

"I'm aware of it," *replied the Englishman*.　"这我知道，"那英国人答道。

3）有时为了修辞上的考虑，表语也可以提前：

Very grateful we are for your help.　我们非常感谢你的帮助。

A very reliable person he is, to be sure.　他是个非常可靠的人，没问题。

So sudden was the attack (that) we had no time to escape.　袭击那样突然，我们没有时间逃走。

Such was his strength that he could bend iron bars.　他力气那么大，连铁棍都能拧弯。

24.3　宾语的位置

24.3.1　宾语通常的位置

1）宾语通常跟在谓语后面：

They are touring *Europe*.　他们在游览欧洲。

He wrote *his first novel* at 17.　他十七岁写出了自己的第一本小说。

2）但在下面情况(如宾语由疑问词表示或修饰等)宾语要放在主语前面：

Who are you talking to?　你在和谁讲话?

How many pages have you read?　你看了多少页?

Here is the man *whom* you want to see.　这就是你想见的人。

What she said impressed me deeply.　她说的话给我留下了深刻印象。

Whatever she did was right.　她做的一切都是对的。

3）在有两个宾语时，一般间接宾语在前，直接宾语在后：

He handed *me those two parcels*.　他把那两个包裹递给了我。

Show *us your papers*.　把证件拿给我们看看。

I'll find *you something to do*.　我给你找点事做。

She sent *me a birthday card*.　她寄给我一张生日贺卡。

24.3.2　一些宾语提前的情况

1）当一个宾语需要强调时，有时可以提前：

This I hope you'll keep in mind.　这一点我希望你记在心里。

We can't afford it. *That* I know.　我们买不起，这一点我是知道的。

These two letters I'd like to send by ordinary mail, and this one by registered mail.　这两封寄平信，这一封寄挂号。

All this we must take fully into account.　这一切我们必须充分考虑。

2) 有些宾语从句，如果需要强调，也可以提到主语前面：

What I'm going to do next, I don't quite know.　下一步该怎么办我还不太清楚。

What he has once heard, he never forgets.　凡是他听过一次的话，他再也不会忘记。

Whether it is a defect or not I don't quite know.　它是否是缺点我不十分清楚。

That she is a good girl I know.　她是个好姑娘我是知道的。

Whatever he does he does well.　他做什么事都很好。

24.3.3　一些其他情况

1) 当宾语 (加上它的修饰语) 较长时，我们常把状语放在它前面以保持句子的平衡：

Here I wish to extend *to you* our warmest welcome.　这里我愿向你表示我们最热忱的欢迎。

These programmes do much to bring home *to people* the serious risks of smoking.　这些节目在让人们认识吸烟的危害方面起到很大作用。

She has translated *into English* a novel by Lao She.　她把老舍的一本小说译成了英文。

He declared *to Jenny* that the trees were in a dreadful condition.　他向珍妮表明那些树状态很糟糕。

She announced *at the meeting* that she was going to resign.　她在会上宣布她准备辞职。

2) 有时宾语的补语可以移到宾语前面：

They found *sitting on the bed* a man dressed like a worker.　他们发现一个工人装束的男子坐在床上。

They found *half hidden among the rocks* a plant which they had never seen before.　他们发现一株从未见过的植物半隐半现在岩石中间。

Many people consider *impossible* what really is possible.　许多人把实际上

可以做到的事认为不可能。

She must have seen *spring up* before her a new hope. 她一定是看见面前出现了新希望。

3）由"及物动词＋副词"构成的成语动词，后面的宾语可以有两个位置：

宾语一般在成语动词后面	宾语较短也可放在副词前面
Put on *your coat*.	Put *it (your coat)* on.
Hand in *your (exercise) books*.	Hand *them* in, please.
Write down *your names* here.	Write *everything (it)* down here.
Shall I turn on *the lights*?	Shall I turn *the lights (them)* on?

24.4　定语的位置

24.4.1　定语通常的位置

1）单词定语一般放在所修饰的词前面(这和汉语一样)：

financial problems　财政问题　　　peaceful construction　和平建设

life insurance　人寿保险　　　　　trade deficit　贸易逆差

developing countries　发展中国家　living conditions　生活条件

由副词表示的定语通常放在所修饰词后面：

The situation *here* is highly explosive. 这里的局势具有高度的爆发性。

The people *there* are very friendly. 那里的人很友好。

I met your sister on my way *home*. 我在回家路上遇见了你妹妹。

Is there anything *on* tomorrow? 明天有什么活动吗？

This was her first day *up*. 这是她起床的第一天。

还有一些单词定语在后面的情况可参阅第 14.3.1 节。

2）下面各类定语都放在所修饰词的后面：

a. 定语从句：

The noise *he made* woke everybody up. 他弄出的响声把大家都吵醒了。

Everyone *who (that) knew him* liked him. 认识他的人都喜欢他。

She gave me this jumper, *which she had knitted herself*. 她给了我这件毛衣，这是她亲手织的。

b. 介词短语：

He was a Doctor of Philosophy *in economics of Yale*. 他是耶鲁大学的经济学博士。

She looked to be a young woman *of twenty*. 她看起来像一个二十岁的青
年女子。

He was hired to illustrate a book *on the birds of the world*. 他受雇为一本
描写世界鸟类的书画插图。

c. 分词短语和不定式短语:

People *waiting for the bus* often shelter in my doorway. 等公共汽车的人
常常在我家门道里躲雨。

Is this the table *reserved for us*? 这是给我们留的桌子吗?

They need a garden *to play in*. 他们需要一座花园好在里面玩耍。

d. 其他作定语的短语:

They saw a building *about sixty stories high*. 他们看见一座六十层左右的
高楼。

Soldiers *normally timid* don't fight well. 平时就胆小的士兵打起仗来也
不行。

She has done a play, *at once educational and witty*. 她写了一个剧本,既
有教育意义,又诙谐幽默。

24.4.2　定语和所修饰词分开的情况

1) 定语有时和它修饰的词分开:

What do you have *to say* in this regard? 关于这一点你有什么要说? (to
say 修饰 what)

All we have *left* is some cold meat. 我们只剩了一些冷肉。

I saw something in the paper *which might interest you*. 我在报上看到一些
东西,你可能会感兴趣。

Can you see who those people are *standing at the gate*? 你能看清楚站在
大门口的那些人都是谁吗?

2) 一个名词有时有两个定语,其中一个就不得不和它修饰的词分开:

This is the book *I bought about space flight*. 这是我买的一本关于太空飞
行的书。

Is there anyone *among you interested in going to the caves*? 你们中谁有兴
趣去参观那些洞穴?

Have you got any novels *by Tolstoy in English translation*? 你有没有托尔
斯泰小说的英译本?

24.4.3 定语的顺序

1）一个名词有几个定语时，大体上按下面顺序排列：

all, both	冠词或其他代词	其他单词定语	名 词
all	the	Chinese	students
both	her	younger	brothers
all	these	new	buildings
both	their	former room	mates
	the	past ten	years
	the	same old	topic
	an	interesting detective	story

2）有个别定语可放在冠词 a(n) 或 the 前面：

such a nice person	so short a time
rather a hard time	too small an income
many a student	quite a lot (number)
half an hour	quite a gentleman
half the distance	twice the amount
double the amount	quite the fashion

3）一个名词有几个形容词修饰时，表示基本品质的词，离所修饰的词最近，其他可大致按品质、大小、形状等特点安排：

代词，冠词	品 质	大小、年岁等	颜 色	国家等	名 词
the	new			French	government
a		young		Korean	dancer
our	numerous	splendid		tourist	attractions
all the	beautiful	small	green	jade	figures
a	calm		blue		sea
a	daring	attractive		American	pilot

　　语言是灵活的，这样的归纳只能作参考，实际情况需要自己观察，关于形容词位置可参阅第 14.3.1 节。

24.5　状语的位置

24.5.1　状语通常的位置

1) 状语通常放在谓语后面：

They work *energetically*.　他们干劲十足地工作。

The train was going *fast*.　火车在飞驰。

She went *straight home*.　她直接回家了。

Turn *right here*.　就在这里拐弯。

2) 若有宾语则放在宾语后面：

She welcomed us *warmly*.　她热情地欢迎我们。

You can dial Rome *directly*.　你可以直接拨电话到罗马。

He denied the accusation *hotly*.　他愤怒地否认这一指责。

He led us *astray*.　他把我们引上了歧路。

3) 在被动结构中状语可放在过去分词前面：

Her little daughter is always *prettily* dressed.　她的小女儿总是打扮得漂漂亮亮的。

He was *rightly* punished.　他受到应得的惩罚。

I was *correctly* informed.　我获得了正确的信息。

The boy was *seriously* injured.　男孩受了重伤。

4) 如果有几个时间或地点状语，一般小单位在前，大单位在后：

He was born at 9:30 on Thursday May 5th 1998.　他于 1998 年 5 月 5 日星期四九点半出生。

She lives at 109 Cork Street, Monrovia, California.　她住在加州蒙诺维亚柯克街 109 号。

24.5.2　状语放在句首的情况

1) 为了强调，状语常可以放在句首：

In union there is strength.　团结就是力量。

After midnight, the party broke up.　午夜之后晚会散了。

On his return from Europe, he set to work in earnest.　欧洲回来之后他认真干了起来。

Gently she put the baby on the bed.　她轻轻地把宝宝放在床上。

2）疑问副词及含有疑问词的状语都放在句首：

Why haven't you been to see me all this time?　为什么这么长时间你没来看我？

How did you enjoy your Spring Festival?　你春节过得怎样？

In which year were you born?　你哪年生的？

For what purpose did you invite me to come here?　你请我来这里是什么目的？

3）句子状语常放在句首：

Quite honestly, she isn't the sort of person we're looking for.　说实话，她不是我们在找的那种人。

Strange to say, he did pass his exam after all.　说也奇怪，他考试竟然真的通过了。

Judging from what you say, he ought to succeed.　从你的话里看，他应当能成功。

In conclusion, I'd like to say how much I've enjoyed staying here.　最后我想说我在这里过得非常愉快。

4）与上文有密切联系的状语常放在句首：

He promised to come and *sure enough* he did.　他答应来，果然来了。

It doesn't seem ugly to me; *on the contrary*, I think it's rather beautiful.　我看它似乎并不丑，相反我认为它还相当美。

The traffic was very heavy and *as a result* I arrived late.　路上车很多，结果我晚到了。

24.5.3　插在主语和谓语之间的状语

1）有些副词可放在主语或谓语之间 (a)，或主要动词或表语前面 (b)：

a. She *quickly* finished the letter.　她迅速把信写完。

He *carefully* began to analyze the problem.　他开始仔细分析这个问题。

Lester *immediately* approved of this.　莱斯特立即同意了这个意见。

Our parents *recently* celebrated their golden wedding anniversary.　我们的父母最近庆祝了他们的金婚纪念日。

b. I've only *recently* begun to learn French.　我最近刚开始学法语。

We'll *just* stay in tonight.　我们今晚就留在家里。

The train was *already* moving.　火车已经开动了。

She was *still* weak after the long illness.　久病之后她身子仍然虚弱。

关于副词的位置可参阅第 15.4.1 — 15.4.3 节。

2) 由短语或词组表示的状语也可放在主语和谓语之间:

This, *in brief,* is the official view of the trade unions.　总之，这是工会的正式看法。

Romeo, *believing that Juliet was dead,* decided to kill himself.　罗密欧以为朱丽叶死了，决定自杀。

Tom, *horrified at what he had done,* could not say anything.　汤姆对自己的行为感到震惊，什么话也说不出来。

Your suggestion, *to be frank,* will only get us into trouble.　你的建议，说实在的，只会给我们找麻烦。

24.5.4　状语从句的位置

1) 和其他状语一样，多数状语从句都放在句子后部 (谓语或宾语后面):

Lanny was worried *because he hadn't had any letter from Diana.*　莱尼很发愁因为他没接到戴安娜的任何来信。

Look *before you leap.* (谚)三思而后行。

I always keep candles in the house *in case there is a power cut.*　我在家里总存些蜡烛以防停电。

We'll go on with the work, *whether we can find the necessary tools.*　不管能不能找到必要的工具，我们都将继续这项工作。

2) 状语从句有时也放在主句前(这时常有一个逗号把它和主句分开):

However cold it is, she always goes swimming.　不管天多冷她都去游泳。

As she sang, tears ran down her cheeks.　她唱着唱着，眼泪顺着她的面颊流了下来。

Though times were changed, Bursley was still Bursley.　尽管时代变了，伯斯利还是伯斯利。

Whether we go or whether we stay, the result is the same.　不管我们是去还是留，结果都一样。

3) 在少数情况下，状语从句也可插在主语和谓语之间，特别是它比较短时(例如有词省略时):

Such things, *whether you like it or not,* do happen from time to time.　这种

事情，不管你喜欢与否，总是时有发生的。

This view, *though understandable*, is wrong. 这种看法，尽管可以理解，却是错误的。

This thing, *if continued*, is going to do him irreparable damage. 这件事如果继续下去，将给他造成无法挽回的损害。

第25章 省略句

25.1 概 说

25.1.1 省略与省略句

1）为了省事，人们常把某些词省掉，特别是在口语中：

(I) Thank you. 谢谢你。

(I'm) Glad to see you. 见到你很高兴。

How nice (it is)! 多好呀！

Really? 真的吗？

(You're) Right. (你是)对的。

这种现象称为 **省略** (Ellipsis)，这种句子称为 **省略句** (Elliptical Sentences)。

2）被省略的部分可能是：

a. 主语：

(I) Hope to see you again. 希望再见到你。

(I) Haven't seen you for ages. 好久不见。

(It) Doesn't matter. 没关系。

(It) Serves him right! 他活该！

(I) Just dropped in to ask you a question. 我只是来问你一个问题。

b. 主语和助动词：

(I've) Got to go now. (我)得走了。

(Do you) Want some? (你)要一点吗？

(Have you) Had your breakfast? 吃早饭了吗？

(Are you) Going to town? 进城去吗？

(Do you) See what I mean? 懂我的意思吗？

(Are you) Looking for me? 你找我？

c. 谓语或谓语的部分：

(Is there) Anything you want to tell me? 有什么事要告诉我吗？

(Is there) Anything wrong? 有什么地方有问题吗？

(Does) Anybody want to go?　有谁要去吗?

(Are) The students still waiting?　同学们还在等吗?

d. 宾语:

Is she back yet?　——I don't know.　她回来了吗?　——我不知道。

Which is better?　——It's hard to tell.　哪一个比较好?　——很难说。

"He's a kind man." "I know."　"他是个好人。" "我知道。"

"Where should we go?" "I don't care. Anywhere you want."　"我们去哪里?""我无所谓,你想去哪就去哪儿。"

3) 有时句子大部分都省略,只剩下:

a. 表语:

(I'm) Sorry!　对不起!

Tired?　你累了?

What a pity (it is) you can't come with us!　真遗憾你不能和我们一道去!

Nice you're back.　你回来了很好。

b. 宾语:

(I beg your) Pardon.　请再说一遍。

How many do you want?　——Just one.　你要多少?　——就一个。

Sorry, (you've dialed the) wrong number.　对不起,你拨错号了。

c. 状语:

(Come) This way, please.　请往这边走。

Did you like the film?　——Oh, very much.　这电影你喜欢吗?　——啊,很喜欢。

When are you going?　——Tomorrow.　你什么时候走?　——明天。

d. 其他:

Are you going to paint it green or red?　——Red, I think.　你打算把它漆成绿色还是红色?　——我想漆成红色。

Is she older than you or younger than you?　——Much younger.　她比你大还是小?　——比我小多了。

(Of) Course that's only a beginning.　当然这只是一个开始。

25.1.2　省略句的意思

1) 省略句有时本身意思很清楚:

I'd help you if I could.　如果我能帮你我会帮的。

Sounds a good idea.　听起来是个好主意。

Got any writing paper? 有信纸吗?

So delighted to see you. 看到你真高兴。

Ready? 准备好了吗?

Good! 挺好!

Waiting for the bus? 在等车吗?

Leaving so soon? 这么快就走?

2) 有时意思需从上下文中推断:

"I don't want to go." "Why?" "我不想去。" "为什么?"

"She opposes the idea." "Does she?" "她反对这想法。" "是吗?"

"How much did you pay for it?" "Twenty dollars." "你付了多少钱?" "20 美元。"

"Where are you from?" "Tianjin." "你是哪儿人?" "天津人。"

"When is he arriving?" "Tonight." "他什么时候到?" "今晚。"

I won't accept their terms, never! 我不会接受他们的条件,绝不会!

"Will they agree to the proposal?" "Not likely." "他们会同意这个建议吗?" "不太可能。"

3) 某些描绘性文字(如小说、日记、摘要等)中,有时也有词省略,但由于有上下文,意思则很清楚:

Then we came to the grasslands. Marshes everywhere. No birds! No trees! No house! Not a soul to be seen! 然后我们来到草地,到处都是沼泽,没有飞鸟!没有树木!没有房舍!荒无人烟!

Another busy day! Went to work by bike. Witnessed a car accident. Got to my office ten minute late. 又一个忙碌的日子!骑车上班。看见一场车祸。到办公室时晚了十分钟。

Born in 1830. Went to a grammar school. Entered Eton. Won several awards during his college days. Became a lawyer in 1860... 1830年出生。上语法学校。升入伊顿(学院)。大学期间获了几次奖。1860年当上了律师…

25.1.3 单部句

有些句子,只包含主语和谓语的一部分,很难说什么词省略,意思却很清楚,如:

My goodness! 我的老天!

Thanks a lot.　非常感谢!

Away with you!　走开!

Out with it!　说出来吧!

No entry.　不得进入!

No parking.　禁止泊车!

Down with tyranny!　打倒暴政!

You naughty boy!　你这个调皮孩子!

Nonsense!　胡说!

这类句子称为 **单部句** (One-member Sentences)。

25.2　简单句中的省略

25.2.1　陈述句中的省略

1) 在日常生活中我们会用到很多省略句:

Happy New Year.　——The same to you.　新年快乐。——也祝你新年快乐。

Many happy returns (of the day).　(生日祝贺语)祝你长寿。

Have a pleasant journey.　祝旅途愉快。

Goodbye and good luck to you!　再见，祝你好运!

What awful luck!　真倒霉!

Must have gone down town.　准是进城了。

How nice to see you!　看到你真高兴!

What a nice day!　多好的天气!

Just wonderful!　好极了!

Hope to see you well soon.　祝你早日康复。

So pleased to have made your acquaintance.　认识了你真高兴。

2) 在回答别人问题时，常可省略某些成分:

Will you join us?　——*Well, I'd love to.*　你愿意参加我们的活动吗?　——愿意。

Have you had your supper?　——*Not yet.*　吃晚饭了吗?　——还没有。

Shall I call a doctor?　——*Do, please.*　我要不要去请医生?　——去请吧。

Are you ready?　——*Not quite.*　准备好了吗?　——没完全好。

"How are things going?"　"*Pretty well.*"　"情况如何?"　"很不错。"

How is the weather?　——*Going to clear up.*　天气怎么样？　——快放晴了。

Are your hungry?　——*Not very.*　你饿吗？　——不太饿。

What's your family name?　——*Johnson.*　你姓什么？　——约翰逊。

How do you feel?　——*Just a bit tired.*　你感觉怎样？　——稍有点累。

Where are you going?　——*To the library.*　你去哪儿？　——图书馆。

3) 在对别人的话作出反映时也可以用省略句：

It looks like rain.　——*Yes, somewhat.*　看来要下雨了。　——是的，有点像。

I guess it's an ancient temple.　——*Very likely.*　我猜那是一座古庙。——很可能。

I'd like to ask one or two questions if I may.　——*Certainly.*　如果可能我想问一两个问题。　——当然可以。

I hope I'm not disturbing you too much.　——*Certainly not.*　希望我没过分打扰你。——当然没有。

I hope you won't mind me joking.　——*Not in the least.*　希望你不介意我的笑话。——一点都不介意。

This is a good solution.　——*Sure.*　这是个很好的解决办法。——是的。

也可提出问句：

George isn't coming.　——*Why?*　乔治不来了。　——为什么？

The conference is to be held next week.　——*Where?*　会议下周开。——在哪里开？

She bought a new car.　——*When?*　她买了一辆新车。　——什么时候买的？

They're going to emigrate to New Zealand.　——*Are they?*　他们准备移民到新西兰。——是吗？

25.2.2　疑问句、祈使句和感叹句中的省略

1) 疑问句有时可以有词省略：

Had your breakfast?　吃过早饭了吗？

Anything I can do for you?　我能帮你做什么吗？

Anybody against it?　有人反对吗？

Going to the supermarket?　到超市去吗？

A nice man, isn't he?　他是个好人，是吧？

Going to be a nice day, isn't it?　今天天气会很好，是吧？

Why bring that up?　为什么要提起此事？

What next?　下一步怎么办？

2）祈使句中也可以有词省略：

Gently, please.　请轻一点。

A little more slowly.　再慢一点。

Quick!　快！

Just a minute.　稍等一会儿。

A strawberry milk-shake, please.　请给我一份草莓奶昔。

Attention!　立正！

Editor-in-chief's office, please.　请接总编辑室。

Quiet, please!　请安静点！

3）感叹句也有省略现象：

What a beautiful picture!　多美的画！

How nice of you to come!　你来了真好！

Very good!　很好！

Excellent!　好极了！

Just wonderful!　太妙了！

Rubbish!　胡说八道！

Such an intelligent girl!　这样聪明的姑娘！

Just lovely!　太美了！

另外，在报纸标题或文章标题中也常常出现省略句：

Senator to Seek Reelection　参议员争取再次当选

A baby born on a plane　飞机上诞生婴儿

What to do in an emergency　紧急情况下怎么办

How to prepare a computer programme　如何进行程序设计

25.3　复合句中的省略

25.3.1　对话中的省略句

1）在对话中有些句子可能有词省略，特别是包含宾语从句的句子：

Will it rain tomorrow?　——I hope not.　明天会下雨吗？　——我希望别下。

Can I use your car tonight?　——Sorry, you can't. I'm using it myself.　今晚我能用你的车吗?　——对不起,不行。我自己要用。

His father came here yesterday.　——Yes, I know.　他爸昨天回来了。——我知道。

"That will cost more money." "I see."　"那样会花更多的钱。""我明白了。"

When will Mum be back?　——Who knows.　妈什么时候回来?　——谁知道。

2) 有时可用 so 代表前面说的话,这不是省略句,但作用接近省略句:

Are we late?　——I'm afraid so.　我们迟到了吗?　——我想是的。

Will it be fine tomorrow?　——I hope so.　明天会是晴天吗?　——我希望会。

Is she coming?　——I think (don't think) so.　她会来吗?　——我想会(不会)来。

Shakespeare was born in 1564, wasn't he?　——I believe so.　莎士比亚是 1564 年生的,对吗?　——我认为是的。

I suppose you'll be going to the meeting?　——Yes, I suppose so.　我想你会参加这次会议的吧?　——是的,我想我会。

这种现象称为 **替代** (Substitution)。

3) 还有一些其他类型的省略复合句:

Is everything going all right?　——Not so well as I expected.　一切都进展顺利吗?　——不像我预期的那样好。

Do they make glass fiber?　——Not any that I know of.　他们生产玻璃纤维吗?　——据我知道不生产。

Did you know anything about it?　——Not until you told me.　这件事你知道吗?　——你告诉我后才知道。

Shall we have our picnic tomorrow?　——Unless it rains.　我们明天去野餐吗?　——要是天不下雨的话。

Shall we stop over in Shenzhen?　——Yes, if time permits.　我们要不要在深圳停留?　——如果时间允许就停留。

25.3.2 状语从句中的省略

状语从句中省略一些词是非常普通的现象。通常省略主语和系动词(如果主语与主句主语相同则可能省略），大部分从句中都可以有省略结构，如：

1) 时间状语从句：

Often she would weep *when* (she was) *alone*. 她一个人时常常哭泣。

He had an accident *while on his way here*. 他在来这里的路上出了车祸。

Even as a girl she showed great promise as a pianist. 她从小就显露出有望成为钢琴家。

Whenever possible, the children should play outside in the fresh air. 任何时间只要可能就该让孩子们到户外玩耍，那里空气新鲜。

A friend is never known *till needed*. 患难之中见真交。

Once in the examination hall, you would forget all such trivialities. 一进考场，这样的细节你都会忘记。

2) 条件状语从句：

If necessary, ring me at home. 如有必要可往我家里打电话。

If in doubt, ask at your local library. 若有疑问，可向当地图书馆查询。

He would never do this *unless compelled*. 他绝不会这样做，除非是被迫。

3) 让步状语从句：

Though not large, the room was well lit. 房间虽不大却很亮堂。

Although still young, he's going very grey. 他虽然年纪还轻，头发却已灰白。

Things were beginning to improve, *even if not quickly enough*. 情况开始改善，尽管速度不够快。

4) 方式状语从句：

As expected, the afforestation movement rapidly spread. 如预料的那样，造林运动迅速展开了。

He glanced about *as if in search of something*. 他四下张望，仿佛在找什么东西似的。

She waited *as though for a reply*. 她等了等，似乎在等候回答。

5) 地点状语从句：

Fill in blanks with articles *where necessary*. 在必要的地方用冠词填空。

They tried to acquire colonies *where possible*. 在可能的地方他们就设法夺取殖民地。

Avoid structures of this kind *wherever possible*. 任何地方只要可能就要避免这种结构。

They believed in the application of force *wherever and whenever necessary*.

在任何地方任何时间，只要必要他们就主张使用武力。

6) 比较状语从句 (省略的方式与其他状语从句不同):

The profits are greater *than the losses (are)*. 利润大于损失。

He has more time *than me (I do)*. 他的时间比我多。

He loved her more *than ever*. 他比过去更爱她了。

It's even hotter today *than yesterday*. 今天比昨天更热了。

He was almost as tall *as his father*. 他几乎有他父亲那样高了。

She was as interested in art *as ever*. 她对艺术的兴趣一如既往。

I shall come along as often *as possible*. 我将尽量多来。

7) 有些让步状语从句有特殊的省略方式:

In our company, everybody is well taken care of, *no matter what his position (is)*. 在我们公司，人人都得到很好的照顾，不管他地位如何。

Anyone, *no matter who (he is)*, may point out our shortcomings. 我们的缺点，不管是什么人，谁向我们指出都行。

The country is always beautiful *whatever the season (is)*. 这一带的田野，不管什么季节，都那样美丽。

We're going to the seaside *whatever the weather*. 不管天气如何，我们都要去海滨。

I refuse, *however favourable the condition*. 不管条件多好我都不接受。

25.3.3 一些其他的省略复合句

1) 有些复合句的主句中有词省略:

(Is there) Anything you want to add? 还有什么你要补充吗?

(Is there) Anyone wishing to join the book club? 有谁想参加读书俱乐部?

(It's) Too bad you can't stay any longer. 你不能再多待真遗憾。

(It's) So nice you're all for the idea. 太好了，你们都赞成这个想法。

(It's) Strange no one knows anything about it. 真奇怪，没人知道这件事。

(I'm) Sorry, the line is busy. 对不起，占线了。

(I) Hope you'll enjoy your stay here. 希望你在这儿过得愉快。

(I) Don't know when she'll be back. 不知道她什么时候回来。

I would (do it) if I could. 如果我能做到我会做的。

2) 一些复合句的从句中可以有词省略:

Will he check in his luggage? —— I believe not. 他的行李会托运吗? ——我想不会。

Will she speak at the meeting? ——I don't think she will. 她会在会上发言吗？ ——我想不会。

Will they accept these terms? ——I guess not. 他们会接受这些条件吗？ ——我猜不会。

At last they did as we told them to. 最后他们照我们的话做了。

We'll do all we can to fulfil our task. 我们将尽一切可能完成任务。

We won't postpone the trip unless we have to. 除非不得已我们不会推迟这次旅行。

We'll raise more fund for the project if we can. 如果可能我们将为这项计划多筹集一点经费。

Don't tell me if you don't want to. 如果你不想告诉我就别说。

I'll pay for the hotel, if you will for the food. 如果你付伙食费，我会付旅馆住宿费。

His opinion, whether right or wrong, should be considered. 他的意见，不管对还是错，都应当考虑。

〔注〕有些句子看上去结构不完整，却表示完整的意思，很难说哪些词语被省略，如：

That he should have left without asking me! 他竟然没征求我的同意就走了！

And to think that I trusted him! 我竟然信任了他！

If only he had had more courage! 他要是再勇敢一点就好了！

Would that I were with her now! 但愿我现在和她在一起！

25.4　并列句中的省略

25.4.1　并列句中的省略

1）并列句中，如果后面分句有词和前面分句的词相同，有时可以省略，以避免重复：

Some of them were injured, *but most of them weren't*. 他们中有些人受伤了，但大部分人没受伤。

She could have applied for that job, but *she didn't*. 她本可申请那份工作，但她没有。

One soldier was killed and *two others wounded*. 有一个士兵被打死，另外两个受了伤。

I work in a factory and *my sister on a farm*. 我在工厂工作，我妹妹在农场工作。

Tom majors in history and *I in computer science*. 汤姆学历史，我则学电脑。

My office is on the ground floor and *hers on the 5th*. 我的办公室在一楼，她的在五楼。

The scenery was beautiful, and *the acting superb*. 布景很漂亮，表演很出色。

She can't speak French and *I can't either*. 她不会讲法语，我也不会。

I didn't see it and *nor did Marry*. 我没看见，玛丽也没看见。

2) 有时并列连词可引导一个短语，也可说有词省略：

You must stop, *and (stop) at once*, this sort of behavior. 你必须停止这种行为，而且是马上停止。

They tried to save her, *but in vain*. 他们试图救活她，但没成功。

I won't stop, *not until I've achieved my ambition*. 我不会停止，直到我实现自己的理想。

She wouldn't go home, *not even when I had asked twice*. 她不肯回家，甚至我劝了她两次仍不肯回去。

第26章　句型的转换

26.1　简单句句型的转换

26.1.1　句型的转换

1) 同一个意思常有许多表达方法。例如"他英文很好"就可以有许多表达方法，如：

He knows English very well.

He has a good knowledge of English.

He has a good command of English.

His English is perfect (superb, wonderful).

这是一种词汇手段。还有一个办法，就是利用不同句型表达同一思想，这是一种语法手段，如"你这样做是对的"这句话可以用不同句型来表示：

You were right to do that.

You were right in doing that.

It was right for you to do that.

It was right of you to do that.

学习用词汇手段来使表达方法多样化是一个漫长的过程，随着语言修养的提高，表达的方法也会逐渐丰富，而用语法手段来提高表达能力相对要容易一些。这种把一种结构改为另一种结构来表达同一思想的做法，可称为 **句型的转换** (Transformation of Sentence Patterns)。适当探讨这个问题，可以丰富我们的表达能力，使我们使用语言更精确。

2) 一个句子有很多成分都可转换为另一种形式，例如：

a. 主语：

Varied methods help to liven up a lesson.

Variety of methods helps to liven up a lesson.

(教学)方法多样化可使课堂生动。

b. 谓语：

He evidently *recieved little benefit* from our advice.

He evidently *benefited little* from our advice.

显然他没从我们的劝告中有所获益。

c. 宾语:

> They marvelled at *our great achievements*.
>
> They marvelled at *the greatness of our achievements*.
>
> 他们对我们的巨大成就感到惊讶。

d. 状语:

> We immediately set out *to pursue the enemy*.
>
> We immediately set out *in pursuit of the enemy*.
>
> 我们立即出动去追击敌人。

e. 定语:

> The question was one *to be debated*.
>
> The question was *a debatable one*.
>
> 这是一个值得争论的问题。

有时整个句子结构都可以改变:

> You are so kind to help us.
>
> It's so kind of you to help us.
>
> 你帮助我们太好了。

26.1.2 主语的转换

1) 主语结构转换时有时对别的部分没有影响:

> There is *nothing inconsistent* in what she said.
>
> There is *no inconsistency* in what she said.
>
> 她的话并无前后矛盾之处。

> *His arrogant manner* made everyone dislike him.
>
> *His arrogance* made everyone dislike him.
>
> 他的傲慢态度使大家都讨厌他。

> *Her late arrival* delayed our departure.
>
> *Her arriving late* delayed our departure.
>
> 她到晚了延误了我们的出发时间。

> *Your denying it* is useless.
>
> *Your denial of* it is useless.
>
> 你的否认没有用。

2) 有时其他部分也需作相应的改动：

Mastery of a language requires painstaking efforts.

It requires painstaking efforts to master a language.

学语言要下苦功。

No amount of persuasion could make her change her mind.

Nothing could persuade her to change her mind.

不管怎样劝说，她都不肯改变主意。

The choice is up to you.

It's up to you to make the choice.

这由你来作选择。

His decision was to have it out with her that night.

He decided to have it out with her that night.

他决定当晚就和她说清楚。

26.1.3 谓语的转换

1) 谓语有时可改为带表语的结构：

These books *can be obtained* at any library.

These books *are obtainable* at any library.

这些书哪个图书馆都有。

Every language *reflects the culture* that produces it.

Every language *is a reflection of the culture* that produces it.

每种语言都反映产生它的文化。

She always *minds her obligation* to others.

She *is always mindful of her obligation* to others.

她总是注意自己对别人的责任。

They *opposed* reform.

They *were opposed to* reform.

他们反对改革。

2) 谓语有时可改成"动词 + 名词"这类结构：

Why didn't you *inquire further* about it?

Why didn't you *make further inquiry* about it?

你为什么没对此作进一步的了解？

He *apologized* for having broken his promise.

He *offered apologies* for having broken his promise.

他为违背诺言而道歉。

She *recited* a poem by Heine.

She *gave a recitation of* a poem by Heine.

她朗诵了海涅的一首诗。

He *applied* for a passport.

He *made an application* for a passport.

他申请一份护照。

3）有时可把表语作某种改动：

Your suggestions are *of great value to us*.

Your suggestions are *very valuable to us*.

你的建议对我们很有价值。

Sunlight is *of great benefit to the human body*.

Sunlight is *quite beneficial to the human body*.

阳光对人体很有好处。

His speech is *of little significance*.

His speech is *not significant at all*.

他的发言毫不重要。

This is *of no use* to us.

This is *not useful* to us.

这对我们没有用处。

4）有些被动结构可换为"be + 介词短语"结构：

The road *is being repaired*.

The road *is under repair*.

马路正在翻修。

The case *is being investigated*.

The case *is under investigation*.

该案正在调查之中。

The scene *couldn't be described*.

The scene *is beyond description*.

那景色无法形容。

His conduct *can't be criticized*.

His conduct *is beyond criticism*.

他的行为无可非议。

5) 有些被动结构可以换为"be ＋形容词"结构：

His bravery *is to be commended.*
His bravery *is commendable.*
他的勇敢值得赞扬。

Her behaviour *ought to be praised.*
Her behaviour *is praiseworthy.*
她的行为值得赞美。

Such expenses *can be avoided.*
Such expenses *are avoidable.*
这种开销是可以避免的。

These practices *can be justified.*
These practices *are justifiable.*
这些做法是有道理的。

26.1.4　宾语的转换

1) 宾语有时也可以转换：

The expansion of the city required *extension of the communication lines.*
The expansion of the city required *extended communication lines.*
城市要扩大就要延长交通线。

The report revealed *the precariousness of their position.*
The report revealed *their precarious position.*
报告透露了他们处境的危险。

They were deeply impressed by *the fluency of her English.*
They were deeply impressed by *her fluent English.*
她流利的英语给他们留下了深刻的印象。

They marvelled at *the beauty of the lake.*
They marvelled at *the beautiful scenery round the lake.*
他们对湖上的美景感到惊讶。

2) 在不少情况下不定式可转换为动名词或分词：

He hated *to see* any bird killed.
He hated *seeing* any bird killed.
他不愿看到鸟被打死。

She loves to *have* a lot of kids round her.

She loves *having* a lot of kids round her.

　她喜欢身边有许多孩子。

I watched him *eat* his breakfast.

I watched him *eating* his breakfast.

　我看着他吃早饭。

Did you notice her *leave* the house?

Did you notice her *leaving* the house?

　你没注意到她离开屋子吗?

3) 有时只有宾语的一部分可以改变:

He advised us *to be vigilant*.

He advised us *to maintain vigilance*.

　他告诫我们要保持警惕。

They always consider themselves *to be right*.

They always consider themselves *to be in the right*.

　他们总认为自己是对的。

I believe him *to be honest*.

I believe him *honest*.

　我相信他是诚实的。

She regarded his conduct as *being totally unacceptable*.

She regarded his conduct as *totally unacceptable*.

　她认为他的行为是完全不能接受的。

26.1.5　状语的转换

1) 副词有时可转换为介词短语:

He laughed *contemptuously*.

He laughed *with contempt*.

　他鄙夷地笑了笑。

She *purposely* ignored me at the party.

She ignored me *on purpose* at the party.

　在晚会上她故意不理会我。

I only met her *accidentally*.

I only met her *by accident*.

　我只是偶然碰到她的。

> The winning team returned home *triumphantly*.
> The winning team returned home *in triumph*.
> 获胜的队得意地回到本国。

2）不定式有时也可转换为介词短语：

> I've come *to get your advice*.
> I've come *for your advice*.
> 我是来征求你的意见的。

> The policemen ran through the street *to pursue the bank robbers*.
> The policemen ran through the street *in pursuit of the bank robbers*.
> 警察在马路上奔跑追逐抢劫银行的人。

> We walked through the woods *to search for the little girl*.
> We walked through the woods *in search of the little girl*.
> 我们穿过树林找寻那个小女孩。

> There's a gentleman asking *to see you*.
> There's a gentleman asking *for you*.
> 有位先生要求见你。

3）分词短语也可转换为介词短语：

> The staff members in the office are all busy *working*.
> The staff members in the office are all busy *at work*.
> 办公室的职员们都在紧张地工作。

> He spent two hours *doing his homework*.
> He spent two hours *on (in doing) his homework*.
> 他用了两小时做作业。

> The books lay *piled up* on the floor.
> The books lay *in piles* on the floor.
> 书一堆堆地放在地板上。

> He entered, *accompanied by* a group of boys.
> He entered *in company with* a group of boys.
> 他和一群男孩一道走了进来。

26.1.6   定语的转换

1）形容词可以转换为介词短语：

It's a very *important* discovery.

It's a discovery *of great importance*.

这是一项重大发现。

She is *an intelligent girl*.

She is a girl *of high intelligence*.

她是个智力很高的姑娘。

She is *a highly imaginative* woman.

She is a woman *of remarkable imagination*.

她是个有丰富想像力的女人。

He has a plan *to overcome the difficulties*.

He has a plan *for overcoming the difficulties*.

他有一个克服困难的计划。

2) 有些不定式也可转换为形容词:

Her fondness of hard work is a trait *to be commended*.

Her fondness of hard work is a *commendable* trait.

她喜欢苦干是一种值得赞扬的品质。

This was indeed a day *to be remembered*.

This was indeed a *memorable* day.

这确实是一个令人难忘的日子。

He is not a man *to be easily excited*.

He is not an *excitable* man.

他不是一个容易激动的人。

We all thought it a deed *to be praised*.

We all thought it a *praiseworthy* deed.

我们都认为这是一个值得赞扬的行为。

26.2 复合句和并列句句型的转换

26.2.1 复合句句型的转换

1) 在改变复合句的句型时，我们可以只改变从句的一部分，如改变其主语(a)、谓语(b)、宾语(c)、状语(d)或定语(e):

a. I guess *their arriving late* will affect our schedule.

I guess *their late arrival* will affect our schedule.

我想他们晚到会影响我们的日程。

I think *their denying our request* is rather impolite.

I think *their denial of our request* is rather impolite.

我认为他们不答应我们的请求很不礼貌。

b. She knew he *could be trusted*.

She knew he *was trustworthy*.

她知道他是可以信赖的。

I hear she always *works hard*.

I hear she *is always hard-working*.

我听说她一向工作努力。

c. Can you tell me *what is required* for this job?

Can you tell me *about the requirements* for this job?

你能否告诉我干这工作有什么要求?

They say he *has a fondness for* his little sister.

They say he *is very fond of* his little sister.

他们说他很喜欢他的小妹妹。

d. She felt uneasy when people looked at her *suspiciously*.

She felt uneasy when people looked at her *with suspicion*.

当人们带着怀疑的眼光看她时, 她感到很不自在。

I felt that he had arrived late *purposely* to annoy me.

I felt that he had arrived late *on purpose* to annoy me.

我觉得他是故意迟到来使我不高兴。

e. This shows that *educational* reform is not an easy task.

This shows that reform *of education* is not an easy task.

这表明教育改革不是一件容易的事。

You see this is a day *never to be forgotten*.

You see this is an *unforgettable* day.

你知道这是一个难忘的日子。

2) 也可以只改变主句的一部分:

The sparkle in her eyes showed how excited she was.

Her sparkling eyes showed how excited she was.

她闪光的眼睛表明她多么兴奋。

The soldiers *resisted so stubbornly* that the enemy were forced to retreat.

The soldiers *put up such a stubborn resistance* that the enemy were forced to retreat.　士兵们顽强抵抗, 敌军被迫撤退。

> She spoke *so sincerely* that I was greatly touched.
>
> She spoke *with such sincerity* that I was greatly touched.
>
> 她讲得那样诚恳,我深受感动。

3) 有时整个句子结构都可以改变:

> Nothing indicates that the weather is changing.
>
> There is no indication that the weather is changing.
>
> 没有迹象表明天气要发生变化。

> The large fantail is a peculiarity of the peacock.
>
> One thing peculiar about the peacock is its large fantail.
>
> 孔雀的一个独特之处就是它的扇形尾巴。

> Completion of the project took three years.
>
> It took three years to complete the project.
>
> 完成这项工程花了三年时间。

26.2.2　并列句句型的转换

并列句的结构也可以转换,通常是改动一个分句的结构:

> She said nothing but her eyes *reproached us*.
>
> She said nothing but her eyes *were reproachful*.
>
> 她没说什么,但眼睛里却有责备的神情。

> He remained modest; no praise or compliments *had any effect on him*.
>
> He remained modest; no praise or compliments *could affect him*.
>
> 他依然很谦虚;赞扬和恭维对他没有影响。

> It was Thursday afternoon; *scarce a soul was about*.
>
> It was Thursday afternoon; *there was scarcely a soul about*.
>
> 这是星期四下午,附近简直没有一个人。

26.3　简单句和复合句的互换

26.3.1　短语和从句的互换

简单句和复合句的互换,实际上是短语和从句的互换。句子成分若是用单词或短语表示,这个句子就是简单句。如有一个或更多成分由从句表示,则这个句子就是复合句。许多句子通过把从句变为短语,即可以由复合句变为简单句。这样转换的成分可以是：

a. 主语：

> It's a pity *we should waste so much time on it* .
>
> It's a pity *to waste so much time on it* .
>
> 在这上面浪费这么多时间真可惜。

b. 表语：

> The question is *how we can raise sufficient fund for it*.
>
> The question is *how to raise sufficient fund for it*.
>
> 问题是如何筹集足够的资金。

c. 宾语：

> He insisted *that she should give him a straightforward answer*.
>
> He insisted *on her giving him a straightforward answer*.
>
> 他坚持要她给他一个直截了当的回答。

d. 定语：

> Those *who wish to go* please sign up here .
>
> Those *wishing to go* please sign up here.
>
> 想去的人请在这里签名。

e. 状语：

> We couldn't build it *because we lacked money*.
>
> We couldn't build it *for lack of money*.
>
> 因为缺钱我们不能修建它。

26.3.2　主语从句和短语的互换

1) 主语从句有时可换为不定式（短语）：

> It's regrettable *that one should be so extravagant*.
>
> It's regrettable *to be so extravagant*.
>
> 这样奢侈浪费是令人遗憾的。

> It's a good thing *that you give us so much support*.
>
> It's a good thing *for you to give us so much support*.
>
> 你给我们这么多支持是一件好事。

> It's nice *you came so early*.
>
> It's nice *of you to come so early*.
>
> 你来这么早很好。

It hasn't been decided *where we should hold the conference*.

It hasn't been decided *where to hold the conference*.

在哪里开这次会议还没有决定。

2）主语从句有时也可转换为动名词短语：

It worries her *that Tom should mix with such people*.

Tom's mixing with such people worries her.

汤姆和这样的人来往令她发愁。

It's strange *that he left so suddenly*.

His leaving so suddenly was strange.

他这样突然离去是很奇怪的。

It doesn't make any difference *whether I'm here*.

It doesn't make any difference *my being here*.

我在不在这里都没有什么关系。

It is a great honour *that you've come to visit us*.

Your coming to visit us is a great honour.

你的来访是我们的一大荣幸。

26.3.3　表语从句转换为短语

1）表语从句有时可转换为不定式短语：

My idea is *that we should rent an apartment*.

My idea is *to rent an apartment*.

我的想法是去租一套房子。

Another plan is *that we go to Hong Kong first*.

Another plan is *for us to go Hong Kong first*.

另一个计划是我们先去香港。

Now the question is *how we could raise so much money*.

Now the question is *how to raise so much money*.

现在的问题是如何筹到这么多资金。

The problem is *that we should find a place quickly*.

The problem is *to find a place quickly*.

问题是赶快找到一个地方。

2）表语从句也可转换为动名词短语：

Our chief worry was *that she lacked enthusiasm*.

Our chief worry was *her lacking in enthusiasm*.

我们主要的担心是她缺乏热情。

Their difficulty was *that they did not have the necessary funds*.

Their difficulty was *their not having the necessary funds*.

他们的困难是没有必要的资金。

My suggestion is *that we make immediate enquiries into the matter*.

My suggestion is *making immediate enquiries into the matter*.

我的建议是马上调查此事。

The trouble is *they could not agree among themselves*.

The trouble is *their not being able to agree among themselves*.

问题是他们内部都不能取得一致意见。

3）表语从句有时也可转换为名词引导的短语：

Our major problem was *that we lacked raw materials*.

Our major problem was *our lack of raw materials*.

我们的主要问题是缺乏原料。

Another difficulty was *that they couldn't communicate with the outside*.

Another difficulty was *their inability to communicate with the outside*.

另一个困难是他们无法与外界联系。

Their trouble is *that they are short of skilled workers*.

Their trouble is *their shortage of skilled workers*.

他们的困难是缺乏熟练工人。

One requirement is *that we should participate in their activities*.

One requirement is *our participation in their activities*.

一个要求是我们应该参加他们的活动。

26.3.4 宾语从句转换为短语

1）宾语从句常常可以转换为动名词短语：

I suggest *we leave early for the airport*.

I suggest *leaving early for the airport*.

我建议早点动身去机场。

I remember *I've heard you speak on that subject*.

I remember *having heard you speak on that subject*.

我记得曾听你说过这个问题。

He denied *that he had made any statement to that effect*.

He denied *making any statement to that effect*.

他否认曾作过那样内容的声明。

She insisted *that I should be there*.

She insisted *on my being there*.

  她坚持要我待在那里。

2）宾语从句还可转换为带不定式的复合宾语:

Do you expect *she will stay after that*?

Do you expect *her to stay after that*?

  出了这事你难道还指望她待下去?

The police ordered *that they should wait right there*.

The police ordered *them to wait right there*.

  警察命令他们就在那里等候。

She told me *where I could shop cheaply*.

She told me *where to shop cheaply*.

  她告诉我在哪里可以买到便宜东西。

I want to show you *how it can be done quickly*.

I want to show you *how to do it quickly*.

  我想告诉你怎样迅速做好这事。

3）宾语从句有时可转换为名词短语:

Dock workers demanded *that they should be paid higher wages*.

Dock workers demanded *higher wages*.

  码头工人要求增加工资。

They requested *that he resign immediately*.

They requested *his immediate resignation*.

  他们请他立即辞职。

The judge ordered *that the prisoner be released*.

The judge ordered *the release of the prisoner*.

  法官命令释放这名囚犯。

26.3.5　定语从句转换为短语

1）定语从句常可以转换为不定式短语:

There are a lot of things *we should do today*.

There are a lot of things *to do today*.

  今天有很多事要做。

There's little *I can say about it*.

There's little *to be said about it*.

对此(我)没有什么可说的。

What's the next problem *we should tackle*?

What's the next problem *to be tackled*?

下一个该解决的问题是什么?

That's nothing *we should feel ashamed of*.

That's nothing *to be ashamed of*.

这不是什么该羞愧的事。

2) 定语从句还常常可以转换为分词短语:

Those *who study there* are mostly disabled children.

Those *studying there* are mostly disabled children.

在那里学习的大多数是残疾儿童。

Only people *who live here* can apply for membership.

Only people *living here* can apply for membership.

只有住在这里的人可以申请入会。

These are the seats *which are reserved for VIP's*.

These are the seats *reserved for VIP's*.

这些是为贵宾们保留的座位。

Are you in favour of the suggestion *Peter put forward*?

Are you in favour of the suggestion *put forward by Peter*?

你赞成彼得提出的建议吗?

3) 定语从句有时还可转换为介词短语 (a) 或名词等 (b):

a. The information *that is in his possession* is strictly confidential.

The information *in his possession* is strictly confidential.

他掌握的情报是绝密的。

He lost his position owing to circumstances *which he couldn't control*.

He lost his position owing to circumstances *beyond his control*.

由于他无法控制的情况, 他失去了自己的职位。

b. Elizabeth, *who was a girl of a strong character*, refused to back down.

Elizabeth, *a girl of a strong character*, refused to back down.

伊丽莎白是个性格坚强的姑娘, 不肯退让。

Her daughter, *who is now already grown-up*, helps out in the store.

Her daughter, *now already grown-up*, helps out in the store.

她的女儿现在已长大成人, 能在店里帮忙了。

26.3.6　状语从句转换为短语

1) 状语从句常可以转换为分词短语：

As she feared something was the matter, she went to the door and listened.

Fearing something was the matter, she went to the door and listened.

她害怕有什么事，走到房门口听了听。

After he had failed twice, he didn't want to try again.

Having failed twice, he didn't want to try again.

他已失败两次，不想再尝试了。

As it had been weakened by storms, the bridge was no longer safe.

Weakened by storms, the bridge was no longer safe.

因受暴风雨侵袭，这座桥不再安全。

As he was convinced that they were trying to poison him, he refused to eat anything.

Convinced that they were trying to poison him, he refused to eat anything.

因认定他们想毒害他，他什么东西都不肯吃。

2) 状语从句有时也可转换为不定式短语：

He wore a mask *so that no one should recognize him*.

He wore a mask *so as not to be recognized*.

他戴了一个面罩以防有人认出他。

She was *so* young *that she couldn't understand such matters*.

She was *too* young *to understand such matters*.

她太年轻不懂这些事。

I'm sorry *I've taken up so much of your time*.

I'm sorry *to have taken up so much of your time*.

对不起占用了你这么多时间。

Who are you *that you should talk like that*?

Who are you *to talk like that*?

你是谁竟然这样讲话？

3) 状语从句有时还可以转换为介词短语：

Don't make any changes *until you get further notice*.

Don't make any changes *until further notice*.

在另接通知之前不要作任何改动。

In case there is a fire, ring this bell.

In case of fire, ring this bell.

如有火警，请按此铃。

If it hadn't been for your support, we would have gone bankrupt.

Without your support we would have gone bankrupt.

要不是有你的支持，我们早都破产了。

I'll write to you when I hear from her.

I'll write to you on hearing from her.

我一收到她的信就写信告诉你。

第27章 标点符号

27.1 概　说

27.1.1 英语中的标点符号

英语中的标点符号有下面这些:

句　号	(.)	Full Stop 或 Period
问　号	(?)	Interrogation Mark 或 Question Mark
感叹号	(!)	Exclamation Mark
逗　号	(,)	Comma
分　号	(;)	Semicolon
冒　号	(:)	Colon
破折号	(—)	Dash
括　号	(())	Brackets 或 Marks of Parentheses
引　号	("" 或 ' ')	Quotation Marks
连字号	(-)	Hyphen
撇　号	(')	Apostrophe

27.1.2 标点符号的作用

标点符号的作用是使句子的意思更加清楚。句号代表较长的停顿,说明句子结束。逗号表示较短的停顿,表示句子尚未结束,但可稍作停顿。各种符号都有一定的意义。英语的标点符号与汉语的标点符号大致相近。只要细心观察,不难掌握标点符号的用法。

27.2 用在句末的标点符号

27.2.1 句号、问号和感叹号

1) 这三种符号都用在句末 —— 陈述句及祈使句结束时加句号:

We have made great advances in the last twenty years. 近二十年我们取得了巨大的进展。

Be careful of what you are doing. 做事要小心。

祈使句如要加强语气,可以加感叹号;陈述句如带有较强的感情色彩也可加感叹号:

Look out! You nearly got hit by that bicycle! 小心! 你差点被那辆自行车撞了!

2) 疑问句都需加问号:

What's all this about? 这都是怎么回事?

What's that? He refuses to come? 怎么? 他不肯来?

You're still waiting here? 你还在这里等?

Any more? 还要一点吗?

3) 感叹句后需加感叹号:

What a lovely baby! 多可爱的小宝宝!

How do you dare say that! 你怎么敢这样讲话!

Thank you so much! 十分感谢!

It's so good of you! 你真好!

27.2.2 引语中的标点符号

1) 在直接引语中,可以用感叹号和问号:

He said, "What a dreadful idea!" 他说,"多可怕的想法!"

"Good!" he exclaimed. "好的!"他叫道。

"Evacuate the area!" ordered the Commander. "撤出这个地区!"司令员命令说。

"I don't know the way. Do you? " he asked. "我不知道路,你知道吗?"他问道。

"I'm going shopping. Can I get you something? " she said. "我去买东西,我能给你买点什么吗?"她说道。

2）如引用词在前，也可用句号：

He said, "If she leaves the house, follow her." 他说，"如果她离开这房子，就跟着她。"

如引用词在后，则不能用句号，而需用逗号：

"I advise cancelling the meeting," he said. "我建议取消这次会议，"他说。

"Let's sell the house," said Tom. "咱们把房子卖掉吧，"汤姆说。

"Please don't drink too much! Remember that you'll have to drive home," she said. "别喝太多酒！记住你还得开车回家，"她说。

27.3　用在句子当中的标点符号

27.3.1　逗号的主要用法

逗号表示一个短促的停顿，它可以用来把下面的这些成分和句子的其他部分隔开：

1）同位语：

This is Li Ying, monitor of Class 4. 这是四班的班长李瑛。

People, old and young, all came out to greet the guests. 老老少少大家都出来欢迎客人。

但限制性同位语前不用加逗号。

We Chinese students find the use of prepositions especially difficult. 我们中国学生感到介词特别难用。

2）插入语：

That's a better solution, don't you think? 这是个比较好的解决办法，你觉得呢？

This, I think, was mainly due to our lack of experience. 这个，我想，主要是由于我们缺乏经验的缘故。

"Tell me," he said, "what did you think of the discussion?" "告诉我，"他说，"你觉得这次讨论怎么样？"

在感叹词后可以用逗号，如感叹情绪很强，就以用感叹号较好：

Well, I must be leaving. 嗯，我得走了。

Ouch! That hurt. 唉哟！真疼。

3）以分词短语或复合结构表示的状语：

Bored with his work, he thought of going home early. 他干烦了，想早

点回家。

She walked slowly, stopping frequently to rest.　她慢慢走着，不时停下休息。

The day being fine, we decided to go swimming.　天气很好，我们决定去游泳。

以分词短语表示的状语，在紧跟它所修饰的动词时，有时可以不用逗号：

For the whole night she lay tossing in bed.　她在床上翻来覆去一夜没睡着。

4）放在句首或插在句子中间的状语从句（或其省略形式）：

When the bell rings, stop writing.　铃响时就不要再写了。

His response, when I questioned him, was a shake of his head.　我问他时，他的反应是摇摇头。

This medicine, taken in time, can be very effective.　这种药如果及时服用是很有效的。

放在句首的状语，如果不长，也可不加逗号：

If you like you may stay.　如果你愿意可以留下。

5）放在句首或插在句子中间的某些其他形式的状语：

To make a long story short, they smoothed away their misunderstanding and became good friends again.　总之，他们消除了误会，重归于好。

The date, however, hasn't been fixed.　但日期还没有确定。

Your argument, in my opinion, is valid.　在我看来，你的论点是站得住的。

6）非限制性定语从句：

That summer, she went to Wuhan, where her husband worked.　那年夏天她去了武汉，她丈夫在那里工作。

The weather may not be good enough tomorrow, in which case we'll have to put the trip off.　明天天气可能不够好，如果那样我们就得延期再去。

27.3.2　逗号的其他用法

1）逗号还可以用来连接一个句子中的平行成分，如：

a. 主语、表语或宾语：

Lao Wu, Xiao Lin and myself were all very enthusiastic about this idea.

老吴、小林和我自己都很支持这个意见。

The main products of the district are wool, cotton, timber and tung-oil. 这个地区的主要产品是羊毛、棉花、木材和桐油。

She sent me some postcards, a few books, a pocket English dictionary and an album of pictures. 她寄给我一些明信片、几本书、一本袖珍英文词典和一本画册。

b. 定语:

We had a long, hard, but interesting journey. 我们做了一次劳累但很有意思的长途旅行。

He was a very lovable man, kind-hearted, easy to get along with and always ready to help others. 他是一个很可爱的人,心地善良,容易相处,总是乐于帮助别人。

有时不需要用逗号:

You naughty little thing! 你这个调皮的小家伙!

c. 谓语或其他以动词表示的成分:

He got up, washed, dressed and hurried to school. 他起床、洗脸、穿衣,然后匆忙赶往学校。

He was fond of skating, boating and playing football. 他喜欢溜冰、划船和踢足球。

d. 状语:

A group of young men were standing there, talking, laughing and teasing each other. 一群年轻人站在那里,又说又笑,互相取乐。

Please read slowly, loudly and clearly. 请慢慢地大声清楚地朗读。

e. 分句:

Everybody was surprised, and Shuzhen, after looking at her for a moment, went up and clasped her hand. 大家都很惊奇,淑贞看了一会儿之后走上前握住她的手。

Ann can't come, she is taking her exam now. 安不能来,她在考试。

平行的成分若只有两个,在多数情况下,它们之间都用 and 而不用逗号。如果有两个以上,则最后两个之间用 and,不用逗号。不过近年来,and 前加逗号的情况也不少,特别是在美国。

2) 除此之外,逗号还可以用来:

a. 表示某些词省略了 (主要是在并列句中):

My room is on the second floor, and hers, on the third one. 我的房间在二

层，她的房间在三层。

b. 表示任何需要停顿的地方：

This mistake can be, and should be, corrected. 这一错误可以也应该改正。

Whether or not she will come, I've no idea. 她究竟来不来我不知道。

c. 标写日期和地址：

The conference is scheduled for the 3rd of July, 2000. 会议定于 2000 年 7 月 3 日召开。

My address is 707 Park Avenue, San Francisco, CA 94037. 我的地址是 加州旧金山派克大道 707 号(邮区 94037)。

27.3.3　分号的用法

分号表示的停顿比句号短，比逗号长，主要用来：

1) 把两个意思上有一定联系的句子连在一起：

It was getting late; she must start back for the village. 时间不早了，她 得动身回村了。

2) 连接两个等立的分句，如果其中一个（或更多）里面含有逗号：

When I started, the sky was clear; but before I had gone two *li*, it began to rain. 我动身时天上明净无云，但走了不到两里路就开始下雨了。

27.3.4　冒号的用法

冒号也是在句子中间使用的，它主要用在：

1) 列举的东西前面：

There are in English two articles: the definite article and the indefinite article. 英语中有两个冠词，即定冠词和不定冠词。

A noun can be used as: 1) subject, 2) object, 3) predicative, 4) an attribute. 名词可以用作：1) 主语，2) 宾语，3) 表语，4) 定语。

2) 引用的句子前面，特别是当这个句子比较长时：

Shakespeare said: "Neither a borrower nor a lender be." 莎士比亚说："既 不要找人借钱，也不要借钱给人。"

3) 一个附加的解释性的分句前面：

You can't count on him to help: he is such a busy man. 你不能指望他 帮忙，他是这样一位大忙人。

在后两种情况下，不用冒号用逗号也可以。

27.3.5　破折号的用法

破折号主要有下面这些用处：

1) 用在一个解释性的分句或句子前面：

It's an environmental issue. — That's not a small matter.　这是个环境保护的问题，这不是一件小事。

How lucky the girls nowadays are! — They can go anywhere, say anything. 今天的女孩子多幸福! 她们哪儿都能去，什么话都能说。

2) 用在一个解释性的插入语的前面和后面(相当于一个括号)：

During my vacation — I must have been insane — I decided I would ski. 假期中，我准是发疯了，我决定去滑雪。

Then the proposals — both Xiao Yang's and mine — were adopted. 后来两个建议 —— 小杨的和我的 —— 都被采纳了。

3) 用在一个引用的句子前面(代替一个冒号，或与分号一起用)：

Uncle Wang laughingly answered — "No, no; stay where you are."　王大叔笑着回答道："不用了，不用了，你就待在你那儿。"

4) 表示意思的突然转折：

"And may I ask — " said Xiao Wu; "but I guess it's better for you to ask him about it."　"我可以问 —— "小吴说；"不过我想还是你问他的好。"

5) 表示迟疑犹豫：

"I — I — I rather think — maybe — Amy has taken it."　"我——我——我想——或许——是艾米拿了。"

6) 总括前面列举的若干东西：

New houses, larger schools, more sheep, more pigs and chickens, more horses and donkeys — everywhere we saw signs of prosperity.　新房子，扩建的学校，更多的羊、猪、鸡，更多的马和驴，到处我们都看到一片繁荣景象。

27.3.6　引号的用法

1) 引号主要用来表示中间包括的成分是引语：

Longfellow wrote, "Life is real! Life is earnest!"　朗费罗写道，"生活是

真实的! 生活是严肃的!"

2) 也可用来加在书名、剧名这类东西的两端:

Tolstoy's "War and Peace" is a great novel. 托尔斯泰的《战争与和平》是一部伟大的小说。

Have you read Lao She's "Tea House"? 你读过老舍的《茶馆》吗?

3) 加在一个词的两头，来引起对它的注意:

What's the difference between "differ" and "differentiate"? differ 和 differentiate 有什么区别?

如果引语中包括另一个引语，常加单引号:

The teacher asked, "Who said, 'Give me liberty or give me death'?" 老师问道,"谁说'不自由毋宁死'?"

_____

27.3.7 括号的用法

1) 括号主要用来表示里面的东西是一个插入的或附加的解释:

No article should be used in such cases. (cf. Chap. 1, Sec. 2) 在这种情况下不用冠词。(参阅第1章第2节)

Quotation marks may be single ('') or double (" "). 引号可以是单引号(''),也可以是双引号(" ")。

2) 方括号可用来注音，如 mine [maɪn]，但现在用斜线的人越来越多了，如 mine /maɪn/。

27.4　用在一个词内部的符号

27.4.1　撇号

撇号可用来:

1) 构成名词所有格:

They worked without a moment's rest. 他们一刻不停地工作。

2) 表示一个或几个字母给省略掉:

"Yes, ma'am," Robert said. 罗伯特说,"是的,夫人。"

'flu, 　　　'cello, 　　　'88

3) 构成字母、数码字等的复数形式:

You mustn't forget to dot your i's and cross your t's. 别忘了在i上加点,在 t 上加横。

How many 5's have you got?　你得了几个五分?

4) 用来构成动词短语的紧缩形式:

I've got something to tell you.　我有事要告诉你。

I'd like to have a try.　我想试一试。

27.4.2　连字号

连字号主要用来构成合成词,如:

water-lily 水莲　　water-melon 西瓜　　water-plane 水上飞机

但有些合成词不用连字号,或连写成一个词,如:

water polo 水球　　waterfall 瀑布　　waterway 航道

印刷时移行也须借助连字号,如:

On further reflection, she set up in business as a book-
　　seller.　再次考虑之后,她做起了书商的生意。

附录 1　常用成语动词

下面列出最常用的成语动词 (黑体部分)，每个给一个例句。关于成语动词的详细用法可参阅《现代英语用法词典》(外研社)。

A

A treasurer must **account for** the money he spends.　财务主管必须说明钱是怎么花的。

The factory must **aim at** increasing production.　工厂必须致力于增加生产。

We must **allow for** the train being late.　我们必须把火车晚点考虑进去。

The situation **allows of** no delay.　形势不容许延误。

If I scold the boy he always **answers back**.　如果我责备这孩子,他总是顶嘴。

Seven candidates **applied for** the position.　有七个人申请这个职位。

I quite **approve of** the idea.　我完全赞成这个想法。

What decision did you finally **arrive at**?　最后你作出了什么决定?

They all **asked after** you.　他们都问你好。

They **ask for** more pay and shorter hours.　他们要求增加工资减少工时。

He often **asked** her **out** in the evenings.　他常常在晚上邀请她出去。

I'll **attend to** it.　我来处理此事。

B

When he took a gun out everyone **backed away** nervously.　当他拿出枪时,大家都紧张地往后退。

He agreed to help but **backed out** when he found how difficult it was.　他同意帮忙,但当他发现这事多么困难时就打退堂鼓了。

I've got to **back** him **up**.　我得支持他。

I'm **against** doing anything (**for** doing nothing) till the police arrive.　在警察到来之前我不赞成做任何事(我主张不做任何事)。

I'm afraid she's **away** for the weekend.　我想她是出去度周末了。

She'll **be back** in half an hour.　她半小时后回来。

I'm afraid we're **in for** a bumpy flight.　恐怕我们的飞行会很颠簸。

The storm **is** now **over**.　暴风雨已经过去。

She **isn't up** yet. 她还没有起床。

After his illness, the Minister **was** no longer **up to** doing the work. 生病之后部长已不能干这工作。

The boys are very quiet. I wonder what they **are up to**. 孩子们都非常安静，我纳闷他们想干什么(调皮的事)。

It **is up to** the government to take action on violence. 该由政府采取行动来对付暴力。

This report **bears out** my theory. 这个报告证实了我的理论。

He **bore up** well against all these misfortunes. 他坚强地承受了这一切不幸。

What has **become of** Jennie? 珍妮怎么样了？

The prisoner **begged for** mercy. 犯人乞求宽恕。

I'll **begin by** telling you an anecdote. 我先给你们讲一件有趣的事。

The concert **began with** the National Anthem. 音乐会以演奏国歌开始。

He **believed in** Darwinism. 他信仰进化论。

Most of them **belong to** the Han nationality. 他们大多数属于汉族。

Beware of pickpockets! 小心扒手！

The wind **blew out** the candle. 风把蜡烛吹灭了。

They **blew up** the bridge so that the enemy couldn't follow them. 他们炸毁了桥梁，使敌人无法追赶他们。

The milk **boiled over**. 牛奶溢了出来。

The firemen had to **break down** the door to get into the burning house. 消防队员只得砸门进入熊熊燃烧的房子。

He **broke down** when telling us about his son's tragic death. 他向我们讲述他儿子的惨死时禁不住哭了出来。

After years of overwork his health **broke down** and he had to retire. 多年过分劳累把他的身体弄垮了，他不得不退休。

The negotiations **broke down** because neither side would compromise. 商谈中断了，因为双方都不肯妥协。

The car **broke down** when we were driving to the airport. 在去机场的路上我们的车坏了。

Thieves **broke in** and stole the jewels. 小偷潜入屋内偷去了首饰。

He took a bar of chocolate and **broke off** a bit. 他拿了一大块巧克力，掰下一小块。

She has **broken off** her engagement to Peter. 她解除了和彼得的婚约。

War **broke out** on December 8. 战争于12月8日爆发。

The meeting **broke up** in confusion.　会议在混乱中结束。

Divorce **breaks up** a lot of families.　离婚使许多家庭破碎。

After a lot of argument **I brought** him **round** to my point of view.　经过长时间的辩论，我使他转而同意我的观点。

She fainted, but a little brandy soon **brought** her **round**.　她昏死过去，但喝了一点白兰地后她苏醒了过来。

She **brought up** her children to be truthful.　她培养孩子们说真话。

Why did you **bring up** that question?　你为什么提出那个问题？

The mob **burnt down** the embassy.　暴民焚毁了大使馆。

C

I'll **call for** you at nine.　我九点钟来接你。

We **called for** the package at the post office.　我们到邮局取包裹。

They **called for** a show of hands.　他们要求举手表决。

I think we ought to **call in** a specialist.　我想我们应当去请一位专家来。

They've **called** the game **off**.　他们取消了这次比赛。

I **called on** Mr. Black this evening.　今天晚上我去拜访了布莱克先生。

They **called on** the workers to oppose it.　他们号召工人反对它。

She **called on** a student to answer the question.　她叫一名学生回答这问题。

The police couldn't control the mob so troops were **called out**.　警察无法控制暴乱的人群，因此请来了军队。

All right, I'll **call up** again.　好的，我回头再打电话来。

That teacher didn't really **care about** his students.　那位教师并不真正关心他的学生。

He doesn't **care for** films about war.　他不喜欢战争片。

The mother **cared for** the sick child day and night.　这位母亲日夜照顾生病的孩子。

We have **carried on** a correspondence for years.　我们相互通信了好多年。

We'll **carry on** our conversation tomorrow.　明天我们继续谈。

Carry on with your work.　继续干你的工作。

He had **carried out** my instruction to the letter.　他严格执行了我的指示。

His courage **carried** him **through**.　他的勇气使他度过了难关。

I started last in the race but I soon **caught up with** the others.　赛跑时我最后一个起跑，但不久我就赶上了其他人。

They **charged** him **with** theft.　他们控告他偷窃。

He had to **choose between** death and dishonour.　他得在死和羞辱之间作出选择。

I must **clean out** the spare room.　我必须把那间备用房收拾干净。

Clean up the yard.　把院子打扫干净。

Could you **clear away** these papers?　你可否把这些报纸收走?

The mist **cleared away** as the sun came out.　太阳出来时雾气就消散了。

He told them to **clear off** or he'd call the police.　他让他们走开,否则他要叫警察了。

He **cleared out** the cupboards.　他把柜子收拾干净了。

The cop told the boys to **clear out**.　警察让那些男孩子走开。

The weather has **cleared up**.　天放晴了。

Clear up the mess.　把这些脏东西清扫掉。

I'd like to **clear up** two or three points.　我想澄清两三点。

I've lots of work to **clear up** by the weekend.　我有大量工作需在周末前完成。

Trade was so bad that many small shops **closed down**.　生意那样不好,许多小商店关门了。

The troops were **closing in on** the enemy.　军队从四面八方向敌人围了上来。

Darkness (Night) **closed in on** us.　夜色向我们逼近。

Perhaps I shall **come across** him in Japan.　或许我在日本会碰到他。

You go now. I'll **come along** later.　你先走,我稍晚就来。

Take every chance that **comes along**.　抓住任何出现的机会。

How is your work **coming along**?　你的工作进展情况如何?

And so Saturday night **came around** again.　于是星期六晚上又来临了。

The crazed man **came at** me with a meat-axe.　那个疯子拿着一把剁肉的斧子向我扑来。

Come away now. It's time to go home.　走吧,该回家了。

How did you **come by** this painting?　这张画你怎么得来的?

The price of meat has **come down** this week.　这星期肉价下降了。

The doctor **came down on** him hard.　医生厉声斥责了他。

He has **come down with** influenza.　他患上了流感。

I've **come for** my belongings.　我来拿我的东西。

Summer is supposed to **come in** during May.　夏天应在五月来临。

The socialists **came in** at the last election.　上次选举社会党人上台了。

She **came in for** a lot of criticism.　她受到很多批评。

The trees are late **coming into blossom** this year.　这些树今年开花很晚。

The treaty will **come into force** next month.　条约将在下月生效。

The present government **came into power** a year ago.　现政府是一年前开始执政的。

He **came of** a poor peasant family.　他出生于一个贫穷的农民家庭。

This **comes of** your carelessness.　这是你粗心大意造成的。

His hair began to **come off**.　他的头发开始脱落。

When does the concert **come off**? 音乐会什么时候举行？

His plans haven't **come off**.　他的计划没有成功。

I hope his plans are **coming on** all right.　我希望他的计划进展顺利。

The wheat was **coming on** nicely.　小麦长势良好。

Winter is **coming on**.　冬天正在来临。

Come on, make haste, or we'll be too late for the party.　来吧，赶快，否则就来不及参加晚会了。

Pulling open a drawer, she **came on (upon)** Jim's diary.　拉开抽屉时她看到了吉姆的日记本。

When did the book **come out**? 这书什么时候出版的？

Some flowers have begun to **come out**.　有些花已经开始绽放了。

She **came out first** in the examination.　她考了第一名。

The truth has **come out** at last.　真相终于大白。

She always **comes out** well in photographs.　她总是很上相。

The men've **come out** (on strike) for more pay.　工人们罢工要求增加工资。

Ink stains don't usually **come out**.　墨水印通常洗不掉。

Many congressmen **came out against (for)** the bill.　许多参议员表示反对(支持)这项法案。

He **came out with** some funny ideas.　他提出了一些滑稽的想法。

You must **come over** some evening.　哪天晚上你一定要到我家来。

A strange feeling **came over** me.　我突然产生一个奇怪的感觉。

I'm very much obliged to you for **coming round**.　你来我家我非常感谢。

The unconscious man slowly began to **come round**.　那个失去知觉的人开始慢慢苏醒过来。

She would **come round** — that was the best of her.　她会回心转意的，这是她最大的优点。

He **came through** the operation on his heart.　他安全经受了心脏手术。

As he **came to** a bridge, he heard a train approaching.　他来到桥头时听到有火车开过来。

The bill **comes to** $ 50.　账单总共是50美元。

In a few moments she suddenly **came to**.　过了一会儿她突然苏醒过来。

We must **come to** a definite decision.　我们必须作出一个明确的决定。

The train **came to a stop**.　火车停了下来。

The summer term had **come to an end**.　夏天的这个学期结束了。

Presently they **came to blows**.　不久他们就打起来了。

He never **came to** anything in the end.　最后他从未取得什么成就。

Don't act so foolishly.　**Come to your senses**.　不要干傻事了,清醒清醒吧。

But Aunt Josephine **came to** his rescue.　但约瑟芬姨母来援救他了。

Don't talk all round the question, **come to the point**.　不要绕圈子,谈正题吧。

While we were talking, a man **came up**.　我们正谈话时一个人走了过来。

The bill **came up** for debate.　法案被提交大家辩论。

You might **come up against** a bit of opposition.　你可能会遭到一点反对。

The concert did not **come up to** expectations.　音乐会没达到预期的水平。

He **came up with** a new suggestion.　他提出了一个新建议。

The poet **compared** her teeth **to** pearls.　诗人把她的牙齿比作珍珠。

He cannot **compare with** Shakespeare.　他不能和莎士比亚相比。

Nothing can **compensate for** the loss of one's health.　丧失了健康什么也不能弥补。

They **competed for** the gold medal.　他们争夺金牌。

We can't hope to **compete with** him.　我们不能指望和他抗衡。

She **complained about** the food (**of** his rudeness).　她抱怨伙食不好(他粗鲁无礼)。

We must **comply with** the rules.　我们必须遵守这些规定。

The school **conferred** a medal **on** him.　学校颁发给他一枚奖章。

I must **confer with** my lawyer first.　我得先和我的律师商量一下。

He **confessed to** having done it.　他承认这是他干的。

All students must **conform to** the rules.　所有学生都要遵守规定。

Carbon dioxide **consists of** carbon and oxygen.　二氧化碳含有碳和氧。

Goodness **consists in** being honest.　善良也包含诚实。

All sorts of difficulties **cropped up**.　产生了各种各样的困难。

If you **cut down** all the trees you will ruin the land.　如果你把所有的树都砍掉,这片地就毁了。

We must **cut down** expenses.　我们必须削减开支。

Could you **cut** the article **down to** 2,000 words?　你能把这遍文章压缩到两千

词吗？

They have **cut off** our electricity supply.　他们切断了我们的电源。

The village was **cut off** by the snow for more than a month.　大雪把村子和外界隔绝了一个多月。

Let's **cut out** the unimportant details.　咱们把不重要的细节删掉。

The boy is **cut out for** an artist.　这男孩天生适合当画家。

He always **cuts up** his food before he eats it.　他总是把食物切碎后再吃。

D

The merchant **deals in** silk goods.　这个商人经营丝织品。

He **deals** fairly **with** all people.　他对待所有的人都很公平。

The town **depends on** the tourist trade.　这座城市依靠旅游业。

The sounds **died away**.　这些声音逐渐消失。

The wind has **died down** a bit.　风停息了一点。

I'm **dying for** a drink.　我迫切想喝点什么。

This kind of bird is **dying out**.　这种鸟濒临绝种。

On one point I **differ from (with)** you.　有一点我和你看法不同。

I want them to **do away with** this barbarous custom.　我希望他们废除这种野蛮的习俗。

We'll get a professional decorator to **do up** the rooms.　我们将请一位职业装饰家来装饰这些房间。

She **did** herself **up** for the occasion.　她打扮了一番来参加这次活动。

She forgot to **do up** her zip.　她忘了拉上拉链。

What did you **do with** the camera you found?　你把你找到的相机怎么样了？

During the war we had to **do without** luxuries.　战时我们只好不用奢侈品。

If there isn't any milk we'll have to **do without** (it).　如果没有牛奶我们只好不喝了。

Everyone **drew back** in alarm.　大家都惊慌地往后退。

Winter is **drawing on**.　冬天正在临近。

The novelist **drew (upon)** his own experience for the plot.　这位小说家从自己的经历中找寻素材来安排故事情节。

I **drew out** a hundred pounds last week.　我上星期取出一百英镑。

We must **draw up** a contract.　我们必须草拟一份合同。

I never **dreamt of** such a thing.　我做梦也没想到会有这样的事。

He **dropped behind** the other runners.　他落在其他赛跑选手后面了。

Drop by any time you're in town.　任何时候你进城时到我家坐坐。

He often **dropped in** for coffee.　他常常到我家喝咖啡。

I **dropped in at** the club on my way home.　回家路上我到俱乐部去看了看。

Sales have been **dropping off** badly.　销售量一直急剧下降。

I **dropped** him **off** at the post office.　我在邮局门口让他下了车。

If you don't like the idea, **drop out**.　如果你不赞成这个想法可以退出。

E

The whale **emerged from** the ocean depths.　鲸鱼从大洋深处浮了上来。

Twelve thousand competitors have **entered for** the next London Marathon.　一万二千名参赛者已报名参加下一次的伦敦马拉松赛。

He **engaged in** a serious study of the problem.　他从事对这问题的认真研究。

She **entered into** a five-year contract.　她签订了一个五年的合同。

We are **entering upon** a new epoch in the history of civilization.　我们正在进入文明史上的一个新时代。

I **entrusted** him **with** my money.　我把我的钱托付给他。

Excuse me **for** coming back.　原谅我又来了。

Will you **excuse** me **from** the meeting?　你能否允许我不参加这次会议?

F

The band moved on and the music **faded away**.　乐队往前行进,音乐慢慢消逝。

He's a clever man, but **fails in** perseverance.　他是个聪明人,但缺乏毅力。

As the enemy advanced they **fell back**.　敌人前进时他们就后退了。

As fresh milk wasn't available, we had to **fall back on** dried milk.　由于买不到鲜奶,我们只好还用奶粉。

He didn't want to **fall behind** in his studies.　他不希望学习落后。

They **fell behind with** the rent.　他们的房租交晚了。

The old lady **fell down** in the street and broke her leg.　老太太在街上摔倒,把腿摔折了。

Dick **fell for** baseball when he was a boy.　狄克从小就爱上了棒球。

He **fell in with** my views at once.　他立即同意了我的意见。

The measure **falls in with** popular demand.　这些措施符合公众的要求。

He **fell into a** dose (a deep sleep).　他打起盹来(陷入沉睡)。

His story **falls into** five parts.　他的故事分为五部分。

The soldiers **fell into line**.　士兵们排好队。

Their enthusiasm seems to be **falling off** a bit.　他们的热情似乎减少了一点。

They **fell on** the enemy vigorously.　他们向敌人猛扑过去。

The responsibility **fell on (upon)** me.　责任落到了我身上。

Fall out!　解散!

Jane and I have **fallen out** again.　简和我又争吵了。

The scheme **fell through**.　计划失败了。

Jennie **fell to** her task in silence.　珍妮静静地开始干她的活。

The chore **fell to** him.　这项家务活落到了他头上。

I'm **fed up** with this wet weather.　我讨厌这样的雨天。

I **feel like** going to bed. I'm tired.　我想去睡觉,我累了。

I don't **feel up to** the journey.　我感到不适合去作这次旅行。

You'll have to **fight against** the difficulties.　你得和困难作斗争。

He told the workers to **fight for** their rights.　他要工人们为自己的权利而斗争。

England **fought with (against)** Germany in the First World War.　在第一次世界大战中英国和德国交战。

I had to **fill in** three forms to get my new passport.　领取新护照我得填三张表格。

When Bill was nineteen he began to **fill out**.　比尔十九岁时开始长胖起来。

Fill up the glass.　把杯子斟满。

The theatre **filled up** rapidly.　戏院很快坐满了人。

In the end I **found out** what was wrong with my hi-fi.　最后我弄清了我的音响出了什么毛病。

Mary was angry when Jane **found out** her secrets.　当简发现了她的秘密,玛丽非常生气。

She **finished up** a painting.　她完成了一张画。

I **finished with** the first draft this morning.　今天早上我完成了第一稿。

It **fits in** well **with** my arrangements.　这很符合我的安排。

Your theory does not **fit with** the facts.　你的理论不符合实际。

We'd better **fix on** a date for the meeting.　我们最好确定一个开会的日子。

We've **fixed up** our little differences.　我们已解决了我们小小的分歧。

Trouble may **flare up** in the big cities.　这些大城市里可能会爆发麻烦事。

Applications **flooded in**.　申请书大批涌来。

Men and women **flooded out** into the streets.　男男女女涌上街头。

The boy **followed out** his father's advice.　那男孩完全照他父亲的话做了。

He's determined to **follow** his plan **through**.　他决心把计划进行到底。

The reporter **followed up** on the story.　那位记者继续报导这个消息。

G

The news of the disaster soon **got about**.　灾害的消息迅速传开。

He has quite recovered and is able to **get about**.　他已完全痊愈,可以随意走动了。

He **got** his meaning **across**.　他把他的意思讲清楚了。

We are **getting ahead** well with the project.　我的研究计划进展良好。

John **got ahead of** the other runners in the race.　约翰跑在其他选手前头了。

How are you **getting along** with your work?　你工作进展情况如何?

They **got along** very nicely.　他们相处得很好。

Bad news **gets around** quickly.　坏消息传得快。

I can't **get at** him on the telephone.　我没能通过电话和他联系上。

I wish I could **get at** the facts in this case.　我希望能弄清案情的真相。

The girls **get away** from work at five p.m.　姑娘们下午五点下班。

The bank robbers used a stolen car to **get away**.　银行劫匪利用偷来的汽车逃跑了。

Not many criminals **get away with** their crimes.　罪犯犯了罪而不受惩罚的很少。

I shall **get back** at 6 o'clock.　我六点钟回来。

He will **get back at** you for this.　他将为此向你报复。

She can't **get by** on such a small income.　她无法靠这微薄的收入生活。

Let's **get down to** the problem.　咱们开始认真讨论这个问题吧。

They **got in** and drove off.　他们坐上车开走了。

I'm **getting in touch** with him right away.　我马上和他联系。

I've **got into** trouble.　我出问题了。

They **got off** the bus and walked away.　他们下了公共汽车走开了。

The plane **got off** on time.　飞机正点起飞了。

You won't **get off** so easily next time.　下次不会这样轻易放过你。

Where did you **get on**?　你在哪儿上车的?

The work is **getting on** splendidly.　工作进展顺利。

It's **getting on for** nine o'clock.　快到九点了。

Old Mrs Ward doesn't **get out** much these days.　这些天沃德老太太不怎么出

门。

The news has **got out** that you are leaving.　有消息说你要走了。

He says that he smokes too much but he can't **get out of** the habit.　他说他烟抽得太多, 但这嗜好他已戒不掉了。

You cannot **get out of** paying your debts.　你没法回避偿还债务。

She seemed to have **got over** her distress.　她似乎已克服她的痛苦情绪。

We are certain that he will **get over** his illness.　我们肯定他的病能够痊愈。

Girls can usually **get round** their fathers.　女孩子常常能哄得父亲做她们想的事。

I meant to visit her, but I never **got round to** it.　我打算去看望她, 但一直没抽出空来。

He **got through** his exam all right.　他顺利通过了考试。

The operator finally **got** me **through.**　接线生最后接通了我的电话。

The new law **got through.**　新法律通过了。

When can we **get together**?　我们什么时能欢聚一次?

Who is going to **get up** the concert?　谁将举办这次音乐会?

She **got** herself **up** as a peasant girl.　她把自己打扮成一个农家姑娘。

He **gave away** most of his fortune to the poor.　他把大部分家财散给了穷人。

Please don't **give** my secrets **away.**　请不要泄露我的秘密。

He didn't want to **give** his friend **away.**　他不想出卖朋友。

Give the book **back** to your brother!　把书还给你弟弟!

The flowers **gave forth** an intoxicating scent.　这些花散发出一种醉人的香味。

But in the end he **gave in.**　但最后他让步了。

The rioters were at last forced to **give in to** the police.　叛乱分子最后被迫向警察投降了。

The flowers **gave off** a sweet fragrance.　这些花散发出芳香。

Our drawing-room **gives on** the garden.　我们的客厅正对着花园。

The teacher **gave out** the examination papers.　教师分发考卷。

They **gave out** the names of the winners.　他们宣布了优胜者的名单。

The fuel **gave out.**　燃料用完了。

She **gave up** her job to look after her invalid mother.　她放弃了工作来伺候她体弱多病的母亲。

He **gave up** cigarettes (smoking).　他戒烟了。

She has **given up** her life to nursing the sick.　她把一生献给照顾病人。

Give up your arms and live!　交枪不杀!

He **went about** doing good.　他到处做善事。

Jennie **went about** her work, but the impression persisted.　珍妮干着她的工作，但那印像仍存留在她脑中。

They both **went after** the same girl.　他们两人都追同一个姑娘。

It **goes against** my principles.　这是违背我的原则的。

You **go ahead** and I'll follow.　你先走，我随后就来。

He's **going around** looking for work.　他到处去找工作。

Don't worry! There's enough coffee to **go around (round)**.　别着急! 有足够的咖啡给大家喝。

He **went at** him with an axe.　他拿着一把斧头向他冲去。

You should see her **go at** the job.　你应当看她干这工作。

Are you **going away** for your holiday?　你准备出去度假吗?

Please **go away**; I can't wrok unless I am alone.　请离开;我一个人才能工作。

I'm never **going back** to that hotel. It is most uncomfortable.　我绝不会回那家旅馆去，它非常不舒适。

He **went back** on his promise to tell nobody about it.　他没遵守他不告诉任何人的诺言。

He **went back on** his friends.　他背弃了他的朋友。

The price **went beyond** our means.　这个价钱超出了我们的经济能力。

Don't let this chance **go by**.　不要错过这个机会。

Shares have **gone down** by ten points.　股票下降了十个点。

Her temperature has **gone down**.　她的烧退了。

I assumed that he had **gone for** a stroll.　我想他是出去遛弯了。

The wounded lion **went for** the hunter.　受伤的狮子向猎人扑去。

Do you **go for** modern music?　你喜欢现代音乐吗?

What sports do you **go in for**?　你从事什么运动?

A man wanted me to **go in for** film work.　有个人要我从事电影工作。

She **went in for** a singing competition.　她参加歌咏比赛。

The police are **going into** the murder case.　警方在调查这宗谋杀案。

He has **gone into** teaching.　他从事教学工作。

The company has **gone into** bankruptcy.　这家公司破产了。

The firecracker **went off** with a bang.　炮仗砰的一声炸开了。

Everything **went off** according to the plan.　一切按计划进行。

He **went off** in a great hurry.　他匆忙走掉了。

Go on till you come to the crossroads.　往前走直到十字路口。

Please **go on** playing it.　请继续弹。

A struggle was **going on** within him.　他心里正进行着一场斗争。

Everything is **going on** all right.　一切都进展顺利。

May I **go on with** my work?　我能继续干我的工作吗?

She has **gone out for** a walk.　她出去散步了。

That expression has **gone out**.　这种说法已经陈旧。

This party may **go out** at the next election.　下次选举这个党派可能下台。

They **went over** the plans again.　他们把计划又审查了一遍。

They **went over** their lessons together at night.　他们晚上一道复习功课。

I'm **going over to** Mary's house.　我现在去玛丽家。

Let's **go round** and ask him.　咱们去问问他。

Will there be enough wine to **go round**?　有足够的酒让大家喝吗?

They **went through** our luggage at the Customs.　海关人员检查了我们的行李。

The auditors **went through** the accounts.　审计员核查了账目。

We have **gone through** the required formalities.　我们已办完必要的手续。

Most families **went through** a lot during the war.　战争期间许多家庭饱受苦难。

I'm resolved to **go through with** it.　我决心把这事进行到底。

Does your son **go to** university?　你的儿子上大学吗?

He **went to** great trouble to make his guests comfortable.　他费了很大功夫让客人们感到舒适。

Cotton has **gone up**.　棉花涨价了。

The temperature is **going up**.　气温正在上升。

New office blocks are **going up** everywhere.　到处在盖办公大楼。

He has **grown into** a fine young man.　他已成长为一个帅小伙。

Arguments often **grow out of** misunderstanding.　争吵常常由误会引起。

I **grew up** on a farm.　我是在一家农场长大的。

H

This legend has been **handed down** from father to son.　这个传说是一代一代传下来的。

I **handed in** my resignation.　我递交了我的辞职信。

He was standing at the door of the theatre **handing out** leaflets. 他站在剧场门口散发宣传单。

The outgoing Minister **handed over** his department to his successor. 离职的部长把他的部门移交给继任者。

The hostess **handed round** coffee and cakes. 女主人把咖啡和蛋糕递给各位客人。

He **hung about (around)** the entrance all day, hoping for a chance to speak to the director. 他在大门口守候了一天, 希望有机会和所长说句话。

Paul **hung back** from taking part in the discussion. 保罗畏缩不前不敢参与议论。

Just **hang on** till I get help. 抓住不放, 直到我找人来帮忙。

It's hard work but if you **hang on** you'll succeed in the end. 这是艰苦的工作, 如果你能坚持, 你最后会取得成功。

Hang on! I'll call him. 别挂(电话)! 我去叫他。

The prospect of war **hung over** the country. 战争的阴云笼罩着这个国家。

I hope we shall all **hang together** in this emergency. 在这紧急关头我希望我们都团结在一起。

Tom **helps out** in the store after school. 放学后汤姆在店里帮忙。

She'll **help** you **with** the chores. 她将帮助你干家务活。

He **hit at** me, but missed. 他朝我打了一拳但没打中。

He **hits back** from the beginning. 他从一开头就进行了回击。

I have **hit on (upon)** a new way of doing it. 我想到一个做这事的新办法。

The MP **hit out at** Government policy on unemployment. 这位国会议员攻击政府关于失业问题的政策。

When danger came, no one **held back**. 危险到来时没人退缩不前。

The police **held back** the crowd. 警察控制住人群。

Do not **hold back** the truth. 不要隐瞒事实真相。

They know very well how to **hold down** the public. 他们很清楚如何控制民众。

We must try to **hold** prices **down**. 我们必须抑制物价。

I hope that the rain **holds off** a few hours more. 我希望雨再延迟几小时下。

Hold on, everything will be all right. 坚持住, 一切都会好的。

Hold on a minute. Mrs. Green will speak to you. 请等一下(别挂), 格林夫人要和你讲话。

The city **held out** for six months under the siege. 这座城遭到围攻, 坚守了

六个月。

She **held out** her hand in welcome. 她伸出手来欢迎。

I still **hold to** my former views. 我仍坚持过去的看法。

We cannot be defeated while we **hold together**. 只要我们团结就不会被打败。

Hold up your right hand. 举起右手。

The traffic was **held up** by an accident. 车祸堵塞了交通。

The thieves **held up** the van and took everything in it. 匪徒抢劫送货车，把里面的东西全拿走了。

The terrorists **held up** the train and kept the passengers as hostages. 恐怖分子劫持了火车，把乘客留作人质。

In this I **hope for** your help. 在这方面我希望得到你的帮助。

I

He **improved on** his invention. 他把他的发明作了改进。

He went to the police and **informed against (on)** the criminals. 他向警察告发了那些犯罪分子。

The pilot **inquired about** the weather conditions. 飞行员询问天气情况。

She **inquired after** my mother (my mother's health). 她问候了我的母亲。

A man has been **inquiring for** you at the office. 有人到办公室要求见你。

The police **inquired into** her background. 警察调查了她的背景。

She **insisted on** writing at once. 她坚持要马上写信。

No one wants to **interfere with** you. 没人想干预你的事。

This would **involve** him in serious trouble. 这会使他陷入很大的麻烦。

Finally they **ironed out** their differences. 最后他们消除了分歧。

J

The girl **joined in** our conversation. 那姑娘参加了我们的谈话。

He **joined up** in the last months of the war. 在战争最后几个月他参了军。

Will you **join with** us and give him a present? 你要不要和我们一道送他一份礼？

Alice **jumped at** the chance of going to Egypt. 阿丽丝立即抓住这个去埃及的机会。

K

He **keeps at** his studies, although he is ill. 他虽然生病仍坚持学习。

Keep away from that woman. 避开那个女人。

I'll **keep** nothing **back** from you. 我不会向你隐瞒任何事。

She couldn't **keep back** her tears. 她控制不住她的眼泪。

You have to be home by 11 o'clock. **Keep that in mind**. 你得在十一点前回家,记住这一点。

Keep off the grass. 勿踩草地。

He **kept on** till the work was finished. 他一直继续到把活干完。

Columbus **kept on** until he saw land. 哥伦布继续往前航行直到看见陆地。

Why do you **keep on** smiling? 为什么你老是笑?

The coat should **keep out** the cold. 这件大衣应该能挡住寒气。

He always **keeps to** his promises. 他向来信守诺言。

She **kept** the news **to** herself. 她没把这消息告诉别人。

I hope the weather will **keep up**. 我希望这天气能继续下去。

We've **kept up** our friendship for over twenty years. 我们保持友谊已达二十多年。

Her spirits **kept up** in spite of all her trouble. 尽管出了许多烦心事她的情绪依然高涨。

She had to run to **keep up with** him. 她得跑着才能跟上他。

It's difficult to **keep up with** medical developments. 要跟上医学发展是困难的。

We're going to **knock down** those old buildings soon. 不久我们将把这些旧楼拆掉。

A bus **knocked** the child **down**. 一辆公共汽车把小孩撞倒了。

What time do you **knock off**? 你什么时候下班?

The boxer **knocked out** his opponent in the second round. 这位拳击手在第二回合就把对手击败了。

They **knocked out** a large number of enemy effectives. 他们歼灭了敌军大批有生力量。

Who **knocked** that bottle **over**? 谁把那瓶子打翻了?

I happened to **know about** him. 我碰巧了解他的情况。

I **know of** a hotel which might suit you. 我知道有一家旅馆可能适合你。

L

I want you to **lay aside** these prejudices. 我希望你放弃这些偏见。

She managed to **lay aside (by)** thirty dollars. 她设法存起了三十美元。

He has **laid down** certain conditions which you must follow.　他规定了一些你必须遵守的条件。

The general told the troops to **lay down** their arms.　将军让士兵们放下武器。

He was willing to **lay down** his life for his country.　他愿为国家而献生。

She **laid in** plenty of food for Christmas.　她为圣诞节储存了大量食物。

The factory has **laid off** workers because of the drop in sales.　由于销售量下降工厂临时解雇了一些工人。

Le Nôtre **laid out** the gardens at Versailles.　勒·诺特设计了凡尔赛的花园。

Bees **lay up** honey for the winter.　蜜蜂储存蜂蜜过冬。

The incident **led to** his resignation.　这一事件导致他辞职。

She **leans on** her husband for advice.　她依靠她丈夫出主意。

When did you **learn of** Mary's divorce?　你什么时候听说玛丽离婚的?

I've **left** my coat **behind** in the bus.　我把大衣落在公共汽车上了。

We **leave for** Madrid by the next plane.　我们坐下一班飞机去马德里。

Has it **left off** raining yet?　雨停了吗?

She **left out** an important detail in her account.　她的叙述漏掉了一个重要细节。

When in doubt, **leave out**.　没有把握时就删掉。

Some disputes among these countries are **left over** by history.　这些国家之间的某些纠纷是历史遗留下来的。

We mustn't **leave** it **to** chance.　我们不能去碰运气。

I won't **let** him **down** in any way.　我怎么也不能做对不起他的事。

The terrorists **let off** a bomb near the building.　恐怖主义分子在大楼附近引爆了一颗炸弹。

I'll **let you off** if you promise never to do it again.　如果你答应不再这样做我就放过你。

Someone has **let** the news **out**.　有人泄露了这消息。

The rain **let up**.　雨渐渐停了。

Let up for a minute, you can't work hard all day.　休息一会儿, 你不能整天苦干。

The doctor advised me to **lie up** for a week.　医生劝我卧床休息一周。

We **listened to** the radio last night.　我们昨晚听收音机了。

She **lives by** sewing.　她靠缝纫为生。

Students of this college are expected to **live in**.　这所大学的学生都应住校。

She still **lives off** her parents.　她仍然靠父母生活。

These people **live on** meat and milk.　这些人靠肉和奶生活。

Students can **live out** if they wish.　学生如果愿意可以走读。

They **lived through** the long famine.　他们度过了长期的饥荒。

She tries to **live up to** her ideals.　她设法按她的理想生活。

Open the door! you've **locked** me **in**.　开门! 你把我锁在屋里了。

People usually **lock up** before they go to bed at night.　通常人们在晚上睡觉前都把屋门锁上。

She **locked up** her papers in the desk.　她把文件都锁在抽屉里。

He **longed for** friendship.　他渴望友谊。

Will you **look after** my parrot when I am away?　我不在家时你可否帮助照看我的鹦鹉?

It's time you **looked ahead** and made plans for your retirement.　现在你该想远一些, 计划一下退休后的生活。

That's the way I **look at** it.　这是我对它的看法。

I like to **look back on** my high-school days.　我喜欢回想我中学的日子。

I wish you wouldn't **look down on** this kind of work.　我希望你不要看不起这种工作。

I have been **looking for** you.　我一直在找你。

I'm **looking forward to** her arrival.　我在盼望她的到来。

I'll **look in** this evening to see how she is.　我今晚将来看看她情况怎样。

On his way downtown, Jim **looked in on** his aunt.　吉姆进城时顺道看望了他的姑姑。

We'll **look into** this matter together.　我们将一道研究这件事。

Richie **looked on**, to improve his chess.　里奇在一旁观看来提高棋艺。

His house **looks on to** the sea.　他家的房子对着大海。

He **looks on** her **as** a child.　他把她当作孩子。

Look out! There's a lorry coming!　当心! 有一辆卡车开过来了!

He looked out his address in the directory.　他在电话簿里查到他的地址。

The teacher will **look over** our tests tomorrow.　老师明天批阅我们的试卷。

I'm going to **look over** a house that I'm thinking of buying.　我准备去看一所我考虑要买的房子。

We went to **look round** the town.　我们去城里游逛。

She began to **look through** photograph albums.　她开始翻阅相册。

Look to your own shortcomings.　注意你自己的缺点。

He **looked to** us **for** support.　他指望我们的支持。

Look up the word in the dictionary.　在词典里查查这个词。

I want to **look** them **up** sometime.　我想什么时候去看望他们。

The weather is **looking up**.　天气正在好转。

She **looked** me **up and down**.　她上下打量我。

Schoolboys usually **look up to** great athletes.　男生通常崇拜优秀运动员。

M

She **majors in** psychology.　她主修心理学。

The robbers **made away** with all the money in the safe.　匪徒把保险柜里的钱全抢走了。

They set off by car and **made for** the nearest town.　他们坐汽车出发向最近的城市开去。

Thoughtfulness **makes for** closer relations.　多为他人考虑有助于建立较亲密的关系。

Thieves **made off** with many of their valuables.　窃贼偷了他们许多贵重物品溜掉了。

I can't **make out** the address, he has written it so badly.　我看不清他的地址，他写得那样潦草。

I couldn't **make out** what he meant.　我不理解他的意思。

Please **make out** a bill for these goods.　请为这些商品开一张账单。

He **makes** himself **out** to be a doctor.　他假称自己是医生。

I have **made over** the farm to my son.　我把农场转给我儿子了。

He **made up** an interesting story for the children.　他给孩子们编了一个有趣的故事。

Mary and Tim quarrelled, but **made up** after a while.　玛丽和蒂姆吵了一架，但过了一会儿又和好了。

I have to **make up** the test I missed last week.　我得把上周缺的测验补上。

The actors were **making up** when we arrived.　我们到达时演员们正在上装。

They **made up** 60 per cent of the people.　他们占人口的百分之六十。

Hard work can often **make up for** a lack of intelligence.　勤能补拙。

Some try to get on by **making up to** the boss.　有些人靠拍老板的马屁向上爬。

He **met with** some difficulties (a warm reception).　他碰到一些困难(受到热情的招待)。

Stop **messing about (around)**.　不要瞎胡闹(混)了。

Her late arrival **messed up** our plans.　她的迟到打乱了我们的计划。

The printers have **missed out** a line.　印刷工人排漏了一行。

The office **mixed up** the flight tickets. John got mine and I got his.　办公室把我们的机票弄混了，约翰拿了我的票，我拿了他的票。

Even the twins' mother **mixes** them **up**.　连双胞胎的母亲都把他们弄混了。

She had **mixed** him **up with** someone else.　她把他和另外一个人弄混了。

The policeman told us to **move along**.　警察让我们往前走(不要逗留)。

They have **moved away**.　他们搬走了。

Our new neighbours have just **moved in**.　我们的新邻居刚搬来。

We're **moving out** of our old house next week.　我们下星期从老住处搬出来。

They are **moving** him **up**.　他们正在提升他。

O

The company has decided to **open up** this area for housing.　这家公司决定开发这个住宅区。

Trade is **opening up** again.　贸易又活跃起来。

He is a retired general and still has the habit of **ordering** people **about**.　他是位退休将军，还有发号施令的习惯。

He **orders** his assistants **around** in a way that is very offensive.　他对他的助手发号施令，那态度很令人不快。

He **owned to** having lied.　他承认撒了谎。

You had better **own up**.　你最好坦白交代。

He **owned up to** the crime (having taken it).　他承认了这罪行(承认拿了它)。

P

People **packed into** the subway car.　人们挤进地铁车厢。

They **packed** her **off** to her aunt's house.　他们把她打发到她姑姑家里去了。

In the meantime he would go home and **pack up**.　与此同时他将回家收拾行李。

He **passed away** at eighty.　他八十岁时去世了。

A policeman **passed by**.　一位警察从旁经过。

She's 40, but I think she could **pass for** 25.　她四十岁了，但我认为她可以冒充二十五岁。

The headache soon **passed off**.　头痛很快好了。

She **passed** herself **off as** an American.　她冒充(自己)是美国人。

I received your message, and have **passed** it **on** to all those whom it concerns.

我收到你的信息，已经传给所有有关的人。

Two women **passed out**. 两位妇女昏厥了。

The father **passed over** the boy's crime. 这位父亲没追究那男孩的罪行。

On our way we had to **pass through** Hudson Street. 在路上我们得经过哈德森街。

Never **pass up** a chance to improve your English. 绝不要错过提高英语的机会。

He **paid** the money **back** promptly. 他很快偿还了那笔钱。

I'll **pay** them **back** for this treatment. 他们这样对待我我要报复。

How much did you **pay for** the book? 买这本书你花了多少钱?

You'll have to **pay for** your crime. 你将不得不为你的罪行付出代价。

Please **pay up** all you owe. 请把你的欠款还清。

They **picked on** him for the work. 他们挑选他干这工作。

Have you **picked out** the movie you want to see? 你选没选出想看的电影?

He **picked up** his suitcase and went out. 他提起箱子走了出去。

Where did you **pick up** your Russian? 你的俄语是在哪里学的?

Pick me **up** at the hotel. 到旅馆来接我。

He gave all the credit to his colleagues, and **played down** his own part in the discovery. 他把功劳都归于同事,轻描淡写自己在这一发现中的作用。

She won by **playing on** his weak points. 她利用他的弱点取胜。

Hogg **plays** himself **up** and plays Shelley down. 霍格抬高自己贬低雪莱。

He always **plays up to** his superiors. 他总是讨好上级。

It is wrong for a man to **play with** a woman's affection. 男人玩弄女人的感情是不对的。

The guide **pointed out** the principal sights of the city. 导游点出了城里的主要景点。

He **pointed out** that the road was not safe in winter. 他指出这条路冬天不安全。

All the evidence **points to** his guilt. 所有证据说明他是有罪的。

Good will **prevail over** evil in the end. 善良终会战胜邪恶。

They **prevailed upon** her to remain a little longer. 他们劝说好她再待长一点时间。

He **provided for** his family by working in a mill. 他在工厂工作来养家糊口。

The old house was **pulled down**. 那所老房子给拆掉了。

We did it, we've **pulled it off**, we've won. 这事我们做了,成功了,胜利了。

With careful nursing the patient **pulled through**.　经过精心护理，病人逐渐康复。

The car **pulled up** at the gate.　车在大门口停了下来。

Don't try to **push** me **around**!　别想对我发号施令!

A group of people are **pushing for** the adoption of the bill.　有一批人在敦促通过这项法案。

They **pushed on** at a rapid pace.　他们快速向前推进。

We must **push on with** our work.　我们必须坚决推行我们的工作。

They're trying to **push** legislation **through**.　他们正设法通过立法。

The wage increase **pushed up** prices.　增加工资使物价上涨了。

Who **put** that lie **about**?　谁散布的这个谎言?

He knew how to **put** his ideas **across**.　他知道怎样把自己的想法讲清楚。

She **put** her needle work **aside**, and we had a talk.　她放下针线活，我们谈了谈。

John **puts** ten dollars **aside** every week.　约翰每星期存十块钱。

Put your toys **away**.　把你的玩具收好。

Put the dictionary **back** on the shelf.　把字典放回到书架上。

The meeting has been **put back** until next week.　会议延迟到下星期开。

Put down that knife before you hurt somebody!　把刀放下别伤了人!

Put down these examples.　把这些例句写下来。

He has **put down** several other revolts.　他还平定过另外几次叛乱。

He **put** it **down to** a piece of bad luck.　他认为这是运气不好。

He **put** the odd weather **down to** nuclear explosions.　他认为天气反常是核爆炸的结果。

The tree **put forth** leaves.　这棵树长出了新叶。

Are you serious in **putting forward** such a view?　你提出这种看法是认真的吗?

The attack had been **put forward** an hour.　进攻提前了一小时。

They have **put in for** membership of the club.　他们申请加入俱乐部。

They **put off** the picnic because of the rain.　由于下雨他们把野餐推迟了。

He could be a good salesman, but his manner **puts** customers **off**.　他本可以是个好推销员，但他的态度让顾客反感。

Why don't you **put on** the dark gray suit today?　你今天怎么不穿那套深灰色的西服?

The actor **put on** a fine performance.　那演员作了精彩的表演。

Mary isn't really sick; she's only **putting on**. 玛丽不是真的生病,她是装病。

He **put out** the light and went out. 他关灯出去了。

The publishers **put out** fifty new books last season. 出版商上个季度出版了五十本新书。

The government will **put out** a new statement next week. 政府将于下星期发表一份新声明。

She was easily **put out** by little things. 她容易为小事生气。

I will **put** your views **to** the committee. 我将向委员会提交你的看法。

I'd rather not **put** you **to** any inconvenience. 我宁愿不给你造成不便。

Put up your hand if you think you know the answer. 认为知道答案的人举手。

They are **putting up** several new houses on this street. 他们正在这条街上盖几座新房。

They **put up** for the night at a farmhouse. 他们在一家农舍过了一夜。

Could you **put** me **up** tonight? 今晚你能留我住一夜吗?

I suppose I must **put up with** my loss. 我想我得忍受我的损失。

R

I **read about** it in the paper. 我是在报上读到这事的。

He spent three years **reading for** a degree in history. 他花了三年读历史学位。

I **read of** his death in yesterday's newspaper. 我在昨天的报上读到他死去的消息。

The boy **read out** his lesson loudly. 男孩大声地朗读课文。

He **read** it **through**, but could make no sense of it. 他看了一遍却看不懂。

I shall have to **read up** on the subject if I am to give a talk about it. 如果我要作一个这学科的报告,我得看些有关的书。

You can **reckon** me **among** your supporters. 你可以把我算作你的支持者。

Can I **reckon on** your support? 我能指望得到你的支持吗?

They **reckoned up** the expenditure of the past week. 他们算出了上星期的开支。

We'll **reckon with** you later. 我们将来要和你算账。

I'll **ring back** in ten minutes. 十分钟后我再打电话来。

I'll find out the address and **ring** you **back**. 我会查一下地址,然后再给你去电话。

We **ring in** the new year with the church bells. 我们以教堂钟声迎接新年。

He **rang off** before I could ask his name. 不等我问他姓名他就把电话挂上

了。

A shot **rang out** in the night. 夜里响起一声枪声。

Could you **ring** me **up** here as soon as he arrives? 等他一到你可否立即给我这儿打电话?

The room **rang with** laughter. 房间里回响着笑声。

They **rolled** the carpet **back**. 他们把地毯卷了起来。

Invitations kept **rolling in**. 邀请信大批涌来。

Roll up that map, please. 请把那张地图卷起来。

He **rounded off** their tour of France by a last call at Paris. 他最后访问巴黎圆满结束了他们的法国之行。

On the day after the riots the police **rounded up** all suspects. 暴乱后的那一天警察搜捕了所有嫌疑分子。

Rub those words **off** the board. 把那些字从黑板上擦掉。

He **rubbed out** what he had written. 他把他写的字擦掉了。

I want you to **rub up** the silver. 我要你把银器擦亮。

I must **rub up** my French. 我得复习我的法语。

I cannot **rule out** the possibility of trouble. 我不能排除出麻烦的可能性。

An emperor is a monarch who **rules over** an empire. 皇帝是统治帝国的君主。

I **ran across** him yesterday. 我昨天碰到了他。

If you **run after** two hares, you will catch neither. (谚)同时追两兔,全都抓不住。

Don't **run away**; I've something to say to you. 别跑(走)开,我有话和你说。

He **ran away** from home and got a job in a garage. 他逃离了家,在一家车库找到一份工作。

His temper **ran away with** him. 他的脾气失去了控制。

Don't **run away with** the idea that you needn't work. 不要以为你不需要工作。

She **ran** the tape **back** after hearing it. 她听了磁带之后把它倒回去。

They love **running** people **down**. 他们喜欢说别人的坏话。

The police **ran** him **down** eventually. 警察最后把他抓到了。

He wants to **run for** governor. 他想竞选州长。

I **ran into** him now and then. 我不时碰到他。

She had **run into** financial difficulties. 她遇到了经济上的困难。

All our supply of food has **run out**. 我们的食品全吃完了。

We **ran out of** petrol yesterday. 昨天我们的汽油用完了。

He nearly **ran over** the dog.　他差点把狗压死。

The water **ran over** the edge of the jug.　水从水杯口上溢了出来。

Run through this article and tell me what you think of it.　把这篇文章快速浏览一遍，然后告诉我你的看法。

He **ran through** the family fortune in a year.　他一年就把家财耗尽了。

The book **runs to** about three hundred pages.　这本书约有三百页。

He **ran up** a bill for over £ 100.　他欠了一百多镑的债。

I've **run up against** a few problems.　我碰到了几个问题。

S

I will **see about** it.　我来处理这事。

I went to the airport to **see** him **off**.　我到机场去给他送行。

I'll **see** you **out**.　我送你到门口。

I'd like to **see over** the house.　我想参观一下这座房子。

I **saw through** his trick (lies).　我看穿了他的诡计(谎言)。

Don't worry about money; I'll **see** you **through**.　不要为钱发愁,我会帮你度过难关。

I've a mass of things to **see to** this morning.　今早我有一大堆事要处理。

Has the car been **seen to** yet?　汽车修了吗?

I'll **see to** it that you are not inconvenienced.　我将留意不给你造成不便。

Your house ought to **sell for** at least £ 12,000.　你的房子至少可以卖12,000镑。

The firm **sold off** its summer stock to be ready for the new winter goods.　这家商号贱价卖掉它的夏季存货,准备购进新的冬季商品。

The shop **sold out** all the shirts.　这家商店把所有衬衫都卖出去了。

Sorry, the tickets are **sold out**.　对不起,票都卖光了。

Bad news **sent** market prices **down**.　坏消息使市场价格下降了。

Have you **sent for** the doctor?　你派人去请医生了吗?

If you want a visa, be sure to **send in** your application in good time.　你如果想要签证,一定要及时把申请书寄去。

Why haven't you got my letter? I **sent** it **off** last week.　为什么你还没收到我的信? 我上星期发出的。

I'll **send on** any letters that come for you.　我将把所有给你的信都转给你。

Some stars **send out** vast quantities of radiation.　有些星星散发出大量的辐射。

Any increase in production costs is bound to **send up** prices. 任何生产成本的增加一定会使价格上涨。

I don't know how to **set about** it. 我不知道怎样着手办这事。

She **set** the children **against** their father. 她让孩子和他们的父亲为敌。

Set down your heavy bags and take a rest. 把你沉重的行李放下休息一会儿。

He tried to **set** his ideas **down**. 他设法把他的想法写下来。

Winter **set in** early. 冬天早早来临了。

Then we shall **set off** together. 然后我们将一道出发。

They **set off** fireworks and make speeches to mark the occasion. 他们燃放烟火并发表演说来纪念这个日子。

They **set out** as the sun was rising. 太阳出来时他们出发了。

They **set out** all their reasons. 他们列举了他们的种种理由。

They **set up** a First Aid Post on the beach. 他们在海滩上建立了一个急救站。

He **set up** a new record for the 1,000 metres. 他创了一千米赛跑的新纪录。

He is **settling down** to his new job. 他正在安下心来干他的新工作。

They have **settled down** very happily in their new home. 他们高兴地在他们的新家定居了。

After some discussion we **settled on** a date in early July. 经过一番讨论我们选定了七月初的一个日子。

Tell me what I owe you and I'll **settle up**. 告诉我该付多少钱，我来结账。

I just can't **shake off** this cold. 这感冒我就是好不了。

Let me **shake up** a cocktail for you. 我来给你调制一杯鸡尾酒。

They were **shooting at** a target. 他们在打靶。

He suddenly **shot out** his fist. 他猛地打出一拳。

The rocket **shot up** into the sky. 火箭射向天空。

Don't **shout at** me. 别冲我嚷嚷。

They **shouted** the speaker **down**. 他们喊叫着把演讲人哄下台。

I shall be delighted to **show** you **around** the place. 我将很高兴带你到处看看。

They only wanted to **show off** their dresses. 他们只是想展示他们的服装。

She loves **showing off**. 她喜欢卖弄。

He was invited, but didn't **show up**. 他受到邀请，但没有来。

They **shut down** their factory. 他们把工厂关闭了。

He **shut** himself **in** his room to think. 他把自己关在屋里进行思考。

Shut the steam **off** — it's getting too warm in here. 把暖气关掉，屋里太暖和了。

He's **shutting** himself **off** from society. 他把自己和社会隔离开来。

These trees **shut out** the view. 这些树挡住了视野。

They **shut** the boy **up** in the cellar. 他们把那男孩关在地窖里。

Oh, **shut up**! I'm tired of your talk. 闭嘴! 你的话我都听厌了。

John wants to **sign up** for the contest. 约翰想报名参加比赛。

His eyes have **sunk in**. 他的眼睛陷下去了。

He **sank into** a deep sleep. 他陷入沉睡之中。

Please **sit down**, all of you. 请大家都坐下。

He **sat for** a schlarship but failed to win it. 他参加奖学金考试但没成功。

We're having a conference and we'd like you to **sit in**. 我们在开会,想请你旁听。

I **sat up** until midnight, writing letters. 我到半夜都没睡,一直在写信。

What others think I do not know. I can only **speak for** myself. 别人怎么想我不知道,我只能谈我自己的意见。

He always **speaks out** against injustice. 他一贯大胆讲话反对不公平的事。

If you thought that wasn't fair, why didn't you **speak up**? 如果你认为那不公平,你为什么不坦率地讲出来?

You can't **stand by** and allow such a thing. 你不能袖手旁观允许发生这样的事。

Our flag **stands for** our country. 我们的旗帜代表我们的国家。

The new President **stood for** honest government. 新总统主张诚实政府。

On this list two names **stand out** particularly. 在这名单上两个名字特别突出。

One should **stand up for** the weak and oppressed. 我们应为弱小受压迫的人说话。

We're determined to **stand up for** our rights. 我们决心维护我们的权力。

A soldier must **stand up to** danger. 军人必须敢于面对危险。

Stay away from dangerous electrical things. 不要靠近危险的电器。

He **stayed behind** to finish some work. 他留下来完成一些工作。

Can you **stay for** dinner? 你能留下吃晚饭吗?

I'm **staying in** tonight to watch television. 我今晚留在家里看电视。

You oughtn't to **stay out** so late. 你不应该在外头待得这么晚。

I **stayed up** reading until midnight. 我看书直到深夜。

When the judge became ill, he had to **step down**. 那位法官生病时不得不让位。

The police had to **step in** to control the outbreak of rioting. 警察不得不进行干预来控制骚乱的爆发。

The factory has **stepped up** production. 工厂已加速生产。

He **sticks at** his work ten hours a day. 他每天坚持工作十小时。

He is **sticking to** his principles in this matter. 在这件事上他是坚持原则的。

I **stopped in** to see her this afternoon. 今天下午我顺路去看了看她。

We'll **stop off** for a few days in Paris to visit my cousins. 我们路上将在巴黎停留几天来看望我的表兄妹。

Leaves **stopped up** the drain. 树叶把下水道堵住了。

He **struck at** the dog with his stick. 他用拐杖打狗。

When he attacked me, naturally I **struck back**. 他袭击我时，我当然反击了他。

They **struck** him **down** and kicked him. 他们把他打倒在地并踢他。

They **struck** him **off** the list of players. 他们把他从球员的名单上划掉了。

He **struck** their names **out**. 他把他们的名字划掉了。

The band **struck up** *Blue Danube*. 乐队奏起"蓝色的多瑙河"。

All his life he has been **struggling against** injustice. 他一生都和不公正的事作斗争。

The poor had to **struggle for** a living. 穷人们只得为生活而挣扎。

All his life he has been **struggling with** illness. 他一生都和疾病作斗争。

He **suffered** a great deal **from** cold and hunger. 他饱受饥寒之苦。

The judge **summed up** the evidence. 法官总结了证词。

This supermarket **supplies** us **with** all we need. 这家超市提供我们所需要的一切。

T

She **was taken aback** at his question. 听了他的问题她大吃一惊。

That boy **takes after** his father. 那男孩长得像他父亲。

He **book** the engine **apart**. 他把发动机拆开了。

I **take back** what I have just said. 我收回我刚才说的话。

The reporter **took down** the speech. 记者把讲的话都记了下来。

I **took** him **for** his brother. 我把他当成他哥哥了。

He had nowhere to go, so I **took** him **in**. 他没地方可去，因此我收留了他。

He **took** me **in** with his story. 他用编的谎言哄骗我。

The boys could not **take in** his meaning. 孩子们听不懂他的意思。

I **take in** a daily paper and a monthly magazine. 我订阅了一份日报和一份周刊。

He **took off** his coat (wet shoes). 他脱下大衣(湿鞋子)。

The plane **took off** on time. 飞机准时起飞了。

Is he willing to **take on** the responsibility? 他愿意承担责任吗？

The college is **taking on** more staff. 那所大学正在雇用更多的职工。

I'll **take** her **out** to the pictures. 我要带她出去看电影。

This large company has **taken over** many small ones. 这家大公司接管了许多小公司。

She has really **taken to** that child. 她真的喜欢上那个孩子了。

Then he **took to** writing plays. 这时他开始喜欢写剧本。

During the flood the people **took to** the hills. 洪水泛滥时居民都逃到山上。

I **took up** mathematics, shorthand and economics. 我选修了数学、速记和经济学。

When he left school, he **took up** journalism. 他毕业后从事新闻工作。

I won't **take up** much of your time. 我不会占用你很多时间。

We must **talk** that matter **over**. 我们得好好谈谈这事。

I couldn't **tear** myself **away** from the television. 我舍不得离开电视。

Did they **tear** the building **down**? 他们把那座楼拆了没有？

He **tore up** the letter angrily. 他生气地把信撕碎。

The teacher could not **tell** the twins **apart**. 老师无法把两个双胞胎区分开。

He **told** them **off** severely. 他严厉地斥责了他们。

What are you **thinking about**? 你在想什么？

He frequently **thought of** Sophia. 他经常想到索菲娅。

She began to **think of** going south. 她开始想到到南方去。

We've got to **think out** a way to explain it. 我们得想出一个办法来解释它。

I would like to **think** it **over**. 我想把这事好好想一想。

He **thought up** a good answer. 他想出了一个好答案。

This is your last chance; don't **throw** it **away**. 这是你最后的机会，别把它抛弃掉。

This has **thrown** everything **into** confusion. 这使一切陷入混乱。

He **threw himself into** his work. 他投入他的工作。

He **threw up** his job. 他放弃了他的工作。

The new baby **tied** her **down**. 她新生的婴孩让她脱不开身。

Tie up the package. 把包裹捆好。

The plane **touched down** at 2 o'clock.　飞机两点钟着陆了。

The boy **touched off** a firecracker.　男孩燃放了一枚炮仗。

The arrest of the men's leaders **touched off** a riot.　逮捕这些人的领导者引发了一场暴乱。

He **touched on** theoretical physics.　他顺带谈到了理论物理。

Thank you for **touching up** my poetry.　谢谢你为我的诗润色。

The book **treated of** the history of Ireland.　这本书论述了爱尔兰的历史。

She **treated** me **to** an ice-cream.　她请我吃了一份冰淇淋。

She was **trying on** a new hat.　她在试一顶新帽子。

Let's **try out** his suggestion.　咱们试试他的建议。

His friend **turned against** him.　他的朋友转而反对他。

The little girl **turned around** and ran to her mother.　小女孩转身向她母亲跑去。

He **turned away** three applicants.　他撵走了三个申请人。

He got tired and **turned back**.　他累了便往回走。

The company **turned down** the suggestion of shorter hours.　公司拒绝了缩短工时的建议。

Turn down the TV.　把电视声音开小点。

Eleven o'clock — Let's **turn in**.　十一点了，咱们去睡觉吧。

I want you to **turn in** a good history paper.　我要你交一篇好的历史论文。

Caterpillars **turn into** butterflies.　幼虫会变成蝴蝶。

Turn off (on) the light.　把电灯关掉(打开)。

The tigress **turned on** the trainer and struck him to the ground.　母老虎转而袭击驯兽人，把他打翻在地。

The examination **turned out** (to be) easy.　考题结果很容易。

It **turned out** that he was George's father.　结果发现他是乔治的爸爸。

This factory **turns out** bicycles.　这家工厂生产自行车。

The whole town **turned out** for the parade.　全镇的人都出来观看游行。

He **turned over** the business to his son.　他把买卖移交给了他儿子。

He **turned over** in bed.　他在床上翻了一次身。

She had no one to **turn to** for advice.　她找不到人帮她出主意。

For some reason he didn't **turn up**.　由于某种原因他没有来(出席)。

Something will **turn up** to get you out of the difficulty.　会发生什么事来帮你摆脱困难的。

She **turned** the sound **up** on the television.　她把电视音量加大了。

Don't bother to look for my umbrella; it will **turn up** some day. 不要费事去找我的雨伞；什么时候它会出来的。

W

The bad news **woke** the country **to** the dangers of war. 这个坏消息让全国意识到战争的危险。

She **waits on** her husband from morning till night. 她从早到晚伺候丈夫。

Wake up! It's seven o'clock. 醒一醒！已经七点了。

The noise **woke** me **up**. 嘈杂的声音把我吵醒。

He **wakened** everyone **up** at 6 a.m. 早上六点钟他就把大家叫醒了。

The workers have **walked out**. 工人们罢工了。

She **warned** me **against** pickpockets. 她叫我提防扒手。

He **warned** us **of** the danger. 他让我们提防这个危险。

I **washed** the dirt **off** (my hand). 我把(手上的)污垢洗掉。

I can't **wash out** the marks from the shirt. 我没法把衬衫上的污渍洗掉。

It's your turn to **wash up**. 今天该你洗碗了。

附录 2　不规则动词表

不定式	过去式	过去分词
arise	arose	arisen
awake	awoke, awaked	awoken, awaked
be	was, were	been
bear (生)	bore	borne, born (用于被动语态)
bear (负，带)	bore	borne
beat	beat	beaten
become	became	become
begin	began	begun
bet	bet, betted	bet, betted
bend	bent	bent
bid	bade, bid	bidden, bid
bind	bound	bound
bite	bit	bitten (偶作 bit)
bleed	bled	bled
blow	blew	blown
break	broke	broken
breed	bred	bred
bring	brought	brought
broadcast	broadcast	broadcast
build	built	built
burn	burnt, burned	burnt, burned

不定式	过去式	过去分词
burst	burst	burst
buy	bought	bought
cast	cast	cast
catch	caught	caught
choose	chose	chosen
cling	clung	clung
come	came	come
cost	cost	cost
creep	crept	crept
cut	cut	cut
deal	dealt	dealt
dig	dug	dug
do	did	done
draw	drew	drawn
dream	dreamt [dremt] (英) dreamed (美)	dreamt (英) dreamed (美)
drink	drank	drunk
drive	drove	driven
dwell	dwelt, dwelled	dwelt, dwelled
eat	ate [英 et, 美 eɪt]	eaten
fall	fell	fallen
feed	fed	fed
feel	felt	felt
fight	fought	fought
find	found	found
flee	fled	fled
fling	flung	flung
fly	flew	flown
forbid	forbade	forbidden

不定式	过去式	过去分词
forget	forgot	forgotten
forgive	forgave	forgiven
freeze	froze	frozen
get	got	got (美有时作 gotten)
give	gave	given
go	went	gone
grind	ground	ground
grow	grew	grown
hang	hung, hanged	hung, hanged
have	had	had
hear	heard	heard
hide	hid	hidden
hit	hit	hit
hold	held	held
hurt	hurt	hurt
keep	kept	kept
kneel	knelt	knelt
know	knew	known
lay	laid	laid
lead	led	led
lean	leant [lent] (英) leaned [li:nd] (美)	leant (英) leaned (美)
leap	leapt [lept] (英) leaped [li:pt] (美)	leapt (英) leaped (美)
learn	learnt, learned	learnt, learned
leave	left	left
lend	lent	lent
let	let	let
lie	lay	lain

不定式	过去式	过去分词
light	lit / lighted	lit / lighted (作定语时较多)
lose [lu:z]	lost [lɒst]	lost
make	made	made
mean [mi:n]	meant [ment]	meant
meet	met	met
mistake	mistook	mistaken
overcome	overcame	overcome
pay	paid	paid
put	put	put
read [ri:d]	read [red]	read [red]
ride	rode	ridden
ring	rang	rung
rise	rose	risen ['rɪzn]
run	ran	run
saw	sawed	sawn (偶作 sawed)
say [seɪ]	said [sed]	said
see	saw	seen
seek	sought	sought
sell	sold	sold
send	sent	sent
set	set	set
shake	shook	shaken
shave	shaved	shaved / haven (主要用作定语)
shed	shed	shed
shine	shone [ʃɒn]	shone
shoot	shot	shot

不定式	过去式	过去分词
show	showed	shown (偶作 showed)
shrink	shrank	{ shrunk shrunken (作定语)
shut	shut	shut
sing	sang	sung
sink	sank	sunk (作定语时为 sunken)
sit	sat	sat
sleep	slept	slept
slide	slid	slid
smell	smelt, smelled	smelt, smelled
sow	sowed	sown, sowed
speak	spoke	spoken
speed	sped, speeded	sped, speeded
spell	spelt, spelled	spelt, spelled
spend	spent	spent
spill	spilt, spilled	spilt, spilled
spin	spun, span	spun
spit	spat	spat
split	split	split
spoil	spoilt, spoiled	spoilt, spoiled
spread	spread	spread
spring	sprang	sprung
stand	stood	stood
steal	stole	stolen
stick	stuck	stuck
sting	stung	stung
stride	strode	stridden
strike	struck	{ struck striken (仅作定语或表语)

不定式	过去式	过去分词
string	strung	strung
strive	strove	striven ['strɪvn]
swear	swore	sworn
sweep	swept	swept
swell	swelled	swollen (偶作 swelled)
swim	swam	swum
swing	swung	swung
take	took	taken
teach	taught	taught
tear	tore	torn
tell	told	told
think	thought	thought
throw	threw	thrown
tread	trod	trodden, trod
understand	understood	understood
upset	upset	upset
wake	woke, waked	woken, waked
wear	wore	worn
weave	wove	woven
weep	wept	wept
win	won [wʌn]	won [wʌn]
wind [waɪnd]	wound [waʊnd]	wound [waʊnd]
write	wrote	written

* * *

注: 这只是常用不规则动词表, 不常用的没有收入。

附录 3 常用语法术语表

1. **Morphology** 词法
   Syntax 句法
   Notional Words 实意词
   Form Words 虚词
   Parts of Speech 词类
   The Noun 名词
   The Pronoun 代词
   The Numeral 数词
   The Adjective 形容词
   The Verb 动词
   The Adverb 副词
   The Article 冠词
   The Preposition 介词
   The Conjunction 连词
   The Interjection 感叹词
   Determiner 限定词
   The Particle 小品词
   Word Building 构词法
   Conversion 转化
   Derivation (Affixation) 派生(词缀法)
   Compounding (Composition) 合成
   Prefix(es) 前缀
   Suffix(es) 后缀
   Compound Words 合成词

2. **Classification of Nouns** 名词的分类
   Common Nouns 普通名词
   Proper Nouns 专有名词

   Individual Nouns 个体名词
   Collective Nouns 集体名词
   Material Nouns 物质名词
   Abstract Nouns 抽象名词
   Countable Nouns 可数名词
   Uncountable Nouns 不可数名词
   The Singular Form 单数形式
   The Plural Form 复数形式
   The Common Case 普通格
   The Possessive Case 所有格
   Gender 性
   The Definite Article 定冠词
   The Indefinite Article 不定冠词

3. **Personal Pronouns** 人称代词
   Possessive Pronouns 物主代词
   Self Pronouns 自身代词
   Demonstrative Pronouns 指示代词
   Interrogative Pronouns 疑问代词
   Conjunctive Pronouns 连接代词
   Relative Pronouns 关系代词
   Reciprocal Pronouns 相互代词
   Indefinite Pronouns 不定代词
   The Absolute Forms of Possessive Pronouns 物主代词的绝对形式
   The Subjective Case 主格
   The Objective Case 宾格
   Cardinal Numerals 基数词
   Ordinal Numerals 序数词
   Fractional Numerals 分数词

The Imperative Mood　祈使语气

The Subjunctive Mood　虚拟语气

Sentences of Real Condition　真实条件句

Sentences of Unreal Condition　虚拟条件句

Conditional Sentences of Mixed Time　错综时间条件句

Sentences of Implied Condition　含蓄条件句

7. Adverbs of Time　时间副词

Adverbs of Place　地点副词

Adverbs of Manner　方式副词

Adverbs of Degree　程度副词

Adverbs of Frequency　频度副词

Relative Adverbs　关系副词

Conjunctive adverbs　连接副词

Interrogative Adverbs　疑问副词

Coordinating Conjunctions　并列连词

Subordinating Conjunctions　从属连词

8. The Sentence　句子

Members of the Sentence　句子的成分

The Subject　主语

Preparatory Subject　先行主语

The Predicate　谓语

The Predicative　表语

The Object　宾语

Retained Object　保留宾语

The Attribute　定语

The Adverbial (Modifier)　状语

The Appositive　同位语

Independent Elements　独立成分

Declarative Sentences　陈述句

Imperative Sentences　祈使句

Exclamatory Sentences　感叹句

Interrogative Sentences　疑问句

General Questions　一般问句

Special Questions　特殊问句

Alternative Questions　选择问句

Disjunctive Questions　反意问句

Simple Sentences　简单句

Compound Sentences　并列句

Complex Sentences　复合句

Compound Complex Sentences　并列复合句

One-member Sentences　单部句

Two-member Sentences　双部句

Elliptical Sentences　省略句

Cleft Sentence　分裂句

9. The Simple Predicate　简单谓语

The Compound Predicate　复合谓语

The Compound Verbal Predicate　表行为的复合谓语

The Compound Nominal Predicate　表性状的复合谓语

The Direct Object　直接宾语

The Indirect Object　间接宾语

The Complex Object　复合宾语

The Cognate Object　同源宾语

Direct Address　呼语

Parenthesis　插入语

Direct Speech　直接引语

Indirect Speech　间接引语

Absolute Constructions　独立结构

10. Phrases　短语

Participial Phrases　分词短语

Prepositional Phrases　介词短语

附录4 关于语法体系的一些说明

近年来语法科学有较大的进展,加深了我们对语言的认识。有些问题值得我们进一步研究。为了帮助读者了解一些有关语法体系的问题,这里作一些简单的介绍和说明。

1. 限定词

近年来不少语法书使用了**限定词** (Determiner)这个名称,有的人把它们作为一个词类,有的人把它们作为某些词类的总称。它们大致包括以下内容:

1) 冠词: Where should we put *the* chairs?

2) 物主代词: Here is *your* luggage.

3) 关系代词: *whose* 和 *which* (用作定语):
This is the lady *whose* husband you met yesterday.
Call again at 11, by *which* time the meeting should be over.

4) 由 ever 构成的连接代词 (用作定语):
Vote for *whichever* proposal you think most favourable.
For *whatever* reason, don't be late again.
Whoseever idea this my be, I don't like it.

5) 作定语用的疑问代词:
What colour?
Which information?
Whose ideas are these?

6) 作定语用的 some, any, no 及 enough:
I want *some* rolls (bread), please.
Have you got *any* stamps (ink)?
The sign said, "*No* parking."
We haven't got *enough* tools (equipment) for the job.

7) 作定语用的指示代词:
Have you read *this* (*that*) book?
Have you seen *these* (*those*) plays?

8) 作定语用的不定代词 each, every, either, neither:
I want to interview each (*every*) student individually.

You can park on *either* side.

Neither party accepted the arbitration proposal.

9）作定语用的不定代词 all, both:

All the girls want to come with us.

Both these cars are sold out.

10）作定语用的不定代词 many, much, little, few 及 several:

He wrote *few* (*a few*) books.

There are too *many* (very *few*) mistakes in your essay.

She has got *little* (hasn't got *much*) money.

Several people volunteered for the work.

11）作定语用的数词及 once, twice, half 等词:

Everything was all right in the *first* two days.

She came down here every *three* months.

He did it in *one-third* the time it took me.

I'll be back in *half* an hour.

这样的区分有一定的好处, 但也造成许多问题。许多词 (特别是代词) 处理起来会更麻烦, 作定语时作为限定词, 作主语、宾语等时作为代词。如果按照旧的体系, 代词大部分都可用作定语, 这样就不必分出来讲了, 因此我们没有把限定词单列出来。许多字典的处理办法也不一致。不少字典把作定语用的这类代词干脆称为形容词。美国字典大多如此。连许多英国字典, 如 *Longman Modern English Dictionary, Chambers Universal Learners' Dictionary* 都这样处理。在大家没有取得一致意见以前, 我们似以沿用传统做法较为妥当。

2. 分词及动名词问题

现在有些语法家主张去掉动名词这一提法, 把现在分词和动名词统称为 -ing 分词 (-ing participle)。把过去分词称为 -ed 分词 (-ed participle), 也同时使用现在分词和过去分词这两个名词。这样实际上只会造成混乱。大量过去分词是不规则的, 根本不是靠加 -ed 构成的, 却把它们称作 -ed 分词, 这是牵强的。现在分词和过去分词在用法上有许多共同之处, 称它们为分词是有道理的, 而动名词却起着完全不同的作用, 硬要把它和现在分词拉在一起, 这是并不科学也不现实的。因此多数语法书仍保留了动名词的名称, 尤其是在中国, 我们使用了 "动名词" 这个名称, 充分说明了它的特点, 即在句中起名词的作用。在实际教学中, 有这个名称很方便, 并不构成负担, 若把它取消, 反倒会造成不便。当然, 我们也要看到动名词和现在分词也有相通之处, 在有些情况下一个动词的 -ing 形式, 说它是动名词或是分词都可以, 如:

I don't remember your *saying* that. (动名词)

I don't remember Lao Wu *saying that.* (说是动名词或现在分词似都可以)

He continued working. (动名词)

He kept (on) *working.* (说是现在分词或动名词都有道理)

这时就不宜细抠。在不少情况下，我们也可避免动名词这个名称，例如可以说，在不少动词后都跟动词的 -ing 形式，如：

I enjoyed working here.

Stop talking.

这样就可省去许多麻烦。

3. 助动词及情态动词问题

有些语法家把助动词和情态动词的讲法作了一些调整。do，have，be 仍称助动词，下面这些统称 **情态助动词** (Modal Auxiliaries)，也称 **情态动词** (Modal Verbs)：

can, could

may, might

shall, should

will, would

must

dare

need

ought to

used to

} 称为 **边缘性情态助动词** (Marginal Modals)

这样做有一定道理。另外他们还增加了一些东西：

1) 情态短语 (Modal Idioms): had better, would rather, would sooner, be to, have got to.

2) 半助动词 (Semi-auxiliaries): have to, be about to, be able to, be bound to, be going to, be likely to, be obliged to, be supposed to, be willing to, be apt to, be due to, be meant to, etc.

3) 关连动词结构 (Catenative Verb Construction): appear to, happen to, seem to, get +过去分词, keep +动词的 -ing形式, get to, come to, turn out to, tend to, manage to, fail to, etc.

这样处理对掌握这类结构有一定帮助，但怎样和助动词及情态动词连系起来还值得研究。我们是在句法部分处理该问题的，把它们和后面跟的不定式称为复合谓语，这样做也可达到同样的目的。这类谓语常可译为一个汉语动词：

How *did you get to know* him? 你怎么认识他的?

You'*ll come to like* the place. 你会喜欢这地方的。

She *failed to turn up*. 她没能来。

We *managed to get a* ticket. 我们设法搞到了一张票。

You'*re supposed to be back* at 9. 你应该在九点钟回来。

I am *willing to help*. 我愿意帮忙。

She *happened to be in*. 她恰好在家。

It *turned out* (*to be*) *quite successful*. 结果很成功。

She'*s due to arrive* tomorrow. 她定于明天到达。

把这类谓语作为整体来看待是符合思维逻辑的。

4. 关于词类的划分问题

关于词类有许多划分方法。现在举出几种分法:

1) 《综合英语语法》的分法 (保留原来例词):

(1) 介词: of, at, in, without, in spite of

(2) 代词: he, they, anybody, one, which

(3) 限定词: the, a, that, every, some

(4) 连词: and, that, when, although

(5) 情态动词: can, must, will, could

(6) 助动词: be, have do (原名为 Primary Verb)

(7) 名词: John, room, answer, play

(8) 形容词: happy, steady, new, large, round

(9) 完全动词 (full verb): search, grow, play

(10) 副词: steadily, completely, really

(11) 数词: one, two, three; first, second, third

(12) 感叹词: oh, ah, ugh, phew

(外加否定词 not, 不定式标记词 to 等特殊词)

2) 《大学英语语法》的分法 (该书的两位作者也是上书的作者):

(1) 名词: John, room, answer, play

(2) 形容词: happy, steady, new, large, round

(3) 副词: steadily, completely, really, very, then

(4) 动词: search, grow, play, be, have, do

(5) 冠词: the, a(n)

(6) 指示词: that, this

(7) 代词: he, they, anybody, one, which

(8) 介词: of, at, in, without, in spite of

(9) 连词: and, that, when, although

(10) 感叹词: oh, ah, ugh, phew

3）美国出的《英语语法与作文》的分法（例词从所给词中挑出）:

(1) 名词: Chicago, girl, army, city

(2) 代词: he, some, who, those

(3) 形容词: green, late, lazy, rich

(4) 动词: lose, grow, will, must

(5) 副词: beautifully, now, usually, how

(6) 介词: across, by, through, toward

(7) 连词: after, if, when, where

(8) 感叹词: ouch, ah, well, hurrah

(另一个美国出的 *Index to Modern English* 也是这样分法。) 通过对比，我们不难看出怎样区分词类比较合理。

5. 关于时态问题

现在某些语法家在讲时态时，提出了三个概念：一是时间，这是客观存在的；二是时态，这是指语言表示动作时间的形式；三是体 (aspect)，指动作表现的方式，如表示它正在进行，则用进行体，表示动作已完成，则用完成体。在观念上这样提还是可以的，但实际上时态还是得一个一个地讲。以《大学英语语法》为例，仍是按下列顺序讲:

1) 现在时: 简单现在时, 现在进行时

2) 过去时: 简单过去时, 过去进行时, 现在完成时, 过去完成时, 过去进行时

3) 完成进行时: 现在完成进行时

4) 将来时

5) 过去将来时

讲得清不清楚不说，也看不出有太大特色。

《交际英语语法》开头提到了"体"，到后来仍是一个个时态讲，仍然使用传统名词 (简单现在时、现在进行时、简单过去进行时、现在完成时等等)。因此在时态的讲解体系上没有必要作大的变动。事实上各个时态的用法都是历史实践中发展过来，用简单的几条去套是困难的。我们的办法是反映实际使用的情况，逐个解决。

6. 关于语气的问题

虚拟语气是一个引起争议的问题。究竟哪些动词形式算虚拟语气？这里我们把几家的说法作个简单的介绍。著名语法学家 Zandvoort 认为以下两类为虚拟语气：

1) 不带 -s 词尾的原形动词：

a. Joanna had insisted that he *come*.

An army lieutenant demanded that the flag *be* lowered.

b. Though everyone *desert* you, I will not.

If two angles of a triangle *be* equal to one another...

Be that as it may, little had been said about her husband.

2) were:

She looked as though she *were* fainting.

I wish it *were* over.

If I *were* you, I should go.

She is, as it *were*, my second self.

他认为虚拟语气表示愿望 (wish)、可能性 (possibility) 和非真实情况 (irreality)。

而 Eckersley 则认为虚拟语气有下列几类：

1) 现在虚拟语气 (The Present Subjunctive)：

(1) 表示愿望和祈祷：

God *save* the Queen.

Heaven *forbid* that...

Heaven *help* us.

Be that as it may...

(2) 用在某些动词后的从句中：

It is our wish that he *do* what he pleases.

She urged that he *write* and *accept* the post.

I propose that the secretary's resignation *be* accepted.

The King ordered that the man *be* released.

(3) 偶尔用在让步状语从句及条件状语从句中：

Though the whole world *condemn* him, I will still believe in him.

This, if the news *be* true, is a very serious matter.

2) 过去虚拟语气 (The Past Subjunctive)：

(1) 用于虚拟条件句：

If I *were* you, I should accept the offer.

What would you say if I *asked* you to join us for a holiday?

(2) 用在某些词语后:

I wish I *were* as handsome as he is.

I wish he *visited* us more often.

Suppose (that) the teacher *caught* us wasting time.

I had rather (that) you *told* him than (that) I *did*.

He ran as if his life *depended* on it.

It is (high) time I *went* home.

3) 过去完成虚拟语气 (The Past Perfect Subjunctive):

I wish I *had been* at the seaside.

虚拟条件句中从句的谓语他认为也是虚拟语气。他说:"在第二类句子 (假想条件句) 中,在 if 引导的从句中用过去虚拟语气,在主句中谓语由 would 或 should 加不定式构成。"他举的例子是:

If the grass *needed* cutting, I would cut it.

If John *had worked* hard, he would have passed the examination.

If our train *were* to arrive punctually, we should have time to visit your sister.

Were John here now, he would explain the whole matter.

Had you *asked* me, I would have told you the answer.

I will go, *should* it be necessary.

从上面介绍的情况看,他心目中的虚拟语气比 Zandvoort 包含得更广一些。

最后再介绍 Quirk 等人在《综合英语语法》中的讲解。他们也提出了:

1) 现在虚拟语气:

If any person *be* found guilty, he shall have the right of appeal.

Whether she *be* right or wrong, she will have my unswerving support.

Though he *be* the President himself, he shall hear us.

Congress has voted that the present law *be* maintained.

We insisted that he *leave* at once.

It is essential that a meeting *be* convened this week.

Our decision is that the school *remain* closed.

2) 过去虚拟语气:

I wish she *were* not married.

If only I *were* not so nervous.

If she *were* here, she would speak on my behalf.

Suppose we *were* lost.

The stuffed dog barked as if it *were* a real one.

I'd rather I *were* in bed.

虚拟条件句中的动词形式,他们称为假想的过去形式 (The Hypothetic Past) 和假想的过去完成形式 (Hypothetic Past Perfect)。但在索引中仍归在虚拟语气下面。

在《如何准备托福考试》(*How to Prepare for the TOEFL*) 一书中,把虚拟语气分为下面几类 (例句都是原书中的):

1) 表示与事实相反的情况 (即虚拟条件句):

If he *were* older, we *could take* him with us.

If I *had* the time, I'*d take* a vacation.

If she *had been* here, she *could have shown* you.

If *I had had* the time, I'*d have taken* the vacation.

2) 表示愿望:

I wish he *were* old enough to go with us.

I wish she *had been* here yesterday.

3) 用于某些句型:

He acts as if he *were* older.

It is important that he *exercise* every day.

他们处理得比较简单,但代表了一般教师的看法。

综上所述,我们处理的办法与他们基本上是一致的。只是范围略为拓宽了一点,把 could, might 等用来表示现在情况的句子也归入此类。这是因为它们不受时态规律的约束,而且接近一个含蓄条件句 (如 *I would like to go with you.* 可改为 *I would like to go with you if I might.*),放在这里处理至少是比较方便的。另外,should + 不定式这种结构,Quirk 等人称为"假定式的 should"(Putative should),把这类结构放在虚拟语气一起讲,可以简化头绪。虚拟语气究竟怎样处理最好,还需要大家来作进一步的研究。

7. 短语和从句的问题

传统语法对短语和从句是有明确的界限的,现在使用的大多数语法和教科书也是这样处理的。但现在有些语法学家却有些新的讲法,他们把许多短语都称作从句,如现在分词从句、过去分词从句及不定式从句等:

Entering the house, he tripped over the mat.

Covered with confusion, she hurriedly left the room.

The best thing would be *to tell everybody*.

The job finished, we went home straight away.

这些他们称作非限定从句 (Non-finite Clauses),下分分词从句、不定式从句等。他们甚至还提出无动词从句 (Verbless Clauses),如:

By then nervous, the men opened the letter.

Long and untidy, his hair waved in the breeze.

The oranges, *when ripe*, are picked and sorted.

他们这样做有一定的道理，这类短语在概念上很接近从句，很多可以改为从句。但谈句法问题时主要还应从结构上去看，如果结构上是短语 (没有自己的主语谓语)，还是以不说成从句为好，否则容易引起混乱。

8. 补语、表语和状语的问题

句中我们称作表语的部分，西方语法学家多数称为补语 (Complement)。我们保留了表语这个名称原因有二，一是它更好表明它的特点 (说明主语的情况)，二是它的英文名称 Predicative 和谓语的英文名称 Predicate 有更紧密的联系。当然叫它补语也未尝不可。不过有些语法学家 (如 Greenbaum 等)，把更多的东西都称作补语，如：

1) 形容词补语 (Adjective Complements)：

She'll be glad $\begin{cases} \textit{(that) you are coming.} \\ \textit{to hear the good news.} \\ \textit{of your success.} \end{cases}$

2) 介词补语 (Prepositional Complements)：

They argued about $\begin{cases} \textit{the change.} \\ \textit{what was to be changed.} \\ \textit{changing the agreement.} \end{cases}$

这样一来补语的概念就不明确了。

系动词后面跟的成分，我们都称作表语，当然也可叫作补语。其中有一种表示地点等的介词短语或副词，有些语法学家称之为状语：

Your children are *outside*.

The next meeting will be on the 5th of February.

He's *off cigarettes*.

The road is *under construction*.

Payment is *by cash only*.

Jack and Nora are *with me*.

Quirk 等人称之为与主语有关的状语 (Subject related adverbial)。有些称为状语是有道理的，如头两个例子，变为问句可用 when, there 开始：

Where are my children?

When will the next meeting be?

后面的句子就难说了。他们自己也认为这种状语和表语的界限很不清楚。因此我们主张不作这样的区分，统统称为表语，对学习可能更有利一些。

9. 状语从句和宾语从句的问题

在"be＋形容词"结构后的从句是宾语还是状语，历来都是一个有争议的问题。主张是宾语的人是从概念上去考虑的，如：

I am sure we are right.

（比较：I know for sure we are right.）

She is convinced (that) you are the right person for the job.

（比较：She believes that you are the right person for the job.）

但这样做有一定的困难，因为只有及物动词才有宾语，be sure 和 be convinced 都不是及物动词。主张作状语的人是从结构上考虑。试比较下面句子：

I was pleased *to see her*. （不定式作状语）

I was pleased *with the result*. （介词短语作状语）

I was pleased *that they had decided to come*.

三者比较起来，说从句作状语似乎更好一些。而且 that 引导从句作状语的时候是很多的，如：

Bring it closer *that I may see it better*.

What was the matter with the fellow *that he looked so happy*.

He ran with such a speed *that I could not catch him*.

当然也可以回避这个问题，Quirk 等提出的办法，称它们为形容词的补语，也许是一个可行的办法。

10. 各类英语的问题

世界上有数以亿计的人使用英语，但不同的人在不同场合使用的英语是不尽相同的。但各类英语都有些共同的东西，可称为共同核心英语 (The Common Core)。我们学英语主要是或者首先是学习这一部分英语。例如 children 这个词就属于这个范畴，学会它之后再了解 kids 在日常口语中可用来代替 children，在较文气的语言中可用 offspring 这个词。另外，比较下面三个句子：

Feeling tired, John went to bed early.

John went to bed early because he felt tired.

John felt tired, so he went to bed early.

第二句属于共同核心英语这个范畴，在书面语和口语中都可以使用。第一句则比较文气，主要用在书面语言中。第三句是比较随便的说法，很可能出现在轻松的谈话之中。本书中大部分属于核心英语范畴，有些则分属书面语或口语范畴。比较突出的都已点出 (如带主语的分词短语)，有些本身就很明显，稍加注意可以看出。

大体说来，学英语时要注意下面这些不同类型的语言：

1）书面语与口语：

一般说来书面语比较规范，结构比较严谨，口语则比较简短，结构比较松散，甚至中间夹有各种插入语，有时只说半句话又转入另一句，省略句较多。有的人还会夹杂俚语方言，这都会构成理解的障碍。

大家只要阅读一本知识性的书（如历史、地理、政治、经济），不难体会书面语的特点。反过来看一些剧本或是读一些小说中的对话，也不难看出口语的特点。

2）正式场合及非正式场合用的英语：

正式场合用的英语，字典及语法中都标为 formal，可以是书面的，如报告、商业书信、条规等中用的语言。比较规范，有时甚至比较文气。口头上也可使用这种语言如演讲、讲课、正式作报告等。非正规场合使用的英语，指的是比较随便的英语，口头上用得最多，写信、甚至写文章也可能用这种语言。字典和语法书上多标作 informal。这里举些例子说明两者的差异：

> When his dad died, Peter had to get another job.
>
> After his father's death, Peter had to change his job.
>
> On the decease of his father, Mr Brown was obliged to seek alternative employment.

第一句为 informal 的语言，第三句为 formal 的语言，第二句介乎两者之间，可说属于 the common core。另外再看下面这几对句子：

> The meeting will commence at 4 p.m. (formal)
>
> The meeting will begin at 4 o'clock. (informal)

> The government is continuing its struggle against inflation. (formal)
>
> The government is keeping up its fight against inflation. (informal)

> The concert concluded with a performance of Beethoven's 5th Symphony. (formal)
>
> They ended the concert with Beethoven's 5th Symphony. (informal)

另外，很多成语动词也都表现了 informal English 的特点，例如：

formal	*informal*
discover	find out
explode	blow up
encounter	come across
invent	make up
tolerate	put up with
investigate	look into

另外在结构上也有些差别，例如：

> She longed for a friend in whom she could confide. (formal)
> She longed for a friend (who) she could confide in. (informal)

> In what country was he born? (formal)
> What country was he born in? (informal)

一般说来，informal language就是指口语体的语言 (Colloquial Language), formal language 多有些文气，书面上用得比较多。但现在书面语言也在变化，有些人写作也多避免太文气的语言，而使文体显得比较轻松随便平易易懂，甚至在大学课堂讲课都比以前更加随便。

3）英国英语及美国英语：

美国英语是从英国英语发展而来的，基本是一种语言，但毕竟还有一些差别，主要表现在下面几方面：

（1）语音：最大的差别是在元音后的 r，在英国英语中不发音，而在美国英语中发音，如 bird，在英国读为 [bɜ:d]，而在美国读为 [bɜ:rd], letter 在英国读为 ['letə]，在美国读为 ['letər]。另外，不少在英国读为 [ɑ:] 的音节，在美国读为 [æ]，如 glass，bathroom 在美国分别读为 [glæs] 和 ['bæθrʊm]。此外，某些元音音素两国的读法也有一定的差别，特别是字母 o 的短音，英语读 [ɒ]，美国接近 [ɑ], 如 God.

（2）语法：总的说来差别不大，但也有少许差别，例如动词 have 的否定及疑问形式，shall，will 的用法，加词尾时 1 是否要双写，两国间是有差别的。又如：

> Have you gotten (got) the tickets for the match? （美）
> Have you got the tickets for the match? （英）

> They suggested that Smith be dropped from the team. （美）
> They suggested that Smith should be dropped from the team. （英、美）

> One cannot succeed unless he tries hard. （美）
> One cannot succeed unless one tries hard. （英）

> Their house is different than ours. （美）
> Their house is different from ours. （英）

随着两国交往的日益密切、电视节目的相互影响，这方面的差别是越来越小了。

（3）词汇：这方面是有些差别的，一是在拼法上有些差别，如 color (美)与 colour (英)；program (美)与 programme (英)；grey (英)与 gray (美)；center (英)与 centre (美)；cheque (英)与 check (美)；axe (英)与 ax (美)等

等。但更多是在用词上的差别，如：

	英国英语	美国英语
商店	shop	store
汽油	petrol	gas
电影院	cinema	movie theater
铁路	railway	railroad
裤子	trousers	pants
单元住宅	flat	apartment
地铁	underground	subway
出租汽车	taxi	cab
出纳员	cashier	teller
罐头	tin	can
分数	marks	grades
飞机	(aero)plane	airplane
(电视)天线	TV aerial	antenna
留声机	gramophone	phonograph
人行道	pavement	sidewalk
钱包	handbag, bag	purse
糖果	sweets	candies
电影	film	movie
球赛	match	game
邮件	the post	the mail
监狱	prison	jail
垃圾	rubbish	garbage
秋天	autumn	the fall
电梯	elevator	lift
车胎	tyre	tire
上衣	jacket	coat
生病	ill	sick
橡皮	rubber	eraser
饼干	biscuit	cookie
药房	the chemist's	the drug store
扳手	spanner	wrench
修理	repair, mend	fix

打电话	phone	call
租用	hire	rent
和…谈话	talk to	talk with
中学	secondary school	high school
在…街	in...street	on...street
五点十分	ten past five	ten after five
两次	twice	two times
(女)理发店	hairdresser's	beauty parlor
休假	on holiday	on vacation
真的吗?	Really?	Is that so?
在周末	at the weekend	on the weekend
住院	in hospital	in the hospital
一杯咖啡	a coffee	a cup of coffee
洗盘子	do the washing up	wash the dishes
没问题，可以	certainly	sure
谢谢	Thanks very much.	Thanks a lot.

　　但这类词汇在整个词汇中占的比重不大。另外有些美国习语英国人是不熟悉甚至不懂的。但这不足为奇。美国南部的话和北部的话也不尽相同，甚至在伦敦一个城市之中不同阶层人说的话，也有不少的差别。因此，既要知道有各种特色的英语，也不必在上面花过多的心思。我们主要是学"大路货"，即大家都通用的语言。

参考书目（Bibliography）

Adams, V. 1973, *An Introduction to Modern English Word-Formation*, London: Longman

Alexander, L. G. 1997, *Longman English Grammar*, Longman

Allerton, D. J. 1979, *Essentials of Grammatical Theory*, London: Routledge

Alter, J. B. 1980, *Essential English Usage and Grammar*, Melbourne: Times Educational

Aronoff, M. 1976, *Word Formation in Generative Grammar*, Cambridge, Mass: MIT Press

Azar, B. S. 1981, *Understanding and Using English Grammar*, New Jersey: Prentice-Hall

Bauer, L. 1983, *English Word-Formation*, Cambridge University Press

Brown, E. K. and J. E. Miller 1982, *Syntax: Generative Grammar*, London: Hutchinson

Close, R. A. 1975, *A Reference Grammar for Students of English*, London: Longman

Collins 1995, *Cobuild English Grammar*, Harper Collins Publishers

Crowell, T. L. 1964, *Index to Modern English*, New York: McGraw-Hill

Culicover, P. W. 1982, *Syntax*, New York: Academic Press

Curme, G. O. 1931, *Syntax, A Grammar of the English Language*, Boston: Heath

Dick, S. C. 1978, *Functional Grammar*, Amsterdam: North Holland

Eckersley, C. E., M. Macaulay and D. K. Swan 1987, *Brighter Grammar*, New Edition, London: Longman

Eckersley, C. E. 1982, *A Concise English Grammar for Foreign Students*, London: Longman

Eckersley, C. E. and J. M. Eckersley 1961, *A Comprehensive English Grammar*, London: Longman

EK, J. A. van, Nico J. Robat 1984, *The Students' Grammar of English*, Oxford: Basil Blackwell

Ferguson, C. A. and S. B. Heath 1981, *Language in the USA*, Cambridge University Press

Givon, T. 1979, *Understanding Grammar*, New York: Academic Press

Greenbaum, S. 1985, *The English Language Today*, Oxford: Pergamon Press

Herndon, J. H. 1976, *A Survey of Modern Grammars*, New York: Holt, Rinehart and Winston

Hornby, A. S. 1954, *A Guide to Patterns and Usage in English* , London: Oxford University Press

Huddleston, R. D. 1984, *Introduction to the Grammar of English*, Cambridge University Press

Jesperson, O. 1909 — 1949, *A Modern English Grammar on Historical Principles* I— Ⅶ, Copenhagen: Munksgaard

Jesperson, O. 1933, *Essentials of English Grammar,* London: Allen and Unwin

Kruisinga, E. 1931—1932, *A Handbook of Present-day English*, Groningen: Noordhoff

Leech, G. 1971, *Meaning and the English Verb*, London: Longman

Leech, G. and Jan Svartvik 1984, *A Communicative Grammar of English*, London: Longman

Lim, Phyllis and Mary Kurtin 1982, *TOEFL Workbook*, New York: Arco Publishing, Inc.

Mathews, P. H. 1974, *Morphology*, Cambridge University Press

Mathews, P. H. 1981, *Syntax*, Cambridge University Press

Murphy, R. 1994, *English Grammar in Use*, Cambridge University Press

Murphy, R. 1990, *Essential Grammar in Use*, Cambridge University Press

Palmer, F. R. 1974, *The English Verb*, London: Longman

Patricia, K. Werner, etc. 1997, *A Communicative Grammar*, McGraw-Hill

Poutsma, H. 1926 — 1929, *A Grammar of Late Modern English*, Groningen: Noordhoff

Quirk, R., S. Greenbaum, G. Leech and J. Startvik 1972, *A Grammar of Contemporary English*, London: Longman

Quirk, R., and S. Greenbaum 1985, *A University Grammar of English*, London: Longman

Quirk R., S. Greenbaum, G. Leech and J. Startvik 1985, *A Comprehensive Grammar of the English Language*, London: Longman

Scheurweghs, G. 1959, *Present-day English Syntax*, Leuven Nauwelaerts

Schibsbye, K. 1979, *A Modern English Grammar*, Oxford University Press

Swan, M. 1980, *Practical English Usage*, Oxford University Press

Sweet, H. 1891—1998, *A New English Grammar*, Oxford University Press

Thomson , A. J. and A. V. Martinet 1999, *A Practical English Grammar*, Oxford University Press

Tracy, R. D. 1980, *Correcting Common Errors in English*, Hong Kong: Times Educational

Warriner, J. E., J. Mersand, H. Town send and F. Griffith 1973, *English Grammar and Composition*, New York: Harcourt Brace Jovanovich

Zandvoort , R. W. 1975, *A Handbook of English Grammar*, London: Longman